Digital
Networks
and
Computer
Systems

Digital Networks and Computer Systems

Second Edition

Taylor L. Booth
Professor of Computer Science
and Electrical Engineering
University of Connecticut
Storrs, Connecticut

John Wiley & Sons, New York · Santa Barbara · London · Sydney · Toronto

Library of Congress Cataloging in Publication Data:

Booth, Taylor L
  Digital networks and computer systems.

  Includes indexes.
  1. Electronic digital computers—Circuits. 2. Electronic digital computers—Programming. I. Title.
TK7888.3.B66 1978   001.6′4   77–10832
ISBN 0-471-08842-0

Printed in the United States of America

10 9 8 7 6 5 4 3 2 1

To
Aline,
Shari,
Michael,
and Laurine

Preface

A major shift has occurred in the field of the design and application of digital systems and computers. Integrated circuit technology has so sharply reduced the price of both digital computers and basic logic modules that many tasks traditionally performed by analogue circuits and systems are now carried out by digital techniques. The programmable hand calculator and microprocessor have become a commonplace engineering tool while the speed and capability of minicomputers have allowed them to replace larger computer systems in a great number of applications. As a result, many engineers and scientists have found it necessary to understand the basic operation of digital systems and how these systems can be designed if they are to carry out particular information-processing tasks associated with their work.

This trend has produced a need for an introductory undergraduate course in the digital-system area designed to provide a unified overview of the interrelationship between digital system design, computer organization, and machine-language-level programming techniques. In 1971 when the first edition of this text was published no book existed that presented such a combination of topics. The broad acceptance of the first edition has proved that the perceived need did exist. Most up-to-date computer science curriculums include one or more basic courses that provide students with an understanding of computer organization. In other areas, such as engineering, the physical or life sciences, similar courses also have been developed to provide the understanding needed to effectively employ digital devices and computers as basic laboratory tools. Students completing an introductory course based on this book are also prepared to go on to more advanced courses that specialize in one particular aspect of digital system design.

This book is organized to provide an integrated overview of the various classes of digital information-processing systems and the interrelationship between the hardware and software techniques that can be used to solve a particular problem. The unifying theme throughout the book is the concept that the steps involved in solving a problem must first be represented by an algorithm. It is then the designers task to choose the best techniques to realize the given algorithm. In some cases it is obvious that either a hardware or a software solution should be used. However, there is an ever-increasing gray area between these two approaches in which many different alternatives must be considered before the best solution can be identified. By giving the student a view of the interdependencies of logic design, digital system design, and machine-level programming, it is possible to provide an appreciation of how all of these different areas of computer technology interact.

At the University of Connecticut this book is used in the first professional-level computer science course. Since the only prerequisite to this course is an introductory programming course, many students from areas such as engineering, mathematics, statistics, the physical sciences, the life sciences, as well as students planning on majoring in computer science take this course. This serves the dual purpose of preparing students for advanced study in the computer science area and of giving other students an overview of digital networks and computers beyond that presented in the introductory programming course.

All computer science and electrical engineering majors take this course as a required course. Because of scheduling considerations, most of these students take the course during the first semester of their sophomore or junior year. However, many freshmen have completed this course without difficulty since there is no specific mathematical background required of the student other than an understanding of high-school-level mathematics.

At other schools this book is suitable for an introductory digital systems course such as envisioned by the COSINE Committee of the Commission on Education of the National Academy of Engineering or for courses I3 or I6 of the ACM Curriculum 68 (Communications of the ACM, March 1968, pp. 151–197). A revised ACM curriculum recommendation is currently being developed and this text would be ideal for course CS-4*, Introduction to Computer Organization, contained in that curriculum.

The sequence in which the material is presented provides an orderly and logical transition from the basic ideas of representing digital information and performing basic logical operations through the idea of complex information processing systems and programs. Chapter 1 gives a brief overview of the various topics discussed in the book and their interrelationships. Chapters 2, 3, and 4 present a discussion of the techniques that can be used to represent and operate upon information in digital form. The material in Chapters 5, 6, and 7 provide an introduction to basic switching theory and combinational logic network design. The main concepts of switching theory are presented in a straightforward manner without excessive formalism. This material also illustrates many of the standard logical circuits encountered in digital systems.

Chapters 8, 9, 10, and 11 deal with the idea of digital networks with memory. Several of the basic memory elements are first discussed and then the idea of a synchronous sequential network is introduced. No attempt is made to treat asynchronous networks. Chapters 10 and 11 are particularly important since they show how the simple digital networks treated in the earlier chapters can be combined to form complex digital systems.

Chapter 12 introduces the general ideas behind the operation of stored program digital computers. In particular, a special simulated educational computer,

* Working report of ACM Committee on Curriculum in Computer Science ACM SIGCSE Bulletin Vol. 9, No. 2, June 1977.

called SEDCOM, is introduced to illustrate these ideas. SEDCOM is then used in Chapter 13 to illustrate the idea of machine-language programming and the various programming techniques that can be used to carry out different types of information processing tasks on a small computer. Chapters 14 and 15 then discuss the general structure of assembler- and procedure-oriented languages and the translator programs that can be used to transfer source-language programs into object-language programs.

At the University of Connecticut we cover the first 14 chapters in detail and briefly discuss the material in Chapter 15 as time permits at the end of the semester. Dr. Bernard Lovell of our faculty has developed a program to simulate SEDCOM on our Computer Center's IBM 360/65. We therefore require our students to actually write and run a number of home problems in Chapters 13 through 15 on this simulated computer. Students can also use special logic breadboards in our digital system laboratory to obtain additional insight into the operation of digital networks.

In order to aid the student and help the independent reader, several simple exercises are included at the end of each section to illustrate the material of that section. The answers to many of these exercises are included in Appendix 2. Several home problems are included at the end of each chapter. These problems are comprehensive in nature; they extend the material contained in the chapter and start the student thinking about one or more new concepts that will be discussed in one of the following chapters. The references at the end of the chapter guide the reader who is interested in the further exploration of a given area. A *Teacher's Manual* is available from the publisher on request for those instructors who adopt the text for classroom use.

I am indebted to the many faculty members who used the first edition of this book and who have sent me helpful suggestions about ways to improve presentations of particular topics or new material to be included. Another very imprtant and continuing source of suggestions and comments have been from my colleagues; Bulent Dervisoglu, Bernard Carey, Yi-Tzuu Chien, Thomas Gilkey, Richard Hart, Ralph Kochenberger, Bernard Lovell, Howard Sholl, and John White who have made many useful comments over the past six years as they have taught from this book. The revision of the text was made much easier by the ability of Mrs. Jean Hayden to transform my rough notes and corrections into manuscript form. Finally, I thank my wife, Aline, for her patience and encouragement throughout the whole revision process.

Storrs, Connecticut, 1977   Taylor L. Booth

Contents

CHAPTER 5 Combinational Logic Circuit Elements 123

CHAPTER 6 Switching Algebra and Logic Network Realization 145

CHAPTER 7 Minimization of Combinational Logic Networks 177

CHAPTER 8 Flip-Flops, Registers and Basic Information Transfers 217

CHAPTER 9 Introduction to the Analysis and Design of Synchronous Sequential Networks 257

CHAPTER 15 Programming Languages and Compilers • 523

APPENDIX 1 Binary Codes for Character Representation 565

APPENDIX 2 Answers to Selected Exercises 569

INDEX 587

1

Introduction to Digital Systems

1. INTRODUCTION

Because of the increasing complexity of civilization, man has been forced to continually develop better and more efficient techniques to process and utilize information. Initial attempts at developing information processing aids centered around improving methods of carrying out mechanical manipulations of numbers. During the 17th century many of the leading mathematicians and scientists developed calculating devices to aid them in their research. As industrial technology developed during the 18th and 19th centuries, these basic ideas were refined and extended to develop complex mechanical devices that could be used to control machines and aid businessmen in performing repetitive calculations and bookkeeping tasks.

In the early 1800's Charles Babbage proposed and attempted to construct a device that he referred to as an analytical engine. Conceptually this device was similar to our modern digital computers. Although he was able to build a simple model of his machine, he was never able to complete the construction of a machine that would handle practical problems. One of the reasons for his failure was that the design called for so many moving mechanical parts that the inherent friction between the various parts prevented satisfactory operation of the complete machine. Even though Babbage failed to build a practical device, many of the concepts that he developed laid the foundation for the design concepts of modern computers.

Computers, as we know them today, have become practical only because we have been able to replace mechanical devices with electronic devices. In the late 1930's and early 1940's a series of relay computers were built through the joint effort of Harvard University, Bell Telephone Laboratories, and IBM. Although these computers operated satisfactorily, they were quickly superseded by electronic computers.

In 1946 J. P. Eckert and Dr. J. W. Mauchly developed the first electronic computer, the ENIAC, at the Moore School of Engineering at the University of Pennsylvania. This computer contained 18,000 vacuum tubes. Vacuum tubes were so unreliable at that time that the predicted mean time to failure was shorter than the mean time to repair the device. Nevertheless the computer did work and was used by the U.S. Army for a number of years.

As the capability of computers and digital systems became better understood, many major technical advances were made. With the introduction of the transistor in the early 1950's, it became possible to design and construct highly reliable computers. Discrete transistor circuits have given way to integrated circuit technology. It is now possible to place thousands of electronic components on a silicon chip that is at most a few centimeters square. The most visible result of this development is the hand calculator, which can be used to carry out complex numerical calculations.

Integrated circuits have had a major impact on both the design and applications of digital networks and computer systems. Their low cost has greatly expanded the areas of application as well as reduced the price of complete computer systems. We have also reached the point where a large number of manufacturers are producing computers of various sizes and capabilities with prices that range from a few thousands to many millions of dollars.

The majority of people who come in contact with computers can be classified as occasional computer users. Their main interest is to use the computer to carry out the routine data processing task or calculations needed as part of their work. By using procedure-oriented languages such as FORTRAN, COBOL, or PL/1, these people are able to carry out data processing tasks without worrying about the internal organization or structure of the computer.

The high information processing rates of modern computers, however, makes it possible to apply computers to a variety of information processing tasks that were not even conceived of before the development of modern computers. Consequently just as engineers or scientists must understand the limitations of the physical laws of nature they must also develop an understanding and appreciation of the laws dealing with the utilization, processing, and transmission of information.

This book has been designed for the person who has reached the point where a computer is viewed as more than a calculating device to solve routine problems. Consequently we first investigate the mathematical techniques that are used to describe and analyze digital networks and systems. Next, the methods that may be used to design combinational and sequential logic networks, which are found in every digital system and computer, are presented. Once the operation of these basic building blocks is understood we then consider how they can be used to form complex data processing devices and general purpose digital computers. Finally, we consider the various types of programming systems that can be used to program a computer and how they are related to the efficiency of the overall information processing system.

2. ALGORITHMIC PROCESSES

Two of the major problems in designing a complex digital information processing system concern:

1. The identification of the various fundamental information processing tasks that must be accomplished.
2. The specification of the component parts of the system needed to carry out these tasks.

From an abstract viewpoint, the complete computational process carried out by any digital information processor or computer can be formally represented by the mathematical relationship

$$F(x) = y$$

where x represents the data presented to the processor, $F(x)$ represents the computation performed on the data and y represents the results of this computation. The computation represented by $F(x)$ can take many forms.

In the simplest case, the processor might be a simple logic network that takes the current value of n input variables, $[x_1, x_2, \ldots, x_n]$, and immediately produces an output $f(x_1, x_2, \ldots, x_n)$. On the other hand, the processor might be a large-scale computer system that measures the status of a chemical production process and produces output signals to control the rate at which certain chemical reactions are allowed to take place.

For each of these information processing tasks or any other tasks that we might wish to perform, there is only one restriction that we must place on the computation represented by $F(x)$. We must be sure that there is an explicit and unambiguous set of instructions that tells us how to perform the computation. This set of rules is called an algorithm for the computation of $F(x)$.

Alogorithm

We say that an *algorithm* for the computation $F(x) = y$ exists if there is an ordered sequence of discrete steps that can be performed mechanically by a device such that given x the device either:

(a) forms $y = F(x)$ by executing these steps in the prescribed order, or
(b) indicates that no y exists that satisfies the conditions of the computation.

The device must require only a finite number of steps to reach one or the other of these decisions.

From this definition we see that if we are to implement an algorithm on a digital device we must reduce the steps of the algorithm to a sequence of elementary operations that can be performed by the device. In some cases the device will consist of a simple digital network constructed to perform the complete computation in one step while in other cases the algorithm for the computation will be so complex that it requires a large number of steps and can only be implemented on a large-scale digital computer. We now investigate the general properties of algorithms as they relate to the design and utilization of digital information processing devices. This will, in turn, allow us to gain an insight into the interrelationship between the organization of digital networks and computers and the computational processes that can be carried out by these devices. Our first task is to define what we mean by an "elementary operation".

We automatically carry out an algorithm every time we perform a particular mathematical or logical operation. However, we seldom give any thought to the form that this algorithm takes. This is because our previous experience has taught us to associate fixed reactions and interpretations to different mathematical symbols. However, if we wish to describe how we carried out a given calculation to someone who does not have our background we must explain, in great detail, how the computation is performed.

For example assume that we wish to compute the sum of the three two-digit numbers

$$A = a_2 a_1 \qquad B = b_2 b_1 \qquad D = d_2 d_1$$

Normally we would probably carry out the addition in our heads, write down the answer

$$Y = A + B + D = y_3 y_2 y_1$$

and consider our problem solved. Most computers cannot simultaneously add three numbers together. They must, instead, perform the calculation in two steps as:

Step 1 $R_1 = A + B$
Step 2 $Y = R_1 + D$

Thus, if we assume that we can use the elementary operation of adding two numbers together, our calculation can be completed by using a two-step algorithm. However, consider what would happen if the computing device that we had could only add two digits at a time. Should this be the case we would have to replace both step 1 and step 2 with a sequence of steps that would describe how the two numbers are to be added together digit by digit.

The elementary operation in this case would be digit addition which can be formally defined by

$$
\begin{array}{r}
u_i \\
v_i \\
\hline
c_i \quad s_i
\end{array}
$$

where s_i is the unit sum of the two digits and c_i is the carry. For example, let $u_i = 9$ and $v_i = 5$. Then

$$\begin{array}{r} 9 \\ 5 \\ \hline 1 \ \ 4 \end{array}$$

and we see that $c_i = 1$ and $s_i = 4$.

It is possible to build a device to compute the two functions

$$s_i = F_1(u_i, v_i)$$

and

$$c_i = F_2(u_i, v_i)$$

If we must use this device to compute

$$Y = A + B + D$$

they we could use the following algorithm:

Algorithm to compute $Y = A + B + D$ First Part Compute $R = A + B$	Example of Calculation Performed Using Algorithm $Y = 25 + 34 + 98$
Step 1 $\quad r_1 = F_1(a_1, b_1)$	$r_1 = 9 = F_1(5, 4)$
Step 2 $\quad c_1 = F_2(a_1, b_1)$	$c_1 = 0 = F_2(5, 4)$
Step 3 $\quad p_2 = F_1(a_2, b_2)$	$p_2 = 5 = F_1(2, 3)$
Step 4 $\quad r_2 = F_1(p_2, c_1)$	$r_2 = 5 = F_1(5, 0)$
Step 5 $\quad m_2 = F_2(a_2, b_2)$	$m_2 = 0 = F_2(2, 3)$
Step 6 $\quad n_2 = F_2(p_2, c_1)$	$n_2 = 0 = F_2(5, 0)$
Step 7 $\quad c_2 = F_1(m_2, n_2)$	$c_2 = 0 = F_1(0, 0)$

Second Part
$Y = R + D$

Step 8 $\quad y_1 = F_1(r_1, d_1)$	$y_1 = 7 = F_1(9, 8)$
Step 9 $\quad c_1' = F_2(r_1, d_1)$	$c_1' = 1 = F_2(9, 8)$
Step 10 $\quad p_2' = F_1(r_2, d_2)$	$p_2' = 4 = F_1(5, 9)$
Step 11 $\quad y_2 = F_1(p_2', c_1')$	$y_2 = 5 = F_1(4, 1)$
Step 12 $\quad m_2' = F_2(r_2, d_2)$	$m_2' = 1 = F_2(5, 9)$
Step 13 $\quad n_2' = F_2(p_2', c_1')$	$n_2' = 0 = F_2(4, 1)$
Step 14 $\quad c_2 = F_1(m_2', n_2')$	$c_2 = 1 = F_1(1, 0)$
Step 15 $\quad y_3 = F_1(c_2', c_2)$	$y_3 = 1 = F_1(1, 0)$

Result

$$Y = y_3 y_2 y_1$$

Result

$$Y = y_3 y_2 y_1 = 157$$

This algorithm actually represents the following very simple addition process.

	Stage 1	0 0			Carry
	Compute $R = A + B$	0	2	5	A
		0	3	4	B
		0	5	9	R

	Stage 2	1 1			Carry
	Compute $Y = R + D$	0	5	9	R
		0	9	8	D
		1	5	7	Y

Thus we see that the set of basic operations that we can use affects the complexity of an algorithm. The example also illustrates how we can solve the problem. When we are working with a system there will usually be a sequence of operations that are used enough times to justify attaching a functional name to them. Thus we could define a function

$$F_S(U, V) = U + V$$

that stands for the steps needed to form the sums in the above algorithm. The algorithm then goes back to

Step 1 $R = F_S(A, B)$
Step 2 $Y = F_S(R, D)$

This idea of taking a sequence of simple operations and defining a new operation to represent this sequence is used repeatedly throughout this book. In this way we can concentrate on the important concepts being presented without worrying about the fine details of how each step of the process is actually implemented.

Flowchart Representation of Algorithms

One of the most convenient ways to represent an algorithm is by means of a *flowchart* or *flow diagram*. A flowchart is a graphical representation of a particular algorithm that indicates the logical sequence of operations that are to be performed by the device that executes the algorithm. The flowchart is basically a collection of specially shaped boxes and directed lines. The contents of each box indicate which operations are to be performed while the lines that interconnect the boxes indicate the sequence in which the instructions are to be performed.

A very elaborate flowchart symbology has been evolved by computer programmers. However, for our needs in this book we will limit our flowchart symbols

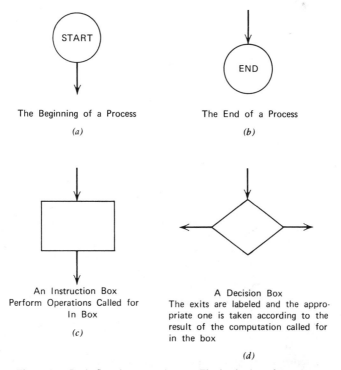

The Beginning of a Process

(a)

The End of a Process

(b)

An Instruction Box
Perform Operations Called for
In Box

(c)

A Decision Box
The exits are labeled and the appropriate one is taken according to the
result of the computation called for
in the box

(d)

Figure 1-1. Basic flowchart notation. (a) The beginning of a process. (b) The end of a process. (c) An instruction box performs operations called for in box. (d) A decision box. The exits are labeled and the appropriate one is taken according to the result of the computation called for in the box.

to those illustrated in Figure 1-1. Reference 5 at the end of this chapter presents an extensive discussion of flowcharting techniques.

Each instruction box and decision box will contain one or more expressions describing how the basic operations are used to carry out the calculations. It is assumed that the reader has been introduced to computer programming in sufficient detail to be aware of how flowcharts are used. The following example will serve to review these ideas.

Assume that we wish to calculate the roots of the equation $ax^2 + bx + c$. If $a \neq 0$ then these roots are given by

$$r_1 = \frac{-b + \sqrt{b^2 - 4ac}}{2a} \qquad r_2 = \frac{-b - \sqrt{b^2 - 4ac}}{2a}$$

The simplest possible flowchart for finding r_1 and r_2 is given in Figure 1-2. However, if we examine this flowchart we see that it is not much different from our

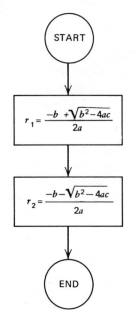

Figure 1-2. A simple flowchart for computing r_1 and r_2.

initial statement of the problem. In particular, it assumes that we have two basic operations corresponding to

$$f_1(a, b, c) = \frac{-b + \sqrt{b^2 - 4ac}}{2a}$$

and

$$f_2(a, b, c) = \frac{-b - \sqrt{b^2 - 4ac}}{2a}$$

that can be evaluated to find r_1 and r_2. Since these two functions are somewhat specialized, it becomes desirable to break the calculation down into smaller parts. Before we can do this, we must consider some of the problems that must be overcome.

First, we note that if $a = 0$ we have

$$r_1 = r_2 = -\frac{c}{b}$$

provided we always assume that b is not also 0. Similarly we note that if $b^2 - 4ac \geq 0$ then the roots are real, while if $b^2 - 4ac < 0$ we have the imaginary roots

$$r_1 = \frac{-b + j\sqrt{4ac - b^2}}{2a} \qquad r_2 = \frac{-b - j\sqrt{4ac - b^2}}{2a}$$

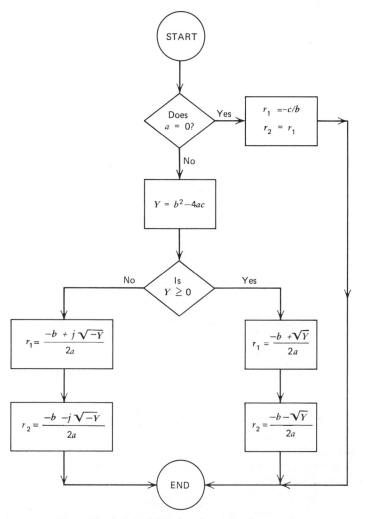

Figure 1-3. A second flowchart for computing r_1 and r_2.

where $j = \sqrt{-1}$. Using these observations let us now formulate a much more comprehensive flowchart description of our computation of r_1 and r_2. This flowchart is given in Figure 1-3.

This flowchart is much more complex than the one in Figure 1-2, but we still find boxes that call for complex computations such as $Y = b^2 - 4ac$. If this were the flowchart for a program that is to be written in a programming language such as FORTRAN, it would be an acceptable computational step because we could leave the translation of this mathematical statement into a form that the computer can use up to the computer's compiler program. Here again it is also possible to construct a digital network that would accept the variables a, b, and c

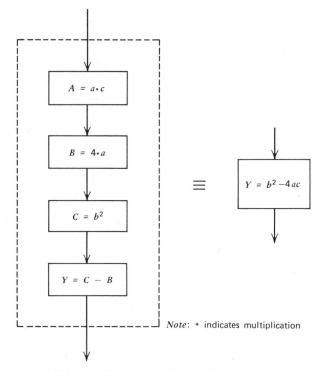

Figure 1-4. Reduction of complex mathematical statement to component operations.

as inputs and produce Y as an output. However, a network of this type is still too specialized to be of much use.

As a final step in our flowchart example let us take the box that contains $Y = b^2 - 4ac$ and replace it by a set of more basic operations. This is done in Figure 1-4. In this flowchart we have used the operations of multiplication and subtraction as our basic mathematical operations. Similarly we could replace each of the larger boxes of Figure 1-3 with a much more detailed flowchart involving basic operations similar to those illustrated in Figure 1-4.

The discussion of this section has presented a survey of the problems involved in studying the way in which the calculations required in a given information processing task can be described in a formal manner. We paid no attention to the physical problem of how these calculations can actually be performed by a realizable digital device. This problem will now be considered.

3. DIGITAL NETWORKS

For every operation called for as part of an algorithm there must be a digital network or system that will perform the operations. As with algorithms, some of these networks perform very simple operations while there are other, much more complex, digital systems that perform extremely complex tasks. In this section we briefly consider the general forms that these networks and systems can take. A much more extensive discussion of these devices is presented in later chapters.

Combinational Logic

The simplest class of networks are combinational logic networks such as are illustrated in Figure 1-5. Logic networks accept input variables which can only take on one of two values. For convenience these values are arbitrarily designated as 0 and 1. Such a signal is said to carry one *bit* of information.

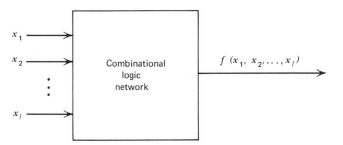

Figure 1-5. General combinational logic network.

If the inputs to the logic network are indicated by the variables $x_1, x_2, \ldots, x_l$, the current output of the network can be expressed as

$$y = f(x_1, x_2, \ldots, x_l)$$

where y takes on the value 0 or 1 depending on the particular values assigned to the current input variables. Networks of this type can be used alone or can be combined with other circuit elements to form much more complex logic networks.

Registers

In addition to being able to operate on digital signals in a logical manner, a digital network must, in many instances, have the ability to store information about the past behavior or the past inputs to the network. To accomplish this required information storage, a wide variety of information storage devices have been developed. At present we will refer to the basic storage element as a *cell* and assume that it can store a signal with a value of either a 0 or a 1. The output of each cell has a value corresponding to the quantity stored in the cell. The content of the cell remains constant until an input signal is received instructing the cell to change its content. Figure 1-6a illustrates the symbolic representation that we use for a cell.

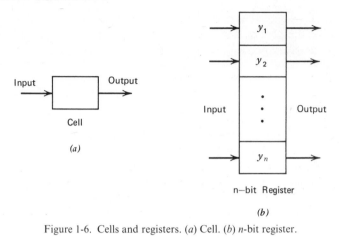

Figure 1-6. Cells and registers. (*a*) Cell. (*b*) *n*-bit register.

Single information storage cells have rather limited storage capabilities since they can only store a single bit of information. If more information must be stored, a collection of cells can be joined together, as shown in Figure 1-6*b*, to form a *register*. A register with *n* cells is said to be an *n-bit register*.

Registers by themselves are of relatively little value. They must be combined with combinational logic networks if the stored information is to be used as part of a computation.

Digital Networks

The behavior of any digital network containing a register is dependent on the way in which the inputs to the register are formed. Figure 1-7 shows a completely general model that can be used to represent a digital network which has the ability to store information. The size of the register in this circuit depends on the amount of information that must be stored while the overall operation of the network depends on the form that the combinational logic network takes.

A digital computer is made up of hundreds of these digital networks. Their design is a straightforward process involving three basic steps.

1. Description of the operation that the network is to perform.
2. Development of a mathematical representation of the logical operations to be performed by the combinational logic network.
3. Realization of the network in terms of a particular set of components.

As long as we are interested in the design of a particular network to carry out a given operation, we must deal with models of the type illustrated in Figure 1-7. However, if we assume that the network is already developed and we wish to

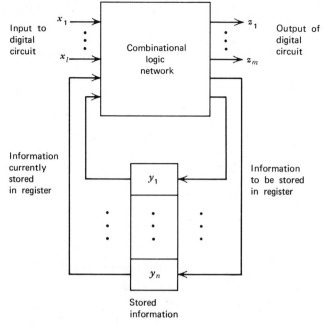

Figure 1-7. General model of a digital circuit.

investigate how it is used in a complete system, we can replace the detailed representation of the network by a block diagram representation such as that illustrated in Figure 1-8. The content of each register is indicated by a capital letter as are the input and output signals. The operation performed on this information is represented by a function such as $F(A, B, C)$. In this way we are aware of the overall behavior of the network without being lost in a mass of details concerning the way that the circuit is constructed.

This approach is becoming a common design technique using integrated circuit technology. Many of the common information processing tasks have been

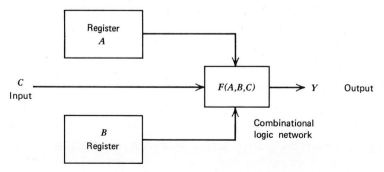

Figure 1-8. Block diagram representation of a digital network.

standardized, and special *medium-scale integrated* circuits (MSI) or *large-scale integrated* circuits (LSI) have been developed by electronic manufacturers to carry out these tasks. Thus a digital system designer can buy these circuits as standard electronic components without having to worry about how they are constructed.

Digital Systems

Complete information processing systems can be constructed using a small number of basic digital networks. For example it is possible to build a digital system that will observe the output of a radio receiver and sound an alarm whenever a particular coded message is received.

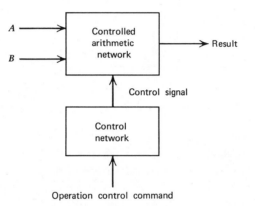

Figure 1-9. A controlled arithmetic processor.

Another type of digital system is illustrated in Figure 1-9. This system is made up of two parts, a control network and an arithmetic unit. An external signal is used to select the arithmetic operation that must be performed on the input signals *A* and *B*. This operation control command is applied to the control network, which then generates the sequence of commands necessary to make the controlled arithmetic network perform the desired operation. Here again we use a block diagram that shows only the operations that we are interested in and omits the particular details of how the networks, which may be integrated circuits, are actually constructed.

Digital Computers

Although computers are constructed from many different electronic and mechanical elements, the basic organization of a computer can be roughly broken down into the five major parts illustrated in Figure 1-10.

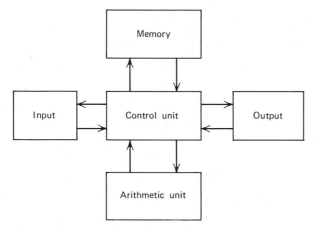

Figure 1-10. A simple block diagram showing the major parts of a computer.

The input to a computer can take many forms depending on the type of information that must be delivered to the computer. In most large data processing applications, the major input devices are punched card, magnetic tape, or paper tape readers. These devices can transfer a large amount of information into the computer in a relatively short period of time.

For other applications it is necessary to provide the capability of man-computer communications. This can be accomplished through the use of such devices as typewriters, display scopes, and graphic position sensors. With devices of this type an operator can guide the operation of a computer by instructing it to perform various operations as intermediate results are made known.

A third type of input situation occurs when the computer is used as part of a complete system such as an automatic flight control system or a chemical processing plant. Applications of this type require the computer to collect input data from a variety of sensor elements. This data might consist of physical quantities such as voltages, temperatures, pressures, or velocity, or the data might be information about the system such as current supply levels, relative anticipated demands for a given system product, or current market prices.

The arithmetic unit of a computer is the center in the computer where the actual operations on the data take place. This unit must be able to hold and manipulate data under the direction of the control unit. The heart of this unit is one or more special registers called *accumulators*, which provide for the temporary storage of information while it is being processed. In addition to these accumulators, this unit also contains the necessary logic circuits to carry out the basic arithmetic and logic operations that the computer has been designed to perform.

A typical computer has four classes of basic operations that can be performed.

1. Arithmetic operations such as addition, subtraction, and multiplication.
2. Logical operations such as greater than, less than, or comparisons.

3. Data manipulation such as shifting the position of data in an accumulator, and transferring data into or out of an accumulator.

4. Decisions on where to take the next instruction in a program based on the form of the data currently stored in a particular accumulator.

One of the first problems that must be solved when a new computer is being designed is that of selecting the specific set of basic operations, called *instructions*, that can be executed by the computer. These instructions must be selected so that all of the information processing tasks that the computer might be asked to perform can be expressed in terms of an algorithm which makes use of these instructions. The sequence of instructions needed to realize a given algorithm is called a *program*.

Each instruction of the program is encoded into digital form and is stored in the main memory unit. This encoded program is called a *machine-language program*. In addition, the data needed to perform the calculations described by the program is also stored in the memory unit. Such data is directly accessible to the computer.

In addition to main memory, many of the larger computers have some form of bulk storage such as magnetic tapes, drums, or disks which allow vast amounts of data and information to be stored. This data is usually not directly available to a computer during a calculation. If some of the information stored on one of these devices is needed, it is necessary to transfer this information into main memory.

The actual execution of a given machine-language program is under the direct supervision of the control unit. The control unit reads the current instruction to be executed from memory, interprets the instruction, and then coordinates the operation of all the parts of the computer so that each step needed to carry out the instruction happens in a logical sequence and at the right time. As soon as the computer finishes the operation called for by the current instruction, the control unit goes on to the next instruction in the machine-language program.

The final major section of a computer is the output device. Data can be transferred from the computer in many forms. For a computer mainly devoted to computations, the output is usually printed or punched on cards. Computers used as an integral part of a much more complex system can have a variety of other forms of outputs.

Control computers usually produce signals that activate some physical process. For example, in a steel mill a computer might control both the amount of raw material and the sequence of operations used in each step of the steel-making process.

The output of a computer might be some form of graphic display so that the user can obtain a dynamic interpretation of the interaction between the various variables of his problem. Outputs of this type are very useful in computer-aided design problems where the operator can vary one parameter of a problem and see how this parameter influences the rest of the problem.

Computer size has been rapidly decreasing in recent years. Integrated circuit technology has reached the point where it is possible to realize a complete computer using only a few integrated circuit modules. Computers of this type are called *microcomputers*. The heart of a microcomputer is usually a *microprocessor*, which is an integrated circuit that realizes the operations carried out by the arithmetic unit and the control unit. Additional integrated circuits are needed for memory and input/output. With this new technology, computer systems that once might have required a large room can be constructed in a few cabinets. Although the size of a computer has been markedly reduced, the theory of operation of a micro-computer is essentially the same as any other computer system.

In this section we have briefly considered the general types of hardware that can be used to carry out various classes of logical operations. As the complexity of the operations that we wished to accomplish increased we saw that it became increasingly desirable to carry out the operation as a controlled sequence of logical steps. This approach led us to the concept of a digital computer where the com-putations carried out by the computer are determined by a program stored in the computer's memory. The problems associated with developing these programs are considered in the next section.

4. COMPUTER PROGRAMMING

One of the basic assumptions in our discussions of algorithms was that a mechani-cal device was available to automatically carry out each step of the algorithm. From the last section we know that each digital computer has a set of basic operations that it can perform under the direction of a control element. We also know that the order in which these operations are performed is determined by a machine-language program. Thus, if we wish to use a digital computer to carry out a given calculation, we must first develop an algorithm, using only the allowable computer instructions, that describes how to perform the desired calculation. We must then encode the algorithm into a machine-language program that can be executed by the computer. This section briefly considers the problems associated with generating these programs.

Machine-Language Programming

Every basic instruction associated with a computer is coded as an n-digit sequence of 0's and 1's. For example the instruction "add A to B" might be encoded as 001010110101. As indicated previously, the set of all the possible encoded instruc-tions is called the machine language of the computer. Any program that is to be executed by a computer must ultimately be expressed in this machine language.

In the earliest computers the machine-language instructions necessary to implement a given algorithm were coded by a programmer directly in the machine language for that computer. For example, the machine-language program to compute

$$Y = A + B - (C + D)$$

might be represented in machine language as

Instruction	Machine-Language Code	Meaning
1	001011010100	Form $S = C + D$
2	011001010101	Form $R = B - S$
3	001010101110	Form $Y = A + R$
4	010000000000	Halt calculation

Obviously a language of this type is very unsatisfactory for general use. There are two major reasons for this conclusion. First, the basic operations that can be performed by the computer are very elementary compared with the operations usually employed in the solution of practical problems. The inclusion of any operation into the set of basic operations of a computer is based on a compromise between the cost of wiring the operation into the computer and the advantages of having this particular operation directly available for use by the computer programmer. This selection process is based primarily on the frequency of use of the operation, and the operational advantage gained by wiring it as an elementary operation, rather than performing it as a sequence of elementary operations. Consequently, the more complex the operation the less likely it is to be included as a basic machine operation. The second problem of writing a program in machine language is that it is just too notationally inconvenient for human use.

Higher Level Programming Languages

Although an experienced programmer is usually familiar with the machine language of the computer with which he works, he would much rather use names or other meaningful symbols to help program a given problem. In addition, he would like to have the computer carry out many of the simple bookkeeping jobs which are necessary in programming. This has been the motivating force behind the creation of all the higher level programming languages, such as FORTRAN and PL/1.

A computer is a symbol-manipulating device. Therefore, it is possible to design a special machine-language program that will take symbolic statements written in a high level language, such as FORTRAN, and convert these statements into a machine-language program that can be executed by the computer.

The initial program written by the programmer in the higher level language is called the *source program*, while the resulting machine-language program is called the *object program*. The special machine-language program that converts the source program to the object program is called a *translator*. There are many different types of translator programs and higher level languages.

Assembler Languages

The simplest improvement that can be made is to use short names, called *mnemonics*, to identify each basic computer instruction and the data terms manipulated by these instructions. For example, the instruction

$$001011010100$$

might be represented in mnemonic form as

$$ADD\ C, D$$

and correspond to the addition of the two data terms C and D. A translator program can be developed to convert a source program, written in mnemonic form, into the corresponding machine-language object program.

A program, written in mnemonic form, to carry out the computation

$$Y = A + B - (C + D)$$

might have the following form

Instruction	Mnemonic Representation	Meaning
1	*S, ADD C, D*	Form $S = C + D$
2	*R, SUB B, S*	Form $R = B - S$
3	*Y, ADD A, R*	Form $Y = A + R$
4	*HLT*	Halt calculation

A translator program can be developed to convert these mnemonic terms into their corresponding machine-language representation and carry out other simple programming tasks. Such a translator is called an *assembler* and the corresponding language is called an assembler language. If the above mnemonic source program were processed by an assembler, the resulting object program might have the following form.

$$001011010100$$
$$011001010101$$
$$001010101110$$
$$010000000000$$

The problem with an assembler language is that the set of basic operations that are represented by this language are essentially the same as those represented by the machine language. Assembler-language programs are very useful to the experienced programmer for developing special programs. However, they are not suitable for the computer user whose main interest is in using a computer to carry out a given task associated with a particular problem. Thus, in order to meet the need for a user-oriented language the concept of higher level programming languages has been developed.

Higher Level Languages

The average computer user does not have the interest, or the time, to master the details of the assembler language or machine language associated with a given computer. A *higher level language* is any language that has been designed so that the statements that make up a program written in that language closely resemble the form of the mathematical statements that are used to describe the problem under investigation. Since these statements cannot be used directly by the computer to carry out the necessary computations, a translation program, called a *compiler*, is used to analyze each source language statement and convert it into the machine-language program used by the computer to carry out the desired computation.

A large number of user-oriented languages have been developed. Among the best known are FORTRAN and ALGOL which are primarily for engineering and scientific applications; COBOL for business applications; LISP, COMIT, and SNOBOL for the processing of lists of information. Recently PL/1 has been introduced which incorporates many of the important features of the above languages.

To solve a problem of adding two numbers, a user-oriented language would use a statement such as the following:

$$Y = A + B - (C + D)$$

The compiler program would then translate this statement into a sequence of machine-language instructions of the form given in the previous examples.

5. SUMMARY

The first digital logic networks and digital computers were very cumbersome and costly relative to the information processing tasks they performed. However, with the advent of modern integrated circuit technology the prices of digital networks and computers have been reduced to the point where it is practical to use digital devices in a wide variety of information processing tasks. This has meant that anyone who wishes to effectively use these devices must fully appreciate their characteristics and limitations.

In this book we will take a comprehensive look at the various aspects of digital circuit and system design. Our approach is designed to provide the insight necessary to understand the relationships that exist between the design considerations and structure of digital devices and the way that these devices can be used. To accomplish this goal we first investigate how information can be represented in digital form. We then investigate the principles involved in logic network design and consider how these networks can be used to carry out specific information processing tasks. This background will then allow us to consider the organization of digital computers and the techniques that can be used to program these computers to carry out specific information processing tasks. Examples and home problems are then used to show how these concepts can be applied to actual digital system design problems.

Since each chapter contains several new and important concepts, the following chapter organization is used to help the reader identify and understand these concepts. At the end of each major section a set of short exercises is inserted to illustrate the important ideas of that section. The answers to many of these exercises are included in the back of the book. In addition, a set of more extensive home problems is included at the end of each chapter. These problems are of a more advanced nature and are designed to further illustrate material contained in the chapter and to relate the current material to that previously considered. The references at the end of each chapter are selected to supplement and indicate the extensions of the material contained in the chapter and home problems.

REFERENCE NOTATION

Computers and digital systems have had a tremendous impact on engineering and science. Tutorial papers relevant to the various areas of computer technology and computer science can be found in *Spectrum*, the survey and tutorial journal of the Institute of Electrical and Electronic Engineers (IEEE), *Computer*, the survey magazine of the IEEE Computer Society, *Computing Surveys*, the survey and tutorial journal of the Association for Computing Machinery (ACM), or in trade publications such as Datamation.

A history of the early development of electronic computers can be found in [4] while [1] gives a very readable overview of many of the tasks modern computers can perform. The idea of an algorithmic process is discussed in detail in [2] while Schriber [5] describes how flowcharts can be effectively used to graphically represent an algorithm. McCracken [3] illustrates how algorithms can be implemented in the FORTRAN IV programming language.

REFERENCES

1. (1966) *Information*, W. H. Freeman Co., San Francisco, Calif.

2. Booth, T. L., and Chien, Y. T. (1974), *Computing: Fundamentals and Applications*, Hamilton Division, John Wiley, New York.

3. McCracken, D. D. (1965), *A Guide to FORTRAN IV Programming*, John Wiley, New York.

4. Rosen, S. (1969), *Electronic Computers: A Historical Survey*, Computing Surveys Vol. I, No. 1, pp. 7–36, March.

5. Schriber, T. J. (1969), *Fundamentals of Flowcharting*, John Wiley, New York.

2

Representation of Information in Digital Form

In describing the properties and characteristics of physical systems, continuous functions are required since the physical quantities of interest can take on a continuum of values. When dealing with devices which process information we find that the same restrictions do not apply. In fact it has been found that discrete valued functions are often more appropriate in the representation of information.

As we have already seen in Chapter 1, many of the signals that we must deal with are already in discrete form. In other cases it is often desirable to use a discrete signal to approximate a continuous information-bearing signal in order to minimize and control the introduction of unwanted distortion and unpredictable errors that may be introduced when the information is being processed. Although there are many possible classes of discrete signals that could be used in this application, it has been found that a variable that can only take on two distinct values is the best type to use as a building block in developing a discrete signal representation of any information-bearing signal. This selection also considerably simplifies the design of the networks that are used to process this class of signal.

In this chapter we investigate the different ways that can be used to represent these digital signals and information. First we introduce the conventions that are used to describe these signals. Then we discuss how various types of numeric and nonnumeric information can be represented in digital form. Finally we consider some of the ways in which continuous information can be encoded into digital form. Throughout this discussion it is unnecessary to refer to any physical device when making any of our definitions. Thus, the results of this chapter can be applied to any system that deals with data in digital form.

2. REPRESENTATION
OF DIGITAL INFORMATION

As we deal with digital circuits and systems we find that it is necessary to be able to differentiate between digital information that is being transmitted between different parts of the system and digital information that is being stored in some manner for later use. The following discussion defines a way of describing these signals and storage units.

Signals

A typical digital network is illustrated in Figure 2-1. This network has two input signals, denoted by X and Y and one output signal Z. Each of these signals is represented by the values assigned to the variables that make up the signal.

Let us consider the input signal X represented by the r-tuple

$$[x_1, x_2, \ldots, x_r]$$

Each variable x_i is assumed to be a *binary variable* that can only assume a value of either 0 or 1. Such a variable is said to represent one *bit* of information. Because of this we see that the signal X can only assume

$$2 \cdot 2 \cdot \ldots \cdot 2 = 2^r$$

different values corresponding to the 2^r different ways that 0 and 1 can be assigned to $[x_1, \ldots, x_r]$.

As an example, let $r = 2$. Then the four possible values of the signal $X = [x_1, x_2]$ are

$$[0, 0], [0, 1], [1, 0], [1, 1]$$

The actual meaning that we associate with the values of X depends on the way X is defined. For example, suppose that we have a situation where we wish to indicate which of two doors is open at a given time. The variable x_i can be used to

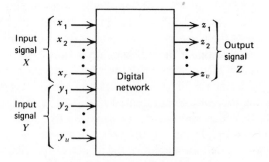

Figure 2-1. Typical digital network.

describe the condition of door i by making the following assignment of values to x_i:

$$x_i = 0 \quad \text{door } i \text{ is closed}$$
$$x_i = 1 \quad \text{door } i \text{ is open}$$

With this convention we then use the 2-tuple $[x_1, x_2]$ to represent the desired information about the two doors. Thus, if we are given the 2-tuple $[1, 0]$ we know that the first door is open and that the second door is closed. This problem is considered in greater detail in Section 3.

Registers

For our present discussion we call any device that can store digital information a *register*. Registers, in this broad sense, can take many forms but, for the current discussion, we treat them in a somewhat abstract sense. Figure 2-2 illustrates the general form of a register.

The basic storage element of a register is a *cell* which can store a value of either 0 or 1. The output of each cell has a value corresponding to the quantity stored in the cell. The contents and output of each cell remain constant until an input signal is received instructing the cell to change its contents.

A collection of cells connected together form a register. If there are n cells in the register, it is called an *n-bit register*.

The variables $y_1, y_2, \ldots, y_n$, corresponding to the content of each cell are called *state variables*. The 2^n distinct values that the n-tuple $[y_1, y_2, \ldots, y_n]$ can take on are called the *states of the register*. For example if $n = 2$ we have two state variables y_1 and y_2. The four distinct states of a two-cell register are

$$[0, 0], \ [0, 1], \ [1, 0], \ [1, 1]$$

When we talk about a register we usually indicate it by a name or a capital letter. For example, we can talk about register A or the Memory Buffer Register,

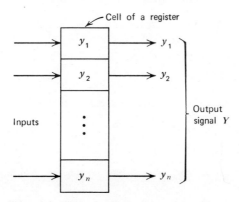

Figure 2-2. General representation of a register Y.

MBR. If Y is a register, we denote the actual contents of the register by $[Y] = [y_1, y_2, \ldots, y_n]$. In some cases we find it convenient to number the cells from left to right while in other cases the cells are numbered from right to left. The actual convention used will be evident from the material under discussion.

3. CODING OF INFORMATION

If the rather abstract representation of digital information presented in the previous section is to be useful we must have some way to attach meaning to the digital information contained in a signal or stored in a register. Thus we must now consider how information can be encoded into a digital form.

Assume that we are given a digital signal $X = [x_1, x_2, \ldots, x_r]$. This signal can carry a maximum of 2^r distinct pieces of information since there are 2^r distinct values that can be assigned to the r-tuple X. The way we assign meaning to these signals depends on the type of information with which we are dealing. Usually we find that this information can be classified as either *logical*, *symbolic*, or *numeric* information. In this section we introduce the basic methods that are used to encode these types of information. These ideas are expanded on throughout the rest of the book as we encounter specific problems where it is necessary to represent information in particular forms.

Encoding Logical Information

A considerable portion of the analytical techniques used in digital system design have evolved from the study of mathematical logic. Basically mathematical logic deals with the truth or falsity of declarative statements. In this case the variable x_i represents the ith statement in a set of r statements. For example, x_i might stand for the statement

$$x_i - \text{``The } i\text{th ball landed inside the box''}$$

This statement will either have a truth-value TRUE (the ball landed in the box) or FALSE (the ball did not land in the box).

We may represent the truth-value of a logical statement as

$$x_i = 1 \qquad \text{The } i\text{th statement is TRUE}$$
$$x_i = 0 \qquad \text{The } i\text{th statement is FALSE}$$

If we have r statements $x_1, x_2, \ldots, x_r$, then $X = [x_1, x_2, \ldots, x_r]$ represents the truth value associated with all the statements. For example if we throw five balls at a box then

$$X = [1,0,1,1,0]$$

represents the fact that balls 1, 3, and 4 landed in the box while balls 2 and 5 did not.

We will find logical statements to be very useful analytical tools in later discussions. There are, however, many other types of information that are not conveniently or efficiently represented by simple logic statements.

Encoding Symbolic Information

Symbolic information can take a variety of forms. For example, we might wish to code the alphabet into a digital form or it might be necessary to indicate the operational status of a machine performing a complex manufacturing operation in terms of a digital signal. The problem of encoding information of this type into digital form can be treated in the following general manner.

Assume that we are given a set S of k distinct quantities. Then we can set up a one-to-one relationship which associates a distinct value of the r-tuple $[x_1, x_2, \ldots, x_r]$ with each element of the set provided that

$$k \leq 2^r$$

This correspondence is not unique. In fact there are

$$(2^r)(2^r - 1)(2^r - 2) \cdots (2^r - k + 1) = \frac{(2^r)!}{(2^r - k)!}$$

distinct ways in which this correspondence can be established.

As an example, let us assume that the set S consists of the three commands given in Table 2-1. Information of this type must often be encoded into digital form for use in digital information processing systems. Two possible ways in which this information can be encoded are illustrated in this table. The first method uses a 2-bit signal since $r = 2$ is the smallest value that can be selected. The second encoding uses 3 bits, which is more than absolutely required. The advantage of using this type of encoding is that we can associate a particular symbol with a particular bit of the encoded signal. Thus if $y_1 = 1$ we know that this indicates the addition operation, while $y_2 = 1$ indicates subtraction and $y_3 = 1$ indicates multiplication.

Table 2-1   Encoded Symbolic Information

Symbolic Information	Encoding Using $[x_1, x_2]$	Encoding Using $[y_1, y_2, y_3]$
+	[0, 0]	[1, 0, 0]
−	[0, 1]	[0, 1, 0]
*	[1, 0]	[0, 0, 1]

The above discussion implicitly assumed that the number of bits necessary to represent a given set of information could be selected arbitrarily. There are many cases where this is not true. For example, the memory of a digital computer can be considered as being made up of a large number of registers with a fixed number of bits. Each register is said to form one *word* of memory and the number of bits in the register is said to be the *word size*. Thus, if someone says that a given computer has a memory capacity of 4096 16-bit words, you know that the computer's memory has 4096 individual registers that make up its memory and that each register has 16-bits. Thus, if information is to be stored in a register of prespecified size, it becomes necessary to define an economical way in which to encode this information.

Standard binary codes have been developed to represent the alphabetic, numeric, and special symbols found in digital systems. The two most common codes are

EBCDIC—Extended Binary Coded Decimal Interchange Code

ASCII—American Standard Code for Information Interchange

The EBCDIC code uses 8 bits to represent each symbol while the ASCII code comes in two forms. The standard ASCII code is a 7-bit code. However an 8-bit modified ASCII code is used with the teletypes found on many small computers. In this modified code the leftmost bit is always 1. This indicates that the next 7 bits form the code word. Appendix 1 gives these codes. There are many other codes that have been developed to code symbolic information but they are used to a lesser extent in modern computer systems.

To illustrate how symbolic information is encoded, consider the following sequence of symbols:

$$\text{ADD} \sqcup 1\emptyset \sqcup \text{TO} \sqcup 6.$$

In this sequence the special symbol $\sqcup$ is used to indicate a space and the period "." is used as an end marker to indicate the end of the symbol sequence.

If we were dealing only with the 26 letters A through Z, the space symbol $\sqcup$, the 10-decimal integers $\emptyset$ through 9, and the end marker ".", then we would have a symbol set of $26 + 1 + 10 + 1 = 38$ elements. This would mean that we would need at least 6 bits to store each character.

However let us assume that we wish to store this symbol sequence in a memory that is made up of 16-bit words and that we wish to use the modified ASCII code described in Appendix 1 to represent each symbol. Since each symbol is represented by an 8-bit code, we see that we can "pack" two 8-bit characters into each 16-bit memory word. The way the above 12-symbol sequence is packed into the memory registers is illustrated in Figure 2-3. The following digital encoding is used to

	First Stored Character								Second Stored Character							
Memory Register 1	1	1	0	0	0	0	0	1	1	1	0	0	0	1	0	0
Memory Register 2	1	1	0	0	0	1	0	0	1	0	1	0	0	0	0	0
Memory Register 3	1	0	1	1	0	0	0	1	1	0	1	1	0	0	0	0
Memory Register 4	1	0	1	0	0	0	0	0	1	1	0	1	0	1	0	0
Memory Register 5	1	1	0	0	1	1	1	1	1	0	1	0	0	0	0	0
Memory Register 6	1	0	1	1	0	1	1	0	1	0	1	0	1	1	1	0

Figure 2-3. Storage of a sequence of symbols.

represent the characters that make up this sequence. The ASCII code for the characters that make up the sequence ADD ⌴ 1∅ ⌴ TO ⌴ 6. are as follows:

Letters		Numbers		Special Characters	
A	11000001	∅	10110000	⌴	10100000
D	11000100	1	10110001	.	10101110
O	11001111	6	10110110		
T	11010100				

Symbolic information is so common in digital systems that the number of bits used to represent a single symbol is called a *byte*. Common usage usually inplies that one byte is 8-bits. However, in a few cases a byte may be taken as 6-bits.

If we wish, we could continue this discussion by considering many of the other techniques that are used to represent symbolic information in digital form. However, many of these techniques are presented in later discussions in a much more meaningful context. Thus, we now turn to the special but very important problem of representing numerical information in digital form.

Number Systems

The problem of representing numerical information in digital form is of central importance in the design and use of digital devices and computers. The following discussion provides a brief description of the various number systems that we encounter in this book, the relationship between these number systems, and the methods of encoding them into digital form.

Decimal numbers are so common to our culture that when we see a symbol such as 632.45 we immediately feel that we understand its numerical meaning. This reaction is so common that we forget that each digit of a decimal number has a place value. Thus 632.45 is really a shorthand way of expressing the number

$$N_{10} = 6(10)^2 + 3(10)^1 + 2(10)^0 + 4(10)^{-1} + 5(10)^{-2} = 632.45_{10}$$

A decimal number is said to be expressed in terms of the base 10 since each digit is multiplied by an appropriate power of 10. The number forming the base of a number system is called the *radix* of the system. When it is important to indicate the radix of a number system we can include it as a subscript. Thus N_{10} indicates that the number N is expressed in the base 10 number system.

The use of 10 as a radix for our number system probably occurred as a natural consequence of the fact that man has 10 fingers. However, as discussed in reference [2], there is no reason why another number could not be used as the base for a number system. In general any number N can be represented in the base r number system as

$$N_r = a_{n-1}(r)^{n-1} + \cdots + a_1(r) + a_0(r)^0 + a_{-1}(r)^{-1} + \cdots + a_{-m}(r)^{-m}$$

If r is selected as the radix then the digits a_i of the number take on integer values between 0 and $r - 1$. Since it is too cumbersome to write a number in the above form, we use the shorthand notation

$$N_r = (a_{n-1}a_{n-2} \cdots a_1 a_0 . a_{-1} \cdots a_{-m})_r$$

to indicate that the number is expressed in terms of the base r.

The number N_r is divided into two parts by the *radix point* that appears between a_0 and a_{-1}. The terms to the right of the radix point represent the *fractional* part of the number while the terms to the left represent the *integer* portion of the number. In our later discussions we often need to treat the integer part of a number differently from the fractional part.

Some of the common radices used in the digital area are given in Table 2-2.

Table 2-2   Summary of Common Number Systems

Radix	Name of Number System	Basic Digits Used in System[a]
2	Binary	0,1
3	Ternary	0,1,2
8	Octal	0,1,2,3,4,5,6,7
10	Decimal	0,1,2,3,4,5,6,7,8,9
16	Hexadecimal	0,1,2,3,4,5,6,7,8,9,A,B,C,D,E,F

[a] The hexadecimal system requires 16 distinct symbols to represent digits. The convention of using the first six letters of the alphabet plus the 10 decimal digits has become common usage.

Suppose that one is given the marks shown below and we wish to indicate the number of marks present.

卌 卌 卌 卌 卌 ||||

This number, writen in the various number systems, would be

$$N_2 = 11101_2 \qquad N_{10} = 29_{10}$$
$$N_3 = 1002_3 \qquad N_{16} = 1D_{16}$$
$$N_8 = 35_8$$

Range of a Number

When dealing with the base r number system, we find that the values of m and n determine the range of values which can be represented by N_r. The integer portion of N_r will have an equivalent decimal value that falls between 0 and $r^n - 1$. Every integer in this interval can be represented exactly by a base r number with n or fewer digits. Thus if we make n large enough, any particular integer can be represented exactly in any given base r number system.

We have a more difficult problem when dealing with the fractional part of a number. A fraction represents a number that falls in the open interval $(0, 1)$. Since this interval represents a continuum of values, there are an uncountable infinite number of points in this interval. However, since m is a finite value, we can only represent $2^m - 1$ fractions in this interval. Thus, as shown in Figure 2-4, there are gaps between each of the fractional points that can be represented. The size of this gap Δ (expressed in base 10 notation) is

$$\Delta_{10} = \left(\frac{1}{r}\right)^m$$

and is called the *resolution interval*. Note that the resolution interval will have a different value for each base.

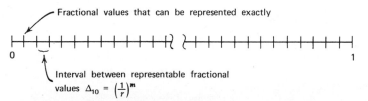

Figure 2-4. Graphical illustration of the finite number of fractional values that can be represented by an m-digit fraction.

If we wish to represent a fraction that does not correspond to one of the allowed values, we must approximate the fraction by the closest allowed value. There are two standard ways of doing this: truncation and rounding.

Assume that we have a fraction of the form

$$F_r = .a_{-1}a_{-2}a_{-3} \cdots a_{-m}a_{-(m+1)} \cdots a_{-(m+u)}$$

and we must represent this fraction by using only m digits. This fraction is said to be *truncated* if we simply drop all the digits to the right of a_{-m}. For example, in a base 10 system $F_{10} = .18763$ would be truncated to $.187$ if $m = 3$. The maximum error introduced by truncation will always be less than the resolution interval. Thus the decimal value of the truncation error ε_T in a base r system is bounded by

$$\varepsilon_T < \left(\frac{1}{r}\right)^m$$

Figure 2-5a illustrates the form that the truncation error takes.

Another way to approximate a fraction is to select the allowed fraction closest to the desired value as the one to represent that variable. This process is called

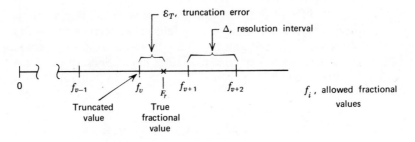

(*a*) Illustration of Truncation Error

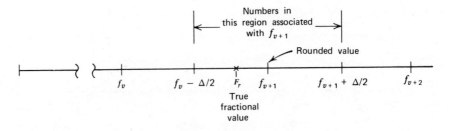

(*b*) Illustration of Rounding Error

Figure 2-5. Errors introduced by uses of finite length fractions.

rounding. Assume that F_r falls between the fractional values f_v and f_{v+1}. Then

$$f_v \text{ approximates } F_r$$

if

$$(F_r - f_v) \leq \frac{\Delta}{2}$$

$$f_{v+1} \text{ approximates } F_r$$

if

$$(F_r - f_v) > \frac{\Delta}{2}$$

The decimal value of the magnitude of the error ε_R in a base r system is bounded by

$$\varepsilon_R \leq \frac{1}{2}\left(\frac{1}{r}\right)^m$$

To illustrate rounding, assume a base 10 system with $m = 3$ and that $F_{10} = .18763$. Then

$$\frac{\Delta}{2} = \frac{1}{2}\left(\frac{1}{10}\right)^3 = .0005$$

Thus since

$$f_v = .187$$
$$f_{v+1} = .188$$

therefore

$$(F_r - f_v) = .00063 > .0005$$

Thus F_r is approximated by the rounded value of .188. Figure 2-5*b* illustrates the rounding process.

Now that we have a general idea of the different number systems that can be used, our next task is to consider how we can convert numbers from one system to another.

An Application of Binary, Octal, and Hexadecimal Numbers

Binary numbers fit naturally into discussions of digital systems since we describe signals and contents of registers by r-tuples $[x_1, x_2, \ldots, x_r]$ of binary-valued variables. Thus, it is often convenient to think of the contents of a register or the value of a signal as a binary integer even if the actual information represented by the r-tuple has some other meaning.

For example if the contents of a register are represented by $[1,0,1,1,0,1,0,1,0]$, it is just as easy to represent this same information as the binary number $N_2 = 101101010$.

The one problem that we have with binary numbers is that they tend to be long and cumbersome to remember. We often find it convenient to use an octal or a hexadecimal number to represent binary information since there is a very easy technique that can be used to convert from one system to the other.

Table 2-3a gives the relationship between the octal digits and their corresponding binary representation and Table 2-3b gives the same correspondence between hexadecimal digits and their binary representation.

It is a very easy process to convert a number from a binary to an octal representation. Starting at the radix point we separately divide the integer portion and the

Table 2-3

(a) Octal-Binary Equivalence		(b) Hexadecimal-Binary Equivalence	
Octal Digit	Equivalent Binary Representation	Hexadecimal Digit	Equivalent Binary Representation
0	000	0	0000
1	001	1	0001
2	010	2	0010
3	011	3	0011
4	100	4	0100
5	101	5	0101
6	110	6	0110
7	111	7	0111
		8	1000
		9	1001
		A (10)	1010
		B (11)	1011
		C (12)	1100
		D (13)	1101
		E (14)	1110
		F (15)	1111

fractional portion of the binary number into groups of three digits and then combine each group of binary digits into a single octal number. The following example illustrates this process.

$$
\begin{array}{c c c c c c c l}
** & 1010111101.11010 & & * & & \text{binary number} \\
001 & 010 & 111 & 101 & . & 110 & 100 & \text{groups of 3 digits} \\
1 & 2 & 7 & 5 & . & 6 & 4 & \text{octal digit equivalent}
\end{array}
$$

$$1010111101.11010_2 = 1275.64_8$$

* Note the zeros added to fill out groups of three binary digits.

To go in the opposite direction we just reverse the process. For each octal digit we write the corresponding 3-digit binary number and then combine all the resulting binary digits into a single binary number. This process is illustrated by the following example.

$$
\begin{array}{c c c c c c l}
1 & 5 & 4 & . & 6 & 3 & \text{octal number} \\
001 & 101 & 100 & . & 110 & 011 & \text{3-digit binary representation}
\end{array}
$$

$$154.63_8 = 1101100.110011_2$$

With a little practice the conversion between binary and octal numbers can be carried out by inspection. The reason behind this conversion process can easily be seen by considering the following steps that we are actually carrying out when we follow this conversion process.

$$
\begin{aligned}
N_2 = 101010.101_2 &= 1(2)^5 + 0(2)^4 + 1(2)^3 + 0(2)^2 + 1(2) + 0(2)^0 \\
&\quad + 1(2)^{-1} + 0(2)^{-2} + 1(2)^{-3} \\
&= [1(2)^2 + 0(2) + 1(2)^0](2)^3 + [0(2)^2 + 1(2) + 0(2)^0] \\
&\quad + [1(2)^2 + 0(2) + 1(2)^0](2)^{-3} \\
&= 5(8)^1 + 2(8)^0 + 5(8)^{-1} = 52.5_8
\end{aligned}
$$

The conversion of a number from binary to hexadecimal form and vice versa is carried out in exactly the same manner except that we form groups of four binary digits rather than groups of three. The following examples illustrate this conversion process. First consider the binary to hexadecimal conversion process.

$$
\begin{array}{c c c c c l}
 & 101011 & . & 101 & & \text{binary number} \\
0010 & 1011 & . & 1010 & & \text{groups of 4 digits} \\
2 & B & . & A & & \text{hexadecimal digit equivalent}
\end{array}
$$

$$101011.101_2 = 2B.A_{16}$$

Next consider the hexadecimal to binary conversion process.

5	A	.	6	hexadecimal number
0101	1010	.	0110	4-digit binary representation
	1011010	.	011	binary equivalent

$$5A.6_{16} = 1011010.011_2$$

The reason the conversion process between binary, octal, and hexadecimal numbers is so easy is that the radix of each number system is a power of 2. The problem of converting between one of these systems and the decimal system requires a little additional work but it is also easily accomplished.

Binary, Octal, and Hexadecimal to Decimal Conversion

The conversion of a binary, octal, or hexadecimal number to a decimal number is not difficult. For a binary number we simply write the expression for the binary number in powers of 2 notation and then expand and collect these terms to obtain the corresponding decimal number. For example,

$$11010.101_2 = 1(2)^4 + 1(2)^3 + 0(2)^2 + 1(2)^1 + 0(2)^0 + 1(2)^{-1} + 0(2)^{-2} + 1(2)^{-3}$$
$$= 16 + 8 + 2 + .5 + .125 = 26.625_{10}$$

We use a similar process for octal to decimal conversion except that we use the radix 8 instead of 2. To illustrate, consider the following example.

$$613.24_8 = 6(8)^2 + 1(8) + 3(8)^0 + 2(8)^{-1} + 4(8)^{-2}$$
$$= 384 + 8 + 3 + .25 + .0625$$
$$= 395.3125_{10}$$

Similarly the conversion from a hexadecimal to a decimal number can be accomplished as illustrated in the following example. Note that it is necessary to convert the digits A through F to their corresponding decimal values of 10 through 15.

$$5A . E_{16} = 5(16) + A(16)^0 + E(16)^{-1}$$
$$= 5(16) + 10(16)^0 + 14(16)^{-1}$$
$$= 80 + 10 + .875 = 90.875_{10}$$

Decimal to Binary, Octal, or Hexadecimal Conversion

The conversion of a decimal number to a binary, octal, or hexadecimal form can also be handled in a straightforward manner. First, we note that any decimal number can be written

$$N_{10} = \langle \text{integer part} \rangle_{10} . \langle \text{fractional part} \rangle_{10}$$

In the conversion process we first convert the $\langle$integer part$\rangle_{10}$ to $\langle$integer part$\rangle_r$ and then we convert $\langle$fractional part$\rangle_{10}$ to $\langle$fractional part$\rangle_r$. These conversions are carried out separately because two different techniques must be employed. After the integer and fractional parts are determined, we can write

$$N_r = \langle \text{integer part} \rangle_r \, . \, \langle \text{fractional part} \rangle_r$$

We will consider the complete details of the conversion from decimal to binary numbers. The extension of the conversion technique to the other number systems will then be illustrated by an example.

Suppose the decimal number is given by

$$N_{10} = d_{n-1}d_{n-2} \cdots d_0 \, . \, d_{-1}d_{-2} \cdots d_{-m} = I_{10} \, . \, F_{10}$$

and we wish to convert it to the binary number

$$N_2 = b_{u-1}b_{u-2} \cdots b_0 \, . \, b_{-1}b_{-2} \cdots b_{-v} = I_2 \, . \, F_2$$

First, we convert the integer part of the decimal number $I_{10} = d_{n-1}d_{n-2} \cdots d_0$ to the corresponding integer part of the binary number $I_2 = b_{u-1}b_{u-2} \cdots b_0$. This is accomplished by observing that

$$I_{10} = b_{u-1}(2)^{u-1} + b_{u-2}(2)^{u-2} + \cdots + b_1 2 + b_0$$

If we divide I_{10} by 2 we find that we obtain an integer quotient Q_1 and a remainder b_0. That is

$$I_{10} = 2Q_1 + b_0$$

where

$$Q_1 = b_{u-1}(2)^{u-2} + b_{u-2}(2)^{u-3} + \cdots + b_1(2)^0$$

Next we see that if we divide Q_1 by 2 we obtain an integer quotient Q_2 and a remainder b_1. That is

$$Q_1 = 2Q_2 + b_1$$

where

$$Q_2 = b_{u-1}(2)^{u-3} + b_{u-2}(2)^{u-4} + \cdots + b_2(2)^0$$

From this we see that we can continue this process until a value of n is reached such that $Q_n = 0$. The remainder terms generated by this process are then read off as the terms of the binary integer that is equivalent to the original decimal integer.

To illustrate this process let $I_{10} = 25$. Then

$$
\begin{array}{ll}
I_{10} = 2(12) + 1 & Q_1 = 12,\ b_0 = 1 \\
Q_1 = 2(6) + 0 & Q_2 = 6,\ b_1 = 0 \\
Q_2 = 2(3) + 0 & Q_3 = 3,\ b_2 = 0 \\
Q_3 = 2(1) + 1 & Q_4 = 1,\ b_3 = 1 \\
Q_4 = 2(0) + 1 & Q_5 = 0,\ b_4 = 1
\end{array}
$$

From this result we have

$$I_{10} = 25 \text{ is equivalent to } I_2 = 11001$$

This process can easily be carried out in the following form:

Thus

$$I_2 = b_4 b_3 b_2 b_1 b_0 = 11001$$

The second step is to convert the fractional part of the decimal number

$$F_{10} = d_{-1} d_{-2} \cdots d_{-m}$$

to the corresponding fractional part of the binary number,

$$F_2 = b_{-1} b_{-2} \cdots b_{-v}$$

There is one difficulty associated with the conversion of fractions that must be pointed out. We often find that a decimal fraction with a finite number of digits will produce a corresponding binary fraction that contains an infinite number of terms. This occurs because the resolution interval is different for binary and decimal numbers. In this situation we must then arbitrarily select a value for the maximum number, v, of digits that we will retain in our binary fraction.

The conversion process is accomplished by observing that

$$F_{10} = b_{-1}2^{-1} + b_{-2}2^{-2} + \cdots + b_{-v}2^{-v} + \cdots$$

Thus if we multiply F_{10} by 2 we have

$$2F_{10} = b_{-1} + b_{-2}2^{-1} + \cdots + b_{-v}2^{-v+1} + \cdots = b_{-1} + C_1$$

where $C_1 < 1$ and b_{-1} is either 1 or 0. Next we multiply C_1 by 2 to obtain

$$2C_1 = b_{-2} + b_{-3}2^{-1} + \cdots + b_{-v}2^{-v+2} + \cdots = b_{-2} + C_2$$

where $C_2 < 1$ and b_{-2} is either 0 or 1. Continuing in this way we finally obtain

$$2C_{v-1} = b_{-v} + C_v$$

where $2^{-v}C_v \le \varepsilon$ and ε is the largest error that we are willing to tolerate in our conversion process. If $C_v = 0$ for some value of v then the conversion is exact. Otherwise the resulting binary fraction is an approximation, to within ε, of the original decimal fraction. The two following examples illustrate both situations.

Exact Conversion	*Approximate Conversion*
	$\varepsilon_{10} = .001$
$F_{10} = .125$	$F_{10} = .3$
$2(.125) = 0 + .250$	$2(.3) = 0 + .6$
$2(.25) = 0 + .5$	$2(.6) = 1 + .2$
$2(.5) = 1 + .0$	$2(.2) = 0 + .4$
$F_2 = .001$	$2(.4) = 0 + .8$
	$2(.8) = 1 + .6$
	$2(.6) = 1 + .2$
	$2(.2) = 0 + .4$
	$2(.4) = 0 + .8$
	$2(.8) = 1 + .6 \quad 2^{-9}(.6) > .001$
	$2(.6) = 1 + .2 \quad 2^{-10}(.2) < .001$
	$F_2 \cong .0100110011$

In many situations it is necessary to specify a value of v that will be used independent of the number being converted. For this case we have

$$\text{(conversion error)} \le 2^{-v}$$

Now that we have an understanding of the conversion process, the following examples illustrate how we can find the octal or hexadecimal equivalent of a decimal number. The first two examples deal with octal conversion.

Exact Conversion   *Approximate Conversion*

$$\varepsilon_{10} = .001$$

$$F_{10} = 25.125 \qquad\qquad F_{10} = 25.3$$

Integer Part	*Fractional Part*	*Integer Part*	*Fractional Part*
8 ⌊25	(8)(.125) = 1 + .0	8 ⌊25	8(.3) = 2 + .4
8 ⌊ 3 1		8 ⌊ 3 1	8(.4) = 3 + .2
0 3		0 3	8(.2) = 1 + .6
			8(.6) = 4 + .8

$$F_8 = 31.1_8 \qquad\qquad F_8 \cong 31.2314_8$$

The next two examples deal with the hexadecimal conversion process.

Exact Conversion   *Approximate Conversion*

$$\varepsilon = .001$$

$$F_{10} = 25.125 \qquad\qquad F_{10} = 25.3$$

Integer Part	*Fractional Part*	*Integer Part*	*Fractional Part*
16 ⌊25	(16)(.125) = 2 + 0	16 ⌊25	(16)(.3) = 4 + .8
16 ⌊ 1 9		16 ⌊ 1 9	(16)(.8) = 12 + .8
0 1		0 1	(16)(.8) = 12 + .8

$$F_{16} = 19.2_{16} \qquad\qquad F_{16} \cong 19.4CC_{16}$$

Symbolic Encoding of Numerical Information

Just as with symbolic information, there are a variety of ways in which numeric information can be encoded into digital form. The simplest method is to take a given number and convert it to its equivalent binary value. This binary number is then taken as the encoded digital value of the given number. However, there are certain restrictions and conventions that must be kept in mind.

If a register contains r cells, then we can only deal with binary numbers that have a maximum of r binary digits. This means that any positive decimal integer between 0 and $2^r - 1$ can be represented in an r-bit register. For example, if a 3-bit register contained [0, 1, 0] then we say that the binary number 010 corresponding to 2_{10} is contained in this register.

When dealing with general binary numbers, we usually do not try to encode the location of the binary point. Instead we assume that the person designing the

Table 2-4 Signed-Magnitude Binary Numbers and Decimal Equivalent

Binary	Decimal
000	$+0$
001	$+1$
010	$+2$
011	$+3$
100	-0
101	-1
110	-2
111	-3

system in which the number appears also keeps track of where the binary point should be placed and makes appropriate allowance for this whenever the encoded numeric information is used. Thus the binary numbers .101, 1.01, 10.1 and 101. are all encoded in a 3-bit register as $[1, 0, 1]$.

If negative, as well as positive, numbers must be encoded we must use one bit of the register to indicate the sign of the number. Thus, if we have an r-bit register, the first bit can be used as a *sign bit* and the other r-1 bits can be used to encode the value of the magnitude of the number. A 1 in the first bit indicates a negative number and a 0 in this position indicates a positive number. Such a representation is called a *signed-magnitude* representation. Table 2-4 shows the relationship between the signed-magnitude binary numbers and the decimal numbers for $r = 3$.

Generalizing on the example presented in Table 2-4 we see that an r-cell register can represent any binary number between $\pm(2^{r-1} - 1)$. In addition, we note that we have a $+0$ and a -0.

There are also other methods of representing negative numbers. However, we will postpone our discussion of these methods until Chapter 4 where we discuss binary arithmetic.

Encoding Decimal Numbers

In the above section we saw that the content of a register could be treated as a binary number. However, we live in a decimal world and it is often desirable to retain the decimal character of a number even after it is encoded into digital form. To do this, various coding schemes have been developed. In this section we briefly consider typical codes that have been developed for this purpose.

To encode a decimal digit into a binary form it is necessary to use a minimum of four binary bits. Thus, if we wish to encode a decimal number with u decimal digits and still retain the identity of each digit, we must use a register that has at least $4u$-bits. These bits would be ordered as follows:

$$
\overbrace{[x_{1,1}, x_{1,2}, x_{1,3}, x_{1,4},}^{\substack{\text{first decimal} \\ \text{digit}}} \overbrace{x_{2,1}, x_{2,2}, x_{2,3}, x_{2,4},}^{\substack{\text{second decimal} \\ \text{digit}}} \ldots, \overbrace{x_{u,1}, x_{u,2}, x_{u,3}, x_{u,4}]}^{\substack{u\text{th decimal} \\ \text{digit}}}
$$

From our previous discussion we know that there are

$$
\frac{2^4!}{(2^4 - 10)!} \cong 2.9 \times 10^{10}
$$

possible ways that the 10 decimal digits can be encoded as a digital 4-tuple.

The choice of a code is important and influences the design of any digital system that must operate on the numbers represented in the code. Some of the important parameters that must be considered are: ease of performing arithmetic operations, economy of storage space, economy of logic circuitry, error detection and correction, and simplicity of use. These considerations are discussed in reference [4] listed at the end of this chapter. For this discussion we will limit ourselves to two representative coding schemes.

Weighted Codes

In a weighted code each bit of the 4-tuple $[x_1, x_2, x_3, x_4]$ is assigned a decimal value w_1, w_2, w_3, w_4 called a *weight*. The decimal number represented by a particular 4-tuple is then given by

$$
N = \sum_{i=1}^{4} w_i x_i
$$

One of the commonest weighted codes is the *Binary Coded Decimal* (BCD) or 8-4-2-1 code. The decimal digits in this code are represented by their 4-digit binary equivalent. This code is given in Table 2-5.

Using this table we can find the BCD representation of any decimal number. For example the BCD representation of $N = 7954$ is

$$
\begin{array}{cccc}
7 & 9 & 5 & 4 \\
0111 & 1001 & 0101 & 0100 = 0111100101010100
\end{array}
$$

There are more than 80 possible weighted codes, 17 of which have all positive weights. Two other typical weighted codes are given in Table 2-6.

Table 2-5 BCD Code Representation of Decimal Digits

Decimal Digit	Weight	BCD Representation			
		8	4	2	1
0		0	0	0	0
1		0	0	0	1
2		0	0	1	0
3		0	0	1	1
4		0	1	0	0
5		0	1	0	1
6		0	1	1	0
7		0	1	1	1
8		1	0	0	0
9		1	0	0	1

Table 2-6 Two Typical Weighted Codes

Decimal Digit	Weight	Code 1				Code 2			
		2	4	2	1	7	4	-2	-1
0		0	0	0	0	0	0	0	0
1		0	0	0	1	0	1	1	1
2		0	0	1	0	0	1	1	0
3		0	0	1	1	0	1	0	1
4		0	1	0	0	0	1	0	0
5		1	0	1	1	1	0	1	0
6		1	1	0	0	1	0	0	1
7		1	1	0	1	1	0	0	0
8		1	1	1	0	1	1	1	1
9		1	1	1	1	1	1	1	0

Unweighted Codes

Sometimes it is desirable, for particular design reasons, to use an unweighted encoding of the decimal numbers. One of the best known unweighted codes is the *excess* 3 code. In this code the decimal digit d is represented by the 4-bit binary

Table 2-7   Three Unweighted Codes

| (a) Excess 3 Code | | (b) | | (c) BCD With Even Parity | |
Decimal Digit	Coded Representation	Decimal Digit	Coded Representation	Decimal Digit	Code 8421P
0	0011	0	0001	0	00000
1	0100	1	0010	1	00011
2	0101	2	0011	2	00101
3	0110	3	0100	3	00110
4	0111	4	0101	4	01001
5	1000	5	0110	5	01010
6	1001	6	1000	6	01100
7	1010	7	1001	7	01111
8	1011	8	1010	8	10001
9	1100	9	1100	9	10010

number corresponding to $d + 3$. This code has the property that every code group has at least a single 1. Table 2-7a illustrates this code.

A second example of an unweighted code is given in Table 2-7b. This code has been designed so that no code group has less than one 1 or more than two 1's. This feature is useful since there is a minimal fluctuation in the 0 and 1 values as the encoded variable changes value.

There are many codes that use more than 4 bits to represent a binary number. One of the simplest is the 5-bit even parity code. A fifth bit is introduced that is set so that the total number of 1's in the representation is even.

For example, a BCD encoding with even parity is shown in Table 2-7c. The leftmost 4 bits represent a standard BCD encoding, and the rightmost bit is the parity bit. Thus the BCD representation

$$0101 \quad \text{becomes} \quad 01010$$

since there are already an even number of 1's while

$$0111 \quad \text{becomes} \quad 01111$$

since the initial encoding has an odd number of 1's.

Reflected Numbers and the Gray Code

One of the main problems in a number system using positional notation is that, when going from one number to the next, more than one digit position may change at the same time. For example, when 0111_2 advances to 1000_2, four digits must change simultaneously. This can cause trouble in systems where we are trying to read information, such as the angle or the position of a platform, into a digital system. To illustrate this idea, let us assume that we must read the position of a shaft using a BCD mechanical encoder as shown in Figure 2-6a. As we pass from the 5 to the 6 region we note that the code goes from 0101 to 0110. However, the sensor that we use to measure the coded signal may have problems in the transition region and it is entirely possible that we might read out some erroneous combination such as 0111 or 0100 while we are going from region 5 to region 6. The coding arrangement shown in Figure 2-6b gets around this problem by only allowing one digit change as we go from region to region. Thus, as we go from region 5 to region 6 the code goes from 0111 to 0101 without any possible erroneous outputs.

The above example illustrates the main feature of a reflected number system. In a reflected number system the coding is set up so that only one digit can change as we go from N to $N + 1$. The way that this is accomplished can be understood if we compare the reflected decimal and binary number systems given in Table 2-8b to the conventional decimal and binary number systems given in Table 2-8a.

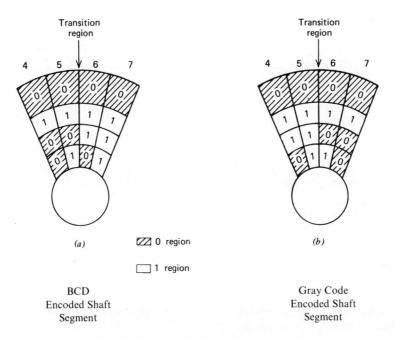

BCD
Encoded Shaft
Segment

Gray Code
Encoded Shaft
Segment

Figure 2-6. Two methods of encoding shaft position.

Table 2-8   Conventional and Reflected
                                                    Decimal and Binary Number Systems

(a) Conventional Number Systems		(b) Reflected Number Systems		
Decimal	Binary	Decimal Value	Reflected Decimal	Reflected Binary
0	0	0	0	0
1	1	1	1	1
2	10	2	2	11
3	11	3	3	10
4	100	4	4	110
5	101	5	5	111
6	110	6	6	101
7	111	7	7	100
8	1000	8	8	1100
9	1001	9	9	1101
10	1010	10	19	1111
11	1011	11	18	1110
12	1100	12	17	1010
13	1101	13	16	1011
14	1110	14	15	1001
15	1111	15	14	1000
16	10000	16	13	11000

Examining these tables we note that in the conventional number systems each column systematically advances through the ordered sequence of symbols to the last symbol and then abruptly returns to the symbol at the head of the list. On the other hand, the reflected number system advances each column systematically through the list of ordered symbols until the end of the list is reached. At that point the column then retreats backward through the sequence of symbols rather than snapping back to the head of the list. The binary reflected number system is often called a *gray code*.

The problem of converting a gray coded number to a regular binary number and vice versa can be handled by the following algorithm. Assume that the regular binary number is represented as $A_n A_{n-1} \cdots A_1$ and the gray coded number is represented as $a_n a_{n-1} \cdots a_1$. Then

1. To find a_k, add modulo 2 (i.e., disregard the carry) the digits A_k and A_{k+1}. Notice that a_n always equals A_n.
2. To find A_k add a_k through a_n, divide by 2, and the remainder is A_k.

To illustate this conversion technique, let

$$A_5 A_4 A_3 A_2 A_1 = 10110$$

$$a_5 = A_5 = 1$$
$$a_4 = A_5 + A_4 = 1 + 0 = 1$$
$$a_3 = A_4 + A_3 = 0 + 1 = 1$$
$$a_2 = A_3 + A_2 = 1 + 1 = 0 + \text{carry } 1 = 0$$
$$a_1 = A_2 + A_1 = 1 + 0 = 1$$

Thus $a_5 a_4 a_3 a_2 a_1 = 11101$

Next let

$$a_5 a_4 a_3 a_2 a_1 = 11010$$

Then

$$A_5 = \frac{a_5}{2} = \frac{1}{2} = 0 + \text{remainder of } 1$$

$$A_4 = \frac{a_5 + a_4}{2} = \frac{2}{2} = 1 + \text{remainder of } 0$$

$$A_3 = \frac{a_5 + a_4 + a_3}{2} = \frac{2}{2} = 1 + \text{remainder of } 0$$

$$A_2 = \frac{a_5 + a_4 + a_3 + a_2}{2} = \frac{3}{2} = 1 + \text{remainder of } 1$$

$$A_1 = \frac{a_5 + a_4 + a_3 + a_2 + a_1}{2} = \frac{3}{2} = 1 + \text{remainder of } 1$$

Thus $A_5 A_4 A_3 A_2 A_1 = 10011$

Floating Point Numbers

Up to this point we have been working with numbers that used a decimal or binary point to separate the integer part of the number from its fractional part. This type of notation, which is called *fixed point notation*, requires that all of the digits that make up the number be written down. When the number of digits or bits needed to represent the number is small, this does not present any problem. However, there are a number of situations where this is an impractical process.

In most scientific applications, it is only necessary to retain a fixed number of significant digits in a calculation. For example, we use 3×10^8 rather than 300,000,000 to represent the speed of light and 9.107×10^{-31} rather than a 9 preceded by 31 zeros to represent the mass of an electron in kilograms. Numbers represented in this form are said to be represented in *floating point* or *scientific notation*. Since floating point notation is in common usage, the following discussion summarizes the properties of binary floating point numbers and indicates how they may be stored in one or more registers.

Floating Point Binary Numbers

In digital systems and computers binary floating point numbers are usually represented as

$$.m_{-1}m_{-2}\cdots m_{-r}2^{\pm e_{k-1}e_{k-2}\cdots e_0} = M2^{\pm E}$$

where M is called the *mantissa* and E is the *exponent* of the number. When dealing with binary numbers both M and E will be represented in binary form.

The first term, m_{-1}, of the mantissa M is always adjusted to be 1. Thus M is a binary fraction with a decimal value in the following range

$$\tfrac{1}{2} \le M_{10} < 1$$

The exponent E is a binary integer that falls in the region $\pm(2^k - 1)_{10}$. This number indicates the number of positions that the binary point should be shifted right $(+E)$ or left $(-E)$ to convert the number to fixed point form.

In digital systems the number E is represented in binary form. However, since most people are more at home working with decimal numbers, E is often given in its decimal form. This method of representation is particularly useful in going back and forth from fixed point to floating point notation. For our discussion E is assumed to be a binary number unless it is specifically indicated as a decimal number.

Some typical binary floating point numbers are

$$.110101\ 2^{1011} = .110101\ 2^{(11_{10})} = 11010100000.$$
$$.1101\ 2^{-101} = .1101\ 2^{-(5_{10})} = .000001101$$

If a binary floating point number is to be stored in a single register then $r + k + 2$ bits are required. This follows since r-bits will be required to represent the magnitude of the mantissa, k-bits will be required to represent the magnitude of the exponent, and 2-bits will be required to represent the signs of these two quantities. Figure 2-7a shows how the information might be organized in a single register.

In other applications two registers are used to represent a binary floating point number. A $(r + 1)$-bit register is used to hold the mantissa and a $(k + 1)$-bit register is used to hold the exponent. Figure 2-7b illustrates this organization.

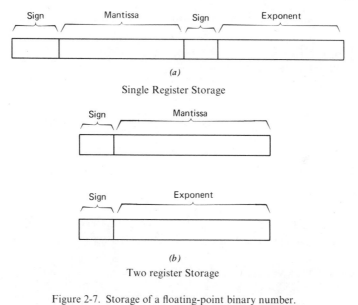

(a)

Single Register Storage

(b)

Two register Storage

Figure 2-7. Storage of a floating-point binary number.

EXERCISES

1. A computer has a 3-bit instruction register that must indicate which one of the five following instructions is currently being executed by the computer. Give a possible coding of this instruction set.
   Instructions
   Add, Multiply, Subtract, Divide, Clear

2. Encode the following numbers into binary form:

$$14.62_8, \ 123.61_{10}, \ A1B.F12_{16}$$

3. Find the BCD representation of 145.64_{10}

4. Convert the following decimal numbers to their equivalent octal and hexa-decimal representation:

$$14.65_{10}, \ 1568.721_{10}$$

5. Find the gray code representation of the following binary numbers:

$$10110101_2, \ 1111111_2$$

6. Find the floating point representation for the following numbers

    (a) 10110.1101
    (b) .00000010110
    (c) 1000000000000

7. Find the fixed point representation of the following floating point numbers

    (a) .101101 2^{-1011}
    (b) .101101 2^{110}
    (c) .11111 2^{1010}

8. How many digits are required in a base r fraction if the truncation error ε_T is to be kept less than 10^{-3}. Let $r = 2,3,4,5,8,10,16$.

4. DIGITAL-TO-ANALOG CONVERSION

Since the physical world normally deals with continous signals there are many situations where information contained in a digital signal must be transformed into an analog or continuous signal before it can be used. The transformation of a digital signal into an analog signal is called a *digital-to-analog* conversion or simply a D/A conversion. A device that performs this operation is called a *digital-to-analog-converter* or DAC.

There are a number of ways in which this conversion can take place. For the current discussion we assume that it can be accomplished by using a general network of the form shown in Figure 2-8. This digital information contained in the

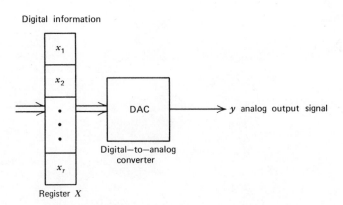

Figure 2-8. General form of a digital-to-analog converter.

register X is processed by the DAC which generates an analog signal that has a numerical value equal to the digital number stored in X.

The digital information to be processed is placed in the X register. For this discussion we will assume that the register represents the binary number

$$\overbrace{b_s}^{\text{sign bit}} \quad \overbrace{b_{u-1}b_{u-2} \cdots b_1 b_0}^{u \text{ bits}} . \overbrace{b_{-1}b_{-2} \cdots b_{-v}}^{v \text{ bits}}$$

where

b_s indicates the sign of the number
$\quad b_s = 0$ indicates a positive number
$\quad b_s = 1$ indicates a negative number
$b_{u-1} \cdots b_1 b_0$ represents the integer portion of the number
$b_{-1}b_{-2} \cdots b_{-v}$ represents the fractional portion of the number

The value of u and v must be selected so that

$$u + v + 1 = r$$

If $v = 0$, then there will be no fractional part of the number, and if $u = 0$, there will be no integer part of the number.

Under these assumptions the digital signal will take on a value in the range

$$\pm([2^u - 1] + [1 - 2^{-v}])$$

The output analog signal will thus assume values in the same range. Since there are only a finite number of distinct values which can be stored in the register X, the output signal will also only take on a set of discrete values. Each value will be separated by an amount equal to 2^{-v}. For example, let $u = 2$, $v = 2$ and $r = 5$. The distinct digital signals and their corresponding analog values are given in Table 2-9.

As long as the signal in the X register remains unchanged, the output remains at a constant value. In many applications, the digital signal will take on a sequence of values. For example, assume that the X register receives a new value every second. If the sequence of values given in Table 2-10 appear in the X register, then the output signal will have the form shown in Figure 2-9.

Examining this figure, we see that the waveform of the output approximates a sine wave. However, the approximation is quite jagged because the output must change in steps of .25 units, since only 2 bits are used in the fractional part of the number.

Table 2-9 An Example of a D/A Conversion

Digital Number	Analog Output	Digital Number	Analog Output
000.00	0.00	100.00	−0.00
000.01	0.25	100.01	−0.25
000.10	0.50	100.10	−0.50
000.11	0.75	100.11	−0.75
001.00	1.00	101.00	−1.00
001.01	1.25	101.01	−1.25
001.10	1.50	101.10	−1.50
001.11	1.75	101.11	−1.75
010.00	2.00	110.00	−2.00
010.01	2.25	110.01	−2.25
010.10	2.50	110.10	−2.50
010.11	2.75	110.11	−2.75
011.00	3.00	111.00	−3.00
011.01	3.25	111.01	−3.25
011.10	3.50	111.10	−3.50
011.11	3.75	111.11	−3.75

The difference between two successive values of the output of a digital-to-analog converter is called the *resolution* of the converter. The *range* of the converter is the distance between the most positive and the most negative value that the converter can generate. The converter in the example of Table 2-10 has a resolution of .25 and a range of 3.75 to −3.75. Many commerical digital-to-analog converters have X registers with 8 to 10 bits. In some cases, the sign bit is not used and the output is assumed to be a positive number.

Table 2-10 Typical Values Placed in X Register

Time	X	Time	X
0	00001	8	10001
1	00010	9	10010
2	00011	10	10011
3	00100	11	10100
4	00011	12	10011
5	00010	13	10010
6	00001	14	10001
7	00000	15	10000

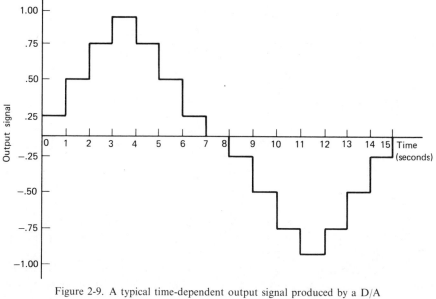

Figure 2-9. A typical time-dependent output signal produced by a D/A converter.

1. What is the range and resolution of a DAC if $u = 4$, $v = 8$?

2. The following values were placed in a 6-bit X register.

$$100100$$
$$110101$$
$$010111$$
$$001010$$
$$101111$$

What will be the value of the output signal for $v = 0, 1, 3, 5$.

5. ANALOG-TO-DIGITAL CONVERSION

There are many situations where the information to be processed by a digital system is initially in continuous or analog form. Thus it is necessary to transform the analog information into digital form. This can be accomplished by using an *analog-to-digital converter* or simply an ADC or *A/D converter*.

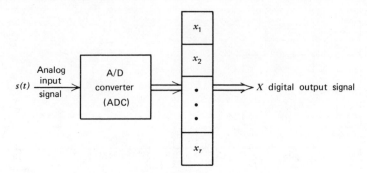

Figure 2-10. General form of an A/D converter.

There are a number of ways that an A/D conversion can be accomplished. For this discussion we assume that a converter can be represented as shown in Figure 2-10.

The input analog signal $s(t)$ is applied to the A/D converter, which generates a digital signal that is stored in the register X. The relationship between the input signal and the value stored in X is illustrated in Figure 2-11. In this example it is assumed that $s(t)$ will fall in the range $\pm.9$ and that the register X has 4 bits. The digital signal is also assumed to be represented in sign-magnitude form.

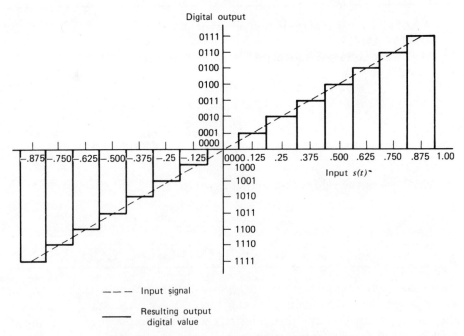

Figure 2-11. Conversion relationship for A/D converter.

Quantization Error

If we examine the input/output relationship illustrated by Figure 2-11, we see that in most cases there will be a conversion error. This error comes about because we cannot exactly represent all values in the continuum $\pm.9$ by the finite number of values that can be represented by the information stored in a 4-bit register. In this example the largest error occurs when the input signal has a value halfway between two adjacent values of X. This is the point where the value in the X register changes and the error corresponds to $\frac{1}{2}(.125) = .0625$ units.

For the general case assume that the digital signal represents the binary number

$$b_s b_{u-1} \cdots b_1 b_0 \cdot b_{-1} b_{-2} \cdots b_{-r}$$

Then the maximum error will be $\frac{1}{2}(2^{-v}) = 2^{-(v+1)}$.

The error introduced by the digital approximation of a continuous signal is called *quantization error*. The only way to reduce this type of error is to increase the number of bits used in the representation of the digital signal. The choice of the number of bits is determined by the accuracy needed to represent $s(t)$.

Sampling

In most applications where we use A/D converters we are interested in reading the value of the signal every T seconds. Thus the output will be a series of values. This process is called *sampling* the input signal.

For example, assume that the input signal given by

$$s(t) = \sin \omega t$$

where

$$\omega = 15 \text{ degrees per second}$$

is to be sampled 11 times in the time interval 0 to 20 seconds. In this case, $T = 2$ and the samples are taken for

$$t = nT \qquad n = 0, 1, \ldots, 10$$

Table 2-11 gives the value of $s(t)$ at these sample points and the corresponding digital value in the output register X. It is assumed that X is a 5-bit register which has a 3-bit fraction part, a 1-bit integer part, and a sign bit.

Table 2-11 Sampled Values of
sin 15t

n	nT	sin 15nT	X(nT)
0	0	0.000	00000
1	2	0.50	00100
2	4	0.866	00111
3	6	1.000	01000
4	8	0.866	00111
5	10	0.50	00100
6	12	0.000	00000
7	14	−0.500	10100
8	16	−0.866	10111
9	18	−1.000	11000
10	20	−0.866	10111

A graphical interpretation of the information in Table 2-10 is given in Figure 2-12. Note that the value of the input signal will change between the sampling points while the value of the digital signal in the output X register remains constant during the time between samples. A much more comprehensive discussion of the sampling process and how it influences the accuracy of the information being used in a given information processing task can be found in reference [3] listed at the end of this chapter.

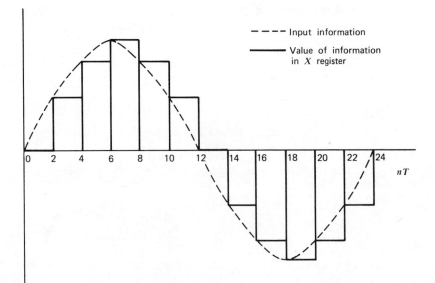

Figure 2-12. Graphical interpretation of the sampling process.

EXERCISES

1. An analog signal with a range of ± 5 units must be converted to a digital signal with a quantization error of less than .01. How many bits are needed in the output register of the A/D Converter?

2. Assume that the signal $s(t)$ given below is to be converted to digital form using an A/D Converter which has a 6-bit digital output. Let the sampling interval be 1 second. Compute the first 10 output values of the digital signal.

$$s(t) = .5 \cos \omega t \qquad \omega = 10 \text{ deg/sec}$$

6. SUMMARY

All information found in a digital system must be represented in binary form. This chapter has presented a summary of the common methods that may be used to represent both numeric and nonnumeric information. Throughout the rest of this book it is assumed that any information under investigation has already been reduced to a suitable digital representation.

In the next chapter we investigate how the different types of digital signals introduced in this chapter can be processed to form new information. Once we have developed an understanding of what operations we might wish to perform on digital information, we can then investigate the techniques that are used to actually perform these operations.

REFERENCE NOTATION

The paper by Gardner [2] provides a very interesting and informative discussion of why various number systems have been used by man as civilization evolved. Chu [1] and Knuth [4] present detailed discussions of various number systems and operations on numbers. A detailed summary of different binary codes can be found in [1]. A/D and D/A conversion is discussed extensively in [3].

REFERENCES

1. Chu, Y. (1962), *Digital Computer Design Fundamentals*, McGraw-Hill, New York.

2. Gardner, M. (1968), "Counting Systems and Their Relationship Between Numbers and the Real World," *Scientific American*, Vol. 219, No. 3, pp. 218–230, September.

3. Hoeschele, David F. Jr. (1968), *Analog-To-Digital/Digital-to-Analog Conversion Techniques*, John Wiley, New York.

4. Knuth, D. E. (1975), *The Art of Computer Programming*, Vol. 1, Addison-Wesley, Reading, Mass.

HOME PROBLEMS

1. An optical character reader has been constructed that is able to recognize 72 different characters. This unit is to be used as an input device to a digital computer.

   (a) If each word of the computer's memory contains 16 bits, what is the maximum number of characters that can be stored in each word?
   (b) One use that will be made of the computer system is to edit printed text. Estimate the number of words of memory that would be required to store one page of a typical textbook.

2. (a) Develop an algorithm that can be used to convert a ternary number directly to an octal number.
   (b) Develop an algorithm that can be used to convert an octal number directly to a ternary number.

3. The output voltage, v_p, of a pressure transducer has a range of 0 to 2.5 volts. This voltage is to be converted to a binary number, using an analog-to-digital converter, before it is transmitted to a central computer for processing. If the maximum allowable error in indicating v_p must be kept below .1 volt, how many bits must the binary number have in order to represent v_p to the desired degree of precision?

4. Although 4 bits are adequate to code a decimal digit, several codes with more than 4 bits are often used in digital systems to simplify logic circuitry or to make it easy to carry out special operations. Derive the code tables for the following codes.

   (a) The 5-4-3-2-1-0 code—the leftmost bit determines if the digit is 5 or greater and a single 1 is placed in one of the other 5 bits to determine the complete value of the digit. This is a weighted code.
   (b) The 5-1-1-1-1 code—the leftmost bit determines if the digit is 5 or greater and the number and position of the 1's in the other 4 bits determine the rest of the value of the digit. This is a weighted code. How many different ways can this code be defined?

5. When digital data is transmitted between two points in a system random errors due to noise may occur. Since the presence of an error can lead to the malfunction of the system, digital information is often encoded in a way that allows the system to detect when a single error has occurred.

   One such code is the odd parity check code. If the original digital signal has n-bits then the transmitted signal has $n + 1$ bits. The extra bit is set to 1 if there are an even number of 1's in the first n-bits. Otherwise this bit is set equal to zero.

   (a) Find the parity check code for the BCD code of Table 2-5.
   (b) An error in transmission of the signal is detected by counting the number of 1's in the received signal. It is known that an odd number of 1's is always transmitted. If the received signal has an even number of 1's, then this indicates that a transmission error has occurred. Is it possible to locate which bit is in error? Explain your answer.

6. A 16-bit register is to be used to store a floating point binary number. The exponent will be stored in the leftmost 6 bits and the mantissa will be stored in the rightmost 10 bits. The quantizing error will not be constant if we try to represent a continuum of values. What is the largest and smallest quantization error and when do these values occur?

3

Representation of Basic Logic Operations

By itself a digital signal X represented by the r-tuple $[x_1, x_2, \ldots, x_r]$ has limited usefulness. However, when we operate on this signal to form a signal Y represented by the r-tuple $[y_1, y_2, \ldots, y_k]$ we perform one of the initial steps in the information processing process. Such an information processing task can be assumed to be performed by a logic network as shown in Figure 3-1. If, in addition, we assume that this network does not contain any memory, then the current value of the output variables $[y_1, y_2, \ldots, y_k]$ depends only on the current value of the input variables $[x_1, x_2, \ldots, x_r]$. Logic networks with this property are called *combinational logic networks*.

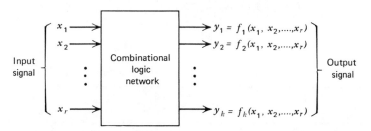

Figure 3-1. General representation of a combinational logic network.

The relationship between the input and the output is determined by the functions $f_j(x_1, x_2, \ldots, x_r)$. In this chapter we examine the basic properties of these functions and show that the behavior of any combinational logic network can be described in terms of a set of simple logical operations. These ideas will then be used throughout the rest of this book to describe the behavior of all classes of digital systems.

2. REPRESENTATION OF LOGICAL FUNCTIONS AND OPERATIONS

Let $[x_1, x_2, \ldots, x_r]$ be an ordered r-tuple of r binary variables. By a *binary function* $f(x_1, x_2, \ldots, x_r)$ of the binary variables $[x_1, x_2, \ldots, x_r]$ we mean a unique correspondence that associates a value of either 0 or 1 to each of the 2^r possible values that the r-tuple $[x_1, x_2, \ldots, x_r]$ can take on. This correspondence can be given by listing, in tabular form, all of the possible values of the arguments and the value of the function associated with each such value. The function can also be expressed as a mathematical expression involving the r variables and a set of basic logical operations. This section will investigate both methods for representing binary functions.

Truth Tables

One way to describe a binary function $f(x_1, x_2, \ldots, x_r)$ is to list $[x_1, x_2, \ldots, x_r]$ and the corresponding value of $f(x_1, x_2, \ldots, x_r)$ for each of the 2^r distinct values of the r-tuple $[x_1, x_2, \ldots, x_r]$. Such a listing is called a *truth table* representation of the binary function $f(x_1, x_2, \ldots, x_r)$. Table 3-1 illustrates how a truth table can be used to represent a typical binary function when $r = 3$.

Expanding this example to the general case we see that a truth table associated with r variables has 2^r rows. The value of the function associated with each row will be either 0 or 1. Therefore if we combine these observations we see that there are $(2)^{2^r}$ possible binary functions of r-variables. Obviously as r becomes large it becomes impractical to list all of the possible binary functions. Fortunately it is also possible to represent any binary function as a mathematical expression involving a small set of logical operations.

Table 3-1   Truth Table (Tabular Representation) of a Particular Binary Function

	x_1	x_2	x_3	$f(x_1, x_2, x_3)$	
	0	0	0	0	
	0	0	1	1	
All possible	0	1	0	1	Corresponding value
3-tuples listed	0	1	1	0	of function
in order of	1	0	0	1	
increasing	1	0	1	0	
binary value	1	1	0	1	
	1	1	1	1	

Basic Unary Logic Operations

If we let $r = 1$, then the input X will be the 1-tuple $[x_1]$ and the binary functions will be of the form

$$y = f(x_1)$$

The value y is thus a function of one variable. There are $2^{2^1} = 4$ such functions. These functions are listed in Table 3-2.

Examining this table we see that the functions $f_1(x) = 0$ and $f_4(x) = 1$ simply assign a constant value to the function while the function $f_2(x) = x$ is simply the *identity function*.

The function $f_3(x)$ is much more interesting. Examining this operation we see that $f_3(x)$ has a value that is opposite to the value of x. For example, assume that x represents the statement

"The door is open"

When this statement is TRUE, x has a value of 1 and when the statement is FALSE, x has a value of 0.

If we apply the function $f_3(x)$ to the statement x, we create the new statement

"The door is *NOT* open"

Since when $x = 1$ then $f_3(x) = 0$, and when $x = 0$, $f_3(x) = 1$.

Because of this, we say that the function $f_3(x)$ represents the unary logical operation NOT. This operation can be formally defined as follows where the names in parenthesis indicate other commonly used names for this operation.

NOT (negation, complement) *Operation*

$$f(x) = \bar{x}$$

x	$f(x)$
0	1
1	0

Alternate notation $f(x) = \neg\, x, \quad f(x) = x'$

As we will soon see the NOT operation is a very important logical operation.

Table 3-2   Unary Function

$[x]$	$f_1(x) = 0$	$f_2(x) = x$	$f_3(x) = \bar{x}$	$f_4(x) = 1$
0	0	0	1	1
1	0	1	0	1

Basic Binary Logic Operations

If we let $r = 2$, then there are 16 possible functions of the form $f(x_1, x_2)$. Several of these functions are used so often that they are given special names. These functions, together with the unary NOT operation just defined, make up the set of basic logic operations that we can use to define arbitrary functions of r variables.

The following listing describes six of the important binary logical operations that are used in later chapters. This listing defines the operations, gives the notational representation that we use to indicate the operation, and gives the name (or names) commonly associated with the operation.

AND Operation (Logical Product)

$$f(x_1, x_2) = x_1 \wedge x_2 = x_1 x_2$$

(Both notations are used extensively in following discussions.)

This operation gives a value of 1 if and only if both x_1 and x_2 equal 1.

Alternate notation $x_1 \cdot x_2$. The notation $x_1 \cdot x_2$ is reserved in this book to indicate the arithmetic multiplication of numbers.

x_1	x_2	$x_1 \wedge x_2$
0	0	0
0	1	0
1	0	0
1	1	1

OR Operation (Logical Sum, Inclusive OR)

$$f(x_1, x_2) = x_1 \vee x_2$$

This operation gives a value of 1 if *either* x_1 or x_2 or *both* are equal to 1.

Alternate notation $x_1 + x_2$. The notation $x_1 + x_2$ is reserved in this book to indicate the arithmetic sum of two numbers.

x_1	x_2	$x_1 \vee x_2$
0	0	0
0	1	1
1	0	1
1	1	1

EXCLUSIVE OR Operation

$$f(x_1, x_2) = x_1 \oplus x_2$$

This operation gives a value of 1 if either x_1 or x_2 but not both equal 1

x_1	x_2	$x_1 \oplus x_2$
0	0	0
0	1	1
1	0	1
1	1	0

COINCIDENCE

$$f(x_1, x_2) = x_1 \odot x_2$$

The output is 1 if and
only if both x_1 and x_2
have the same value

x_1	x_2	$x_1 \odot x_2$
0	0	1
0	1	0
1	0	0
1	1	1

NAND Operation (Sheffer Stroke)

$$f(x_1, x_2) = x_1 \uparrow x_2$$

This operation equals 1
unless x_1 and x_2 equal 1.

Alternate notation $x_1 | x_2 \quad \overline{x_1 x_2}$.

x_1	x_2	$x_1 \uparrow x_2$
0	0	1
0	1	1
1	0	1
1	1	0

NOR Operation (Pierce Arrow)

$$f(x_1, x_2) = x_1 \downarrow x_2$$

This operaton equals 1
if and only if both x_1
and x_2 equal 0.

Alternate notation $(\overline{x_1 \lor x_2})$.

x_1	x_2	$x_1 \downarrow x_2$
0	0	1
0	1	0
1	0	0
1	1	0

These basic operations can now be used to define the more complex functions of r variables.

Composition of Functions

So far we have been taking the arguments of the operations to be arbitrary variables. However, a function is itself a binary variable so any argument in an operation can be replaced by an arbitrary function. For example, if $f(x_1, x_2, \ldots, x_r)$, $g(y_1, y_2, \ldots, y_k)$, and $h(z_1, z_2)$ are three functions, then $h[f(x_1, x_2, \ldots, x_r), g(y_1, y_2, \ldots, y_k)]$ is also a function. The resulting function is said to be the *composition* of the two functions f and g by the function h.

To illustrate this idea let

$$f(x_1, x_2) = x_1 \oplus x_2$$
$$g(x_2, x_3) = x_2 \downarrow x_3$$
$$h(z_1, z_2) = z_1 \lor z_3$$

Then

$$h[f(x_1, x_2), g(x_2, x_3)] = h(x_1, x_2, x_3) = (x_1 \oplus x_2) \vee (x_2 \downarrow x_3)$$

From this example we see that it is very easy to generate rather complex functions. In fact, any function of r variables can be represented by an expression involving only the operations of AND, OR, and NOT. However, before we can prove this assertion we must further examine some of the basic properties of composite functions.

Evaluation of Composite Functions

The value of a composite function, $f(x_1, x_2, \ldots, x_r)$ for particular values of $[x_1, x_2, \ldots, x_r]$ can be obtained by substituting these values in the expression describing the function and then carrying out the indicated operations.

As in any mathematical system, the order in which operations are performed is important. If we include parentheses around all pairs of terms in an expression that are to be operated on by a given operator, we have no problem in determining the order in which the operators are to be applied. For example, the expression

$$f(x_1, x_2, x_3) = (x_1 \uparrow x_2) \oplus (x_2 \downarrow x_3)$$

is evaluated by first evaluating $y_1 = x_1 \uparrow x_2$ and $y_2 = x_2 \downarrow x_3$. These results are then used to finally evaluate

$$f(x_1, x_2, x_3) = y_1 \oplus y_2$$

Thus if $[x_1, x_2, x_3] = [1, 1, 0]$, then

$$y_1 = 1 \uparrow 1 = 0 \qquad y_2 = 1 \downarrow 0 = 0$$

and

$$f(x_1, x_2, x_3) = 0 \oplus 0 = 0$$

As long as we are dealing with expressions that involve the EXCLUSIVE OR, NAND, or NOR operations it is best to use parentheses to indicate the two operands that the particular operator operates on. However, in digital logic most expressions only involve the operations of AND, OR, and NOT. If we were to include parentheses around all the pairs of terms in an expression that are to be operated on by an operator we would have a very cumbersome expression. To overcome this problem a set of rules has been established to indicate the *precedence* or order in which these logical operations are to be applied. These rules are as follows.

1. Evaluation of logical expressions without parentheses is accomplished by first applying all instances of the NOT operation to variables in a left-to-right order, then applying all instances of the AND operation in a left-to-right order, and then applying all instances of the OR operation in a left-to-right order.

2. If parentheses are present, this evaluation procedure is applied within the parentheses, and the resulting value entered as an evaluated variable in further evaluation.

3. The NOT operator applied over an expression has the effect of enclosing the expression in parentheses.

For example $\overline{x_1 x_2} \lor x_3$ is equivalent to $\overline{(x_1 x_2)} \lor x_3$

4. When in doubt, always use parentheses to establish the proper order of evaluation.

To illustrate how these rules are applied, let us assume that we wish to evaluate

$$f(x_1, x_2, x_3, x_4) = (\overline{\overline{x_1 x_4} \lor \bar{x}_1 x_3}) x_2 \lor x_1 x_2 x_4 \lor \bar{x}_1 x_2 x_3$$

for $x_1 = 0$, $x_2 = 1$, $x_3 = 0$, and $x_4 = 1$.

First we evaluate $\overline{x_1 x_4}$ which gives $\overline{x_1 x_4} = 1$. Then the term $\overline{(1 \lor \bar{x}_1 x_3)}$ gives 0. Finally we evaluate the whole expression by performing the NOT operation first, then the AND operation, and finally the OR operations. The resulting value is

$$f(x_1, x_2, x_3, x_4) = 0$$

These rules give rise to the following widely used conventions. When dealing with a sequence of AND operations such as

$$x_1 \land (x_2 \land x_3) \qquad \text{or} \qquad x_1(x_2 x_3)$$

we can omit the parentheses to give

$$x_1 \land x_2 \land x_3 \qquad \text{or} \qquad x_1 x_2 x_3$$

Similarly

$$(x_1 x_2 x_3) \lor ((x_1 \bar{x}_2 x_3) \lor (\bar{x}_1 \bar{x}_2 \bar{x}_3))$$

can be written as

$$x_1 x_2 x_3 \lor x_1 \bar{x}_2 x_3 \lor \bar{x}_1 \bar{x}_2 \bar{x}_3$$

Logical Equivalence of Functions

Two functions $f(x_1, \ldots, x_r)$ and $g(x_1, \ldots, x_r)$ defined for the same arguments are *logically equivalent* if and only if

$$f(x_1, \ldots, x_r) = g(x_1, \ldots, x_r)$$

for all possible combinations of the r-tuple $[x_1, \ldots, x_r]$. This is one of the situations where the idea of a truth table representation of a function is very handy. All that we have to do to show that two functions are equivalent is to form the truth table for both functions and see if they compare. If they compare then we know that the two functions are logically equivalent. Otherwise, they are not. The following example illustrates this idea.

Let

$$f(x_1, x_2, x_3) = (x_1 \oplus x_2)(x_2 \lor x_3)$$
$$g(x_1, x_2, x_3) = \bar{x}_1 x_2 \bar{x}_3 \lor \bar{x}_1 x_2 x_3 \lor x_1 \bar{x}_2 x_3$$

The following truth table compares these two functions.

x_1	x_2	x_3	$x_1 \oplus x_2$	$x_2 \lor x_3$	$f(x_1, x_2, x_3)$	$\bar{x}_1 x_2 \bar{x}_3$	$\bar{x}_1 x_2 x_3$	$x_1 \bar{x}_2 x_3$	$g(x_1, x_2, x_3)$
0	0	0	0	0	0	0	0	0	0
0	0	1	0	1	0	0	0	0	0
0	1	0	1	1	1	1	0	0	1
0	1	1	1	1	1	0	1	0	1
1	0	0	1	0	0	0	0	0	0
1	0	1	1	1	1	0	0	1	1
1	1	0	0	1	0	0	0	0	0
1	1	1	0	1	0	0	0	0	0

Thus we see that $f(x_1, x_2, x_3)$ and $g(x_1, x_2, x_3)$ are logically equivalent.

Similarly we can show that $f(x_1, \ldots, x_r)$ is not logically equivalent to $g(x_1, \ldots, x_r)$ by finding one possible value of the r-tuple $[x_1, \ldots, x_r]$ for which the two functions are not equal.

For example

$$(x_1 \odot x_2) \lor x_3$$

is not equivalent to

$$(x_1 \oplus x_2) \land x_3$$

since if $[x_1, x_2, x_3] = [0, 0, 0]$ then

$$(0 \odot 0) \lor 0 = 1$$

but

$$(0 \oplus 0) \land 0 = 0$$

which proves that the two functions are not equivalent.

EXERCISES

1. Show that

(a) $x_1 \downarrow x_2 = \overline{(x_1 \vee x_2)} = \bar{x}_1 \bar{x}_2$

(b) $x_1 \uparrow x_2 = \overline{(x_1 \wedge x_2)} = \bar{x}_1 \vee \bar{x}_2$

(c) $x_1 \wedge x_2 = \overline{((\overline{x_1 x_2})(\overline{x_1 x_2}))}$

(d) $(x_1 \vee x_2) \vee x_3 = x_1 \vee (x_2 \vee x_3)$

(e) $(x_1 \wedge x_2) \wedge x_3 = x_1 \wedge (x_2 \wedge x_3)$

2. Show that $f(x_1, x_2, x_3, x_4) = g(x_1, x_2, x_3, x_4)$ if

$$f(x_1, x_2, x_3, x_4) = (x_1 \vee x_3 \vee \bar{x}_2)(x_1 \vee x_3 \vee \bar{x}_4)$$

$$g(x_1, x_2, x_3, x_4) = x_1 \vee x_3 \vee \bar{x}_2 \bar{x}_4$$

3. Let $g(x_1, x_2) = \overline{(x_1 x_2 \vee \bar{x}_1)}$

$$f(x_2, x_3) = (x_2 \vee x_3) \uparrow (x_2 x_3)$$

$$h(y_1, y_2) = y_1 y_2 \vee \bar{y}_1 \bar{y}_2$$

Find the truth table for

$$m(x_1, x_2, x_3) = h[g(x_1, x_2), f(x_2, x_3)]$$

3. CANONICAL FORMS OF BINARY FUNCTIONS

In the last section we saw that it was possible to describe a binary function by using a truth table to list the value of the function for all possible values of its arguments. Similarly, it was shown that we could easily obtain the truth table of a function if the function was expressed in terms of the basic logic operations AND, OR and NOT. In this section we reverse this process and show how to obtain a mathematical expression to represent a function that is described by a truth table.

Minterms and Maxterms

Before considering the general problem we define two special types of functions. Let us assume that we are dealing with a function of r variables $[x_1, x_2, \ldots, x_r]$.

A *product term* is a function that is defined to be the logical AND (logic product) of a set of terms that are either variables x_i or their negation $\bar{x}_i$. No variable can appear more than once in a product term. For example, if $r = 5$ three typical product terms would be

$$x_1 \bar{x}_2 x_3 x_4 \bar{x}_5, \qquad \bar{x}_1 \bar{x}_2 x_4 x_5, \qquad x_3 x_4$$

A product term in which all variables appear once and only once is called a *minterm*. Some typical minterms for $r = 5$ are

$$x_1 x_2 x_3 x_4 x_5, \qquad x_1 \bar{x}_2 \bar{x}_3 x_4 x_5, \qquad x_1 x_2 x_3 \bar{x}_4 \bar{x}_5$$

The reason that these terms are called minterms is that they have a value of 1 for only one of the 2^r possible values of the r-tuple $[x_1, \ldots, x_r]$ and zero for all other values. The following truth table illustrates the form of three typical minterms.

Row Number	x_1	x_2	x_3	$m_7 = x_1 x_2 x_3$	$m_5 = x_1 \bar{x}_2 x_3$	$m_1 = \bar{x}_1 \bar{x}_2 x_3$
0	0	0	0	0	0	0
1	0	0	1	0	0	1
2	0	1	0	0	0	0
3	0	1	1	0	0	0
4	1	0	0	0	0	0
5	1	0	1	0	1	0
6	1	1	0	0	0	0
7	1	1	1	1	0	0

In the above table we have assigned decimal row numbers to each row of the table corresponding to the binary number represented by the input combination associated with the row. These decimal numbers can be used to indicate particular minterms. If we wish to obtain a minterm that has a value of 1 in row d all that we need do is convert d to its equivalent binary number and then express this number in logical form. This minterm is indicated as m_d. To accomplish this we let each 1 value indicate the unnegated form of the variable and each 0 its negated form. For example let $r = 3$. Then

$$m_7 = x_1 x_2 x_3 \text{ because } 7_{10} = 1\,1\,1_2$$
$$m_5 = x_1 \bar{x}_2 x_3 \text{ because } 5_{10} = 1\,0\,1_2$$
$$m_1 = \bar{x}_1 \bar{x}_2 x_3 \text{ because } 1_{10} = 0\,0\,1_2$$

Note that $m_7 = 1$ if and only if $x_1 = 1$ and $x_2 = 1$ and $x_3 = 1$. Similarly $m_5 = 1$ if and only if $x_1 = 1$ and $x_2 = 0$ and $x_3 = 1$. (How about m_1?)

A sum term is a function that is defined to be the logical OR (logical sum) of a set of terms that are either variables x_i or their negation $\bar{x}_i$. No variable can appear more than once in a sum term. For example, if $r = 5$, three typical sum terms would be

$$x_1 \vee \bar{x}_2 \vee x_3 \qquad x_1 \vee x_2 \vee x_3 \vee x_4 \qquad x_1 \vee x_5$$

A sum term in which all variables appear once and only once is called a *maxterm*. Some typical maxterms for $r = 5$ are

$$(x_1 \vee x_2 \vee x_3 \vee x_4 \vee x_5) \qquad (\bar{x}_1 \vee x_2 \vee x_3 \vee \bar{x}_4 \vee \bar{x}_5)$$

The reason that these terms are called maxterms is that they have a value of 0 for only one of the 2^r possible values of the r-tuple $[x_1, \ldots, x_r]$ and 1 for all other values. The truth table below illustrates the form of three typical maxterms.

To indicate a maxterm we can also make use of row numbers. In this case the row number is used to indicate the row in which the 0 value of the term is to appear. Thus we must convert the binary number corresponding to that row into a sum term that has a value of zero when evaluated using these values for the variables.

Row Number	x_1	x_2	x_3	$M_7 = (\bar{x}_1 \vee \bar{x}_2 \vee \bar{x}_3)$	$M_5 = (\bar{x}_1 \vee x_2 \vee \bar{x}_3)$	$M_1 = (x_1 \vee x_2 \vee \bar{x}_3)$
0	0	0	0	1	1	1
1	0	0	1	1	1	0
2	0	1	0	1	1	1
3	0	1	1	1	1	1
4	1	0	0	1	1	1
5	1	0	1	1	0	1
6	1	1	0	1	1	1
7	1	1	1	0	1	1

To accomplish this we let each 0 value indicate the unnegated form of the variable and each 1 value indicate the negated form of the variable. The maxterm corresponding to row d is indicated as M_d. For example, let $r = 3$. Then

$$M_7 = (\bar{x}_1 \vee \bar{x}_2 \vee \bar{x}_3) \text{ because } 7_{10} = 1\,1\,1_2$$
$$M_5 = (\bar{x}_1 \vee x_2 \vee \bar{x}_3) \text{ because } 5_{10} = 1\,0\,1_2$$
$$M_1 = (x_1 \vee x_2 \vee \bar{x}_3) \text{ because } 1_{10} = 0\,0\,1_2$$

Note that $M_7 = 0$ if and only if $x_1 = 1$, $x_2 = 1$, $x_3 = 1$.

Canonical Representation of Logic Expressions

Now that we have defined the concept of a minterm and a maxterm, we can use these functions as a set of basic building blocks to represent any arbitrary function that is described by a truth table. The following example illustrates how we can do this.

Assume that a function $f(x_1, x_2, x_3)$ is given by the following truth table and we wish to obtain an expression that describes this function. Examining this truth table we see that the function takes on a value of 1 in row 1 *or* row 3 *or* row 5

Row Number	x_1	x_2	x_3	$f(x_1, x_2, x_3)$
0	0	0	0	0
1	0	0	1	1
2	0	1	0	0
3	0	1	1	1
4	1	0	0	0
5	1	0	1	1
6	1	1	0	0
7	1	1	1	1

or row 7. Therefore, we can represent this function as

$$f(x_1, x_2, x_3) = m_1 \lor m_3 \lor m_5 \lor m_7 = \bar{x}_1\bar{x}_2x_3 \lor \bar{x}_1x_2x_3 \lor x_1\bar{x}_2x_3 \lor x_1x_2x_3$$

This function is said to be represented in the *canonical sum-of products form* or *disjunctive normal form*. Any binary function can be represented by a unique canonical sum-of-product expression.

A second way to represent a function in a canonical form is to use *maxterms*. Suppose we wish to represent $f(x_1, x_2, x_3)$ in this manner. We note that this function is 0 for row 0 *and* row 2 *and* row 4 *and* row 6. Therefore we can represent this function as

$$f(x_1, x_2, x_3) = M_0 \land M_2 \land M_4 \land M_6$$

This function is said to be represented in the *canonical product-of-sum form* or *conjunctive normal form*. Any binary function can also be represented by a unique canonical product-of-sum expression.

The above discussion has shown that any binary function of r variables can be represented in terms of the AND, OR, and NOT operations. Therefore, we can conclude that we do not need to introduce any other special operations to represent any binary function in terms of a logical expression.

EXERCISES

1. For $r = 4$ find the following minterms and maxterms:

$$m_0, m_1, m_2, m_4, m_{11}, m_{13}, m_{15}$$
$$M_0, M_1, M_2, M_4, M_{11}, M_{13}, M_{15}$$

2. Find the canonical sum-of-product and product-of-sum representation for the following truth table.

x_1	x_2	x_3	x_4	$f(x_1, x_2, x_3, x_4)$
0	0	0	0	1
0	0	0	1	1
0	0	1	0	0
0	0	1	1	0
0	1	0	0	1
0	1	0	1	0
0	1	1	0	1
0	1	1	1	1
1	0	0	0	0
1	0	0	1	0
1	0	1	0	0
1	0	1	1	1
1	1	0	0	0
1	1	0	1	1
1	1	1	0	1
1	1	1	1	0

3. Show the canonical forms for the binary operations

(a) $x_1 \uparrow x_2$
(b) $x_1 \downarrow x_2$
(c) $x_1 \oplus x_2$

4. REDUCTION OF LOGICAL SPECIFICATIONS TO LOGICAL EXPRESSIONS

The discussion in the previous section assumed that we were given the truth table representation of a given function and all that we were asked to do was to find an expression to represent this truth table. This is a rather special situation. In most cases we are given a (rather vague) word description of what we would like a logic network to do and we are then required to translate this word description into a truth table description.

One form of this problem is illustrated in Figure 3-2. Assume that we have formulated a word description of a logical process that we would like carried out by a logic network in this form. We can reduce this word description to a truth table description by carrying out the following steps.

1. Identify all of the input terms A, B, . . . , F and then output term Z.
2. Establish the exact relationship that must hold between the inputs and the outputs.
3. Code (if necessary) the input and output terms into digital form.
4. Using the information from steps two and three, develop a truth table representation of the process.
5. Obtain the logical expressions describing the process.

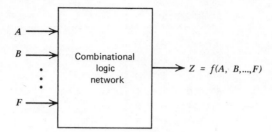

Figure 3-2. General representation of logic network.

The following examples will illustrate how this technique is applied.

Assume that we are given two 2-bit registers A and B and we wish to form the absolute value of the difference between the number stored in A and the number stored in B. From the statement of the problem we know that we can represent A and B as

$$[A] = [a_1, a_2] \quad [B] = [b_1, b_2]$$

Thus A and B will have a decimal value of 0, 1, 2, or 3. Now the output must be

$$Z = |A - B|$$

where the contents of A, B, and Z are taken to be binary numbers. From this we see that Z will never be larger than 3_{10}. Thus the output Z can be represented as

$$[Z] = [z_1, z_2] = [f_1(a_1, a_2, b_1, b_2), f_2(a_1, a_2, b_1, b_2)]$$

Combining this information we find that we can use a network of the form shown in Figure 3-3 to carry out the desired computation. The following truth table for

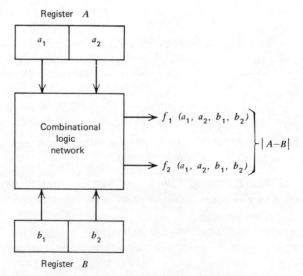

Figure 3-3. A logic network to compute $Z = |A - B|$.

f_1 and f_2 describes the logical expressions that must be realized by the combinational logic network.

a_1	a_2	b_1	b_2	$f_1(a_1, a_2, b_1, b_2)$	$f_2(a_1, a_2, b_1, b_2)$
0	0	0	0	0	0
0	0	0	1	0	1
0	0	1	0	1	0
0	0	1	1	1	1
0	1	0	0	0	1
0	1	0	1	0	0
0	1	1	0	0	1
0	1	1	1	1	0
1	0	0	0	1	0
1	0	0	1	0	1
1	0	1	0	0	0
1	0	1	1	0	1
1	1	0	0	1	1
1	1	0	1	1	0
1	1	1	0	0	1
1	1	1	1	0	0

For example, if A has a decimal value of 2 and B has a decimal value of 3, then $|A - B|$ has a decimal value of 1 and

$$[A] = [1,0], \quad [B] = [1,1], \quad [Z] = [0,1]$$

Thus

$$f_1(a_1, a_2, b_1, b_2) = 0 \qquad f_2(a_1, a_2, b_1, b_2) = 1$$

Examining this table, we see that

$$f_1(a_1, a_2, b_1, b_2) = m_2 \lor m_3 \lor m_7 \lor m_8 \lor m_{12} \lor m_{13}$$
$$f_2(a_1, a_2, b_1, b_2) = m_1 \lor m_3 \lor m_4 \lor m_6 \lor m_9 \lor m_{11} \lor m_{12} \lor m_{14}$$

In this example, all the input and output variables were specified in a manner so that they could easily be identified and represented in digital form. This is not always the case as illustrated by the next example.

Assume that you are working for a company that has three parking lots. Originally each employee was assigned to a specific lot and issued a specially coded card that indicated where he could park. However, it was found that many employees were disregarding these assignments, thus causing a very serious parking problem.

The management has decided to erect a gate at the entrance to each lot. To enter the lot an employee will be required to insert his card in a special slot at the gate. If the card entitles the employee to use the lot the gate will open. Otherwise nothing happens.

The following parking assignments have been made.

Employee Class	Parking Area Allowed		
Company officers	1	2	3
Managers	1	2	
Engineers	1	3	
Secretaries	2	3	
Machinists	1	2	
Electricians	1	3	
Accountants	2		

Your job is to develop a logic network that can be used to decide, based on the output from the card sensor, if a gate should be opened.

Examining this problem we see that we must design three combinational logic networks. The input to each network will be a coded digital signal that either indicates no one has inserted a card or indicates which class of employee is seeking admittance. The output will be a 1 if the gate is to open or a 0 if it is to remain closed.

The first task is to assign a coding to the seven different employee groups and the "no input" condition. This coding, which requires at least three bits, can be assigned in an arbitrary manner. Once this coding is completed the final task is to derive the logic expressions describing the outputs of each network. The following table indicates one possible solution to this problem.

Employee Class	Digital Coding			Output		
	x_1	x_2	x_3	Gate 1	Gate 2	Gate 3
No input	0	0	0	0	0	0
Company officers	0	0	1	1	1	1
Managers	0	1	0	1	1	0
Engineers	0	1	1	1	0	1
Secretaries	1	0	0	0	1	1
Machinists	1	0	1	1	1	0
Electricians	1	1	0	1	0	1
Accountants	1	1	1	0	1	0

The final task is to obtain a logical expression describing each output. Using maxterms, these expressions become

Gate 1

$$f_1(x_1, x_2, x_3) = M_0 \wedge M_4 \wedge M_7$$
$$= (x_1 \vee x_2 \vee x_3) \wedge (\bar{x}_1 \vee x_2 \vee x_3) \wedge (\bar{x}_1 \vee \bar{x}_2 \vee \bar{x}_3)$$

Gate 2

$$f_2(x_1, x_2, x_3) = M_0 \wedge M_3 \wedge M_6$$
$$= (x_1 \vee x_2 \vee x_3) \wedge (x_1 \vee \bar{x}_2 \vee \bar{x}_3) \wedge (\bar{x}_1 \vee \bar{x}_2 \vee x_3)$$

Gate 3

$$f_3(x_1, x_2, x_3) = M_0 \wedge M_2 \wedge M_5 \wedge M_7$$
$$= (x_1 \vee x_2 \vee x_3) \wedge (x_1 \vee \bar{x}_2 \vee x_3)$$
$$\wedge (\bar{x}_1 \vee x_2 \vee \bar{x}_3) \wedge (\bar{x}_1 \vee \bar{x}_2 \vee \bar{x}_3)$$

Problem Decomposition

The examples given thus far deal with truth tables that have a reasonable number of rows. However, consider the problem of developing a truth table for a function

$$Z = F(A, B)$$

when the information associated with A and B are represented by the r-tuples

$$[a_1, a_2, \ldots, a_r] \quad \text{and} \quad [b_1, b_2, \ldots, b_r]$$

respectively.

The truth table representation of $F(A, B)$ will require 2^{2r} rows. If $r = 2$ we need 16 rows, if $r = 3$ we need 64 rows, and if r equals 5 we need 1024 rows. Obviously if we are dealing with $r > 2$, it is not practical to try to write down a truth table which represents $F(A, B)$.

To solve this problem we must be able to break the task represented by $F(A, B)$ into component parts. Let us assume that Z is an n-tuple $[z_1, z_2, \ldots, z_n]$. Then the statement

$$Z = F(A, B)$$

really means that there exist n-binary functions $f_i(a_1, a_2, \ldots, a_r, b_1, b_2, \ldots, b_r)$ such that

$$z_1 = f_1(a_1, a_2, \ldots, a_r, b_1, b_2, \ldots, b_r)$$
$$z_2 = f_2(a_1, a_2, \ldots, a_r, b_1, b_2, \ldots, b_r)$$
$$\vdots$$
$$z_n = f_n(a_1, a_2, \ldots, a_r, b_1, b_2, \ldots, b_r)$$

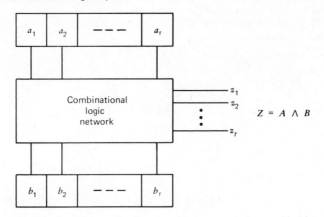

Figure 3-4. Realization of a function using one complex combinational logic network.

This does not appear to be an improvement. However, when we examine the definition of $F(A, B)$, we may find that the binary function f_i is dependent on only a small number of the variables in the set $(a_1, a_2, \ldots, a_r, b_1, b_2, \ldots, b_r)$. The following examples illustrate this idea.

Assume that we wish to carry out the operation

$$Z = A \wedge B$$

where A and B are two r-bit registers and the output Z is to be the bit by bit ANDing of the contents of each register. For example, if

$$A = [1, 0, 1, 1] \qquad B = [0, 1, 1, 0]$$

then

$$Z = [1, 0, 1, 1] \wedge [0, 1, 1, 0] = [0, 0, 1, 0]$$

In this situation we note that since A and B are represented by r-tuples then Z will be represented by an r-tuple $[z_1, z_2, \ldots, z_r]$. To realize this operation using a single combinational logic network would require a network of the form shown in Figure 3-4.

A truth table for this network, even for $r > 3$, would be an impossible task. However, consider the binary function that describes each z_i. Since $A \wedge B$ represents the bit by bit ANDing of the two r-tuples, this means that

$$z_1 = a_1 \wedge b_1 = f_1(a_1, \ldots, a_r, b_1, \ldots, b_r) = f_1(a_1, b_1)$$
$$z_2 = a_2 \wedge b_2 = f_2(a_1, \ldots, a_r, b_1, \ldots, b_r) = f_2(a_2, b_2)$$
$$\vdots$$
$$z_r = a_r \wedge b_r = f_r(a_1, \ldots, a_r, b_1, \ldots, b_r) = f_r(a_r, b_r)$$

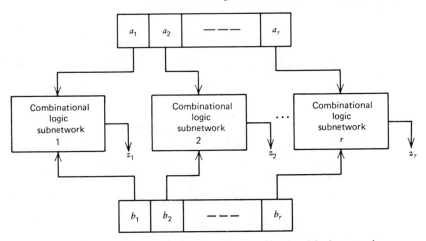

Figure 3-5. Decomposition of a complex combinational logic network into subnetworks.

Thus the complex combinational network of Figure 3-4 can be decomposed into r subnetworks as shown in Figure 3-5. The ith subnetworks computes

$$f_i(a_i, b_i) = a_i \wedge b_i$$

Each subnetwork can thus be represented by a much simpler truth table with only 2^2 rather than 2^{2r} rows.

A Controlled Combinational Logic Network

There are many applications where we want to control the operation performed by a combinational logic network. This can be accomplished by using an organization like that shown in Figure 3-6. The system consists of two r-bit registers A and B and a third register I which we call an instruction register. We wish to build a logic network that carries out the operations listed below, where [0] indicates that the output should be identically zero.

Contents of Instruction Register	Operation to be Performed	Meaning
0	$Z = A \wedge B$	Bit by bit AND
1	$Z = A \vee B$	Bit by bit OR
2	$Z = \bar{A}$	Bit by bit NOT
3	$Z = [0]$	Each output bit 0

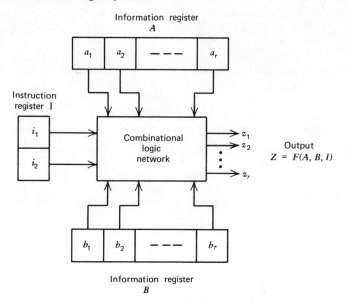

Figure 3-6. Controlled combinational logic network.

From the above we see that the register I must have 2 bits, since there are four different instructions. Thus the general form of the logic network that operates on the jth bits of the A and B registers to form z_j can be represented as shown in Figure 3-7.

The truth table representing the function $f_j(i_1, i_2, a_j, b_j)$ is as follows.

i_1	i_2	a_j	b_j	$f_j(i_1, i_2, a_j, b_j)$	*Operation Performed*
0	0	0	0	0	
0	0	0	1	0	
0	0	1	0	0	$A \wedge B$
0	0	1	1	1	
0	1	0	0	0	
0	1	0	1	1	
0	1	1	0	1	$A \vee B$
0	1	1	1	1	
1	0	0	0	1	
1	0	0	1	1	
1	0	1	0	0	$\bar{A}$
1	0	1	1	0	
1	1	0	0	0	
1	1	0	1	0	
1	1	1	0	0	[0]
1	1	1	1	0	

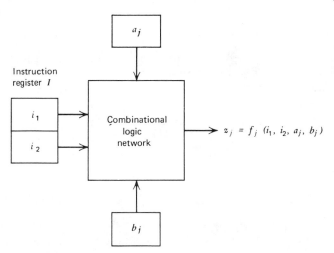

Figure 3-7. Component part of a register logic network.

Examining this truth table we see that

$$f_j(i_1, i_2, a_j, b_j) = m_3 \lor m_5 \lor m_6 \lor m_7 \lor m_8 \lor m_9$$

Thus if we build r logic networks, each of which carries out the above logical operation, we will have a complete network that carries out the desired set of logic operations on the information contained in the registers A and B.

EXERCISES

1. It is desired to build a combinational logic network that will convert numerical information encoded in a 3-bit gray code into conventional binary number form. Find the logical expressions that will describe this network. (*Hint:* see Table 2-8 of Chapter 2).

2. Let A and B be two r-bit registers and I an instruction register. Find the logical expression that describes the logic network that will carry out the following operations

Contents of Instruction Register	Operation to Be Performed
0	$\overline{A \land B}$
1	$\overline{A \lor B}$
2	$A \lor B$
3	$A\bar{B} \lor \bar{A}B$

5. SUMMARY

In this chapter we have established the different fundamental logic operations that can be used to process information in digital form. Our first application of these ideas was to the problem of describing the operations performed by simple combinational logic networks. In the next chapter we extend these ideas to much more complex information-processing tasks. However, no matter how complex the device we are considering, we will find that the analysis of the operation of the device is carried out by applying the basic logic operations developed in this chapter.

HOME PROBLEMS

1. Error-checking codes are used extensively in digital systems to detect when an error occurs in an information transfer operation. One of the simplest ways to introduce this feature is to introduce an extra bit called a parity bit in the digital representation of the information for the sole purpose of checking for an error. In one code the parity bit is chosen so that the number of 1's (including the parity bit) in the digital representation of the information is even. A way for generating the parity bit is shown in Figure P3-1. Define the logical expression for the parity bit generator network.

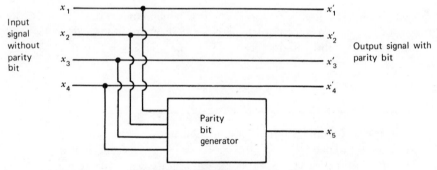

Figure P3-1. Generation of parity bit.

2. Let $g(x_1, x_2, x_3, x_4)$ be any logical expression. Give a general method that may be used to find either the canonical sum-of-product or product-of-sums expression for this expression.

3. Let A be a digital signal corresponding to a decimal number between 0 and 9 encoded by a 4-bit gray code. This signal is applied to a logic network that has 10 output lines. Line y_i is connected to a lamp that lights whenever $y_i = 1$. Develop the logic expression for y_i such that the ith lamp will light if and only if the input corresponds to the decimal number i.

4. A combinational logic network has 10 input lines and 4 output lines. At any time, one and only one of the inputs must be set to 1. If input $x_i, i = 0, 1, \ldots, 9$,

is 1 then the output must be the BCD encoded representation for the decimal number i. Develop the logic expressions that describe this network.

5. A complex logic network of the form shown in Figure P3-5 can be used to detect if the contents of the A register and the contents of the B register are equal. Define the logic expression g_i, which describes the r-identical combinational logic networks used to realize the whole network.

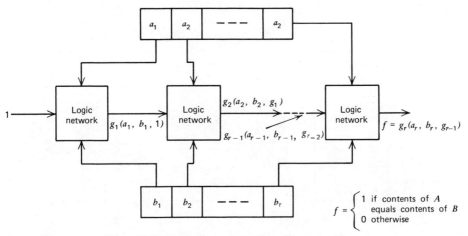

Figure P3-5. Network to test equality of two quantities.

6. A multiplexer network of the form shown in Figure P3-6 is to be realized. Give the logical expressions that describe this network, where

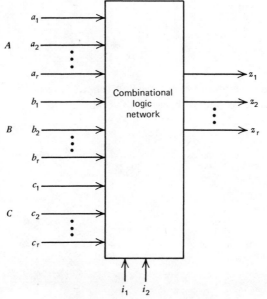

Figure P3-6. A multiplexer network.

$$Z = [0] \quad \text{if} \quad [i_1, i_2] = [0, 0]$$
$$Z = A \quad \text{if} \quad [i_1, i_2] = [1, 0]$$
$$Z = B \quad \text{if} \quad [i_1, i_2] = [0, 1]$$
$$Z = C \quad \text{if} \quad [i_1, i_2] = [1, 1]$$

7. Numeric displays of the type found on hand calculators are realized using 7-segment displays of the form shown in Figure P3-7a.

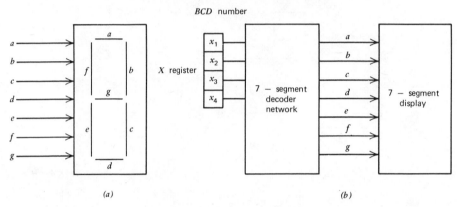

Figure P3-7. Numeric display.

When a 1 is placed on one of the input leads, the corresponding bar in the display lights up. The numbers 0 through 9 are then formed as

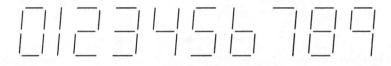

Give the logic expressions for the combinational logic functions that describe the 7-segment decoder of Figure P3-7b. The input is a BCD encoded number.

4

Operations on Digital Information

In Chapter 3 we investigated the analytical techniques that we can use to represent the behavior of combinational logic networks. From this discussion it might appear that each of these networks must be custom-designed for a particular application. Fortunately this is not true. We can use the analytical techniques that we have developed to define a collection of standard operations which can be performed on digital information.

In fact, many of the operations that we will consider are available as predesigned integrated circuit modules. Thus it is quite easy to construct complex information processing systems by using these modules.

Our major purpose in this chapter is to concentrate on the flow or processing of information at the system level without becoming too involved with the fine details of how this processing is carried out. Logic networks of the type shown in Figure 4-1a and b are represented at the system level by black boxes of the form shown in Figure 4-1c and d.

In this representation the input and output consist of appropriately encoded digital signals X, Y, and Z. The relationship between the output signal Z and the input information represented by the signals X and Y depends on the operations indicated by the functions $F(X)$ and $G(X, Y)$ instead of on the encoding. It is only when we wish to proceed from the system level to the logic level that we must introduce a particular encoding of the information and a representation of the system functions by the individual functions

$$f_i(x_1, \ldots, x_r) \qquad \text{and} \qquad g_i(x_1, \ldots x_r, y_1, \ldots, y_s).$$

In this chapter we begin to introduce the notational conventions that we will use in later chapters to design complex digital networks. We also introduce the fundamental system level operations needed to describe common information processing tasks. Finally we show how these operations can be described in terms of basic logic expressions.

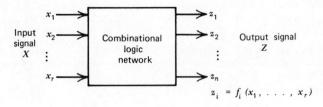

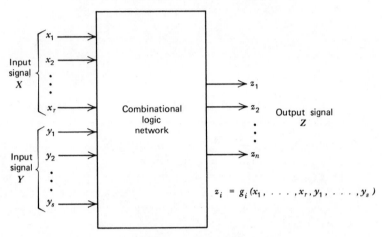

$$z_i = f_i(x_1, \ldots, x_r)$$

(a)

One-Input-Signal Combinational-Logic-Network

$$z_i = g_i(x_1, \ldots, x_r, y_1, \ldots, y_s)$$

(b)

Two Input Signal Combinational Logic Network

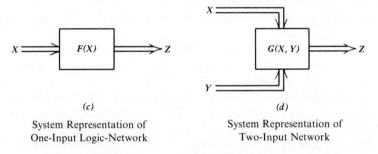

(c)

System Representation of
One-Input Logic-Network

(d)

System Representation of
Two-Input Network

Figure 4-1. General system representation of high-level processing tasks.

2. NOTATIONAL CONVENTIONS

Currently, a number of different conventions are used to describe the operations that can be performed on signals in digital systems. The following discussion introduces the conventions used in this book. Other notational conventions that are also in general use are described in the references listed at the end of this chapter.

Operands

The information found in signals and registers form the basic operands used in all of our calculations. No matter what coding is used, each operand is represented by an ordered r-tuple of binary variable such as $[x_1, x_2, \ldots, x_r]$. Normally individual binary variables are represented by lowercase letters while operands are represented by capital letters. When an individual variable is considered by itself, it is called a *scalar*.

Assume that X represents an operand. The value of the operand is indicated as $[X]$, which is a shorthand notation for the r-tuple $[x_1, x_2, \ldots, x_r]$.

When we are dealing with an operand, the individual variables that make up the r-tuple representing the operand will be numbered from left to right. In some cases the numbering will be 1 through r while in other cases it is convenient to use 0 through $r - 1$. Both conventions are in common usage.

Specification or Definition

Figure 4-2 illustrates how we can process one or more input operands to produce an output signal Z. In this situation we say that Z is *defined* or *specified* to have a particular relationship to the operands. To indicate this, we use the following operation.

$$\langle \text{operand} \rangle := \langle \text{value} \rangle$$

where the operation $:=$ is used to indicate that the quantity on the left-hand side of $:=$ is specified or defined to have the value given by the quantity on the right-hand side. We use this special symbol instead of the equal sign $=$ since, as is discussed shortly, the equal sign has another meaning.

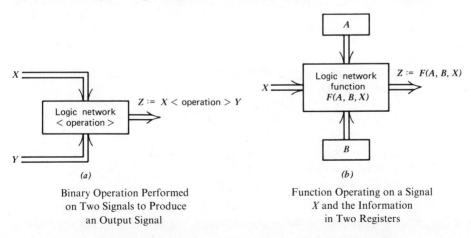

(a)	*(b)*
Binary Operation Performed on Two Signals to Produce an Output Signal	Function Operating on a Signal X and the Information in Two Registers

Figure 4-2. Schematic representation of basic information processing operations.

The term ⟨value⟩ may be either a constant or it may be obtained by carrying out a particular information processing operation on one or more input operands. Some of the typical forms that this operation can take are

$$A := B + C$$
$$A := [20]$$
$$Z := A \land X$$

The meaning of these statements will be discussed in the sections that follow.

The value of the quantity on the left-hand side of the definition operation is assumed to remain unchanged as long as all of the operands used to form that value remain unchanged.

Constants

As we know from Chapter 2, an operand can represent a wide variety of information. Thus the form that constants may take depends on the particular task we are dealing with.

The simplest situation occurs when we wish to specify that an operand has a particular value. For example, if X is a 4-tuple, then

$$X := [1, 1, 0, 1]$$

means that a particular value has been specified for the operator X.

In many situations we are interested in the value of a unit of information but not in the particular coding used to represent that information. The following conventions are used to represent numerical or character constants.

Assume that an operand is to take on the numerical value n. This is represented as

$$X := [n]$$

where it is assumed that an appropriate encoding has been used. If the base b of the number system is important, we can indicate this as

$$X := [n_b]$$

if the base is not obvious from the context of the discussion.

In particular the notation

$$X := [0]$$

is used to indicate that all of the operand's binary variables are identically 0. Thus

$$X := [0]$$

is equivalent to

$$X := [0, 0, \ldots, 0]$$

Similarly character constants are indicated as

$$X := ['AB']$$

The single quotes around the character string AB indicate that the constant is an appropriately encoded version of these characters. For example, if the modified ASCII code were used, then

$$X := ['AB']$$

would be equivalent to

$$X := [1, 1, 0, 0, 0, 0, 0, 1, 1, 1, 0, 0, 0, 0, 1, 0]$$

Expressions

The value used in a specification can be obtained by the evaluation of an expression such as

$$X := A + B$$

An expression is a formula constructed from a set of basic operations that tell us how to combine a collection of operands and constants to obtain a value. Many system level operations can be defined. In the rest of this chapter we investigate a number of these basic operations and show how they can be used. We also show how these system level operations can be represented in terms of the basic logic operations discussed in Chapter 3.

3. LOGIC OPERATIONS

The basic logic operation discussed in Chapter 3 can easily be extended to information represented in the form of r-tuples. For example, assume that X and Y are represented by the r-tuples $[x_1, x_2, \ldots, x_r]$ and $[y_1, y_2, \ldots, y_r]$ respectively. Then we may define the basic logic operations on these r-tuples as shown in Table 4-1.

Table 4-1   Logic Operations Defined on r-tuples

Operation	Representation	Meaning
NOT	$Z := \bar{X}$	$z_i = \bar{x}_i \quad i = 1, 2, \ldots, r$
AND	$Z := X \wedge Y$	$z_i = x_i \wedge y_i \quad i = 1, 2, \ldots, r$
OR	$Z := X \vee Y$	$z_i = x_i \vee y_i \quad i = 1, 2, \ldots, r$
EXCLUSIVE OR	$Z := X \oplus Y$	$z_i = x_i \oplus y_i \quad i = 1, 2, \ldots, r$
COINCIDENCE	$Z := X \odot Y$	$z_i = x_i \odot y_i \quad i = 1, 2, \ldots, r$
NAND	$Z := X \uparrow Y$	$z_i = x_i \uparrow y_i \quad i = 1, 2, \ldots, r$
NOR	$Z := X \downarrow Y$	$z_i = x_i \downarrow y_i \quad i = 1, 2, \ldots, r$

Examining this table we see that the result of applying the operation is a result Z corresponding to the r-tuple $[z_1, z_2, \ldots, z_r]$. The output is obtained by applying the indicated operation bit-by-bit to the input operands. Operations of this type are referred to as *vector* operations, since the input operands are r-tuples (or vectors) and the output is an r-tuple (or vector).

These basic operations can be expanded to provide more complex expressions. For example,

$$Z := (A \vee B) \oplus ((C \vee D) \odot (A \wedge D))$$

is such a complex expression where parenthesis have been used to indicate the order of evaluation. If A, B, C, and D were the 3-tuples $[1, 0, 1], [1, 1, 0], [0, 1, 0],$ $[1, 1, 1]$ respectively, then the expression would become

$$
\begin{aligned}
Z :&= ([1, 0, 1] \vee [1, 1, 0]) \oplus (([0, 1, 0] \vee [1, 1, 1]) \odot ([1, 0, 1] \wedge [1, 1, 1])) \\
:&= ([1, 1, 1]) \oplus ([1, 1, 1] \odot [1, 0, 1]) \\
:&= ([1, 1, 1]) \oplus ([1, 0, 1]) \\
:&= [0, 1, 0]
\end{aligned}
$$

Mixed-Mode Operations

In many situations we wish to combine a scalar x (i.e., a 1-tuple) and an r-tuple Y given by $[y_1, y_2, \ldots, y_r]$ where $r \geq 1$. To do this we define special mixed-mode logic operations according to the following convention:

Operation

$$Z := x \left\langle \begin{array}{c} \text{logical} \\ \text{operator} \end{array} \right\rangle Y$$

Meaning

$$z_i = x \left\langle \begin{array}{c} \text{logical} \\ \text{operator} \end{array} \right\rangle y_i \qquad i = 1, 2, \ldots, r$$

Table 4-2   **Some Basic Mixed Mode Operations**

Operation	Representations	Meaning	Observations
AND	$Z := x \wedge Y$ or $Z := xY$	$z_i = x \wedge y_i$ $i = 1, 2, \ldots, r$ $z_i = xy_i$ $i = 1, 2, \ldots, r$	$Z := \begin{cases} [0] & \text{if } x = 0 \\ Y & \text{if } x = 1 \end{cases}$
OR	$Z := x \vee Y$	$z_i = x \vee y_i$ $i = 1, 2, \ldots, r$	$Z := \begin{cases} Y & \text{if } x = 0 \\ [1, 1, \ldots, 1] & \\ & \text{if } x = 1 \end{cases}$
EXCLUSIVE OR	$Z := x \oplus Y$	$z_i = x \oplus y_i$ $i = 1, 2, \ldots, r$	$Z := \begin{cases} Y \text{ if } x = 0 \\ \bar{Y} \text{ if } x = 1 \end{cases}$

From this definition we see that the scalar x is combined with each bit of Y according to the rules associated with $\left\langle \begin{array}{c} \text{logical} \\ \text{operator} \end{array} \right\rangle$.

This convention introduces the interesting situations shown in Table 4-2.

Note that the result Z of a mixed-mode operation is an r-tuple if Y is an r-tuple. Because of this it is possible to combine the results of mixed-mode operations. For example, consider the expression:

$$Z := (a_1 \wedge W) \vee (a_2 \wedge X) \vee (a_3 \wedge Y)$$

If $a_1 = 0$, $a_2 = 0$, $a_3 = 1$, then

$$Z := Y$$

Similarily if $a_1 = 0$, $a_2 = 1$, $a_3 = 0$, then

$$Z := X$$

The scalar term in a mixed-mode expression can also be a logical expression. For example

$$Z := (a_1 \bar{a}_2 a_3 \wedge W) \vee (a_1 a_2 \bar{a}_3 \wedge X) \vee (a_1 a_2 a_3 \wedge Y)$$

has the result

$$Z := \begin{cases} W \text{ if } a_1 = 1, a_2 = 0, a_3 = 1 \\ X \text{ if } a_1 = 1, a_2 = 1, a_3 = 0 \\ Y \text{ if } a_1 = 1, a_2 = 1, a_3 = 1 \\ [0] \text{ for all other triples } a_1, a_2, a_3 \end{cases}$$

Control of Operations

Mixed-mode operations are particularly useful if we wish to use a control signal to define which operation is to be performed by a combinational logic network. Networks of this type are quite common in digital systems, and they have the typical form illustrated in Figure 4-3.

In this network the value of the control signal T determines which operation is to be performed to produce the output signal Z. For example, suppose that this network is to be designed to carry out the following tasks:

Value of Control Signal $T := [t_1, t_2]$	Value of Output Signal Z
$[0, 0]$	$[0]$
$[0, 1]$	$A \vee B$
$[1, 0]$	$\overline{A}$
$[1, 1]$	$A \wedge B$

The following mixed-mode expression can be used to define Z:

$$Z := (\bar{t}_1 t_2 \wedge (A \vee B)) \vee (t_1 \bar{t}_2 \wedge \overline{A}) \vee (t_1 t_2 \wedge (A \wedge B))$$

Note that in this expression for Z we do not need the term

$$\bar{t}_1 \bar{t}_2 \wedge [0]$$

since this term is, by definition, [0] for all input conditions.

We will find this ability to provide such a compact representation for a combinational logic network very useful in later discussions.

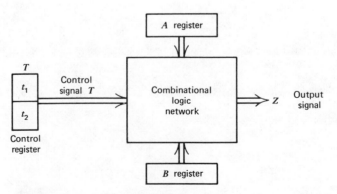

Figure 4-3. A typical controlled information processing network.

EXERCISES

1. Let $A := [1, 0, 1]$, $B := [1, 1, 0]$, $C := [0, 0, 1]$.
   Find Z for the following logical specification operations.

   (a) $Z := A \oplus (B \oplus C)$
   (b) $Z := (A \vee B) \oplus (\bar{A} \vee \bar{B})$
   (c) $Z := (A \downarrow B) \downarrow (A \downarrow B)$

2. Assume that the characters are encoded using the modified ASCII code and that Z is represented by an 8-tuple. Find Z.

   (a) $Z := ['A'] \vee [17_{10}]$
   (b) $Z := ['1'] \wedge [7_8]$
   (c) $Z := ['A'] \odot ['B']$

3. Give the mixed-mode expression that will compute Z for the following conditions.

Control Signal $T := [t_1 t_2]$	Value of Z
$[0, 0]$	A
$[0, 1]$	$\bar{A} \vee \bar{B}$
$[1, 0]$	$A \oplus C$
$[1, 1]$	$(A \downarrow B) \oplus C$

4. ADDITION AND SUBTRACTION

We are all familiar with the basic arithmetic operations of addition and subtraction as they are carried out using decimal numbers. From an abstract viewpoint we can represent addition and subtraction as

(a) Addition

$$Z := X + Y$$

(b) Subtraction

$$Z := X - Y$$

However to fully appreciate how these operations are performed and the limitations imposed on these operations by the system, we must consider the following questions.

(a) What method of encoding is used to represent the numerical information?
(b) How are negative numbers represented?
(c) How many bits are used in the digital representation of the information?

In this section we first consider the addition and subtraction of binary numbers. This discussion is then extended to other number systems and methods of encoding.

Binary Addition

Binary addition is carried out in the same way as decimal addition except that we use the following relationships.

$$
\begin{array}{cccc}
0 & 0 & 1 & 1 \\
+0 & +1 & +0 & +1 \\
\hline
0 & 1 & 1 & 10
\end{array}
$$

                                              ↖Carry digit

The carry digit becomes important when adding two multiple digit binary numbers. The following example illustrates this point

$$
\begin{array}{cccccc}
 & 1 & 1 & & & & \text{Carry} \\
 & 1 & 0 & 1 & 1 & 0 & \text{Augend number} \\
+ & 0 & 0 & 1 & 1 & 1 & \text{Addend number} \\
\hline
 & 1 & 1 & 1 & 0 & 1 & \text{Sum}
\end{array}
$$

The dotted arrows indicate that a carry was generated and brought over to be added to the next column. We have also used the relationship that

$$1 + 1 + 1 = 10 + 1 = 11$$

If we add two r-bit binary numbers the result will be a binary number of no more than $r + 1$ bits. For example

$$
\begin{array}{cccccc}
1 & 1 & 1 & 1 & & \text{Carry} \\
1 & 0 & 1 & 1 & 0 & \text{Augend number} \\
0 & 1 & 1 & 1 & 0 & \text{Addend number} \\
\hline
1 & 0 & 0 & 1 & 0 & 0 & \text{Sum}
\end{array}
$$

Thus we see that the sum of two 5-bit numbers produces a result that requires 6 bits to represent it.

As long as we place no restriction on the number of bits that we can have in a binary number, we have no problem in carrying out the addition of two or more numbers. However, now let us consider the problem that arises if each of the binary numbers involved in the addition process must fit into an r-cell register. Without loss of generality we consider, initially, only integer valued numbers.

From our previous discussion we know that any number that we encounter must fall between 0 and $2^r - 1$. If we add two numbers that give a sum which does not exceed $2^r - 1$ there is no problem. However, if the sum does exceed $2^r - 1$, then we lose the higher order bit. In particular, assume that we form the sum $A + B$ and this gives us a number larger than $2^r - 1$. The number that we will actually form, since we do not retain the $r + 1$th bit will be $A + B - 2^r$. The following example illustrates this. Assume that $r = 3$, $A_{10} = 6$, and $B_{10} = 4$. Then in binary notation we have

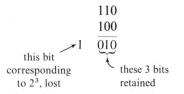

$$
\begin{array}{r}
110 \\
100 \\
\hline
010
\end{array}
$$

this bit corresponding to 2^3, lost

these 3 bits retained

The highest order bit is lost since we can only retain 3 bits. Thus we find that the answer is $(6 + 4)_{10} - (2^3)_{10} = 2_{10} = 010_2$. If we have a means for detecting the fact that we have an extra bit, we can detect that the sum is too large to store in our register. Such a situation is referred to as an *overflow* of our register.

Modular Number System

The above is an example of modular arithmetic which we encounter when we have to work with finite length registers. Normally we can represent numbers as a set of ordered points on a line as illustrated in Figure 4-4. Addition then simply consists of connecting line segments together as shown.

When we deal with numbers stored in an r-bit register we must use a different graphical representation. In this case we are dealing with the finite set of numbers between 0 and $2^r - 1$. Graphically we can represent the distinct numbers of this set as points on the circumference of a circle.

For example if $r = 3$ this representation has the form shown in Figure 4-5.

Addition can be represented as before by connecting line segments. The only difference, in this case, is that the line segments lie along the circumference of the circle. If A and B are two r-bit numbers such that their sum is less than 2^r, then addition in this system is the same as before. However, if the sum is equal to or greater than 2^r we have the situation illustrated in Figure 4-6. The resulting number is the remainder we obtain by subtracting 2^r from the sum. This phenomenon can be formalized in the following manner.

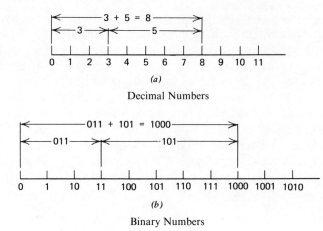

(a)

Decimal Numbers

(b)

Binary Numbers

Figure 4-4. Graphical method of representing the addition of numbers on a linear scale.

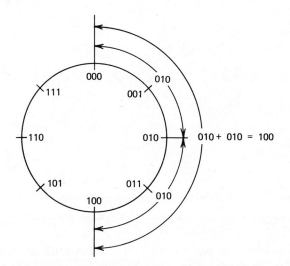

Figure 4-5. Circular representation of numbers stored in 3-bit register.

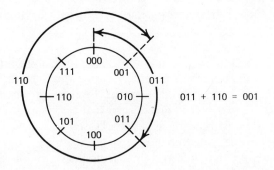

Figure 4-6. An example of addition involving fixed-length registers.

The numbers A and B are said to be *equivalent modulo* N if the remainder obtained when A is divided by N is the same as the remainder that is obtained when B is divided by N. This is indicated by writing

$$A \equiv_N B$$

For example if

$$A = 10 \quad \text{and} \quad B = 18$$

then we say that

$$A \equiv_8 B$$

since

$$10 = 1 \cdot 8 + \overset{\text{remainder}}{2} \qquad \text{and} \quad 18 = 2 \cdot 8 + \overset{\text{remainder}}{2}$$

In a modular number system we have

$$0 \equiv_N N$$
$$1 \equiv_N N + 1$$
$$\vdots$$
$$N - 1 \equiv_N N + N - 1 = 2N - 1$$

Addition in a modular number system is thus the same as the addition process illustrated in Figures 4-5 and 4-6.

When we deal with numerical information represented by r-bit binary numbers all of our arithmetic operations are carried out modulo 2^r. With a little practice it is as easy to carry out the arithmetic operations modulo 2^r as it is to carry out the same operations in the standard manner.

For example, the addition table for numbers modulo 4 is given by Table 4-3. Thus, if we wish to add 2 and 3 we go to the table and find that $2 + 3 = 5 \equiv_4 1$.

Table 4-3   Addition Table For Addition Modulo 4

+	0	1	2	3
0	0	1	2	3
1	1	2	3	$4 \equiv_4 0$
2	2	3	$4 \equiv_4 0$	$5 \equiv_4 1$
3	3	$4 \equiv_4 0$	$5 \equiv_4 1$	$6 \equiv_4 2$

Binary Subtraction

Binary subtraction is carried out in essentially the same way that we carry out decimal subtraction. There is no problem in carrying out the following subtractions.

$$
\begin{array}{ccc}
0 & 1 & 1 \\
-0 & -0 & -1 \\
\hline
0 & 1 & 0
\end{array}
$$

However, when we try to form $0 - 1$ we find that we cannot carry out this operation unless we introduce a borrowing process. For this case we assume that we have

$$
\begin{array}{r}
10 \\
-1 \\
\hline
01
\end{array}
$$

The extra 1 that we used is borrowed from the next higher order column by subtracting 1 from that column. For example to form $11011 - 01101$ we proceed in the following manner

$$
\begin{array}{ccccccl}
-1 & -1 & & & & & \text{Borrow} \\
1 & 11 & 10 & 1 & 1 & & \text{Minuend} \\
- & 0 & 1 & 1 & 0 & 1 & \text{Subtrahend} \\
\hline
0 & 1 & 1 & 1 & 0 & & \text{Difference}
\end{array}
$$

In this example the answer is positive because the subtrahend is smaller than the minuend. However, if the reverse condition were true, we would have to account for this by subtracting the minuend from the subtrahend and then assign a negative sign to the answer.

This form of arithmetic is easily handled when we are making hand calculations. However, if we wish to build a computer to carry out both addition and subtraction using this form of arithmetic, we need separate logic networks for each operation. If we wish to minimize the number of logic networks we can use a special property of modular number systems to replace the subtraction operation by an addition operation.

2's Complement Representation of Negative Numbers

A number B is said to be the negative of a number A if

$$
A + B = 0
$$

If we are dealing with a regular number system we have the unique relationship

$$
B = -A
$$

However, let us consider what happens if we are dealing with the set of numbers modulo N. In this case

$$A + B \equiv_N 0$$

implies that B is the negative of A. But B is not unique. In fact any B such that

$$B = kN - A \qquad k = 0, 1, \ldots$$

satisfies the condition that B is the negative modulo N of A. For $k = 0$ we have the standard relationship. However, we have a very interesting situation for the case $k = 1$.

If A is less than N, then $B = N - A$ is seen to be a positive number less than N. Thus, as far as all our calculations are concerned, we can use $B = N - A$ in any calculation calling for $-A$ as long as all the operations are performed modulo N. Thus the calculation

$$C = D - A$$

is equivalent (modulo N) to

$$C = D + (N - A)$$

Therefore if we can find an easy way to find $(N - A)$, not involving subtraction we see that the subtraction operation can be replaced by addition. We now show how this can be accomplished.

If we are carrying out our operations using r-bit binary integers, then

$$N = 2^r$$

We can represent this N in binary form as

$$N = \overbrace{1000 \cdots 0}^{r + 1 \text{ terms}} = \overbrace{111 \cdots 1}^{r \text{ terms}} + \overbrace{00 \cdots 0\,1}^{r - 1 \text{ terms}}$$

Now let $A = a_{r-1}, a_{r-2}, a_{r-3} \cdots a_0$ be any r-bit number. Forming $(N - A)$ we have

$$N - A = (1 - a_{r-1}), (1 - a_{r-2}), (1 - a_{r-3}), \ldots, (1 - a_0) + 000 \cdots 01$$

But a_j is either 1 or 0. Thus $(1 - a_j)$ is 0 if a_j is 1 and 1 if a_j is 0. For example, let $r = 3$ and $A = 010$. Then

$$N = 1000 = 111 + 001$$

and

$$N - A = 1000 - 010 = 111 - 010 + 001 = (1 - 0), (1 - 1), (1 - 0) + 001$$
$$= 101 + 001 = 110$$

The quantity $(N - A)$ is called the *2's complement* of A. The 2's complement of any r-bit binary number A is found by applying the following algorithm.

1. Set each bit of A to its opposite value by forming $\bar{A}$.
2. Add 1 to the rightmost digit of the result and propagate any carry generated.

For example let $r = 5$ and $A = 01000$. Then the 2's complement of A is formed as follows.

Step 1   10111
Step 2 $+00001$
2's complement of A $\overline{11000}$

Table 4-4 gives the binary representation of the decimal numbers between $+7$ and -7. The negative numbers are represented in 2's complement form.

Examining this table we see that we have used 4 bits to represent the numbers. Any number in the table can be represented as

$$A = a_3 a_2 a_1 a_0$$

If a_3 is 0, then A is a positive integer, while if a_3 is 1, then A is a negative integer. Generalizing this observation we see that the leftmost bit always represents the sign of the number no matter what value of r is used.

Table 4-4 Binary Representation of Numbers Between $+7$ and -7 with 2's Complement Representation of Negative Numbers

Binary Number	Decimal Number
0111	7
0110	6
0101	5
0100	4
0011	3
0010	2
0001	1
0000	0
1111	-1
1110	-2
1101	-3
1100	-4
1011	-5
1010	-6
1001	-7

We also note that if we take the 2's complement of $(N - A)$ we have

$$N - (N - A) = A$$

Thus the relation $-(-A) = A$ also holds true for the 2's complement representation of negative numbers.

2's Complement Subtraction

The 2's complement representation for negative numbers allows us to carry out subtraction by using addition. To see this assume that A and B are two r-bit binary numbers which may represent a decimal value between $\pm(2^{r-1} - 1)$. It is also assumed that negative numbers are represented in 2's complement form.

Assume that we wish to compute $A - B$ where A and B may themselves be positive or negative. To perform this calculation we use the result that

$$A + (N - B) \equiv_N A - B$$

where $N = 2^r$. Thus to form $A - B$ we first form the 2's complement of B and then add the result to A. The following examples illustrate this type of calculation for several different cases.

1. $A = 0111_2 = 7_{10} \qquad B = 0110_2 = 6_{10}$
    $A - B = 0111 + 1010 = 10001 \equiv_{2^4} 0001$

2. $A = 0011_2 = 3_{10} \qquad B = 1101_2 = -3_{10}$
    $A - B = 0011 + 0011 = 0110$

3. $A = 1101_2 = -3_{10} \qquad B = 0100_2 = 4_{10}$
    $A - B = 1101 - 1100 = 11001 \equiv_{2^4} 1001$

In the above examples we note that whenever we have an overflow (i.e., the result is expressed as a 5-bit number) we disregard the overflow bit to obtain the result of our computation. This observation can be generalized to:

Whenever a carry is generated in performing 2's complement arithmetic this carry is ignored.

This generalization assumes that the true result of the calculation falls within the range $\pm(2^{r-1} - 1)$.

When carrying out arithmetic operations using 2's complement arithmetic we must always make sure that all of the terms involved in the computation are represented as r-bit numbers. For example, let us find $A - B$, where $A = 1101.10$ and $B = 10.111$, using 2's complement arithmetic. To carry out this calculation we must first decide on the proper value for r and then find the 2's complement for B. Writing out $A - B$ gives

add extra 0 to provide for sign bit

note that we must line up
binary point

$$A = \quad 01101.100$$

add a 0

$$-B = -00010.111$$

add extra 0's

In forming the expression for $A - B$ we note that before we can determine r we must first line up the binary points and then add 0's to make sure each number has the same number of positions. Finally, we add an extra 0 on the left to allow for the sign digit. After finishing this preliminary organization we can then find r by counting the number of digits in either number. Carrying out this process we find that $r = 8$. Thus the 2's complement of B is

$$N - B = 11101.000 + 00000.001 = 11101.001$$

Thus

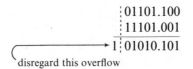

$$\begin{array}{r} 01101.100 \\ 11101.001 \\ \hline 1\,01010.101 \end{array}$$

disregard this overflow

Therefore

$$A - B = 1010.101$$

which is a positive number, since the sign bit has a value of zero. In performing this type of arithmetic operation, one should be very careful to account for all of the bit positions *including the sign-bit position*.

1's Complement Representation of Negative Numbers

In forming the 2's complement of a number we had to perform two steps. First we negated each digit of the number and then we added 1 to the result. If we omit the last step, we form what is known as the *1's complement* of the number. For example the 1's complement of

0101 is 1010.

Table 4-5 presents the binary representation of the positive and negative integers between $+7$ and -7 where a 1's complement representation is used for the negative numbers.

Table 4-5 Binary Representation of
Numbers Between +7 and −7 with
1's Complement Representation of
Negative Numbers

Binary Number	Decimal Number
0111	+7
0110	+6
0101	+5
0100	+4
0011	+3
0010	+2
0001	+1
0000	+0
1111	−0
1110	−1
1101	−2
1100	−3
1011	−4
1010	−5
1001	−6
1000	−7

Examining this table we see that we have both a positive and a negative zero and that this table differs from Table 4-5 only by the fact that an extra one must be added to the negative numbers to form the 2's complement.

1's Complement Subtraction

To carry out the subtraction process using 1's complement subtraction we proceed in the same way as for 2's complement subtraction except that we do not neglect the carry at the left end if one is generated. This is illustrated in the following example.

Suppose we wish to calculate $A - B$ where $A = 1101.10$ and $B = 10.111$. This is carried out in the following manner with $r = 8$.

```
              01101.100    A
              11101.000    1's complement of B
              ─────────
carry       1 01010.100
              │
              ↓
              ┆---------► 1    add in carry
              ─────────
              01010.101
```

This example has illustrated the fact that whenever a carry is generated, it is added to the least significant digit of the sum generated by the addition operation. This is known as an *end-around carry*.

To show why we need to include the end around carry assume that X and Y are both positive r-bit numbers. The 1's complement of Y is represented (in decimal notation) as

$$-Y \equiv_{2^r} 2^r - Y - 1$$

To perform the addition $X + (-Y)$ we have

$$X + (1\text{'s complement of } Y) = X + 2^r - Y - 1$$
$$= 2^r + (X - Y) - 1$$

We must now consider two possibilities

1. If $X \geq Y$ then $X - Y \geq 0$ and the sum will be a positive number with a carry. If this carry is added to the result this gives

$$[(X - Y) - 1 + \overset{\overset{\text{carry added in}}{\frown}}{1}]$$

   which is $(X - Y)$ the desired result.

2. If $X < Y$ then the sum will be $2^r - (Y - X) - 1$ with no carry, which is the 1's complement of the positive number $(Y - X)$.

Finally we must consider the addition of $(-X)$ to $(-Y)$. This is represented as

$$(2^r - X - 1) + (2^r - Y - 1) = 2^r + [2^r - (X + Y) - 1] - 1$$

Thus the carry represented by the first 2^r can be added in to eliminate the last -1 leaving the result

$$[2^r - (X + Y) - 1]$$

which is the 1's complement representation of $-(X + Y)$.
Note that we have assumed that $2^r - 1 \geq X + Y \geq 0$.

Realization of an Adder Logic Network

The basic task performed in the previous discussion is that of addition. Thus let us consider how we can describe the behavior of a combinational logic network that will carry out the operation

$$Z := A + B$$

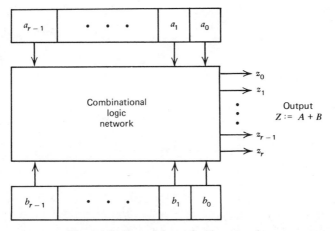

Figure 4-7. General form of adder network.

where A and B correspond to two r-bit registers that hold two binary numbers. This network can be assumed to have the form shown in Figure 4-7. Note that the output Z is assumed to be represented by $r + 1$ bits.

The direct method of using a truth table to represent the behavior of the whole network cannot be easily used except for $r \leq 2$. Instead we must look at the addition process in greater detail. As a first step let us write out the general addition operation in symbolic form. Doing this we have

$$
\begin{array}{cccccccc}
c_{r-1} & c_{r-2} & c_{r-3} & & c_1 & c_0 & & \text{Carry} \\
a_{r-1} & a_{r-2} & \cdots & a_2 & a_1 & a_0 & \\
b_{r-1} & b_{r-2} & \cdots & b_2 & b_1 & b_0 & \\
\hline
z_r & z_{r-1} & z_{r-2} & z_2 & z_1 & z_0 & & \text{Sum}
\end{array}
$$

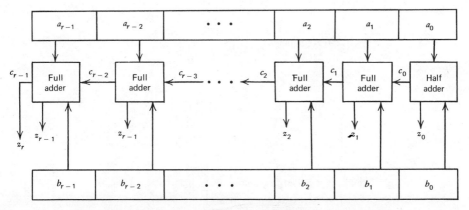

Figure 4-8. Adder network realization using subnetworks to carry out the intermediate summation process.

Table 4-6   Truth
Table for Half Adder

a_0	b_0	z_0	c_0
0	0	0	0
0	1	1	0
1	0	1	0
1	1	0	1

In this form the z_i's are the sums and the c_i's are the carries produced at the ith stage. Examining this example we see that we can decompose the general addition network into a collection of subnetworks as shown in Figure 4-8.

The first subnetwork is called a *half adder*, since all it has to do is compute z_0 and c_0 from a_0 and b_0. All of the rest of the subnetworks are called *full adders*, since they must not only form the sum of a_i and b_i but also must include the carry information from the previous stage in forming the sum. To complete the specification of this network, we must now develop the truth tables for both the half adder and the full adder.

For the half adder we note that there are two inputs to this subnetwork and two outputs. Thus the table will have 2^2 rows. The table is given by Table 4-6.

Examining this table we find that z_0 and c_0 are given by

$$z_0 = \bar{a}_0 b_0 \vee a_0 \bar{b}_0 = m_1 \vee m_2 \qquad c_0 = a_0 b_0 = m_3$$

where m_1, m_2, and m_3 are the minterms associated with the table. Similarly the truth table for the full adder has the form given by Table 4-7.

Table 4-7 Truth Table for Full Adder

a_i	b_i	c_{i-1}	z_i	c_i
0	0	0	0	0
0	0	1	1	0
0	1	0	1	0
0	1	1	0	1
1	0	0	1	0
1	0	1	0	1
1	1	0	0	1
1	1	1	1	1

Examining this table we see that the values of z_i and c_i are given by

$$z_i = \bar{a}_i \bar{b}_i c_{i-1} \vee \bar{a}_i b_i \bar{c}_{i-1} \vee a_i \bar{b}_i \bar{c}_{i-1} \vee a_i b_i c_{i-1} = m_1 \vee m_2 \vee m_4 \vee m_7$$

$$c_i = \bar{a}_i b_i c_{i-1} \vee a_i \bar{b}_i c_{i-1} \vee a_i b_i \bar{c}_{i-1} \vee a_i b_i c_{i-1} = m_3 \vee m_5 \vee m_6 \vee m_7$$

where the m_i's again represent the minterms necessary to represent each expression. To complete the design we note that

$$z_r = c_{r-1}$$

Complement Arithmetic in the Decimal Number System

Although binary arithmetic is very important in digital system design, we often find that some type of decimal encoding of the decimal numbers is used in systems that perform numerical calculations. We could use standard decimal addition and subtraction. However, just as for the binary system, it is easier to use complement arithmetic to perform subtraction. The following discussion describes complement arithmetic in the decimal number system.

Let

$$D = d_{n-1} d_{n-2} \cdots d_0$$

$$n \text{ terms}$$

be an n-digit decimal integer. Then the largest value of D is $\overbrace{999 \cdots 9}$.
In particular we note that

$$10^n = \overbrace{999 \cdots 9}^{n \text{ terms}} + \overbrace{00 \cdots 01}^{n-1 \text{ terms}} = \overbrace{1000 \cdots 0}^{n \text{ terms}}$$

The *10's complement* of an n-digit decimal number is thus

$$10^n - D = c_{n-1} c_{n-2} \cdots c_0 + 000 \cdots 01$$

where $c_i = (10 - 1) - d_i = 9 - d_i$.
To form the 10's complement of a decimal number $A = d_{n-1} d_{n-2} \cdots d_0$

(a) Subtract each d_i from 9 to give

$$(9 - d_{n-1}), (9 - d_{n-2}), \ldots, (9 - d_0)$$

(b) Add 1 to the resulting number.

For example if $n = 6$ and $D = 273245$, then the 10's complement of D is

$$10^6 - D = (9 - 2), (9 - 7), (9 - 3), (9 - 2), (9 - 4), (9 - 5) + 000001$$
$$= 726754 + 000001 = 726755$$

If we use 10's complement arithmetic then the positive numbers correspond to the numbers between $\overbrace{00 \cdots 0}^{n \text{ terms}}$ and $\overbrace{499 \cdots 9}^{n - 1 \text{ terms}}$ while the negative numbers correspond to the numbers between $\overbrace{99 \cdots 9}^{n \text{ terms}}$ (corresponds to -1) and $50 \cdots 01$ (corresponds to $-499 \cdots 9$). The number $50 \cdots 0$ serves as a dividing line between the positive and negative numbers.

To illustrate how we can perform arithmetic operations using 10's complement addition let

$$A = 22763.425$$

$$B = 13621.2$$

and compute $C = A - B$. This is carried out as follows

$$
\begin{array}{ll}
22763.425 & A \\
86378.800 & \text{10's complement of } B \\
\hline
1\ 09142.225 &
\end{array}
$$

disregard overflow

Answer 9142.225

Note that whenever there is a carry in 10's complement addition the carry is disregarded.

We can also form the *9's complement* of a decimal number. In this case we form the 10's complement of the number but do not add the 1 to the lowest order digit. When we perform a subtraction, any carry must be added into the lower order digit as we did for 1's complement arithmetic.

For example, let A and B be defined as above. Then

$$
\begin{array}{ll}
22763.425 & A \\
86378.799 & \text{9's complement of } B \\
\hline
109142.224 & \\
\cdots\cdots\cdots\to 1 & \\
\hline
09142.225 & \text{Answer 9142.225}
\end{array}
$$

End around
carry

Hardware Realization of a Decimal Adder

The hardware realization of a decimal adder is much more complex than a binary adder. Assume that a register D contains an encoded decimal number. Each decimal digit is represented by 4 binary bits. Thus the decimal number $d_{n-1}d_{n-2} \cdots d_0$ would require a representation of the form shown in Figure 4-9.

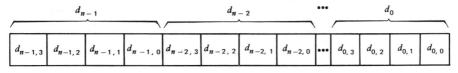

Figure 4-9. Encoded decimal number.

Thus if we wish to add two numbers, say D and E, represented in this form, we could use a logic network of the form shown in Figure 4-10.

The only difference in this network from the binary adder is the design of the subnetworks that carry out the digit-by-digit addition. In this case the network has the form shown in Figure 4-11.

By examining this figure we see that the network will have $4 + 4 + 1 = 9$ inputs and $4 + 1 = 5$ outputs. Thus a truth table with $2^9 = 512$ rows would be required to formally design this network. In addition, we must specify the coding used to represent the decimal numbers.

At this point we must end this discussion, since we have not yet developed enough design tools to complete our design except for the brute force manner of using a truth table. We will encounter this problem later. However, it is possible to purchase an integrated circuit module that will carry out this BCD addition task.

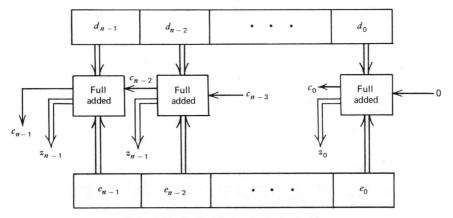

Figure 4-10. General form of a decimal adder.

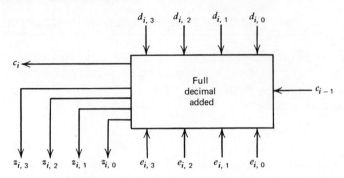

Figure 4-11. General form of a full decimal adder.

Complements in Number Systems with Radix r

The two systems of complements that we have just considered are special cases of general complement arithmetic. If the base of the number system is r the r's complement or the true complement of the n-digit number

$$D = d_{n-1}d_{n-2} \cdots d_0$$

is

$$r^n - D = c_{n-1}c_{n-2} \cdots c_0 + 000 \cdots 01$$

where $c_i = (r - 1) - d_i$.

For example, if

$$r = 8 \quad \text{and} \quad D = 157513 \text{ then the 8's complement is}$$
$$620264 + 000001$$
$$= 620265$$

If we do not add the 1 to the lowest order digit when we form the r's complement we form the (radix $-$ 1) complement. Thus the 7's $=$ $(8 - 1)$'s complement of 157513 is 620264. The arithmetic operations using true complements or (radix $-$ 1) complements is carried out in the same manner as that used for the decimal and binary cases. For example, assume that $A = 3763$ and $B = 104$ are two octal numbers. Then $A - B$ can be obtained by forming the 8's complement of B and adding A. This calculation gives the following results

$$
\begin{array}{r}
A \quad 3763 \\
-B \quad 7674 \\
\hline
1\ 3657
\end{array}
$$

carry ignored

$$A - B = 3657$$

Similarly the same computation performed using 7's complement arithmetic is

$$
\begin{array}{rr}
A & 3763 \\
-B & 7673 \\
\hline
& 13656 \\
\text{End around} & \cdots\!\!\rightarrow 1 \\
\text{carry} & \overline{3657}
\end{array}
$$

The result of the 8's complement calculations is positive, since it falls in the range 0000 to 3777. If it had fallen in the range 4000 to 7777, the result would be a negative number represented in 8's complement form.

Similarly the result of the 7's complement calculation is positive, since it falls in the range 0000 to 3777. If it had fallen in the range 4000 to 7777, the result would have been a negative number represented in 7's complement form.

Addition and subtraction are the keys to many of the more complex computational tasks performed in a digital system. For example, multiplication involves a sequence of addition operations, and division requires a sequence of subtractions. Complex operations of this type are considered in later chapters.

EXERCISES

1. Find the r's complement and the (radix $-$ 1) complement of the following numbers, which are all assumed to be positive.

   (a) $r = 2$ 10101.11
   (b) $r = 3$ 121.11
   (c) $r = 8$ 2721.63
   (d) $r = 16$ A6315

2. Compute $A - B$. A and B are assumed to both be positive. Use both r's complement and (radix $-$ 1) arithmetic.

   (a) $r = 2$ $A = 101.110$ $B = 11.01011$
   (b) $r = 3$ $A = 212.21$ $B = 22.22$
   (c) $r = 8$ $A = 7644.24$ $B = 77654.21$

5. DECISIONS AND RELATIONS

In our previous discussion we concentrated on the operations that can be used to form complex expressions. The arguments of these expressions and the resulting values were n-tuples. In any complex information processing task we must also be able to control the sequence of a calculation by first testing the current status of

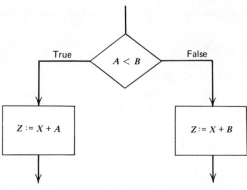

Figure 4-12. Use of a decision in a calculation.

one or more quantities and then performing the next step of the calculation based on the result of this test. An example of such a situation is illustrated in Figure 4-12. To perform this computational task the following steps must be performed.

(a) Compare the numerical value of A to the numerical value to B.
(b) If it is TRUE that $A < B$ then compute Z as $X + A$.
(c) If it is FALSE that $A < B$ then compute Z as $X + B$.

Observing this example, we note that we have introduced a new type of an expression. The expression $(A < B)$ has n-tuple arguments, the quantities A and B, but has a scalar result that has a value either TRUE or FALSE (or equivalently 1 or 0). The operator $<$ is called a *relational operator*.

Relational Operators

In many information processing tasks we find it necessary to compare two items of information and make the logical decision that either

(a) "it is TRUE that the two items compare in the required manner"
or
(b) "it is FALSE that the two items compare in the required manner"

Mathematically the task of making such a comparison is carried out by using a binary relational operator $\mathcal{R}$. Let X and Y be the two items of information to be compared. Then a relational operation has the general form

$$z := X \mathcal{R} Y$$

where z is a scalar that has the value 1 (TRUE) if the comparison indicated by $\mathcal{R}$ is satisfied. Otherwise z has the value 0 (FALSE).

The relational operations given in Table 4-8 are in common usage in the design of digital systems.

Table 4-8   The Basic Relational Operations

$<$ Less than	$>$ Greater than
$\leq$ Less than or equal	$\geq$ Greater than or equal
$=$ Equal	$\neq$ Not equal

These relational operations provide all of the tools that we need to define any decision process which we might desire to carry out in a digital system. Thus we must be very explicit in their definition if we are to make certain they are used properly.

The information contained in X and Y is represented by bit patterns. To employ relational operations of the type given in Table 4-8, we make the following assumptions.

(a) X and Y have the same number of bits in their representation.
(b)   The information represented by X and Y is assumed, for the purpose of comparison, to be numeric.

To illustrate these assumptions assume that X and Y are 8-tuples and that

$$X := [11000001]$$

$$Y := [11000101]$$

Then in the relational operation

$$z := X < Y$$

z has the following values depending on the meaning we assign to X and Y.

(a) X, Y represent unsigned binary numbers

$$z := 1 \qquad (X_{10} = 193, Y_{10} = 197)$$

(b) X, Y represent sign-magnitude binary numbers

$$z := 0 \qquad (X_{10} = -65, Y_{10} = -69)$$

(c) X, Y represent ASCII encoded letters

$$z := 1 \qquad (X = [`A'], Y = [`E']; X_{10} < Y_{10})$$

In some applications, one of the operands in a relational operation can be a constant. For convenience we usually give the constant in its uncoded form and assume that proper encoding is obvious from the context. For example

$$z := X < [108_{10}]$$

$$z := Y > [`A']$$

$$z := Z = [5_8]$$

will all have a value of $z := 1$ if $X = 82_{10}$, $Y = {}'B'$ and $Z = 5_8$. Similarly

$$z := X > [108_8]$$
$$z := Y = ['A']$$
$$z := Z > [25_8]$$

will all produce $z := 0$ for the same values assigned to X, Y, and Z.

Collating Sequence

If the relational operations are applied to character information we must define a "natural ordering" that indicates how relations such as $<$ or $>$ are to be interpreted. This ordering depends on the code used to represent the characters and is referred to as the *collating sequence* of the character set. The collating sequence for the two standard character codes is given below

Collating sequence ASCII code

$$\sqcup < 0 < 1 < 2 < \cdots < 8 < 9 < A < B < \cdots < X < Y < Z$$

Note: $\sqcup$—blank

Collating sequence EBCDIC code

$$\sqcup < A < B < \cdots < X < Y < Z < 0 < 1 < 2 < \cdots < 8 < 9$$

Once the collating sequence is established for a given system, the ordering of any two character sequences can be decided very easily. Starting on the left of both sequences a character-by-character comparison is carried out until two dissimilar characters are found. The two character sequences are then ordered according to these two characters. For example

$$['ABC'] < ['DEF']$$
$$['ABC'] < ['ABF']$$

both have a value of 1 while

$$['AC'] > ['BC']$$

has a value of 0.

We must, however, be careful in working with relational operations. For example, the value of z in the expression

$$z := ['2A'] < ['A2']$$

is 1 if an ASCII code is used and is 0 if an EBCDIC code is used.

Relational Expressions

When we apply a relational operator, the resulting value is a scalar. But scalars can be combined by using the standard logic operations of AND, OR, NOT, etc. Thus we can use this property to define complex relational expressions.

For example

$$z := ((A < B) \wedge (A < C)) \vee ((B < C) \wedge (B < A))$$

would be such a relational expression where A, B, and C represent n-tuples and the result z is a scalar.

Mixed-Mode Expressions and Control

As we learned in Section 3, we can use mixed-mode operations to control the behavior of a logic network. Since the value of a relational expression is a scalar, we can substitute a relational expression for a scalar term in a mixed mode expression. This means that we can use relational expressions to control the behavior of a computation. For example, consider the decision illustrated in Figure 4-12. The computation represented by the partial flowchart of that figure can be described by the following specification statement.

$$Z := ((A < B) \wedge (X + A)) \vee ((A \geq B) \wedge (X + B))$$

From this we see that the operation performed will depend on the values of A and B.

Realization of Relational Operations

A logic expression to represent the basic relational operations can easily be derived. For example, let us consider the relationship $=$. Assume that the two arguments A and B are represented by the n-tuples $[a_{n-1}, a_{n-2}, \ldots, a_0]$ and $[b_{n-1}, b_{n-2}, \ldots, b_0]$ respectively. In this case

$$A = B \quad \text{if and only if } a_i = b_i \quad \text{for} \quad i = 0, 1, \ldots, n - 1$$

The COINCIDENCE binary operation can be applied on a bit-by-bit basis to carry out this test. Thus the relational operation

$$z := A = B$$

can be carried out by a combinational logic network that realizes the following logical expression

$$z := (a_{n-1} \odot b_{n-1}) \wedge (a_{n-2} \odot b_{n-2}) \wedge \cdots \wedge (a_0 \odot b_0)$$

As a somewhat more complex example consider the relation $<$. This operation can be realized by a combinational logic network of the form shown in Figure 4-13. The comparison needed to evaluate

$$z := A < B$$

is carried out on a bit-by-bit basis by the subnetworks N, which are defined according to the following rules:

$$d_i = 1 \quad \text{if (a) } a_i = 0, b_i = 1$$
$$\text{(b) } d_{i-1} = 1, a_i = 0, b_i = 0$$
$$\text{(c) } d_{i-1} = 1, a_i = 1, b_i = 1$$
$$d_i = 0 \quad \text{all other cases}$$

These rules are based on the fact that we can scan A and B from left-to-right until we find 2 bits that are not equal. If $a_i = 0$ and $b_i = 1$, then we know that $A < B$

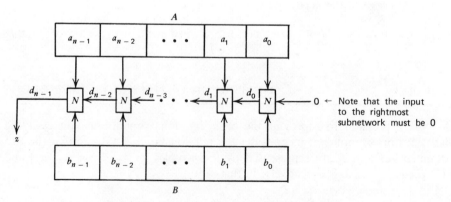

Figure 4-13. Network to realize relational operation.

and we set $d_i = 1$ and propagate this value to the output to give the result that z is 1. If $a_i = 1$ and $b_i = 0$, then we know that A is not less than B, and we set $d_i = 0$ and propagate that to the output to give the result that z is 0. Note that the input to the rightmost subnetwork must be 0. For example, consider the following cases:

A	B	d_2	d_1	d_0	z
[0, 1, 1]	[0, 1, 1]	0	0	0	0
[0, 1, 0]	[0, 1, 1]	1	1	1	1
[0, 1, 0]	[1, 1, 0]	1	0	0	1

Using these results, we generate the truth table for the network N shown in Table 4-9.

Table 4-9 Truth Table for Network N

a_i	b_i	d_{i-1}	d_i
0	0	0	0
0	0	1	1
0	1	0	1
0	1	1	1
1	0	0	0
1	0	1	0
1	1	0	0
1	1	1	1

This means that

$$d_i = \bar{a}_i\bar{b}_id_{i-1} \vee \bar{a}_ib_i\bar{d}_{i-1} \vee \bar{a}_ib_id_{i-1} \vee a_ib_id_{i-1}$$

Similar types of logic expressions can be obtained for the other basic logic operations.

Control of a Logic Network

To illustrate how we can use mixed-mode relational expressions to control a logic network, consider the network shown in Figure 4-14.

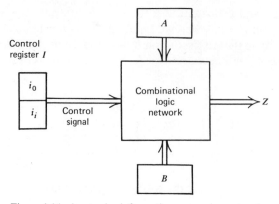

Figure 4-14. A complex information processing network.

The operations performed on A and B are determined by the control register I. The operations to be performed are defined by Table 4-10.

The behavior of this network can be described by the mixed-mode expression

$$Z := ((I = [0]) \wedge [0]) \vee ((I = [1]) \wedge (A + B)) \vee ((I = [2]) \wedge \bar{A})$$
$$\vee ((I = [3]) \wedge (\bar{A} \vee \bar{B}))$$

However, we note that the first term $(I = [0]) \wedge [0]$ is not needed, since it is always the zero term. Thus the expression reduces to

$$Z := ((I = [1]) \wedge (A + B)) \vee ((I = [2]) \wedge \bar{A}) \vee ((I = [3]) \wedge (\bar{A} \vee \bar{B}))$$

In this case we have given each task a number and have used our relational operations to relate the task number to the task performed. Many information processing tasks performed by complex combinational logic networks can often be very compactly represented by using the techniques presented in this chapter.

Table 4-10   Operations To Be Performed by Network of Figure 4-14

Task Number	$[i_1, i_0]$	Operation
0	$[0, 0]$	$Z := [0]$
1	$[0, 1]$	$Z := A + B$
2	$[1, 0]$	$Z := \bar{A}$
3	$[1, 1]$	$Z := \bar{A} \vee \bar{B}$

EXERCISES

1. Use the ASCII code (see Appendix 1) to indicate the collating sequence for the following symbols

$$+, \,-, \,^*, \,?, \,/, \,=, \,<, \,'$$

2. Redesign the network N of Figure 4-12 to allow for the evaluation of

$$z := A \leq B$$

3. Give the mixed-mode expression that describes a 4-input, 1-output multiplexer. The inputs are $X0$, $X1$, $X2$, $X3$ and the control is $T = [t_1, t_2]$. The input signal Xi is connected to the output Z when the binary value of the control has the decimal value i.

6. SUMMARY

In this chapter we have investigated how some of the basic information processing operations can be represented by simple combinational logic networks. These operations will form, in later chapters, the basic building blocks from which we will construct complex systems.

Solid state electronic techniques have been developed to the point where it is possible to buy very low cost integrated circuits to carry out both the logic operations discussed in Chapter 3 and the more complex information processing operations discussed in this chapter. Some of the more important properties of these devices are discussed in the next chapter. Because of the availability of these devices, it is possible to design complete digital systems, using operations of the type discussed in this chapter, without considering the details of the electronic techniques that are necessary to realize the particular operation. This is the approach we follow in the rest of this book.

REFERENCE NOTATION

Several different methods have been developed to represent information-processing operations. The language APL developed by Iverson [5] has had a strong influence in the development of various information transfer design languages. Hellerman [3] uses it extensively, and Hill and Peterson [4] modify it for hardware applications. Other variations of information transfer languages are used in [1], [2], and [6].

REFERENCES

1. Bell, C. G., and A. Newell (1971), *Computer Structures: Reading and Examples.* McGraw-Hill, New York.

2. Chu, Y. (1972), *Computer Organization and Microprogramming*, Prentice-Hall, Englewood Cliffs, N. J.

3. Hellerman, H. (1973), *Digital Computer System Principles*, Second Edition, McGraw-Hill, New York.

4. Hill, F. J., and G. R. Peterson (1973), *Digital Systems: Hardware Organization and Design*, John Wiley, New York.

5. Iverson, K. E. (1962), *A Programming Language*, John Wiley, New York.

6. Sloan, M. E. (1976), *Computer Hardware and Organization*, SRA, Chicago.

HOME PROBLEMS

1. Use a network similar to the one of Figure 4-8 to realize a binary subtractor using regular binary subtraction. Give the logical expressions describing the subnetworks.

2. Develop a network to realize the following computation

$$Z := [(I = [1]) \wedge (A + B)] \vee [(I = [2]) \wedge (A - B)]$$

The addition is a binary addition and subtraction is assumed to be 2's complement subtraction. Give the logic expression that describes all subnetworks.

3. Develop a network similar to that of Figure 4-12 to realize the relational operation $>$. That is

$$z := A > B$$

4. Develop a network similar to that of Figure 4-13 to realize the following mixed-mode expression

$$z := [(I = [0]) \wedge (A = [0])] \vee [(I = [1]) \wedge (A < [0])] \vee [(I = [2])$$
$$\wedge (A > [0])] \vee [(I = [3]) \wedge (A \geq [0])]$$

5. Give the logic expressions that will describe a network which carries out the following transformation.

Input: $X := [x_1 x_2 x_3 x_4]$ represents a BCD encoded number
Output: $Y := [y_1 y_2 y_3 y_4]$ the equivalent Gray code of the input. (For example, if the input is 0101 the output would be 0111.) (See Table 2-8.)

This transformation is represented by

$$Y := G(X)$$

6. Give a general design, complete with all important logic expressions, that will realize the following computation

$$Z := \text{MAX}(X, Y)$$

where X and Y are r-bit binary numbers and Z is to be the maximum of the two.

5

Combinational Logic Circuit Elements

1. INTRODUCTION

In the previous chapters we have considered the general problem of describing digital signals and the various types of operations that can be performed on these signals. This discussion was kept as general as possible so that we could concentrate on the various ways that the information could be represented in digital form. Because of this, no attempt was made to describe how these signals are actually represented and operated on by physical circuit elements.

The three general problems considered in this chapter are:

1. What are the actual physical forms that digital signals can take?
2. What are the actual physical forms that the combinational logic elements can take?
3. What are the constraints imposed on digital networks by the physical characteristics of the signals and components that make up these networks?

There are a wide variety of devices that can be used to form logic networks. We do not attempt to make an exhaustive catalog of these devices and their characteristics. Instead we concentrate on the basic physical properties that must be considered when selecting logic elements and how these properties influence the overall behavior of a logic network built from these devices.

2. LOGIC CIRCUIT SYMBOLS

In order to talk about a network we must introduce a set of logic circuit symbols that can be used to describe the basic logic operations. At one time several different sets of logic circuit symbols were used in the literature. A set of standard symbols

Table 5-1   Standard Logic Circuit Symbols

Operation	Symbol
NOT (Inversion)	
AND	
OR	
NAND	
NOR	
EXCLUSIVE OR	
COINCIDENCE	or

have now been established to represent the basic logic operations (military service standard MIL-STD-8063, American National Standard ANSI Y32.14-1973). The symbols used in this book are given in Table 5-1 and correspond to this standard.

The standard multiple input logic elements are often called *gates*. Thus one might speak of an AND gate, an OR gate or a NAND gate when talking about a particular hardware element used in a circuit. The NOT logic element is usually called an *inverter*.

The basic elements can easily be expanded to account for any number of inputs. For example, assume that we have the logic expression

$$f(x, y, z) = xy \lor \bar{x}\bar{z} \lor x\bar{y}z$$

This expression can be realized by the network shown in Figure 5-1a if it is assumed that we have the quantities x, $\bar{x}$, y, $\bar{y}$, z, and $\bar{z}$ available as inputs. A network of this

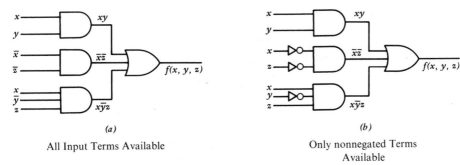

(a)

All Input Terms Available

(b)

Only nonnegated Terms
Available

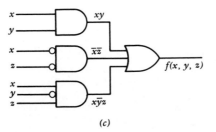

(c)

Shorthand Notation Indicating Inverters
on Input

Figure 5-1. Various representations of $f(x, y, z) = xy \vee \bar{x}\bar{z} \vee x\bar{y}z$.

type is called a *two level logic* circuit, since only two stages of logic are used. If $\bar{x}$, $\bar{y}$, and $\bar{z}$ are not available, then these quantities must be generated by using inverters as shown in Figure 5-1b.

Sometimes when we wish to indicate that the negation of an input term is needed we use the notation shown in Figure 5-1c. If the input line associated with a given term ends in a circle, then that term is negated before the operation indicated by the element symbol is performed. In most instances, an actual inverter, as shown in Figure 5-1b, would have to be included in the logic circuit to account for the indicated negation if the negated value of the term is not available as an input. Any line without a circle is assumed to transmit the variable associated with that line directly to the element.

A slightly different situation occurs when the circle is associated with the output of an element. The operation indicated by the element is performed and then, the resulting output is negated. For example, the logic network of Figure 5-2a realizes

$$g(x, y, z) = \overline{(x \vee y \vee z)}$$

To illustrate how both of these conventions are used, consider the circuit diagram shown in Figure 5-2b. By examining this diagram, we can immediately write down the equation for the network as

$$h(x, y, z) = xy \vee \overline{(x\bar{z})}$$

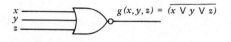

$$g(x, y, z) = \overline{(x \lor y \lor z)}$$

(a)

Illustration of Output Negation Convention

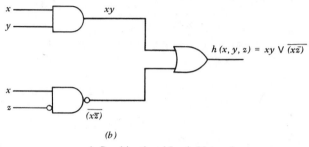

(b)

A Combinational Logic Network

Figure 5-2. Logic circuit description.

We see that we can derive the equation for this network by starting on the left and by forming the partial results as we pass each logic element. These results are then combined to produce the final answer.

EXERCISE

1. Draw a logic circuit representation for

$$f(w, x, y, z) = (w\bar{x} \lor \bar{y}z)(x \lor \bar{y}z)$$

(a) Assuming negated inputs available.
(b) Assuming negated inputs not available.

3. ELECTRONIC LOGIC DEVICES

In a digital system the binary variables can be represented in a wide variety of physical forms. Sometimes the physical form used to represent a variable is dictated by the way in which the variable is generated, while in other cases it is up to the logic designer to select the best physical representation for the variable. In this section we discuss many of the standard physical representations that are found in digital systems, indicate how they are associated with binary variables, and describe some of the physical limitations that must be considered in each type of realization.

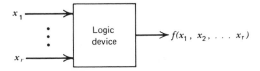

Figure 5-3. General representation of a logic device.

Any physical device or phenomenon that exhibits the property of having at least two distinct and reproducible physical states can be used to represent binary information. A detailed analysis of all the possible physical devices that are found in digital networks and computers requires more space than we have available in this book. Instead we take a modular viewpoint in discussing the various logical devices. Each device is considered to be a "black box" with a set of input and output terminals. We then discuss the observable external behavior of the device, rather than the physical processes that take place inside the device. This approach is fully consistent with the current design practice of using logic modules in the construction of digital networks. The references listed at the end of this chapter present an extensive analysis of the internal design and behavior of the devices discussed.

Most of the logic elements in large digital systems and computers are electronic devices. This is because they are the only devices that can operate fast enough to keep pace with the information processing speeds required for the satisfactory operation of these systems. Integrated circuit technology has now reached the point where one or more logic operations are performed in a single microelectronic circuit that can hardly be seen by the unaided eye. This observation reinforces our assumption that we can disregard the internal structure of the circuit and only investigate the circuit's external characteristics.

A typical logic device can be represented as shown in Figure 5-3. The input signals to the device are voltages and the output is a voltage which can be described as a particular function of the input voltages. In studying this device we must investigate the way it behaves when the input signals remain at a constant value (*steady state behavior*) and what happens when one or more of the input signals change value (*transient behavior*).

Representation of Logical Variables

There are two modes of operation that are found in logic networks. In some cases the different variables are represented by voltage levels that remain constant until the value of the variable changes to a new value. A signal of this type is represented in Figure 5-4a. When dealing with voltage levels time is not a central parameter. However, many digital networks operate on pulse signals such as are illustrated in Figure 5-4b and c. When a variable x_1 is used to describe signals of this type it

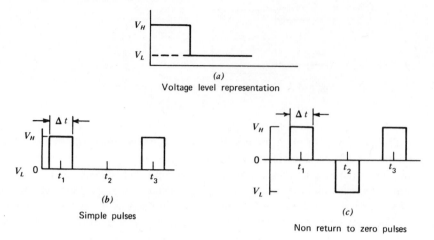

(a)
Voltage level representation

(b)

Simple pulses

(c)

Non return to zero pulses

Figure 5-4. Typical voltage waveforms. (a) Voltage level representation.
(b) Simple pulses. (c) Nonreturn to zero pulses.

is implicitly assumed that the signal is defined for a time interval Δt seconds long centered at the time instants $t_1, t_2, \ldots$, etc.

In all these cases we distinguish two distinct values of voltage, V_H corresponding to the higher of the two voltages and V_L corresponding to the lower of the two voltages. There are two ways in which we can assign binary values to these voltages. The first method is called a *positive logic* assignment and it assigns a logical value of 1 to V_H and a value of 0 to V_L. The second method, which is called a *negative logic* assignment, is to let V_H represent the logical value 0 and V_L represent the logical value of 1.

The choice of either a positive logic or negative logic convention is up to the system designer. The following example, however, illustrates the effect of choosing one or the other assignment.

Let us assume that we have a logic network, such as illustrated in Figure 5-5 where $V_H = 0$ and $V_L = -5$ volts respectively. The relationship between the input and output voltages for this device is given by Table 5-2. If we use a positive logic assignment we obtain the truth table representation of this device given by Table 5-3a while we obtain the truth table representation given by Table 5-3b if we use a negative logic assignment. Examining these two tables we see that our device is an OR logic element if we use positive logic and it is an AND logic element if we use negative logic.

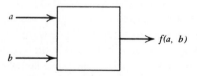

Figure 5-5. A logic device.

		Table 5-2 Voltage Levels		
a	b	$f(a, b)$		
0	0	0		
0	-5	0		
-5	0	0		
-5	-5	-5		

Table 5-3   Truth Table Representation of Device

(a) Positive Logic			(b) Negative Logic		
a	b	$f(a, b)$	a	b	$f(a, b)$
1	1	1	0	0	0
1	0	1	0	1	0
0	1	1	1	0	0
0	0	0	1	1	1

All devices behave in a nonideal manner. Thus we must indicate the range of operating parameters that can be expected when using a particular logic element. The above discussion of logic levels was based on the fact that we could distinguish two distinct voltage levels V_H and V_L. In reality, these voltage levels are nominal values and we must, in practice, indicate a range of voltages we will accept as V_H and V_L. Figure 5-6 illustrates this idea. Inside of the bands representing V_L or V_H the voltage is recognized as representing a specific binary value. However, in the region between these two bands the logical value of the signal is undefined. This transition region is usually very small in most electronic devices.

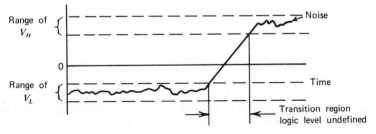

Figure 5-6. Typical waveform of digital signal.

Every signal has some fluctuations in value that we call noise. The ranges assigned to V_H and V_L should be large enough so that a signal that belongs in one range is not driven outside that range by this unwanted noise. Similarly, the two bands should be sufficiently separated so that there is no problem in distinguishing a V_H level from a V_L level even if unwanted noise is present.

Fan-In and Fan-Out Capabilities

When two or more logic circuits are connected together, the output signal of one network is the input signal to one or more following networks. If information is to be propagated through a network we must have a transfer of energy from the driving logic circuit producing the signal to the receiving logic circuit that is accepting this information. In order to simplify the design of logic networks, input loading (i.e., the amount of energy absorbed by a given input) and output drive capability can be specified in terms of a unit load. When we do this we can describe the ability of a logic network to receive and transmit information in terms of its fan-in and fan-out capabilities.

The maximum number of independent input variables that can be used by a logic circuit is called the maximum *fan-in* of the circuit. For example, a commercial logic circuit might have five input leads available for use by the network designer. This device then has a fan-in of five.

The number of unit loads that can be driven by a given logic circuit is limited by the way the circuit is constructed. The maximum number of unit loads that can be driven by a particular circuit is called its *fan-out* capability. Usually the input to a logic circuit represents a unit load. Therefore, the fan-out ability of a logic circuit is also a measure of the number of logic circuits that can be driven by the logic circuit under consideration.

Fan-in and fan-out limitations are very important parameters to keep in mind when logic networks are being designed. No logic circuit can be employed in a manner which would require more inputs or outputs than the circuit can accommodate.

Dynamic Behavior

All logic devices contain energy storage elements as an integral part of their construction. Therefore the effect of a change in the input to the device cannot instantly appear at the output. For example, consider the AND circuit shown in Figure 5-7a. The a input is initially set to 1 and the input to the b terminal is shown in figure 5-7b.

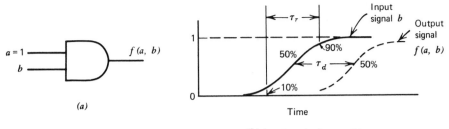

(a)

(b) Input, output response

Figure 5-7. Dynamic response of logic circuit.

Examining the input signal we see that it is initially zero producing a steady-state output signal of zero. The *b* input then changes to a 1 value but this cannot happen instantaneously. The time τ_r that it takes the signal to go from 10% to 90% of its final value is called the *rise time* of the input signal and it is a measure of the speed at which the input can change. The output, which must become a 1, does not respond instantaneously to this input signal. Instead there is a delay of τ_d seconds before the output responds to the input change, measured between the 50% points on the input and output waveforms.

The inherent delay found in all logic elements is important in determining the maximum operating speed of a logic network. If we must consider this problem we can approximate the dynamic properties of a given logic element by the circuit diagram shown in Figure 5-8. Figure 5-8*b* shows a typical model of an AND element.

In this model the logic elements are assumed to be ideal. Thus they introduce no delay. The delay in the circuit is introduced by the ideal delay element, which delays the output signal from the ideal logic element τ_d seconds before it appears at the

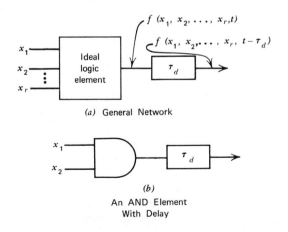

(a) General Network

(b)
An AND Element
With Delay

Figure 5-8. Logic network with inherent delay. (a) General network. (b) An AND element with delay.

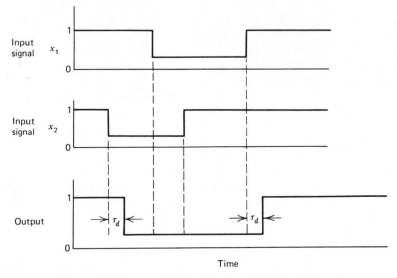

Figure 5-9. An example of the delay in an AND logic element.

output terminal. Figure 5-9 illustrates the type of signals we are dealing with if we use this ideal model for an AND element. Note that the delay is important only when the output changes value.

Timing Diagrams

The delay introduced by each logic element in a logic network contributes to the overall delay of the network. In some cases it becomes very important to know the exact effect that each element has on the transient behavior of the complete network. We can study this behavior by using a timing diagram which provides a time history of each important signal that is found in the network.

The timing diagram for the network shown in Figure 5-10a is shown in Figure 5-10b where it is assumed that $\tau_2 > \tau_1$.

The delays in any logic element are determined by the physical structure of the element and can vary quite markedly from element to element of the same type. The delays included in any timing diagram are thus representative values that characterize the average behavior of each element.

The operating speed of any logic network is determined by the total time it takes for the network's output to reach a steady state value after a change in the input signal. In the example illustrated in Figure 5-10, it takes $\tau_1 + \tau_3$ seconds for the network to reach a stable condition after a change in an input to the upper path through the network and $\tau_2 + \tau_3$ seconds after a change in an input to the lower path through the network. Since $\tau_2 > \tau_1$ the overall operating speed of the network is limited by the delay of $\tau_2 + \tau_3$ seconds. Thus the input to this network should be limited to fewer than $1/(\tau_2 + \tau_3)$ changes per second.

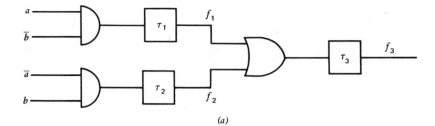

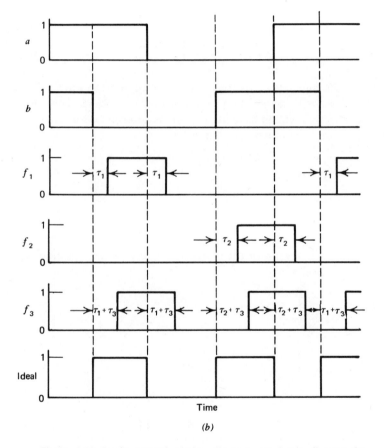

Figure 5-10. Logic network timing diagram. (*a*) Logic diagram for $a\bar{b} \vee \bar{a}b$. (*b*) Timing diagram.

EXERCISES

1. The voltage levels associated with a given logic circuit are given in the following table. What logic operation does this device perform if we use (a) negative logic? (b) positive logic?

a	b	$f(a, b)$
$-5v$	$-5v$	$3v$
$-5v$	$3v$	$-5v$
$3v$	$-5v$	$-5v$
$3v$	$3v$	$-5v$

2. AND and OR logic elements that have a fan-in and fan-out of 5 cost $0.25 each and those with a fan-in and fan-out of 3 cost $0.15 each. What is the minimum cost that we can have for a 5-input, 3-output two-level logic network that will realize the following function?

$$f_1(x_1, x_2, x_3, x_4, x_5) = x_1 x_2 x_3 x_4 \lor x_2 x_5 \lor x_1 x_3 x_4 x_5$$

$$f_2(x_1, x_2, x_3, x_4, x_5) = x_2 x_3 x_5 \lor x_1 x_3 x_4 x_5$$

$$f_3(x_1, x_2, x_3, x_4, x_5) = x_1 x_3 x_4 x_5 \lor x_2 x_5$$

3. Sketch a timing diagram for the following logic network. Assume $\tau_2 < \tau_1$.

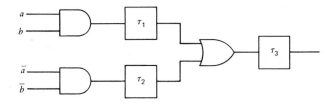

4. INTEGRATED CIRCUITS

A very important technological advance in digital system design occurred in the late 1960's. Instead of building the individual logic elements from discrete electronic components, it became possible to place a large number of logic elements on a semi-conductor chip a few milimeters square. With this development, the price of digital logic dropped from the range of dollars per logic operation to cents per logic operation. In addition, the amount of space needed to construct a digital system was drastically reduced.

Small-Scale Integration (SSI)

The first result of this breakthrough was the development of logic packages that contained from 1 to 12 individual logic elements. The most common way to produce these circuits is in a 14-pin *dual inline package* (DIP), which has the general form shown in Figure 5-11a. The leads to the logic elements are brought out to the pins. For example, the type SN7408 Quad 2-input AND gate has the internal organization shown in Figure 5-11b.

A very large family of SSI circuits are available to the designer. All of the logic networks discussed in this book can be realized by using integrated circuits of this type. References [5] and [7] at the end of this chapter give further details about the types of circuits available and how they are used to construct logic networks. It should be emphasized that very little electronic background is needed to construct digital systems using these integrated circuits.

(a)

Typical DIP Package

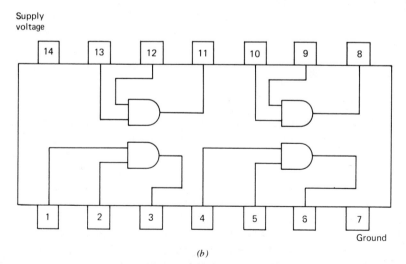

(b)

Typical Internal Organization of a DIP

Figure 5-11. A typical SSI package.

Medium-Scale Integration (MSI)

As integrated circuit technology developed, it became possible to develop devices that carried out much more complex tasks. Networks containing the equivalent of 13 to 99 logic elements are called *medium-scale integrated* (MSI) circuits. Some of the typical tasks performed by MSI units are decoders, adders, comparators, and multiplexers.

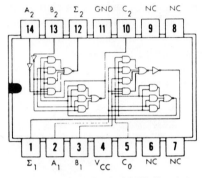

Figure 5-12. A Typical MSI Circuit.

MSI units are usually packaged in 14- to 16-pin DIP's. Figure 5-12 shows a typical configuration for a 2-bit binary full adder. Reference [7] describes many of the common MSI networks available for system design.

Large-Scale Integration (LSI)

Integrated circuit technology has now reached the point where it is possible to place the equivalent of hundreds of logic units on a single chip. Integrated circuits with more than 99 logic elements are called *large-scale integrated* (LSI) circuits. Depending on the particular function carried out, a circuit might be packaged in a 16-, 24-, 40- or even more lead package.

LSI devices generally perform complete tasks. Thus they are usually much more complex than SSI and MSI devices. These devices have made possible such things as the programmable hand calculator, digital watches, and TV games. Many of the digital systems that we discuss in later chapters can be realized by using LSI devices. Their major impact on the digital system designer has been to make it easier and less expensive to build digital systems. The basic design techniques necessary to specify these systems remain the same.

5. MECHANICAL DEVICES

The classical logic circuit is a circuit made up of a number of switches that may be activated by a lever, a pushbutton, or an electromagnet. Before the advent of the electronic computers and logic networks, relays were used extensively in telephone switching systems. However, the importance of relay networks has declined in recent years. Nevertheless there are several logical control functions that are still more economical to perform using mechanical rather than electronic devices.

A *switch* is any mechanical device by means of which two (or more) electrical conductors can be conveniently connected or disconnected. The status of the mechanical contact, which can be opened or closed, can be represented by a variable x_i. Normal practice is to assign a logical value to x_i as follows:

$$x_i = 0 \text{ switch open}$$

$$x_i = 1 \text{ switch closed}$$

Thus if a set of switches is interconnected as shown in Figure 5-13 we can write the following logical expression to describe the condition that there is a closed path between the terminals a, b.

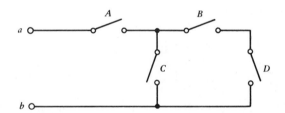

Figure 5-13. A typical switching circuit.

The logical expression is

$$f_{a,b}(A, B, C, D) := A(C \vee BD)$$

A relay is a switch operated by an electromagnet. When a current of sufficient strength is applied to the magnet's coil, a magnetic force displaces the arm of the relay, which in turn causes a set of contacts to either open or close. The position of the switch contacts when the relay is not energized is known as the *normal position* of the relay. Thus a relay can have both *normally open* (NO) and *normally closed* (NC) contacts. Figure 5-14 illustrates the general form of a relay. To indicate

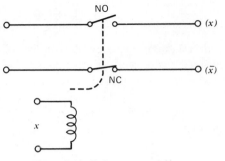

Figure 5-14. Relay representation.

the operation of a relay circuit we can assign the following logical values to the input to the relay.

$$x = 1 \text{ relay energized}$$
$$x = 0 \text{ relay not energized}$$

These logical values are then transferred to the status of the contacts as indicated in Figure 5-14. A NO contact takes the logical value x, since it is closed only if the relay is energized. Similarly, the NC contact takes the value $\bar{x}$, since it is closed only if the relay is not energized.

A typical relay network is illustrated in Figure 5-15. The variables corresponding to each contact are used to represent the contact.

Examining this network we see that

$$f(A, B, C, D, E) := (A\bar{B} \vee C\bar{D})E$$

represents the logic expression that describes when the output path is a closed circuit.

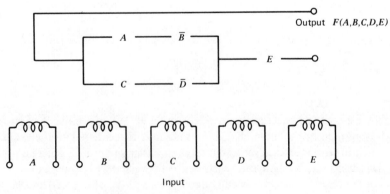

Figure 5-15. A typical relay network.

There is an extensive literature that discusses the analysis and synthesis of relay logic networks. Several of the references listed at the end of this chapter contain an extensive discussion of this problem. However, because of their relative unimportance in the type of problems considered in this book, we do not consider this class of network in any detail.

EXERCISE

1. Find the logic function for the following network.

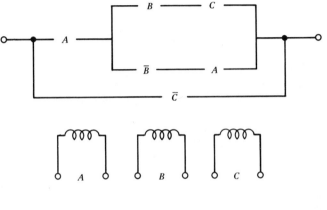

6. SUMMARY

The briefness of this chapter should not be taken as a sign that the hardware which makes up a digital system is of little importance. This is certainly not the case. What we have attempted to do is to indicate the parameters of a digital logic element that influence the performance of that element when it is incorporated into a logic network. For our purposes in the following chapters, this is an entirely satisfactory approach. However, anyone who plans to participate in the design of digital devices must become much better acquainted with the internal operations of these devices. The references listed below provide detailed discussion of the internal structure of many different types of logic networks.

REFERENCE NOTATION

Extensive discussions concerning the construction and design of digital circuits and logic networks can be found in [2], [3], and [4]. Wickes [6] presents a discussion of integrated circuit logic networks. Caldwell [1] presents an extremely comprehensive treatment of relay switching networks. Modern integrated circuit technology is discussed in [5] and [7].

REFERENCES

1. Caldwell, S. H. (1958), *Switching Circuits and Logical Design*, John Wiley, New York.

2. Harris, J. N., Gray, P. E., and Seale, C. L. (1966), *Digital Transistor Circuits*, Semiconductor Electronics Education Committee, Vol. 6, John Wiley, New York.

3. Lo, A. W. (1967), *Introduction To Digital Electronics*, Addison-Wesley, Reading, Mass.

4. Millman, J., and Taub, H. (1965), *Pulse, Digital and Switching Waveforms*, McGraw-Hill, New York.

5. Morris, R. L. and Miller, J. R. (eds.) (1971), *Designing with TTL Integrated Circuits*, McGraw Hill, New York.

6. Wickes, W. E. (1968), Logic Design With Integrated Circuits, John Wiley, New York.

7. *The TTL Data Book* (Latest Edition), Texas Instrument, Dallas, Tex.

HOME PROBLEMS

1. Prove that the two logic networks shown in Figures P5-1*a* and P5-1*b* realize the same logical expression.

2. Smaller logic networks are often interconnected to form larger logic networks. A typical arrangement of this type is shown in Figure P5-2. Assume that the outputs c_i and d_i of the ith sublogic network do not reach a stable steady state value until τ_1 seconds after the inputs to the network reach a steady value.
   (a) How long will it be necessary to wait after an input has been applied before we can be sure that the output of the complete network has reached a steady-state value?
   (b) How many input changes per second can be processed by this network without encountering errors due to this time delay?

3. Assume that the subnetworks shown in Figure P5-2 are full adders and that $N = 3$. Let

$$A = [0 \ 1 \ 1]$$
$$B = [0 \ 0 \ 1]$$

and assume that the inputs are applied at $t = 0$. Draw a set of timing diagrams that shows the values of the variables c_i and d_i as a function of time. Assume that the delay τ associated with each network is 10^{-6} seconds.

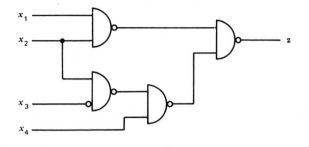

(a)

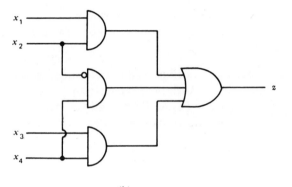

(b)

Figure P5-1.

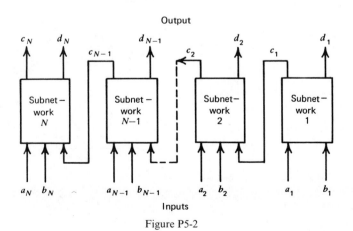

Output

Inputs

Figure P5-2

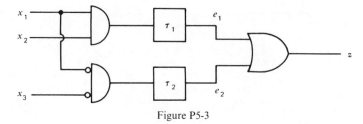

Figure P5-3

4. In the logic circuit shown in Figure P5-3 $z = 1$ will be the steady-state value of the output for both $[x_1, x_2, x_3]$ equal to $[0, 1, 0]$ and $[1, 1, 0]$. However when the input is $[0, 1, 0]$, $e_1 = 0$ and $e_2 = 1$ while for the input $[1, 1, 0]$, $e_1 = 1$ and $e_2 = 0$. Thus when the input changes from $[0, 1, 0]$ to $[1, 1, 0]$ or from $[1, 1, 0]$ to $[0, 1, 0]$ there exists a possibility that z_1 will momentarily go to zero. This spurious output produced during such a change in the input is called a *static hazard*. Use a timing diagram to show that a static hazard will exist whenever $\tau_1 \neq \tau_2$.

5. Switches are bidirectional devices while electronic logic networks are unidirectional devices. This bidirectional property can be used to form a bridge circuit of the form shown in Figure P5-4. Find the logic expression that indicates when there will be a closed path between a and b.

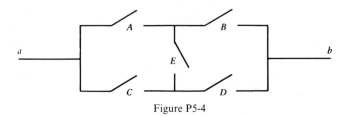

Figure P5-4

6. Assume that the input signals x_1 and x_2 shown in Figure P5-5a are applied to the logic circuit shown in Figure P5-5b. Initially $z = 0$. If $\tau_1 = 1$, sketch $z(t)$ as a function of t.

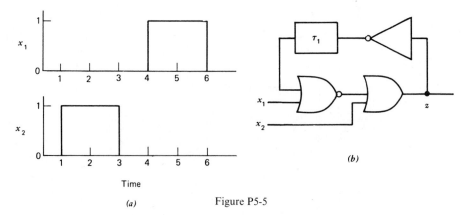

Time

(a)   Figure P5-5

7. Give an AND-OR combinational logic network realization of a full adder (see Table 4-7).

8. Give an AND-OR combinational logic network that will realize the relational operation

$$Z := A > B$$

where A and B are r-bit positive binary numbers.

6

Switching Algebra and Logic Network Realization

1. INTRODUCTION

The previous chapters have provided us with an insight into how digital information is represented in a digital device and how we can operate on this information. However, if we are to make extensive use of these new ideas, we must develop the algebraic properties associated with these operations. That is our purpose in this chapter.

In the first part of the chapter we investigate the properties of switching algebra. This is a system of mathematical logic that can be used to manipulate the logical expressions which describe the behavior of logic networks.

The second part of this chapter illustrates how these techniques can be used to design complex combinational logic networks.

2. SWITCHING ALGEBRA

In the mid-1800's George Boole introduced a system of mathematics that provided an algebraic treatment of logic. This algebra, which has become known as Boolean algebra, has a great many interesting applications in mathematics, engineering, and the sciences. Our interest, however, is not in the general theory of Boolean algebra, but in the special class of problems associated with investigating the algebra of binary functions of the type we encountered in Chapter 3. A general treatment of Boolean algebra as it applies to general problems can be found in several of the references listed at the end of this chapter.

Boolean algebra, like any other algebra, is composed of a set of symbols and a set of rules for manipulating these symbols. In our case, the set of symbols is taken to be the set of binary valued variables and the operations are taken to be the operations of AND, OR, and NOT developed in Chapter 3. This introductory discussion can be formalized by stating the above ideas in terms of the following basic postulates for our particular form of Boolean algebra, which is called *switching algebra*.

Basic Postulates of Switching Algebra

Postulate 1 A Boolean variable, x, has two possible values, 0 and 1. These values are exclusive, that is

$$\text{if } x = 0 \quad \text{then } x \neq 1$$
$$\text{if } x = 1 \quad \text{then } x \neq 0$$

Postulate 2 The NOT operation " $-$ " is defined as

$$\bar{0} = 1 \qquad \bar{1} = 0$$

Postulate 3 The logical operations $\wedge$ AND, and $\vee$ OR are defined as

$$0 \wedge 0 = 0 \qquad 0 \vee 0 = 0$$
$$1 \wedge 0 = 0 \qquad 0 \vee 1 = 1$$
$$0 \wedge 1 = 0 \qquad 1 \vee 0 = 1$$
$$1 \wedge 1 = 1 \qquad 1 \vee 1 = 1$$

NOTE: When there will be no confusion we use the notation $x_1 x_2$ to indicate the AND operation $x_1 \wedge x_2$.

Using this set of postulates we can build a set of useful theorems that will allow us to manipulate and simplify the logical expressions that we use to represent binary functions. For switching algebra there are two general methods of proof that we can use to prove theorems.

Proof by Perfect Induction

The first method, called *proof by perfect induction*, is a brute force technique. Let us suppose that we wish to prove a theorem which states that the logical expression $f(x_1, \ldots, x_r) = g(x_1, \ldots, x_r)$ is true for all $(x_1, \ldots, x_r)$. Since the variables used in this expression can take on only one of two values at a given time, all that we have to do to test if $f(x_1, \ldots, x_r) = g(x_1, \ldots, x_r)$ is to form the truth table for each function. If the two functions are equal for each entry in the truth table then the theorem is true. Otherwise, it is false. This method of proof, which we have already used in Chapter 3, is best used when the number of variables is small.

Proof by Deduction

The second method of proof, called *proof by deduction*, is to show that a given expression is true by showing that the expression can be derived by starting with the basic set of postulates and known theorems and then applying mathematical deduction to obtain the desired expression. This method of proof is effective if the expression under investigation is indeed true. However, if the expression is false, the best method of showing this is to find a counter example which shows that the expression is false.

One of the problems that arises when someone first encounters switching algebra is the great similarity between switching algebra and ordinary algebra. This leads to a tendency to automatically apply concepts from ordinary algebra to similar situations in switching algebra. Unfortunately there are several differences between the two algebraic systems and this approach can lead to erroneous results. The following discussion will establish the rules that we can use to manipulate and simplify logical expressions.

Basic Properties of Switching Algebra

The amount of work necessary to evaluate a logical expression can often be reduced by applying one or more of the following algebraic relations that hold true for switching algebra. In the following, x can represent a single variable or a general logical function.

1. Special properties of 0 and 1

$$0 \vee x = x \qquad 0 \wedge x = 0$$
$$1 \vee x = 1 \qquad 1 \wedge x = x$$

2. The idempotence laws

$$x \vee x = x \qquad x \wedge x = x$$

3. Complementation laws

$$x \vee \bar{x} = 1 \qquad x \wedge \bar{x} = 0$$

4. Involution

$$\overline{(\bar{x})} = x$$

5. Commutative laws

$$x \vee y = y \vee x \qquad x \wedge y = y \wedge x$$

6. Associative laws

$$x \vee (y \vee z) = (x \vee y) \vee z \qquad x \wedge (y \wedge z) = (x \wedge y) \wedge z$$

7. Distributive laws

$$x \wedge (y \vee z) = (x \wedge y) \vee (x \wedge z)$$
$$x \vee (y \wedge z) = (x \vee y) \wedge (x \vee z)$$

8. Absorption laws

$$x \vee (x \wedge y) = x \qquad x \wedge (x \vee y) = x$$
$$x \vee (\bar{x} \wedge y) = x \vee y \qquad x \wedge (\bar{x} \vee y) = x \wedge y$$

If we examine the above relationships we see that there are many identities that are not found in regular algebra. The proof of these relationships is straightforward for our particular form of Boolean algebra. In fact all of these laws are easily proved by the method of perfect induction. For example, let us prove that

$$x \vee \bar{x} = 1$$

The truth table for this expression is

x	$x \vee \bar{x}$	1
0	1	1
1	1	1

Similarly the absorption law

$$x \vee (x \wedge y) = x$$

is proved by using the following truth table

x	y	$(x \wedge y)$	$x \vee (x \wedge y)$	x
0	0	0	0	0
0	1	0	0	0
1	0	0	1	1
1	1	1	1	1

These basic relations can also be proved by deduction. In this case we start off with the expression we wish to prove and then, using only previously proven results, try to show that one side of the equation can be reduced to the other side of the equation. For example, let us prove the absorption law

$$x \lor (\bar{x} \land y) = x \lor y$$

under the assumption that the relationships 1 to 7 have been established. The following steps illustrate the method of proof:

Initial statement	$x \lor (\bar{x} \land y)$
Distributive law	$x \lor (\bar{x} \land y) = (x \lor \bar{x}) \land (x \lor y)$
Complementation law	$(x \lor \bar{x}) \land (x \lor y) = 1 \land (x \lor y)$
Special property of 1	$1 \land (x \lor y) = x \lor y$

Simplification of Logic Expressions

One of our greatest applications of the above relationships is to the problem of simplifying logical expressions. For example, assume that we wish to find a logical expression to represent the following truth table.

x_1	x_2	x_3	$f(x_1, x_2, x_3)$
0	0	0	1
0	0	1	1
0	1	0	0
0	1	1	0
1	0	0	0
1	0	1	1
1	1	0	0
1	1	1	0

From our discussion of Chapter 3 we know that we can represent this function in the following canonical form.

$$f(x_1, x_2, x_3) = \bar{x}_1 \bar{x}_2 \bar{x}_3 \lor \bar{x}_1 \bar{x}_2 x_3 \lor x_1 \bar{x}_2 x_3$$

However, this function can be simplified by using the above relationships. This simplification process proceeds as follows:

1. Use the idempotence law to add $\bar{x}_1 \bar{x}_2 x_3$.

$$f(x_1, x_2, x_3) = \bar{x}_1 \bar{x}_2 \bar{x}_3 \lor \bar{x}_1 \bar{x}_2 x_3 \lor \bar{x}_1 \bar{x}_2 x_3 \lor x_1 \bar{x}_2 x_3$$

2. Combine the first two and last two terms using the distributive law.

$$f(x_1, x_2, x_3) = \bar{x}_1 \bar{x}_2 (\bar{x}_3 \vee x_3) \vee \cdot (\bar{x}_1 \vee x_1) \bar{x}_2 x_3$$

3. Use the complementation law.

$$f(x_1, x_2, x_3) = \bar{x}_1 \bar{x}_2 \vee \bar{x}_2 x_3$$

4. Use the distributive law again.

$$f(x_1, x_2, x_3) = (\bar{x}_1 \vee x_3) \wedge \bar{x}_2$$

This is as far as we can reduce this expression.

Obtaining the Canonical Forms of an Expression

A second problem that we often encounter is that of obtaining a canonical representation of a given logical expression. We could, of course, derive the truth table for the expression and then obtain the canonical representation from the truth table. However, it is also possible, and in most cases easier, to obtain the canonical form of a given expression in a purely algebraic manner.

Assume that we wish to obtain the canonical representation of a given logical expression in the canonical sum-of-product form. To do this we first reduce the expression to a sum-of-product form and then we use the complementation law and the distributive law to transform each product term into its corresponding minterm representation. The following example will illustrate this technique.

Let

$$f(x_1, x_2, x_3) = (\bar{x}_1 \vee x_2)(x_1 \vee \bar{x}_3)$$

be the given function. The canonical sum-of-products representation is obtained by the following steps.

1. Use the distributive law to obtain a sum-of-product representation of the expression.

$$f(x_1, x_2, x_3) = \bar{x}_1 x_1 \vee \bar{x}_1 \bar{x}_3 \vee x_1 x_2 \vee x_2 \bar{x}_3 = \bar{x}_1 \bar{x}_3 \vee x_1 x_2 \vee x_2 \bar{x}_3$$

2. Use the complementation law to transform each product term into a corresponding minterm representation.

(a) $\bar{x}_1 \bar{x}_3 = \bar{x}_1 (x_2 \vee \bar{x}_2) \bar{x}_3 = \bar{x}_1 x_2 \bar{x}_3 \vee \bar{x}_1 \bar{x}_2 \bar{x}_3$

(b) $x_1 x_2 = x_1 x_2 (x_3 \vee \bar{x}_3) = x_1 x_2 x_3 \vee x_1 x_2 \bar{x}_3$

(c) $x_2 \bar{x}_3 = (x_1 \vee \bar{x}_1) x_2 \bar{x}_3 = x_1 x_2 \bar{x}_3 \vee \bar{x}_1 x_2 \bar{x}_3$

Thus

$$f(x_1, x_2, x_3) = \bar{x}_1 x_2 \bar{x}_3 \vee \bar{x}_1 \bar{x}_2 \bar{x}_3 \vee x_1 x_2 x_3 \vee x_1 x_2 \bar{x}_3 \vee x_1 x_2 \bar{x}_3 \vee \bar{x}_1 x_2 \bar{x}_3$$
$$= \bar{x}_1 x_2 \bar{x}_3 \vee \bar{x}_1 \bar{x}_2 \bar{x}_3 \vee x_1 x_2 x_3 \vee x_1 x_2 \bar{x}_3$$

A similar technique can be used to obtain the canonical product-of-sum representation of a function.

Principle of Duality

If we examine the above postulates and algebraic relationships we see that there are two forms for each law. This would seem to imply that we would have to prove both forms. However, the *principle of duality* simplifies our effort. This principle states that each theorem has a dual which can be obtained by:

1. Interchanging the OR and AND operations of the expression.
2. Interchanging the 0 and 1 elements of the expression.
3. Not changing the form of the variables.

To illustrate the use of this property, we note that applying the principle of duality to

$$0 \vee x = x \qquad \text{replace 0 with 1}$$

gives the dual relationship $\updownarrow \ \updownarrow$ and

$$1 \wedge x = x \qquad \text{replace } \vee \text{ with } \wedge$$

while

$$x \wedge (x \vee y) = x$$

gives the dual relationship

$$x \vee (x \wedge y) = x$$

As a final example consider

$$\bar{x}_1 \bar{x}_3 \vee \bar{x}_1 x_2 \vee x_2 x_3 = \bar{x}_1 \bar{x}_3 \vee x_2 x_3$$

Then the dual of this expression is

$$(\bar{x}_1 \vee \bar{x}_3)(\bar{x}_1 \vee x_2)(x_2 \vee x_3) = (\bar{x}_1 \vee \bar{x}_3)(x_2 \vee x_3)$$

WARNING: If the expression $g(x_1, x_2, \ldots, x_r)$ is the dual of the expression $f(x_1, x_2, \ldots, x_r)$ this *does not* imply that these two expressions are equal. The truth of this warning is easily verified.

In particular if

$$g(x_1, x_2, x_3) = \bar{x}_1 \bar{x}_3 \vee x_2 x_3$$

then its dual is

$$f(x_1, x_2, x_3) = (\bar{x}_1 \vee \bar{x}_3) \wedge (x_2 \vee x_3)$$

However

$$g(0, 0, 0) = 1$$

while

$$f(0, 0, 0) = 0$$

Thus, $g(x_1, x_2, x_3) \neq f(x_1, x_2, x_3)$.

The principle of duality lets us establish two theorems for the effort of one proof. If we can prove, through a series of logical steps, that a given theorem is true, then we immediately know that the dual of the theorem is also true, since the dual of the logical steps that proved the original theorem proves the dual theorem.

DeMorgan's Theorem

DeMorgan's theorem is a very important and interesting theorem and is one that has many useful applications. In particular, we will find it helpful when dealing with the design of logic networks constructed from NAND and NOR logic elements. This theorem states:

$$\overline{(x \vee y)} = \bar{x} \wedge \bar{y}$$

$$\overline{(x \wedge y)} = \bar{x} \vee \bar{y}$$

The proof of this theorem for our switching algebra is easily accomplished by using the following truth table.

x	y	$\overline{(x \vee y)}$	$\bar{x} \wedge \bar{y}$
0	0	1	1
0	1	0	0
1	0	0	0
1	1	0	0

Thus we see that

$$\overline{(x \vee y)} = \bar{x} \wedge \bar{y}$$

By the principle of duality we then have the dual theorem

$$\overline{(x \wedge y)} = \bar{x} \vee \bar{y}$$

DeMorgan's theorem can easily be extended to give

$$\overline{(x_1 \vee x_2 \vee \cdots \vee x_n)} = \bar{x}_1 \wedge \bar{x}_2 \wedge \cdots \wedge \bar{x}_n$$

and

$$\overline{(x_1 \wedge x_2 \wedge \cdots \wedge x_n)} = \bar{x}_1 \vee \bar{x}_2 \vee \cdots \vee \bar{x}_n$$

Or for a general function we have

$$\overline{f(x_1, \ldots, x_n, \vee, \wedge)} = f(\bar{x}_1, \ldots, \bar{x}_n, \wedge, \vee)$$

The following example illustrates the application of this theorem. If

$$f(x_1, x_2, x_3) = \overline{(x_1 \wedge x_2)} \vee \bar{x}_1 \vee (x_2 \wedge \bar{x}_3)$$

Then the complement of this function is

$$\overline{f(x_1, x_2, x_3)} = (\bar{x}_1 \vee \bar{x}_2) \wedge x_1 \wedge (\bar{x}_2 \vee x_3)$$

Another interesting result that can be proved by using DeMorgan's theorem is that the NAND operation is a universal operation. By this we mean that any logic expression can be represented only using the NAND operator. To prove this statement, we start with the fact that any logic expression $f(x_1, x_2, \ldots, x_n)$ of n variables can be represented in canonical form using the operations of NOT, AND, and OR. All that we have to do is show that each one of these operations can be represented in terms of the NAND operation

(a)   The NOT Operation

$$\overline{(x \wedge x)} = \bar{x} \vee \bar{x} = \bar{x}$$

(b)   The AND operation

$$\overline{\overline{(x \wedge y)} \wedge \overline{(x \wedge y)}} = (x \wedge y) \vee (x \wedge y) = x \wedge y$$

(c)   The OR operation

$$\overline{\overline{(x \wedge x)} \wedge \overline{(y \wedge y)}} = (x \wedge x) \vee (y \wedge y) = x \vee y$$

This proof is in the form of an existence proof. It shows that we can always express a canonical sum-of-product expression by using only the NAND operation. The direct application of this result is very cumbersome. In Section 3 we present an easy way to carry out this conversion. By the principle of duality it is also possible to show that the NOR operation is also a universal operation.

In the next section we use these results to reduce the complexity of combinational logic networks. The reader should be very careful not to confuse the general statement of DeMorgan's theorem with the general statement of the principle of duality.

EXERCISES

1. Prove the commutative and associative laws using perfect induction.

2. Prove by deduction that the following logical expressions are true.

   (a) $x_1 \bar{x}_2 \vee \bar{x}_1 x_2 = \overline{(x_1 x_2 \vee \bar{x}_1 \bar{x}_2)}$
   (b) $x_1 x_2 \vee \bar{x}_1 \bar{x}_3 = (\bar{x}_1 \vee x_2)(x_1 \vee \bar{x}_3)$
   (c) $x_2 \bar{x}_3 \vee x_1 \bar{x}_3 \vee x_2 x_3 \vee x_1 x_3 \vee \bar{x}_1 x_2 \vee (\bar{x}_1 \vee \bar{x}_2) = \overline{(\bar{x}_1 \bar{x}_2)}$

3. Find the canonical sum-of-product and product-of-sum representations for the following logical functions

   (a) $f(x_1, x_2, x_3) = \overline{(x_1 x_2 \vee \bar{x}_1 \bar{x}_3)}$
   (b) $f(x_1, x_2, x_3) = \overline{(\bar{x}_1 \bar{x}_2 \vee x_1 x_3)}$
   (c) $f(x_1, x_2, x_3) = (x_1 x_2 \vee x_3)(x_1 \bar{x}_2 \vee \bar{x}_3)$

3. LOGIC NETWORK REDUCTION USING BOOLEAN ALGEBRA

As we have seen in our previous discussions, the binary function describing any combinational logic network can always be represented by a logic expression in canonical form. These expressions can, in turn, be realized by simple two-level logic networks. However, in many cases, the canonic logic expressions can be reduced in complexity by the use of algebraic techniques. In general, if the number of occurrences of variables or terms in a given expression describing a function is reduced by these calculations, a reduction in the number of logic circuit elements will be possible when realizing the logic network that represents this function. This process of shortening an expression describing a specific function is called *simplifying* or *minimizing* the expression. The minimization process is complicated by the different forms in which a given expression may be written, by the cost of the different types of elements required to construct the networks, and by the operational characteristics of the logic circuit elements that are to be used in the network. In this section we consider some of the general characteristics of these reduction processes.

Simplification of Canonic Networks

In order to see how we can apply Boolean algebra to the simplification of a logic network let us assume that we are dealing with a binary function described by the following truth table.

x_1	x_2	x_3	$f(x_1, x_2, x_3)$
0	0	0	1
0	0	1	1
0	1	0	0
0	1	1	0
1	0	0	1
1	0	1	1
1	1	0	0
1	1	1	1

This function can be represented in either the sum-of-product or product-of-sum canonical form as

$$f(x_1, x_2, x_3) = \bar{x}_1\bar{x}_2\bar{x}_3 \vee \bar{x}_1\bar{x}_2 x_3 \vee x_1\bar{x}_2\bar{x}_3 \vee x_1\bar{x}_2 x_3 \vee x_1 x_2 x_3$$
$$= m_0 \vee m_1 \vee m_4 \vee m_5 \vee m_7$$
$$= (x_1 \vee \bar{x}_2 \vee x_3)(x_1 \vee \bar{x}_2 \vee \bar{x}_3)(\bar{x}_1 \vee \bar{x}_2 \vee x_3)$$
$$= M_2 \wedge M_3 \wedge M_6$$

These two representations of the function $f(x_1, x_2, x_3)$ give rise to the two possible two-level logic networks shown in Figure 6-1. Examining these two networks we see that the product-of-sum representation appears to require fewer logic elements. However, let us see what happens when we apply our algebraic relationships to both canonical forms.

First, we consider the sum-of-product representation. We can reduce this function using the distributive, complementation, and absorption laws as follows.

$$f(x_1, x_2, x_3) = \bar{x}_1\bar{x}_2\bar{x}_3 \vee \bar{x}_1\bar{x}_2 x_3 \vee x_1\bar{x}_2\bar{x}_3 \vee x_1\bar{x}_2 x_3 \vee x_1 x_2 x_3$$
$$= \bar{x}_1\bar{x}_2 \vee x_1\bar{x}_2 \vee x_1 x_2 x_3$$
$$= \bar{x}_2 \vee x_1 x_3$$

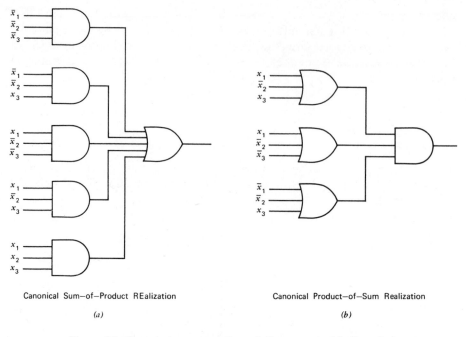

Canonical Sum—of—Product REalization

Canonical Product—of—Sum Realization

(a)

(b)

Figure 6-1. Canonical representation of $f(x_1, x_2, x_3)$, (a) Canonical sum-of-product realization. (b) Canonical product-of-sum realization.

Thus we have reduced the network of Figure 6-1a to that of Figure 6-2a.

It is also possible to reduce the product-of-sum expression using the idempotence, complementation, and distributive laws as follows.

$$
\begin{aligned}
f(x_1, x_2, x_3) &= (x_1 \vee \bar{x}_2 \vee x_3)(x_1 \vee \bar{x}_2 \vee \bar{x}_3)(\bar{x}_1 \vee \bar{x}_2 \vee x_3) \\
&= (x_1 \vee \bar{x}_2 \vee x_3)(x_1 \vee \bar{x}_2 \vee \bar{x}_3)(x_1 \vee \bar{x}_2 \vee x_3)(\bar{x}_1 \vee \bar{x}_2 \vee x_3) \\
&= (x_1 \vee \bar{x}_2 \vee x_3\bar{x}_3)(x_1\bar{x}_1 \vee \bar{x}_2 \vee x_3) \\
&= (x_1 \vee \bar{x}_2)(\bar{x}_2 \vee x_3)
\end{aligned}
$$

Thus we have reduced the network of Figure 6-1b to that of Figure 6-2b. These two networks realize the same logic function since, because of the distributive law, we have

$$\bar{x}_2 \vee x_1x_3 \equiv (\bar{x}_2 \vee x_1)(\bar{x}_2 \vee x_3)$$

However, we also note that the product-of-sum now requires one more logic element than the sum-of-product realization.

If the variables x_i and their negation $\bar{x}_i$ are available, we can always construct a two-level logic network to realize any given binary function. These networks have the fastest operating speed since there is a maximum of two delays between any input variable and the output. However, when we work with integrated circuit logic

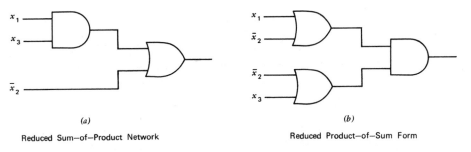

(a)

Reduced Sum—of—Product Network

(b)

Reduced Product—of—Sum Form

Figure 6-2. Representation of $f(x_1, x_2, x_3)$ in reduced form. (a) Reduced sum-of-product network. (b) Reduced product-of-sum form.

modules we often have other considerations which must be included in the design process.

For example, assume that we are working with a family of integrated circuit logic elements that only have 2-input OR or 2-input AND elements available. Suppose that we wish to realize a logic network with the following sum-of-product form.

$$f(x_1, x_2, x_3, x_4) = x_1 x_2 \bar{x}_3 \vee x_1 x_2 x_4 \vee x_2 \bar{x}_3 x_4$$

This function cannot be constructed from our logic elements as long as it remains in this form. However, we can factor this function into a more desirable form by applying the commutative, distributive, and idempotence laws in the following manner

$$\begin{aligned} f(x_1, x_2, x_3, x_4) &= x_1 x_2 \bar{x}_3 \vee x_1 x_2 x_4 \vee x_1 x_2 x_4 \vee x_2 \bar{x}_3 x_4 \\ &= x_1 x_2 (\bar{x}_3 \vee x_4) \vee x_2 x_4 (x_1 \vee \bar{x}_3) \end{aligned}$$

which can be realized by a network of 2-input logic elements as shown in Figure 6-3.

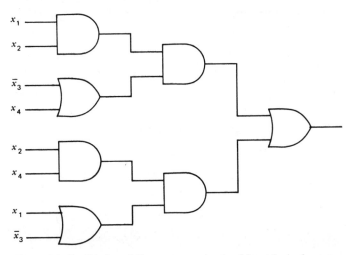

Figure 6-3. Realization of $f(x_1, x_2, x_3, x_4)$ using 2-input logic elements.

Factoring a logic expression usually reduces the fan-in requirements while increasing the number of logic levels and the number of logic elements in the circuit. The larger the number of levels in the resulting circuit, the greater the total delay time of the complete network. However, in some design problems it is much more important to use standard elements rather than to minimize network delay.

The design of logic networks is an art that depends on many things beside switching algebra. If only a few copies of the network are to be constructed it is not economical for a designer to spend a large amount of time trying to obtain an optimum minimum network. This is true since the cost of logic elements usually represents a small fraction of the total design cost while the logic designer's time may often be a major part of the design cost. On the other hand, the optimization of the network is very important if the network is to be mass produced. In either case, the availability of algorithmic procedures that can be used to eliminate unnecessary terms and variables can make any minimization process easier to handle. Procedures of this type are presented in Chapter 7.

Logic Network Design Using NAND and NOR Circuit Elements

All of our discussion of switching algebra and logic network design has, so far, assumed that we are working with circuits that can perform the basic logical operations of AND, OR, or NOT. Anyone familiar with the integrated circuit logic elements that are currently available might wonder why we take this approach, since the basic integrated circuit logic elements are NAND and NOR circuits, which have the general form shown in Figure 6-4.

As we previously proved, any binary function $h(x_1, x_2, \ldots, x_r)$ can be realized using only NAND elements or NOR elements. In particular, we now show how any sum-of-product expressions can be realized by a 2-level network involving only NAND elements and how any product-of-sum expressions can be realized by a

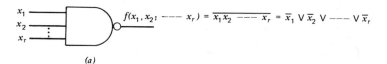

$$f(x_1, x_2; \text{---} x_r) = \overline{x_1 x_2 \text{---} x_r} = \overline{x}_1 \vee \overline{x}_2 \vee \text{---} \vee \overline{x}_r$$

(a)

General Form of NAND Logic Element

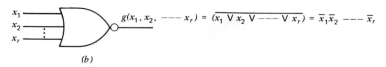

$$g(x_1, x_2, \text{---} x_r) = \overline{(x_1 \vee x_2 \vee \text{---} \vee x_r)} = \overline{x}_1 \overline{x}_2 \text{---} \overline{x}_r$$

(b)

General Form of NOR Logic Element

Figure 6-4. NAND and NOR logic elements.

2-level network involving only NOR elements. The following discussion deals only with the sum-of-product realization using NAND elements. The arguments for a NOR element realization of a product-of-sum expression follow from the principle of duality.

From our previous discussion we know that any function $h(x_1, x_2, \ldots, x_r)$ can be represented in a canonical sum-of-product form. We can then apply, if desired, the basic properties of switching algebra to obtain a minimal sum-of-product realization of the function. The following example will show how any sum-of-product function can be realized using only NAND elements.

Assume that we are given a function $h(x_1, x_2, x_3)$ in canonical sum-of-product form:

$$h(x_1, x_2, x_3) = \bar{x}_1 \bar{x}_2 \bar{x}_3 \vee \bar{x}_1 \bar{x}_2 x_3 \vee x_1 \bar{x}_2 \bar{x}_3 \vee x_1 x_2 \bar{x}_3 \vee x_1 x_2 x_3$$

This canonical expression can be reduced to

$$h(x_1, x_2, x_3) = \bar{x}_1 \bar{x}_2 \vee \bar{x}_2 \bar{x}_3 \vee x_1 x_2$$

The 2-level AND-OR realization is given in Figure 6-5.

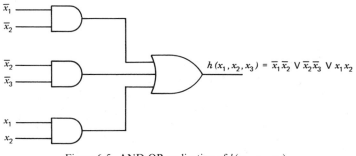

Figure 6-5. AND-OR realization of $h(x_1, x_2, x_3)$.

Now let us consider how we can realize $h(x_1, x_2, x_3)$ as a 2-level NAND network. Using involution we note that

$$h(x_1, x_2, x_3) = \overline{\overline{h(x_1, x_2, x_3)}}$$
$$= \overline{\overline{(\bar{x}_1 \bar{x}_2 \vee \bar{x}_2 \bar{x}_3 \vee x_1 x_2)}}$$

Applying DeMorgans theorem then gives

$$h(x_1, x_2, x_3) = \overline{(\overline{\bar{x}_1 \bar{x}_2} \wedge \overline{\bar{x}_2 \bar{x}_3} \wedge \overline{x_1 x_2})}$$

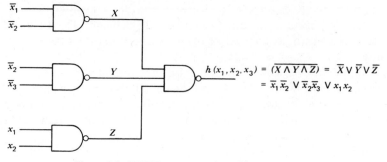

Figure 6-6. NAND representation of $h(x_1, x_2, x_3)$.

However, if we examine this expression we can write

$$h(x_1, x_2, x_3) = (\overline{X \wedge Y \wedge Z})$$

where

$$X = (\overline{\bar{x}_1 \bar{x}_2}) \qquad Y = (\overline{\bar{x}_2 \bar{x}_3}) \qquad Z = (\overline{x_1 x_2})$$

Thus we see that we can realize $h(x_1, x_2, x_3)$ using NAND elements as shown in Figure 6-6.

A graphical proof that the NAND network of Figure 6-6 is equivalent to the AND-OR network of Figure 6-5 is presented in Figure 6-7. The key to the conversion process is shown in Figure 6-7a where the NAND element is converted to an OR element with all of its inputs negated.

From this example we see that the NAND network realization follows directly from the sum-of-product representation. There is one special situation that we must be careful to handle properly. Assume that we have a function such as

$$f(x_1, x_2, x_3) = \bar{x}_1 \vee x_2 x_3$$

to realize. The product term $\bar{x}_1$ involving a single variable must be handled very carefully if a mistake is to be avoided. The NAND network corresponding to $f(x_1, x_2, x_3)$ is given in Figure 6-8.

Initially we need a NAND element to realize the term $\overline{\bar{x}_1}$ as shown in Figure 6-8a. However, a single input NAND element is an inverter that performs the NOT operation. Thus we can eliminate this NAND element as shown in Figure 6-8b if x_1 is available as an input.

Using the principle of duality, we can realize a product-of-sum expression using NOR elements in a similar manner. For example, the network shown in Figure 6-9 will realize the function

$$g(x_1, x_2, x_3) = (x_1 \vee x_2)(x_1 \vee \bar{x}_3)(\bar{x}_2 \vee \bar{x}_3)$$

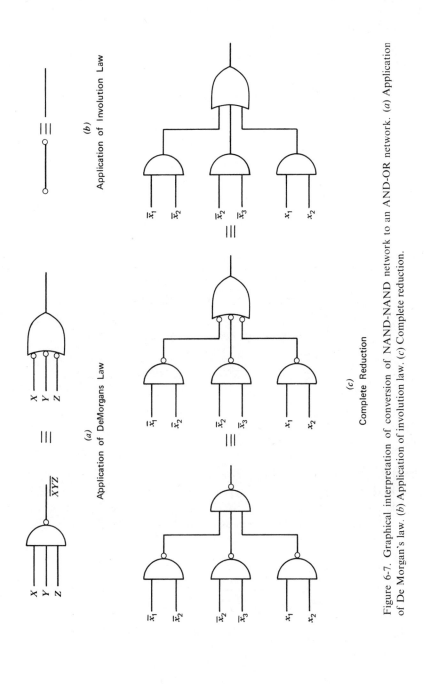

Figure 6-7. Graphical interpretation of conversion of NAND-NAND network to an AND-OR network. (*a*) Application of De Morgan's law. (*b*) Application of involution law. (*c*) Complete reduction.

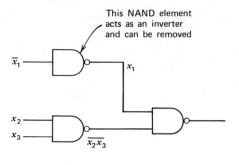

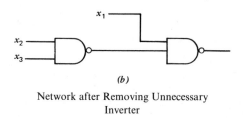

(a)

Formal NAND Network Realization

(b)

Network after Removing Unnecessary
Inverter

Figure 6-8. Treatment of single variable product terms.

We can prove that this realization gives the desired logic function in exactly the same way that we did for the previous example. These calculations are left as an exercise.

WARNING The above relationships are true only if we are dealing with 2-level sum-of-product or product-of-sum expressions. If logic networks with more than two levels are used the situation is considerably more complicated. A complete discussion of the logic design problem using NAND or NOR circuits can be found in reference [7] listed at the end of this chapter.

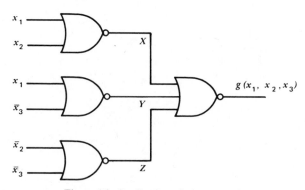

Figure 6-9. Realization of $g(x_1, x_2, x_3)$.

EXERCISES

1. Find a minimal AND-OR, OR-AND, NAND, and NOR realization for the following truth table

x_1	x_2	x_3	$f(x_1, x_2, x_3)$
0	0	0	1
0	0	1	0
0	1	0	1
0	1	1	1
1	0	0	0
1	0	1	0
1	1	0	1
1	1	1	0

2. Find an equivalent network using only AND, OR, and NOT circuits for the following network

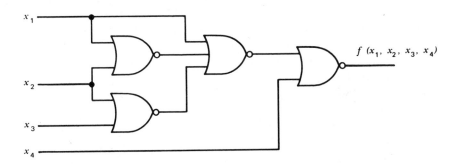

3. Prove that the circuit shown in Figure 6-9 realizes the logic function $g(x_1, x_2, x_3)$.

4. SWITCHING ALGEBRA AND THE DESIGN OF COMPLEX COMBINATIONAL LOGIC NETWORKS

In Chapter 4 we investigated the problem of developing logic expressions and truth tables to represent the behavior of combinational logic networks. Switching algebra can often be very useful in this type of design process. For some networks, switching algebra will allow us to reduce the complexity of the logic needed to realize a given network. In other cases the actual logic expression necessary to describe a given network can be written down directly from the description of the task that the network must perform without the necessity of first deriving the truth table which describes the network's performance.

This section presents a number of design examples that illustrate how switching algebra is used. We assume that a statement describing the operational requirements of a given combinational logic network is given. Using this statement, we must identify the inputs that must be supplied to the network and the required outputs. From this information we then define the exact relationships that must exist between these quantities.

At this point we must decide if the network can be realized by a single combinational logic network or as an interconnection of several subnetworks. If this selection is not obvious at this stage it is often desirable to try several different network configurations. Each configuration should be evaluated and those that appear to be the most desirable are retained for the next stage of the design process.

Once we have developed a general specification for the network we must reduce the specification to a set of logical expressions that can be used to define the logic circuits necessary to realize the network. If the input and output quantities are not already in digital form we first assign a digital representation for each input and output quantity. Using this digital representation for the input and output and the specification of the function to be performed by each network, we then form the logical expressions or truth table that describes the operation of the network.

The design process, up to this point, is highly dependent on the ability and past experience of the designer. However, once we obtain a truth table or logical expression description of a given combinational logic network we know that there are several standard analysis techniques we can apply to obtain a logic circuit representation of the network.

Example 1   An Automatic Toll Collector

Automatic toll collectors have been introduced on many toll highways to speed up traffic flow. Let us assume that we were asked to build a logic network that is part of an automatic toll collector. This logic network is to count the amount of change placed into the collector. If fifteen cents is deposited (nickels and dimes only) then the go light is flashed on and a change collect signal is sent out to collect the coins. Otherwise, the stop light is to remain on.

Examining the problem statement we see that there are two input signals and one output signal. They are:

N number of nickels deposited

D number of dimes deposited

C command to the signal light and collection control

These signals will take on the following integer and logical values.

$$0 \le N \le 3 \quad \text{number of nickels}$$
$$0 \le D \le 1 \quad \text{number of dimes}$$
$$C = 0 \quad \text{15 cents not in change holder}$$
$$C = 1 \quad \text{15 cents in change holder}$$

It is assumed that the information concerning the number of coins deposited shows up at the same time so that the network does not have to have a "memory."

The first task is to encode the input and output information. One such encoding is

$$N = [n_1, n_2] \quad [0, 0] \ 0 \ \text{nickels}$$
$$[0, 1] \ 1 \ \text{nickel}$$
$$[1, 0] \ 2 \ \text{nickels}$$
$$[1, 1] \ 3 \ \text{nickels}$$
$$D = [d_1] \quad [0] \quad 0 \ \text{dime}$$
$$[1] \quad 1 \ \text{dime}$$

The output of the network $C = [c_1]$ is 1 if we have at least [three nickels] or [1 nickel and 1 dime]. We also decide that if the driver puts in more than the minimum amount we give a go signal but no change. (After all, we can give him fair warning by putting up a sign saying "Exact Change Only").

Now that we have identified the inputs, the outputs and the logical relationships that describe the operation of the network our final step is to find the logical expressions that describe the logic circuitry necessary to realize this network. Since there are only three input variables $[n_1, n_2]$ and $[d_1]$ we can do this by using the following truth table.

n_1	n_2	d_1	c_1
0	0	0	0
0	0	1	0
0	1	0	0
0	1	1	1
1	0	0	0
1	0	1	1
1	1	0	1
1	1	1	1

Examining this table we can write the following logical expression for c_1

$$c_1 = \bar{n}_1 n_2 d_1 \lor n_1 \bar{n}_2 d_1 \lor n_1 n_2 \bar{d}_1 \lor n_1 n_2 d_1$$

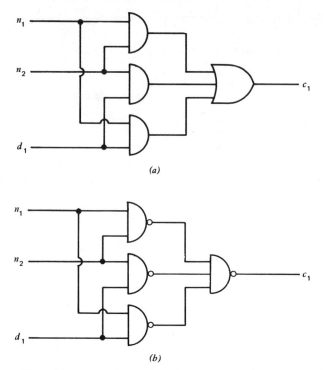

Figure 6-10. Two realization of logic network for toll collector.

Using our algebraic techniques this expression reduces to

$$c_1 = n_2 d_1 \ \lor \ n_1 n_2 \ \lor \ n_1 d_1$$

Two possible realizations of the desired logic network are shown in Figure 6-10.

This example has served to illustrate our design process when only a small number of input and output variables are involved. The next example will illustrate how we can handle much more complex problems.

Example 2   Bus Information Distribution

In many computers and microprocessors it is necessary to be able to transmit a digital signal to a particular output terminal. Such an arrangement is called an *information transmission bus* or *bus* for short. The general structure of a bus is shown in Figure 6-11.

In this system the select line indicates which output terminal of the k possible output terminals is to output the information placed on the information bus. (In this example we assume that only one terminal can be selected at a time, but this

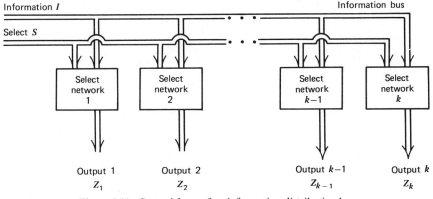

Figure 6-11. General form of an information distribution bus.

is not a necessary restriction). The select network uses the information on the select line to determine if the information on the information bus is to be transmitted to the network's output. The first step in the design is to determine the form of the signals in the system.

The select signal must be able to indicate the terminal to be selected. Thus the select signal must be an r-tuple where r is selected so that

$$2^r \geq k$$

Let $[s_1, s_2, \ldots, s_r]$ correspond to the select signal S.

The information signal I will be assumed to be represented by the u-tuple $[i_1, i_2, \ldots, i_u]$ and the output of the jth select network, Z_j will be indicated by the u-tuple $[z_{j,1}, z_{j,2}, \ldots, z_{j,u}]$. The value of u depends on the particular system being investigated.

The next problem is to decide on a coding for the select signal. One obvious coding is that when the select signal S has a binary value j, then the jth select network is activated. For all other r-tuples the select network is not activated. With this convention we can define the select function as

$$F_j(S, I) = \begin{cases} I & \text{if } S = [j] \\ [0] & \text{if } S \neq [j] \end{cases}$$

Thus

$$Z_j := F_j(S, I) \quad \text{or} \quad Z_j := (S = [j]) \wedge I$$

One way to develop a logic expression representation for $F_j(S, I)$ would be to write down a truth table. Such a table would have 2^r rows and u output columns. Thus, except for very small values of u and r, this would be an impractical approach.

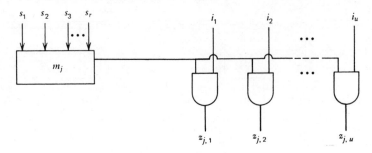

Figure 6-12. The general form of the jth select network.

A description of $F_j(S, I)$ can be developed in a much more logical manner using switching algebra. First, we note that the r-tuple minterm m_j has the property that $m_j = 1$ for $S = [j]$ and $m_j = 0$ for all other cases. Thus we can define Z_j as

$$Z_j := m_j \wedge I = [m_j \wedge i_1, m_j \wedge i_2, m_j \wedge i_3, \ldots, m_j \wedge i_n]$$

By using this result, we see that the select network has the general form shown in Figure 6-12. The network m_j is an appropriate network necessary to realize m_j. For example, if $r = 3$ and $j = 5$, then

$$m_5 = s_1 \bar{s}_2 s_3$$

and the m_5 network would have the form shown in Figure 6-13.

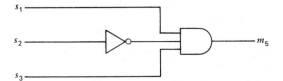

Figure 6-13. Minterm network m_5 for a 3-tuple select signal.

Example 3 Processing of Information in Registers

The next problem is typical of the type of problems that we encounter as part of the design of digital computers or other complex data processing systems. Assume that we have two r-bit registers A and B and that we wish to perform the information processing tasks described in Table 6-1 on the information contained in these

Table 6-1   Required Information Processing Tasks

Task	Representation	Explanation
T_0	$Z := A + B$	Form binary sum of binary numbers in A and B
T_1	$Z := A \wedge B$	AND the contents of A and B term by term
T_2	$Z := A \vee B$	OR the contents of A and B term by term
T_3	$Z := \bar{A}$	Form the negation of the contents of A

registers. We can then use a controlled combinational logic network organized as shown in Figure 6-14 to accomplish this task.

The control signal T has four values, T_0 through T_3, corresponding to the tasks that must be performed. The output can then be described by the following expression:

$$Z := ((T = T_0) \wedge (A + B)) \vee ((T = T_1) \wedge (A \wedge B)) \vee ((T = T_2)$$
$$\wedge (A \vee B)) \vee ((T = T_3) \wedge (\bar{A}))$$

Since there are four tasks to be performed, we can encode T by the 2-tuple $[t_1, t_2]$ as follows:

$$[0, 0] \text{ Task } T_0 \quad . \quad [1, 0] \text{ Task } T_2$$
$$[0, 1] \text{ Task } T_1 \quad [1, 1] \text{ Task } T_3$$

If we try to design the network as a single unit, then we would have to work with $2r + 2$ input signals. Since this is an unnecessary complication, we can decide to divide the network into subnetworks as shown in Figure 6-15.

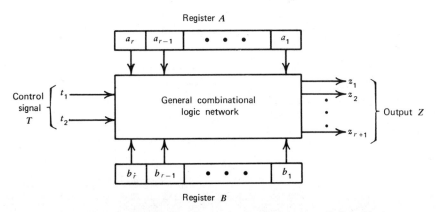

Figure 6-14. Representation of general network to carry out information processing tasks of Table 6-1.

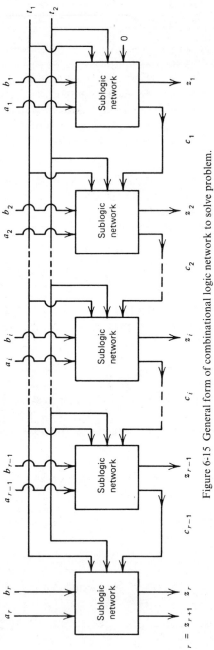

Figure 6-15 General form of combinational logic network to solve problem.

By examining this figure we see that each sublogic network has five inputs and two outputs. We could write down a truth table for each subnetwork. However, it would contain 32 rows and would be very tedious to work with. Therefore, we first try to write a logic expression that describes the operation of the subnetwork directly from the problem statement. As a starting point we use the above expression for Z.

The following two expressions can be used to represent the two outputs

$$c_i := [(T = T_0) \land \text{CARRY}(a_i, b_i, c_{i-1})] \qquad i = 1, 2, \ldots, r$$

$$z_i := [(T = T_0) \land \text{SUM}(a_i, b_i, c_{i-1})] \lor [(T = T_1) \land (a_i \land b_i)]$$
$$\lor [(T = T_2) \land (a_i \lor b_i)] \lor [(T = T_3) \land (\bar{a}_i)] \qquad i = 1, 2, \ldots, r$$

There are two special cases

$$c_0 := 0 \qquad z_{r+1} := c_r$$

Using these expressions, we can now reduce the above general expressions to specific logic expressions.

First we note that the addition operation $A + B$ is carried out by using full adders. From Chapter 4 we know that the SUM and CARRY operations are defined as

$$\text{SUM}(a_i, b_i, c_{i-1}) := \bar{a}_i \bar{b}_i c_{i-1} \lor \bar{a}_i b_i \bar{c}_{i-1} \lor a_i \bar{b}_i \bar{c}_{i-1} \lor a_i b_i c_{i-1}$$

$$\text{CARRY}(a_i, b_i, c_{i-1}) := \bar{a}_i b_i c_{i-1} \lor a_i \bar{b}_i c_{i-1} \lor a_i b_i \bar{c}_{i-1} \lor a_i b_i c_{i-1}$$

However, we note that the expression for $\text{CARRY}(a_i, b_i, c_{i-1})$ can be reduced to give

$$\text{CARRY}(a_i, b_i, c_{i-1}) := a_i b_i \lor a_i c_{i-1} \lor b_i c_{i-1}$$

(the proof of this is left as an exercise)

Next we note that the term $T = T_i$ corresponds to the two variable minterm m_i. For example, $T = T_1$ is equivalent to $\bar{t}_1 t_2 = m_1$.

Using these results and the form of the network shown in Figure 6-15 we obtain the following expression to describe the behavior of the ith sublogic network:

$$z_i = m_0(\bar{a}_i \bar{b}_i c_{i-1} \lor \bar{a}_i b_i \bar{c}_{i-1} \lor a_i \bar{b}_i \bar{c}_{i-1} \lor a_i b_i c_{i-1}) \lor m_1(a_i \land b_i)$$
$$\lor m_2(a_i \lor b_i) \lor m_3 \bar{a}_i \qquad i = 1, 2, \ldots, r$$

$$c_i = m_0(a_i b_i \lor a_i c_{i-1} \lor b_i c_{i-1}) \qquad i = 1, 2, \ldots, r + 1$$

$$z_{r+1} = c_r$$

Using the above logic expressions for the c_i's and the z_i's, we can easily develop the logic networks necessary to realize each of the subnetworks in Figure 6-15.

EXERCISES

1. Let X_8 represent the octal representation of the contents of a 3-bit register. Design a combinational logic network that will carry out the following operations:

   (a) If $X_8 \geq 5$ turn on a red light

   (b) If $X_8 \leq 3$ turn on a green light

   (c) If $3 < X_8 < 5$ turn on a yellow light

2. Prove

$$\text{CARRY} \, (a_i, b_i, c_{i-1}) := a_i b_i \lor a_i c_{i-1} \lor b_i c_{i-1}$$

5. SUMMARY

This chapter has served to introduce the analytical techniques that we can use to work with combinational logic. We have seen that there is a direct relationship between the logic operations involved in switching algebra and the form of the logic networks used to realize particular logic expressions.

Although switching algebra is a completely consistent mathematical system, it is sometimes difficult to directly deal with the analysis of a complex logic network as a single unit. To overcome this problem we saw that we can often decompose a complex network into an interconnection of subnetworks that are designed to carry out specific tasks. Not only does this approach allow us to more easily analyze the behavior of a given network, it also gives us additional insight into how the network processes information.

We also saw that the problems of describing the required behavior of a given logic network could be handled in a variety of ways. The simplest situations occur when a truth table representation can be formed to describe the network. However, we found that this was often an impractical approach for the more complex networks. For these networks we must identify the elementary component tasks that are to be performed by the network, the interrelationship between these tasks, and the networks' overall performance.

Our next task will be to develop systematic techniques that can be used to carry out some of the calculations necessary to find minimal logic expressions to represent the behavior of logic networks. This problem is tackled in the next chapter. The results of this work will then allow us to understand the design and operation of much more complex logic and information processing devices.

REFERENCE NOTATION

A comprehensive discussion of Boolean algebra and its mathematical properties can be found in [1] and [4]. Applications of Boolean algebra to switching circuits can be found in [1], [2], [5], and [6]. A discussion of logic circuit design is found in [2] and [7]. An extensive discussion of how integrated circuit logic elements can be used to realize given logic functions is presented in [7].

REFERENCES

1. Brzuzowski, J. A. and Yoeli, M. (1976), *Digital Networks*, Prentice-Hall, Englewood Cliffs, N.J.

2. Dietmeyer, D. L. (1971), *Logic Design of Digital Systems*, Allyn and Bacon, Boston.

3. Flegg, H. C. (1964), *Boolean Algebra and Its Application*, John Wiley, New York.

4. Hohn, F. E. (1966), *Applied Boolean Algebra—An Elementary Introduction*, MacMillan, New York.

5. Krieger, M. (1967), *Basic Switching Circuit Theory*, MacMillan, New York.

6. McClusky, E. J. (1965), *Introduction to the Theory of Switching Circuits*, McGraw-Hill, New York.

7. Wickes, W. E. (1968), *Logic Design with Integrated Circuits*, John Wiley, New York.

HOME PROBLEMS

1. From our discussion in Chapter 4 we know that any logical function $f(x_1, x_2, \ldots, x_n)$ of n variables can be represented in canonical form using the Boolean operations of AND, OR, and NOT applied to the variables.
   (a) Show, using DeMorgan's theorem, that any logical function of n variables can be represented by a Boolean expression involving only the operations of AND and NOT.
   (b) State the dual of this result.

2. Is the NAND operation
   (a) Commutative?
   (b) Associative?
   (c) Distributive with respect to AND?
   Prove each result. State the dual of these results.

3. The cancellation law of regular algebra says that if

$$a + b = a + c$$

then

$$b = c$$

Prove, by giving a counter example, that if

$$a \vee b = a \vee c$$

then

$$b = c$$

is a false assumption. Thus the cancellation law does not hold true in Boolean algebra.

4. Convert the networks shown in Figure P6-1 to corresponding networks that use only NAND gates without changing the general organization of the network.

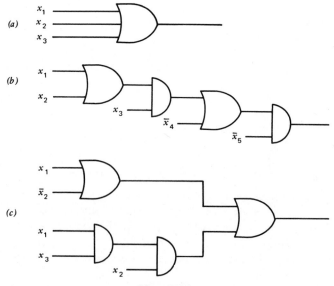

Figure P6-1

5. Networks of the general form shown in Figure P6-2 are quite common in digital systems. Design a logic network to realize the following values for c_1, c_2 and c_3.

$c_1 = 1$ when the contents of A is an even binary number

$c_2 = 1$ when the contents of A is a binary number corresponding to the decimal numbers 3 or 6

$c_3 = 1$ when the contents of A is a binary number corresponding to the decimal numbers 1, 3, 5, or 7.

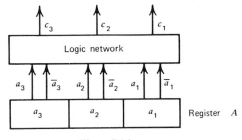

Figure P6-2

6. Assume that A, B, C, D are r-bit signals and S is a 2-bit control signal. Give the logic expression that realizes the following information processing task.

$$Z := [(S = [0]) \wedge A] \vee [(S = [1]) \wedge B] \vee [(S = [2]) \wedge C] \\ \vee [(S = [3]) \wedge D]$$

7. Assume that A, B, C are r-bit signals. Give the logic expression that realizes the following information processing task.

$$Z := [(A = B) \wedge (B + C)]$$

7

Minimization of Combinational Logic Networks

The final step in the design of a combinational logic network involves the realization of the network from standard logic elements. This step can be carried out in a variety of ways depending on the types of logic elements that are to be used and other constraints that are placed on the network. In this chapter we consider the problem of building a combinational logic network of the form shown in Figure 7-1. The inputs to the network are the binary variables $x_1, x_2, \ldots, x_r$ and the

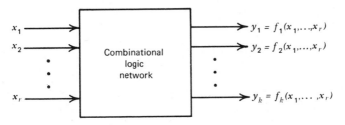

Figure 7-1. General form of combinational logic network.

outputs are the binary variables $y_1, y_2, \ldots, y_k$ which are defined by the functions $f_1(x_1, \ldots, x_r), \ldots, f_k(x_1, \ldots, x_r)$. These functions are assumed to be defined by either a truth table or a logic expression. Our task is to specify a two-level logic circuit, using a minimum number of logic elements, to realize the desired logic network.

Completely Specified and
Incompletely Specified Transmission Functions

The variables x_i are called *input-variables*, the variables y_j are called *output variables*, and the functions $y_j = f_j(x_1, x_2, \ldots, x_r)$ are called *transmission functions*. A transmission function is said to be *completely specified* if $f_j(x_1, x_2, \ldots, x_r)$ is assigned a value for all possible values of the r-tuple $[x_1, x_2, \ldots, x_r]$. If, on the other hand, there are values of $[x_1, x_2, \ldots, x_r]$ that never occur because of the way in which the variables are generated, then the function $f_j(x_1, x_2, \ldots, x_r)$ need not be defined for these values. Such a situation is called a "*don't care*" condition and the transmission function is said to be *incompletely specified*.

Incompletely specified functions are quite common in digital system design. For example, assume that the input to the logic network represents a decimal number encoded in BCD form. Then only 10 of the 4-tuples $[x_1, x_2, x_3, x_4]$ would be specified and the other 6 would correspond to don't care conditions. The following truth table (Table 7-1) also illustrates another incompletely specified function. The don't care entries in this table are indicated by d.

Table 7-1 Typical Incompletely Specified Function

x_1	x_2	x_3	$g(x_1, x_2, x_3)$
0	0	0	1
0	0	1	1
0	1	0	d
0	1	1	1
1	0	0	0
1	0	1	0
1	1	0	d
1	1	1	0

A Preview of the Minimization Problem

There are several methods of finding a minimal representation of the transmission function. In the next few sections we present two of the standard minimization techniques; the map method and the prime implicant method. However, before proceeding, let us try to obtain an understanding of the minimization problem by finding a minimal representation for two transmission functions.

First consider the completely specified function given by

$$f(x_1, x_2, x_3) = \bar{x}_1 x_2 \bar{x}_3 \vee x_1 \bar{x}_2 \bar{x}_3 \vee x_1 \bar{x}_2 x_3 \vee x_1 x_2 \bar{x}_3 \vee x_1 x_2 x_3$$

If we were to realize this function directly we would need a logic network with five AND elements and one OR element. However, we can continually apply the laws

$$\bar{x}y \vee xy = y \qquad \text{and} \qquad x \vee \bar{x}y = x \vee y$$

to produce the reduced function

$$f(x_1, x_2, x_3) = x_1 \vee x_2 \bar{x}_3$$

This function can be realized with one AND element and one OR element.

Next let us consider the case where the truth table description of the transmission function contains a don't care condition. The function represented by Table 7-1 is an example of such a situation. Since the 3-tuples $[0, 1, 0]$ and $[1, 1, 0]$ never occur as input combinations, we can assign any value that we want to $g(0, 1, 0)$ and $g(1, 1, 0)$. There are four possible ways in which values could be assigned. If we do this we obtain the following four possible representations of $g(x_1, x_2, x_3)$ that differ only for the don't care values of $[x_1, x_2, x_3]$.

Case 1

$$g(0, 1, 0) = g(1, 1, 0) = 0$$

$$g_1(x_1, x_2, x_3) = \bar{x}_1 \bar{x}_2 \bar{x}_3 \vee \bar{x}_1 \bar{x}_2 x_3 \vee \bar{x}_1 x_2 x_3$$

Case 2

$$g(0, 1, 0) = 1 \qquad g(1, 1, 0) = 0$$

$$g_2(x_1, x_2, x_3) = \bar{x}_1 \bar{x}_2 \bar{x}_3 \vee \bar{x}_1 \bar{x}_2 x_3 \vee \bar{x}_1 x_2 x_3 \vee \bar{x}_1 x_2 \bar{x}_3$$

Case 3

$$g(0, 1, 0) = 0 \qquad g(1, 1, 0) = 1$$

$$g_3(x_1, x_2, x_3) = \bar{x}_1 \bar{x}_2 \bar{x}_3 \vee \bar{x}_1 \bar{x}_2 x_3 \vee \bar{x}_1 x_2 x_3 \vee x_1 x_2 \bar{x}_3$$

Case 4

$$g(0, 1, 0) = 1 \qquad g(1, 1, 0) = 1$$

$$g_4(x_1, x_2, x_3) = \bar{x}_1 \bar{x}_2 \bar{x}_3 \vee \bar{x}_1 \bar{x}_2 x_3 \vee \bar{x}_1 x_2 x_3 \vee \bar{x}_1 x_2 \bar{x}_3 \vee x_1 x_2 \bar{x}_3$$

If we apply the reduction laws to these four functions we find that

$$g_1(x_1, x_2, x_3) = \bar{x}_1 \bar{x}_2 \vee \bar{x}_1 x_3$$

$$g_2(x_1, x_2, x_3) = \bar{x}_1$$

$$g_3(x_1, x_2, x_3) = \bar{x}_1 \bar{x}_2 \vee \bar{x}_1 x_3 \vee x_1 x_2 \bar{x}_3$$

$$g_4(x_1, x_2, x_3) = \bar{x}_1 \vee x_2 \bar{x}_3$$

Examining the minimal form of these four possible representations of $g(x_1, x_2, x_3)$ we see that $g_2(x_1, x_2, x_3) = \bar{x}_1$ is the simplest expression. Therefore, if we arbitrarily assign the values

$$g(0, 1, 0) = 1 \qquad g(1, 1, 0) = 0$$

to the don't care condition of Table 7-1 we obtain a very simple transmission function to represent $g(x_1, x_2, x_3)$ for all those values of $[x_1, x_2, x_3]$ where $g(x_1, x_2, x_3)$ is defined. This example has illustrated that it is often possible to obtain a simpler minimal expression if we make use of the flexibility provided by the freedom of assigning any value we wish to the don't care entries.

In these two examples we have used algebraic techniques to obtain the minimal expressions. This was easy to do because it was fairly obvious which reduction should be applied to each expression. When there are more variables or when the expressions take on a more complex form, this is not as easy to do. Several minimization algorithms have been developed which, in theory, allow us to handle any minimization problem in a mechanical manner.

2. MINIMIZATION BY THE MAP METHOD

Sometimes the most difficult problem one encounters in trying to reduce logical expressions to minimal form by algebraic means is to identify the terms in the expression that can be combined to form a new term with fewer variables. The map method of minimization uses a visual representation of the expression under investigation to aid us in selecting the terms that can be combined to obtain a simpler expression. This map is called a *Karnaugh map*.

Forming the Map

Basically the Karnaugh map of a transmission function is a visual way of presenting the same information contained in the truth table representation of the function. A map for a function $f(x_1, x_2, \ldots, x_r)$ of r variables contains 2^r squares, there being a square on the map for every possible value of the r-tuple $[x_1, x_2, \ldots, x_r]$. Assume that $[e_1, e_2, \ldots, e_r]$ is a particular value of $[x_1, x_2, \ldots, x_r]$. Then the square corresponding to this particular input assignment is labeled $f(e_1, e_2, \ldots, e_r)$. Under this convention a 1 is placed in each square representing a combination for which an output of 1 is desired; a 0 is placed in each square representing a combination for which an output of 0 is desired; and a d is entered in those squares corresponding to don't care input conditions.

The two basic algebraic laws that we make use of in the map method of reduction are

$$xy \vee \bar{x}y = y \qquad \text{and} \qquad x \vee \bar{x}y = x \vee y$$

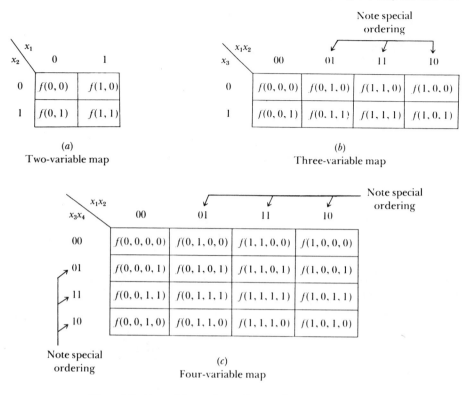

Figure 7-2. General form of two, three, and four variable maps.

Therefore when we construct a map of a given transmission function we must arrange the map in such a way that we can apply these laws by inspection. This condition is satisfied, for functions of two, three, or four variables, if we arrange the maps as shown in Figure 7-2. Note that any two adjacent squares in the map correspond to r-tuples which differ in only one variable. Also note that the r-tuple corresponding to the leftmost square of any row differs in only one variable from the r-tuple corresponding to the rightmost square of that row. Similarly the top square of any column differs in only one variable from the bottom square of the column. The significance of this ordering will become evident shortly.

Figure 7-3 gives specific examples of maps corresponding to two, three, and four variables. There are two possible interpretations that we can give to a map. If we concentrate on the 1 and d entries, then the resulting minimal function that we obtain will be in the sum-of-product form. This is true because the 1 entries of a map correspond to the minterms of the function.

However, because of the duality of switching algebra, we can also concentrate on 0 and d entries of a map. In this case the 0 entries correspond to the maxterms of a given function and the resulting minimal function that we obtain will be in the product-of-sum form.

x_1	x_2	$f(x_1, x_2)$
0	0	0
0	1	1
1	0	0
1	1	1

x_1	x_2	x_3	$f(x_1, x_2, x_3)$
0	0	0	1
0	0	1	1
0	1	0	d
0	1	1	1
1	0	0	0
1	0	1	0
1	1	0	d
1	1	1	0

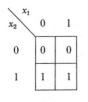

(a)

Two-variable function

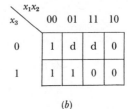

(b)

Three-variable function

x_1	x_2	x_3	x_4	$f(x_1, x_2, x_3, x_4)$
0	0	0	0	1
0	0	0	1	1
0	0	1	0	0
0	0	1	1	1
0	1	0	0	0
0	1	0	1	0
0	1	1	0	0
0	1	1	1	1
1	0	0	0	0
1	0	0	1	1
1	0	1	0	1
1	0	1	1	0
1	1	0	0	0
1	1	0	1	0
1	1	1	0	1
1	1	1	1	0

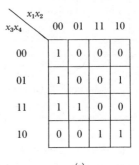

(c)

Four-variable function

Figure 7-3. Example of two, three, and four variable maps.

Minimal Sum-of-Product Functions

To find a minimal sum-of-product function we visualize the map as a representation of the function in its canonical sum-of-product form. Each 1 or *d* entry will correspond to possible minterms that can be combined to simplify our expression. Since we are not interested in the 0 entries in the map we will adopt the convention that

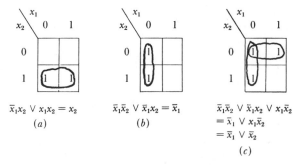

$$\bar{x}_1 x_2 \vee x_1 x_2 = x_2$$

(a)

$$\bar{x}_1 \bar{x}_2 \vee \bar{x}_1 x_2 = \bar{x}_1$$

(b)

$$\bar{x}_1 \bar{x}_2 \vee \bar{x}_1 x_2 \vee x_1 \bar{x}_2$$
$$= \bar{x}_1 \vee x_1 \bar{x}_2$$
$$= \bar{x}_1 \vee \bar{x}_2$$

(c)

Figure 7-4. Three typical reductions.

these entries are left blank in order to reduce the clutter in a map. The maps of Figure 7-4 illustrate this convention.

Our reduction process is based on the use of the following identities,

$$xy \vee \bar{x}y = y \quad \text{and} \quad x \vee \bar{x}y = x \vee y$$

to combine and simplify the product terms. The application of these identities is facilitated by the convention that we have used to set up our map. Any two adjacent squares correspond to minterms that differ in only one variable. In one square this variable appears in the negated form and in the other square it appears in its unnegated form.

For example, the map of Figure 7-4a has two adjacent minterm entries $m_1 = \bar{x}_1 x_2$ and $m_3 = x_1 x_2$. The two terms m_1 and m_3 differ in that the variable x_1 appears in its negated form in m_1 and its unnegated form in m_3. From this we see that we can combine these two terms to obtain

$$\bar{x}_1 x_2 \vee x_1 x_2 = x_2$$

This simplification is noted on the map by drawing a circle around the two squares that we combined to form the simpler expression.

Two other examples are shown in Figure 7-4b and c. In particular the reduction shown in Figure 7-4c should be considered in detail. This reduction has made use of the fact that the minterm $m_0 = \bar{x}_1 \bar{x}_2$ can be combined with both the minterm $m_2 = x_1 \bar{x}_2$ and the minterm $m_1 = \bar{x}_1 x_2$. It should also be noted that it is not possible to combine minterms such as m_1 and m_2 that fall along the diagonal of the map.

Next consider the case of functions of three or four variables. Maps of these functions will have two or four rows respectively and we can combine either two, four, or eight squares at a time to obtain a reduced function. Figure 7-5 shows some of the possible forms that the four-square at a time combinations can take. The two-square at a time combinations take the same form as in Figure 7-4. Note the use of the top-bottom and left-right combinations on the columns and rows respectively.

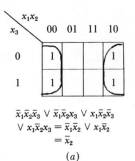

$$\bar{x}_1\bar{x}_2\bar{x}_3 \lor \bar{x}_1\bar{x}_2x_3 \lor x_1\bar{x}_2\bar{x}_3$$
$$\lor\, x_1\bar{x}_2x_3 = \bar{x}_1\bar{x}_2 \lor x_1\bar{x}_2$$
$$= \bar{x}_2$$

(a)

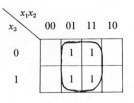

$$\bar{x}_1x_2\bar{x}_3 \lor x_1x_2\bar{x}_3 \lor \bar{x}_1x_2x_3 \lor x_1x_2x_3$$
$$= x_2\bar{x}_3 \lor x_2x_3$$
$$= x_2$$

(b)

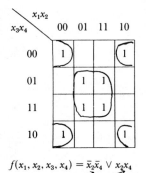

$$f(x_1, x_2, x_3, x_4) = \bar{x}_2\bar{x}_4 \lor x_2x_4$$

Corner terms   Center terms
Combination at corners and center

(c)

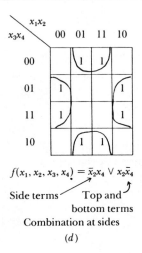

$$f(x_1, x_2, x_3, x_4) = \bar{x}_2x_4 \lor x_2\bar{x}_4$$

Side terms   Top and
bottom terms
Combination at sides

(d)

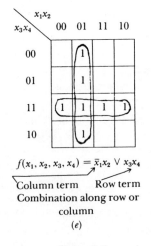

$$f(x_1, x_2, x_3, x_4) = \bar{x}_1x_2 \lor x_3x_4$$

Column term   Row term
Combination along row or
column

(e)

Figure 7-5.

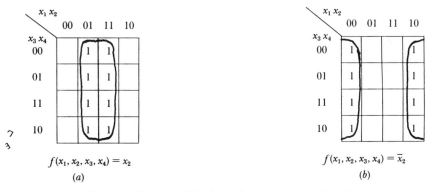

Figure 7-6. Some possible eight adjacent square combinations.

Figure 7-6 shows some of the ways that eight adjacent squares can be combined.

So far we have shown the methods of combining blocks of either two, four, or eight adjacent squares to identify the terms that can be combined to minimize a given function. Often we find patterns in which we can combine adjacent squares in a number of different ways. To decide which combinations should be made we can formulate the following general rules.

1. Every one-square must be accounted for at least once.
2. Any combination should be as large as possible. Thus a one-square should not be taken by itself if it can be taken as part of two adjacent squares; a group of two adjacent squares should not be combined if they can be combined in a group of four adjacent squares; etc.
3. All one-squares should be accounted for in the minimum number of groups of adjacent squares.

Figure 7-7 illustrates these general rules. The map of Figure 7-7a is formed in a straightforward manner. Although the two-square term corresponding to $x_2 \bar{x}_3 x_4$

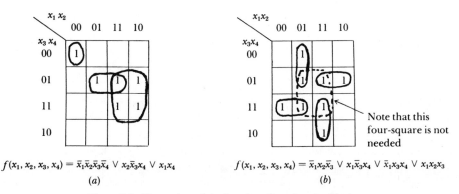

Figure 7-7. Illustration of the forming of overlapping blocks.

overlaps the four-square term corresponding to $x_1 x_4$, both terms are required to cover the map. However, consider the map given in Figure 7-7b. It appears that we should include the four-square indicated by the dotted line. But if we examine the map carefully we see that every square in that particular four-square is already contained in a two-square which cannot be eliminated; thus the term $x_2 x_4$, corresponding to the four-square is redundant and does not have to be included in the expression for $f(x_1, x_2, x_3, x_4)$.

Reading a Map

Each set of minterms that are combined on a map correspond to a product term that can be formed by algebraically combining these minterms. Each time two minterms are combined we eliminate one of the variables in the product term. The variable that is eliminated is the one that appears in its negated form in one minterm and in its unnegated form in the other minterm. Similarly when four minterms are combined we eliminate two variables and when we combine eight minterms we eliminate three variables.

To find the product term corresponding to any combined set of minterms is easily accomplished if we use the above observation. The rows and columns of a map are labeled so that only one variable changes value as we go from row-to-row or column-to-column. Thus if we combine minterms in adjacent rows or adjacent columns we see that we are actually eliminating the variable that changes value from one row to the other or one column to the other.

For example in Figure 7-7a consider the two minterms in row 01 and columns 01 and 11. These two terms are combined. We note that the x_1 variable is the variable that changes when we go from column 01 to column 11. Thus x_1 is the variable eliminated from the product term. The three other variables remain 1, 0, and 1 respectively. Thus we see that the resulting product term is $x_2 \bar{x}_3 x_4$. Similarly we see that the four minterms in rows 11 and 01 and columns 11 and 10 can be combined into a single product term. In this case the variables x_2 and x_3 are the ones that change value and can thus be eliminated. The two variables x_1 and x_4 remain 1 and 1 respectively. Thus the product term corresponding to this grouping is $x_1 x_4$.

The Reduction Process

Now that we have developed an understanding of how we can use a map to locate the minterms that can be combined into single product terms, our next task is to see how these techniques can be used to find a minimal map of a given function. The reduction process that we use involves the systematic grouping of minterms into the largest group possible. Sometimes this grouping will be unique. At other times we will find that more than one grouping can be found. Whenever this occurs we know that there will be several possible minimal representations of a function.

Case I. Unique Minimum Map

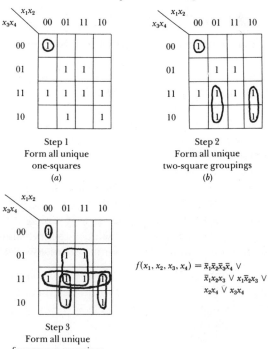

Step 1
Form all unique
one-squares
(a)

Step 2
Form all unique
two-square groupings
(b)

Step 3
Form all unique
four-square groupings
(c)

$$f(x_1, x_2, x_3, x_4) = \bar{x}_1\bar{x}_2\bar{x}_3\bar{x}_4 \vee$$
$$\bar{x}_1 x_2 x_3 \vee x_1 \bar{x}_2 x_3 \vee$$
$$x_2 x_4 \vee x_3 x_4$$

Case II. Nonunique map

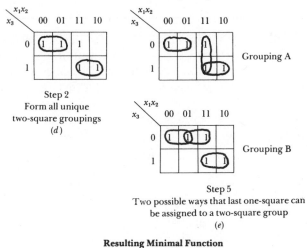

Step 2
Form all unique
two-square groupings
(d)

Grouping A

Grouping B

Step 5
Two possible ways that last one-square can
be assigned to a two-square group
(e)

Resulting Minimal Function

Grouping A $f(x_1, x_2, x_3) = \bar{x}_1\bar{x}_3 \vee x_1 x_3 \vee x_1 x_2$
Grouping B $f(x_1, x_2, x_3) = \bar{x}_1\bar{x}_3 \vee x_1 x_3 \vee x_2\bar{x}_3$

Figure 7-8. Illustration of minimal map algorithm.

The following algorithm can be used to find a minimal map of a given function.

Algorithm for Finding Minimal Map

1. Identify and circle all one-squares that cannot be combined with any other squares.
2. Identify all one-squares that can be combined with only one other square. Use these pairs to form two-square groupings. Leave any square which can be combined in more than one way until later.
3. Identify all squares that can be combined in groups of four in only one way provided all of the squares are not already covered by the groupings of step 2. Use these squares to form four-square groups. Leave any squares that can be combined in more than one way until later.
4. Repeat the combination process for groups of eight squares provided all the squares in the group are not already covered.
5. Next investigate any squares not assigned to a grouping. Arbitrarily form the largest group that can be formed that includes the most uncovered squares. Add just enough terms until all the one-squares are covered.

The steps of this algorithm are illustrated in Figure 7-8. Two examples are shown. The first example given by Figure 7-8a to c illustrates the case where there is no problem in deciding how to assign the blocks. The second example given by Figure 7-8d and e shows the situation where there is no unique assignment of blocks to cover the one-square corresponding to $f(1, 1, 0)$. Either of the two assignments are equally valid.

Don't Care Condition

The extension of the above minimization process to the case where the function has one or more don't care conditions associated with it is straightforward. As indicated before, don't care conditions are shown by a d entry in the map. In combining squares we use a d entry whenever possible to form larger blocks of squares. However, any d-square not needed to create a larger block is neglected. To illustrate the case, consider the map given in Figure 7-9. The d-square corresponding to $f(0, 1, 0)$ is used to form a four-block while the d-square corresponding to $f(1, 1, 0)$ is not used.

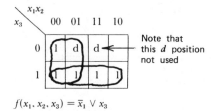

$$f(x_1, x_2, x_3) = \bar{x}_1 \vee x_3$$

Figure 7-9. Use of don't care conditions in the map minimization process.

Minimal Product-of-Sum Functions

As was indicated previously, we can find a minimal product-of-sum function representation for a given map by visualizing the map as a representation of the function in the canonical product-of-sum form. In this case we concentrate on the 0 entries in the map rather than the 1 entries. Each 0 entry corresponds to one of the maxterms of the function. For example, the map shown in Figure 7-10 where the 0 rather than the 1 entries have been retained, corresponds to the logical expression

$$f(x_1, x_2, x_3) = (x_1 \lor x_2 \lor x_3)(x_1 \lor \bar{x}_2 \lor x_3)(x_1 \lor \bar{x}_2 \lor \bar{x}_3)$$

where each sum term corresponds to one of the maxterms associated with a 0 entry. The reduction process makes use of laws of the form

$$(x \lor y)(x \lor \bar{y}) = x \qquad \text{and} \qquad (x \lor y)(x \lor z \lor \bar{y}) = (x \lor y)(x \lor z)$$

to simplify the map.

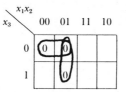

Figure 7-10. A map set up for product-of-sum evaluation.

We proceed in exactly the same manner as in the discussion for sum-of-product functions except that we try to enclose the largest number of 0's into groups. The map shown in Figure 7-10 admits two enclosures corresponding to the following applications of the above laws

$$f(x_1, x_2, x_3) = (x_1 \lor x_2 \lor x_3)(x_1 \lor \bar{x}_2 \lor x_3)(x_1 \lor \bar{x}_2 \lor \bar{x}_3)$$
$$= (x_1 \lor x_3)(x_1 \lor \bar{x}_2 \lor \bar{x}_3) = (x_1 \lor x_3)(x_1 \lor \bar{x}_2)$$

As another example, consider the map shown in Figure 7-11. This map has three sum terms in the product. The resulting minimal function for this map is

$$f(x_1, x_2, x_3, x_4) = (x_2 \lor x_4)(\bar{x}_2 \lor x_3 \lor \bar{x}_4)(\bar{x}_1 \lor x_2)$$

The minimal product-of-sum expression can be realized by a two-level OR-AND logic network. For the function given by the map in Figure 7-11 the resulting network would require three OR elements and 1 AND element.

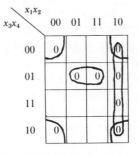

Figure 7-11. A maxterm map.

Prime Implicants

The map method of minimization can be extended to five and even six variables. However, the added complexity involved is usually not worth the bother and the tabular method to be presented in the next section is easier to use for more complex problems. In particular, the tabular technique can be used to develop computer programs that carry out the more tedious aspects of the reduction process.

Besides giving us a quick way to reduce logic expressions of up to four variables, the map of a function has another useful feature. It gives us a visual understanding of an important relationship that exists between logic terms which we use in the next section.

When we use the map method to find a minimal sum-of-product representation of a logic function we try to combine all adjacent one-squares into groups of $2^n (n = 0, 1, \ldots)$ one-squares. Each such group of squares that we can form *that is not properly contained* in a larger group of squares is a graphical example of what we call a *prime implicant*. To illustrate this idea consider the map shown in Figure 7-12. There are four prime implicants as indicated in this figure.
They have been formed by continually applying the reduction rule $xy \lor x\bar{y} = x$ to the product terms found in the sum-of-product expression until no new reductions can be made. For example

$$\bar{x}_1 x_2 = \bar{x}_1 x_2 \bar{x}_3 \bar{x}_4 \lor \bar{x}_1 x_2 \bar{x}_3 x_4 \lor \bar{x}_1 x_2 x_3 x_4 \lor \bar{x}_1 x_2 x_3 \bar{x}_4$$

is such a prime implicant.

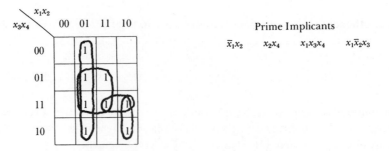

Figure 7-12. Illustration of prime implicants.

If we examine Figure 7-12 we see that although the function represented by the map can be represented as

$$f(x_1, x_2, x_3, x_4) = \bar{x}_1 x_2 \lor x_2 x_4 \lor x_1 x_3 x_4 \lor x_1 \bar{x}_2 x_3$$

in reality we do not need the prime implicant $x_1 x_3 x_4$ since the block represented by this term contains only one-squares that are already contained in other blocks that must be used in the representation of the function.

In the next section we show how these prime implicants can be found using a tabular method and how we can go about selecting the smallest set of these prime implicants that we need to represent a function.

EXERCISES

1. Find all minimal sum-of-product and product-of-sum expressions for the following truth tables

x_1	x_2	x_3	$f(x_1, x_2, x_3)$	$g(x_1, x_2, x_3)$
0	0	0	1	1
0	0	1	1	d
0	1	0	0	d
0	1	1	1	0
1	0	0	0	1
1	0	1	0	d
1	1	0	1	0
1	1	1	1	0

x_1	x_2	x_3	x_4	$h(x_1, x_2, x_3, x_4)$
0	0	0	0	1
0	0	0	1	0
0	0	1	0	1
0	0	1	1	0
0	1	0	0	1
0	1	0	1	0
0	1	1	0	0
0	1	1	1	d
1	0	0	0	1
1	0	0	1	1
1	0	1	0	d
1	0	1	1	1
1	1	0	0	1
1	1	0	1	d
1	1	1	0	0
1	1	1	1	0

2. Find the prime implicants of the functions defined in Figure 7-8 and by Table 7-2 in Section 3.

3. The transmission function for the sum and carry output of a full adder is described by the two functions (see Table 4-7, Chapter 4):

$$s_i = \bar{a}_i \bar{b}_i c_{i-1} \vee \bar{a}_i b_i \bar{c}_{i-1} \vee a_i \bar{b}_i \bar{c}_{i-1} \vee a_i b_i c_{i-1}$$

$$c_i = \bar{a}_i b_i c_{i-1} \vee a_i \bar{b}_i c_{i-1} \vee a_i b_i \bar{c}_{i-1} \vee a_i b_i c_{i-1}$$

Use the map method to minimize these functions.

3. MINIMIZATION BY THE TABULAR METHOD

The tabular method of simplification, also called the Quine–McCluskey method, consists of a systematic enumerative technique for reducing functions initially in the sum-of-product form to minimal form. It is based on the relationship $xy \vee x\bar{y} = x$ where x is any product expression representing one or more variables and y is a single variable.

The minimization process is carried out according to the following algorithm.

1. Form the canonical sum-of-product representation of the function to be minimized.
2. Examine all product terms and apply the reduction $xy \vee x\bar{y} = x$ as many times as possible. All of the new product terms so formed will have one less variable than the original terms.
3. Take the new set of product terms and repeat step 2 on this new set of terms. When no further reductions are possible all of the product terms that were generated by steps 1 and 2 and which cannot be further reduced are the prime implicants associated with the function to be minimized.
4. The set of prime implicants are then inspected to choose a minimal set that can be ORed together to represent the function.

The advantage of the Quine–McCluskey method is that it provides an algorithmic technique that can be used to generate all of the prime implicants associated with a given transmission function. Once all of the prime implicants are found, the second stage of the process allows us to generate all of the possible minimal expressions that represent the function. The following example explains the steps of this simplification technique.

Assume that we are given the function described by the truth table given by Table 7-2. The sum-of-product representation of this function is

$$f(x_1, x_2, x_3, x_4) = \bar{x}_1 \bar{x}_2 \bar{x}_3 \bar{x}_4 \vee \bar{x}_1 x_2 \bar{x}_3 \bar{x}_4 \vee \bar{x}_1 x_2 \bar{x}_3 x_4 \vee \bar{x}_1 x_2 x_3 \bar{x}_4$$
$$\vee x_1 \bar{x}_2 x_3 x_4 \vee x_1 x_2 \bar{x}_3 \bar{x}_4 \vee x_1 x_2 \bar{x}_3 x_4$$
$$\vee x_1 x_2 x_3 \bar{x}_4 \vee x_1 x_2 x_3 x_4$$

Table 7-2   Truth Table Representation of $f(x_1, x_2, x_3, x_4)$

x_1	x_2	x_3	x_4	$f(x_1, x_2, x_3, x_4)$
0	0	0	0	1
0	0	0	1	0
0	0	1	0	0
0	0	1	1	0
0	1	0	0	1
0	1	0	1	1
0	1	1	0	1
0	1	1	1	0
1	0	0	0	0
1	0	0	1	0
1	0	1	0	0
1	0	1	1	1
1	1	0	0	1
1	1	0	1	1
1	1	1	0	1
1	1	1	1	1

To apply the reduction process we must identify all product terms which differ in only one variable. That variable is negated in one expression and not in the other. All other variables have the same form. The two terms $\bar{x}_1 \bar{x}_2 \bar{x}_3 \bar{x}_4$ and $\bar{x}_1 x_2 \bar{x}_3 \bar{x}_4$ are two such product terms which we can combine to form $\bar{x}_{1\,-}\,\bar{x}_3 \bar{x}_4$. The blank indicates that one variable has been eliminated from the product.

We now form a special table that allows us to identify the product terms that can be combined in this manner. The 0, 1 representation of each product term, where 0 indicates a negated and 1 an unnegated variable, is used in this table.

First we list all terms that do not contain any 1's, then all terms that contain only one 1, then all terms that have two 1's, and so on until the last part of the list contains the term with all 1's if it is present. Table 7-3 shows this listing and the corresponding product term.

Instead of examining all possible pairs of product terms to apply the relationship $xy \vee x\bar{y} = x$, all that we have to do is examine the adjacent groups of the table that were formed by counting the number of 1's in a row. If two rows are to be combined they can differ in only one column. In that column one row contains a 1 and the corresponding column in the other row must contain a 0. When we locate two rows that can be combined we make the following reduction

$$0\,0\,0\,0 \qquad 0\,\_\,0\,0$$
$$0\,1\,0\,0$$

The "_" indicates that the variable has been eliminated by application of the relation $xy \vee x\bar{y} = x$.

Table 7-3 First Step in Tabular Reduction Process

Product Terms		0, 1 Representation
$\bar{x}_1\bar{x}_2\bar{x}_3\bar{x}_4$	0000	Terms with no 1 per row
$\bar{x}_1 x_2 \bar{x}_3 \bar{x}_4$	0100	Terms with one 1 per row
$\bar{x}_1 x_2 \bar{x}_3 x_4$	0101	
$\bar{x}_1 x_2 x_3 \bar{x}_4$	0110	Terms with two 1's per row
$x_1 x_2 \bar{x}_3 \bar{x}_4$	1100	
$x_1 \bar{x}_2 x_3 x_4$	1011	
$x_1 x_2 \bar{x}_3 x_4$	1101	Terms with three 1's per row
$x_1 x_2 x_3 \bar{x}_4$	1110	
$x_1 x_2 x_3 x_4$	1111	Terms with four 1's per row

Note that the product terms are only included in this example for illustrative purposes. They are usually not included in forming the table.

Table 7-4 shows how we use this technique to carry out the first step of the reduction process for the function described in Table 7-3. The first reduction is obtained by combining 0000 with 0100 to give 0_00 which is entered in the column labeled first reduction. This says that $\bar{x}_1\bar{x}_2\bar{x}_3\bar{x}_4 \lor \bar{x}_1 x_2 \bar{x}_3 \bar{x}_4 = \bar{x}_1\bar{x}_3\bar{x}_4$ is a possible simplification. A " $\checkmark$ " mark is placed alongside the rows 0000 and 0100 to indicate that they are not prime implicants. Next we take the row 0100 and try to combine

Table 7-4 Illustration of Reduction Process

				First Reduction				Second Reduction			
x_1	x_2	x_3	x_4	x_1	x_2	x_3	x_4	x_1	x_2	x_3	x_4
0	0	0	0$\checkmark$	0	_	0	0*	_	1	0	_*
0	1	0	0$\checkmark$	0	1	0	_$\checkmark$	_	1	_	0*
0	1	0	1$\checkmark$	_	1	0	0$\checkmark$	1	1	_	_*
0	1	1	0$\checkmark$	0	1	_	0$\checkmark$				
1	1	0	0$\checkmark$	_	1	0	1$\checkmark$				
1	0	1	1$\checkmark$	_	1	1	0$\checkmark$				
1	1	0	1$\checkmark$	1	1	0	_$\checkmark$				
1	1	1	0$\checkmark$	1	1	_	0$\checkmark$				
1	1	1	1$\checkmark$	1	_	1	1*				
				1	1	_	1$\checkmark$				
				1	1	1	_$\checkmark$				

it with the rows containing two 1's. Combining 0100 with 0101 gives 010_ which is the second entry in our second column. Similarly 0100 combines with 1100 to give _100. The terms 0101 and 1100 are checked to indicate that these two rows are not prime implicants. It should be noted that even when a row is checked it is still used to try to find reduced terms. This is because of the law $x \lor x = x$. Continuing in this manner we obtain the table labeled "First Reduction" in Table 7-4. We also see that all of the terms in the original table have been checked so that none of them are prime implicants. If any row had not been checked that row would have corresponded to one of the prime implicants that we are looking for.

The next step is to compare the rows in the new table, labeled "First Reduction," to find new reductions. Again, for two rows to combine, they must differ in only one column. All other columns must be identical. Thus 0_00 and _101 cannot combine because they differ in the first, second, and fourth column. However _100 and _101 can be combined to give _10_.

The _'s speed up the reduction process since, in particular, it can be seen that two terms cannot be combined if the _'s do not appear in the same place in both rows. For example 0_00 in the first group of the second table cannot combine with any of the terms in the second group because all three of these terms have a 1 in the x_2 column.

Applying the reduction rules to the table we obtained in the first reduction we obtain the new table labeled "Second Reduction." Here again we observe some interesting properties. We note that _10_ can be obtained by combining either 010_ and 110_, or _100 and _101. Thus all four of these terms are checked as not being prime implicants. We also note that the terms 0_00 and 1_11 cannot be combined. These terms, which are prime implicants, are starred (*).

Finally we examine the last table and see that the terms _10_, _1_0, and 11__ are also prime implicants since they cannot be combined. Thus we have completed the first stage of the reduction process and we have identified the five product terms $\bar{x}_1 \bar{x}_3 \bar{x}_4$, $x_1 x_3 x_4$, $x_2 \bar{x}_3$, $x_2 \bar{x}_4$, and $x_1 x_2$ as prime implicants. Figure 7-13 is a map of the function under investigation with the prime implicants indicated.

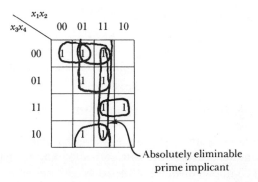

Absolutely eliminable
prime implicant

Figure 7-13. A map representation of the prime implicants.

Table 7-5   Table of Choice

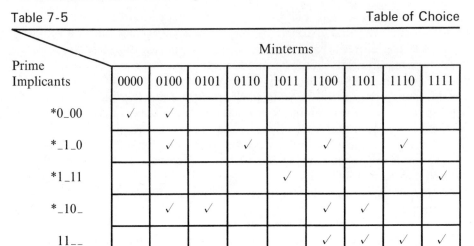

Prime Implicants	Minterms								
	0000	0100	0101	0110	1011	1100	1101	1110	1111
*0_00	✓	✓							
*_1_0		✓		✓		✓		✓	
*1_11					✓				✓
*_10_		✓	✓			✓	✓		
11__						✓	✓	✓	✓

Now that we have identified all the prime implicants, our final step is to select, enough prime implicants to account for all of the original product terms. This is accomplished by constructing a table of choice. Each column of the table corresponds to one of the minterms in the original sum-of-product expression we started with and each of the rows corresponds to one of the prime implicants that we have found in the previous step. For each prime implicant, a check mark is placed in the columns of those minterms accounted for by that prime implicant. For example consider the column headed by 1100 corresponding to the minterm $x_1 x_2 \bar{x}_3 \bar{x}_4$. This minterm was used to form the prime implicants _1_0 corresponding to $x_2 \bar{x}_4$, _10_ corresponding to $x_2 \bar{x}_3$, and 11__ corresponding to $x_1 x_2$. Thus we place a check in this column whenever one of the three rows corresponding to these prime implicants intersect the column. Table 7-5 gives the complete table of choice for our example.

Examining this table we can make the following observations:

1. A prime implicant with no _'s accounts for only 1 minterm, a prime implicant with one _ accounts for 2 minterms, and in general a prime implicant with u_'s accounts for 2^u minterms.

2. It is possible to have one or more minterms that are accounted for by one and only one prime implicant. Prime implicants of this type are called *essential* or *core* prime implicants. These prime implicants are starred in the table.

In the above example 0_00, _1_0, 1_11, and _10_ are essential prime implicants.

3. A prime implicant is an *absolutely eliminable prime implicant* if all of the columns that are checked in the row corresponding to that prime implicant are also checked in one or more of the rows corresponding to the core prime implicants.

In the above example $11\_\_$ is an absolutely eliminable prime implicant. The reason for this is also graphically illustrated in Figure 7-13.

4. The set of prime implicants that are not essential prime implicants or absolutely eliminable prime implicants is called the *set of eligible prime implicants*. A subset of this set must be used together with the core prime implicants to form the minimal logic expression representation of the given function.

In the above example we see that all the prime implicants are either core prime implicants or absolutely eliminable. Therefore there is only one minimal logic expression to represent the function. That expression is

$$f(x_1, x_2, x_3, x_4) = \bar{x}_1\bar{x}_3\bar{x}_4 \lor x_2\bar{x}_4 \lor x_1x_3x_4 \lor x_2\bar{x}_3$$

The next example illustrates the case where we have a set of eligible prime implicants.

Don't Care Conditions

When we have don't care conditions present in the truth table representation of the logic function we wish to synthesize, we proceed in the same way as before except for one small modification. In forming our table for the reduction process we include all the product terms that correspond to the don't care conditions and then proceed with our reduction process. After we have found the prime implicants we then form our table of choice. However, we do not include any columns in the table for the product terms corresponding to the don't care conditions.

In this case the don't care conditions are only used for the generation of prime implicants with the fewest number of variables. The following example illustrates this process. Assume that we wish to realize the function described in Table 7-6. The reduction process is carried out in Table 7-7. The two-product terms 0000 and 0010 corresponding to the don't care conditions are included when we find the prime implicants but not when we form the table of choice.

Examining the table of choice we see that there is only one essential prime implicant, $\_1\_1$. The other five prime implicants form an eligible set and our final problem is to decide which prime implicants actually need to be selected from this set in order to complete our expression. There are a number of possible selections. The only requirement is that the prime implicants must provide checks in those columns that are not accounted for by any of the essential prime implicants. To aid in making this choice we can use a reduced table of choice such as illustrated in Table 7-7c. This table is obtained by eliminating the rows corresponding to the essential prime implicants and the columns containing checks associated with the essential prime implicants.

Table 7-6   A Function with Don't Care Conditions

x_1	x_2	x_3	x_4	$f(x_1, x_2, x_3, x_4)$
0	0	0	0	d
0	0	0	1	0
0	0	1	0	d
0	0	1	1	1
0	1	0	0	0
0	1	0	1	1
0	1	1	0	0
0	1	1	1	1
1	0	0	0	1
1	0	0	1	0
1	0	1	0	1
1	0	1	1	1
1	1	0	0	1
1	1	0	1	1
1	1	1	0	0
1	1	1	1	1

Table 7-7

(a) Prime Implicant Calculations

	x_1	x_2	x_3	x_4	x_1	x_2	x_3	x_4	x_1	x_2	x_3	x_4
Don't care	0	0	0	0✓	0	0	_	0✓	_	0	_	0*
conditions	0	0	1	0✓	_	0	0	0✓	_	0	1	_*
included	1	0	0	0✓	0	0	1	_✓	_	_	1	1*
only for	0	0	1	1✓	_	0	1	0✓	_	1	_	1*
selection	0	1	0	1✓	1	0	_	0✓				
or Prime	1	0	1	0✓	1	_	0	0*				
Implicants	1	1	0	0✓	0	_	1	1✓				
	0	1	1	1✓	_	0	1	1✓				
	1	0	1	1✓	0	1	_	1✓				
	1	1	0	1✓	_	1	0	1✓				
	1	1	1	1✓	1	0	1	_✓				
					1	1	0	_*				
					_	1	1	1✓				
					1	_	1	1✓				
					1	1	_	1✓				

Table 7-7 (*continued*)

(b) Table of Choice (Note that 0000 and 0010 corresponding to don't care conditions are not included as minterms)

Prime Implicants	Minterms								
	0011	0101	0111	1000	1010	1011	1100	1101	1111
1_00				✓			✓		
110_							✓	✓	
_0_0				✓	✓				
_01_	✓				✓	✓			
__11	✓		✓			✓			✓
*_1_1		✓	✓					✓	✓

(c) Reduced Table of Choice Associated with the Eligible Set

Eligible Set		Minterms				
		0011	1000	1010	1011	1100
A	1_00		✓			✓
B	110_					✓
C	_0_0		✓	✓		
D	_01_	✓		✓	✓	
E	__11	✓			✓	

By examining this table we see that any one of the following four possible sets of prime implicants from the eligible set can be used, together with the essential prime implicant to represent the logic function of the example.

Set 1	Set 2	Set 3	Set 4
1_00	1_00	110_	110_
_01_	_0_0	_0_0	_0_0
	__11	_01_	__11

Examining this set we see that set 1 has the fewest terms so we can select this set of terms to complete our expression. The resulting minimum logic expression is

$$f(x_1, x_2, x_3, x_4) = x_2 x_4 \vee x_1 \bar{x}_3 \bar{x}_4 \vee \bar{x}_2 x_3$$

In many cases the selection of the subset of the eligible set necessary to complete the minimal expression representation of a function is obvious. However in some situations it is desirable to have an algorithm that can be used to find the desired expressions. We now consider this problem.

Algebraic Solution of Reduced Choice Table

To find all of the combinations of prime implicants that can be formed from the eligible set to complete our expression we assign a variable to each element of the eligible set. This is illustrated in Table 7-7c.

For each column in the reduced table of choice we write a logical expression indicating which prime implicants contribute a check to that column. For example, consider the column corresponding to the product term 0011. Both rows D and E contribute a check to that column. Thus we can say that in the final expression we must have the prime implicant D *OR* the prime implicant E. This condition is indicated by writing $(D \vee E)$. For each column we can form the following logical sums describing the conditions that give a check in that column.

Column	Logical Sums
0011	$(D \vee E)$
1000	$(A \vee C)$
1010	$(C \vee D)$
1011	$(D \vee E)$
1100	$(A \vee B)$

Next we note that we must select our prime implicants so that we have at least one check in each column. For an n column table this can be stated logically as (there must be one check in column 1) *AND* (one check in column 2) *AND* .... *AND* (one check in column n). To satisfy this logical condition all we have to do is to form the logical product of the logical sum terms describing each column.

For our example the resulting logical expression associated with Table 7-7c is found to be

$$(D \vee E)(A \vee C)(C \vee D)(D \vee E)(A \vee B) = F(A, B, C, D, E)$$

But this is a logical expression. Thus we can use our laws of switching algebra to reduce and expand this expression to a sum-of-product form. The steps of this process are given below for our example.

In this reduction we make use of the logical relationship

$$(x \vee w)(x \vee v) = (x \vee xv \vee xw \vee wv) = (x \vee wv)$$

Applying this relationship to our function gives

$$
\begin{aligned}
F(A, B, C, D, E) &= (D \vee E)(A \vee C)(C \vee D)(D \vee E)(A \vee B) \\
&= (A \vee C)(A \vee B)(D \vee E)(D \vee C) \\
&= (A \vee CB)(D \vee EC) \\
&= AD \vee AEC \vee CBD \vee CBE
\end{aligned}
$$

When we obtain the sum-of-product form, as in the above example, we look at each of the product terms. The prime implicants corresponding to the variables in each of the product terms are the ones that form the subsets of the eligible set that we are looking for. Thus we see that $F(A, B, C, D, E)$ tells us there are four sets which are

Set 1	Set 2	Set 3	Set 4
A 1_00	A 1_00	C _0_0	C _0_0
D _01_	E __11	B 110_	B 110_
	C _0_0	D _01_	E __11

These sets are the same sets that we have found previously.

EXERCISES

1. Use the tabular method to minimize the following logical expressions.

($m_i = i$th minterm)
(a) $f(x_1, x_2, x_3) = m_0 \vee m_2 \vee m_3 \vee m_4 \vee m_7$
(b) $f(x_1, x_2, x_3, x_4, x_5)$
$\quad = m_0 \vee m_2 \vee m_4 \vee m_6 \vee m_8 \vee m_{12} \vee m_{16} \vee m_{19} \vee m_{29} \vee m_{30}$

4. MULTIPLE OUTPUT LOGIC NETWORKS

Up to this point we have limited our discussion to logic networks with only a single output. Most of the logic networks that we deal with have multiple outputs. One method of approach would be to design a separate logic network for each transmission function. Such an approach would generate a network with the general

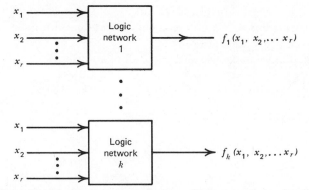

Figure 7-14. A simple realization of a multiple transmission function network.

form shown in Figure 7-14. For many of the simpler logic networks this approach is a realistic solution to the problem.

However, as the transmission functions become more complex we often find that it is possible to share part of the logic network circuitry among many of the transmission functions, thereby reducing the overall cost of the network. In this section we investigate two design techniques that can be used to design two-level AND-OR, multiple-output logic networks that share as many logic circuit elements as possible.

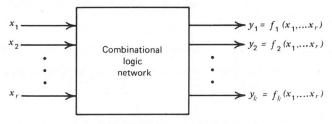

Figure 7-15. Multiple output logic network.

A general multiple output logic network has the form shown in Figure 7-15. As we know from our previous discussions, each transmission function can be represented in canonical sum-of-products form as

$$f_1(x_1, \ldots, x_r) = m_{1,1} \vee m_{1,2} \vee \cdots \vee m_{1,n_1}$$

$$f_2(x_1, \ldots, x_r) = m_{2,1} \vee m_{2,2} \vee \cdots \vee m_{2,n_2}$$

$$\vdots$$

$$f_k(x_1, \ldots, x_r) = m_{k,1} \vee m_{k,2} \vee \cdots \vee m_{k,n_k}$$

where the terms $m_{i,j}$ are the minterms associated with the transmission function $f_i(x_1, \ldots, x_r)$. The larger the number of minterms that are common to two or more transmission functions, the greater will be our chance to share logic circuit elements.

Switching Matrix

One quite common method of realizing a multiple output network is to actually realize the canonical expressions that represent each transmission function. The resulting network is called a *switching matrix* and is very easily constructed.

Table 7-8   Truth Table for a Multiple Output Network

x_1	x_2	x_3	$f_1(x_1, x_2, x_3)$	$f_2(x_1, x_2, x_3)$	$f_3(x_1, x_2, x_3)$
0	0	0	0	1	0
0	0	1	1	1	0
0	1	0	1	0	1
0	1	1	0	0	0
1	0	0	0	1	1
1	0	1	1	1	1
1	1	0	0	0	0
1	1	1	1	0	0

To illustrate this method, assume that we wish to realize a network that is described by the truth table given in Table 7-8. The transmission functions associated with this table are as follows:

$$f_1(x_1, x_2, x_3) = m_1 \lor m_2 \lor m_5 \lor m_7$$
$$f_2(x_1, x_2, x_3) = m_0 \lor m_1 \lor m_4 \lor m_5$$
$$f_3(x_1, x_2, x_3) = m_2 \lor m_4 \lor m_5$$

The switching matrix representation of this function is given in Figure 7-16.

The complete circuit diagram for a switching matrix can become rather cluttered. An alternative representation of the switching matrix of Figure 7-16 is shown in Figure 7-17. In this representation the minterm generator generates only those minterms necessary to realize the transmission functions.

The output is then formed by selecting the minterms for each output function. When a minterm is needed it is "or"ed to the output, and this is indicated by the fact that the minterm line and output line are connected by the special symbol —▷— shown in Figure 7-17.

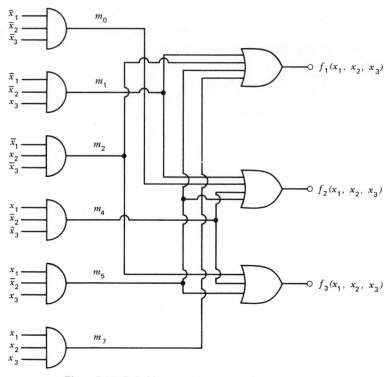

Figure 7-16. Switching matrix representation of Table 7-8.

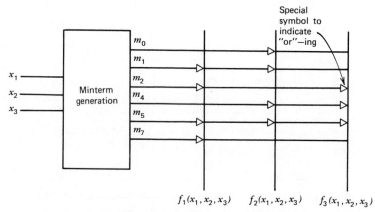

Figure 7-17. Simplified representation of a switching matrix.

Programmable Logic Arrays

Special integrated circuits, called *programmable logic arrays* (PLA), have been developed which makes it very easy to realize a switching matrix. A typical PLA as produced by a manufacturer has a form as shown in Figure 7-18a. This array has not been programmed so that it initially does not realize any transmission function.

When the designer completes the specification for a network, the array can be programmed by using special equipment that will make the necessary inter-connections. Usually this is accomplished by applying special voltages or currents that "burn out" unwanted connections or "burn in" desired connections. These operations are quite easy to accomplish and can be carried out under computer control or by hand by a very careful technician.

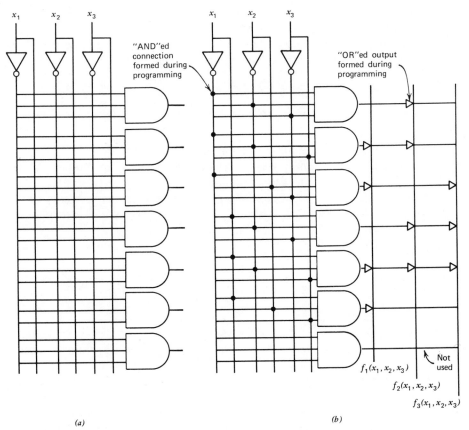

(a)

Unprogrammed PLA

(b)

Programmed PLA

Figure 7-18. Illustration of use of a PLA to realize a switching matrix for functions in Table 7-8.

For example, the PLA shown in Figure 7-18a can be programmed to represent the switching matrix of Figure 7-16 by making the connections as shown in Figure 7-18b. Note that all of the possible product terms do not have to be used.

PLA's are particularly useful in the realization of multiple-output networks that do not require many product terms. If we have an n input network, there are 2^n possible minterms. Assume that we need K minterms to realize a given network. If $n > 5$, $K \ll 2^n$, then a PLA can easily be used to realize functions with these characteristics.

The switching matrix approach to the realization of multiple-output logic networks does not make any attempt to simplify the logic expressions that describe the transmission functions. There are, however, instances where it is desirable to minimize the number of logic elements that appear in the network. A considerable simplification can often be obtained if we use techniques similar to those of the last section to simplify the transmission function while we also try to retain as much commonality as possible between functions. The following discussion outlines the algorithm that can be used to reduce multiple output networks. This process becomes very tedious if it is carried out by hand. Computer programs have been developed to carry out this reduction process and are often available where a large amount of logic network design is carried out.

Tabular Reduction of Multiple Output Networks

The main difference between the reduction process of this section and the tabular reduction of single output networks is that we must include a method that allows us to determine which product terms can be used in the realization of more than one transmission function. Although this reduction process can be presented in a completely general manner, we deal only with the design of a logic network with r input variables $x_1, x_2, \ldots, x_r$ and three output variables

$$y_1 = f_1(x_1, \ldots, x_r) = m_{1,1} \vee m_{1,2} \vee \cdots \vee m_{1,n_1}$$

$$y_2 = f_2(x_1, \ldots, x_r) = m_{2,1} \vee m_{2,2} \vee \cdots \vee m_{2,n_2}$$

$$y_3 = f_3(x_1, \ldots, x_r) = m_{3,1} \vee m_{3,2} \vee \cdots \vee m_{3,n_3}$$

The approach that we use is fully evident from this discussion and its extension to the case of four or more output variables is quite straightforward.

When we dealt with a single transmission function our first step was to obtain the set of prime implicants associated with the function. We then eliminated all absolutely eliminable prime implicants from the set. From the remaining set of prime implicants we selected the minimal number that we needed to represent the transmission function. Each prime implicant so chosen corresponded to one of the product terms in the minimal sum-of-product representation for the transmission function.

For the multiple output case the same general procedure is applied except that we are now looking for product terms that can be used as part of the representation for more than one transmission function. To find these product terms we make the following observation.

A product term can be used in the minimal representation of the transmission functions $f_i(x_1, \ldots, x_r)$ and $f_j(x_1, \ldots, x_r)$ only if the term is a prime implicant of the function.

$$f_{i,j}(x_1, \ldots, x_r) = f_i(x_1, \ldots, x_r) \wedge f_j(x_1, \ldots, x_r)$$

Similarly, a product term can be used in the minimal representation of the transmission functions $f_1(x_1, \ldots, x_r)$ and $f_2(x_1, \ldots, x_r)$ and $f_3(x_1, \ldots, x_r)$ only if the term is a prime implicant of the function

$$f_{1,2,3}(x_1, \ldots, x_r) = f_1(x_1, \ldots, x_r) \wedge f_2(x_1, \ldots, x_r) \wedge f_3(x_1, \ldots, x_r)$$

From this observation we see that we must evaluate the prime implicants for the functions $f_{1,2}(x_1, \ldots, x_r), f_{1,3}(x_1, \ldots, x_r), f_{2,3}(x_1, \ldots, x_r)$, and $f_{1,2,3}(x_1, \ldots, x_r)$ as well as for the functions $f_1(x_1, \ldots, x_r), f_2(x_1, \ldots, x_r)$, and $f_3(x_1, \ldots, x_r)$. Once we have obtained these prime implicants, using the methods described in the previous sections, we form a multiple-output table of choice that has the general organization illustrated in Table 7-9.

The columns of this table are partitioned into three groups corresponding to the three transmission functions. Within each group there is a column headed by each of the minterms associated with the given transmission function. The rows of the table correspond to the prime implicants of the seven functions f_1 through $f_{1,2,3}$. The rows are also grouped so that all the prime implicants associated with a given function are in the same group.

A large X is placed in the areas of the table where the prime implicants of a given group cannot be associated with the minterms of a given transmission function. For each prime implicant in the remainder of the table, a check mark is placed in the columns of the minterms accounted for by that prime implicant. Once we complete the table of choice we proceed in the same manner as for the single output case, except that we disregard that portion of the table that has been X-ed out.

The multiple table of choice can often be simplified if we make the following observation.

1. If p_a is a prime implicant of $f_{i,j}$ then p_a may also be a prime implicant of f_i and f_j. Should this be true then p_a need not be included in the f_i and f_j rows of the multiple table of choice.
2. If p_a is a prime implicant of $f_{i,j,k}$ then p_a may also be a prime implicant of $f_i, f_j, f_k, f_{i,j}, f_{ik}$, and $f_{j,k}$. Should this be the case p_a need only be included in the $f_{i,j,k}$ rows of the multiple table of choice.

Table 7-9 General Form of a Multiple Output Table of Choice

		Function $f_1(x_1, \ldots, x_r)$			Function $f_2(x_1, \ldots, x_r)$			Function $f_3(x_1, \ldots, x_r)$		
	Minterms — Prime Implicants	$m_{1,1}$	$m_{1,2} \cdots m_{1,n_1}$		$m_{2,1}$	$m_{2,2} \cdots m_{2,n_2}$		$m_{3,1}$	$m_{3,2} \cdots m_{3,n_3}$	
f_1	$p_{1,1}$ ⋮ p_{1,u_1}									
f_2	$p_{2,1}$ ⋮ p_{2,u_2}									
f_3	⋮									
$f_{1,2}$	⋮									
$f_{1,3}$	⋮									
$f_{2,3}$	⋮									
$f_{1,2,3}$	⋮									

The reasoning behind these two observations should be clear if the definition of $f_{i,j}$ and $f_{i,j,k}$ is examined. For example, assume that two minterms, m_a and m_b, in $f_{i,j}$ can be combined to form a prime implicant p_a of $f_{i,j}$. These two minterms are also included in f_i and f_j and can also be combined. The resulting product term p_a will be a prime implicant of f_i if there is no other pair of minterms of f_i that are not in $f_{i,j}$ and which can be combined with p_a to form a product term $\hat{p}_a$ which is a reduction of p_a. To illustrate this case assume that

$$f_1 = x_1 x_2 \bar{x}_3 \vee x_1 \bar{x}_2 \bar{x}_3 \vee x_1 \bar{x}_2 x_3 \vee x_1 x_2 x_3$$
$$f_2 = x_1 x_2 \bar{x}_3 \vee x_1 \bar{x}_2 \bar{x}_3 \vee \bar{x}_1 x_2 x_3$$

then

$$f_{1,2} = x_1 x_2 \bar{x}_3 \lor x_1 \bar{x}_2 \bar{x}_3$$

Thus we see that

$$p_a = x_1 \bar{x}_3$$

is a prime implicant of $f_{1,2}$. Examining f_1 we see that p_a is not a prime implicant of f_1 since

$$\hat{p}_a = x_1 = p_a \lor x_1 x_3$$

However the prime implicants of f_2 are

$$p_a = x_1 \bar{x}_3 \qquad p_b = \bar{x}_1 x_2 x_3$$

Thus in our multiple table of choice we would have $\hat{p}_a$ as the only prime implicant entry for f_1, p_b as the only prime implicant entry for f_2 and p_a as the only prime implicant entry for $f_{1,2}$.

The following example illustrates our method of approach. Assume that we wish to realize a three-output logic network that is represented by the truth table given by Table 7-10.

Table 7-10   Truth Table for Three Output Logic Network

Minterm	x_1	x_2	x_3	x_4	y_1	y_2	y_3
m_0	0	0	0	0	0	0	1
m_1	0	0	0	1	0	0	0
m_2	0	0	1	0	0	0	0
m_3	0	0	1	1	1	0	0
m_4	0	1	0	0	0	0	1
m_5	0	1	0	1	1	1	0
m_6	0	1	1	0	0	0	0
m_7	0	1	1	1	1	1	0
m_8	1	0	0	0	0	0	0
m_9	1	0	0	1	0	0	0
m_{10}	1	0	1	0	0	1	1
m_{11}	1	0	1	1	0	0	0
m_{12}	1	1	0	0	0	0	0
m_{13}	1	1	0	1	1	1	0
m_{14}	1	1	1	0	1	1	1
m_{15}	1	1	1	1	1	1	1

The corresponding transmission functions are

$$y_1 = f_1(x_1, x_2, x_3, x_4) = m_{1,3} \lor m_{1,5} \lor m_{1,7} \lor m_{1,13} \lor m_{1,14} \lor m_{1,15}$$

$$y_2 = f_2(x_1, x_2, x_3, x_4) = m_{2,5} \lor m_{2,7} \lor m_{2,10} \lor m_{2,13} \lor m_{2,14} \lor m_{2,15}$$

$$y_3 = f_3(x_1, x_2, x_3, x_4) = m_{3,0} \lor m_{3,4} \lor m_{3,10} \lor m_{3,14} \lor m_{3,15}$$

Using these functions we find that

$$
\begin{aligned}
f_{1,2}(x_1, x_2, x_3, x_4) &= f_1(x_1, x_2, x_3, x_4) \land f_2(x_1, x_2, x_3, x_4) \\
&= m_5 \lor m_7 \lor m_{13} \lor m_{14} \lor m_{15}
\end{aligned}
$$

$$f_{1,3}(x_1, x_2, x_3, x_4) = m_{14} \lor m_{15}$$

$$f_{2,3}(x_1, x_2, x_3, x_4) = m_{10} \lor m_{14} \lor m_{15}$$

$$f_{1,2,3}(x_1, x_2, x_3, x_4) = m_{14} \lor m_{15}$$

If we go through the standard reduction process we find that the prime implicants for these functions are

Function	Prime Implicant
f_1	0_11, 111_, _1_1
f_2	1_10, 111_, _1_1
f_3	0_00, 1_10, 111_
$f_{1,2}$	111_, _1_1
$f_{1,3}$	111_
$f_{2,3}$	111_, 1_10
$f_{1,2,3}$	111_

Examining this set of prime implicants we see that several of them can be eliminated. For example, 111_ is a prime implicant of $f_{1,2,3}$. Thus it is not necessary to include this term as a prime implicant of the other six functions. Similarly, since 1_10 is a prime implicant of $f_{2,3}$, we do not need to retain 1_10 as a prime implicant of f_2 or f_3. Continuing in this manner we obtain the following reduced set of prime implicants.

Function	Prime Implicant
f_1	0_11
f_2	none
f_3	0_00
$f_{1,2}$	_1_1
$f_{1,3}$	none
$f_{2,3}$	1_10
$f_{1,2,3}$	111_

Using these results we obtain the multiple output table of choice given by Table 7-11. The rows corresponding to f_2 and $f_{1,3}$ are omitted.

Now that we have the table of choice we must select the prime implicants that can be used in forming a minimal representation for our transmission functions.

Table 7-11   Multiple Output Table of Choice for Network

Prime Implicants	Minterms	$f_1(x_1,x_2,x_3,x_4)$						$f_2(x_1,x_2,x_3,x_4)$						$f_3(x_1,x_2,x_3,x_4)$				
		m_3	m_5	m_7	m_{13}	m_{14}	m_{15}	m_5	m_7	m_{10}	m_{13}	m_{14}	m_{15}	m_0	m_4	m_{10}	m_{14}	m_{15}
f_1	0_11	✓		✓														
f_3	0_00													✓	✓			
$f_{1,2}$	$\_1\_1$		✓	✓	✓		✓	✓	✓		✓		✓					
$f_{2,3}$	1_10									✓		✓				✓	✓	
$f_{1,2,3}$	$111\_$					✓	✓					✓	✓				✓	✓

To do this we start off in the standard manner. First we locate all columns that have only one ✓ in them. The row that contains the ✓ thus corresponds to an essential prime implicant. If all of the columns cannot be covered by essential prime implicants we are then free to choose, from the remaining prime implicants, enough additional prime implicants to complete our covering of the multiple table of choice. This is done in the manner described at the end of the last section except that we try to select those prime implicants that can be used in forming the maximum number of transmission functions.

Up to this point our selection process has concentrated on the whole multiple table of choice. Our final task is to select the prime implicants that are actually needed to realize each transmission function. The final step then is to examine the columns associated with each transmission function and select the minimal number of prime implicants needed to cover each function.

If we examine Table 7-11 we see that all the prime implicants are essential prime implicants. The logical expressions for f_1 and f_3 can be read directly from the table. However, if we examine the columns of the table associated with f_2 we see that the prime implicant $111\_$ is not needed to cover this function. Thus only the prime implicants $\_1\_1$ and 1_10 are needed to realize f_2. From this we find that the three transmission functions can be represented by the following logical expressions.

$$f_1(x_1, x_2, x_3, x_4) = x_1 x_2 x_3 \lor x_2 x_4 \lor \bar{x}_1 x_3 x_4$$

$$f_2(x_1, x_2, x_3, x_4) = x_2 x_4 \lor x_1 x_3 \bar{x}_4$$

$$f_3(x_1, x_2, x_3, x_4) = x_1 x_2 x_3 \lor x_1 x_3 \bar{x}_4 \lor \bar{x}_1 \bar{x}_3 \bar{x}_4$$

The logic network corresponding to these expressions is given by Figure 7-19.

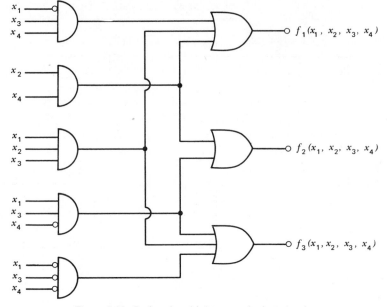

Figure 7-19. Reduced multiple output logic network.

A PLA can also be used to realize a network of this type. Figure 7-20 shows the PLA realization. Observe that instead of realizing the minterms of the function, we realize the product terms corresponding to the prime implicants needed to represent the output functions.

This discussion has been of an introductory nature. There are several very detailed algorithms that can be used to design a minimum logic representation of multiple-output networks. References [1], [6], and [7] give a much more extensive discussion of this problem.

EXERCISE

1. Find a minimal two-level logic network that will realize the following functions.

$$f_1(x_1, x_2, x_3, x_4) = m_{1,0} \vee m_{1,2} \vee m_{1,5} \vee m_{1,6} \vee m_{1,13} \vee m_{1,14}$$

$$f_2(x_1, x_2, x_3, x_4) = m_{2,0} \vee m_{2,5} \vee m_{2,8} \vee m_{2,13} \vee m_{2,15}$$

$$f_3(x_1, x_2, x_3, x_4) = m_{3,0} \vee m_{3,3} \vee m_{3,8} \vee m_{3,12}$$

Show how these functions are realized using a PLA.

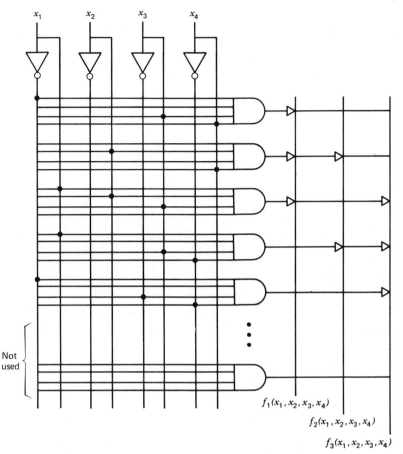

Figure 7-20. A PLA realization of a minimized multiple output network.

5. SUMMARY

In some ways the problem of finding a minimal logic circuit realization of a given function is not as critical as it once was. Before the development of integrated circuit elements, each logic element involved a relatively high cost, both in terms of money and equipment considerations. The availability of integrated circuits has considerably altered this picture. Integrated circuit logic elements are very cheap and one logic package may contain several identical logic elements.

Reduction of logic circuits now becomes important in order to simplify the organization of the circuits and the number of interconnections necessary to construct a given network. However, this is not the only reason that we study the minimization processes.

Our ability to apply and use logic networks in an efficient manner and to understand their behavior requires us to fully understand how the various components of a logic network interact to realize a given logical expression. This insight is one of the major side products of our present investigation.

From this point it is assumed that any logic network that is needed as part of a system can be designed by the techniques that have been developed in this and the preceding chapters.

REFERENCE NOTATION

There are a large number of books available that discuss the design and minimization of logic networks. Caldwell [2] presents an extensive discussion of the problem, which was not even considered in this chapter, of reducing relay switching circuits. References [3], [4], [5], and [6] are at an intermediate level of complexity while reference [7] and [8] give a much more theoretical treatment of switching theory. Bartee, Lebow, and Reed give a particularly extensive discussion of the general minimization problem.

REFERENCES

1. Bartee, T. C., Lebow, I. L., and Reed, I. S. (1962), *Theory and Design of Digital Machines*, McGraw-Hill, New York.

2. Caldwell, S. H. (1958), *Switching Circuits and Logical Design*, John Wiley, New York.

3. Hill, F. J., and Peterson, G. R. (1974), *Introduction to Switching Theory and Logical Design*, John Wiley, New York.

4. Krieger, M. (1967), *Basic Switching Circuit Theory*, MacMillan, New York.

5. Marcus, M. P. (1962), *Switching Circuits for Engineers*, Prentice Hall, Englewood Cliffs, N.J.

6. McCluskey, E. J. (1965), *Introduction to the Theory of Switching Circuits*, McGraw-Hill, New York.

7. Miller, R. E. (1965), *Switching Theory*, Vol. I, John Wiley, New York.

8. Wood, P. E., Jr., (1968), *Switching Theory*, McGraw-Hill, New York.

HOME PROBLEMS

1. Information is transferred in a digital system using a 4-bit code. Bits 1 through 3 are information bits and bit 4 is a parity bit. The value of the parity bit is chosen so that the number of 1's (including the parity bit) in the 4-bit representation of the information is odd. Design a minimum 2-level AND-OR logic

network that will indicate (with a 1 output) whenever an error is present in the received information.

2. Let A and B be two 3-bit binary numbers and let T be a 2-bit control signal. Design a logic network that computes

$$z := ((T = [0]) \wedge (A < B)) \vee ((T = [1]) \wedge (A = B))$$
$$\vee ((T = [2]) \wedge (A > B))$$

3. Let A be a BCD encoded decimal digit. Design a logic network that will give a 1 output if the decimal value of A is a nonzero multiple of 3 and 0 otherwise.

4. A digital counter contains a 3-bit register. The counter counts from $0 = [0,0,0]$ to $7 = [1,1,1]$ and then resets and starts all over again. This counter is used, as indicated in Figure P7-1, to generate 3 control signals c_1, c_2, c_3. These signals take a value of 1 as indicated by the following conditions.

$$c_1 = 1 \text{ for a count of } 0, 1, 3, 5, 7$$
$$c_2 = 1 \text{ for a count of } 0, 3, 5, 6$$
$$c_3 = 1 \text{ for a count of } 0, 3, 4, 7$$

They are 0 for all other conditions. Design a minimal logic network that will generate c_1, c_2, and c_3.

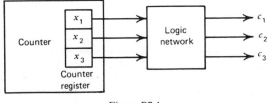

Figure P7-1

5. The minimal logic network shown in Figure P7-2 has a static hazard. (See Home Problem 4, Chapter 5). Use a three-variable map to explain why this hazard exists. How can the addition of an extra AND gate to this network eliminate this hazard?

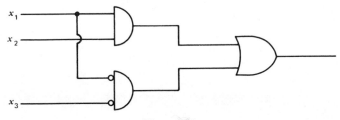

Figure P7-2

6. The discussion of multiple output logic networks in Section 4 assumed that all output logic expressions were completely specified. Extend the analysis techniques presented in that section to treat the situation where one or more of the logic expressions are incompletely specified.

7. Let A and B be two 3-bit binary numbers and let S be a 2-bit control signal. Design a logic network that will form the signal Z given by

$$Z := [(S = [0]) \wedge [0]] \vee [(S = [1]) \wedge (A + B)]$$
$$\vee [(S = [2]) \wedge (A + B)] \vee [(S = [3]) \wedge (\overline{AB})]$$

8. Design a PLA network to realize a 7-segment decoder network (see Home Problem 7, Chapter 3).

9. A BCD adder to add two BCD encoded digits can be realized as shown in Figure P7-3. The two BCD digits are $[a_3, a_2, a_1, a_0]$ and $[b_3, b_2, b_1, b_0]$. Complete the design of this adder.

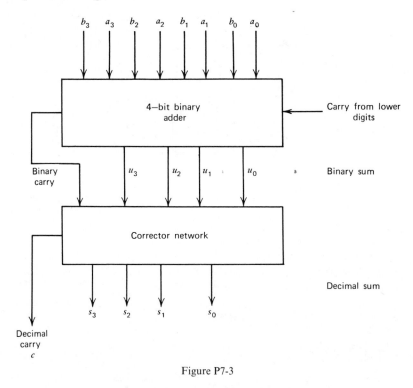

Figure P7-3

8

Flip-Flops, Registers, and Basic Information Transfers

1. INTRODUCTION

Up to this point we have been concentrating on the operation and design of combinational logic networks. These networks are important, since they are used to carry out many of the basic information-processing tasks in a digital system. They are, however, memoryless elements, since their current output depends only on their current input.

There are many situations where we must be able to store information and then use this stored information to influence the future behavior of a given information-processing task. If a system is to possess memory we must have a system element to supply this capability. In digital systems, registers serve this purpose.

The idea of a register was introduced in Chapter 2. In that discussion we indicated that a register was made up of r cells, and that each cell stored one bit of information. We are now ready to start investigating the characteristics of these cells and how they are used to form registers. First, we introduce the basic concept of a flip-flop and show how it can store a single bit of information. Next we consider the common types of flip-flops found in digital systems and how they are used to form different types of registers. The final portion of this chapter is devoted to a discussion of some of the basic information transfers that can be implemented by using registers.

No attempt is made to present a detailed description of the electronic realization of the various flip-flops. Our main concern is with the external properties of these components and how they are used in the design of digital networks and systems.

2. FLIP-FLOPS

A wide variety of devices can be used as cells to store digital information. The only requirement such a device must satisfy is that it have two easily distinguished internal conditions. Each such condition is called a *state of the cell*.

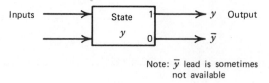

Note: $\bar{y}$ lead is sometimes
not available

Figure 8-1. Basic model of a cell.

The state of a cell is indicated by a *state variable y*, which we usually assume can take on the value of either 0 or 1. When $y = 0$ we say that the cell is in the zero-state, and when $y = 1$ we say the cell is in the one-state.

To change the state of the cell, we must have some type of input signal. The form of the input signal and the way that it causes the state of the cell to change usually serves to characterize the cell.

A cell has the general representation shown in Figure 8-1. Two output leads are usually available, one corresponding to the value of the state variable y and the other corresponding to $\bar{y}$. Having both y and $\bar{y}$ available is a very useful feature particularly when the information is used as the input to a combinational logic network that may require both y and $\bar{y}$ as variables. The cell remains in a fixed state until an activation condition appears on the input that causes the cell to change state. After the change the output remains at a constant value until the next change occurs.

Cells can be realized in a number of different ways. One important group of devices that can be used are called flip-flops. In this section we examine the basic structure of flip-flops and some of the forms that they can take.

Set-Reset (S-R) Flip-Flops

All the logic networks that we have considered so far had the property that the signals were propagated from the input terminals to the output terminals without any feedback paths. For this class of networks the inherent delays in the logic elements were not of particular importance in considering the logical behavior of the network. However, let us consider the simple logic network shown in Figure 8-2a where the inherent delay, Δt, of each NOR logic element is indicated. Examining this circuit we see that there exists a feedback path from the output of each NOR element to the input to the other element. Because of these feedback paths the current state of the network depends on its past history.

Let us assume that the network is in an initial steady state condition of $R = 0$, $S = 0$, $y = 0$, and $\bar{y} = 1$. At time t_1 assume that a 1 is applied to the S input and the R input remains 0. When this input occurs the output of NOR element 2 goes to 0 and after Δt seconds $\bar{y}$ goes to 0. This in turn drives the output of NOR element 1 to 1 and after another Δt seconds y goes to 1. Now if S goes to 0 and if R remains 0, the complete network will hold the condition $y = 1$, $\bar{y} = 0$. When this happens we say that the network is in the 1 state.

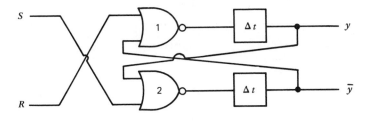

Logic Circuit

(a)

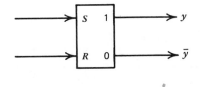

Symbolic Representation

(b)

Figure 8-2. Basic *S-R* flip-flop. (*a*) Logic circuit. (*b*) Symbolic representation.

Next consider what happens when an input condition of $S = 0$, $R = 1$ occurs while this flip-flop is in the 1 state. When this happens the output of logic element 1 becomes 0 and the output of logic element 2 becomes 1. Thus the state variable has a value of $y = 0$ and we say that the flip-flop is in the 0 state.

A complete timing diagram illustrating the dynamic behavior of this circuit is shown in Figure 8-3. Note that after the change of state occurs the inputs can both be set to 0 and the outputs hold at a constant value. The only requirement is that the inputs remain applied for a time greater than $2\Delta t$ seconds.

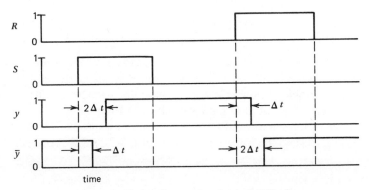

Figure 8-3. Timing diagram for simple *S-R* flip-flop.

Table 8-1   Transition Table for S-R Flip-Flop

Input at Time t		Current State $y(t)$	Next State $y(t + \tau)$
$S(t)$	$R(t)$		
0	0	0	0
0	0	1	1
0	1	0	0
0	1	1	0
1	0	0	1
1	0	1	1
This input condition must never be allowed to occur { 1	1	0	indeterminate
1	1	1	indeterminate

This simple circuit is called a *set-reset flip-flop*, or *S-R* flip-flop for short,* since a 1 on the *S* input *sets* the circuit to the 1 state while a 1 applied to the *R* input *resets* the circuit to the 0 state. It should be noted that the input condition $S = 1$, $R = 1$ is an indeterminate condition and should never be allowed to occur. The reason for this restriction can be understood if we examine Figure 8-2. If $S = R = 1$, we see that

$$y = \bar{y} = 0$$

which is inconsistent with our convention that y represents the state of the flip-flop.

The behavior of an *S-R* flip-flop can be described by a transition table of the form given by Table 8-1 or by the logical expression

$$y(t + \tau) = S(t) \lor y(t)\bar{R}(t)$$

where $y(t + \tau)$ is the state of the flip-flop τ seconds after the input is applied at time t and $y(t)$ is the initial state of the flip-flop. It is also assumed that $\tau > 2\Delta t$.

As a simple example of how information might be transferred into a particular *S-R* flip-flop consider the digital network shown in Figure 8-4.

The transfer of information into the *S-R* flip-flop is controlled by the control signal $U = [u_1, u_2]$ and the values of a and b. Table 8-2 describes the transfer rules.

---

* Flip-flops of this type are also referred to as *R-S* flip-flops and sometimes as *C-S* (clear-set) flip-flops.

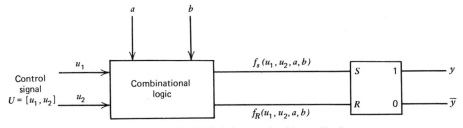

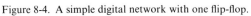

Figure 8-4. A simple digital network with one flip-flop.

Table 8-2   Transfer Operations

Control Signal U	Action
[0, 0]	Value of y remains unchanged
[0, 1]	$y(t + \tau) = a(t)$
[1, 0]	$y(t + \tau) = b(t)$
[1, 1]	$y(t + \tau) = a(t)\bar{b}(t) \vee \bar{a}(t)b(t)$

Table 8-3 Truth Table for Control Network

u_1	u_2	a	b	f_S	f_R
0	0	0	0	0	0
0	0	0	1	0	0
0	0	1	0	0	0
0	0	1	1	0	0
0	1	0	0	0	1
0	1	0	1	0	1
0	1	1	0	1	0
0	1	1	1	1	0
1	0	0	0	0	1
1	0	0	1	1	0
1	0	1	0	0	1
1	0	1	1	1	0
1	1	0	0	0	1
1	1	0	1	1	0
1	1	1	0	1	0
1	1	1	1	0	1

Using the information contained in Table 8-2 and the known behavior of S-R flip-flops, we can define the truth-table that describes the functions f_S and f_R. This table is given by Table 8-3.

By using standard minimization techniques, we obtain the following minimal expressions:

$$f_S(u_1, u_2, a, b) = \bar{u}_1 u_2 a \lor u_2 a \bar{b} \lor u_1 \bar{a} b \lor u_1 \bar{u}_2 b$$

$$f_R(u_1, u_2, a, b) = \bar{u}_1 u_2 \bar{a} \lor u_2 \bar{a} \bar{b} \lor u_1 u_2 a b \lor u_1 \bar{u}_2 \bar{b}$$

The realization of the complete digital network is shown in Figure 8-5.

If we examine this network closely, we see that a change in the input which causes a change in f_S and/or f_R will immediately be acted on by the flip-flop. In many networks the input signals will fluctuate before the final desired value is reached. These fluctuations may be large enough to cause the flip-flop to make an unwanted transition. We now investigate how these unwanted changes can be eliminated.

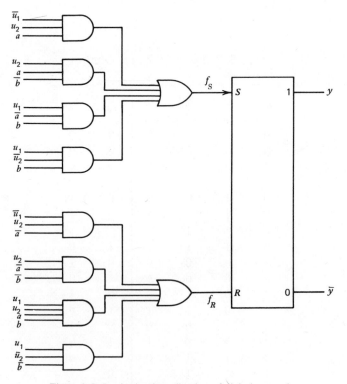

Figure 8-5. Logic circuit realization of digital network.

Clocked S-R Flip-Flops

To make sure that the flip-flop is not activated at the wrong point, an AND gate can be introduced in the S and R lines as shown in Figure 8-6a. After sufficient time has been allowed for f_S and f_R to reach a steady-state value a pulse, called a *clock pulse* or *transfer pulse*, can be applied to the other input of the AND gate and the S-R flip-flop is activated. Such a circuit is called a clocked S-R flip-flop. The pulse must last for a sufficient time to allow the flip-flop to assume its new state.

Many of the integrated circuit flip-flops contain a clock pulse input as part of their basic design. Therefore, we will assume, when necessary, that all flip-flops are internally connected for clocked operation and have an input terminal for a clock pulse. Figure 8-6b shows the symbol that we will use to indicate a clocked S-R flip-flop.

When a flip-flop is initially placed into service, it is often necessary to make certain that it is in a known initial state. Two inputs are provided to do this as shown in Figure 8-7a. A 1 on the PRESET input places the flip-flop in the 1-state while a 1 on the CLEAR input places it in the 0-state. The symbolic representation of this flip-flop is shown in Figure 8-7b. These particular inputs are not usually included in a logic diagram unless needed.

S-R flip-flops can be realized in a number of different forms. The actual construction of flip-flops is not of importance to our discussion. However, it is important for us to know the relationship between the inputs and outputs of the flip-flop and the shape of the clock pulse.

For the very simple S-R flip-flop presented in Figure 8-6 the output starts to change Δt seconds after the clock pulse is applied and a new steady-state output appears in $2\Delta t$ seconds. If the inputs change while the clock pulse is on, the final state of the flip-flop may not be the one that is expected. Several methods have been developed to overcome this problem.

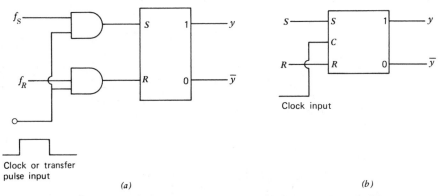

(a)

Clocked Input S-R Flip-Flop

(b)

Representation of Clocked S-R Flip-Flop

Figure 8-6. S-R flip-flop.

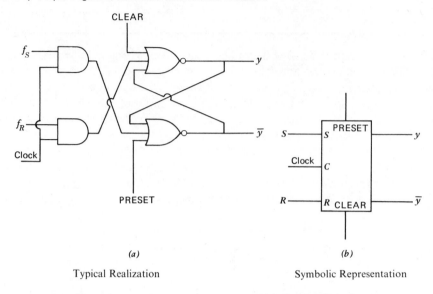

(a)

Typical Realization

(b)

Symbolic Representation

Figure 8-7. A S-R clocked flip-flop with PRESET and CLEAR.

Edge Triggered Flip-Flops

One way to avoid this problem is to make sure that the clock pulse has a width of $2\Delta t$ seconds and that the input remains constant for this period. Since the width of the actual clock pulses in a network may be greater than $2\Delta t$, a pulse shaping circuit can be used in the clock line as shown in Figure 8-8.

The pulse shaping network detects the $0 \rightarrow 1$ transition of the leading edge of the clock pulse. This transition causes the pulse shaping network to generate an

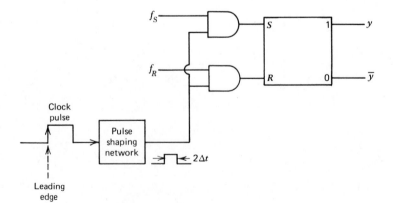

Figure 8-8. A clocked S-R flip-flop with a pulse shaping network.

output pulse of width $2\Delta t$. Since it is assumed that the signals f_S and f_R remain constant in this interval, the output goes to the desired state no matter how long the clock pulse remains on.

Master-Slave Flip-Flop

A second method to overcome the problem of unwanted transitions is shown in Figure 8-9. This circuit, which is called a *master-slave S-R flip-flop*, is basically two S-R flip-flops in series. When the clock pulse goes to 1 the first S-R flip-flop is activated by the input but the inverter in the clock lead cuts the second S-R flip-flop off from the first. Thus the output y is not affected by the input. The clock pulse then goes to 0 and cuts off the input to the first flip-flop. However, the second stage is now connected to the output of the first stage and the intermediate information stored in the first flip-flop causes the second flip-flop to change to the proper state. Thus the output y does not change until after the clock pulse has returned to zero. The timing diagram shown in Figure 8-10 illustrates the operation of this circuit.

We do not use any special symbol to indicate that a given S-R flip-flop is a master-slave flip-flop. However, when we actually try to design a circuit using commercially available flip-flops we must check the manufacturer's specifications to determine the switching characteristics of the flip-flop before we start the overall circuit design. All of the flip-flops that we use in the following chapters are assumed to be of the master-slave type unless we specifically state otherwise.

We now investigate some of the other types of flip-flops that can be found in digital networks. In each case we could develop a complete logic diagram to illustrate how they operate. However, this would add little to our discussion so we only present the general switching characteristics of each of the following flip-flops and show how they can be constructed from S-R flip-flops. Here again, each of these flip-flops is available in integrated circuit form and the actual circuit that is used to construct the flip-flop will be considerably different from the one we present for discussion purposes.

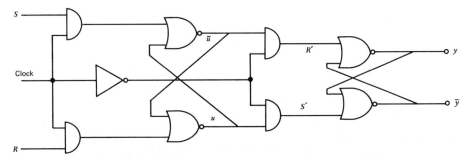

Figure 8-9. Master-slave S-R flip-flop.

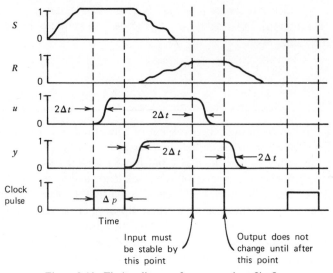

Figure 8-10. Timing diagram for master-slave flip-flop.

The D Flip-Flop

One way of making sure that the indeterminate inputs to an S-R flip-flop never occur is to provide only one input to the flip-flop. The D flip-flop, illustrated in Figure 8-11, is a flip-flop of this type. The input at the time that the clock pulse occurs completely determines the output until the next clock pulse. Thus if $D = 1$, the next state of the flip-flop will become $y = 1$ when the clock pulse appears regardless of the value of y before the clock pulse. The transition table for this flip-flop is given in Table 8-4. Examining this table we see that the following logical expression can be used to describe the input-output relationships of this flip-flop

$$y(t + \tau) = D(t)$$

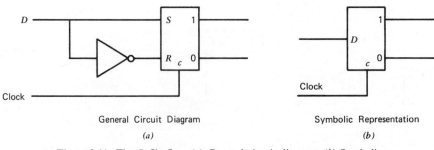

General Circuit Diagram

(a)

Symbolic Representation

(b)

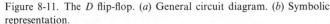

Figure 8-11. The D flip-flop. (*a*) General circuit diagram. (*b*) Symbolic representation.

Table 8-4 Transition Table for *D*
Flip-Flop

Input $D(t)$	Current State $y(t)$	Next State $y(t + \tau)$
0	0	0
0	1	0
1	0	1
1	1	1

where τ is greater than the delay needed for the flip-flop to change its state. This type of flip-flop is useful when transferring data from one source to another. It is also often referred to as a delay flip-flop since it has the property of delaying the input information one clock period.

The *J-K* Flip-Flop

The *J-K* flip-flop has become an extremely popular flip-flop circuit in recent years because integrated circuit technology has brought their price into the same range as any of the other types of flip-flop. The operation of the *J-K* flip-flop is exactly the same as the *S-R* flip-flop except when both inputs are 1. When this occurs the state of the flip-flop changes when the clock pulse occurs. This type of operation can be achieved by modifying the *S-R* flip-flop as shown in Figure 8-12. Examining this circuit we see that the *J* input is equivalent to the *S* input and the *K* input is equivalent to the *R* input of an *S-R* flip-flop. The feedback paths give us the extra flexibility because they ensure that the inputs to the *S-R* flip-flop will never both be 1 at the same time.

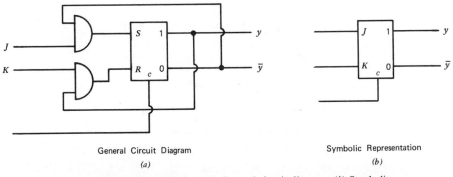

General Circuit Diagram

(a)

Symbolic Representation

(b)

Figure 8-12. The *J-K* flip-flop. (*a*) General circuit diagram. (*b*) Symbolic representation.

Table 8-5   Transition Table for *J-K* Flip-Flop

Input		Current State	Next State
J	*K*	$y(t)$	$y(t + \tau)$
0	0	0	0
0	0	1	1
0	1	0	0
0	1	1	0
1	0	0	1
1	0	1	1
1	1	0	1
1	1	1	0

The transition table for this flip-flop is given in Table 8-5. Examining this table we see that the following logical expression describes the input-output relationship of this flip-flop

$$y(t + \tau) = \bar{y}(t)J(t) \lor y(t)\bar{K}(t)$$

where τ is greater than the delay needed for the flip-flop to change its state.

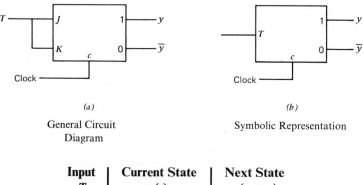

           (a)   (b)

General Circuit   Symbolic Representation
Diagram

Input	Current State	Next State
T	$y(t)$	$y(t + \tau)$
0	0	0
0	1	1
1	0	1
1	1	0

(c)

Truth Table

Figure 8-13. The *T* flip-flop.

Toggle or *T* Flip-Flop

The *toggle* or *T Flip-Flop* is another type of flip-flop that is in common use particularly for counting circuits. One way to form a *T* flip-flop is to use a *J-K* flip-flop that is connected as shown in Figure 8-13. As long as the *T* input has a 0 value the state of the flip-flop does not change. However, when *T* becomes 1 the state of the flip-flop is negated each time a clock pulse appears. The transition table for this flip-flop, which is included in Figure 8-13, shows that the input-output relationship for a *T* flip-flop is

$$y(t + \tau) = \overline{T}(t)y(t) \lor T(t)\overline{y}(t)$$

The Clock Signal

The clock pulse applied to the clock input of a flip-flop can be derived in a number of different ways. In the simplest case we have a special source of clock pulses called a *clock*. The clock generates a sequence of clock pulses that are normally equally spaced and of equal duration as indicated in Figure 8-14.

Figure 8-14. A clock pulse sequence.

The pulse width T_p is usually selected as small as possible to be consistent with the operating characteristics of the flip-flop and the *period T* is selected according to the speed that the network must operate. The only restriction is that T-T_p must be large enough to allow the flip-flop to shift to its new state before the next clock pulse occurs. For modern digital systems, T can vary anywhere from seconds down to the nanosecond range (1 nanosecond $= 10^{-9}$ seconds).

The operation of any logic network constructed from flip-flops can be controlled by proper use of the clock pulse line. Whenever we wish to activate an information transfer, we allow the clock pulse to pass through to the network. Otherwise we prevent it from reaching the network. A simple way to accomplish this is shown in Figure 8-15. When the control signal is on (has a value of 1), the clock pulses pass through the AND gate and are available to activate the operation of the network. When the control signal is off (has a value of 0), the clock pulses are blocked and thus the network does not receive any activation signal.

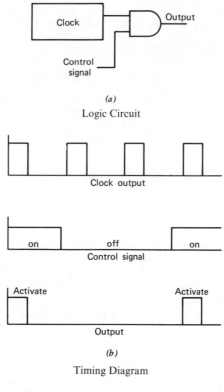

(a)

Logic Circuit

(b)

Timing Diagram

Figure 8-15. Control of clock pulses.

Transfer Pulse

In many design situations the pulse applied to the clock line is generated by another portion of the system under design. Since these pulses may not have a regular period, we usually refer to them as *transfer pulses* rather than clock pulses. When we use this convention it is assumed that a transfer pulse will be generated when it is needed to carry out the task of transferring information into the flip-flop. The terminology clock pulse and transfer pulse is often used interchangeably in the digital system design area.

Special Use of Clock Input

Signal levels, as well as pulses, can be applied to the clock input of some but not all flip-flops. In the simple flip-flops a signal level of 1 allows any input control signals to activate the flip-flop while a signal level of 0 deactivates the flip-flop. A much more interesting situation occurs when we are dealing with a master-slave flip-flop.

Inputs are both 1

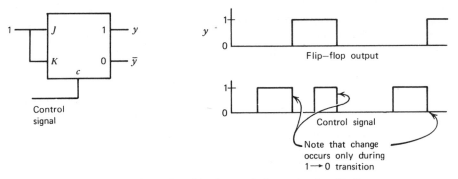

Figure 8-16. Illustration of level control of a master-slave flip-flop.

In this situation the output of the flip-flop will not change state until the signal at the clock input undergoes a transition from 1 to 0. This situation is indicated in Figure 8-16 for a *J-K* flip-flop in which the *J* and *K* inputs are both 1.

There are a number of situations where this type of operations is useful. However, for the purpose of this book we restrict our discussions to digital networks, which are constructed from clocked flip-flops. Some of the other classes of networks are discussed in the references listed at the end of this chapter.

Modes of Operation

Originally flip-flops were constructed from discrete components and they were made as simple as possible to minimize their cost. However, with the development of integrated circuits, it is now possible for a manufacturer to design and produce very complex logic circuits that, in many cases, are not any more expensive than single transistors. Consequently, there are a large number of variations possible in the type of flip-flop integrated circuits that one can use in the design of a system.

In the following discussion we present some of the general applications of flip-flops to various information processing tasks. Most of the circuits that we discuss are *clocked* or *synchronous sequential networks*. In this class of networks the contents of the flip-flops that make up the network do not change until an activation signal or clock pulse occurs. Thus we find it easier to analyze and understand the behavior of these networks.

There are many applications where the input information to a network appears in the form of pulses rather than as voltage levels. In this situation the flip-flops in the network must be activated only when the pulses carrying the input information are present. Digital networks of this type are referred to as *pulse-mode* circuits. It is also possible to design circuits where the flip-flops do not have any clock inputs. Transitions take place as soon as the inputs to the flip-flop change to a value that requires the flip-flop to change states. Such circuits are called *level-mode sequential circuits*.

Both pulse-mode and level-mode circuits are somewhat harder to design because care must be exercised to ensure that the sequence of operations that control these circuits occur in the proper order required for correct operation. The operation of level-mode and pulse mode sequential circuits will not be considered in this book since their design is more complex than synchronous networks.

EXERCISES

1. Let X be a 3-bit binary number. Design the input logic needed to set a clocked S-R flip-flop to the 1 state if X has an odd number of 1's and to the 0 state otherwise. Repeat this problem for clocked D and J-K flip-flops.

2. Describe the operation of the following logic circuits.

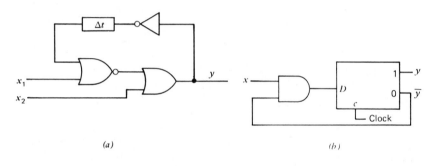

(a)   (b)

3. REGISTERS AND BASIC
TRANSFER OF INFORMATION

One of the major uses of the flip-flops is to form registers which are used to store information during some portion of an information processing task. In this section we investigate the basic properties of registers and introduce some of the notational conventions we use to describe the basic information transfer operations associated with registers.

Representation

A register is made up of n cells. If each cell is a clocked flip-flop, then we can represent a register as shown in Figure 8-17.
The input signal is assumed to be in the form needed by the type of flip-flop used and the transfer pulse, τ, is applied simultaneously to all the flip-flops and is used to transfer information into the register.

The contents of the register X corresponds to the n-tuple $[x_1, x_2, \ldots, x_n]$. We use X to represent both the contents of the register and the register itself. Thus if

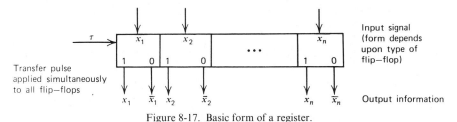

Figure 8-17. Basic form of a register.

we say "the register X" we mean the register that we have named X, while if we say "the contents of X" we mean the particular value assigned to the x_i's of the n-tuple $[x_1, x_2, \ldots, x_n]$.

When we discussed a flip-flop we said that the value of the state-variable x_i represented the state of a flip-flop. Similarly, the *state of a register* corresponds to the particular values assigned to the x_i's. Thus an n-bit register has 2^n states. For example, let $n = 3$. Then the eight states of the register $X = [x_1, x_2, x_3]$ are

$$[0, 0, 0] \quad [1, 0, 0]$$
$$[0, 0, 1] \quad [1, 0, 1]$$
$$[0, 1, 0] \quad [1, 1, 0]$$
$$[0, 1, 1] \quad [1, 1, 1]$$

There are essentially two ways that information can be loaded into a register: parallel transfer and serial transfer. These operations are two of the most basic tasks needed to realize more complex information-processing operations.

Parallel Transfer

Suppose that we are given a signal A represented by the n-tuple

$$[a_1, a_2, \ldots, a_n]$$

and we wish to transfer this information into a register. If A represents an external signal, then the transfer can be accomplished by using an arrangement like that shown in Figure 8-18a. When the transfer pulse τ is applied, the state of the register X is set to the value represented by A.

One way to transfer information between two registers is illustrated in Figure 8-18b. In this case we wish to transfer information from the A register to the X register. When the transfer pulse τ appears, each flip-flop of the X register is set to the value contained in the corresponding flip-flop of the A register.

Many other variations of these basic information transfer networks are possible, depending on the type of flip-flops used and the form of the information to be transferred.

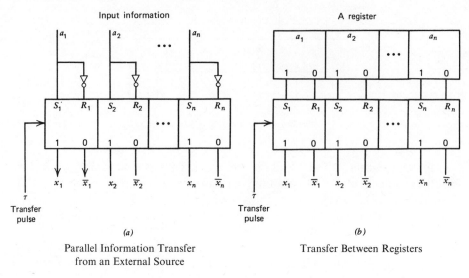

(a)

Parallel Information Transfer
from an External Source

(b)

Transfer Between Registers

Figure 8-18. Two methods of parallel information transfer.

The Assignment Operation

To indicate the transfer of information at transfer time τ we use the *assignment operation* notation:

$$\tau: X \leftarrow A$$

This notation means that when the transfer pulse τ occurs, the value of the information represented by A is transferred into register X. It is assumed that the value of A does not change until the transfer has been completed.

When we work with digital systems, it is not necessary to know all of the details concerning the actual logical structure of a register. In that case we can use the representation shown in Figure 8-19 to indicate a general parallel information transfer.

Serial Transfer

There are many situations in digital systems where information must be transmitted serially one bit at a time instead of using a parallel transfer.

Transfers of this type are easily accomplished. For example, Figure 8-20 illustrates how such a serial transfer can be accomplished using S-R flip-flops. Whenever a 1 input is applied at the x input, the first flip-flop is set to the 1 state when the clock or transfer signal τ is applied. If the input is 0 the first flip-flop is set to 0.

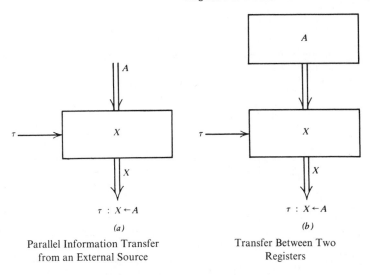

$\tau : X \leftarrow A$

(a)

Parallel Information Transfer
from an External Source

$\tau : X \leftarrow A$

(b)

Transfer Between Two
Registers

Figure 8-19. Register level representation of parallel information transfer.

The next state of flip-flop 2 is dependent on the current state of flip-flop 1 when τ is applied. If $a_1 = 1$, flip-flop 2 will go into the 1 state, while if $a_1 = 0$ it will go into the 0 state. From this we see that the equations describing the operation of a serial transfer are

$$a_1(t + T) = x(t)$$
$$a_2(t + T) = a_1(t)$$
$$a_3(t + T) = a_2(t)$$
$$\vdots$$
$$a_r(t + T) = a_{r-1}(t)$$

where t is the time of occurrence of the current transfer pulse and $t + T$ is the time of occurrence of the next pulse. (Since we are assuming all flip-flops are master-slave flip-flops, the state of each flip-flop does not change until the transfer pulse returns to zero).

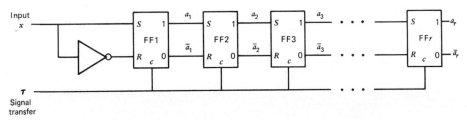

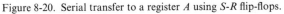

Figure 8-20. Serial transfer to a register A using S-R flip-flops.

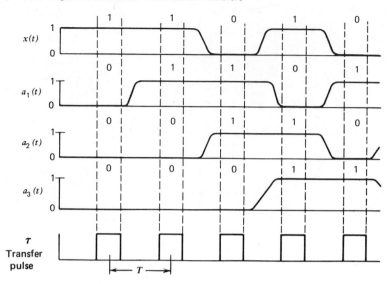

Figure 8-21. Typical time sequence for 3-bit shift register.

Figure 8-21 is a timing diagram illustrating a serial transfer into a 3-bit register.

Another way to look at the operation of a serial transfer is to consider the input at the time that the transfer pulse occurs and the contents of the register after the register has responded to the pulse. Figure 8-22 illustrates this method of describing a serial transfer into a 3-bit register.

Transfer Pulse τ_i	Input When Transfer Pulse Occurs	Contents of Register After It Has Responded To Transfer Pulse. Register Initially Contains All Zeros		
τ_1	1	1	0	0
τ_2	0	0	1	0
τ_3	0	0	0	1
τ_4	1	1	0	0
τ_5	1	1	1	0
τ_6	0	0	1	1

$\rightarrow$
Direction
of Shift

Figure 8-22. Illustration of a shift right serial transfer.

Shift Registers

Registers that have been designed to handle the serial transfer of information are called *shift registers*. They come in a variety of forms. In the previous example, information was entered at the left end of the register and shifted to the right. It is just as easy to construct a register that will receive information from the right and shift left. The following assignment operation notation will be used to describe the serial transfer or shifting operations.

Assume that A is a register formed from the individual cells $A_1, A_2, A_3, \ldots, A_n$. The contents of A is $[a_1, a_2, a_3, \ldots, a_n]$ and the contents of A_i is $[a_i]$. Also assume that X is the input signal $[x]$. Using these conventions, we now define the following basic shift operations.

(a) Shift right operation SR

$$\tau: A \leftarrow SR(X, A)$$

The contents of A are shifted one cell to the right. The value of X is shifted into the leftmost cell of A. The initial contents of A_n is lost.

$$\tau: A \leftarrow SR(X, A) \qquad \begin{cases} A_{i+1} \leftarrow A_i & i = 1, 2, \ldots, n-1 \\ \\ A_1 \leftarrow X \end{cases}$$

Example Initial values $A := [1, 0, 1, 0]$ $\qquad X := [1]$

$$\tau: A \leftarrow SR([1], [1, 0, 1, 0])$$

Final value $A := [1, 1, 0, 1]$.

(b) Shift left operation SL

$$\tau: A \leftarrow SL(A, X)$$

The contents of A are shifted one cell to the left. The value of X is shifted into the rightmost cell of A. The initial contents of A_1 is lost.

$$\tau: A \leftarrow SL(A, X) \qquad \begin{cases} A_{i-1} \leftarrow A_i & i = 2, 3, \ldots, n \\ \\ A_n \leftarrow X \end{cases}$$

Example Initial values $A := [0, 1, 0, 1]$ $\qquad X := [1]$

$$A \leftarrow SL([0, 1, 0, 1], [1])$$

Final value $A := [1, 0, 1, 1]$.

(c) Special case—no input.

If there is no input to a register then the shift operations can be represented as

$$\tau: A \leftarrow SR(A) \qquad \text{Right shift}$$

$$\tau: A \leftarrow SL(A) \qquad \text{Left shift}$$

where the input signal has been omitted as an argument (i.e., it is assumed to be zero).

Using these basic operations it is possible to describe a number of different types of serial information transfer. For example, assume that we wish to serially transfer information from an X register to an A register as shown in Figure 8-23. Initially

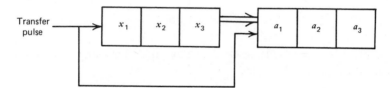

Figure 8-23. Serial transfer between two registers.

we assume that the A register contains $[0, 0, 0]$ and that X register contains $[u_1, u_2, u_3]$. After the transfer we wish that A contains $[u_1, u_2, u_3]$ and X contains $[0, 0, 0]$.

The desired transfer, which requires three transfer-clock pulses, is described as follows:

$$\tau_1: X \leftarrow SR(X) \qquad A \leftarrow SR(X_3, A)$$

$$\tau_2: X \leftarrow SR(X) \qquad A \leftarrow SR(X_3, A)$$

$$\tau_3: X \leftarrow SR(X) \qquad A \leftarrow SR(X_3, A)$$

To illustrate assume that initially $X := [1, 0, 1]$ and $A := [0, 0, 0]$. Then

Transfers	**Contents of X and A after transfer**	
	X	**A**
$\tau_1: X \leftarrow SR([1, 0, 1]),\ A \leftarrow SR([1], [0, 0, 0])$	$[0, 1, 0]$	$[1, 0, 0]$
$\tau_2: X \leftarrow SR([0, 1, 0]),\ A \leftarrow SR([0], [1, 0, 0])$	$[0, 0, 1]$	$[0, 1, 0]$
$\tau_3: X \leftarrow SR([0, 0, 1]),\ A \leftarrow SR([1], [0, 1, 0])$	$[0, 0, 0]$	$[1, 0, 1]$

Register Output

The output of a register is constant except during the period where an information transfer is taking place. For example, consider the timing diagram of Figure 8-21. Since we assumed that the register was constructed from masterslave flip-flops, the output of each cell does not change until just after the transfer-clock pulse has gone to zero.

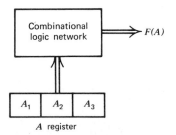

Figure 8-24. Operating on the information contained in A register.

We can use the information contained in a register as an input to a combinational logic network. For example, assume that the register A shown in Figure 8-24 is a 3-bit register and we wish to detect when the octal number stored in this register is between 2_8 and 6_8. The combinational logic network is described by Table 8-6.

This gives the following logical expression for $F(a_1, a_2, a_3)$.

$$F(a_1, a_2, a_3) := \bar{a}_1 a_2 \lor a_1 \bar{a}_2 \lor a_2 \bar{a}_3$$

The corresponding logic circuit realization of this complete network is shown in Figure 8-25.

Table 8-6 Truth Table for Output Network

A_1	A_2	A_3	$F(a_1, a_2, a_3)$
0	0	0	0
0	0	1	0
0	1	0	1
0	1	1	1
1	0	0	1
1	0	1	1
1	1	0	1
1	1	1	0

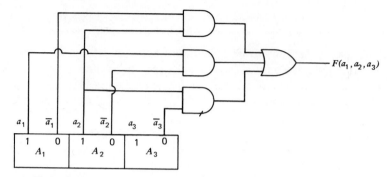

Figure 8-25. Logic diagram of combinational logic network realization of $F(a_1, a_2, a_3)$.

If we examine the logic network in Figure 8-25 we see that we do not need any inverters in the combinational logic network, since both a_i and $\bar{a}_i$ are available as outputs from the ith flip-flop. We also note that as long as the values of the state variables, a_i, remain constant the output value is constant. Thus the output value in this case changes only when the state of the register is changing.

EXERCISES

1. Give the series of information transfer operations if the 1's complement of the contents of register X is to be serial transferred into the register A.

2. Assume that A and B are 4-bit registers designed from D flip-flops. Design a network that will carry out the following information transfer:

$$\tau: B \leftarrow ((T = [0]) \wedge \bar{A}) \vee ((T = [1]) \wedge (A))$$

4. CONTROLLED INFORMATION TRANSFERS

The basic information transfer operations discussed in Section 3 can easily be extended to cover a number of different information processing tasks. In this section we investigate some of these tasks and determine how they are carried out. To do this we make extensive use of the notational conventions introduced in Chapter 4 to represent the basic operations on digital information.

Multiplexed Information Transfer

A *multiplexer* is the equivalent of a multiposition switch. A set of n input signals are applied to the network. The control signal then indicates which one of the n-input signals is to appear at the output. Figure 8-26a indicates the task of a multiplexer. Figure 8-26b illustrates a typical application where the switch is replaced by a combinational logic network and the output information is to be transferred into a register.

In this network the signal T serves as a control signal that determines if one of the input signals A, B, or C are to be transferred into the register X or if the contents of X is to remain unchanged. To describe the information transfer action, define the following scalar functions of T.

$$f_0(T) = (T = [0]) = m_0 \qquad f_2(T) = (T = [2]) = m_2$$

$$f_1(T) = (T = [1]) = m_1 \qquad f_3(T) = (T = [3]) = m_3$$

where m_i is the ith minterm associated with T. With this terminology the information transfer statement describing the network of Figure 8-26 is

$$\tau : X \leftarrow f_0(T)X \vee f_1(T)A \vee f_2(T)B \vee f_3(T)C$$

The way that the network of Figure 8-26 is realized depends on the type of flip-flop used to form the X register and the form of the signals A, B, and C. If S-R flip-flops are used then the network can be realized by using n copies of the network shown in Figure 8-27a. In particular remember that if both the S and the R inputs are 0 then the contents of the flip-flop does not change.

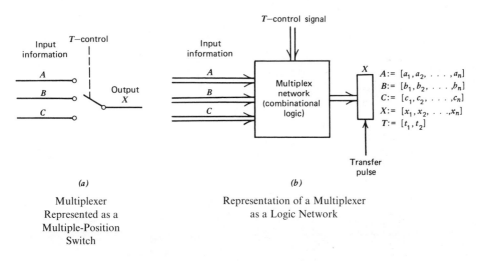

(a)

Multiplexer
Represented as a
Multiple-Position
Switch

(b)

Representation of a Multiplexer
as a Logic Network

Figure 8-26. Multiplexed information transfer.

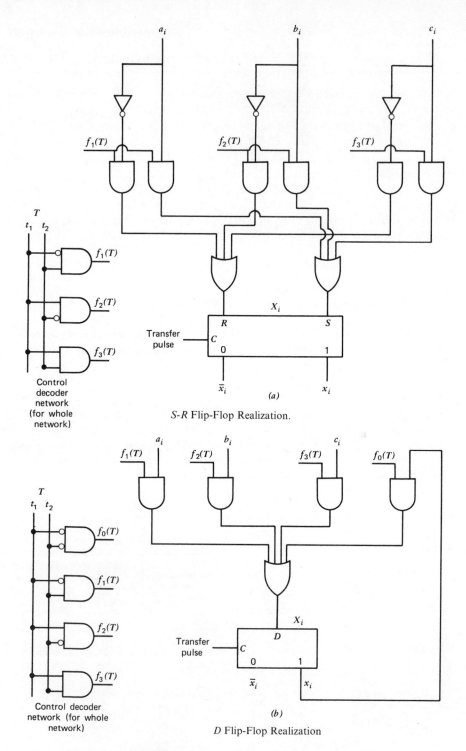

S-R Flip-Flop Realization.

(a)

D Flip-Flop Realization

(b)

Figure 8-27. Multiplex logic network to realize one-bit of the transfer network of Figure 8-26.

Thus no special provision is needed to accommodate the transfer

$$X \leftarrow X$$

corresponding to the control-signal value $f_0(T)$.

If D flip-flops are used a some what different organization is needed as shown in Figure 8-27b. In this case we note that if the D-input to the flip-flop is 0, then the flip-flop will be set to 0. Thus, to accommodate the condition

$$X \leftarrow X$$

corresponding to the control-signal value $f_0(T)$, it is necessary to provide a feedback path from the flip-flops output to its input as shown.

The signal actually transferred into the register depends on the value of the control signal T. In this example the four control values are encoded as a 2-bit signal $[t_1, t_2]$. Thus to generate the scalar functions $f_i(T)$, it is necessary to use a control signal decoder network as shown.

Transfer Pulse Control

Another possible way to realize the controlled transfer when flip-flops such as D flip-flops are used is illustrated in Figure 8-28. When the control signal is $[0, 0]$ we prevent the transfer pulse from reaching the clock input. Thus the contents of

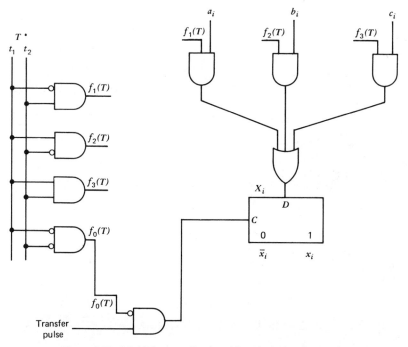

Figure 8-28. Multiplexer realization using clock signal control.

the flip-flop do not change. The control of the transfer pulse signal is particularly useful in complex networks where only a subset of all registers are to carry out an information transfer during a given transfer interval. We discuss this type of operation in greater detail later.

As long as we are interested only in the information transfers being carried out, there is no need to become too concerned with the actual form of the logic networks used to realize these transfers. These problems only become important when we reach the point in the design process where we must define the hardware realization of these networks. Since we already have spent considerable time in the preceding chapters on methods for developing combinational logic networks, in the rest of this discussion we will deal mainly with the information transfer level of operations of a digital network. Examples will occasionally be given to indicate one possible logic circuit that might realize a given transfer. It should be emphasized, however, that this is probably not a unique realization and many other types of logic circuits could be used to carry out the same task.

Demultiplexor Networks

The reverse operation from a multiplexer is a demultiplexer. In this case a single input signal is switched to one or more of n output lines, depending on the value of the control signal T. A typical demultiplexer is shown in Figure 8-29.

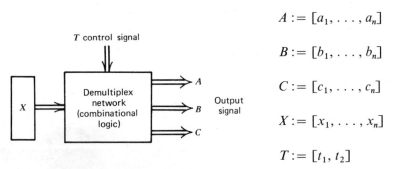

$$A := [a_1, \ldots, a_n]$$

$$B := [b_1, \ldots, b_n]$$

$$C := [c_1, \ldots, c_n]$$

$$X := [x_1, \ldots, x_n]$$

$$T := [t_1, t_2]$$

Figure 8-29. A typical multiplexed output from A register.

For illustrative purposes assume that we have three output lines, A, B, C, and a 2-bit control signal T. If we define the scalar functions $f_i(T)$ as in the discussion of the multiplexer, then one possible set of output equations for the demultiplexer might be

$$A := (f_1(T))X$$
$$B := (f_2(T) \vee f_3(T))X$$
$$C := (f_0(T) \vee f_1(T))X$$

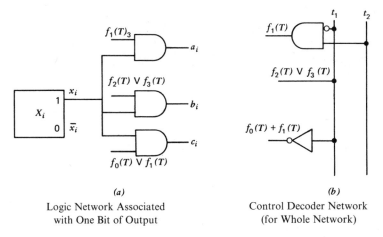

(a)

Logic Network Associated
with One Bit of Output

(b)

Control Decoder Network
(for Whole Network)

Figure 8-30. Output of demultiplexer logic network of Figure 8-29.

(Note that the actual equations needed to define these signals depends on the particular application being considered). The logic network to realize the ith bit of these equations is shown in Figure 8-30.

The multiplexer and demultiplexer networks just discussed can be represented symbolically as shown in Figure 8-31. Single lines represent the scalar quantities while double lines represent vector information. The generalized logic operation is indicated by the proper logic symbol. The scalar functions, which act as control signals, are often generated by decoding networks that may or may not be part of the multiplexer network. In some instances the scalar function control signals will be supplied directly while in others they will be in the form of an encoded control signal that must be decoded by the decoding network.

Bus Data Transfer

In many systems information must be transferred between a number of registers. One low-cost way to carry out this transfer is illustrated in Figure 8-32. This figure shows a system that can be used to transfer information from register X, Y, or Z to one or more of the registers A, B, or C.

The bus consists of a single set of data lines. Information can be placed on the bus by setting one and only one of the control signals f_i to 1. The data in the register associated with this signal is then applied to the bus through the OR gate. This information is then said to be *on-the-bus*. If a transfer of information is to be made to a given register, a transfer pulse g_i must be generated. When the transfer pulse occurs, the information on the bus is transferred into the given register. If no transfer pulse is applied to a register, then no information transfer takes place and the register does not change its state.

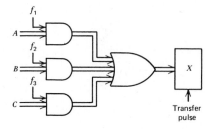

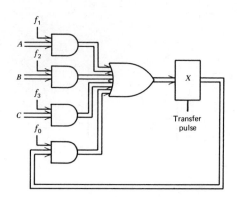

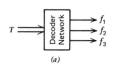

T → Decoder Network → f_1, f_2, f_3

(a)

S-R Flip-Flop

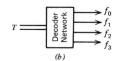

T → Decoder Network → f_0, f_1, f_2, f_3

(b)

D-Flip-Flop

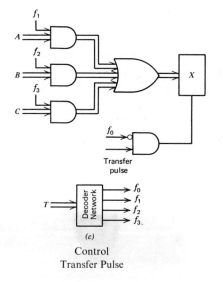

T → Decoder Network → f_0, f_1, f_2, f_3

(c)

Control
Transfer Pulse

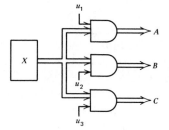

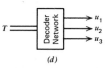

T → Decoder Network → u_1, u_2, u_3

(d)

Output Circuitry
for Demultiplexer

Figure 8-31. Symbolic representation of multiplexer and demultiplexer networks.

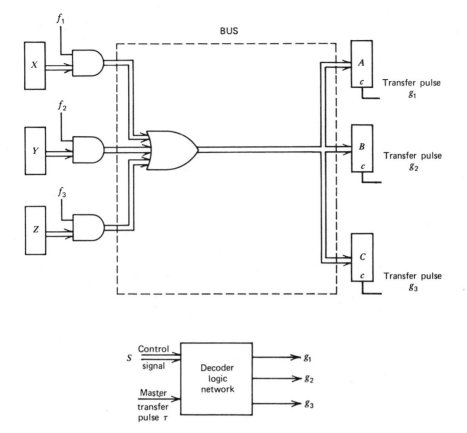

Figure 8-32. Illustration of a data bus. *Note*: 1. At most only one f_i can be nonzero at any time. 2. The control signal S defines which register will receive information from the bus.

The information transfers that can take place are described by the following expressions:

$$\tau: \begin{cases} A \leftarrow f_1 g_1 X \vee f_2 g_1 Y \vee f_3 g_1 Z \vee \bar{g}_1 A \\ B \leftarrow f_1 g_2 X \vee f_2 g_2 Y \vee f_3 g_2 Z \vee \bar{g}_2 B \\ C \leftarrow f_1 g_3 X \vee f_2 g_3 T \vee f_3 g_3 Z \vee \bar{g}_3 C \end{cases}$$

Since we have insisted that at most one f_i can equal 1 at any given time, there is no conflict in these equations.

Much more elaborate busing arrangements are possible. For example, we can expand the number of input and output registers with little difficulty. Similarly it is possible to use one (or more) of the output registers as illustrated in Figure 8-33. We will find the concept of a data bus very useful in our later discussions.

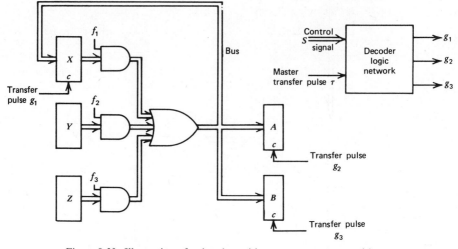

Figure 8-33. Illustration of a data bus with a common output and input register. *Note*: All registers considered to be constructed from *S-R* or *J-K* flip-flops.

EXERCISES

1. Give the information transfer equations that describe the operation of the network shown in Figure 8-33.

5. GENERAL OPERATIONS

The basic register transfer operations just discussed can be easily extended to more general situations. For example, assume that we have three registers A, B, and C as shown in Figure 8-34. The combinational logic network receives input information from registers A and B and forms the output function $F(A, B)$. When the

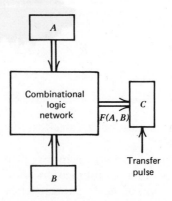

Figure 8-34. A more complex information transfer situation.

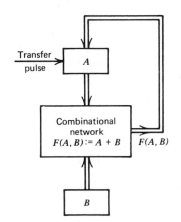

Figure 8-35. Forming the binary sum of two quantities.

transfer pulse occurs, this information is transferred into register C. Symbolically this transfer is indicated as

$$\tau : C \leftarrow F(A, B)$$

Sometimes the register C, which receives the information, is actually one of the registers that supplies one of the initial arguments to the function. For example, consider the network shown in Figure 8-35. The combinational logic network forms the binary sum of the numbers stored in registers A and B. When the transfer pulse occurs, the resulting sum is transferred to register A replacing the previous value stored in A.

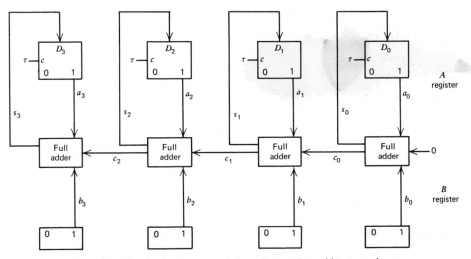

Figure 8-36. Logic circuit representation of network to add two numbers.

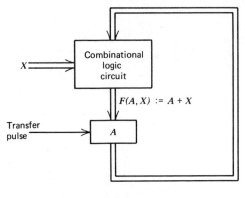

(a)

Logic Network

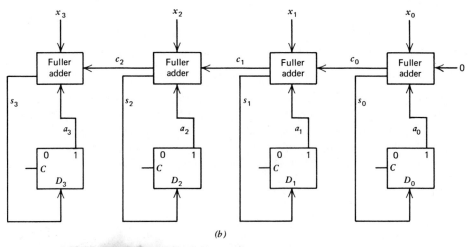

(b)

Logic Circuit

Figure 8-37. A logic network with input.

To illustrate how this transfer is carried out, consider the logic network shown in Figure 8-36. Here the registers are assumed to be made up of D flip-flops, and it is also assumed, for simplicity, that the sum will never require more than 4 bits. Using four full adders, the sum $[s_3, s_2, s_1, s_0]$ is formed. When the transfer pulse occurs, the sum is then transferred into the A register. This network realizes the operation

$$\tau: A \leftarrow A + B$$

Networks with Inputs

Digital networks with inputs can also be handled in a similar manner. For example, consider the system shown in Figure 8-37a, which performs the binary addition of the input X with the contents of A. Symbolically the operation of this network is indicated as

$$\tau : A \leftarrow A + X$$

The logic network corresponding to this computation is shown in Figure 8-37b. Here, again, D flip-flops are used to form the A register, and no overflow is considered.

Controlled Networks

In our discussion of the different types of information transfer we learned that we could use a control signal to influence how the transfer was carried out. Similarly, we can develop complex information processing networks that can carry out a number of different operations. A typical network of this type might have the form shown in Figure 8-38.

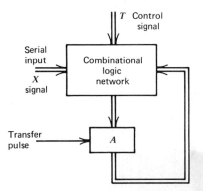

Figure 8-38. A typical network with a control signal.

To illustrate how such a network might be realized, let us assume that we wish to construct a network with the following properties.

Control Signal $[t_1, t_2]$		Operation
[0, 0]	$A \leftarrow A$	Contents of Register A remains constant
[0, 1]	$A \leftarrow SR(X, A)$	Shift information right
[1, 0]	$A \leftarrow SL(A, X)$	Shift information left
[1, 1]	$A \leftarrow [0]$	Clear A (i.e., set contents of A to 0)

These four tasks can be described by the transfer statement

$$\tau: A \leftarrow f_0(T)A \vee f_1(T)SR(X, A) \vee f_2(T)SL(A, X)$$

where

$$f_0(T) = \bar{t}_1\bar{t}_2 = m_0 \qquad f_1(T) = \bar{t}_1 t_2 = m_1 \qquad f_2(T) = t_1\bar{t}_2 = m_2$$

are the minterms associated with T. Note that if T has the value $[1, 1]$, then the right-hand side of the expression is 0 and this is the value transferred into A.

To realize this network, we must make some assumptions about the type of flip-flops that we will use for A. If we assume that we are using D flip-flops, then the logic network will have the general form shown in Figure 8-39a. The need for feedback paths occur because of the shift left operation and the need to be able to retain the contents of A.

Using the information transfer statement as a starting point we can obtain the following logic expressions for $D1$, $D2$, and $D3$.

$$D1 = f_0(T)a_1 \vee f_1(T)x \vee f_2(T)a_2$$
$$D2 = f_0(T)a_2 \vee f_1(T)a_1 \vee f_2(T)a_3$$
$$D3 = f_0(T)a_3 \vee f_1(T)a_2 \vee f_2(T)x$$

These expressions define the logic network shown in Figure 8-39b.

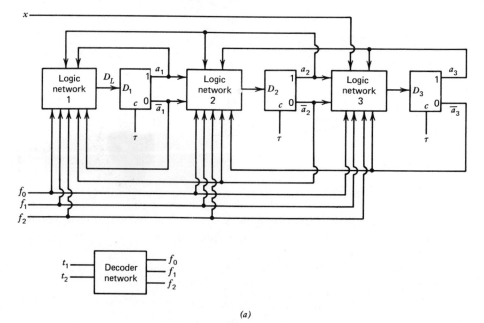

(a)

General Block Diagram

Figure 8-39. A controlled information processing network.

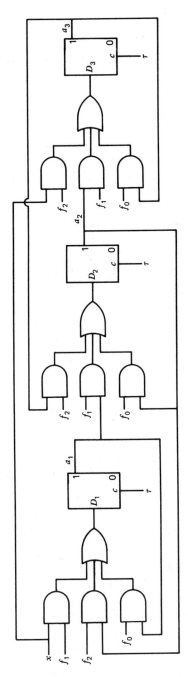

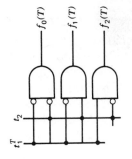

(b)

Logic Network

Figure 8-39 (continued).

EXERCISES

1. Assume that we wish to build a controlled network of the form shown below that will perform the following operations:

T	Operation
[0, 0]	$A \leftarrow \bar{A}$
[0, 1]	$A \leftarrow A \vee X$
[1, 0]	$A \leftarrow B \wedge X$
[1, 1]	$A \leftarrow X$

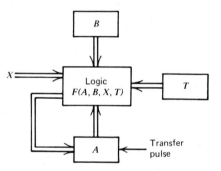

Give the expression that describes the operation of this network.

2. Assume that the registers are constructed using D flip-flops. Design the logic network necessary to realize this controlled network.

6. SUMMARY

The ability of a digital network to store information about its past behavior or the ability of a digital system to store information concerning the sequence of tasks it is to perform makes it possible to use these networks and systems to carry out time dependent information processing tasks. In this chapter we have concentrated on the basic operation and characteristics of flip-flops and registers, since they form the basic building blocks of digital systems.

Now that we have an understanding of the operation of these devices, our next task is to investigate how more complex information-processing tasks which involve memory can be accomplished. In the next chapter we generalize the concepts presented in this chapter and introduce a method for describing the behavior of more complex networks. Once we have developed these concepts, we will then be able to design general digital systems and computers.

REFERENCE NOTATION

Flip-flops currently used in digital systems are purchased as integrated circuits. Wickes [6] presents a good discussion of these flip-flops while their actual electronic structures are discussed in [1]. Some of the practical problems of using integrated circuit components are discussed in [4]. The use of register transfer notation to describe the flow of information is discussed in [2], [3], and [5]. The various types of flip-flop operating modes are discussed in [3].

REFERENCES

1. Harris, J. N., Gray, P. E., Searle, C. L. (1966), *Digital Transistor Circuits*, Vol. 6, Semiconductor Electronic Education Committee, John Wiley, New York.

2. Hellerman, H. (1973), *Digital Computer System Principles*, McGraw-Hill, New York.

3. Hill, F. J., Peterson, G. R. (1973), *Digital Systems: Hardware Organization and Design*, John Wiley, New York.

4. Larsen, D. G., Rony, P. R. (1974), *The Bugbook*, Vol. I, II, III, E. L. Instruments, Derby, Conn.

5. Sloan, M. E. (1976), *Computer Hardware Organization*, SRA, Chicago.

6. Wickes, W. E. (1968), *Logic Design with Integrated Circuits*, John Wiley, New York.

HOME PROBLEMS

1. An input of $S = 1$, $R = 1$ is inadvertently applied to an S-R flip-flop of the type shown in Figure 8-2. If at $t = 0$, S, and R both go from 1 to 0, to what state will the flip-flop go if the upper delay is greater than the lower delay. Draw a timing diagram to show the behavior of the flip-flop.

2. Let A, B be 3-bit registers constructed from J-K flip-flops, and let X be a 3-bit signal. Design a system that will perform the following information transmission task.

$$\tau : \begin{cases} A \leftarrow [(A < B) \wedge X] \vee [(A \geq B) \wedge A] \\ B \leftarrow [(A \leq B) \wedge B] \vee [(A > B) \wedge X] \end{cases}$$

3. Consider the network shown in Figure 8-36 to add two numbers. Assume that the flip-flop delay Δt equals τ_a seconds and that the full adder attains a constant output value τ_b seconds after all of the inputs assume a constant value. Derive, as a function of τ_a and τ_b, the smallest period T the transfer pulse can have. If $\tau_a = \tau_b = 10^{-6}$ seconds, how many additions can be performed a second?

4. Consider a network of the form shown in Figure P8-4.

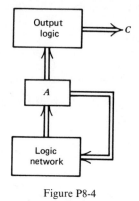

Figure P8-4

Design this circuit to carry out the following tasks. Assume that A has the initial value $[0, 0, 0]$.

$$\tau_1 : A \leftarrow A + [1] \qquad C := [1, 0, 1]$$
$$\tau_2 : A \leftarrow A + [1] \qquad C := [1, 1, 0]$$
$$\tau_3 : A \leftarrow A + [1] \qquad C := [1, 0, 0]$$
$$\tau_4 : A \leftarrow A + [1] \qquad C := [0, 1, 0]$$
$$\tau_5 : A \leftarrow A + [1] \qquad C := [0, 1, 1]$$
$$\tau_6 : A \leftarrow [0] \qquad\quad C := [0, 0, 0]$$

9

Introduction to the Analysis and Design of
Synchronous Sequential Networks

1. INTRODUCTION

Our discussion in Chapter 8 showed that it is possible to construct digital networks that have the ability to store information temporarily during an information processing task. Such networks are called *sequential networks*. The networks that we discussed were easily related to some of the basic information processing tasks that we need to perform a complex computation. The ability of a network to receive input information and then produce output information, which is a function of both the current input and the past behavior of the network, is a property that is of fundamental importance in digital system design. Networks of this type can take on a variety of forms. In this chapter we concentrate on *synchronous sequential networks*. A synchronous sequential network is a sequential network in which the contents of the basic information storage elements can change only during the occurrence of a clock pulse. Between clock pulses logical operations are performed on the input and stored information but there is no change in the information contained in the information storage elements.

In Chapter 8 we concentrated on the basic operating characteristics of the different types of flip-flops and how these flip-flops can be used to form registers. In this chapter we generalize this discussion. First, we show how the operation of a given sequential network can be analyzed. We then go on, using the insight that we obtain from this analysis, to consider the problem of designing a sequential network to carry out specific information processing tasks. The design processes presented are of an introductory nature. They are, however, sufficient to carry out many of the simple design problems encountered in the development of digital systems. The references listed at the end of this chapter show how these ideas can be extended to more sophisticated design problems.

2. ANALYSIS
OF SYNCHRONOUS
SEQUENTIAL NETWORKS

Any synchronous sequential network can be represented in the general form shown in Figure 9-1. The register, which can be constructed from any of the flip-flops discussed in Chapter 8, acts as an internal information storage device, or memory, that keeps track of the important past input events that influence the future behavior of the network. The combinational logic network has two important functions. First, it forms, as a function of the input variables $x_1, \ldots, x_u$ and the variables $y_1, \ldots, y_r$ associated with the storage register, the inputs $i_1, \ldots, i_r$ to the register necessary to modify the register's contents when the next clock pulse occurs. Second, the combinational logic network forms the output of the network as a function of the same variables.

Since this is a clocked network the value of all variables must be constant at the time the clock pulse appears. After the clock pulse occurs, the content of the register changes to a new value which depends on the inputs to the register at the time the clock pulse occurred. Similarly the input may change in the interclock interval. Both of these changes cause the outputs of the combinational logic network to change. The next clock pulse can occur at any time after these outputs have reached a steady value.

State Variables and States

From this we see that the current state of each flip-flop at the time the clock pulse occurs influences the current output of the sequential network and the next state of the flip-flop. The variables $y_1, \ldots, y_r$ are the *state variables* of the sequential

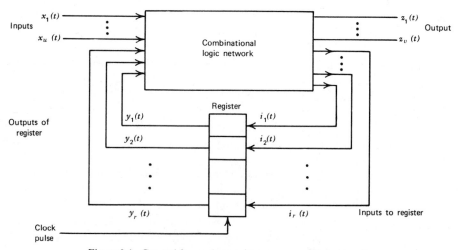

Figure 9-1. General form of a synchronous sequential network.

network and the distinct values that the r-tuple $Y = [y_1, \ldots, y_r]$ can take on are the states of the network.

For example, if $r = 3$, the system has three state variables y_1, y_2, and y_3 and it has eight states corresponding to the 3-tuples $[0, 0, 0]$ through $[1, 1, 1]$. The distinct states of the network correspond to the different items of information that can be "remembered" by the network. The *current-state* of a synchronous sequential network corresponds to the state (i.e., contents of) of the register at the time the clock pulse appears. Similarly we say that the inputs $[x_1, \ldots, x_u]$, outputs $[z_1, \ldots, z_v]$ and control signals $[i_1, \ldots, i_r]$ at the time the clock pulse appears represent the *current-input*, the *current-output*, and the *current-control* signals, respectively.

When the clock pulse occurs the content of the register remains constant until after the clock pulse is completed. At that time the content of the register changes to a new value. This new value is called the *next-state* of the network.

In the following discussion it is extremely important to keep the relative time relationship between the current-input, current-output, current-state, and next-state in mind. When it is necessary to indicate the relative order of the signals in a network we use the notation

$$x_i(t), y_j(t)$$

to indicate the tth value of x_i and y_j. Similarly the complete input or output signal may be represented as

$$X(t) := [x_1(t), x_2(t), \ldots, x_u(t)]$$
$$Z(t) := [z_1(t), z_2(t), \ldots, z_v(t)]$$

while the tth state of the network may be represented as

$$Y(t) := [y_1(t), y_2(t), \ldots, y_r(t)]$$

To illustrate these relationships, consider the simple sequential network shown in Figure 9-2. At $t = 0$ assume that

$$\text{current input } X(0) := [x_1(0)] = [1]$$
$$\text{current state } Y(0) := [y_1(0), y_2(0)] = [0, 0]$$

If we examine the network we see that the following logical expressions

$$z(t) = x(t) \vee y_2(t)$$
$$D_1(t) = y_1(t) \vee \bar{y}_2(t)$$
$$D_2(t) = x(t) y_1(t)$$

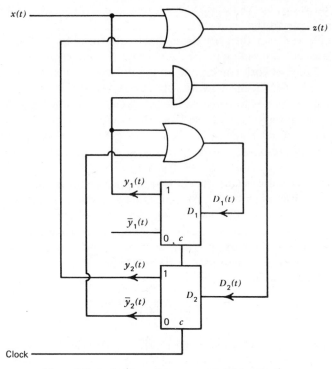

Figure 9-2. A simple synchronous sequential network.

represent the current output and current control signals, respectively. From Chapter 8 we know that the next state of a D flip-flop is given by

$$y(t + 1) = D(t)$$

Thus the next state of this network is given by

$$y_1(t + 1) = D_1(t)$$
$$y_2(t + 1) = D_2(t)$$

Using these expressions we see that for $t = 0$ we have

current input	$x(0) = 1$
current state	$[y_1(0), y_2(0)] = [0, 0]$
current output	$z(0) = 1$
current control	$D_1(0) = 1 \quad D_2(0) = 0$
next state	$[y_1(1), y_2(1)] = [1, 0]$

These observations concerning the behavior of synchronous sequential networks can now be generalized.

Fundamental Equations of Operation

The behavior of any sequential network is defined by three sets of equations called the *output equations*, the *next state equations*, and the *flip-flop control equations*. These equations have the following form where it is assumed that the clock pulses occur at $t = 0, 1, 2, \ldots$.

Output Equations

$$z_1(t) = F_{z_1}[x_1(t), \ldots, x_u(t), y_1(t), \ldots, y_r(t)]$$
$$\vdots$$
$$z_v(t) = F_{z_v}[x_1(t), \ldots, x_u(t), y_1(t), \ldots, y_r(t)]$$

The next state of each flip-flop in the register is dependent on the particular class of flip-flops used to form the register. The control and next state equations for S-R, D, and J-K flip-flops are defined as follows.

Next State Equations

S-R Flip-Flops

$$y_1(t + 1) = S_1(t) \vee y_1(t)\bar{R}_1(t)$$
$$\vdots$$
$$y_r(t + 1) = S_r(t) \vee y_r(t)\bar{R}_r(t)$$

Note $R(t)S(t) = 1$ not allowed

D Flip-Flops

$$y_1(t + 1) = D_1(t)$$
$$\vdots$$
$$y_r(t + 1) = D_r(t)$$

J-K Flip-Flops

$$y_1(t + 1) = \bar{y}_1(t)J_1(t) \vee y_1(t)\bar{K}_1(t)$$
$$\vdots$$
$$y_r(t + 1) = \bar{y}_r(t)J_r(t) \vee y_r(t)\bar{K}_r(t)$$

*Control Equations**

S-R Flip-Flops

$$i_1(t) = \begin{cases} S_1(t) = f_{S_1}[x_1(t), \ldots, x_u(t), y_1(t), \ldots, y_r(t)] \\ R_1(t) = f_{R_1}[x_1(t), \ldots, x_u(t), y_1(t), \ldots, y_r(t)] \end{cases}$$

$$\vdots$$

$$i_r(t) = \begin{cases} S_r(t) = f_{S_r}[x_1(t), \ldots, x_u(t), y_1(t), \ldots, y_r(t)] \\ R_r(t) = f_{R_r}[x_1(t), \ldots, x_u(t), y_1(t), \ldots, y_r(t)] \end{cases}$$

D Flip-Flops

$$i_1(t) = D_1(t) = f_{D_1}[x_1(t), \ldots, x_u(t), y_1(t), \ldots, y_r(t)]$$

$$\vdots$$

$$i_r(t) = D_r(t) = f_{D_r}[x_1(t), \ldots, x_u(t), y_1(t), \ldots, y_r(t)]$$

J-K Flip-Flops

$$i_1(t) = \begin{cases} J_1(t) = f_{J_1}[x_1(t), \ldots, x_u(t), y_1(t), \ldots, y_r(t)] \\ K_1(t) = f_{K_1}[x_1(t), \ldots, x_u(t), y_1(t), \ldots, y_r(t)] \end{cases}$$

$$\vdots$$

$$i_r(t) = \begin{cases} J_r(t) = f_{J_r}[x_1(t), \ldots, x_u(t), y_1(t), \ldots, y_r(t)] \\ K_r(t) = f_{K_r}[x_1(t), \ldots, x_u(t), y_1(t), \ldots, y_r(t)] \end{cases}$$

Let $X(t)$ denote the input u-tuple $[x_1(t), \ldots, x_u(t)]$, $Z(t)$ denote the output v-tuple $[z_1(t), \ldots, z_v(t)]$, $I(t)$ denote the r-tuple $[i_1(t), \ldots, i_r(t)]$, and $Y(t)$ denote the state of the network $[y_1(t), \ldots, y_r(t)]$ at time t. Then the behavior of the sequential network can be expressed as

Output Function

$$Z(t) := F_Z[X(t), Y(t)]$$

Flip-Flop Control Function

$$I(t) := F_I[X(t), Y(t)]$$

Next-State Function

$$Y(t + 1) := F_Y'[I(t)] = F_Y[X(t), Y(t)]$$

---

* Note that for *S-R* and *J-K* flip-flops, two control equations are needed to represent $i(t)$ for each flip-flop.

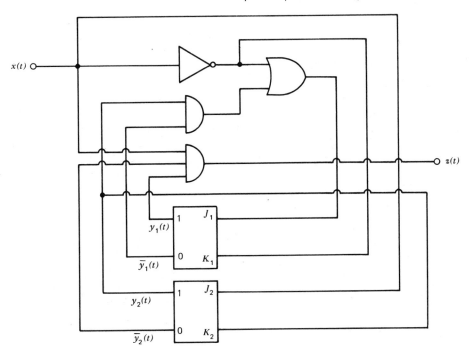

Figure 9-3. A typical sequential network.

The next-state function shows that the $(t + 1)$st state of the system is a function of both the tth state and the input of the network. The following example further illustrates these ideas.

Assume that we wish to analyze the operation of the circuit shown in Figure 9-3. Examining this circuit we find that it can be described by the following equations.

$$z(t) = x(t) y_1(t) \bar{y}_2(t)$$

$$J_1(t) = \bar{x}(t) \vee \bar{y}_1(t) y_2(t) \qquad K_1(t) = \bar{x}(t)$$

$$J_2(t) = x(t) \qquad\qquad K_2(t) = y_2(t)$$

$$y_1(t + 1) = \bar{y}_1(t)\bar{x}(t) \vee \bar{y}_1(t) y_2(t) \vee y_1(t)x(t)$$

$$y_2(t + 1) = \bar{y}_2(t)x(t) \vee y_2(t)\bar{y}_2(t) = \bar{y}_2(t)x(t)$$

These equations can be evaluated as shown in Table 9-1. Although the information presented in Table 9-1 completely describes the behavior of the network, this information is usually presented in a somewhat different form.

Table 9-1   Tabular Representation of Behavior of Sequential Network Shoen in Figure 9-3

		$F_I[X(t), Y(t)]$				$F_Y[X(t), Y(t)]$		$F_Z[X(t), Y(t)]$
Current Input $x(t)$	**Current State** $y_1(t)$ $y_2(t)$	**Current Control FF1** $J_1(t)$ $K_1(t)$		**FF2** $J_2(t)$ $K_2(t)$		**Next State** $y_1(t+1)$ $y_2(t+1)$		**Current Output** $Z(t)$
0	0 0	1	1	0	0	1	0	0
0	0 1	1	1	0	1	1	0	0
0	1 0	1	1	0	0	0	0	0
0	1 1	1	1	0	1	0	0	0
1	0 0	0	0	1	0	0	1	0
1	0 1	1	0	1	1	1	0	0
1	1 0	0	0	1	0	1	1	1
1	1 1	0	0	1	1	1	0	0

State Diagrams and Transition Tables

The next-state function $F_Y[X(t), Y(t)]$ and output function $F_Z[X(t), Y(t)]$ can be described by a graphical representation called a *state transition diagram* or a tabular representation called a *transition table*. Both of these representations are now considered.

The transition table representation of a sequential network displays the properties of the next state and output functions in tabular form. The columns of the table correspond to the possible input symbols and the rows correspond to the possible states of the network. The entry found at the intersection of the kth row and the jth column is

Next State/Current Output

For example, the information presented in Table 9-1 concerning the next state and current output of the network shown in Figure 9-3 can be represented by the transition table given by Table 9-2.

When discussing sequential networks it is often more convenient to indicate the states in symbolic form. For example, we could denote the four distinct states in the above example as q_0, q_1, q_2, and q_3, respectively. This symbolic representation is usually easier to work with when we must deal with networks that have a large number of state variables. We also find this representation useful in later sections where we talk about the design of sequential networks.

Table 9-2 Transition Table for Network of Figure 9-3

Current State	Current Input x 0	1
[0, 0]	[1, 0]/0	[0, 1]/0 Next state
[0, 1]	[1, 0]/0	[1, 0]/0
[1, 0]	[0, 0]/0	[1, 1]/1 Current
[1, 1]	[0, 0]/0	[1, 0]/0 output

The transition table of Table 9-2 can also be expressed in terms of the symbolic representation of the states. In this case we call the resulting table a *state table* for the network. The state table corresponding to Table 9-2 is given by Table 9-3.

The trouble with transition tables and state tables is that it is often hard to visualize the behavior of the network under different input conditions.

State transition diagrams provide a graphical representation of the operation of a sequential network. Each diagram consists of a set of vertices labeled to correspond to the states of the network. For each ordered pair of (not necessarily distinct) states, q_i and q_j, a directed edge connects vertex q_i to q_j if and only if there exists a value, a_k, of the input signal such that

$$q_j = F_Y(a_k, q_i)$$

If a directed edge connects q_i to q_j when the input is a_k, then the edge is labeled as $a_k/F_Z(a_k, q_i)$. Thus the vertices of the transition diagram correspond to the current

Table 9-3 State Table Representation of Transition Table

Current State	Current Input 0	1
q_0	$q_2/0$	$q_1/0$ Next state
q_1	$q_2/0$	$q_2/0$ Current
q_2	$q_0/0$	$q_3/1$ output
q_3	$q_0/0$	$q_2/0$

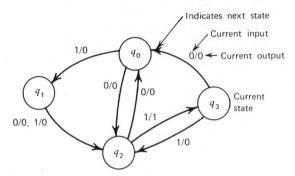

Figure 9-4. State transition diagram corresponding to Table 9-3.

state of the network; the label on the edge indicates the current input and the current output. An arrowhead on each edge is used to indicate the next state of the network. Figure 9-4 is the state transition diagram that corresponds to the state table given by Table 9-3.

Input, Output and State Sequences

When we are dealing with a sequential network that forms part of a complex system we are usually interested in the network's external behavior. In particular, if we apply an input sequence

$$x(0), x(1), x(2), \ldots, x(k)$$

we would like to know what the resulting output sequence

$$z(0), z(1), z(2), \ldots, z(k)$$

will be. The answer to this question is not unique but depends on the initial state of the network at $t = 0$.

For example consider the network represented by the transition diagram of Figure 9-3. Assume that the input sequence

$$x(0) = 1 \qquad x(1) = 0 \qquad x(2) = 1 \qquad x(3) = 0 \qquad x(4) = 0$$

is applied to this network. If the initial state is q_0 then we see from the transition diagram that the network will go from q_0 to q_1 at $t = 0$, from q_1 to q_2 at $t = 1$, from q_2 to q_3 at $t = 2$, from q_3 to q_0 at $t = 3$, and finally from q_0 to q_2 at $t = 4$. The output sequence corresponding to this input sequence and state sequence, which can also be read from the transition diagram, is seen to be

$$z(0) = 0 \qquad z(1) = 0 \qquad z(2) = 1 \qquad z(3) = 0 \qquad z(4) = 0$$

Next consider what happens when the initial state is q_1 instead of q_0. In this case the state sequence is

$$q_1 \rightarrow q_2 \rightarrow q_0 \rightarrow q_1 \rightarrow q_2 \rightarrow q_0$$

and the output sequence is

$$z(0) = 0 \qquad z(1) = 0 \qquad z(2) = 0 \qquad z(3) = 0 \qquad z(4) = 0$$

Thus we obtain a different output sequence and state sequence if we start in a different initial state.

From this discussion we see that the problem of analyzing the behavior of a given sequential network can be handled in a straightforward manner. Although the analytical techniques that we have developed are of importance in themselves, this discussion has also served another important purpose: that of providing the background material that we need to consider the problem of designing a synchronous sequential network to carry out a specific task. The rest of this chapter considers this problem.

EXERCISES

1. Find the transition table and state diagram for the sequential network of Figure P9-1.

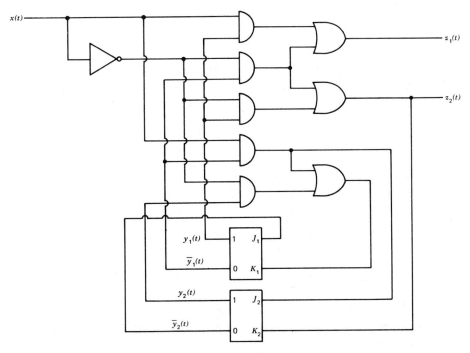

Figure P9-1

2. Find the state sequence and output sequence for the network of Exercise 1 for the following initial state q_I and input sequence $X(t)$

(a) $q_I = [0, 0]$ $X(t) = 1011010$
(b) $q_I = [1, 0]$ $X(t) = 10010101$

3. DESIGN OF SYNCHRONOUS SEQUENTIAL NETWORKS

The problem of analyzing the behavior of a given synchronous sequential network is easily accomplished provided we have a circuit diagram of the network. The reverse problem, that of designing a sequential network to perform a desired information processing operation, is considerably harder to solve. In this situation we assume that we are given a description of the operations that must be performed by the network and are asked to develop a sequential network that carries out these operations.

For example we might wish to design a sequential network which will compute the correct change to return to a customer of a coin operated vending machine. In that case the input consists of the sequence of coins deposited into the machine and the output is a command to return the specific change that the customer expects. Sequential networks also serve as control units in many digital systems where they control the sequence in which the information processing tasks in the system are performed.

The design of a sequential network to carry out a given operation is both an art and a science. At several stages of the process the designer must call on heuristic procedures and past experience to make decisions about the best way to proceed, while at other stages straightforward algorithmic procedures may be employed to carry out the design steps associated with that stage. Every design problem can be broken down into the following stages.

Stage 1. Description of Desired Network Operation   A complete set of specifications must be prepared describing the operation of the network. All inputs and outputs must be identified and the relationship between the quantities must be defined in a consistent manner.

Stage 2. Determination of State Table   Using the specification established at stage 1, an initial state table or state transition diagram is defined for the network. The state table is checked to make sure that it satisfies all design criteria.

Stage 3. State Table Minimization   In the process of developing a state table to satisfy a given set of operational requirements an unnecessarily large number of states may be introduced. Since the number of information storage elements in a circuit increases as the number of states increases, it is often desirable to remove redundant states from the state table.

Stage 4. State Assignments The information contained in the state table must be encoded into binary form. This is not a unique process and the encoding used can considerably influence the complexity of the resulting circuit. The result of this stage is to transform the state table into a transition table.

Stage 5. Network Realization Once a transition table has been constructed, and a decision made concerning the type of storage elements to be used, the logic expressions relating the input and present state to the output and control signals can be obtained.

In the above design process, only stages 3 and 5 can be carried out in a completely algorithmic manner. The state assignment problem of stage 4 could, in theory, also be carried out in an algorithmic manner by simply trying all the possible state assignments and then selecting the best one according to some criteria. Unfortunately the number of possible state assignments is so large that this is an unrealistic approach. Heuristic and advanced analytical techniques have been developed to assist in the solution of this problem.

Except for very simple situations, the first two stages of the design process cannot be handled in a completely algorithmic manner. As a designer gains experience a set of heuristic procedures are learned that have previously proved useful in carrying out these stages of the design process. Fortunately the initial learning process needed to develop a useful set of heuristics usually can be accomplished by solving three or four typical problems.

In this section we concentrate on the last stage of the design process since the desired behavior of many of the networks that are used in complex digital systems and computers can be specified directly in terms of a transition table. The next section will briefly discuss the rest of the design process.

For the rest of this section we assume that we are given a transition table in which all of the inputs, outputs, and states of the network have been identified and encoded into digital form. Our job is to select the types of flip-flops to be used, if they have not already been specified, and to design the combinational circuits necessary to realize the complete network.

Excitation Tables for Flip-Flops

Our initial discussion of flip-flops in Chapter 8 emphasized the response of the different types of flip-flops to various combinations of input signals. This information is very important in analyzing the behavior of a sequential network or in working with flip-flops when there is no feedback information present in the network. However, when we are designing a sequential network we know the current state and the desired next state for each flip-flop under each input condition. This information must then be used to determine the control signals that must be supplied to each flip-flop in order to achieve the desired operation.

Table 9-4   Excitation Tables for *S-R*, *D*, and *J-K* Flip-Flops

Current State $y(t)$	Next State $y(t+1)$	Input Required $S(t)$	$R(t)$	Current State $y(t)$	Next State $y(t+1)$	Input Required $D(t)$
0	0	0	d	0	0	0
0	1	1	0	0	1	1
1	0	0	1	1	0	0
1	1	d	0	1	1	1

S-R Flip-Flop		*D* Flip-Flop
(*a*)		(*b*)

Current State $y(t)$	Next State $y(t+1)$	Input Required $J(t)$	$K(t)$
0	0	0	d
0	1	1	d
1	0	d	1
1	1	d	0

J-K Flip-Flop
(*c*)

The transition table description of flip-flops used in Chapter 8 can be rearranged to form an *excitation table* that relates the known state transitions to the control signals necessary to produce the transitions. Table 9-4 gives the excitation tables associated with *S-R*, *D*, and *J-K* flip-flops. These tables are interpreted in the following manner.

Consider the *S-R* flip-flop and assume that we want to go from the initial state $y(t) = 0$ to the final state $y(t + 1) = 0$. Looking in the first row of Table 9-4a we see that $S(t)$ must be 0 but $R(t)$ can be either 0 or 1 (i.e., a don't care condition) since both values for $R(t)$ will result in $y(t + 1) = 0$. Thus $R(t)$ is indicated as d in this situation. Now consider the case where we want to go from the initial state $y(t) = 0$ to the final state $y(t + 1) = 1$. Looking at the second row of Table 9-4a we see that $S(t)$ must be 1 in order to set the flip-flop to the 1 state and $R(t)$ must be 0 since $S(t) = 1$, $R(t) = 1$ is a prohibited input combination for an *S-R* flip-flop.

Similar considerations also hold for the *J-K* flip-flop as can be seen by inspecting Table 9-4c. These don't care conditions in the excitation tables of both the *S-R* and *J-K* flip-flops allow us greater flexibility in the design of the combinational logic networks that control these flip-flops.

Network Realization

The realization of a sequential network requires us to design a combinational logic network that generates the proper output signals and control signals to the flip-flops. The following example illustrates how we can carry out this design process.

Assume that we wish to construct a sequential network that is described by the transition table given by Table 9-5. This network has three states that are important to its operation and one state [1, 1] that never occurs. The presence of this state means that there will be several don't care entries in the transition table.

Table 9-5 Transition Table for a Sequential Network

Current State	Current Input x_1	
	0	**1**
y_1, y_2		
0, 0	0, 0/0	0, 1/0
0, 1	0, 0/0	1, 0/0
1, 0	0, 0/0	1, 0/1
1, 1	$d, d/d$	$d, d/d$ don't care state

To realize this network we need two flip-flops. Thus the first problem we must consider is what type of flip-flops should we use. Here again the proper choice of flip-flops determines the complexity of the logic circuit that we need. At this point we arbitrarily choose to use two J-K flip-flops. Later on we investigate the type of results we can obtain by using other types of flip-flops. Under this assumption our sequential network has the form shown in Figure 9-5, and we must find the logical expressions that describe the combinational logic network.

The five logical expressions that we must find are easily obtained if we use a modified truth table of the form shown in Table 9-6. Beside the standard input signals, we also include the next state of the network that is associated with these signals. We can now use the information in the J-K flip-flop excitation table to derive the desired logical expression.

For example consider the second row of Table 9-6. The first flip-flop remains in the 0 state, and the second flip-flop goes from the 1 to the 0 state when the input is 0. Looking at the J-K flip-flop excitation table of Table 9-4c we see that this means that $J_1 = 0$, $K_1 = d$, $J_2 = d$, and $K_2 = 1$. The output $z = 0$ is found by examining Table 9-5.

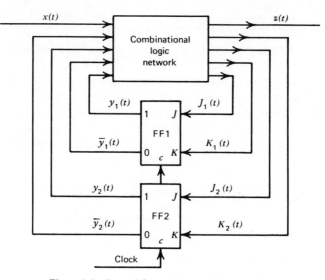

Figure 9-5. General form of sequential network.

The final task in our design process is to obtain the logical expressions describing the combinational logic network. The simplest approach, and the one that we will use, is to treat each expression separately. If we go through the standard minimization process, we obtain the following logical representation for z, J_1, K_1, J_2, and K_2.

$$z = xy_1$$

$$J_1 = xy_2 \qquad J_2 = x\bar{y}_1$$

$$K_1 = \bar{x} \qquad K_2 = 1$$

Table 9-6   Truth Table for Combinational Network

Input x	Current State y_1	y_2	Next State		FF1 J_1	K_1	FF2 J_2	K_2	Output Z
0	0	0	0	0	0	d	0	d	0
0	0	1	0	0	0	d	d	1	0
0	1	0	0	0	d	1	0	d	0
0	1	1	d	d	d	d	d	d	d
1	0	0	0	1	0	d	1	d	0
1	0	1	1	0	1	d	d	1	0
1	1	0	1	0	d	0	0	d	1
1	1	1	d	d	d	d	d	d	d

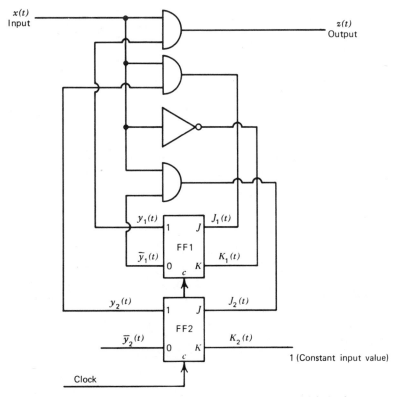

Figure 9-6. Logic diagram of network using individual term minimization.

Using these equations we obtain the network shown in Figure 9-6. This network could be drawn in a much more compact form but it was drawn in this manner to correspond to the general form of sequential networks presented in Figure 9-1.

Flip-Flop Selection

Unfortunately there is no general algorithm that can be used to determine which class of flip-flops will yield the minimum complexity realization for a given design problem.

The selection of which class of flip-flops to use to realize a given network depends on many factors. In some cases the flip-flops are specified by the fact that only one particular type of flip-flop is available to the designer. At other times the designer is free to choose the flip-flop that produces the simplest circuit according to some minimization criterion, such as the minimum number of total circuit elements or the minimum number of connections needed between circuit elements.

To illustrate these considerations let us design a circuit to realize the network described by Table 9-5 using D flip-flops and then one using S-R flip-flops. The

Table 9-7   Truth Table for Realization of
                                                    Sequential Network Using D and S-R

Input x	Current State y_1	y_2	Next State y_1	y_2	(a) D Flip-Flop Realization FF1 D_1	FF2 D_2	(b) S-R Flip-Flop Realization S_1	R_1	S_2	R_2	Output
0	0	0	0	0	0	0	0	d	0	d	0
0	0	1	0	0	0	0	0	d	0	1	0
0	1	0	0	0	0	0	0	1	0	d	0
0	1	1	d	d	d	d	d	d	d	d	d
1	0	0	0	1	0	1	0	d	1	0	0
1	0	1	1	0	1	0	1	0	0	1	0
1	1	0	1	0	1	0	d	0	0	d	1
1	1	1	d	d	d	d	d	d	d	d	d

truth table for the D flip-flop realization is given by Table 9-7a and the truth table for the S-R flip-flop realization is given by Table 9-7b.

Going through our standard minimization process we obtain the following logical expressions:

Case I *Using* D *Flip-Flops*

$$D_1 = xy_2 \lor xy_1$$
$$D_2 = x\bar{y}_1\bar{y}_2$$
$$z = xy_1$$

Case II *Using* S-R *Flip-Flops*

$$S_1 = xy_2 \qquad S_2 = x\bar{y}_1\bar{y}_2 \qquad z = xy_1$$
$$R_1 = \bar{x} \qquad R_2 = y_2$$

If we examine these expressions and compare them to the expressions we obtained for the previous example where we used J-K flip-flops, we see that the network using the J-K flip-flops is minimal both in terms of the number of logic elements used and the number of connections required to construct the circuit. Again it is important to note that there is no general algorithm that can be used to determine which class of flip-flops give us a minimal realization. It is simply a combination of trial and error plus design experience.

EXERCISES

1. It is desired to realize the following sequential network.

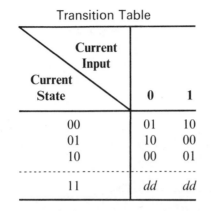

Transition Table

Current State	Current Input 0	1
00	01	10
01	10	00
10	00	01
11	*dd*	*dd*

Design a circuit that will realize this network using (a) *S-R* flip-flops, (b) *D* flip-flops, (c) *J-K* flip-flops. No outputs are given for this network.

2. Which of the circuits of Exercise 1 has the minimal number of logic elements?

4. SPECIFICATION OF TRANSITION TABLES AND STATE TABLES

Once we obtain an assigned transition table description of a given sequential network it is a straightforward process to obtain a circuit that will realize the network. The general problem of obtaining an assigned transition table is, unfortunately, not as straightforward. In fact there is no general algorithmic procedure for going from a word description of what a network must do to an assigned transition table. The main reason for this is that a word description is usually not a formal description of the network's action. Consequently, the designer must use personal insight and past experience to supplement and expand on the initial word description.

For many of the simpler networks that we encounter in digital system design it is possible to go directly to a transition table representation of the network's operation. There are, however, many situations where the first design step consists of formulating a state table or a state transition diagram representation of the operations that the network must perform.

This section briefly investigates how both transition tables and state tables can be developed to meet a specific design requirement. Of necessity, this discussion is heuristic instead of algorithmic since the actual design process must rely extensively on the designer's previous experience and understanding of the operations that the desired network must perform.

Autonomous Networks

A small but important class of sequential networks operate without any input signals. Such networks are called *autonomous networks*. Figure 9-7 illustrates the general form that autonomous networks take. Examining this figure we see that both the network's next state and the output depend only on the current state of the network. Therefore, the transition table or state table representing this network will only have one column.

Autonomous networks are used extensively to generate standard periodic control signal sequences for use in various information processing tasks. In fact, an autonomous network is, in reality, a generalized counter.

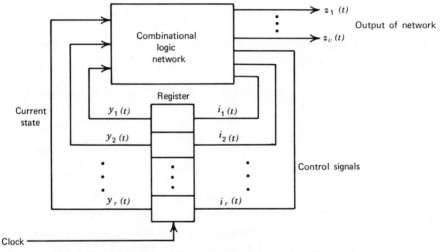

Figure 9-7. General form of autonomous sequential network.

Counters

Counters are important building blocks in digital systems and they can take on a variety of forms depending on the application for which they are used.

A counter will count through a sequence of numbers, then reset itself to an initial value, and then repeat the counting process. The simplest types of counters are binary counters built from r flip-flops. These counters start at 0 and count to $2^r - 1$ and then reset to 0. For example, if $r = 3$, a counter will count through the successive binary numbers 0 through 7. Figure 9-8 gives a transition diagram representation of this counting process. The corresponding transition table representation for

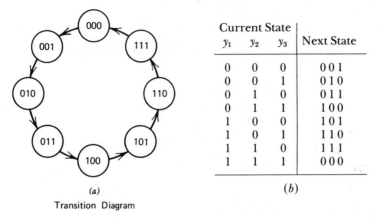

Current State			
y_1	y_2	y_3	Next State
0	0	0	0 0 1
0	0	1	0 1 0
0	1	0	0 1 1
0	1	1	1 0 0
1	0	0	1 0 1
1	0	1	1 1 0
1	1	0	1 1 1
1	1	1	0 0 0

(a)
Transition Diagram

(b)

Figure 9-8. Representation of binary modulo 8 counter. (a) Transition diagram. (b) Transition table.

this network is also shown. Counters of this type are called *binary up counters* or *modulo 2^r counters*.

Several standard circuits are available to realize counters and many manufacturers are currently manufacturing integrated circuits that are complete counters. The design of the necessary logic circuits to realize a counter can be accomplished using the techniques of the last section. For example, let us design the counter of Figure 9-8 using D flip-flops. The control equations for this case are described by Table 9-8. Using the information in this table we find that

$$D_1 = \bar{y}_1 y_2 y_3 \lor y_1 \bar{y}_3 \lor y_1 \bar{y}_2$$
$$D_2 = \bar{y}_2 y_3 \lor y_2 \bar{y}_3$$
$$D_3 = \bar{y}_3$$

Table 9-8

Control Signals Necessary
to Realize a Modulo 8 Counter

Current State			Next State			Control Signals		
y_1	y_2	y_3	y_1	y_2	y_3	D_1	D_2	D_3
0	0	0	0	0	1	0	0	1
0	0	1	0	1	0	0	1	0
0	1	0	0	1	1	0	1	1
0	1	1	1	0	0	1	0	0
1	0	0	1	0	1	1	0	1
1	0	1	1	1	0	1	1	0
1	1	0	1	1	1	1	1	1
1	1	1	0	0	0	0	0	0

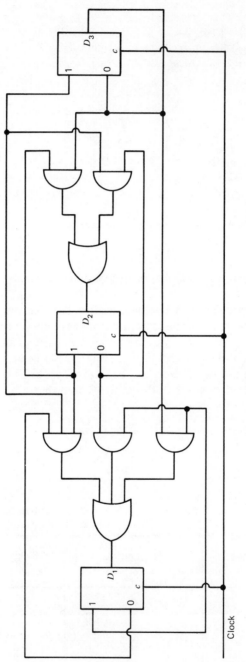

Figure 9-9. Realization of modulo 8 counter using D flip-flops.

The resulting logic diagram is given in Figure 9-9. It is left as an exercise to show that a simpler network is required if *J-K* flip-flops are used to build this counter.

There is, of course, no reason why we must limit ourselves to a modulo 2^r counter or that we even count in the standard binary order. For example, assume that we have a machining process that requires five steps and that there are three possible operations that can be performed at each step. These operations, which are all performed during the interclock interval of the control network, are

c_1 drill
c_2 move drill right 1 unit
c_3 move drill up 1 unit

When no operation is indicated (i.e., all $c_i = 0$) the machine performing the machining operation returns to its starting position.

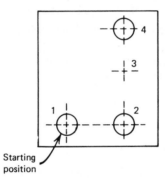

Figure 9-10. Diagram of plate after drilling operation.

The machining process to be carried out is to drill a plate as indicated in Figure 9-10. The operating sequence necessary to accomplish this task is described by the following steps.

Step 1 Initialization of machining operation—position drill in lower left-hand corner.
Step 2 Drill hole 1.
Step 3 Move drill to position 2 and drill hole.
Step 4 Move drill to position 3 do not drill.
Step 5 Move drill to position 4 and drill hole.

This sequence of operations can be controlled by a counter that will generate the successive values of the 3-tuple $[c_1, c_2, c_3]$ where $c_i = 1$ indicates that an operation is performed and $c_i = 0$ indicates that no operation is performed. In this case the state variables of the counter are identical to the outputs of the counter. The actual

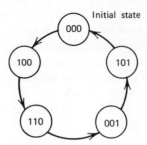

Figure 9-11. Transition diagram and transition table representation of control sequence.

sequence that the counter must go through is illustrated by the transition diagram and transition table of Figure 9-11.

Since the output of the network is assumed to be identical to the value of the current state of the control network, the final step in the design of the control unit is to realize an autonomous sequential network that has the behavior described by the transition table of Figure 9-11. Assume that this network is to be realized using $S\text{-}R$ flip-flops. Then the flip-flop control signals necessary to realize this network are given in Table 9-9. Using this information and our standard logic network realization techniques we obtain the following expressions for the flip-flop control signals:

$$S_1 = \bar{y}_1 \qquad\qquad S_2 = y_1 \bar{y}_2 \bar{y}_3 \qquad S_3 = y_2$$

$$R_1 = y_1 y_3 \lor y_2 \qquad R_2 = y_2 \qquad\qquad R_3 = y_1 y_3$$

The actual circuit of this sequential network is easily obtained from these expressions and is omitted.

Table 9-9   Flip-Flop Control Signals
Necessary to Realize Control Sequences

| Current State | | | Next State | | | Flip-Flop Control Signals | | | | | |
y_1	y_2	y_3	y_1	y_2	y_3	S_1	R_1	S_2	R_2	S_3	R_3
0	0	0	1	0	0	1	0	0	d	0	d
0	0	1	1	0	1	1	0	0	d	d	0
0	1	0	d	d	d	d	d	d	d	d	d
0	1	1	d	d	d	d	d	d	d	d	d
1	0	0	1	1	0	d	0	1	0	0	d
1	0	1	0	0	0	0	1	0	d	0	1
1	1	0	0	0	1	0	1	0	1	1	0
1	1	1	d	d	d	d	d	d	d	d	d

Up to this point the problems have had a form that allowed us to go directly to a transition table description of the network. This, of course, is not always possible since there are many situations that occur where the desired operation of the network is described in terms of a word statement. The design process then involves first obtaining a state table description of the network. Next the state table is turned into a transition table by assigning a digital coding to the state, input, and output symbols associated with the state table. The resulting transition table is then used to complete the design of the network. Thus our next task is to consider how a state table or a state transition diagram can be obtained.

State Tables from Word Statements

The process of defining a state table can be divided into two stages.

1. Determine how many different pieces of information about the past history of the network must be "remembered" by the network. Each such piece of information is represented by a state of the network.
2. Define, for each input and state condition, the next state and output that occurs.

The first stage of this process is probably the hardest since it requires the designer to have the ability to identify the past events that must be remembered and to classify these events into the smallest number of classes possible. This is basically a heuristic process that becomes easier as the designer gains experience.

The problem of forming a state table is not as difficult as it might initially seem. The reason for this is that there are a number of state tables that correspond to the same network performance. Thus all we must do is find one of these tables. In some of the complex problems we often inadvertently include more states than necessary. We will not investigate this problem, however, since it is usually possible to uniquely identify the states we need to represent the stored information in the types of networks that we will be discussing. Although we will not explore this problem, algorithmic procedures do exist that can be used to remove redundant states from a state table or that can transform one state table into another state table without changing the corresponding network performance. The following examples will illustrate how we can define simple state tables.

A Subsequence Detector

Assume that we wish to observe a sequence of 0's and 1's and take the following action based on the patterns observed.

Whenever three consecutive 1's are observed an output $z = 1$ must be produced when the third 1 is applied. Otherwise the output will be $z = 0$.

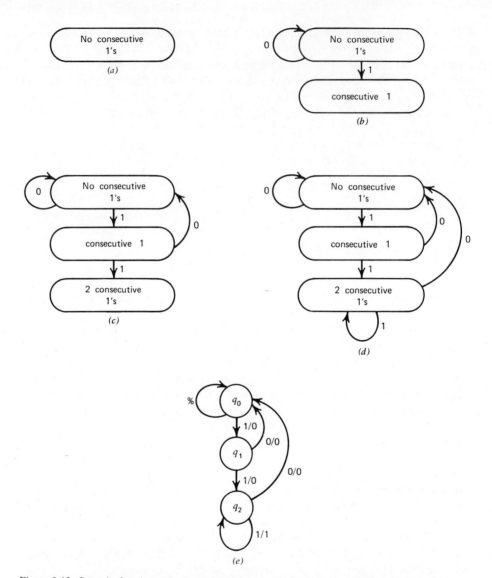

Figure 9-12. Steps in forming state transition diagram. (a) Initial state. (b) Information added by receiving information while in initial state. (c) Information added by receiving information while in state "1 consecutive 1." (d) Information added by receiving information in state "2 consecutive 1's." (e) Final state transition diagram.

In examining this problem statement we observe that we are checking the sequence $x(t-2)$, $x(t-1)$, $x(t)$ to see if the three values are all 1. Since $x(t)$ is the current input we only need to remember information about $x(t-2)$ and $x(t-1)$. In particular we note that all we need to know about the past inputs is "how many consecutive 1's have we had prior to $x(t)$."

One of the easiest ways to investigate the interrelationship between the input information and the information that must be stored by the network is to use a state transition diagram. We start out with an "initial node" corresponding to the assumed initial condition of the network when it starts operating. We then consider each possible input and add new states as needed when the input changes the amount of information we have about the input process. This process of constructing a state transition diagram continues until we reach the point where we have a complete diagram or when we cannot add any additional states. This method is illustrated by Figure 9-12.

Initially we assume that the network starts with no stored information. This condition coincides with the initial state "no consecutive 1's" indicated in Figure 9-12a. Next we consider what happens if we receive an input. If the input is 0 we still have the condition "no consecutive 1's." However a 1 input requires an additional state which will store the information that we have received "1 consecutive 1." This additional state allows us to expand our state transition diagram as shown in Figure 9-12b. We next consider what happens if we are in this new state and we receive an input. If the input is 0 we go back to our initial state while an input of 1 requires us to introduce an additional state to store the information that we have received "2 consecutive 1's." The expanded state transition diagram is shown in Figure 9-12c.

Continuing with this reasoning, we complete our state transition diagram as shown in Figure 9-12d. Our final task is to indicate what outputs occur during each transition. We do this in Figure 9-12e where we have labeled the states as

q_0—no consecutive 1's (initial state)

q_1—1 consecutive 1

q_2—2 consecutive 1's

Using this information, we form the state table given by Table 9-10 for this network

Table 9-10 Transition Table for 111 Sequence Detector

State	Input 0	1
q_0	$q_0/0$	$q_1/0$
q_1	$q_0/0$	$q_2/0$
q_2	$q_0/0$	$q_2/1$

A Controlled Counter

As a second example, assume that we wish to design a special counter that is controlled by three input control signals c_1, c_2, and c_3 in the following manner.

Control Signal	State Behavior Action
c_1	Counter is incremented by 1 each time a clock occurs unless the current count is 4 or 7. If the current count is 4 or 7 when the clock pulse occurs the counter is reset to 0.
c_2	Counter is incremented by 2 each time a clock pulse occurs if the current count is not 5, 6, or 7. If the current count is 5, 6, or 7 when the clock pulse occurs the counter is set to 0, 1, and 2 respectively.
c_3	Counter is decremented by 1 each time a clock pulse occurs. If the count is 0 when the clock pulse occurs the counter is set to 7.

Output Behavior

The output is 0 whenever the current state indicates an even count and 1 whenever the current state indicates an odd count.

Examining these requirements we see that we must remember counts between 0 and 7. Thus we need 8 states that we can label q_i corresponding to "the current count is i." With this convention we can describe the operation of the counter by the state transition diagram shown in Figure 9-13. We have made one slight change

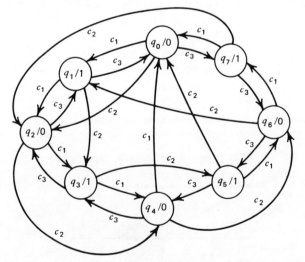

Figure 9-13. State transition diagram representing special counter. *Note*: Label of each node is q_i/z_i where q_i is the current state and z_i is the current output.

Table 9-11 State Table for Special Counter

Current State \ Input	c_1	c_2	c_3	Current Output
q_0	q_1	q_2	q_7	0
q_1	q_2	q_3	q_0	1
q_2	q_3	q_4	q_1	0
q_3	q_4	q_5	q_2	1
q_4	q_0	q_6	q_3	0
q_5	q_6	q_0	q_4	1
q_6	q_7	q_1	q_5	0
q_7	q_0	q_2	q_6	1

in the form of our diagram. Instead of indicating the output as a label on a branch, we have included this information as part of the node label. We do this to emphasize the fact that the output is to depend only on the current state of the network and not the current input. Using the information contained in this diagram, we obtain the state table given by Table 9-11. Since the output does not depend on the input but only on the current state of the network, we include a separate column in the transition table indicating the output.

The Assignment Problem

As we have seen, the state table that we obtain from a word description of the desired behavior of a network is often in a symbolic form that must be encoded into binary notation before we can carry out the rest of the design process. This is known as the *assignment problem*. For a sequential network any encoding that labels each distinct state, input, and output with a unique binary code can be used to solve the assignment problem. However, the choice of a particular coding assignment can have a very profound effect on the number of logic elements needed to realize the network. Thus it would be desirable to have an algorithm that would tell us which coding assignment would result in the most economical circuit.

One algorithm would simply consist of forming all the possible coding assignments and then selecting the most economical circuit from all those that were formed. Unfortunately, this is not a practical approach even though in theory this algorithm always gives us a minimum circuit. In order to see why this algorithm breaks down, all we have to do is investigate the number of distinct codings that are possible for a transition table with m states.

When we make up a state table we concentrate on relating the states of the network to the events that we wish to remember. To construct a sequential network corresponding to this table we must relate the states of the table to the state variables of the flip-flops which make up the network. If we have a network with r flip-flops we know that the 2^r-values of the r-tuple $[y_1, \ldots, y_r]$ represent the possible states of the circuit. Assume that the state table has m states, then the only restriction is that r must be selected such that

$$m \leq 2^r$$

so that it is possible to have a unique assignment between the states of the state table and the r-tuple $[y_1, y_2, \ldots, y_r]$.

For every value of m and r there are many different state assignments that can be used. If we disregard the symmetries that are present between different codings, there are

$$\frac{2^r!}{(2^r - m)!}$$

different ways that we can assign the 2^r-combinations of state variables to the m states. McCluskey and Unger have shown (see reference 4) that this number can be reduced by taking into account certain symmetries and other special properties of logic circuits. With these restrictions included there are

$$\frac{(2^r - 1)!}{(2^r - m)!r!}$$

distinct assignments of r state variable to m states.

Table 9-12 lists the number of distinct assignments for values of r from 1 to 4 and m from 2 to 9. Examination of this table shows that the brute force method of enumerating all of the possible state assignments would only be feasible for

Table 9-12   Table of the Number of Distinct State Assignments

Number of States, m	Number of State Variables, r	Number of Distinct Assignments
2	1	1
3	2	3
4	2	3
5	3	140
6	3	420
7	3	840
8	3	840
9	4	10, 810, 800

values of m up to 4. For values of m of 9 or greater it becomes a completely unreasonable approach, even if a digital computer were available, to carry out the enumeration. A similar problem also occurs when it is necessary to encode the input and/or the output signal of a network.

Several analytical and rule-of-thumb procedures have been developed to find acceptable, if not optimal solutions to the assignment problem. Computer programs have also been developed to help the designer with this problem. Many of these techniques are discussed in detail in references [1], [3], and [5]. Fortunately, for the type of networks that we are interested in, the selection of a satisfactory solution to the assignment problem can usually be obtained by making use of the behavioral description of the network.

For example, consider the special counter described by Table 9-11. In this case the states represent the counts 0 through 7. Thus a natural assignment would be

$$q_0 = [0, 0, 0] \qquad q_4 = [1, 0, 0]$$
$$q_1 = [0, 0, 1] \qquad q_5 = [1, 0, 1]$$
$$q_2 = [0, 1, 0] \qquad q_6 = [1, 1, 0]$$
$$q_3 = [0, 1, 1] \qquad q_7 = [1, 1, 1]$$

Similarly an assignment for the input could be

$$c_1 = [0, 0] \qquad c_2 = [0, 1] \qquad c_3 = [1, 0]$$

The state table of Table 9-11 can now be rewritten in terms of this new coding, and the resulting information can be used to find a logic circuit realization for this counter.

A Change Calculator

As a final example of how one might design a sequential network that will carry out a specific time-dependent task, consider the following problem.

Assume that you work for a vending machine manufacturer. The item sold by the machines produced by the company may cost either 10 cents or 15 cents depending on where the machine is installed. The machine will accept nickles, dimes, and quarters one at a time and give the correct change. A sequential network is to be designed that can be used to compute the amount of change to be returned to each customer. There must be a way to control the operation of the network so that the same network can be used if the items price is 10 cents or 15 cents.

Examining this problem statement, we must first identify the input information that may be applied to the sequential network and the output information we can expect from the network. To do this, it is helpful to draw a diagram of the form shown in Figure 9-14, indicating the information we know about the problem.

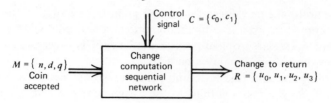

Figure 9-14. General form of network.

The meaning of the symbols shown in Figure 9-14 are as follows:

M Value of coin deposited	C Control signal	R Change returned
n Nickle	c_0 Item costs 10 cents	u_0 0 cents u_2 10 cents
d Dime	c_1 Item costs 15 cents	u_1 5 cents u_3 15 cents
q Quarter		

Now that we have identified the input and output, our next task is to formulate the state transition diagram for this network.

The states of the network serve to remember the amount of money that has been deposited before it is necessary to make change. Thus the initial state, q_0, corresponds to the condition "no money received." Starting with this state and going through all of the possible input combinations provides the state transition diagram shown in Figure 9-15.

Examining this diagram, we see that there are a number of don't care conditions. For example, if we reach state q_1, we assume that the input (c_0, d) would not occur, since the item only costs a dime and thus the person would not have deposited a nickle first. We similarly note that the only time that we will be in state q_2 is when

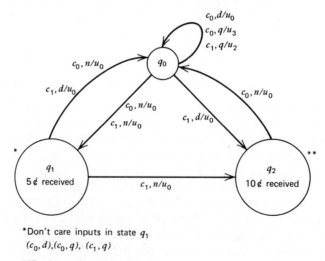

*Don't care inputs in state q_1
$(c_0, d), (c_0, q), (c_1, q)$

**Don't care inputs in state q_2
$(c_0, n), (c_0, d), (c_0, q), (c_1, d), (c_1, q)$

Figure 9-15. State transition diagram for coin change calculator.

Table 9-13 ⠀⠀⠀⠀⠀⠀⠀ **State Transition Table For Coin Change Calculator**

State \ Input	c_0			c_1		
	n	d	q	n	d	q
q_0	q_1/u_0	q_0/u_0	q_0/u_3	q_1/u_0	q_2/u_0	q_0/u_2
q_1	q_0/u_0	$-/-$	$-/-$	q_2/u_0	q_0/u_0	$-/-$
q_2	$-/-$	$-/-$	$-/-$	q_0/u_0	$-/-$	$-/-$

the item costs 15 cents. Thus the inputs $\{(c_0, n), (c_1, d), (c_2, d)\}$ never occur in that state.

The state table associated with this network is given by Table 9-13.

The next step in the design process consists of the binary encoding of the input, output, and state information. At this point the designer's experience and insight into the problem will be very important. As we discussed previously, many distinct encodings are possible. The one chosen should be as straightforward as possible to minimize the complexity of the signal.

If we look at the input information, we see that we have six input conditions. ([2 control values] × [3 coin values]) Thus we need 3 bits to encode the input signal. The input consists of two subparts; one corresponding to the coin received, and one corresponding to the price of the item being sold. This suggests the following encoding.

Definition of Input X

$$[x_1, x_2, x_3]$$

$x_1 = 0$ item costs 10 cents ⠀⠀⠀ $x_2, x_3 = [0, 1]$—input a nickle

$x_1 = 1$ item costs 15 cents ⠀⠀⠀ $x_2, x_3 = [1, 0]$—input a dime

⠀⠀⠀⠀⠀⠀⠀⠀⠀⠀⠀⠀⠀⠀⠀⠀ $x_2 x_3 = [1, 1]$—input a quarter

The output signal may take on four possible values. Two bits are sufficient to encode this information. The following encoding is suggested

$$Z = [z_1, z_2]$$

$u_0 = [0, 0]$ no change ⠀⠀⠀⠀⠀ $u_2 = [1, 0]$ 10 cents change

$u_1 = [0, 1]$ 5 cents change ⠀⠀⠀⠀ $u_3 = [1, 1]$ 15 cents change

Table 9-14   Transition Table for Coin Change Calculations

X / Y	000	001	010	011	100	101	110	111
00	$-/-$	$0,1/0,0$	$0,0/0,0$	$0,0/1,1$	$-/-$	$0,1/0,0$	$1,0/0,0$	$0,0/1,0$
01	$-/-$	$0,0/0,0$	$-/-$	$-/-$	$-/-$	$1,0/0,0$	$0,0/0,0$	$-/-$
10	$-/-$	$-/-$	$-/-$	$-/-$	$-/-$	$0,0/0,0$	$-/-$	$-/-$
11	$-/-$	$-/-$	$-/-$	$-/-$	$-/-$	$-/-$	$-/-$	$-/-$

In this encoding, z_1 can be thought of as an indication that 10 cents should be returned and z_2 can be thought of as an indication that 5 cents should be returned.

The three states can be encoded as

$$Y = [y_1, y_2]$$

$q_0 = [0, 0]$ no money received $q_2 = [1, 0]$ 10 cents received

$q_1 = [0, 1]$ 5 cents received

Using this information we can now generate the transition table of Table 9-14 corresponding to the state table of Table 9-13.

At this point we see that a very large number of don't care conditions exist. Our final task is to reduce this transition table to a sequential network. The final·logic network necessary to realize this sequential machine can be obtained in the standard manner once we decide on the type of flip-flops we will use. The details of this computation are left as an exercise.

EXERCISES

1. Design a modulo 8 counter using J-K flip-flops.

2. Find the state table of a network that counts $\hookrightarrow 0 \to 1 \to 2 \to 3 \to$ at each clock pulse if the input is 0 and $\hookrightarrow 0 \to 3 \to 2 \to 1 \to$ if the input is 1. This is an example of an up-down counter.

3. Find a state assignment for the state table of Exercise 2 and design a sequential network, using J-K flip-flops, that will realize the table.

4. Realize the sequential network described by Table 9-14 using D flip-flops.

5. SUMMARY

In this chapter we have investigated, in an introductory manner, the problems that must be solved when designing a sequential network to handle a specific information processing task. There is an extensive body of knowledge concerning techniques that can be used to design sequential networks. Many of these techniques have been reduced to a set of computer programs, thereby reducing the amount of tedious calculations required of the designer. Unfortunately, the hardest part of many design processes, the problem of actually describing the operations that must be performed by the particular network under investigation, cannot be automated to any great extent.

However, many of the networks required to carry out standard information processing operations have reached the point where they are so common that several standardized designs are already available. In fact, some of these networks are available as standard integrated circuits. As integrated circuit technology advances, it can be expected that a greater range of complete sequential networks will become available. The system designer will then be able to concentrate on the design of a complete system and not have to worry about the details of defining the design of the standard subsystem modules.

REFERENCE NOTATION

All the references listed have extensive discussions concerning the analysis of sequential networks. Hennie [2] discusses many of the theoretical aspects of deriving state tables from word descriptions of the information processing tasks that a network must perform. References [1], [3], [4], and [6] provide an intermediate treatment of the state reduction problem and the behavior of other classes of sequential networks. The state assignment problem is treated extensively in [5].

REFERENCES

1. Dietmeyer, D. L. (1971), *Logic Design of Digital Systems*, Allyn and Bacon, Boston, Mass.

2. Hennie, F. C. (1968), *Finite-State Models for Logical Machines*, John Wiley, New York.

3. Hill, J. H., and Peterson, G. R. (1974), *Introduction to Switching Theory and Logical Design*, John Wiley, New York.

4. McCluskey, E. J. (1965), *Introduction to the Theory of Switching Circuits*, McGraw-Hill, New York.

5. Miller, R. E. (1965), *Switching Theory*, Vol. II, John Wiley, New York.

6. Mowle, F. J. (1976), *A Systematic Approach to Digital Logic Design*, Addison Wesley, Reading, Mass.

HOME PROBLEMS

1. A widget production line has two conveyer belts. To maintain a balanced production schedule a checkpoint is introduced to monitor the flow of widgets on each conveyer belt. If the number of widgets that passed the checkpoint on belt i exceed the number of widgets that passed the checkpoint on belt j by three then belt i must stop until three additional widgets are detected on belt j. As soon as the three additional widgets are detected, belt i is started. A sequential network is to be used to control this operation. Find a transition table for this network.

2. In a number of digital systems it is necessary to have a controllable counter. Design a synchronous sequential network using *J-K* flip-flops that will have the following characteristics.

Input Signal

X_1	X_2	Operation
0	0	No change of state
0	1	Modulo 3 counter
1	0	Modulo 5 counter
1	1	Modulo 7 counter

3. A sequential network with the following transition table is to be constructed using *D* flip-flops. The two state assignments given below are proposed. Which state assignment requires the minimal number of logic elements?

Transition Table

State	Input 0	1
q_1	q_3	q_2
q_2	q_4	q_1
q_3	q_1	q_4
q_4	q_2	q_3

Assignment 1
$q_1 = [0, 0]$ $q_2 = [0, 1]$
$q_3 = [1, 0]$ $q_4 = [1, 1]$

Assignment 2
$q_1 = [0, 0]$ $q_2 = [0, 1]$
$q_3 = [1, 1]$ $q_4 = [1, 0]$

4. Design a BCD decade counter. Every time that the input clock pulse occurs, the count will increase by 1 until 9 is reached. The counter then resets to 0 and a carry output of 1 is generated. Show how four of these counters can be used to form a 4-digit BCD counter.

5. Design a digital combination lock that can only be opened if the proper sequence of 5 buttons on a 10-button keyboard have been pushed. Explain how the combination can be changed.

10

Input, Output, and Memory Elements

1. INTRODUCTION

The digital networks considered in the previous chapters have been designed to carry out a number of important information processing tasks. To complete our understanding of the components that make up digital systems, we must consider the general techniques that can be used to:

(a) Input information to a system.
(b) Output information after a system has completed a computation.
(c) Store the large quantities of information needed by the system to perform a computation.

    In this chapter we investigate the general properties of the devices that are used to carry out these tasks. Our discussion emphasizes the information flow that takes place instead of the specific details of how individual devices operate. Several examples are, however, presented to illustrate the way the various tasks can be used. A much more comprehensive discussion of the internal design of individual devices can be found in the references listed at the end of this chapter.

2. THE INTERFACE PROBLEM

Modern digital systems can process information at a very high rate. Unfortunately the outside world cannot always keep pace with this capability. For example, a typical input to a digital system might be a typewriter with a maximum information transmission rate of 10 characters per second. However, even the slowest digital

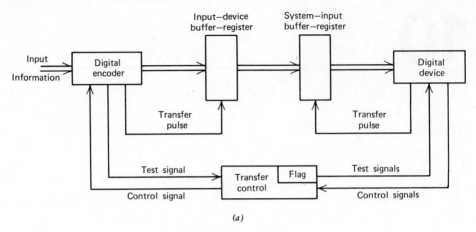

(a)

Input Interface

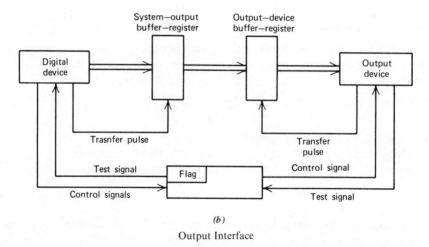

(b)

Output Interface

Figure 10-1. General form of parallel interface.

system can process hundreds of characters a second. If the digital device is to communicate effectively with the outside world through a typewriter, special techniques must be used to match the operating speed of the input/output device (the typewriter) to the operating speed of the digital device.

The problem of matching the operational characteristics of an input or output device to that of a digital processor is referred to as an *interface problem*. Two methods of handling the interface problem are shown in Figure 10-1. In this case it is assumed that information is transferred in parallel between the input or output device and the digital system. A similar type of interface using serial transfer of information could also be developed.

Input Interface

The input interface system shown in Figure 10-1*a* receives information from the outside world that may or may not be in digital form. The input information passes through the digital encoder, which transforms it into an appropriate digital form and then loads the information into the input-device buffer-register.

A special 1-bit register, called a *flag*, is present in the transfer control unit associated with the input device. Normally this flag has a value of 0. However, when the input signal is loaded into the input buffer-register, the flag is set to 1 to indicate that the input information is ready for transfer to the digital system.

As soon as the digital device is ready to receive information, it looks at the value of the flag. When it finds that the flag has a value of 1, it issues the control signals necessary to transfer the information from the device buffer-register to the system-input buffer-register. This transfer command also sets the flag bit to 0, which indicates to the input device that the next input signal can be prepared for transmission. Thus the digital device can control the number of input transfers that takes place but the rate of transfer is determined by the speed of the input device.

Output Interface

The output interface shown in Figure 10-1*b* operates in a manner similar to the input interface. Initially, before any output transfer has occurred, the flag in the output device is set to 1, indicating that it is ready to receive information. The information to be transferred to the output device is placed in the system-output buffer-register. As soon as the digital device detects the 1 value for the flag, a control signal is issued that causes the transfer of the information from the system-output buffer to the output-device buffer. At the same time the output flag is set to 0. When the output device sees that the flag is 0, it knows that it can use the information in the output-device buffer to generate an appropriate output (for example, print a character). As soon as this output operation has been completed, the output device resets the flag to 1 to indicate that it is ready to process the next output.

Here again we see that the number of transfers is controlled by the digital system but that the rate of transfer is governed by the speed with which the output device can process the data it finds in the output-device buffer.

Interface design depends on the type of information that must be transferred and the operating speeds of the two devices to be interconnected. The following examples illustrate some of the different forms an interface may take.

A Keyboard Input

The simplest type of input device is a switch. If we assume that we are using positive logic, then the arrangement shown in Figure 10-2*a* can be interpreted as generating

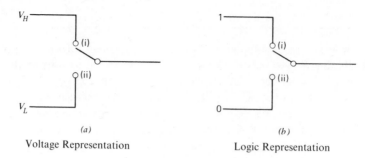

(a)

Voltage Representation

(b)

Logic Representation

Figure 10-2. Generation of a digital signal using a switch.

an input signal as shown in Figure 10-2b. When the switch is in position (i), it has an output value of 1. Similarly, it has an output of 0 when it is in position (ii).

The idea of a switch can be easily extended to a keyboard, such as the one illustrated in Figure 10-3. Each character on the keyboard is assigned a unique digital code, such as the EBCDIC code given in Appendix 1. When a key is pushed, a signal is applied to the decoding network that produces the 8-bit code associated with that key. We also assume that a transfer pulse is generated that can be used to control the transfer of information into a buffer-register. If we assume that the letter A is pressed, then a timing diagram showing the output of the decoder network might have the form shown in Figure 10-4.

Using this information, an input interface unit of the form shown in Figure 10-5 can be used with this input device. The input-device buffer is constructed from D flip-flops.

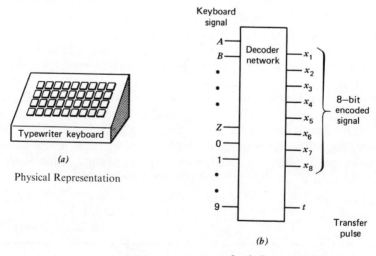

Figure 10-3. A keyboard input device.

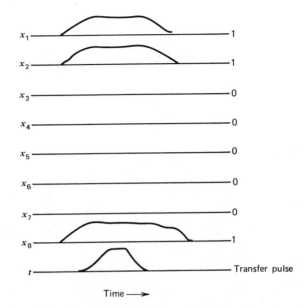

Figure 10-4. Timing diagram of a typical output of keyboard decoder network.

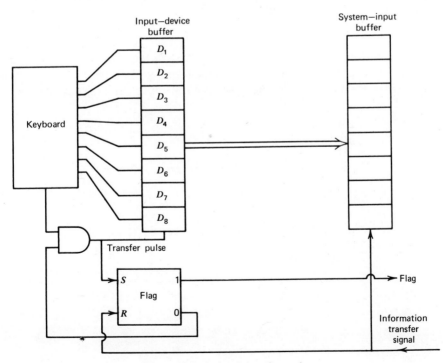

Figure 10-5. A simple interface unit.

Initially, assume that the flag is in the 0 state. When a key is pressed on the keyboard, an input transfer pulse is generated that is applied, through the AND gate, to the clock input on the input-device buffer. The code corresponding to the pressed key is loaded into the register and the flag, which is a simple unclocked S-R flip-flop, is set to 1. This prevents any other information from being loaded into the input-device buffer.

The digital system then observes that the flag has a value of 1 and knows that input information is ready for transmission to the system-input buffer. An information transfer signal is sent out by the digital system. The contents of the input-device buffer is then transferred into the system-input buffer, and the flag is reset to 0. This completes the information transfer sequence, and the next key on the keyboard can be pressed.

This whole transfer sequence usually occurs within, at most, a few milliseconds after the keyboard key is pushed. The person using the keyboard will probably take a tenth of a second or more to push the next key. Thus the user assumes that the system is accepting the keyboard information as fast as the keys can be pushed.

Printer/Punch Output

A common type of output produced by a digital system is a printed record or a punched card. This type of output is essentially the reverse of the input process just discussed. Figure 10-6 shows the form that a printing output device might take.

The code for the character to be printed is placed in the buffer-register. The printing operation is then started by applying a 1 to the start-print input of the printing unit. After the unit has completed the printing of the character, it emits a printing-complete pulse, which indicates that it is ready to print the next character.

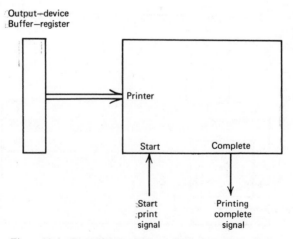

Figure 10-6. General organization of printing output device.

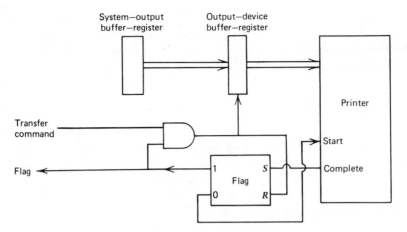

Figure 10-7. An output device interface.

A typical interface for this type of output device is shown in Figure 10-7. Initially the flag is set to 1 indicating that the printer is ready to receive data. The system-output information is placed in the system-output buffer-register. When the system detects that the flag is 1, it transmits a transfer command that transfers the information in the system-output buffer-register into the output-device buffer-register and sets the flag, again a simple unclocked S-R flip-flop, to 0. As soon as the flag goes to 0, the printer is commanded to print the character corresponding to the coded information contained in the output-device buffer-register. On completion of the printing operation the printer issues a printing-complete pulse that sets the flag to 1. This completes the printing cycle and the next character can be transmitted for printing.

These two examples illustrate how the interface problem can be solved in digital systems. Although we can add additional refinements to an interface unit to handle special problems, the basic behavior of any interface corresponds to the description we have just given. In the following chapters we learn how these concepts are employed in designing complete digital systems.

EXERCISES

1. Suppose that the digital device processing the information received from the keyboard interface takes 10^{-4} seconds to process the information. If the keyboard can only generate 10 characters per second how much time does the digital system spend waiting between inputs?

2. Redesign the interface system of Figure 10-7 if a serial information transfer must take place between the system-output buffer-register and the buffer-register of the printer. Assume that the buffer is an 8-bit register.

3. ANALOG/DIGITAL AND DIGITAL/ANALOG CONVERSION

Many of the signals processed by digital systems are initially in analog or continuous form. Thus before the system can operate on the signal, it must be converted into a digital encoded signal. Such a conversion is called *analog-to-digital* or *A/D Conversion*.

Similarly there are many instances where the output signal from a digital system must be converted into analog form before it can be used. Such a conversion is called *digital-to-analog* or *D/A Conversion*.

We have already briefly considered the problem of A/D and D/A conversion in Chapter 2. In the following discussions we investigate the way typical A/D and D/A converters are constructed.

D/A Converters

The digital-to-analog conversion process is the easiest to realize. Figure 10-8 illustrates the general structure of a D/A converter. It is assumed that the number to be converted is represented as a sign-magnitude binary fraction. This number is placed in the D/A buffer register. The content of this register is

$$[x_0, x_{-1}, x_{-2}, \ldots, x_{-n}]$$

where x_0 represents the sign bit (0 corresponds to plus and 1 to minus) and $x_{-1}, x_{-2}, \ldots, x_{-n}$ represents the magnitude ($.x_{-1}x_{-2} \cdots x_{-n}$) of the binary fraction. The output of each bit of the buffer register drives an electronic switch that connects an appropriate voltage to the resister network. The organization of the switches and the decoding network is shown in Figure 10-9 for $n = 4$ and an input of [01010].

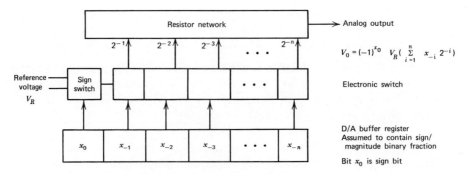

$$V_0 = (-1)^{x_0} \; V_R \left(\sum_{i=1}^{n} x_{-i} \, 2^{-i} \right)$$

Figure 10-8. General form of D/A converter.

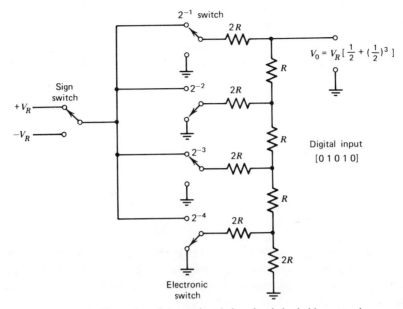

Figure 10-9. Illustration of electronic switch and resistive ladder network.

The resistor network shown in Figure 10-9 can be generalized for the case where the magnitude is represented by n bits. In this case the expression for the output voltage becomes*

$$V_0 = (-1)^{x_0} V_R \left(\sum_{i=1}^{n} x_{-i} 2^{-i} \right)$$

Conversion Rate

The settling time of a D/A converter is the time it takes for the output voltage to reach a steady value after the command is given to load the digital signal into the buffer register. Current D/A converters have settling times in the range of a few microseconds.

If we let t_s represent the settling time for a D/A converter, then the maximum conversion rate is

$$C_{max} = 1/t_s \text{ samples per second}$$

In many cases this conversion rate will be much faster than needed, and the operating conversion rate will depend on how fast the digital system delivers information to the D/A converter.

---

* This formula can be derived by using standard circuit theory analysis techniques. See the reference at the end of this chapter.

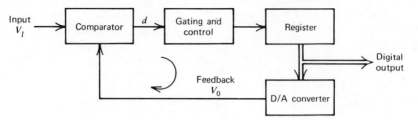

Figure 10-10. General form of A/D feedback converter.

A/D Converters

Analog-to-digital converters can take on a number of forms. The most popular types, and the one that we will discuss, are classified as feedback converters. They have the general form shown in Figure 10-10. This unit operates by generating a sequence of digital values in the register. The content of the register then drives the D/A converter network to produce an output analog voltage V_0. The voltage V_0 is compared to the input voltage V_I in the comparator, which produces an output signal

$$d = \begin{cases} 1 & V_0 \geq V_I \\ 0 & V_0 < V_I \end{cases}$$

Using this value of d, the gating and control network decides on the next value to be placed in the register. This sequence of operations continues until the gating and control network decides that the signal in the register is a satisfactory approximation to V_I.

Counter A/D Converters

The simplest way to realize a feedback A/D converter is to use the register as a counter and count up until a value is reached where $V_0 \geq V_I$. When this condition occurs, the number in the register is the digital approximation to V_I. Figure 10-11 shows the general form of this type of A/D converter. For illustrative purposes it is assumed that the input analog signal is always positive.

The counter is a standard binary counter with a clear input and an increment input. When a pulse is applied to the clear input, the counter is set to 0, and when a pulse appears on the increment input, the count increases by 1. Operation starts when a start pulse is applied to the start line. This clears the counter and sets the control flip-flop to the 1 state. As long as $V_0 < V_I$ the gate will allow the clock pulses to be applied to the increment input. Thus the counter will start to count up, which in turn increases the value of V_0. This operation continues until $V_0 \geq V_I$ at which time $d = 1$, the AND gate opens, and the control flip-flop is reset to 0 indicating that the conversion is complete. The digital value in the counter is the digital approximation to V_I.

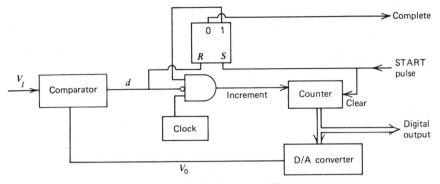

Figure 10-11. A simple counter A/D converter.

The conversion operation is illustrated in Figure 10-12. The time frame of operation has been exaggerated somewhat to show the details of operation. However, the figure does show the important characteristics of a counter A/D converter.

First we note that the value of the digital output will always equal or exceed the value of the input at the time the conversion is ended. Second we see that the conversion time is variable. The larger the magnitude of the signal, the larger the conversion time.

The speed of a counter A/D converter depends on the settling time τ of the D/A converter that generates V_0. If the magnitude of the signal is to be represented by n bits, then the conversion time t_c will fall in the range of

$$\tau \le t_c < 2^n\tau$$

For example, if $\tau = 2$ microseconds and $n = 10$, then t_c would fall in the range of

$$2 \text{ microseconds} \le t_c < 2048 \text{ microseconds}$$

For many applications the simplicity of operation of a counter A/D converter outweighs this wide variation in conversion time. However, for high-speed applications a different conversion method must be used to reduce conversion time.

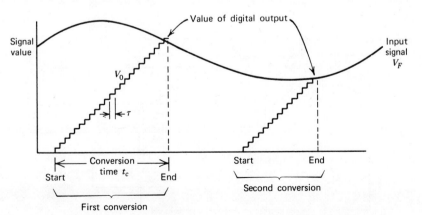

Figure 10-12. Illustration of the operation of a counter D/A converter.

Successive Approximation A/D Converters

In the successive approximation A/D converter we try to match the input signal by successively dividing the possible interval in which the input may fall into smaller and smaller size. To understand the operation of this converter, consider the 4-bit converter shown in Figure 10-13. The register together with the control logic makes up a sequential network. When the start signal is received, the register is driven to [1000]. The output of the D/A converter becomes $V_0 = (V_R/2)$. If

$$\frac{V_R}{2} \le V_I$$

then $d = 0$ and the next state of the register is [1100]; otherwise

$$\frac{V_R}{2} > V_I$$

which means $d = 1$ and the next state of the register becomes [0100]. Again V_0 is compared to V_I and if $V_0 \le V_I$, bit x_{-2} is not changed and x_{-3} is set to 1. Otherwise x_{-2} is set to 0 and x_{-3} is set to 1. The comparison then continues to the point where the values for x_{-3} and x_{-4} are fixed. A complete enumeration of all the possible testing sequences is illustrated by the transition diagram shown in Figure 10-14. Examining this diagram we see that if the converter register has n-bits, then exactly n-steps are needed to complete the conversion after the start signal is given.

The way in which a 4-bit successive approximation A/D converter would process an input signal is illustrated in Figure 10-15. Here we see that if the settling time

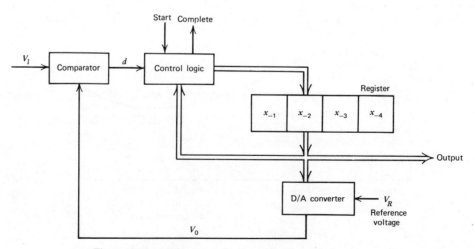

Figure 10-13. A 4-bit successive approximation A/D converter.

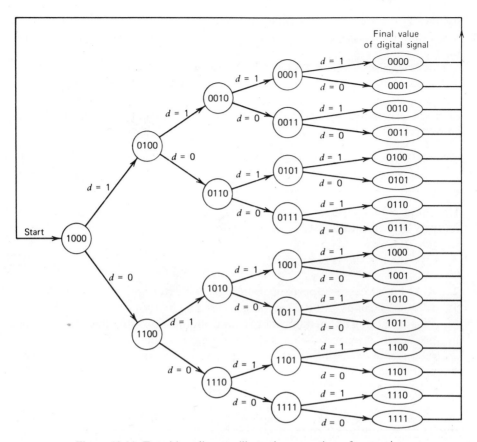

Figure 10-14. Transition diagram illustrating operation of successive approximation D/A converter.

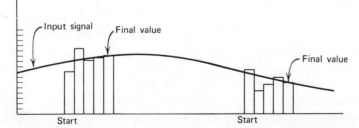

Figure 10-15. Illustration of conversion process for successive approximation A/D converter.

for the D/A converter is τ seconds and if the register has n-bits, then the total conversion time is always $(n + 1)\tau$ seconds independent of the magnitude of the input.

This brief discussion of A/D and D/A converters has introduced the common techniques employed by digital systems to interface digital and analog or continuous systems. The references listed at the end of this chapter give a much more extensive discussion of the organization, construction, and use of A/D and D/A converters.

EXERCISES

1. For an n-bit converter, what is the size of the maximum conversion error that may be introduced in an A/D conversion.
   (a) If a sign bit is present.
   (b) If a sign bit is not present.

2. A 12-bit successive approximation D/A converter with a settling time τ of 1.5 microseconds (1.5×10^{-6} seconds) is used as an output of a digital network. What is the maximum number of distinct output values that this converter may produce in a second? What is the maximum frequency sine wave that can be produced if we assume that we must produce 10 values per period (or cycle) of the sine wave?

4. MEMORY DEVICES

In computers and other digital systems there is often a need to store a large amount of information in a small space at a low cost. We have already seen that registers constructed from flip-flops can be used to store information. There are, however, many other ways in which information can be stored. This discussion introduces some of the different types of memory units that can be found in digital systems and indicates their general organization and operation.

Read-Only Memory

The simplest type of memory devices are *read-only memories* or, as they are usually referred to, *ROMs*. These memories store a fixed collection of information that is required by a digital system to perform a given task.

A read-only memory is used to represent a mapping from a set X to a set Y. This mapping can be represented by

$$Y := F(X)$$

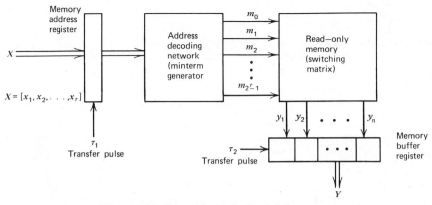

Figure 10-16. General form of a Read-Only memory.

where X is an r-bit input signal and Y is an n-bit output signal. The relationship between X and Y, given by the function F, can be described by a truth table.

As we know from our discussion in Chapter 7 we can realize any truth table by a multiple output switching network where there is a one-to-one correspondence between the rows of the truth table and the rows of the switching network. If we now provide a way to relate X and Y, we have realized a read-only memory (ROM).

Figure 10-16 illustrates the general structure of a ROM. Two registers, the memory address register (MAR) and the memory buffer register (MBR), serve to interface the ROM to the rest of the digital system. The operation of this unit can be described by the following two information transfer statements:

$$\tau_1: \text{MAR} \leftarrow X$$

$$\tau_2: \text{MBR} \leftarrow F(X)$$

From these statements, we see that X is first transferred into the MAR by applying the transfer pulse τ_1. The information in the MAR is decoded in the address decoding network to select the proper row of the switching matrix that makes up the read-only memory. When the second transfer pulse τ_2 is applied, assuming that the output of the switching matrix has reached a steady value, the value for $F(X)$ is transferred into the MBR, where it is now available for use by the rest of the system.

Each row of the switching matrix that makes up the ROM is referred to as a *word*. If the output Y has n-bits, then the ROM is said to be made up of *n-bit words*. The minterm associated with a given row is called the *address* of the row, or the address of the memory word associated with that row.

ROMs have become very important devices in digital system design because of their relative low cost, and the ease with which they can be used to carry out specialized tasks. The following example illustrates one such application.

Output Display Driver

In many digital systems we wish to display the output as a multiple digit decimal number. A common way to display a decimal digit is to use a seven-segment display that has the form shown in Figure 10-17a. When an activate signal (logical 1) is applied to one of the segments of the display, that segment glows. By using this result it is possible to form the digits 0 through 9, the letter E (to indicate an error), and the minus sign as shown in Figure 10-17b.

Each display has seven input leads. If we wish to display the digital value of a BCD encoded number, we can use a ROM as the decoding network. In this case, X is the 4-bit BCD encoded information and Y is the signal needed to activate the corresponding display pattern.

To design the ROM, we must first develop the truth table that describes the relationship F between the input X and the output Y. This is given by Table 10-1. Since there are 16 possible addresses associated with the 4-bit input and only 13 output characters (the 12 characters shown in 10-17b and a blank) to be displayed, we have arbitrarily decided to assign an output of E to all unused input values. This will indicate that an error has occurred if one of these inputs is ever generated by the system.

This table can be used to realize a ROM as shown in Figure 10-18. In this realization the memory buffer register is realized from D flip-flops. The switching matrix is the actual "memory." It has sixteen 7-bit words. Each word is accessed by activating (placing a 1) on the appropriate line. The output then appears on the output or *sense* lines.

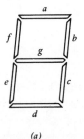

(a)

Segment Organization of Seven-Segment Display

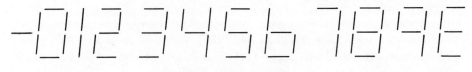

(b)

Character Representation

Figure 10-17. Seven-segment display.

Table 10-1   Programming of Seven-Segment Display Decoder

BCD Input X				Decoded Output Y							Display Output
d_3	d_2	d_1	d_0	a	b	c	d	e	f	g	
0	0	0	0	1	1	1	1	1	1	0	0
0	0	0	1	0	1	1	0	0	0	0	1
0	0	1	0	1	1	0	1	1	0	1	2
0	0	1	1	1	1	1	1	0	0	1	3
0	1	0	0	0	1	1	0	0	1	1	4
0	1	0	1	1	0	1	1	0	1	1	5
0	1	1	0	0	0	1	1	1	1	1	6
0	1	1	1	1	1	1	0	0	0	0	7
1	0	0	0	1	1	1	1	1	1	1	8
1	0	0	1	1	1	1	0	0	1	1	9
1	0	1	0	0	0	0	0	0	0	1	–
1	0	1	1	0	0	0	0	0	0	0	Blank
1	1	0	0	1	0	0	1	1	1	1	E
1	1	0	1	1	0	0	1	1	1	1	E
1	1	1	0	1	0	0	1	1	1	1	E
1	1	1	1	1	0	0	1	1	1	1	E

To illustrate the operation of this system, assume that the input X is [0101]. When τ_1 is applied, X is loaded into the MAR. The decimal value of X is 5. Thus the value we are interested in is in memory word 5. As soon as X is loaded, the address decoding network activates line m_5 and the output [1011011] appears on the output sense lines of the switching matrix. The transfer pulse τ_2 transfers this output into the MBR. Finally the display uses the output of the MBR to form the digit 5 on the display.

Read-only memories come in a number of different forms. The simplest consists of semiconductor arrays in which the 0-bits in a word are realized by actually "burning out" the connection associated with that element. ROMs of this type cannot be changed after they are programmed. If a change in the contents of such a ROM must be made, a completely new ROM must be produced.

To overcome this problem a special class of ROMs have been developed called *Programmable Read-Only Memories* called PROMs. Instead of "burning" out a connection in a PROM we electronically alter the connections in the switching

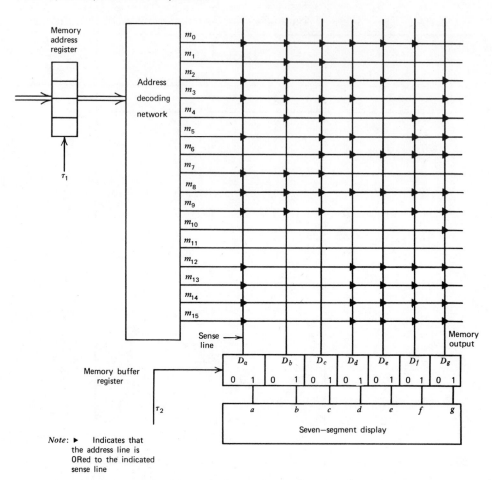

Figure 10-18. Read-Only memory realization of seven-segment decoder.

matrix by applying special conditioning signals that are much different than the normal operating signals. Once the PROM is programmed, it acts just like a ROM. PROMS can be reprogrammed without destroying the memory.

Read/Write Memories

If we wish to be able to dynamically change the information stored in a given memory location, we must use some type of register. Figure 10-19 illustrates a simple arrangement for introducing registers as the information storage element.

Here each memory register is formed from n D flip-flops. If we wish to place information into the ith memory register, we use τ_1 to place the binary number

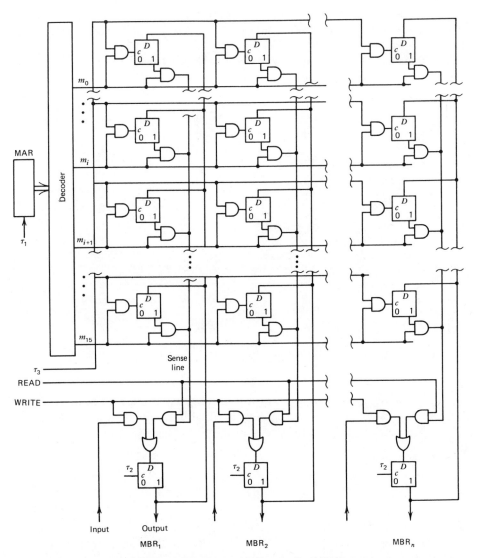

Figure 10-19. A possible organization of a Read/Write memory.

corresponding to i in the MAR. The ith minterm m_i goes to 1, which selects the ith memory register. Since we are going to write information into memory we place a 1 on the write line and transfer the information which is to be written into memory into the MBR by applying a transfer pulse τ_2. Finally we apply the pulse τ_3 which causes the contents of the MBR to be written into memory word i.

To read information out of the ith memory word we first use τ_1 to place the address of the word into the MAR. The decoder then sets m_i to 1 which connects the output lines to the sense lines. A one is placed on the Read input and then the transfer pulse τ_2 is used to read the information on the sense line into the MBR.

For this particular arrangement the contents of the ith word is not changed. Since the contents of the memory word is not changed, this type of read operation is called a *nondestructive read*.

The sequence of operations can be characterized by the following sequence of information transfer operations.

Write Operations
$$WRITE = 1 \qquad READ = 0$$

Transfer Pulse	Transfer
$\tau_1, \tau_2:$	MAR $\leftarrow \langle$address$\rangle$, MBR $\leftarrow \langle$input information$\rangle$
$\tau_3:$	$M_{[MAR]} \leftarrow$ MBR

Read Operation
$$WRITE = 0 \qquad READ = 1$$

Transfer Pulse	Transfer
$\tau_1:$	MAR $\leftarrow \langle$address$\rangle$
$\tau_2:$	MBR $\leftarrow M_{[MAR]}$

The notation $M_{[MAR]}$ is used to indicate the memory word indicated by the contents [MAR] of the memory address register while $\langle$address$\rangle$ and $\langle$input information$\rangle$ are used to indicate external information supplied to the system.

Random Access Memories (RAM)

Read/write memories are called *random access memories* or RAMs, since each memory register is directly accessible by placing its address in the MAR. Several different technologies can be used to construct RAMs. Figure 10-20 illustrates the general representation that can be used to describe the external operation of a RAM.

The memory portion of a RAM can be realized in a number of different ways. Two main classes of memory elements exist; semiconductor memories and magnetic core memories. The RAM illustrated in Figure 10-19 is representative of a semiconductor memory. These memories are available as LSI integrated circuits. A typical LSI semiconductor memory will be made up of two or three separate modules. One module will be used to implement the MAR; another will implement the MBR; and a third module will be the actual memory together with the address decoder and control circuitry.

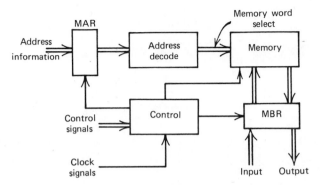

Figure 10-20. General representation of RAM organization.

Semiconductor memories are realized using semiconductor devices similar to those used to realize flip-flops. They have the advantage of high operating speeds and relatively low cost. Their main disadvantage is that once the power supply voltage is removed the information stored in memory is lost. Such a memory is called a *volatile* memory.

A second class of memory device is the *magnetic core memory*. Before modern integrated circuit technology lowered the cost of semiconductor memory, core memory was the dominant memory technology. Magnetic core memory tends to be slower than semiconductor memory and more expensive. It does, however, have the important feature that the contents of memory is not destroyed when the system's power supply is turned off. Thus it is a *nonvolatile* memory.

Magnetic Cores*

A core is a small, donut-shaped element of magnetic material, generally ferrite, that is capable of assuming one of two magnetized states. Figure 10-21 illustrates the general form of a core. The three wires that pass through the core's center are used to obtain information about the magnetization status of the core or to change its status.

In any magnetic core the total flux (the quantity that describes the magnetization of the core) is dependent on the magnitude and direction of the total current in the lines associated with the core. This relationship is given by a hysteresis loop of the form shown in Figure 10-22. When no current is present in the control lines, the core

---

* The discussion in this section assumes that the reader has some familiarity with magnetic field theory. Readers unfamiliar with this material should concentrate on the general ideas of how information is loaded into, stored, and read out of a core and not worry about understanding the details of the physics involved.

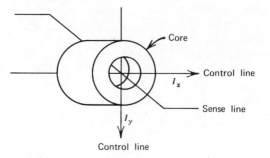

Figure 10-21. Illustration of a magnetic core.

will be either at point *a* corresponding to the 1 state of the core or point *b* corresponding to the 0 state of the core. As long as no current flows, the magnetization of the core will not change.

Now let us assume that the core is initially in the 0 state and a net positive current $I_x + I_y > I_m$ is applied. When this happens the magnetization of the core follows the hysteresis curve from point *b* to point *c* and stays at point *c* until the current $I_x + I_y$ is removed. At that time the magnetization of the core goes from *c* to *a* and the core takes on the magnetization state we associate with a 1. If another positive input current is applied the magnetization would move back to point *c* until the current was removed and then it would return to point *a*. From this we see that if the core is in the zero state a net positive current of magnitude $I_x + I_y > I_m$ will set the core to a 1 state. On the other hand if $I_x + I_y < I_m$ there will not be enough magnetization force to change the state of the core and the core will remain in the 0 state after the current is removed.

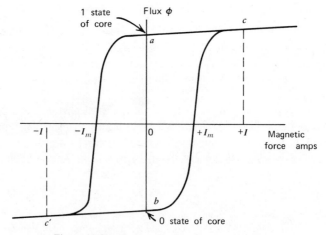

Figure 10-22. Hysteresis loop of a magnetic core.

A similar situation occurs when the core is in the 1 state and a net negative current $-I_x - I_y$ is applied. The core will be set to the 0 state if $-I_x - I_y < -I_m$, otherwise it will remain in the 1 state.

To obtain information about the current state of the core we must make use of the law

$$e = -K \frac{d\phi}{dt}$$

This law says that a voltage is induced in any wire running through the core and that this voltage is proportional to the rate of change of the core flux with respect to time. In particular, this voltage will be induced in the sense line. For example, if we are in the 1 state and a net current of $-I$ is applied we would get a large pulse of voltage as the core changed states because of the rapid change of flux as we go from a to c' to b in the hysteresis loop. However, if we are initially in the 0 state we would only get a small output voltage if we applied a net current of $-I$. This is because there is only a small change in flux as we go from b to c' and back to b.

The above discussion has demonstrated two interesting properties of a core as a storage element. First, we note that if we wish to determine what information is stored in the core we must destroy this information as we read it out of the core. Because of this we say that core storage is a *destructive readout memory device*. Second, we note that if we have two control lines it is the sum of the currents that flow in the control lines that determines if the core changes state or not. For example, assume that the core is in the 0 state. If $I_m/2 < I_x < I_m$ and $I_y = 0$ or if $I_m/2 < I_y < I_m$ and $I_x = 0$ there will be no change in the magnetization of the core. However, if $I_m/2 < I_x, I_y < I_m$ then the net current $I_y = I_x + I_y$ will exceed I_m and there will be a change in state from 0 to 1 when the current is applied.

To overcome the destructive readout problem we introduce the idea of a *read* and a *write* cycle. During the read cycle we find out the state of the core by applying a net current pulse $-I$. If we observe a large output voltage pulse on the sense line we say that the output is 1; otherwise, the output is zero. We also observe that after the read pulse is applied the core is in the zero state. Thus if we wish to retain the information that we just read out of the core we must reset the core to the state that was present before the read pulse was applied. To do this we must apply a net write current pulse $+I$ if we wish to store a value of 1 in the core and no pulse if we wish to store 0 in the core.

Core Memory Systems

Since the technique for reading information in or out of a core is much different than that used for a semiconductor flip-flop, a core memory system has a different organization than a semiconductor memory. The general organization of a core memory is shown in Figure 10-23. The words in a core memory are arranged something like a collection of post office boxes. Each word contains n-bits and the

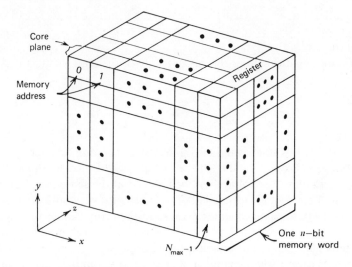

Figure 10-23. Basic organization of a random access memory.

address of each word is indicated by a number between 0 and $N_{max} - 1$ where N_{max} is the number of words in memory. Usually N_{max} is a power of 2. For example, many small computers have $N_{max} = 2^{12} = 4096$ words of memory.

To locate a given word in memory we must give its x and y coordinates. All of the cores that correspond to the jth bit of a word are said to fall on the jth core plane. We first consider how information can be read into or written from a core plane. Then we show how a collection of core planes can be used to form a complete core memory.

Figure 10-24 illustrates the basic control signals necessary to operate a core memory system.

To read a word from memory we place the address of the word in the memory address register. When a read command is received, the word stored in the location

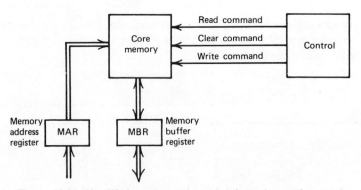

Figure 10-24. Simplified representation of information and control signals in a core memory.

specified by the memory address register is transferred to the memory buffer register. This automatically sets all bits of that memory word to zero. If we wish to retain this information in memory we must then give a write command that will cause the information in the memory buffer register to be rewritten into memory at the proper location.

If a word is to be written into memory, it is placed in the MBR and the address at which the word is to be stored is placed in the MAR. Before we write the information into memory, a clear command must be given to clear the old information out of the selected memory word. Next a write command is given that transfers the information in the MBR into the selected memory word.

Each bit in a core memory is stored in a unique core. Thus it becomes very important that we develop an efficient way to interrogate each core in the memory. One way to do this is to use *coincident current selection*.

Coincident Current Selection of Memory Location

To introduce the idea of coincident current selection we use the simple 16-core core-plane array shown in Figure 10-25 and show how we can individually interrogate any one of the 16 cores. If we examine this figure we see that each core encloses a unique x and a unique y control line. For example, core 5 encloses the pair of lines x_1, y_1.

Let us assume that core 5 is in the 0 state and we wish to set it to the 1 state. We can do this by placing a current of $I/2$ amps on both line x_1 and line y_1. The net current flowing through core 5 will be $I/2 + I/2 = I$ amps. If $I > I_m$ the core will be set to a 1. We also note that the current flowing through cores 4, 6, 7, and 1, 9, 13 will be $I/2 < I_m$ so that these cores will not change state. Thus we have selected core 5 to receive a 1 and all of the other cores are unchanged.

If we examine Figure 10-25, we see all the other cores can be selected in a similar manner if the proper control lines are excited by the decoding logic network selectors.

Information can be read out of a core by a similar technique. Again assume that we are dealing with core 5 and we wish to find out what is stored in this core. This time we send a current pulse of $-I/2$ amps along the x_1 and y_1 lines. If core 5 is in the 1 state it will be switched to the 0 state and an output pulse will be induced in the sense line. This pulse will be sensed by the sense/inhibit unit and the one bit memory buffer register will be set to the 1 state. If core 5 is in the 0 state no pulse will be generated. For this case the memory buffer is set to 0.

The writing of information into a core is usually handled in a somewhat different manner than just described. The information to be written into a core, say core 5, is loaded into the memory buffer register. If the contents of this register is 1, then core 5 is set to 1 by the current pulses of $I/2$ amps applied to the x_1 and y_1 lines. However, if the contents of the register is 0 an additional current pulse of $I/2$ is sent along the sense line. Because of the way the sense line is wound this pulse of

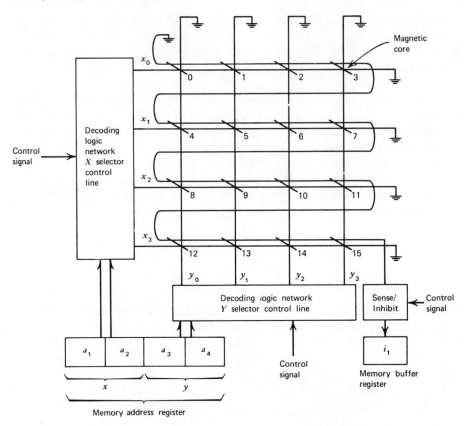

Figure 10-25. Coincident current selection of individual cores.

$I/2$ amps creates a magnetic force that cancels out the $I/2$ amp current pulse on the x_1 line. Thus the net magnetic force acting on core 5 is $I/2 + I/2 - I/2 = I/2$ which is too small to set the core to the 1 state. This inhibiting current causes the core to remain in the 0 state. In most coincident current memories a separate inhibit line is used. This simplifies the operation of the memory unit.

The address of the core being acted on is indicated by the contents of the memory address register. This register can be thought of as being partitioned into two equal subregisters which indicate the X select and Y select lines respectively. Line x_j will be selected if the binary equivalent of j is contained in the X subregister and y_k will be selected if the binary equivalent of k is contained in the Y subregister. Thus if core 5 is to be selected, the memory buffer register would contain 0101 corresponding to x_1, y_1. Similarly if the register contained 1100, core 12 would be selected since lines x_3, y_0 would be the two control lines activated.

The actual decision to read information from a given core or to write information into it is determined by an external control unit. The control unit sends control signals to all the appropriate parts of the memory system and these signals are used

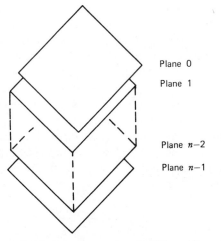

Plane 0

Plane 1

Plane $n-2$

Plane $n-1$

Figure 10-26. Core plane arrangement for n-bit words.

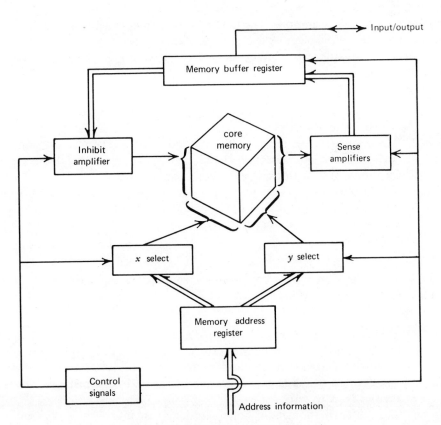

Figure 10-27. Block diagram of memory unit.

to send the current pulses in the proper direction along the lines selected by the memory address register.

Each memory plane of the form shown in Figure 10-25 contains one core corresponding to each possible memory address. If we wish to store an n-bit word in a memory, we must use n memory planes arranged as shown in Figure 10-26.

Suppose that we wish to construct a memory with $4096 = 2^{12}$ 16-bit words. Then each plane would contain 4096 cores arranged in a 64 by 64 array and there would be 16 planes. The memory address register would be a 12-bit register. The first 6 bits would serve to select the proper X control line and the last 6 bits would select the Y control line. The memory buffer register would contain 16 bits. A general block diagram indicating the general arrangement of this memory unit is shown in Figure 10-27.

The Complete Memory Cycle

To read information from or write information into a core memory requires a specific sequence of operations. The time necessary to complete this sequence of operations is called the memory cycle time of the core memory.

To read information from the memory the following sequence of operations must take place.

Step 1 The address of the core memory location to be read is placed in the memory address register.

Step 2 The content of the memory location indicated by the memory address register is read into the memory buffer register. The content of this memory location is 0 since the read operation is destructive.

Step 3 The content of the memory buffer register is rewritten back into the memory location indicated by the memory address register. In addition, the content of the memory buffer register can be used to set other registers in the system.

To write information into the core memory from an external device, the following sequence of operations must take place.

Step 1 The address of the memory location that is to receive information is placed in the memory address register. The information to be written into core memory is placed in the memory buffer register.

Step 2 The content of the memory location indicated by the memory address register is set to zero.

Step 3 The content of the memory buffer register is read into the memory location indicated by the memory address register.

Memory Terminology

Memories can take on a wide range of forms. The three most critical parameters are word size, memory size, and memory cycle time. The word size depends on the particular application. Microcomputers have a word size of 4, 8, and 16 bits. Most minicomputers have a word size of 16 bits although some have a word size of 12 bits or even 32 bits. Larger computers usually have larger word sizes. Some typical sizes are 32, 48, 64, or 128 bits.

The number of words in a memory is usually measured as a multiple of $1024 = 2^{10}$, which is denoted by K. A $4K$ memory is a memory with $4 \times 1024 = 4096$ words while a $64K$ memory has $64 \times 1024 = 65,536$ words.

If numerical information is to be stored in a computer word, it is desirable to have the largest word possible consistent with other system requirements. However, if character information is to be stored, it is now common practice to represent characters by an 8-bit code, such as the modified ASCII or EBCDIC codes. The number of bits needed to store one character is referred to as a *byte*. Some manufacturers now specify the memory size of their computers in bytes rather than words. Thus a minicomputer with a 16-bit word size might have a $4K$ memory if we talk about the number of words in memory, or an $8K$ memory if we consider the number of bytes that can be stored in memory.

The memory cycle time is the time necessary to read information from memory or write information into memory. Core memories tend to be slower than semiconductor memories. Current memory technology can easily produce core memories with memory cycle times in the order of 300 nanoseconds to 1 microsecond. Some semiconductor memories operate at cycle times of the order of 50 nanoseconds to 250 nanoseconds.

This discussion of the basic characteristics of different memories is sufficient for our current needs. We have concentrated on the properties that are needed to understand how a memory operates as a system element. The references at the end of this chapter present a much more extensive discussion of memory technology.

EXERCISES

1. Which core will be selected in Figure 10-25 if the address is 1011?

2. Modify the switching array of Figure 10-18 so that the following input/output pairs are realized

Input	Output Character	Segments
1101	$\square$	a, b, g, f
1110	Γ	a, f
1111	—	d

5. SUMMARY

This chapter has introduced several basic digital system elements which are needed to construct large-scale digital systems. Now that we have an understanding of the operation of these devices, our next task is to investigate how we can use them, along with the concepts presented in the preceding chapters, to design complete information processing systems and computers. We undertake this task in the next chapter.

REFERENCE NOTATION

The general problem of interfacing digital systems is discussed in [3] and [4]. Reference [5] contains a number of articles that deal with interfacing and memory elements and their applications. Reference [2] provides a detailed discussion of the physical properties of memories, and [1] is a very extensive discussion of the design and use of A/D and D/A converters.

REFERENCES

1. Hoeschele, D. F., Jr. (1968), *Analog-to-Digital. Digital-to-Analog Conversion Techniques*, John Wiley, New York.

2. Poppelbaum, W. J. (1972), *Computer Hardware Theory*, McGraw-Hill, New York.

3. Sloan, M. E. (1976), *Computer Hardware and Organization*, SRA, Chicago.

4. Soucek, B. (1976), *Microprocessors and Microcomputers*, John Wiley, New York.

5. Stone, H. S. (ed.) (1975), *Introduction to Computer Architecture*, SRA, Chicago.

HOME PROBLEMS

1. As shown in Figure HP10-1, three keyboards are available for people to send information to a computer system. Design, at the register level, a bus system and a control unit that will allow information to be transmitted to the computer as soon as a flag is raised by any keyboard. The control unit should select the keyboard signal that is to be transmitted. How will the control unit operate if more than one flag is up at any given time? How will the computer know which keyboard generated the input information?

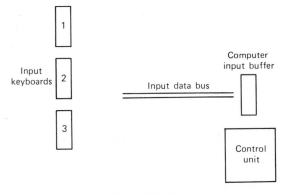

Figure HP10-1

2. Because of the large operating speed difference between $I/0$ devices and digital-systems, local buffer-memories are often built into the $I/0$ devices. One such arrangement is shown in Figure HP10-2 for a line printer.

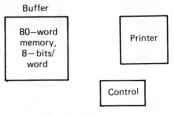

Figure HP10-2

The digital system deposits one line of characters (80 characters including blanks) into the buffer memory at a very high speed. The system then gives a command to the controller to send these 80 characters to the printer. When the printing is completed, the controller informs the system that it is ready to print the next 80 characters. Complete the register level design of this system.

3. An A/D converter is being used to convert the signal

$$g(t) = 1 - \sin(\omega t) \qquad \omega = 2\pi f$$

into digital form. If we are to preserve the general shape of $g(t)$, we should take at least 10 samples for each period of $g(t)$. For example, if the frequency f is 10 kHz (10^4 cycles per second) then we should sample $g(t)$ every

$$T = \frac{1}{10f} = 10^{-5} \text{ seconds} = 10 \text{ microseconds}$$

Assume that 25 values of $g(t)$ are to be obtained for $f = 10$ kHz.
(a) Plot the sampled values of $g(t)$. Compare the resulting waveform with the input signal.
(b) By mistake the input to the A/D converter had a value of $f = 55$ kHz. Plot the values of $g(t)$ and comment on the results.
(c) Assume that f was 110 kHz. Plot the value of $g(t)$ and comment on the results.

4. Four 256-word LSI RAM's are available. Each RAM has 8 address bits. Show how these four RAM's can be used to construct a 1024-word RAM.

5. A magnetic core memory has 256 12-bit words. We wish to design a special system that has three signals which determine how the information is to be written into memory. The following tasks must be performed:

Write Command

W_0	$M_{[MAR]} \leftarrow 0$
W_1	$M_{[MAR]} \leftarrow$ MBR
W_2	$M_{[MAR]} \leftarrow \overline{\text{MBR}} + [1]$
W_3	$M_{[MAR]} \leftarrow \overline{\text{MBR}} + [1]$ (i.e., 2's complement)

Design, at the register level, this special memory system.

11

Digital System Representation and Design

Our discussion in the previous chapters has concentrated on the various ways in which logic and sequential networks can be constructed and how they can be used to process various types of information. We have also investigated the techniques that can be used to represent information in digital form and we have considered some of the typical operations that can be performed upon this information. These investigations have concentrated on what might be considered the microscopic or circuit level behavior of digital systems.

In this chapter we begin our investigation of the macroscopic behavior of digital systems. In particular we concentrate on the problem of how registers and sequential networks can be interconnected to carry out complex information processing tasks. Thus our main interest is directed toward the flow of information, control of information, and transformation of information rather than on the details of how the circuits that perform these tasks are constructed. We assume that we can always, if necessary, use the techniques of the previous chapters to design these circuits.

To describe the systems we expand on the information transfer notation first presented in Chapter 4 so that we can represent the sequencing of the information transfer and processing tasks necessary to carry out a complex multiple-step computation. This notation will allow us to develop a "hardware program" that describes the operation of each system we investigate. In fact, by the end of this chapter the very strong similarity between hardware design and software design will be clear.

2. BASIC MODEL
OF A DIGITAL SYSTEM

Although digital systems take on a variety of forms, we can always reduce system design to two major units or tasks as shown in Figure 11-1. This figure shows that we must distinguish two very important and related tasks in the design of any digital system.

First, we note that any system must have an information processing unit that carries out the basic information processing tasks performed by the system. The structure of the information processing unit defines the operations that may be performed on the data being processed by the system and how the data is transferred between the various registers that are part of the unit. By itself the information processing unit cannot perform any computation.

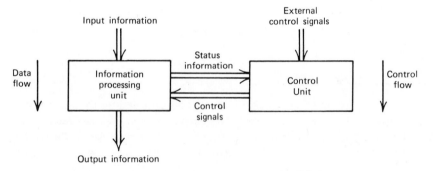

Figure 11-1. General structural components of a digital system.

To carry out a computation, a sequence of operations must be performed on the data. Although the information processing unit contains the necessary hardware to perform these operations, the sequence in which these operations are to be performed is determined by the control unit. As each step in the computation is reached, the control unit sends the appropriate control signals and transfer pulses to the information processing unit indicating that a given set of operations are to be performed. When these operations are complete, the control unit then goes to the next processing step. Sometimes this next step depends on the current status of the information being processed by the information processing unit. Thus the control unit also receives status information from the information processing unit that it can use to guide the computational sequence being performed.

In this section we illustrate how a number of typical information processing systems are described using our register transfer notation. We then show how these systems can be reduced to their equivalent logic circuit representation.

The Basic Tasks

There are three basic types of information processing tasks that are performed by the information processing units. They are:

(a) Information transfer
(b) Operations
(c) Decisions

Information transfer occurs when information is transmitted to a register from outside of the system or when information is moved from register-to-register. When the form of the information must be modified or when two or more items of information must be combined, then we use one of the predefined operations built into the system. Both of these actions can be initiated by the receipt of a control signal commanding that the action take place.

Both transfers and operations are performed internally in the information processing unit. At many points in a computation, the next step will depend on the status of one or more data elements. To report on this status, we must be able to carry out a test that involves one or more data elements and must transmit, through the status information signal, the results of the test to the control unit. Usually these tests are reported as a logical value of 1 if the condition is TRUE or as 0 if the condition is FALSE.

We have already discussed the detailed techniques that can be used to design the digital modules necessary to carry out each of these tasks. Our attention now is directed to the problem of designing complex digital systems by making use of these modules. To do this, we use the following notational conventions.

Information Transfer

For design purposes we assume that transfer operations can be represented as illustrated in Figure 11-2. The control signal T will determine how the information contained in the input signal is to be transferred to the output. It is assumed that

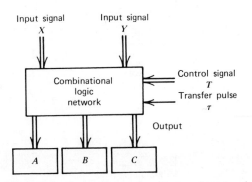

Figure 11-2. Typical representation of a transfer network.

Table 11-1   Specification Table for the Network of Figure 11-2

Control Signal	t_0	t_1	t_2	t_3	t_4
Action (when transfer pulse τ is applied)	No operation	$A \leftarrow X$ $C \leftarrow Y$	$A \leftarrow X$ $B \leftarrow X$ $C \leftarrow Y$	$A \leftarrow Y$ $B \leftarrow X$	$C \leftarrow X$

the values of all the input and control signals are set before the transfer pulse τ occurs. When the transfer pulse occurs, the designed transfer takes place and the input and control signals can change values to prepare for the next transfer pulse.

For convenience we will let the control signal T take on values from a set $\{t_0, t_1, \ldots, t_r\}$ where each distinct value is assumed to represent a particular operation. The actual digital coding of these signals is unimportant at this level of design.

We could use a set of mixed-mode expressions to describe the transfer operations. However, it is often less confusing if we use a *specification table* to describe the properties of a network. Table 11-1 illustrates how the behavior of the network shown in Figure 11-2 could be represented by using a specification table. Each column of the table corresponds to one of the distinct values of the control signal and indicates the transfer operation called for by that signal. The contents of all registers not referenced in the description are assumed to remain unchanged.

As long as we are only interested in the external behavior of a module, the specification table gives us enough information to carry out a system design. When we must design the module, the specification table can be used to write the logic expressions necessary to specify the module's logic level design.

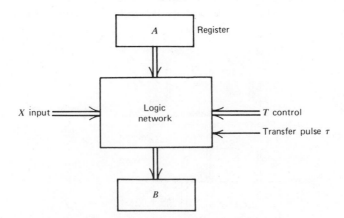

Figure 11-3. An operation network.

Operations

Operations can be performed on information as it passes through the information processing unit. For example, consider the situation illustrated in Figure 11-3. In this case the input signal X and the information in A are combined to produce a result that is placed in the register B. The specification table for the network shown in Figure 11-3 is given by Table 11-2.

Table 11-2

Specification Table for Network Shown in Figure 11-3

Control Signal	t_0	t_1	t_2	t_3
Operation	No operation	$B \leftarrow X + A$	$B \leftarrow X - A$	$B \leftarrow X$

There is no reason why the A and B registers must be distinct registers. For example, consider the network shown in Figure 11-4. In this example the output of the A register is the input to the logic network. This represents no problem, however, since the output of the A register remains constant until the pulse τ goes to 0. At that time the output of the A register goes to the new values, and the next value to be transferred into the A register can be formed.

The operation of this network might be represented by a specification table like Table 11-3.

The network of Figure 11-4 can easily be realized by using standard logic circuits.

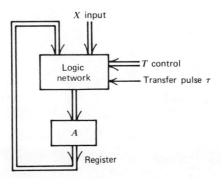

Figure 11-4. Operation network with feedback.

Table 11-3   Specification Table for Network of Figure 11-4

Control Signal	t_0	t_1	t_2	t_3
Operation	No operation	$A \leftarrow X + A$	$A \leftarrow X - A$	$A \leftarrow X$

Decisions

In all but the simplest computations, it is necessary to have the ability to alter the computation sequence by carrying out tests to indicate the current status of the data being processed. This testing process generates the status information that is transmitted to the control unit. The control unit evaluates this information before deciding on the next step in the calculation.

A typical network that generates a status signal is shown in Figure 11-5.

Let us assume that the control signal T has a value from the set $\{t_0, t_1, t_2, t_3\}$ and that the status signal S has a value from the set $\{s_1, s_2, s_3\}$. The behavior of networks of this type are governed by the following rules.

1. The status signal S is not a function of the control signal T.
2. The control unit may use the current value of the status signal S in determining the current value of the control signal T.
3. The information transfer pulse τ is applied only when the control unit has had enough time to generate the proper control signal T after receiving the current value of the status signal S.

When a network generates a status signal, we must specify the conditions that determine the various values of the status signal as well as the actions taken by the network in response to the control signal T. However, any relation between the value of S and the resulting value of T is completely determined by the control unit. Thus the specification table must contain two parts to describe the behavior of the

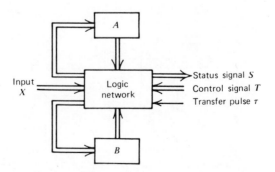

Figure 11-5. An operational network with a status signal S.

Table 11-4　　　　　　　Specification Table for Network of Figure 11-5

Control Signal

Control Signal T	t_0	t_1	t_2	t_3
Operation	No operation	$A \leftarrow X + A$ $B \leftarrow A$	$A \leftarrow X$ $B \leftarrow A + B$	$A \leftarrow [0]$ $B \leftarrow X$

Status Signal

Condition	Status Signal S
$A = B$	s_1
$A < B$	s_2
$A > B$	s_3

network. The first part is used to indicate the response of the network to the different control signals, while the second part indicates the conditions that give rise to the different values of the status signal.

For example, the behavior of the network shown in Figure 11-5 might have a specification table of the form given by Table 11-4.

To emphasize the fact that the status information is independent of the control signal, we can redraw the network shown in Figure 11-5 as shown in Figure 11-6. Note that two combinational logic networks are used. One network computes the value of the status signal while the other network computes the new values for the A and B registers. Observing this organization, we see that the complete system can easily be represented by standard logic circuits.

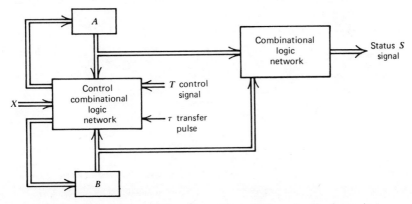

Figure 11-6. An expanded representation of the network shown in Figure 11-7.

The Control Unit

The control unit can take on several different forms. At this point we are interested only in its general behavior with respect to the behavior of the information processing unit. Thus we concentrate on the tasks that the unit must carry out, and will discuss the design of a control unit later.

From a somewhat simplistic viewpoint a simple control unit can be represented as shown in Figure 11-7. The state $Q(t)$ of the control unit at any given time t corresponds to the contents of the control register. The state of this register can change only when a clock-pulse τ occurs. The next state of the register after the application of τ depends on the type of flip-flops that are used to construct the register and the value of $G(t)$. If we assume that the flip-flops are of the master-slave type, then the next state of the register occurs only after the pulse τ goes to zero.

The combinational logic network has the current status information $S(t)$ from the information processing units and the current state information $Q(t)$ as an input. This input information is in the form of signal levels and immediately generates the output control signal $T(t) := F_T(S(t), Q(t))$ and the next-state signal $G(t) := F_G(S(t), Q(t))$. Both of these signals are assumed to have the desired values before the pulse τ occurs.

Since τ is the same pulse signal that is applied to the transfer pulse input of the information processing units, we see that the tasks specified by the control signal $T(t)$ are carried out at the same time that the control unit goes to its next state. Similarly we note that the current status information $S(t)$ influences both the current control signal which is applied to the information processing units and the next state of the control unit.

The computation performed by a complete digital system involves a sequence of steps, each step consisting of executing one or more of the operations or information transfers present in the information processing unit. It is the responsibility of the control unit to make certain that each step is executed properly. The design of the control unit can thus be thought of as the development of the "hardware" program necessary to carry out the desired computation. In the next section we investigate how this is accomplished.

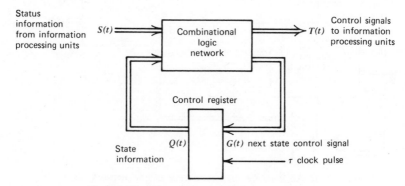

Figure 11-7. General form of a simple control unit.

EXERCISES

1. Give the assignment statements which describe the behavior of the networks shown in Figure 11-2 and Figure 11-3.

2. Give the assignment statements that describe the behavior of the network shown in Figure 11-5 and the specification statement that describes the status signal S.

3. THE COMPUTATION PROCESS

Any but the most trivial computational task requires a number of distinct steps. If we are working with a digital system, we will have a set of basic operations that are defined by the structure of the information processing unit. To carry out a computation, we must design an algorithm, using these basic operations, that describes the exact sequence of steps necessary to perform the computation. Using this algorithm, we then specify the properties of the control unit.

In this section we explore the techniques that can be used to describe such an algorithm. These results will be used in the next section to discuss how a complete digital system can be designed.

Sequential Operation

As an introductory example, consider the digital system shown in Figure 11-8. When the pulse τ is applied, the sum $A + B$ is transferred into register A.

If we are to carry out a multiple-step computation we must know the exact time that each operation or transfer takes place. To indicate that a particular task was

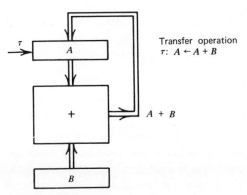

Figure 11-8. Forming the sum of the two quantities.

performed when the ith pulse occurred, we use the following symbolic representation

Transfer Pulse	Information Transfer
τ_i:	$A \leftarrow A + B$

Now suppose that we wish to use the network of Figure 11-8 to add B to itself five times. This would be indicated as

$$\tau_1 : A \leftarrow A + B$$
$$\tau_2 : A \leftarrow A + B$$
$$\tau_3 : A \leftarrow A + B$$
$$\tau_4 : A \leftarrow A + B$$
$$\tau_5 : A \leftarrow A + B$$

which indicates that five transfers are required to carry out this task. To illustrate the performance of this system, assume that A and B are both 3-bit registers with A initially set at $[0, 0, 0]$ and B set at $[0, 1, 0]$. The sequence above would then become

$$\tau_1 : A \leftarrow [0, 0, 0] + [0, 1, 0]$$
$$\tau_2 : A \leftarrow [0, 1, 0] + [0, 1, 0]$$
$$\tau_3 : A \leftarrow [1, 0, 0] + [0, 1, 0]$$
$$\tau_4 : A \leftarrow [1, 1, 0] + [0, 1, 0]$$
$$\tau_5 : A \leftarrow [0, 0, 0] + [0, 1, 0]$$

Note that, since the size of A is limited to 3-bits, we are actually performing our addition operation modulo 2^3.

Now that we have partially developed a symbolic method to express the computation performed by a digital system, let us consider another simple example of how this symbology can be used to describe a complete task.

A Serial Adder

In Section 4 of Chapter 4 we developed a logic network that could carry out the simultaneous addition of two r-bit binary numbers. The logic network required r full-adder logic subnetworks. Sometimes, when the speed with which we must carry out the addition is not important, we can use a serial adder of the form shown in Figure 11-9. The two r-bit numbers are placed in the A and B registers. The addition

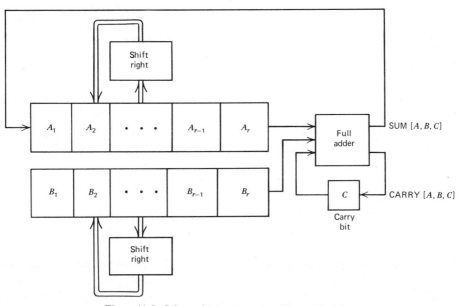

Figure 11-9. Schematic representation of a serial adder.

is carried out one binary digit at a time until all r-digits have been processed. The result appears in the A register and if there is an overflow, it appears in the 1-bit carry register C.

To implement this adder we must first define the basic operations that are carried out by the component units of the network. This requires an understanding of how the addition is performed.

The operation of the serial adder can be studied if we assume that the first number

$$u = u_{r-1}u_{r-2} \cdots u_1u_0$$

is stored in register A and the second number

$$v = v_{r-1}v_{r-2} \cdots v_1v_0$$

is stored in register B. To add these two numbers we must form, in succession, the following calculations.

First Calculation	Second Calculation	Third Calculation	rth Calculation
u_0	c_0	c_1	c_{r-2}
v_0	u_1	u_2	u_{r-1}
	v_1	v_2	v_{r-1}
c_0s_0	c_1s_1	c_2s_2	$c_{r-1}s_{r-1}$

Table 11-5   Basic Operations and Information
                                             Transfers Needed To Realize Serial Adder

Operation	Definition
Full Adder	
1. $A_1 \leftarrow \text{SUM}[A, B, C]$	$A_1 \leftarrow A_r \oplus B_r \oplus C$
2. $C \leftarrow \text{CARRY}[A, B, C]$	$C \leftarrow (A_r \wedge B_r) \vee (A_r \wedge C) \vee (B_r \wedge C)$
Shift	
1. $A \leftarrow SR(A)$	$A_{i+1} \leftarrow A_i \quad i = 1, \ldots, r-1$ $A_1 \leftarrow 0$
2. $B \leftarrow SR(B)$	$B_{i+1} \leftarrow B_i \quad i = 1, \ldots, r-1$ $B_1 \leftarrow 0$

where c_i is the carry and s_i is the $(i + 1)$st term of the sum. As the addition progresses we must provide a way to store the current carry digit c_i and all of the sums s_0 through s_i. The 1-bit C register is used to store the carry information.

A separate register could be used to store the sums. However, in order to carry out the serial addition we must shift the contents of the A and B registers right one bit after we perform each calculation. Thus we can use the vacated space in the A register to store the sums s_0 through s_i.

Table 11-6   Information Transfer
                                                  Sequence Associated with Serial Adder

Initial Conditions

$[A] = [u_{r-1}, u_{r-2}, \ldots, u_1, u_0]$
$[B] = [v_{r-1}, v_{r-2}, \ldots, v_1, v_0]$
$[C] = [0]$

Clock Pulse	Transfer	
$\tau_1:$	$A_1 \leftarrow \text{SUM}[A, B, C]$ $A \leftarrow SR[A]$	$C \leftarrow \text{CARRY}[A, B, C]$ $B \leftarrow SR[B]$
$\vdots$		$\vdots$
$\tau_i:$	$A_1 \leftarrow \text{SUM}[A, B, C]$ $A \leftarrow SR[A]$	$C \leftarrow \text{CARRY}[A, B, C]$ $B \leftarrow SR[B]$
$\vdots$		$\vdots$
$\tau_r:$	$A_1 \leftarrow \text{SUM}[A, B, C]$ $A \leftarrow SR[A]$	$C \leftarrow \text{CARRY}[A, B, C]$ $B \leftarrow SR[B]$

Table 11-7   Illustration of the
Operation of a 3-Bit Serial Adder

Initial Conditions

$[A] = [1, 1, 0]$ $[B] = [0, 1, 1]$ $[C] = 0$

Clock Pulse	Before Clock Pulse			After Clock Pulse		
	$[A]$	$[B]$	$[C]$	$[A]$	$[B]$	$[C]$
τ_1:	$[1, 1, 0]$	$[0, 1, 1]$	$[0]$	$[1, 1, 1]$	$[0, 0, 1]$	$[0]$
τ_2:	$[1, 1, 1]$	$[0, 0, 1]$	$[0]$	$[0, 1, 1]$	$[0, 0, 0]$	$[1]$
τ_3:	$[0, 1, 1]$	$[0, 0, 0]$	$[1]$	$[0, 0, 1]$	$[0, 0, 0]$	$[1]$

Final Result

$[A] + [B] = [0, 0, 1]$ $[C] = [1]$

Answer   1001

To carry out this computation we must use the basic operations and information transfers defined by Table 11-5. Using these results we can describe the operation of the serial adder by the sequence of transfers given in Table 11-6.

Examining this table we see that r identical information transfer operations must be performed to carry out the complete addition process. If the two r-bit numbers are large enough, the resulting sum will be an $r + 1$ bit number. In that case we have an overflow. This condition is indicated when the carry register is 1 at the end of the addition sequence. The actual operation of a typical 3-bit serial adder is summarized in Table 11-7. In particular we see that an overflow occurred since in the final result $C = [1]$.

This example illustrates a very simple computation. The only function of the control element is to supply the r pulses necessary to carry out the complete task. We now investigate how more complex computations can be performed by several simple expansions in the organization of the control unit.

Autonomous Control Units

The simplest type of control unit is the autonomous control unit that has the organization shown in Figure 11-10. This class of unit is useful if a single repetitive information processing task must be performed. The controller steps through a prespecified sequence of control signals that cannot be modified. When it reaches the end of the sequence, it either stops or reinitializes itself and repeats the sequence.

As an example of how an autonomous controller might be used consider the system shown in Figure 11-11, consisting of two r-bit registers A and B and a 1-bit

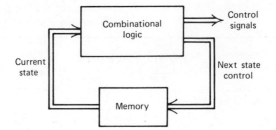

Figure 11-10. General organization of an autonomous control unit.

overflow register C. The system operation is described by the following four-step algorithm.

Step 1   Load value of X into B register.
Step 2   Transfer information from B register to A register. Set contents of register C to 0. (The value of the input signal changes during this operation.)
Step 3   Load new value of X into B register.
Step 4   Form the sum of the numbers contained in A and B and store the result in A. If there is an overflow set register C to 1. Otherwise, leave it set to 0.

Examining the operations that must be performed we see that we need three distinct control signals. One signal must cause the value of X to be loaded into register B, one signal must transfer the contents of register B to register A and set the content of register C to 0, while the third signal must control the addition operation. Denote these signals as s_1, s_2, and s_3. The operations carried out by N_1 and N_2 are described in Table 11-8. Using these operations we find that the control

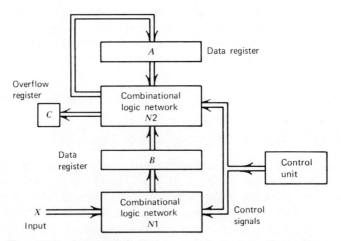

Figure 11-11. A typical information processing system with an autonomous control unit.

Table 11-8   Specification Table of Networks N_1 and N_2

Network N_1

Control Signal	s_1	s_2	s_3
Action	$B \leftarrow X$	No operation	No operation

Network N_2

Control Signal	s_1	s_2	s_3
Action	No operation	$A \leftarrow B$ $C \leftarrow [0]$	$A \leftarrow A + B$ $C \leftarrow$ OVERFLOW$[A, B]$

signal sequence described in Table 11-9 must be generated to carry out the desired information processing task.

The information contained in Table 11-9 indicates that the controller must provide a control sequence s_1, s_2, s_1, s_3. If we assume that this information processing operation must be constantly repeated without stopping, then the control sequence can be provided by an autonomous sequential network which is described by the state transition table given in Table 11-10.

The actual design and realization of the logic networks N_1 and N_2 and the controller can be accomplished using the techniques that have been developed in the previous chapters.

In many applications the sequence of steps involved in a computation are altered according to the status of the information in the processing unit. The next level of control unit complexity is thus a controller with inputs as well as outputs.

Table 11-9   Control Sequence Necessary
to Operate Data Processing Network

Clock Pulse	Control Signal When Clock Pulse Occurs	Operations Performed When Clock Pulse Occurs	Notes
τ_1	s_1	$B \leftarrow X$	Value of X
τ_2	s_2	$A \leftarrow B \quad C \leftarrow [0]$	changes between
τ_3	s_1	$B \leftarrow X$	clock pulse
τ_4	s_3	$A \leftarrow A + B$ $C \leftarrow$ OVERFLOW$[A, B]$	τ_1 and τ_3

Table 11-10 State Transition Table for Controller

Current State	Next State/Current Output
q_1	q_2/s_1
q_2	q_3/s_2
q_3	q_4/s_1
q_4	q_1/s_3

Controllers with Status Input Information

When a controller must use status information to decide on the next set of control signals to apply to the information processing unit, it is equivalent to a sequential machine with an input. Such a controller has the form shown in Figure 11-12.

As an example of this type of computation, consider the digital system shown in Figure 11-13. This system is a modification of the one shown in Figure 11-11 where we have introduced an input and an output device of the type discussed in Chapter 10.

In this system the input device loads a value into the buffer register X and sets the flag $F1$ to 1. When the control unit sees this flag, the contents of X is transmitted to register B and then to register A. In the meantime a new input value is placed in X. This value is placed into B and then the sum $A + B$ is computed and placed into A. If the output flag $F2$ is 1, then the contents of A is transferred to the output buffer Y. The whole sequence is then repeated. The detailed algorithm for this system is shown in Figure 11-14.

In examining this algorithm we see that the control unit receives an input from $F1$ and $F2$ and sends control signals S to network $N1$ and $N2$, control signals T to the output device, and control signals U to the input device.

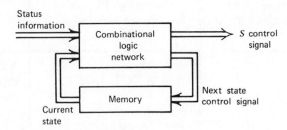

Figure 11-12. Controller with status information input.

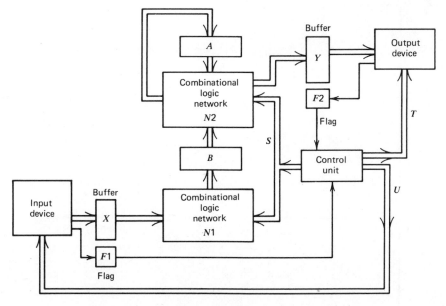

Figure 11-13. A network with an input and an output device.

The operation tables for the networks $N1$ and $N2$ as well as for the input and output devices are given by Table 11-11.

Using the information in the flowchart and the specification tables, we can develop the transition table for the control unit. The input will be the 2-tuple $[F1, F2]$ and the output will be the form $[s_i, t_j, u_k]$. (Note that s_i must be encoded as a 3-bit signal). Each block of the flowchart represents a task that must be performed during a given clock period. Thus each block corresponds to one state of the control unit. The diamonds represent decision points and do not correspond to states.

The resulting state transition table is given by Table 11-12. The control unit starts in state q_1. It stays in state q_1 as long as $F1 = 0$. When $F1$ goes to 1, the controller sends out the control signals necessary to set $F1$ to 0 and to transfer information from the input register X into the B register and goes into state q_2. The contents of B is then transferred to register A and the controller goes to state q_3. It stays in q_3 until $F1$ goes to 1. The transfers $B \leftarrow X$ and $F1 \leftarrow [0]$ are then carried out and the controller goes to q_4. This type of operation continues until the controller reaches state q_5, which represents the end of the cycle. It then resets to q_1 and repeats the whole process.

The system behavior of this digital network is now completely defined. If we wish to realize this network, we can use our logic design techniques from the previous chapters to reduce this system to a logic circuit design.

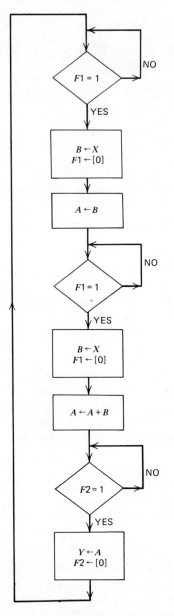

Note: a new input is generated
when $F1$ is set to 0.

Note: the output device generates
the output when $F2$ is set
to 0.

Figure 11-14. Flowchart of algorithm to be executed by the system of
Figure 11-12.

Table 11-11   Tables For Networks of Figure 11-13

Network $N1$

Control Signal	s_0	s_1	s_2	s_3	s_4
Action	No operation	$B \leftarrow X$	No operation	No operation	No operation

Network $N2$

Control Signal	s_0	s_1	s_2	s_3	s_4
Action	No operation	No operation	$A \leftarrow B$	$A \leftarrow A + B$	$Y \leftarrow A$

Output Device

Control Signal	t_0	t_1
Action	No operation	$F2 \leftarrow [0]$ (start output operation)

Note: Output device sets $F2$ to 1 at completion of output operation. No action from the controller is required.

Input Device

Control Signal	u_0	u_1
Action	No operation	$F1 \leftarrow [0]$ (next input is processed)

Note: Input device sets $F1$ to 1 when the next input value has been placed in buffer register X.

The networks in the two examples just considered are able to carry out a single information processing task. If a new task or a change in the way the task is to be executed is needed, then a new control unit must be specified. This observation, therefore, suggests that if we had an easy way to change the control sequence generated by the control unit, then we would be able to carry out many information processing operations using the same digital system.

Table 11-12

State Transition Table
for Controller of Figure 11-13

Input [F1, F2] State	[0, 0]	[0, 1]	[1, 0]	[1, 1]
q_1	$q_1/(s_0, t_0, u_0)$	$q_1/(s_0, t_0, u_0)$	$q_2/(s_1, t_0, u_1)$	$q_2/(s_1, t_0, u_1)$
q_2	$q_3/(s_2, t_0, u_0)$	$q_3/(s_2, t_0, u_0)$	$q_3/(s_2, t_0, u_0)$	$q_3/(s_2, t_0, u_0)$
q_3	$q_3/(s_0, t_0, u_0)$	$q_3/(s_0, t_0, u_0)$	$q_4/(s_1, t_5, u_1)$	$q_4/(s_1, t_0, u_1)$
q_4	$q_5/(s_3, t_0, u_0)$	$q_5/(s_3, t_0, u_0)$	$q_5/(s_3, t_0, u_0)$	$q_5/(s_3, t_0, u_0)$
q_5	$q_5/(s_0, t_0, u_0)$	$q_1/(s_4, t_1, u_0)$	$q_5/(s_0, t_0, u_0)$	$q_1/(s_4, t_1, u_0)$

Instruction-Controlled Controller

One way in which to increase the flexibility of an information processing system is to use a control unit with a separate instruction register like that shown in Figure 11-15.

The instruction register provides an additional input to the control network. Suppose that the instruction register is an r-bit register. Each of the 2^r distinct

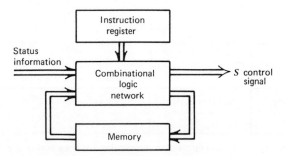

Figure 11-15. An instruction-controlled control-unit.

values that can be placed in the register can be used to indicate a different computational task.

To indicate how an instruction-controlled controller can expand the information processing capabilities of a digital system, we use a system similar to the one shown in Figure 11-11. However, instead of just adding two numbers, we ask that the system be able to carry out four different tasks. The system under consideration is shown in Figure 11-16.

This system has two r-bit information registers A and B, a 1-bit overflow register C, and a 2-bit instruction register I. Two control signals T and S, instead of one, are shown. A single control signal could be used but it is more convenient for this system to use one control signal T to control information transfer between parts of the system and the second control signal S to control the information processing operations. The status signal Y checks the status of the information in the A register.

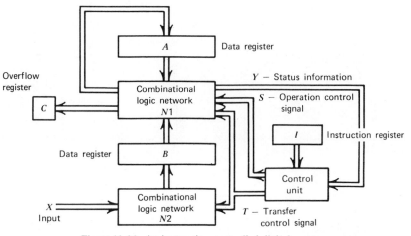

Figure 11-16. An instruction-controlled digital system.

The instruction register can indicate four distinct instructions to the control unit. These instructions, and the desired information processing tasks associated with each instruction are indicated by the flow charts of Figure 11-17.

Examining the flow diagrams shown in Figure 11-17 allows us to identify the information transfer and logical operations that must be carried out. These operations are summarized in Table 11-13.

The control unit must generate the control signals necessary to carry out the different information processing tasks. The particular task actually carried out is determined by the contents of the instruction register. Table 11-14 presents the state transition table that describes the operation of the control unit. Examining this table we see that the number of steps needed to carry out each instruction is different. For example, the information processing task associated with i_0 requires four steps, that with instruction i_1 requires five steps, that with instruction i_3 requires three steps while the task associated with instruction i_2 requires a variable number of steps. We also note that many of the states may serve different purposes depending on the particular instruction being executed.

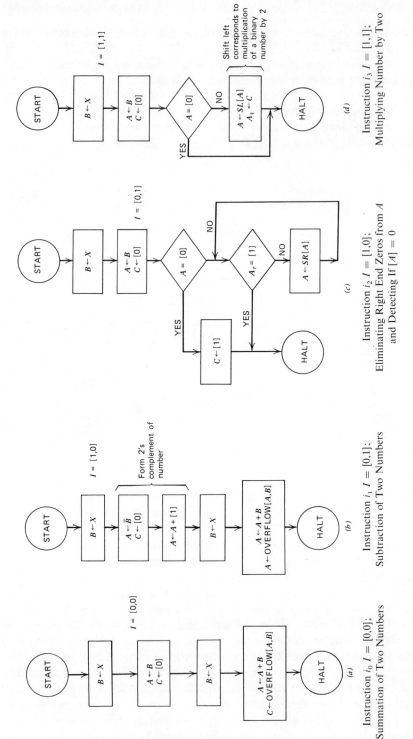

Figure 11-17. Flow diagram describing the four information processing tasks performed by system shown in Figure 11-16.

Table 11-13   Specification Table for Figure 11-16

Transfer Tasks

Control Signal T	t_0	t_1	t_2	t_3
Transfer	No operation	$B \leftarrow X$	$A \leftarrow B$ $C \leftarrow [0]$	$A \leftarrow \bar{B}$ $C \leftarrow [0]$

Operations

Control Signal S	s_0	s_1
Operation	No operation	$A \leftarrow A + B$ $C \leftarrow \text{OVERFLOW}[A, B]$

Operations (continued)

Control Signal S	s_2	s_3	s_4	s_5
Operation	$A \leftarrow A + [1]$	$C \leftarrow [1]$	$A \leftarrow \text{SR}[A]$	$A \leftarrow \text{SL}[A]$

Status Signal Y

Condition	Value of Y
No special status $A = [0]$ $A_r = [1]$	y_0 y_1 y_2

Note: $SR[A]$ is shift right operation; $SL[A]$ is shift left operation.

For example, the state q_0, corresponding to the initial state, always corresponds to the task of reading the first value of X into the B register and the state q_4 always corresponds to the terminal or halt state that indicates that the information processing task is completed. However, the other states correspond to different tasks depending on the values associated with I and Y.

All the examples that we have investigated so far in this chapter have been designed to illustrate one or more of the concepts being discussed. The problem that we actually face in designing a digital system is that of deciding how we should organize a complete digital system to carry out a particular information processing task. We consider this problem in the next section.

Table 11-14 — State Transition Table Describing Operation of Control Unit for Digital System of Figure 11-15

Instruction	i_0	i_1	i_2			i_3	
Current State ╲ Y	y_0,y_1,y_2	y_0,y_1,y_2	y_0	y_1	y_2	y_0,y_2	y_1
q_0	$q_1/t_1, s_0$	$q_1/t_1, s_0$	$q_1/t_1, s_0$	$q_1/t_1, s_0$	$q_1/t_1, s_0$	$q_1/t_1, s_0$	$q_1/t_1, s_0$
q_1	$q_2/t_2, s_0$	$q_5/t_3, s_0$	$q_2/t_2, s_0$	$q_2/t_2, s_0$	$q_2/t_2, s_0$	$q_2/t_2, s_0$	$q_2/t_2, s_0$
q_2	$q_3/t_1, s_0$	$q_3/t_1, s_0$	$q_2/t_0, s_4$	$q_4/t_0, s_3$	$q_4/t_0, s_0$	$q_4/t_0, s_5$	$q_4/t_0, s_0$
q_3	$q_4/t_0, s_1$	$q_4/t_0, s_1$	$-/-$	$-/-$	$-/-$	$-/-$	$-/-$
q_4	$q_4/t_0, s_0$	$q_4/t_0, s_0$	$q_4/t_0, s_0$	$q_4/t_0, s_0$	$q_4/t_0, s_0$	$q_4/t_0, s_0$	$q_4/t_0, s_0$
q_5	$-/-$	$q_2/t_0, s_2$	$-/-$	$-/-$	$-/-$	$-/-$	$-/-$

EXERCISES

1. Define the information transfer sequence that would be associated with an r-bit serial comparator network. This network must serially compare the contents of two registers, A and B, and give a 1 output if the contents are equal and a 0 output if they are not.

2. For the system shown in Figure 11-16 assume that $r = 3$ and that

$$X(1) := [1, 1, 0] \qquad X(2) := [0, 1, 1]$$

where $X(1)$ is the first input signal and $X(2)$ is the second input signal. Illustrate the operation of this network, for each of the four possible instructions, by forming an operating sequence table similar to the one given by Table 11-7.

4. DESIGN OF DIGITAL SYSTEMS

The design of digital systems is much more complex than designing combinational logic networks or sequential networks. One of the main reasons for this is that there are usually a large number of systems that can be defined to carry out a given task and the designer must be able to identify these possible systems and select the "best" one to do the job. Unfortunately there are no algorithms that tell the designer how to find all of the possible systems or how to evaluate them to see which one is the most desirable.

Digital system design thus becomes a heuristic process that relies heavily on the experience and know-how of the designer. This section presents a discussion of the various stages of the design process and indicates some of the techniques which can be used to handle the problems that must be solved at each step.

Problem Specification

The first stage of any design process consists of developing a detailed description of the information processing task and selecting an algorithm which provides a detailed description of the steps that must be performed to carry out the task. For all but the simplest task, there will be more than one possible information processing algorithm.

Sometimes the algorithm to be used is suggested by the task that is to be performed while at other times the designer will be required to develop special data handling methods so that the task can be carried out within certain operational or equipment constraints imposed on the designer by other system requirements. For example, the designer must take into consideration such factors as the types of logic units that might be used in constructing the system, the operations that these units can perform, their operating speed, and the way that the information is encoded.

After one or more possible algorithms describing the way in which the task can be performed are developed, the designer must then decide which algorithm best meets the set of design conditions imposed by the problem specifications. This decision will probably involve minimizing some "cost" criterion that balances the need for special hardware features against the cost of implementing these features and the time required to perform the information processing task. Sometimes it is not possible, at this stage, to select a single algorithm that is obviously better than all other algorithms. In that situation more than one algorithm is retained for additional evaluation.

Initial System Organization

Each algorithm implies a general sequence of data processing steps. The next stage of the design process consists of actually specifying how these steps are carried out. At this point, it is necessary to decide how the information is to be stored while it is being processed, the basic information transfer and processing operations that are to be performed, and the way the components of the system must be interconnected.

Each algorithm carried over from the first stage of the design process will suggest one or more system organizations. All designs are then evaluated and a selection is again made concerning the "best" realization. The goal in this selection is again to obtain the system that comes nearest to the design goals within the constraints imposed by costs and other performance requirements. A single system organization is usually selected at this point since the following stages of the design process involve a considerable amount of detailed design effort.

Control System Specification

Once the basic system organization is established, the next step is to design the control sequence necessary to regulate the sequence of information transfers and processing operations implied by the algorithm describing the system's overall operation. This can be done by developing a flowchart that indicates the exact information transfer and processing operations that must be performed at each step of the process as well as the status information that must be supplied to the control unit. The information contained in this flowchart is then used to develop the state transition table for the control unit.

Final System Realization

At this point in the design process the operational characteristics of all the basic logic units and the control unit have been defined. Thus the final stage of the design process is to use these specifications to carry out the logic circuit design of each unit in the system. Since this phase of the design process uses techniques of the type presented in previous chapters, we will not consider this step in any further detail.

Design of a Digital Multiplier

Previous examples have shown that it is relatively easy to build a logic network to add two binary numbers in a single step. However, if we were to try to use the same techniques to build a logic circuit to multiply two binary numbers in a single step we would find that, in general, the resulting logic circuitry is much more complex and costly. Therefore, multiplication is almost always carried out by a specially designed digital system. We now consider how such a system could be designed. This example considers the basic problem of developing a system to multiply two r-bit positive binary numbers. References [4] and [6] at the end of the chapter discuss the problem of designing a general multiplier in detail.

A digital multiplier performs multiplication by carrying out a series of shifting and addition operations. However, before we consider the actual techniques that we might use, let us investigate how we would carry out a manual multiplication using paper and pencil. The steps of this process are shown in Table 11-15.

This example illustrates the basic features that we must account for in designing a multiplier. First, we note that if we are multiplying two r-bit numbers the result

Table 11-15   An Example of Manual
                                              Multiplication of Two Binary Numbers

		Multiplier digit
1 1 0 1 0	multiplicand	
1 0 1 1 0	multiplier	
0 0 0 0 0	1st partial product	0
1 1 0 1 0	2nd partial product	1
1 1 0 1 0	3rd partial product	1
0 0 0 0 0	4th partial product	0
1 1 0 1 0	5th partial product	1
1 0 0 0 1 1 1 1 0 0	product = sum of partial products	

has at most $2r$ digits. Second, we note that there must be a relative shift of one bit between each partial product. Finally, we note that the ith partial product is set to zero if the ith bit of the multiplier is zero.

In the above example we first formed all the partial products and then added them all together at the same time to form the product. However, it is easier to construct a digital network that only has to add two numbers at a time. Therefore, we can modify the multiplication process as shown in Table 11-16 to accommodate this requirement. The register that holds these partial sums will be called the accumulator.

Examining Table 11-16 we see that as each new partial product is formed it is added to the partial sum already in the accumulator. We also note that the $(i + 1)$th partial product is either zero if $y_i = 0$ or equal to the multiplicand shifted i bits to the left if $y_i = 1$.

Table 11-16   Multiplication Using
                                                 Accumulation of Partial Product

1 1 0 1 0	multiplicand $= x_4 x_3 x_2 x_1 x_0$
1 0 1 1 0	multiplier $= y_4 y_3 y_2 y_1 y_0$
0 0 0 0 0 0 0 0 0 0	initial contents of accumulator
0 0 0 0 0	bit y_0 is 0, 1st partial product zero
0 0 0 0 0 0 0 0 0 0	first partial sum
1 1 0 1 0	bit y_1 is 1, 2nd partial product
0 0 0 0 1 1 0 1 0 0	second partial sum
1 1 0 1 0	bit y_2 is 1, 3rd partial product
0 0 1 0 0 1 1 1 0 0	third partial sum
0 0 0 0 0	bit y_3 is 0, 4th partial product
0 0 1 0 0 1 1 1 0 0	fourth partial sum
1 1 0 1 0	bit y_4 is 1, 5th partial product
1 0 0 0 1 1 1 1 0 0	final product = fifth partial sum

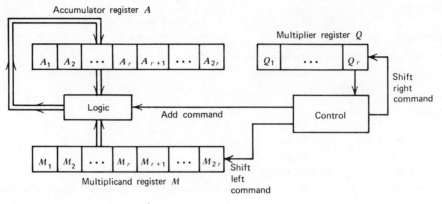

Accumulator register *A*

(a)

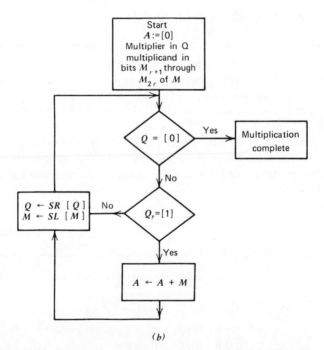

(b)

Figure 11-18. Organization operation of simple multiplier. (*a*) Multiplier organization. (*b*) Multiplication algorithm flow chart. *Note:* SR[*Q*] = shift contents of *Q* right one bit; SL[*M*] = shift contents of *M* left one bit.

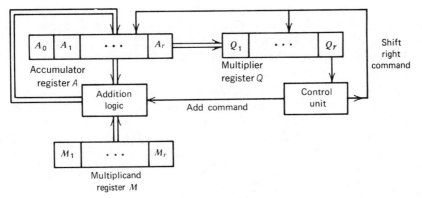

Accumulator
register A

Multiplier
register Q

Addition
logic

Add command

Control
unit

Shift
right
command

M_1 $\cdots$ M_r

Multiplicand
register M

(a)

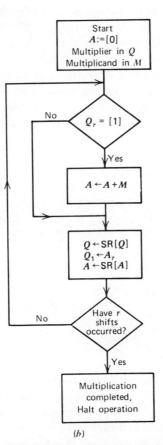

Start
$A := [0]$
Multiplier in Q
Multiplicand in M

$Q_r = [1]$

No

Yes

$A \leftarrow A + M$

$Q \leftarrow SR[Q]$
$Q_1 \leftarrow A_r$
$A \leftarrow SR[A]$

Have r
shifts
occurred?

No

Yes

Multiplication
completed,
Halt operation

(b)

Figure 11-19. Multiplier making more efficient use of registers. (a) Multiplier organization. (b) Multiplication algorithm flow chart.

The simplest realization of a multiplier is shown in Figure 11-18. In this arrangement the multiplier is placed in the Q register, the multiplicand is placed in the r rightmost bits of the M register, and the accumulator is set to 0. The multiplication then takes place according to the algorithm given by the flow chart of Figure 11-18b. This method of multiplication, which is essentially a direct implementation of the operations shown in Table 11-16, is extremely simple and easy to control. However, it makes very inefficient use of the registers. For example, the multiplicand register is a double-length register even though it only holds a single-length operand.

A second method of realizing a multiplier is shown in Figure 11-19. In this system the accumulator register has $r + 1$ bits, A_0 through A_r, and the multiplier register has r bits. The leftmost bit, A_0, of the accumulator is needed to handle overflow information during the addition sequence.

The accumulator and multiplier registers do double duty. Instead of shifting the contents of the multiplicand register to the left after we have formed the partial sum we shift the contents of the accumulator and multiplier registers, treated as a single $2r + 1$ digit register, to the right. In particular the contents of the bit at the right end of the accumulator is transferred to the bit at the left end of the multiplier register. Thus, we use the multiplier register for the double purpose of holding the multiplier at the beginning of the operation and for holding the r least significant digits of the product at the end of the multiplication operation. Except for this change in the direction of information transfer, the operation of the multiplier shown in Figure 11-19 is the same as the operation of the one shown in Figure 11-18. The r highest order bits of the final answer are found in the r rightmost bits of A and the r lowest order bits are contained in Q.

Since the multiplier of Figure 11-19 requires smaller registers, we select this multiplier organization to complete our design. The next step is to define the control signal sequence that must be generated by the control unit.

By examining Figure 11-19, we see that the control unit receives one status input signal which indicates if $Q_1 = [0]$ or if $Q_1 = [1]$, and it must generate three distinct output commands. They are:

$$s_0 \quad \text{no operation}$$

$$s_1 \quad A \leftarrow A + M$$

$$s_3 \quad Q \leftarrow SR[Q], Q_1 \leftarrow A_r, A \leftarrow SR[A]$$

We also see that the control unit must count the number of times the register, made up of the combined A and Q registers, has been shifted. When r shifts have taken place the multiplication operation is complete. The steps of the multiplication algorithm are represented by the flowchart of Figure 11-19b. Using the information contained in this flowchart, we can form the state transition table shown in Table 11-17 to describe the operation of the control unit. Examining this table we see that whenever $Q_r = [0]$ we skip the addition operation and shift the contents of the combined A and Q registers right. However, when $Q_r = [1]$ we need an extra

Table 11-17 State Transition Table for Multiplier of Figure 11-19

Current State \ Current Input	$[Q_r] := 0$	$[Q_r] := 1$
q_1	q_3/s_2	q_2/s_1
q_2	$-/-$	q_3/s_2
q_3	q_5/s_2	q_4/s_1
q_4	$-/-$	q_5/s_2
$\vdots$ $\approx$	$\vdots$	
q_i	q_{i+2}/s_2	q_{i+1}/s_1
q_{i+1}	$-/-$	q_{i+2}/s_2
$\vdots$ $\approx$	$\vdots$	
q_{2r-1}	q_{2r+1}/s_2	q_{2r}/s_1
q_{2r}	$-/-$	q_{2r+1}/s_2
q_{2r+1}	q_{2r+1}/s_0	q_{2r+1}/s_0

clock pulse to carry out the addition operation before we carry out the shift. The time required to carry out a multiplication is variable. If the multiplier register Q contains k 1's then we need $r + k$ clock pulses to carry out the multiplication operation.

A Drilling Machine Controller

The previous example illustrates one of the common types of digital networks used in a computer. However, it is quite common to find digital networks that control the operation of nondigital devices. The example that we now consider is designed to illustrate how a digital controller can be used to control the operation of a nondigital device.

For this example we assume that we are given a drilling machine of the type illustrated in Figure 11-20. The unit to be drilled is placed on the work table in a prespecified position, and a sequence of drilling and positioning operations are performed on the unit. It is desired that these operations be carried out automatically.

In order to automate the drilling operation, the manufacturer of the drilling machine has put three position control motors on the machine to adjust the x and y position of the work table and the height of the drill. A stepping motor has also been included to allow the selection of any one of four drill sizes. Initially the manufacturer provided levers that an operator could use to operate these motors

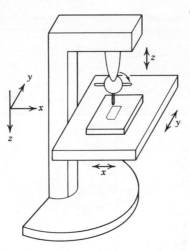

Figure 11-20. A digitally controllable drilling machine.

and indicators to show the current status of each variable. It is now desired to design an automatic control unit which will be able to carry out a preprogrammed sequence of operations. The programmed sequence of operations are to be encoded on a paper tape and the control unit must interpret this information and send appropriate commands to the drilling machine. Our task is to design this control unit and specify how the instructions needed to carry out a given sequence of drilling operations are to be encoded.

The initial step in the design process is to determine the characteristics of each of the devices that we must work with. For this problem there are two devices that are prespecified; the drilling machine and the paper tape reader. The drilling machine is assumed to have the following characteristics.

Work Table Position Characteristics of Drilling Machine

The position of the work table can be adjusted in the x and y direction in increments of 0.1 inch. The x and y position is adjustable between 0.0 and 9.9 inches. The actual value of x or y is indicated by an 8-bit BCD encoded number of the form

inch   0.1 inch
digit   digit

XXXX . XXXX

Two 2-bit control signals CX and CY are used to change the x and y position of the table, respectively. The allowed commands are encoded in the following manner.

Control Signal	CX		CY	
	0 0	no motion	0 0	no motion
	0 1	increase x	0 1	increase y
	1 0	decrease x	1 0	decrease y
	1 1	no motion	1 1	no motion

Drill Selection and Drill Depth Characteristics

The drilling machine has four different size drills mounted as shown in Figure 11-19. The drill mount is rotated in a clockwise direction by a stepping motor. The four drill positions on the mount are numbered 0 through 3 in a clockwise direction. A 2-bit signal M is available to indicate which drill is currently positioned over the work surface.

The rotation of the drill mount is controlled by a 1-bit control signal CM defined as follows:

Control Signal CM	
0	Do not rotate drill mount
1	Rotate drill mount clockwise to the next drill position

Each drill is mounted in the drill mount so that its tip is 0.5 inches above the work table. It can be lowered, under the control of a control signal CD, in increments of 0.01 inches until it touches the work table. The actual displacement, z, of the drill from its at-rest position is indicated by an 8-bit BCD encoded number, Z, of the form:

$$\underbrace{.DDDD}_{\substack{0.1 \text{ inch} \\ \text{digit}}} \underbrace{DDDD}_{\substack{0.01 \text{ inch} \\ \text{digit}}}$$

The actual displacement is controlled by the 2-bit control signal CD according to the following encoding:

Control Signal CD	
0 0	no motion
0 1	increase z
1 0	return drill to zero displacement
1 1	no motion

Block Diagram Representation of Drilling Machine

From the above specifications we develop the block diagram shown in Figure 11-21 to represent the important information and control signals associated with the drilling machine.

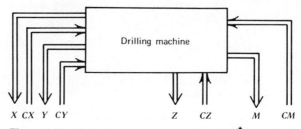

Figure 11-21. Block diagram representation of drilling machine.

Next we investigate the properties of the paper tape reader before we start designing the system.

The Paper Tape Reader

Information is recorded on paper tape by use of punched holes as illustrated in Figure 11-22. Each column of a paper tape has eight channels and a maximum of eight holes can be punched in each column. The presence of a hole in a given channel indicates a 1 and the absence of a hole corresponds to a 0.

The general organization of the paper tape reader unit can be represented by the block diagram shown in Figure 11-23. When a read command, NR, is received the

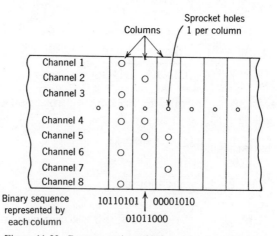

Figure 11-22. Representation of information on paper tape.

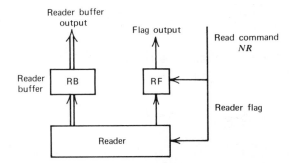

Figure 11-23. Block diagram representation of paper tape reader.

reader flag, *RF*, is set to 0 and the next column on the tape is moved under the reading head. The sprocket hole generates a pulse as soon as the reading head is centered over the column. This pulse causes the information contained in the column to be read in parallel into the 8-bit reader-buffer register, *RB*. At the same time the reader flag is set to 1. The tape position remains fixed until the next read command is received. When the reader is first tuned on, the contents of the reader buffer is set to zero and the reader flag is set to 1.

Now that we have an idea of the operation of the drilling machine and the reader we must turn to the problem of designing the control unit.

A Typical Control Problem

To obtain an idea of the operations that the controller must perform let us consider the sequence of steps necessary to drill the pattern of holes shown in Figure 11-24 in a 0.25 inch thick piece of steel plate. To carry out this drilling operation would

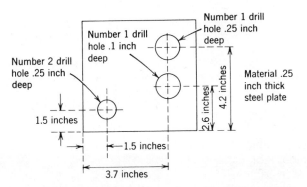

Figure 11-24. A typical task to be performed by drilling machine.

require the following steps. It is assumed that the drilling machine can execute only one step at a time.

Drill hole 1   (a)   Set x to 1.5 in.
                   (b)   Set y to 1.5 in.
                   (c)   Select drill 2
                   (d)   Lower drill .5 in.
                   (e)   Raise drill

Drill hole 2   (a)   Set x to 3.7 in.
                   (b)   Set y to 2.6 in.
                   (c)   Select drill 1
                   (d)   Lower drill .35 in.
                   (e)   Raise drill

Drill hole 3   (a)   Set y to 4.2 in.
                   (b)   Lower drill .5 in.
                   (c)   Raise drill
                   End of drilling operation.

In examining the above list, we see that we must be able to vary the sequence of operations. In particular we note that in the drilling of hole 3 we did not have to repeat the x position operation or the drill selection operation, since they were the same as those used for the drilling of hole 2.

From this observation we can conclude that the controller must have a control unit with an instruction register. We also note that each step of the drilling operation requires the controller to perform two distinct types of operations.

1.   Determine which drilling operation is the next one to be performed.
2.   Generate the commands necessary to cause the drilling machine to execute the indicated drilling operation.

The next stage of the design process thus consists of determining how these two tasks can be performed.

Generation of Drilling Machine Commands

If we examine the specifications for the drilling machine we note that we must control the following variables:

(a) x position of table
(b) y position of table
(c) z depth of drill
(d)   drill selection

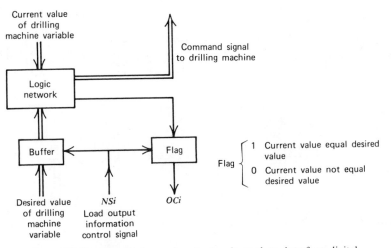

Figure 11-25. General form of output unit used to interface digital drilling control unit to drilling machine.

Since we have sensors on the drilling machine that provide us with the current value of each of these variables, we can use an arrangement of the form shown in Figure 11-25 to generate the necessary control signals to change the value of each variable.

When the flag signal, OCi, is a 1 this indicates that the machine is ready to receive a new position signal. The load-output information-control-signal NSi, transmits the desired value of the machine variable into the buffer register and sets the flag to 0. As long as the value of the current variable is not equal to the desired value of the variable, there is an error. An appropriate drilling machine command is generated to change the value of the current variable in such a way as to reduce this error to zero. When the two values match, the flag is set to 1 and no further changes are called for in the value of the variable being controlled.

Using this type of approach, we obtain the partial organization of the controller shown in Figure 11-26. The signals X, Y, Z, and M are the actual values of the drilling machine variables while the signals DX, DY, DZ, and DM are the respective desired values of the same variable and CX, CY, CZ, and CM are the generated control signals. The signals $OC1$ through $OC4$ are the values of the flags and the signals $NS1$ through $NS4$ are the transfer control signals.

The next problem we must consider is that of determining how the signals DX, DY, DZ, and DM are generated. There are two ways in which this problem can be solved.

The value of each signal will be read from the paper tape into the buffer register of the paper tape reader. One approach would be to use this signal directly as an input for the appropriate control logic network. The second approach would be to introduce a separate signal buffer register for the intermediate storage of each signal. In this case the information in the reader buffer would be transferred into

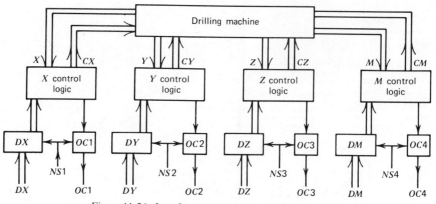

Figure 11-26. Interface organization of drilling machine.

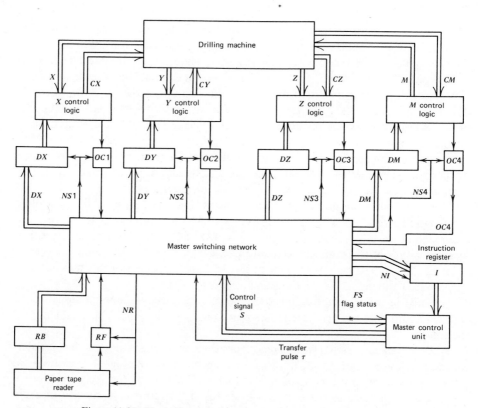

Figure 11-27. Block diagram of complete drilling machine controller.

the appropriate signal buffer register. The output of each such buffer register would then provide the necessary signal input for each control logic network.

Of the two approaches the second would be more expensive, since four additional buffer registers would be required. Since it is necessary to only perform one operation at a time, we decide to use the reader-buffer register as the signal source for each control logic network. This decision requires that we have some way to control which input line is connected to the buffer register.

The necessary switching between different input lines can be accomplished by using a switching network between the reader buffer and the inputs to the control logic networks. This unit is illustrated in Figure 11-27. We must also have a master control unit that selects which input line is connected to the reader buffer. Such a master control unit is also indicated in Figure 11-27. This master control unit must include an instruction register, since the order in which the different drilling tasks are performed can vary from job to job.

The transfer pulses NR and $NS1$ through $NS4$ needed to control the interfaces will also be generated by switching the transfer pulse produced by the control unit in the master control unit. Similarly the value of the different flags will be available to the master controller from the signal FS, which is the 5-tuple

$$FS = [RF, OC1, OC2, OC3, OC4]$$

Now that we have generated a block diagram showing the general operation of the controller, we must next specify the exact operation of each unit in the block diagram.

The Instruction Set

Before we can discuss the operation of the individual units of the controller we must first define the type of instructions that can be interpreted by the master control unit and the method of encoding these instructions. If we examine the types of operations that must be performed we note that there are two general types of instructions that must be implemented. The first type involves a change of a particular drilling machine variable to a new value that must be specified by an instruction. The second type involves taking some action that does not require the specification of a new value of a drilling machine variable. The particular instructions that must be implemented are summarized in Table 11-18.

Examining this list we see that there are seven different instructions. In instructions i_1, i_2, and i_3 we need 8 bits to represent X, Y, and Z information, and we need 2 bits to represent drill number information in i_4. Instructions i_0, i_5, and i_6 do not require any such information.

All of these instructions must be encoded in such a way that they can be placed on a paper tape. Since each column on a paper tape has a maximum of 8 bits, this means that instructions i_1, i_2, and i_3 will require more than one column to encode.

	Instruction	Variable To Be Specified	I	Assigned Code
(a)	No operation	None	i_0	000
(b)	Move X	New value of X	i_1	001
(c)	Move Y	New value of Y	i_2	010
(d)	Drill hole	New value of Z	i_3	011
(e)	Select drill	Drill number	i_4	100
(f)	Raise drill	None	i_5	101
(g)	Halt	None	i_6	110

	Instruction		Encoding Channel Number							
			1	2	3	4	5	6	7	8
(a)	No operation	First column	0	0	0	0	0	0	0	0
(b)	Move x	First column	0	0	1	0	0	0	0	0
		Second column	X	X	X	X	X	X	X	X
	Second column 8 bit BCD representation of DX									
(c)	Move y	First column	0	1	0	0	0	0	0	0
		Second column	Y	Y	Y	Y	Y	Y	Y	Y
	Second column 8 bit BCD representation of DY									
(d)	Drill hole	First column	0	1	1	0	0	0	0	0
		Second column	D	D	D	D	D	D	D	D
	Second column 8 bit BCD representation of DZ									
(e)	Select drill	First column	1	0	0	0	0	0	M	M
	MM binary equivalent of drill number									
(f)	Raise drill	First column	1	0	1	0	0	0	0	0
(g)	Halt	First column	1	1	0	0	0	0	0	0

Direction of tape motion

Columns

7 6 5 4 3 2 1

	7	6	5	4	3	2	1
Channel 1	O	O		O			
Channel 2		O		O			
Channel 3			O	O	O		O	O
(sprocket)	o	o	o	o	o	o	o	o	o	o	o	o	o
Channel 4								
Channel 5						O		
Channel 6				O				
Channel 7					O			
Channel 8				O		O		

Figure 11-28. Typical instruction sequence encoded on paper tape.

To encode each instruction we must provide 3 bits to indicate which type of instruction we are dealing with and either 0, 2, or 8 bits to indicate information needed by the system to execute the instruction. The codes assigned to each instruction are indicated in Table 11-19. Table 11-19 shows how each type of instruction is encoded on the paper tape.

To illustrate how this information actually appears on the paper tape, consider the following five instructions:

(1) Move x $x = 2.9$ in.
(2) Select drill $M = 2$
(3) Drill hole $z = .25$ in.
(4) Raise drill
(5) Stop operation

These instructions are encoded as shown in Figure 11-28. We are now ready to complete our design process by specifying the operation of each of the major units of the controller.

Specification of the Master Switching Network

The master switching network serves to interconnect the input information contained in the reader buffer and the rest of the system. Three tasks must be accomplished. They are:

1. The reader information must be connected to the proper control or information register.
2. The flag status information must be delivered to the master control unit.
3. The information transfer pulse must be applied to the proper point in the system.

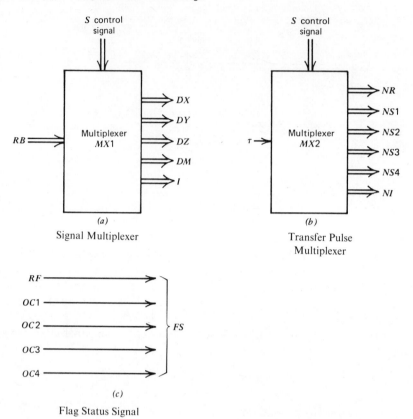

(a)
Signal Multiplexer

(b)
Transfer Pulse
Multiplexer

(c)
Flag Status Signal

Figure 11-29. Decomposition of master switching network into sub-networks.

To realize these tasks the master switching network can be realized by the three subnetworks shown in Figure 11-29. It is assumed that an appropriate multiplexer network is available to accomplish the switching.

The control signal S applied to the master switching network is assumed to have values indicated as s_0 through s_7. These values are associated with the following tasks:

s_0 No operation
s_1 Input operations
s_2 Transfer of information to instruction register
s_3 X control operations
s_4 Y control operations
s_5 Z control operations
s_6 Drill select operations
s_7 Raise drill to initial position

Table 11-20   Specification of Multiplexer Network

Task

Multiplexer \ Signal S	s_0	s_1	s_2	s_3
$MX1$	No operation	No operation	$I := RB_{1,3}$	$DX := RB$
$MX2$	No operation	$NR := \tau$	$NI := \tau$	$N1 := \tau$

Task (continued)

	s_4	s_5	s_6	s_7
$MX1$	$DY := RB$	$DZ := RB$	$DM := RB_{7,8}$	$DZ := [0]$
$MX2$	$NS2 := \tau$	$NS3 := \tau$	$NS4 := \tau$	$NS3 := \tau$

Note: $RB_{1,3}$ is bits 1 through 3 of RB; $RB_{7,8}$ is bits 7, 8 of RB.

The actual tasks performed by the multiplexers $MX1$ and $MX2$ are defined by Table 11-20.

The Master Control Unit

The master control unit is a sequential network with two inputs FS and I and two outputs S and τ. The control signal S is a level signal, but τ will be a clock pulse that causes the appropriate transfers to take place. The general operations performed by the master control unit are specified by the flowchart shown in Figure 11-30.

This figure shows that the control unit has two distinct phases of operations. During the fetch phase the control unit waits until all motion of the drilling machine has been completed and then it reads the information in bits 1 through 3 of the reader buffer into the instruction register. At this point the control unit is ready for the execution phase of operation.

The control unit uses the value in the instruction register I to decide which task to perform. If no additional information is needed (instructions i_0, i_4, i_5, i_6) the control unit sends out the necessary commands. However, if the instruction requires additional information (instructions i_1, i_2, i_3), a second read sequence

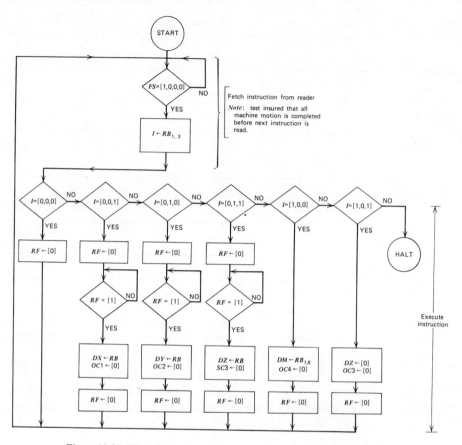

Figure 11-30. Flowchart representing operation of master control unit.

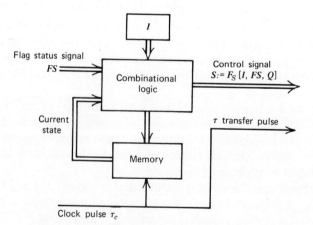

Figure 11-31. General structure of master control unit.

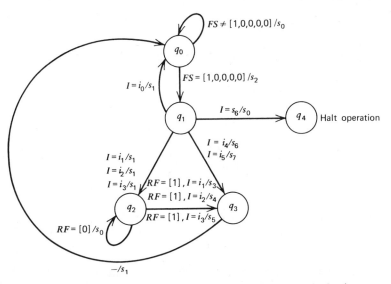

Figure 11-32. General state transition diagram of master control unit.

occurs before the instruction can be completed. The sequence of operation continues until the halt instruction is encountered. The control system stops operation at this point.

The master control unit will have a general organization of the form shown in Figure 11-31. The control signal S will be used to set up the master switching network. The transfer pulse τ will be generated by the clock signal. Transfers in the system take place only when a transfer pulse τ is generated.

The actual behavior of the sequential network, which makes up the heart of the master control unit, can be represented by the state transition table shown in Figure 11-32. The initial state is q_0 and the final state indicating that the drilling operation is completed is state q_4. There are two inputs I and FS and one output S. Since $I = \{i_0, i_1, i_2, i_3, i_4, i_5, i_6\}$, $S = \{s_0, s_1, s_2, s_3, s_4, s_5, s_6\}$ and $FS = [NRF, OC1, OC2, OC3, OC4]$, we can indicate the input output condition as

$$\text{Input condition}/s_a$$

where "input conditon" indicates the input condition needed for a transfer and the output represents the control signal applied to the switching network.

With the specification of the master control unit we have completed the general design of the controller for the drilling machine. Our next task would be to reduce this information to a set of logical expressions that would actually describe the logic circuitry necessary to construct the controller.

This design is not unique. There are many other ways that we could have proceeded. However, the design is simple and would probably be economical to construct.

EXERCISES

1. Let $r = 2$. Show how the multipliers described in Figure 11-18 and 11-19 operate by showing the contents of each register during the multiplication sequence for the following initial conditions.

   (a) Multiplier 10   Multiplicand 11
   (b) Multiplier 11   Multiplicand 11

2. Write out the binary coded representation of the instructions needed to drill the holes in the steel plate shown in Figure 11-24.

5. SUMMARY

In this chapter we have concentrated on the techniques that can be used to describe the information processing operations that take place within complex digital systems. We have seen that it is not necessary, in many cases, to worry about the actual circuit construction of a particular device if we can represent the information processing tasks performed by the device.

The concept of a control unit that can be used to control the operation of a large number of other information processing and transfer devices is of particular importance. In simple systems this control unit is completely responsible for determining the sequence of information processing tasks performed by the system. Thus the design of the control unit is almost completely determined by the algorithm describing the computation that the system must perform.

As the complexity and number of information processing tasks that must be handled by a system increases we find that it is no longer practical to have a system in which the control unit is constrained to one fixed sequence of operation. By introducing the idea of a programmable control unit, we saw that we could greatly increase the flexibility of our system. Thus we are able to increase the overall flexibility of the system with only a small increase in the complexity of the control unit.

Now that we have an understanding of how a programmed control unit operates, our next task is to investigate how this concept can be used to represent a complete computer system. This is done in the next chapter.

REFERENCE NOTATION

The references listed include a wide range of topics related to the material presented in this chapter. References [1], [5], and [6] develop the idea of information transfer. References [4] and [7] give extensive discussions of how various arithmetic operations can be performed using logic networks. Eadie [3] and Stone [8] give a general overview of many different information processing units and how these units can be interconnected to form complete information processing systems. Gschwind [4] and Chu [2] give a somewhat more advanced treatment of the same general material.

REFERENCES

1. Bartree, T. C., Lebow, I. L., and Reed, I. S. (1962), *Theory and Design of Digital Machines*, McGraw-Hill, New York.

2. Chu, Y. (1962), *Digital Computer Design Fundamentals*, McGraw-Hill, New York.

3. Eadie, D. (1968), *Introduction to the Basic Computer*, Prentice-Hall, Englewood Cliffs, N. J.

4. Gschwind, H. W. and McCluskey, E. J. (1975), *Digital Design of Digital Computers*, Springer-Verlag, New York.

5. Hellerman, H. (1973), *Digital Computer System Principles*, Second Edition McGraw-Hill, New York.

6. Hill, F. J. and Peterson, G. R. (1973), *Digital Systems: Hardware Organization and Design*, John Wiley, New York.

7. Mowle, F. J. (1976), *A Systematic Approach to Digital Logic Design*, Addison-Wesley, Reading, Mass.

8. Stone, H. S. (ed.) (1975), *Introduction to Computer Architecture*, SRA, Chicago.

HOME PROBLEMS

1. Design the logic and sequential networks necessary to realize the information processing system shown in Figure 11-16. Assume that all combinational logic must be realized using NAND logic elements and that all flip-flops are *J-K* flip-flops. The *A* and *B* registers are also assumed to be 6-bit registers.

2. Two 10-bit signals *X* and *Y* are available as the output of an analog-to-digital converter. These signals must be added together. After the addition operation is completed the sum must be transferred to a sum buffer register *SB*. The contents of *SB* remains fixed until a new sum is ready to be loaded into *SB*.

At the time a new sum is loaded into *SB* new values of *X* and *Y* are being generated by the analog-to-digital converter.

Design this system. It is not necessary to develop the logic networks required to realize the system.

3. Design a digital system that will automatically test the operation of the combinational logic network shown in Figure P11-1.

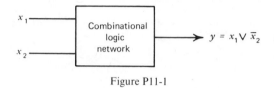

Figure P11-1

4. Design a digital system that will divide the binary number *A* by the binary number *B*.

5. Assume that a 16-bit word memory unit is available to hold a program for the drilling machine shown in Figure 11-20. Redesign the control system for the drilling machine by replacing the program on the paper tape with a program in the memory unit.

6. Hand calculators often use serial operations to carry out the standard arithmetic operations. Design a serial binary multiplier.

12

Stored Program Information Processors and Computers

From our previous discussion we know that any information processing task can be represented by an algorithm involving a sequence of elementary information processing operations. If the task is simple enough we can construct a digital system that will automatically execute the desired sequence of operations under the control of a fixed control unit. Unfortunately, any change in the algorithm requires us to redesign our control unit.

To overcome this problem we introduced the idea of a control unit with an instruction register. This innovation allowed us to select which one of a number of possible information processing tasks that the digital system would perform. Although this approach greatly increases the flexibility of a particular system, there is still a rather severe practical limit on the complexity of the tasks which can be performed by systems of this type.

If we must design a system to carry out a complex task, we could, of course, identify the elementary operations needed to perform the task and then develop a digital system that carries out each of these operations under the control of a control unit with an instruction register. Since each of the different elementary operations would be indicated by a unique code we could carry out the desired information processing task by manually loading the code for each elementary operation into the instruction register as it was required during the execution of the algorithm.

This is a very pragmatic approach except that there is no reason why we cannot extend the design of the control unit to the point where it can automatically sequence through a series of operations. All that we have to do is provide a means for the control unit to have access to a list that indicates the order in which the operations must be performed. A simple system of this type was considered at the end of the last chapter.

A digital system with a control unit which can automatically execute a sequence of basic operations that are contained on an external list is called a programmed information processor. Computers are, of course, one of the most common form of programmed information processors. However, there are many other systems, such as those used to control the operation of machines or the flow of information, which can also be so classified.

In this chapter we first investigate the general structure of a programmed information processor and the operational characteristics of the units that make up the processor. Using this information we then discuss the organization and operation of a simple digital computer in order to obtain an understanding of the typical types of elementary operations that are included in computers. This computer is also used in Chapter 13 to investigate the problem of developing programs to carry out complex information processing tasks.

2. SYSTEM ORGANIZATION

Every programmed information processor is designed so that it can be used to carry out any calculation that belongs to a particular class of calculations. Thus if we are to design such a system, we must:

1. Identify the basic operations that must be available for use by the system in making these calculations.
2. Define how the sequence of steps that make up the task are going to be represented.
3. Define how the processor is going to know which step it must perform at each point in a given calculation.
4. Define how information needed by the processor is to be obtained.

Although the final organization of a given system will be strongly influenced by the type of processing tasks it must perform, most systems have the general organization shown in Figure 12-1.

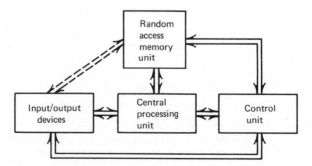

Figure 12-1. Major units of a programmed information processor.

The random access memory unit, of the type discussed in Chapter 10 can be used to store both the sequence of instructions needed by the control unit to carry out a given computation and the information needed by the central processing unit to make the computation. The central processing unit, usually called the CPU, consists of a collection of registers and the associated logic networks necessary to carry out the basic logic and arithmetic operations that can be employed by the system.

The control unit governs the operation of the overall system. It has two main functions. First, it must control the order in which the instructions that describe a given computation are executed. Second, it must control the operation of the CPU and other parts of the system during the execution of a particular instruction.

The input/output section of a system can be made up of a number of different I/O devices. These devices serve as an interface between the system and the outside world. Sometimes I/O information flows through the CPU and at other times information transfer takes place directly between the memory unit and a particular I/O device.

Now that we have an idea of how a programmed information processor is organized, we must determine the behavior of each part of the system and how it contributes to the operation of the overall system. Here again we concentrate on the information flow in the various units rather than on the details of how these units are constructed.

Random Access Memory Control and Organization

The random access memory is usually made up of 2^k r-bit registers which are numbered 0 through $2^k - 1$. The number associated with each register is called its *address*. Each register stores one *word of information*.

A typical memory may be organized as shown in Figure 12-2. The part of the memory reserved for instruction words and the part reserved for data words are

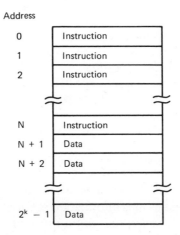

Figure 12-2. Representation of the contents of a random access memory.

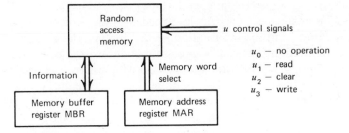

Figure 12-3. Representation of random access core memory.

usually flexible and can easily be reassigned as necessary to carry out a given calculation. In fact, there are many situations where only a portion of the memory is used and the information contained in the rest of the memory words is of no interest.

In order to read data or instruction words into or out of memory we can use an arrangement of the type illustrated in Figure 12-3. As shown, we have an r-bit memory buffer register and a k-bit memory address register associated with the memory unit. The operation of the memory unit depends on the type of memory technology being used. If we use a semiconductor memory, then the read operation is nondestructive. If we use a magnetic core memory, the read operation is destructive and we must rewrite the read data back into memory. For this discussion we will assume that the memory is a magnetic core memory, since the operations involved are slightly more complex. Four memory control signals are needed to control the operation of core memory units. If we indicate the different registers of the memory system as

MBR   memory buffer register
MAR   memory address register
$M_{[MAR]}$ memory location indicated by contents of MAR

then these signals are

u_0 No operation
u_1 Read $M_{[MAR]}$ into MBR
         (This operation also sets $M_{[MAR]}$ to 0)
u_2 Clear $M_{[MAR]}$ (i.e., set $M_{[MAR]}$ to 0)
u_3 Write MBR into $M_{[MAR]}$

To read information into or out of memory requires a three-step process. Table 12-1 summarizes these steps in terms of our information transfer conventions.

The function of a memory unit is to store information that is presented to it and to deliver information to external devices. As long as the proper control signals are presented to the memory unit it will carry out the requested information transfer without regard to the use that this information is put to in the rest of the system. Thus our next task is to consider some of the different ways that this information is used.

Table 12-1   Read and Write Information
Transfer Sequence for Random Access Memory

Read Operation

Clock Pulse	Memory Control Instruction	Transfer Operation	Comments
τ_1	u_0	$\text{MAR} \leftarrow \langle \text{Address Information} \rangle$	Address information introduced from external source
τ_2	u_1	$\text{MBR} \leftarrow \text{M}_{[\text{MAR}]}, \text{M}_{[\text{MAR}]} \leftarrow [0]$	Reading information from $\text{M}_{[\text{MAR}]}$ sets this word to 0
τ_3	u_3	$\text{M}_{[\text{MAR}]} \leftarrow \text{MBR},$ $\langle \text{External Use} \rangle \leftarrow \text{MBR}$	Restore information in $\text{M}_{[\text{MAR}]}$

Write Operation

Clock Pulse	Memory Control Instruction	Transfer Operation	Comments
τ_1	u_0	$\text{MAR} \leftarrow \langle \text{Address Information} \rangle$ $\text{MBR} \leftarrow \langle \text{Information to be stored} \rangle$	Information from external sources to set up registers
τ_2	u_2	$\text{M}_{[\text{MAR}]} \leftarrow [0]$	Clear out old information
τ_3	u_3	$\text{M}_{[\text{MAR}]} \leftarrow \text{MBR}$	Write new information

The Central Processing Unit

Most of the actual information processing tasks performed on data are carried out in the central processing unit. This unit consists of a collection of registers and the associated logic networks necessary to accomplish the basic logic, arithmetic, and information transfer operations that can be employed by the system to carry out a given information processing task. For simpler systems, the heart of this unit is

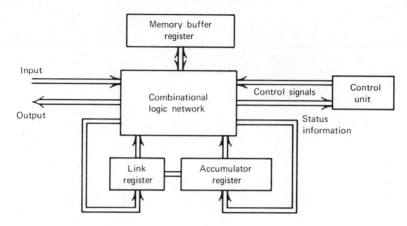

Figure 12-4. Organization of a simple central processing unit.

a special register called an *accumulator*. This register is used to retain the result of logical and arithmetic operations for the interim period between each operation, or it is used to temporarily store information during an information transfer. More sophisticated systems may have a CPU with a number of accumulators or one or more additional registers for the intermediate storage of information that is needed in performing particular operations.

For ease of understanding we will deal with central processing units that have an organization of the type shown in Figure 12-4. The accumulator register, denoted by AC, is an r-bit register where r is the word size associated with the memory register. The link register, denoted by L, is a 1-bit register that serves a number of purposes. In arithmetic operations it serves as a flag to indicate that an overflow occurred, while in other cases it serves as a 1-bit extension of the accumulator. The operation of this register will become more evident as our discussion progresses.

In this particular system, the memory buffer register serves as an intermediate storage point for the transfer of data into and out of memory. For those operations involving two operands, one operand is assumed to be in the accumulator and the other is in the memory buffer register. The result of the operation is retained in the accumulator and possibly the link.

The particular operation performed at a given time depends on which control signals are received from the control unit. Some of the typical types of logical and data manipulation operations that might be performed are given below.

1. *Load the accumulator.* The contents of the memory buffer register are transferred into the accumulator at the end of the memory read cycle.
2. *Deposit the contents of the accumulator.* The contents of the accumulator are transferred into the memory buffer register so that the information can be deposited into memory during the write cycle.

3. *Boolean operations.* Different Boolean operations, such as AND, OR, or EXCLUSIVE OR are performed by logically combining (bit by bit) the contents of the accumulator with the contents of the memory buffer register.

4. *Complement.* Form the 1's complement (logical complement) or the 2's complement of the binary number stored in the accumulator.

5. *Transfer data.* Data can be transferred into the accumulator from an external source or transferred out of the accumulator to an external register.

6. *Rotation.* The contents of the $r + 1$ bit register made up of the link and the accumulator can be rotated one or more bits to the right or left.

7. *Test status of accumulator or link.* The content of the accumulator can be checked to see if it is positive, negative, or zero. The content of the link can be checked to see if it is 0 or 1. The resulting status information is reported to the control unit.

8. *Set register contents to fixed values.* The link can be set to 0 or 1. The accumulator can be cleared, set to all 1's or set to a specific binary number.

The number of arithmetic operations that can be performed in a simple CPU of the type we are considering is usually quite limited. In fact the only arithmetic operation that might be present is addition. In this case the contents of the memory buffer register and the contents of the accumulator are added together and the result is left in the accumulator. If there is an overflow carry, this is placed in the link. (It is assumed that the link was set to 0 before the addition was performed.)

Subtraction is usually accomplished by representing negative numbers in 1's or 2's complement form. The addition operation can thus be used to also perform subtraction.

As we have seen, it is also possible to carry out multiplication as a hardware operation. However, additional registers are needed. If the expense of this additional hardware is not justified, the multiplication operation can be carried out by executing a sequence of addition, rotation, and information transfer operations. Division and other special arithmetic operations such as trigonometric function evaluation or finding the logarithm of a number could also be realized as hardware operations if the CPU were increased in complexity and additional registers were added. The added cost is often not warranted for simple information processors since operations of this type can also be performed as a sequence of simple operations. However, in special situations or in large computer systems it would be practical and even desirable to have a number of these more complex operations actually available as hardware operations.

From our previous discussion we know that the CPU can be implemented using standard logical design techniques once the actual operations that must be performed by the unit have been selected. The choice of these operations represents a compromise between the desirability of having a given operation when carrying out a particular information processing task and the cost of including the hardware necessary to implement that operation. A much more detailed discussion of how different operations can be implemented can be found in references [3] and [2] at the end of this chapter.

Input/Output Section

Every information processing system must have some means to transfer information between the outside world and the information processor. There are two general ways that this transfer can occur.

Information transfers involving the slower speed input/output devices such as paper tape readers and punches, card reader and punches, printers and teletypes, and analogue-to-digital converters are often accomplished by connecting the device to the CPU. Input information is transferred, under the direction of the control unit, from the input device to a register in the CPU while output information is transferred from a particular CPU register to a given output device. The general form that systems of this type take is illustrated in Figure 12-5.

When it becomes necessary to transfer information the control unit sends a signal to the device selector that connects the desired input or output device to the CPU. The control signals necessary to carry out the given information transfer are then generated by the control unit. Information transfers of this type are called *programmed data transfers* because the complete information transfer sequence is under the control of the control unit.

In addition to programmed data transfer, some systems provide for the direct transfer of information between an external device and memory without waiting for special signals from the control unit. In effect, the peripheral device takes over the operation of the system while the data transfer is taking place. Figure 12-6 illustrates how this is accomplished.

Assume that a condition has occurred where it is necessary to exchange information between the system and a high-speed peripheral device. The exchange sequence

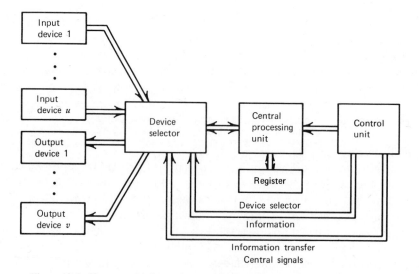

Figure 12-5. Slow-speed information transfer between I/O devices and CPU.

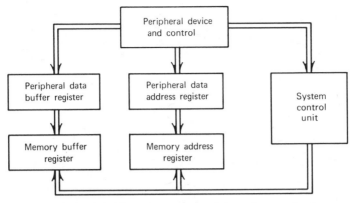

Figure 12-6. Direct memory access information transfer.

is initiated when the device signals the control unit that it is ready to start a data exchange between itself and the system. The control unit then enters the direct memory access mode of operation (which usually means the suspension of other operations) and turns control over to the control unit in the external device. If data is to be transferred into the computer the external device generates the memory address where the first data word is to be deposited and loads this address into the memory address register. At the same time the data information is transferred into the memory buffer register. A memory write cycle is then initiated and the data is entered into memory. This sequence of operations is continued until the peripheral control unit determines that the data transfer is complete. Then the control is returned to the system's control unit. A similar technique is used for data transfer from memory to a peripheral device. This method of information transfer is used for such devices as magnetic tape units, magnetic drums and disks, and cathode-ray-tube displays.

The Control Unit

So far we have considered the function of every unit except the control unit. From our discussion we see that the control unit must serve two purposes: that of controlling the sequence of information processing tasks that must be carried out by the system and that of making sure that each unit of the system carries out a specific operation at a specific time. Since the control unit is of central importance in the design of any system, we devote the next section to a consideration of the major operations that it must perform.

EXERCISE

1. How will the operations of Table 12-1 be changed if the memory is semiconductor rather than magnetic core memory?

3. THE CONTROL UNIT

When we design an information processor, we must select a set of basic computational and information transfer operations that the CPU can carry out. To carry out a complex computation we must then develop an algorithm that describes how this computation can be performed using only those operations that can be executed by the CPU. The algorithm is then reduced to a sequence of basic instructions that the control unit can interpret. This sequence of instructions is called a *machine language program*. To understand how a control unit executes such a program, we must investigate how the instructions that describe a given information processing task are encoded and how they are used by the control unit.

There are two general classes of instruction: those that involve the operation of the CPU and the other parts of the system, and those that influence the sequence in which the instructions that make up the program are executed. Each instruction is stored in memory. To execute the program the control unit must read the instruction from memory, determine the operation called for by the instruction, and then generate the control signals necessary to carry out the operation.

Any data needed to execute a given instruction may be stored in memory, in one of the registers of the CPU, or it may come from an input device connected to the system. When data is needed to execute a given instruction, the control unit must know where to find it and how it is to be used during the execution of the instruction. In some cases this knowledge is designed into the control unit while in others the instruction being processed by the control unit must supply this information.

If the control unit is to execute a program, it must be able to interpret each of the instructions that make up the program. Thus we must define how the information describing each instruction is encoded. Most system designers have evolved their own philosophy concerning the types of instructions they need in their systems, and the way that these instructions should be encoded. Therefore, the following discussion deals only with the basic classes of instructions that are needed in any system and how these instructions might be encoded.

Structure of Instructions

An instruction is partitioned into sections that contain specific types of information. This is accomplished by assigning special meaning to particular groups of non-overlapping bits of an instruction. Each such subsection of an instruction is called a *field*. In an instruction, separate fields might be assigned to indicate the operation to be performed, to indicate the address of data words, to indicate how a word at a given location is to be interpreted, or to indicate that some basic operation is or is not to be performed.

The first type of field that must be included in an instruction is an *operation code field*. This field identifies the instruction to the control unit. If this field has c-bits then the system will have a maximum of 2^c different basic instructions. The remaining bits in the instruction are assigned a meaning depending on which instruction

Operation Code
Field

Information Needed
by Control Unit to
Execute Instruction

i_1	i_2	$\cdots$	i_c	i_{c+1}	$\cdots\cdots$	i_r

Figure 12-7. General form of encoded instruction.

is indicated by the contents of the operation code field. The general structure of a typical instruction is shown in Figure 12-7.

There are three general classes of instructions that must be considered.

1. Memory Reference Instructions
2. Register Reference Instructions
3. Input/Output Control Instructions

The various types of instructions are encoded in different ways depending on the type of information that must be supplied to the control unit.

Memory Reference Instructions

Memory reference instructions involve operations that require information which is stored in one or more memory locations. These instructions are used to carry out such tasks as:

1. Reading data into or out of memory.
2. Performing logical and arithmetic operations involving data stored in memory and data stored in CPU registers.
3. Changing the order in which a program instruction sequence is executed.

The organization of a memory reference instruction can take on a variety of forms depending on the type of system used. A typical memory reference instruction must provide enough information so that the system can execute operations of the form:

Compute ⟨operand 1⟩⟨operation⟩⟨operand 2⟩ and place result in ⟨destination location⟩

To execute such operations the instruction must provide the system with the following information.

1. The operation or transfer to be formed.
2. The addresses of the operands or quantities to be operated on.
3. The location to which the result is to be sent.
4. The location of the next instruction.

Operation Code	First Operand Address	Second Operand Address	Result Address	Next Instruction Address

Four-Address Instruction

(a)

Operation Code	First Operand Address	Second Operand Address	Result Address

Three-Address Instruction

(b)

Operation Code	First Operand Address	Second Operand Address

Two-Address Instruction

(c)

Operation Code	Operand Address

One-Address Instruction

(d)

Operation Code	Tag	Operand Address

One-Address Instruction with a Tag Field

(e)

Figure 12-8. Some typical field organizations of memory address instructions.

All of this information could be coded into an instruction by using a field arrangement like that shown in Figure 12-8a. In this arrangement all of the information needed to execute a given instruction is contained in the instruction. This method of encoding instruction information is very inefficient. For example, if the memory has $2^{12} = 4096$ memory locations, then each address field would require 12 bits. The instruction would thus need 48 bits for address information alone.

If each instruction were encoded into a single memory word, this would mean that each word would have to be greater than 48 bits just to handle address information. An instruction could be encoded by using multiple words. For example, one word could be used for the operation code and a separate word could be used for each address field. Both of these approaches do not make effective use of memory and are only practical for very large computers. Fortunately this structure can be simplified by making use of the general properties of the system.

All the instructions associated with a given calculation can be stored in sequential address positions. If we include a special register, called a *program counter* or *instruction address register*, to point to the next instruction to be executed, then there is no need to include a next-instruction-address address field in the instruction word. The disadvantage of this omission is that we must introduce additional instructions that can be used to alter the sequence in which a set of program instructions are executed. Figure 12-8b illustrates the organization of a three-address instruction.

Every time that we must read information into or out of memory we must go through a memory cycle. One way to reduce the number of memory cycles is to assume that the result of any operation is placed in a fixed register, possibly one that is dependent on the particular operation code used, in the CPU or control unit. By doing this, we can eliminate the result address field and have a word organization such as is illustrated in Figure 12-8c.

By using similar reasoning we can always assume that one of the operands is always present in a fixed register, such as the accumulator, and that the result is left in another fixed register on completion of the operation. Under this convention only one operand address is needed. Such single address instructions require fewer bits and are easier to execute. Because of this, many small computers and information processing systems use single address instructions. Figure 12-8d illustrates this type of instruction.

Some systems may include several hardware registers in their CPU. In such cases we must indicate which register is to be used in conjunction with the operation specified by the operation code. This is accomplished by introducing a *tag field* in the instruction word to convey the necessary information as to which register is to be used. Figure 12-8e illustrates an instruction word with a tag field.

The number of bits assigned to each field in the instruction word determines the amount of information that can be stored in that field. For example, if the address field contains u-bits then exactly 2^u locations in memory can be addressed directly. If the memory contains no more than 2^u locations then there is no problem. However, if the memory contains more than 2^u locations then we cannot directly address every memory location.

One way around this problem is to introduce a separate register, called an *index register*, that can be used to store a number that indicates the "general area" of memory in which we are working. The *effective* address of the information referenced by a memory reference instruction is then the address obtained by summing the number in the index register and the number in the address field of the instruction. A tag field can be used to indicate when the index register is to be used.

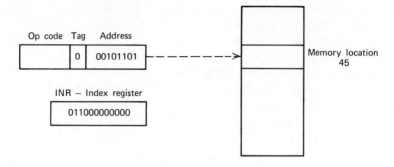

(a)

Direct Addressing Tag = 0

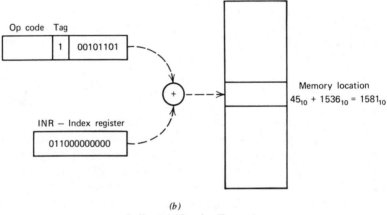

(b)

Indirect Addressing Tag = 1

Figure 12-9. Illustration of the use of an *a* index register to expand address range.

To illustrate how an index register is used, consider Figure 12-9. Assume that the instruction is stored in a 12-bit word with an 8-bit address field and a 1-bit tag field. Since $2^8 = 256$, we can only reference 256 different memory locations. If our memory contains $4096 = 2^{12}$ locations, we can use an index register as an aid in addressing any word in memory. Let INR be a 12-bit index register.

When the tag bit is set to 0, as shown in Figure 12-9a, we take the address as the absolute address of the word that we are interested in. However, when we set the tag bit to 1, then the memory address is formed by adding the number in the index register to the number stored in the address field. This is illustrated in Figure 12-9b. Since the index register may contain any value between 0 and $2^{12} - 1 = 4095$ this means that we can now address all 4096 memory locations.

The number that we place in the index register serves to establish a region in memory, and the address information is used to access memory locations in that region. The main drawback in using this type of addressing is that we must provide additional instructions to service the index register.

Register Reference Instructions

The CPU and control unit in a given system contain a number of registers that store information of different types during a calculation. Register reference instructions can be used to carry out operations such as:

(a) Set the contents of specific registers to specific values.
(b) Add a constant to or subtract it from the quantity stored in a given register.
(c) Transfer the contents of one register to another.
(d) Modify the content of a register using a logical operation.
(e) Test the contents of a register for some property, or compare the contents of two registers.
(f) Shift or rotate the contents of a register.
(g) Perform operations on data stored in two registers and store the results in a specified register.
(h) Alter the program sequence by instructing the control unit to take the next instruction from a different memory location than originally indicated.

From this list it is obvious that there are a wide variety of tasks that can be performed. The field structure for different types of instructions takes different forms. In some cases one instruction is needed to carry out a particular operation while in other cases one instruction can be structured in such a way that it can be used to implement a number of operations. Some typical instruction organizations are given in Figure 12-10.

Figure 12-10a shows the form of an instruction that could be used to change the instruction sequence being executed. Such an instruction tells the control unit to take the next program instruction from the location specified by the content of the address field. Instructions of this type are needed in systems that use one and two address memory reference instructions.

Figure 12-10b illustrates the form an instruction might take if it were dealing with information stored in registers. For example, the instruction might be to compare the contents of register 1 and register 2 to see if they are equal. If they are, the next instruction should be taken from a location determined by the contents of the field labeled action. Otherwise the program sequence is not changed. To execute this instruction, the control unit would instruct the CPU to make the required comparison. If the comparison is true then the contents of the action field are used to change the program sequence. Otherwise the sequence is left unchanged.

Several of the operations that we might wish to perform do not require elaborate encodings. For example, the code necessary to complement a predesignated register or to increment it by 1 does not require a complete instruction word. We can greatly

Controlled Program Sequence Modification
(a)

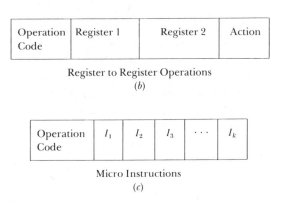

Register to Register Operations
(b)

Micro Instructions
(c)

Figure 12-10. General types of register reference instructions.

expand the number of operations if we group a selection of these simple instructions into a class and indicate this class by a single operation code. We then divide the rest of the instruction into fields as shown in Figure 12-10c. The k-fields I_1, through I_k are assumed to be 1-bit in size and each field corresponds to a particular operation. For example I_1 might correspond to "clear the accumulator," I_2 might correspond to "complement the accumulator," I_3 might correspond to "increment the accumulator,"..., and I_k might correspond to "skip the next instruction if contents of accumulator is 0." If we wish the instruction corresponding to field I_j executed we place a 1 in the field; otherwise it is left 0. Finally we note that several of these instructions could be executed by the control unit during a given execution sequence if we specified the order in which the operations indicated by the fields are to be executed. Let us assume that the control unit executes the fields in natural order. Thus if we wished to form the 2's complement of the number held in the accumulator we would set field I_2 and I_3 to 1 and all other fields to 0. When the control unit encountered this instruction it would first complement the number in the accumulator and then increase it by 1. The net result is the 2's complement of the number originally stored in the accumulator. Instructions of this type are called *micro-coded or micro-programmed instructions*.

Input/Output Instructions

The final class of instructions are those that can be used to transfer information between the system and the various peripheral devices which interface the system to the outside world. An input/output (I/O) instruction must:

1. Indicate the external device associated with the instruction.
2. Supply control information necessary to execute information transfer.

Each device can be assigned a number; thus we can indicate a device by giving its number. The problem of supplying control information to the device is much more complicated since each device has different control requirements. For some devices a single instruction will service a given device while other devices will require a complex program to control information transfer.

Operation Code	Device Selector	Device Control

Figure 12-11. General form of input/output instructions.

The general structure of an input/output instruction is indicated in Figure 12-11. The operation code indicates that the instruction is an I/O instruction and the contents of the device selector field indicates which device is referenced by the instruction. The rest of the instruction word makes up the device control field. This field contains the coded instructions necessary for correct operation of the I/O device referenced by the device selector field.

Now that we have established how the different classes of instructions can be encoded, our next task is to consider how the control unit can make use of these instructions. Control units can take on a variety of forms depending on the final form that is selected for the set of instructions that can be executed by the information processing system. In particular, the decision concerning the organization of memory reference instructions strongly influences the control unit's organization and sequence of operation. For simplicity, the following discussion deals with a control unit that is designed to interpret single address memory reference instructions.

The Control Unit

The control unit of the information processor governs the operation of the complete system. It must not only control the execution of each of the basic operations that make up a given instruction, but it must also control the sequence in which these operations are performed.

One general organization of a control unit and its relationship to the rest of the system is shown in Figure 12-12. As discussed in Chapter 11, the control unit is

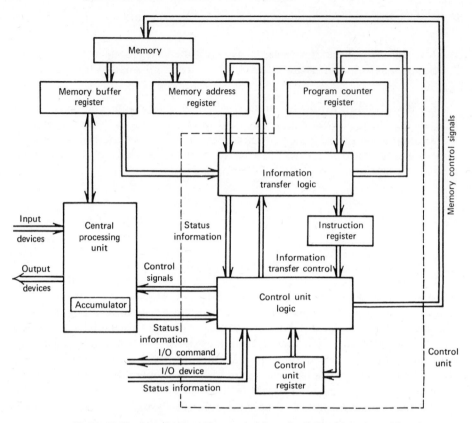

Figure 12-12. Organization of control unit and relationship to rest of system.

responsible for generating the signals that activate the operations performed by the rest of the system. The following discussion is based on the assumption that all of the memory reference instructions in the instruction set are single address instructions.

Assume that the instructions for a given program are stored sequentially in memory locations N through $N + M$. To execute this program the control unit reads the first instruction from memory location N and then initiates the sequence of hardware operation necessary to carry out that instruction. Next it goes to memory location $N + 1$ and executes that instruction in a similar manner. This sequence of operations continues until the control element encounters an instruction that tells the control unit to halt operation or to go to another memory location to find the next sequence of instructions.

From this we see that the control unit must perform two main functions. First, it must fetch the instructions from memory in the proper sequence and second, it must ensure that each instruction is executed properly. Thus we can identify two phases of operation of the control unit.

1. The fetch phase
2. The execute phase

The program counter register is used to keep track of which instruction is to be executed by the system. During the execute phase of operation the memory address from which the next instruction is to be taken is stored in the program counter register.

When the control unit enters the fetch phase of operation a memory read cycle is initiated. The contents of the program counter are transferred into the memory address register. The word stored at this location, which is assumed to be an instruction word, is then read into the memory buffer register. The information in the operation code field of the instruction word is then transferred to the control unit's instruction register and the control unit increases the contents of the program counter by one so that it will be ready when the next instruction is needed. This completes the fetch phase and the control unit enters the execute phase of operation.

During the execute phase the contents of the instruction register together with the status information from the various parts of the system determine the sequence of control signals generated by the control unit. Each type of instruction requires a different control sequence.

If the operation code in the instruction register calls for a memory reference instruction then the execute sequence must:

1. Transfer the address field information contained in the instruction word stored in the memory buffer register into the memory address register.
2. If data must be read from memory this data is read into the memory buffer register. The data is then used by the CPU to perform the indicated operation. The result of the operation is left in the accumulator.
3. If data must be transferred from the CPU into memory this data is first transferred into the memory buffer register. Then the data is written into the memory location indicated by the address stored in the memory buffer register.

If the operation code indicates a register reference instruction then the control unit must use the status information from the different fields of the instruction stored in the memory buffer register together with the status information from the other parts of the system to generate the control signals necessary to execute the called-for operation. The number of steps needed to carry out the operation will depend on the operation and the way that the system is organized.

The input/output instructions set up the control unit to interact with external devices. If the contents of the instruction register indicate an input/output operation is to be performed, then the control unit must use the device selector field

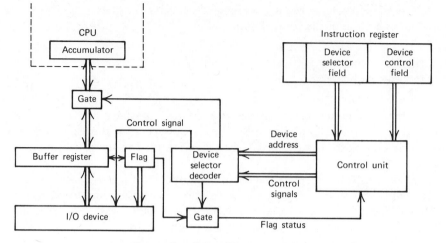

Figure 12-13. Programmed data transfer.

information of the instruction word stored in the memory buffer register to determine which I/O device is to be used for the information transfer. The information transfer sequence is then initiated under the control of the information contained in the device control field of the instruction word.

Each step of a programmed data transfer is under the control of the control unit and is in response to information contained in the device control field of the instruction field. A typical method of programmed information transfer is to transfer data between the CPU's accumulator and the external device in a manner illustrated by Figure 12-13.

When an instruction calls for the transfer of data between an external device and the computer the control element transmits the device address code to all peripheral devices along the device address line. The device selector decoder in each device decodes this information. If the device is the device addressed, it puts out a signal which enables the gates on both the device buffer register and the flag register. If the unit is ready to accept or transmit data the flag is set to 1. This is sensed by the control unit and data transfer between the CPU and the peripheral device is accomplished.

Thus far, we have discussed the general structure of a programmed information processor. In the next section we introduce a very simple, hypothetical, digital computer system in order to give a specific example of how these ideas are applied.

EXERCISE

1. A system has a 1024 word memory. If an instruction word requires a 4-bit operation code field, what is the minimum instruction word size that can be used if all memory locations are to be directly addressable?

4. SEDCOM*

SEDCOM (Simulated EDucational COMputer) is a hypothetical small computer that has been developed to illustrate the general concepts presented in this chapter and to serve as a representative computer for our discussion of machine language programming discussed in the next chapter. This computer can be simulated on any available commercial computer. If such a simulation is available, the reader can actually experimentally explore the programming techniques necessary to carry out a given information processing task without having to use the much more complicated instruction set of the commercial computer.

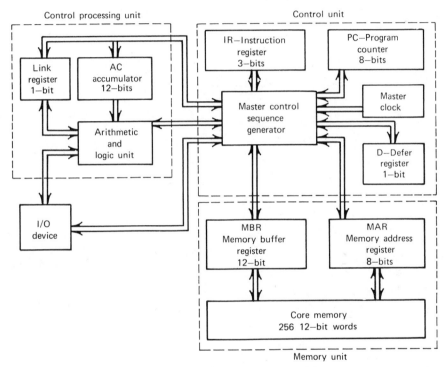

Figure 12-14. General block diagram of SEDCOM.

SEDCOM has a memory of 256 12-bit words. A block diagram showing the general organization of SEDCOM is given in Figure 12-14. All the operations performed by SEDCOM are carried out in a simple and a straightforward manner. An actual computer would have a larger memory size and would probably combine

---

* SEDCOM has been modeled after the Digital Equipment Corporation PDP-8. The logical organization is similar, but not identical to the PDP-8. The instruction set of SEDCOM is compatible with the PDP-8 except that in the PDP-8 memory location 200_8 through 377_8 cannot be directly addressed by memory reference instructions in locations 0 through 177_8. The mnemonics used to represent all the instructions except the input/output instructions are identical to those used on the PDP-8.

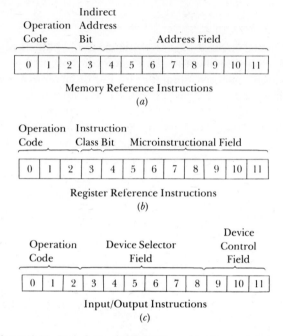

Figure 12-15. Basic form of SEDCOM machine-language instructions.

many of the operational steps that SEDCOM performs into a single step. However, for our purposes it is easier to understand the behavior of the computer if we keep the data flow sequence as simple as possible.

There are three general classes of instruction: memory reference instructions, register reference instructions, and input/output instructions. Each instruction fits into one 12-bit word and the instruction words are divided into fields as indicated in Figure 12-15. The actual form of each instruction is discussed after we explore the general operation of the computer.

Indirect Addressing

The memory reference instruction illustrated in Figure 12-15a includes a 1-bit field called the indirect address bit. When this bit is 0 the memory reference instruction carries out an operation that involves the memory location indicated by the address field of the instruction. However, as we will find shortly, the memory location that we might wish to use may be dependent on some previous calculation. One way to handle this problem would be to actually modify the information in the address field of the instruction. This is usually considered to be poor programming practice. A second and better alternative is to use indirect addressing.

In *indirect addressing* the address information that we want to use is stored in a particular memory location and the address of this special location is placed in the address field of the memory reference instruction. The fact that the instruction deals with an indirect address is indicated by setting the indirect address field bit to 1. Instructions of this type are interpreted in the following manner.

When the control unit sees that the indirect address bit is 1, it places the address field information into the memory address register. It then reads the number stored in the location indicated by the contents of the memory address register into the memory buffer register. This information is now used by the control unit as the effective address referenced by the instruction. The need for this particular form of addressing will become clearer as we become more familiar with the operation of SEDCOM.

General Operation of SEDCOM

We have already considered the general organization of a stored program information processor in the previous section. Therefore, we can now concentrate on the particular operations performed by SEDCOM.

The program executed by SEDCOM and the data needed by the program are stored in the memory. The control unit carries out the dual task of fetching each instruction from memory and then executing the instruction. The master clock, which we assume generates a clock pulse once every 0.5 microsecond, controls the timing of the various information transfers and logical operations performed by the computer.

The master control sequence generator controls the order in which the various internal operations are performed. A complete cycle of fetching an instruction from memory and executing the instruction takes either six clock pulses (3 microseconds) if a direct memory reference is called for, or nine clock pulses (4.5 microseconds) if an indirect memory reference is required. The relative timing of these operations is illustrated in Figure 12-16. We now follow the general operations involved at each step in the fetch and defer portion of the control sequence. The operations

Instruction Not Requiring   Instruction Requiring
     Indirect Addressing   Indirect Addressing

      Clock Pulse   Clock Pulse

                  ⎧ 1   ⎧ 1
        Fetch   ⎨ 2   Fetch   ⎨ 2
                  ⎩ 3   ⎩ 3
                  ⎧ 4   ⎧ 1D
      Execute   ⎨ 5   Defer   ⎨ 2D
                  ⎩ 6   ⎩ 3D
                                                    ⎧ 4
                                        Execute   ⎨ 5
                                                    ⎩ 6

Figure 12-16. Relative timing of control sequence generated by control unit.

involved in the execute portion of the control sequence will be postponed until we discuss the properties of each machine language instruction.

We use the following notational conventions in the discussion of the operation of the control unit.

MBR   memory buffer register
MAR   memory address register
PC   program counter
IR   instruction register
D   defer register
AC   accumulator
L   link register
$M_{[MAR]}$ memory location indicated by contents of MAR

At the beginning of the fetch sequence the program counter register contains the memory address of the instruction that the computer will execute during the execute portion of the control sequence. The sequence of operations performed during the fetch sequence is given in Table 12-2.

Examining this sequence we see that at the occurrence of the first clock pulse the address stored in PC is transferred to MAR. During the second clock period the contents of the memory location indicated by the MAR is transferred to MBR. The fetch sequence is completed at the third clock pulse by reading the operation code field into IR, reading the indirect address bit into D, restoring the contents of $M_{[MAR]}$ and incrementing the contents of the program counter by 1.

The next portion of the control sequence is determined by the contents of IR and D. If the operation code in IR represents a memory reference instruction and if D contains 1, then the instruction read during the fetch sequence involves an indirect address. Thus the control unit must initiate a defer sequence to obtain the address of the information that is needed to execute the operation indicated by the contents of IR before going on to the execute sequence. Otherwise the control unit goes directly to the execute sequence.

The defer operation sequence is indicated by Table 12-3. Examining this table we see that the address information in bits 4 through 11 of MBR are transferred to MAR when the first clock pulse of the defer cycle appears. The contents of the addressed memory location are written into MBR by the second clock pulse of the defer cycle and rewritten into $M_{[MAR]}$ during the third clock pulse of the defer

Table 12-2   Operations Performed During Fetch Sequence

Clock Pulse	Operations Performed
1	$MAR \leftarrow PC$
2	$MBR \leftarrow M_{[MAR]}, M_{[MAR]} \leftarrow [0]$
3	$IR \leftarrow MBR_{0,2}, D \leftarrow MBR_3, M_{[MAR]} \leftarrow MBR, PC \leftarrow PC + [1]$

Table 12-3   Operations Performed During Defer Sequence

Clock Pulse	
1D	$MAR \leftarrow MBR_{4,11}$
2D	$MBR \leftarrow M_{[MAR]}, M_{[MAR]} \leftarrow [0]$
3D	$M_{[MAR]} \leftarrow MBR$

cycle. At the end of the defer sequence the address of the memory location to be used by the control unit during the execute sequence is stored in MBR.

The execute sequence will depend on the operation code stored in IR. As indicated in Figure 12-15 each instruction occupies one 12-bit word. The first 3 bits of an instruction word correspond to the operation code field and the other 9 bits contain the information needed by the computer to carry out the operation called for by the operation code. Memory reference instructions will be indicated by operation codes between 000 and 101, input/output instructions will be indicated by an operation code of 110, and register reference instructions will be indicated by an operation code of 111.

The content of any instruction word or register will be given in octal form. Thus if the binary contents of a word is 011 001 111 110, then this word will be indicated as containing the octal number 3176. The memory addresses will also be given in octal form. Thus the first memory location will be 000 and the 256th location will be 377_8 which corresponds to the decimal number 255_{10}. We adopt this convention since it allows us to write all basic instructions in octal form and eliminates having to convert decimal numbers before we insert the address information into a memory reference instruction. *It should be remembered that the digits 8 and 9 never appear in an octal number.* Using these conventions we now investigate the memory reference instructions, then the register reference instructions, and finally the input/output instructions. The way in which these instructions are used in writing programs is discussed in the next chapter.

The Memory Reference Instructions

We have allotted six operation code values for memory reference instructions. Although it might appear that this small number of instructions would restrict the type of computations that we can perform, this is not the case. The six operations, together with their operation codes and mnemonics are listed in Table 12-4. A mnemonic is a name that we assign so that we can easily discuss the operation.

We now discuss the details of each of these instructions and also the control sequence performed by the control unit to execute each instruction. Each instruction is written in octal form as

CAAA

Table 12-4   SEDCOM Memory Reference Instructions

| | Operation Code | | |
Instruction	Binary	Octal	Mnemonic
Logical AND	000	0	AND
Two's Complement Add	001	1	TAD
Increment and Skip if Zero	010	2	ISZ
Deposit and Clear the Accumulator	011	3	DCA
Jump to Subroutine	100	4	JMS
Jump (Unconditional)	101	5	JMP

where C is an octal number between 0 and 5 that specifies the operation code and AAA is a 3-digit octal number that defines the memory address referenced by the instruction.

This number is defined as follows. If AAA is between 0 and 377 then bit 3, the indirect bit, is 0 and the operation called for is carried out in the direct address mode. If AAA is between 400 and 777 then bit 3 is 1 and the operation called for is carried out in the indirect address mode.

The exact definition of the information transfers and operations performed during the execution cycle for each memory reference instruction is given in Table 12-5. In writing a program at the machine-language level, it is very important that we know the exact definition of each instruction. For example, consider the 2's complement add operation. We should note that if there is an overflow the link bit is *negated* rather than automatically being set to 1. If the link is 1 when an overflow occurs, it will be set to 0. This small point may cause strange errors in a program when the person using the instruction does not realize that the link is negated but, instead, assumes that any overflow automatically sets the link to 1.

The reason for this is that the link and the accumulator form a 13-bit register when we are carrying out addition. Thus if the link is 1 and there is a carry from the accumulator, this is added to the 1 in the link to give 0. The carry out of the link is lost.

Register Reference Instructions

Register reference instructions are used to manipulate or test information that is stored in the accumulator or the link register. Since there is no need to specify a memory address, we can use the bits that make up the memory address field in a memory reference instruction to indicate if a particular register reference instruction should or should not be performed.

Table 12-5

Formal Definition of the
Memory Reference Instructions

1. Logical AND   0AAA   Mnemonic AND

   Definition: The content of the memory location specified by AAA is ANDed
   bit-by-bit to the contents of the accumulator.

   Example:

	Instruction	0123	000 001 010 011
	Initial [AC]	2035	010 000 011 101
	$[M_{123}]$	5124	101 001 010 100
	Final [AC]	0024	000 000 010 100

   Control Sequence:

Clock Pulse	Operations Performed During Execution Sequence
4	$MAR \leftarrow MBR_{4,11}$
5	$MBR \leftarrow M_{[MAR]}, M_{[MAR]} \leftarrow [0]$
6	$AC \leftarrow AC \wedge MBR, M_{[MAR]} \leftarrow MBR$

2. 2's Complement Add   1AAA   Mnemonic TAD

   Definition: The content of the memory location specified by AAA is added
   2's complement to the number stored in the accumulator. If there
   is an overflow the link register L is negated.

   Example:

	Instruction	1256	001 010 101 110
	Initial [AC]	3767	011 111 110 111
	Initial [L]	0	0
	Initial $[M_{256}]$	5705	101 111 000 101
	Final [AC]	1674	001 110 111 100
	Final [L]	1	1

   Control Sequence:

Clock Pulse	Operation Performed During Execution Sequence
4	$MAR \leftarrow MBR_{4,11}$
5	$MBR \leftarrow M_{[MAR]}, M_{[MAR]} \leftarrow [0]$
6	$AC \leftarrow AC + MBR, M_{[MAR]} \leftarrow MBR$
	$L \leftarrow (((AC + MBR) \leq (7777_8)) \wedge L)$
	$\vee (((AC + MBR) > (7777_8)) \wedge \bar{L})$

3. Increment and Skip if Zero   2AAA   Mnemonic ISZ

   Definition: The content of memory location AAA is incremented by 1. If the
   result is zero the instruction following the increment and skip
   instruction is skipped. Otherwise this instruction is performed.

   Example: Instruction   2150   010 001 101 000

   Note: the above instruction assumed to be in location 50

Table 12-5 (*continued*)

Case I—no skip

Initial [PC]	051	00	101	001
Initial [M_{150}]	1177	001 001	111	111
Final [M_{150}]	1200	001 010	000	000
Final [PC]	051	00	101	001

Case II—skip

Initial [PC]	051	00	101	001
Initial [M_{150}]	7777	111 111	111	111
Final [M_{150}]	0000	000 000	000	000
Final [PC]	052	00	101	010

Control Sequence:

Clock Pulse	Operation Performed During Execution Sequence
4	$MAR \leftarrow MBR_{4,11}$
5	$MBR \leftarrow M_{[MAR]} + 1, M_{[MAR]} \leftarrow [0]$
6	$M_{[MAR]} \leftarrow MBR, PC \leftarrow ((MBR = [0]) \wedge (PC + [1]))$ $\vee ((MBR \neq [0]) \wedge PC)$

4. Deposit and Clear the Accumulator   3AAA   Mnemonic DCA

Definition: Deposit the contents of the accumulator in the memory location specified by AAA. The contents of the accumulator are 0000 after this operation.

Example:

Instruction	3255	011	010	101	101
Initial [AC]	3750	011	111	101	000
Initial [M_{255}]	3617	011	110	001	111
Final [AC]	0000	000	000	000	000
Final [M_{255}]	3750	011	111	101	000

Control Sequence:

Clock Pulse	Operations Performed During Execution Sequence
4	$MAR \leftarrow MBR_{4,11}$
5	$MBR \leftarrow AC, AC \leftarrow [0], M_{[MAR]} \leftarrow 0$
6	$M_{[MAR]} \leftarrow MBR$

5. Jump to Subroutine   4AAA   Mnemonic JMS

Definition: This instruction transfers operation from the main program to a subroutine. The value of PC (the address of the jump to subroutine instruction + 1) is temporarily stored in the address indicated by AAA. The next instruction (the first instruction in the subroutine) is taken from the memory location following that indicated by AAA.

Example:
Instruction at location 50	4150	100 001 101 000
Initial [PC]	051	00 101 001
Initial [M_{150}]	0000	000 000 000 000
Final [PC]	151	01 101 001
Final [M_{150}]	0051	000 000 101 001

Control Sequence:

Clock Pulse	Operations Performed During Execution Sequence
4	MAR ← $MBR_{4,11}$
5	$MBR_{0,3}$ ← [0], $MBR_{4,11}$ ← PC
	PC ← MAR + [1], $M_{[MAR]}$ ← [0]
6	$M_{[MAR]}$ ← MBR

6. Jump 5AAA Mnemonic JMP

Definition: The next instruction is taken from the memory location indicated by AAA.

Example:
Instruction	5155	101 001 101 101
Initial [PC]	050	00 101 000
[$MBR_{4,11}$]	155	01 101 101
Final [PC]	155	01 101 101

Control Sequence:

Clock Pulse	Operation Performed During Execution Sequence
4	PC ← $MBR_{4,11}$
5	No operation
6	No operation

An operation code of $111_2 = 7_8$ will indicate that a given instruction is a register reference instruction. In addition we divide the set of register reference instructions into two groups by using bit 3 as an indicator bit. When bit 3 is set to 0 this indicates that the instruction is a Group I instruction; if bit 3 is set to 1 it is a Group II instruction. Group I instructions are used to manipulate the contents of the accumulator and link register while Group II instructions are used to perform tests on these same registers. These two groups of instructions are implemented by making use of the technique of micro-coding, which was discussed in the last section.

In a register reference instruction, bits 4 through 11 are used to indicate the operation to be performed by the instruction. Theoretically we could realize $2^8 = 256$ different instructions in each group. However, the amount of logic circuitry necessary to decode such a large number of different instructions would be quite complex. This problem can be avoided if we associate a specific task with each bit. Such a task is called a *micro-instruction* and bits 4 through 11 are said to form the micro-instruction field of a register reference instruction.

The basic Group I instructions are indicated in Figure 12-17, and their characteristics are summarized in Table 12-6. Each micro-instruction requires only one clock interval in the execution sequence to carry out the instruction. The clock pulse that causes the instruction to be executed is also indicated in Table 12-6.

Table 12-6   Group I Micro-Instructions

---

1. Clear the Accumulator   Mnemonic CLA

    Definition: If bit 4 is a 1 the contents of the accumulator are set to all zeros.
    Example: Instruction   7200   111 010 000 000
               Initial [AC]   3165   011 001 110 101
               Final [AC]   0000   000 000 000 000
    Control Sequence: Clock Pulse 4   AC ← [0]

2. Clear the Link Register   Mnemonic CLL

    Definition: If bit 5 is a 1 the content of the link register is set to zero.
    Example: Instruction   7100   111 001 000 000
               Initial [L]   1   Final [L]   0
    Control Sequence: Clock Pulse 4   L ← [0]

3. Complement the Accumulator   Mnemonic CMA

    Definition: If bit 6 is a 1 the contents of the accumulator are complemented.
    Example: Instruction   7040   111 000 100 000
               Initial [AC]   3671   011 110 111 001
               Final [AC]   4106   100 001 000 110
    Control Sequence: Clock Pulse 5   AC ← $\overline{AC}$

4. Complement the Link Register   Mnemonic CML

    Definition: If bit 7 is a 1 the content of the link register is complemented.
    Example: Instruction   7020   111 000 010 000
               Initial [L]   1   Final [L]   0
    Control Sequence: Clock Pulse 5   L ← $\overline{L}$

5. Rotate the Accumulator and Link One Bit Right   Mnemonic RAR

    Definition: If bit 8 is a 1, the following illustration defines this operation.

    L   AC
    Initial [L] and [AC] |1| |0|1|1|0|1|0|1|1|1|0|0|0|→

    Final [L] and [AC] |0| |1|0|1|1|0|1|0|1|1|1|0|0|

This operation takes place during clock pulse 5.
Instruction: 7010

6. Rotate the Accumulator and Link One Bit Left   Mnemonic RAL

Definition: If bit 9 is a 1 the following illustration defines this operation.

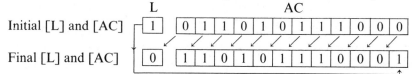

Initial [L] and [AC]

Final [L] and [AC]

This operation takes place during clock pulse 5.
Instruction: 7004

7. Repeat the Rotate Instruction

Definition: Case I Rotate Two Right   Mnemonic RTR
If bit 10 is a 1 and bit 8 is a 1 the accumulator and link are rotated two places right.
        Case II   Rotate Two Left   Mnemonic RTL
If bit 10 is a 1 and bit 9 is a 1 the accumulator and link are rotated two places left (i.e., the indicated rotate instruction is repeated).
Example: Case I
        Instruction   7012   111 000 001 010
        Initial [AC]   7164   111 001 110 100
        Initial [L]   1
        Final [AC]   3635   011 110 011 101
        Final [L]   0

        Case II
        Instruction   7006   111 000 000 110
        Initial [AC]   7164   111 001 110 100
        Initial [L]   1
        Final [AC]   4723   100 111 010 011
        Final [L]   1
Control Sequence: Clock Pulse 5   First rotation
                  Clock Pulse 6   Second rotation

8. Increment Accumulator   Mnemonic IAC

Definition: If bit 11 is a 1, one is added to the contents of the accumulator.
Example: Instruction   7001   111 000 000 001
            Initial [AC]   7631   111 110 011 001
            Final [AC]   7632   111 110 011 010
Control Sequence: Clock Pulse 6   AC ← AC + [1]

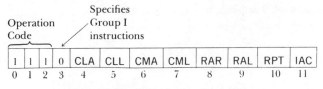

Figure 12-17. Group I micro-instructions.

The basic Group II instructions* are indicated in Figure 12-18 and their characteristics are summarized in Table 12-7. Each micro-instruction requires only one clock interval in the execution sequence to carry out the instruction. The clock pulse that causes the instruction to be executed is given in Table 12-7.

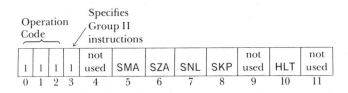

Note: All bits not used should be set to 0.

Figure 12-18. Group II micro-instructions.

Micro-instructions in any group can be combined to form new instructions provided that they are not mutually contradictory. For example, let us assume that we wish to form the 2's complement of the number currently in the accumulator. To accomplish this operation we can combine the two Group I micro-instructions CMA and IAC. Examining the definition of these two instructions in Table 12-6 we see that the accumulator is complemented during clock pulse 5 and then incremented during clock pulse 6. Thus we can define the instruction

Complement and Increment Accumulator

CIA

7041 111 000 100 001

Group II instructions can also be combined. For example, we can define the instruction

Skip on minus accumulator or nonzero link

SMA ∨ SNL

7520 111 101 010 000

by combining the Group II instructions SMA and SNL. It should be noted, however, that Group I and Group II instructions cannot be combined into a single

---

* For simplicity a number of Group II micro-instructions available on the PDP-8 are not included in SEDCOM. The given instructions form a subset of the PDP-8 instruction set.

Table 12-7   Group II Micro-Instructions

1. Skip on Minus Accumulator   Mnemonic SMA

    Definition: The next instruction is skipped if bit 0 of the accumulator is 1
                  (i.e. bit 0 is assumed to be the sign bit).
    Example: Instruction   7500   111 101 000 000
                 [AC]   7610   111 110 001 000
                 Initial [PC]   150   01 101 000
                 Final [PC]   151   01 101 001
    Control Sequence: Clock Pulse 4 $PC \leftarrow (\overline{AC_0} \wedge PC)$
                                                     $\vee \ (AC_0 \wedge (PC + [1]))$

2. Skip on Zero Accumulator   Mnemonic SZA

    Definition: The next instruction is skipped if the accumulator is zero.
    Example: Instruction   7440   111 100 100 000
                 [AC]   0000   000 000 000 000
                 Initial [PC]   150   01 101 000
                 Final [PC]   151   01 101 001
    Control Sequence: Clock Pulse 4 $PC \leftarrow ((AC = [0]) \wedge (PC + [1]))$
                                                     $\vee \ ((AC \neq [0]) \wedge PC)$

3. Skip on Nonzero Link   Mnemonic SNL

    Definition: The next instruction is skipped if $L = [1]$.
    Example: Instruction   7420   111 100 010 000
                 [L]   1
                 Initial [PC]   150   01 101 000
                 Final [PC]   151   01 101 001
    Control Sequence: Clock Pulse 4 $PC \leftarrow (\overline{L} \wedge PC) \vee (L \wedge (PC + [1]))$

4. Unconditional Skip   Mnemonic SKP

    Definition: The next instruction is skipped. Bits 5, 6, and 7 must all be zero.
    Example: Instruction   7410   111 100 001 000
                 Initial [PC]   150   01 101 000
                 Final [PC]   151   01 101 001
    Control Sequence: Clock Pulse 4 $PC \leftarrow PC + [1]$

5. Halt   Mnemonic HLT

    Definition: The operation of the computer halts.
                  Instruction   7402
    Control Sequence: Clock Pulse 6   Computer halts

instruction. Finally, we note that if none of the micro-instruction bits are set to 1 then we just introduce a delay of 3 microseconds in the program. This is indicated as

$$\text{NOP} \quad 7000 \quad \text{or} \quad 7400$$

Input/Output Instructions

The final class of instructions that we must define are the input/output instructions that are used to transfer information between SEDCOM's accumulator and a particular external device. In general an I/0 instruction must supply the following information:

1. The external device involved in the information transfer.
2. The transfer operations to be performed.
3. Timing information.

We assume, for simplicity, that SEDCOM has only a single input device, a reader, and a single output device, a printer. This assumption does not place any limitation on the following discussion.

Figure 12-19 gives a general block diagram representation of the input or output process. Each I/0 device has a buffer register that contains the information to be transmitted to SEDCOM or receives the information transmitted from SEDCOM. The information is transferred in parallel between the buffer register in the I/0 device and SEDCOM's accumulator. The flag is a 1-bit register that indicates if the I/0 device is ready for the information transfer to take place. If the flag is set to 1 the transfer can be initiated; otherwise, the computer must wait until the flag is set to 1 to indicate that the I/0 device is ready.

The actual I/0 device that the program calls for is indicated by the content of the device selector field of the I/0 instruction. This information is simultaneously transmitted to each I/0 device. If the number in the device selector field corresponds to the number assigned to a given device, the device selector network detects this and allows the proper control signals to be applied to the device to carry out the desired information transfer.

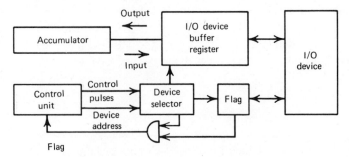

Figure 12-19. General input/output system.

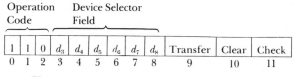

Figure 12-20. General structure of I/0 instruction.

The structure of the I/0 instructions is indicated in Figure 12-20. An operation code of $6_8 = 110_2$ indicates that the instruction is an I/0 instruction. The 6 bits that make up the device selector field indicate which device is referenced by the instruction. For SEDCOM we use the code

$$[d_3, d_4, d_5, d_6, d_7, d_8] = [000011]$$

for the input reader and the code

$$[d_3, d_4, d_5, d_6, d_7, d_8] = [000100]$$

for the output printer.

Both the reader and the printer use the modified ASCII 8-bit code given in Table 12-8 to represent each input or output character. Thus both devices contain an 8-bit

Table 12-8

Selected Characters from modified ASCII 8-Bit Teletype Code in Octal Form (the Full Code Is Given in Appendix 1)

Character	8-Bit Code (Octal)	Character	8-Bit Code (Octal)	Character	8-Bit Code (Octal)
A	301	N	316	0	260
B	302	O	317	1	261
C	303	P	320	2	262
D	304	Q	321	3	263
E	305	R	322	4	264
F	306	S	323	5	265
G	307	T	324	6	266
H	310	U	325	7	267
I	311	V	326	8	270
J	312	W	327	9	271
K	313	X	330	+	253
L	314	Y	331	−	255
M	315	Z	332	=	275
.	256	(	250	space ⌴	240
/	257	)	251	*	252
LINE FEED	212	Carriage RETURN	215		

buffer register. Input information is transferred, in parallel, from the reader buffer to bits AC_4 through AC_{11} of the accumulator. Similarly output information is transferred, in parallel, from bits AC_4 through AC_{11} of the accumulator to the printer buffer.

Reader Operation

When the reader buffer contains information that is to be read by the computer, the reader sets the reader flag to 1. When the computer program is ready to accept data from the reader it uses an I/0 instruction to check if the reader flag is 1. If it is, the program then uses another I/0 instruction that causes the information to be transferred from the reader buffer to the accumulator and at the same time it sets the reader flag to 0. If the reader flag is 0, the program goes into a wait sequence until the flag is set to 1 by the reader.

The instructions associated with the reader are described in Table 12-9.

Printer Operation

The operation of the printer is essentially the same as the reader. When the printer is ready to receive data from the computer it sets its flag to 1. When the computer's program wishes to print data it checks to see if the printer flag is 1. If it is, the program causes the information in bits $AC_{4,11}$ of the accumulator to be transferred

Table 12-9   Reader Instructions

1. Check Reader Flag   Mnemonic CRF*

   Definition: Check the reader flag RF. If it is 1 skip the next instruction. Otherwise execute the next instruction.
   Instruction: 6031   110 000 011 001
   Control Sequence: Clock Pulse 4 $PC \leftarrow ((RF = [1]) \wedge (PC + [1]))$
                                           $\vee ((RF = [0]) \wedge (PC))$

2. Read Reader Data   Mnemonic RRD*

   Definition: The accumulator is cleared. The contents of the reader buffer RB is transferred to bits $AC_{4,11}$ of the accumulator. The reader flag RF is set to 0.
   Instruction: 6036   110 000 011 110
   Control Sequence: Clock Pulse 5 $RF \leftarrow [0], AC \leftarrow [0]$
                                  6      $AC_{4,11} \leftarrow RB$

* The mnemonics used for the I/0 instructions do not correspond to the PDP-8 mnemonics.

Table 12-10   Printer Instructions

1.   Check Printer Flag   Mnemonic CPF*

     Definition: Check the printer flag PF. If it is 1 skip the next instruction. Otherwise execute the next instruction.
     Instruction: 6041   110 000 100 001
     Control Sequence: Clock Pulse 4 $PC \leftarrow ((PF = [1]) \wedge (PC + [1]))$
                                                      $\vee ((PF = [0]) \wedge (PC))$

2.   Send Printer Data   Mnemonic SPD*

     Definition: The contents of bits $AC_{4,11}$ of the accumulator are transferred in parallel to the printer's buffer PB. The printer flag PF is set to 0. The accumulator is not cleared.
     Instruction: 6046   110 000 100 110
     Control Sequence: Clock Pulse 5 $PF \leftarrow [0]$
                                            6      $PB \leftarrow AC_{4,11}$

---

* The mnemonics used for the I/0 instructions do not correspond to the PDP-8 mnemonics.

to the printer buffer and at the same time the printer's flag is set to 0. This flag stays at 0 until the printer is ready to receive the next character to be printed. If the printer flag is 0 the program goes into a wait sequence until the flag is set to 1 by the printer.

The instructions associated with the printer are described in Table 12-10.

Any other I/0 devices that might be associated with SEDCOM would have a similar set of instructions. The way that the above instructions are used is discussed in detail in the next chapter.

The speed with which a reader can deliver information to the reader buffer and the speed with which a printer can print information contained in the printer buffer determines the rate at which information can be transferred between the computer and the outside world. Usually a computer operates much faster than the external devices attached to the computer. For SEDCOM we assume that the reader has a maximum input transmission rate of 10 characters per second and that the printer has a printing rate of 10 characters per second.

Execution of a Program

It is assumed that any sequence of instructions that make up a program are placed in sequential locations in SEDCOM's memory. However, the way in which these instructions are placed in memory is not of particular importance to this discussion.

To execute a program, the address of the first instruction to be executed is placed in the PC register. It is then assumed that a hypothetical " start " button is pushed and the control unit carries out the necessary fetch-execute sequence to read and execute the first program instruction. This operation continues until a halt instruction is encountered. At that point the control unit stops operation and it is assumed that the computation described by the program has been completed.

The Instruction Set

The preceding discussion has fully explained the operation of each instruction. For convenience, Table 12-11 summarizes the basic instructions set of SEDCOM.

Table 12-11   Basic Instruction Set of SEDCOM

Memory Reference Instruction

Instruction	Operation Code (Octal)	Mnemonic
1. Logical AND	0	AND
2. Two's Complement Add	1	TAD
3. Increment and Skip If Zero	2	ISZ
4. Deposit and Clear Accumulator	3	DCA
5. Jump to Subroutine	4	JMS
6. Jump (Unconditionally)	5	JMP

I/0 Instructions

Instruction	Octal Representation	Mnemonic
1. Check Reader Flag	6031	CRF
2. Read Reader Data	6036	RRD
3. Check Printer Flag	6041	CPF
4. Send Printer Data	6046	SPD

Basic Register Reference Instructions

Group I Instructions

Instruction	Octal Representation	Mnemonic	Execution Time
1. Clear Accumulator	7200	CLA	4
2. Clear Link Register	7100	CLL	4
3. Complement Accumulator	7040	CMA	5
4. Complement Link Register	7020	CML	5
5. Rotate Accumulator Right	7010	RAR	5
6. Rotate Accumulator Left	7004	RAL	5
7. Rotate Accumulator Two Right	7012	RTR	5, 6
8. Rotate Accumulator Two Left	7006	RTL	5, 6
9. Increment Accumulator	7001	IAC	6
10. No Operation	7000	NOP	

Group II Instructions

Instruction	Octal Representation	Mnemonic	Execution Time
1. Skip on Minus Accumulator	7500	SMA	4
2. Skip on Zero Accumulator	7440	SZA	4
3. Skip on Nonzero Link	7420	SNL	4
4. Skip	7410	SKP	4
5. Halt	7402	HLT	6
6. No Operation	7400	NOP	

EXERCISES

1. The following information is contained in the indicated registers at the beginning of the fetch cycle. What will be in these same registers at the end of the execute cycle?

   (a) $[PC]$ $[150]$ (b) $[PC]$ $[150]$
   $[AC]$ $[7634]$ $[AC]$ $[7634]$
   $[M_{150}]$ $[0170]$ $[M_{150}]$ $[0570]$
   $[M_{170}]$ $[0324]$ $[M_{170}]$ $[0100]$
   $[M_{100}]$ $[2432]$ $[M_{100}]$ $[2361]$
   $[L]$ $[0]$ $[L]$ $[0]$

   (c) $[PC]$ $[150]$ (d) $[PC]$ $[150]$
   $[AC]$ $[7634]$ $[AC]$ $[7634]$
   $[M_{150}]$ $[7041]$ $[M_{150}]$ $[7500]$
   $[L]$ $[1]$

2. Define a Group I micro-instruction that will place 7777 in the accumulator and set the Link register to 1.

3. What will happen if $[AC_{4,11}] = [305]$ and the next instruction executed is 6046?

5. SUMMARY

The main purpose of this chapter has been to show how a stored program information processor can be constructed as an interconnection of a number of standard logic networks such as we have studied in earlier chapters. Now that we have an idea of how a simple computer operates our next task is to investigate how programs can be developed for the computer in order that it can carry out a complete information processing task. This is done in the next chapter.

REFERENCE NOTATION

The references provide a wide range of topics related to the material presented in this chapter. Reference [1] provides a historical overview of the development of computer designs while [5] provides a summary of the properties of many of the standard microprocessors and microcomputers offered by manufacturers. Various aspects of computer design are discussed in [2], [3], [4], and [6]. As indicated, SEDCOM is based on the PDP-8 computer manufactured by Digital Equipment Corp. A comprehensive discussion of the PDP-8 can be found in [7] while a short summary of its properties is included in [4].

REFERENCES

1. Bell, G. C., and Newell, A. (1971), *Computer Structures: Readings and Examples*, McGraw-Hill, New York.

2. Chu, Y. (1972), *Computer Organization and Microprogramming*, Prentice Hall, Englewood Cliffs, N.J.

3. Hill, F. J., and Peterson, G. R. (1973), *Digital Systems: Hardware Organization and Design*, John Wiley, New York.

4. Sloan, M. E. (1976), *Computer Hardware and Organization: An Introduction*. SRA, Chicago.

5. Soucek, B. (1976), *Microprocessors and Microcomputers*, John Wiley, New York.

6. Stone, H. S. (ed.) (1975), *Introduction to Computer Architecture*, SRA, Chicago.

7. [1975] *Introduction to Programming*, Digital Equipment Corp., Maynard, Mass.

HOME PROBLEMS

1. A magnetic core memory unit consisting of 1024 12-bit words is to be used to store data taken during a measurement process. A block diagram of this system is shown in Figure P12-1.

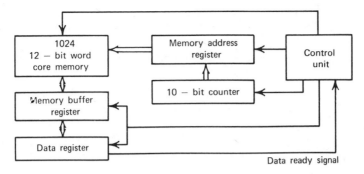

Figure P12-1. Data taking system.

This system operates in the following sequence.

Initially the 10-bit counter is set to 0. When data is present in the data register it sends a 1 signal to the control unit. The control unit then loads the data into memory in the following sequence.

Step 1   The contents of the 10-bit counter are loaded into the memory address register and the contents of the data register are loaded into the memory buffer register.

Step 2   The contents of the memory buffer register are loaded into the memory location indicated by contents of the memory address register. The 10-bit counter is incremented by 1 and the data register is cleared.

Step 3   The system waits until it receives a data ready signal and then repeats the process.

This sequence of operations continues until 1024 data items have been stored in memory. At that point it halts operation.

Assuming that the system is a clocked system and that all the necessary registers are already designed, design the control unit that will control the operation of this system.

2.   In Chapter 11 a controller for a single drilling machine was designed. There are many production situations where more than one drilling machine is used to carry out the same drilling operation. One such situation is illustrated in Figure P12-2.

The drilling program is stored in the random access memory. Each time one of the drilling machines completes an operation the drilling machine requests the next instruction from the system controller. The system controller then obtains the next instruction from memory. If the system controller is servicing another request the new request is postponed until the system controller is free.

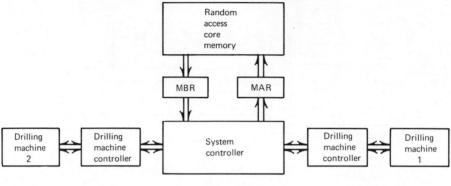

Figure P12-2

Design the system controller and the modifications necessary in the drilling machine controller so that this multiple drilling control system will operate properly.

3. The following sequence of instructions are loaded into the indicated SEDCOM memory locations. The program counter is set to 001 and the start button is pushed.

   (a) How long will this program run before it halts?
   (b) What will be contained in memory locations 100, 101, 102, and 103 and the accumulator when the program halts?

Address	Content of Memory
001	7200
002	1100
003	1101
004	1102
005	3103
006	7402
100	0150
101	0112
102	0500
103	0000

4. The following sequence of instructions are loaded into the indicated SEDCOM memory locations. The program counter is set to 001 and the start button is pushed.

   (a) What will the printer output be when the program halts?
   (b) How long will the computer run before it halts? What factor is most

important in determining the amount of time required to complete the execution of this program?

Address	Content of Memory
001	7200
002	1420
003	6041
004	5003
005	6046
006	2020
007	2021
010	5001
011	7402
020	0100
021	7774
100	0317
101	0313
102	0256
103	0240

5. Assume that SEDCOM has 4096 words of memory instead of 256 words. All of these memory locations cannot be referenced directly by SEDCOM's memory reference instructions.

(a) How could the indirect addressing capability of SEDCOM be used to work with data found any place in memory?

(b) What modifications would be necessary in the hardware structure of SEDCOM to implement this use of indirect addressing?

6. What modifications would be required in the operation of SEDCOM if a hardware multiplication instruction were to be included as one of the basic machine instructions? How many clock pulses would be required to execute the multiplication operations?

13

The Computing Process and Machine-Language Programs

Our introductory discussion in Chapter 1 indicated that any complex information processing task that can be automatically carried out by a computing device must be representable as a sequence of elementary operations that we call a program. The discussion in the preceding chapters has concentrated on the hardware techniques that are used to carry out these elementary operations and on the way in which a stored program computer can be constructed to execute a preprogrammed sequence of information processing tasks. We now switch our investigation from the way in which digital systems can be constructed to a study of how particular information processing algorithms can be reduced to a program that can be executed by a digital system.

As we have seen, there are a variety of ways that the computations called for by an algorithm can be realized by a digital device. For example, in a sequential network the steps of the algorithm are fixed by the way the network is constructed while in a digital computer the steps in the computation are controlled by a program stored in the computer's memory. Our task in this chapter is to investigate the ways a computation can be organized to carry out various information processing tasks rather than to study the hardware that actually performs the computation. This allows us to gain an insight into the interrelationship between the structure of the computational process and the organization of the digital devices that carry out these computations.

Although it would be possible to investigate the structure of the computational process independent of any computing device, this approach would not give us any insight into the practical limitations that must be considered when working with such a device. Therefore for the purpose of this chapter we assume that our programs will be executed by the SEDCOM computer discussed in Chapter 12. In this way we can explore the relationship between how the hardware operations of a computer are implemented and the way in which a program can be executed using these operations.

The first part of this chapter presents the basic programming techniques that are needed in developing any type of program. These techniques are then used to develop programs that perform both numeric and nonnumeric information processing tasks. Throughout this discussion our main concern is in identifying the basic techniques and concepts that are common to all information processing tasks rather than developing advanced programming skills.

A large number of minicomputers and microprocessors are available. SEDCOM was selected as the instructional computer because it has an extremely simple structure and also has all of the important features one must understand in programming at the machine-language level. Once you have mastered the programming concepts presented in this chapter, it is a straightforward process to learn how to use a particular minicomputer or microprocessor.

The discussion in this chapter assumes that the reader has previous programming experience in a higher level language such as PL/I, FORTRAN, or BASIC. It is also assumed that the algorithm necessary to represent a given computational task has been developed and that our task is to create the SEDCOM program necessary to realize the algorithm. Our goal is to develop an insight into the problems associated with programming at the machine level that are hidden from the user when a higher level programming language is used.

2. BASIC PROGRAMMING CONCEPTS

The instruction set of a computer is called its *machine language* and any program that is expressed in terms of these instructions is called a *machine-language program.* When writing machine-language programs in this section we use both the numerical (octal) and mnemonic (symbolic) representation for the various machine-language instructions. Each computer instruction must ultimately be represented in digital form if it is to be interpreted by the computer's control unit. However, the parallel octal/mnemonic representation of the same information makes it easier for us to understand and remember the corresponding digitally represented instructions.

Initially all computer programs were written in machine language. However, the writing of machine-language programs is a tedious task and more advanced programming techniques using higher level programming languages were soon developed. Consequently machine-language programming is rarely used except in developing small programs or making corrections in larger programs that have been developed using some of the higher level languages to be discussed in the following chapters. The reason that we are spending time working with this type of program is that it gives us a better insight into how certain of the basic operations behave and it also serves to illustrate why we need automatic programming techniques.

The Programming Process

The development of a machine-language program for a computer, once the algorithm describing the general structure of the computation has been defined, can be handled in a straightforward manner. The first step in the programming process is to decide how the data and instructions are to be organized in memory. This means that we must assign memory locations for each piece of data that must be stored during the execution of the program and a memory location for each machine-language instruction in the program.

The organization of the program in memory must be considered next. At this point the intermediate computations called for by the different parts of the algorithm are converted into a sequence of machine-language instructions that carry out the computation. As this process progresses we assign additional locations in memory for the intermediate data that is generated during the execution of the program.

A complete program often appears to be a very complex structure. However, most programs are developed by repeatedly applying a few simple programming techniques. In particular, we must be able to carry out the following five basic tasks.

1. Input information.
2. Perform sequential computations.
3. Make decisions.
4. Repeat a fixed procedure a number of times (looping).
5. Output information.

If we can understand how to perform these tasks by using the instructions available in the instruction set of the computer being programmed, then it is relatively easy to develop a program to carry out a particular task.

Straight Line Computation

A straight-line computation is a program sequence that does not involve any decisions or looping. As a simple example, consider the following program specification that describes a task which can be carried out as a straight-line computation.

Figure 13-1a is the flowchart of the algorithm used to compute Y. It is assumed that the values of $X1$, $X2$, and $X3$ are already in the proper memory locations. To carry out this computation we first initialize the accumulator by setting its contents to zero. We then add the three numbers and place the result in location 103.

The machine-language program and its corresponding mnemonic representation is given in Figure 13-1b. Remember that all of the numbers representing both memory locations and machine-language instructions are given by octal numbers.

Program Specification

PROGRAM 1

Task: Sum three numbers (modulo 2^{12})

$$Y = X1 + X2 + X3$$

Input:

X_1 is in location 100
X_2 is in location 101
X_3 is in location 102

Output:

Y is to be placed in location 103

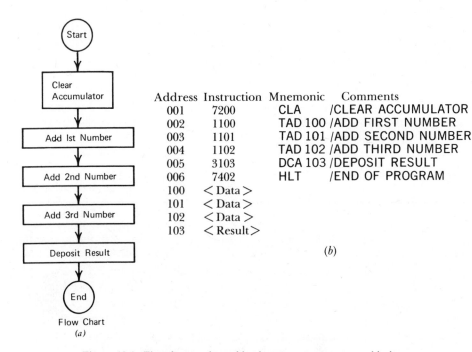

Address	Instruction	Mnemonic	Comments
001	7200	CLA	/CLEAR ACCUMULATOR
002	1100	TAD 100	/ADD FIRST NUMBER
003	1101	TAD 101	/ADD SECOND NUMBER
004	1102	TAD 102	/ADD THIRD NUMBER
005	3103	DCA 103	/DEPOSIT RESULT
006	7402	HLT	/END OF PROGRAM
100	< Data >		
101	< Data >		
102	< Data >		
103	< Result>		

(b)

Flow Chart
(a)

Figure 13-1. Flowchart and machine-language program to add three numbers. (a) Flowchart. (b) Machine-language program.

Decisions

The ability to select the next step of a calculation based on the current status of the calculation is a very important feature of a computer. At the machine level we have a set of instructions that allow us to make several basic tests.

For example, in SEDCOM we have the various skip instructions that tell us to skip the next instruction if a certain condition holds. We can use these instructions, together with the jump instruction, to carry out various types of decision processes.

The skip instructions that we can use are:

ISZ   Increment (a given memory location) and skip the next instruction if the result is zero.

SMA   Skip the next instruction if the contents of the accumulator is minus.

SZA   Skip the next instructions if the contents of the accumulator is zero.

SNL   Skip the next instruction if the link is 1.

SKP   Skip the next instruction (unconditional skip).

The general way that these instructions are used is shown in Figure 13-2a. The box preceding the decision point makes any necessary computation to establish the result that will be tested. The general program organization needed to accomplish this testing process is shown in Figure 13-2b.

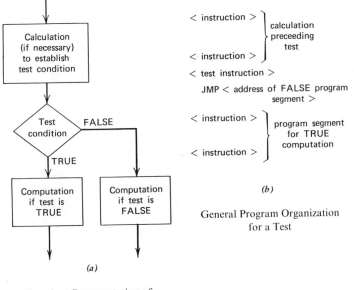

(a)

Flowchart Representation of
a Test

(b)

General Program Organization
for a Test

Figure 13-2. The decision process.

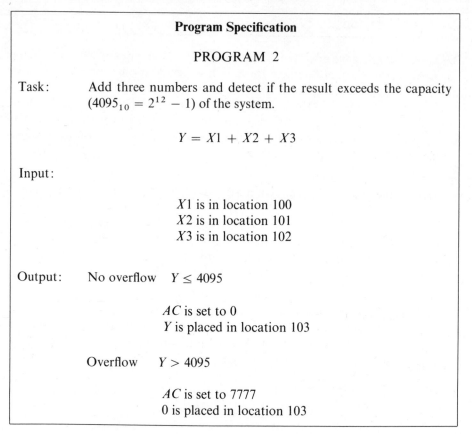

Program Specification

PROGRAM 2

Task: Add three numbers and detect if the result exceeds the capacity $(4095_{10} = 2^{12} - 1)$ of the system.

$$Y = X1 + X2 + X3$$

Input:

X1 is in location 100
X2 is in location 101
X3 is in location 102

Output: No overflow $Y \le 4095$

AC is set to 0
Y is placed in location 103

Overflow $Y > 4095$

AC is set to 7777
0 is placed in location 103

To illustrate how this testing process might be used, we develop Program 2, which will add three numbers and detect if there is an overflow.

Examining this problem statement we see that we must detect when an overflow occurs. This can be done by checking for a nonzero link after each addition. Figure 13-3a gives the flowchart of the algorithm needed to realize this program. The link and accumulator are both initialized to zero at the start of the program.

The machine-language program corresponding to the flowchart of Figure 13-3a is given in Figure 13-3b. If we examine this program, we see that we carry out two tests. If we detect that the link is 1, we set the AC to 7777 and halt. Otherwise we continue our computation.

The jump instruction JMP is a very important instruction in realizing a decision, since it allows us to transfer control to another part of the program. You must, however, be very careful not to overuse the jump instruction because it becomes very difficult to follow the operation of a program if we indiscriminantly transfer control from one section of the program to another. Every attempt should be made to minimize the number of times the jump instruction is used even if this means that a few additional instructions of another type are needed.

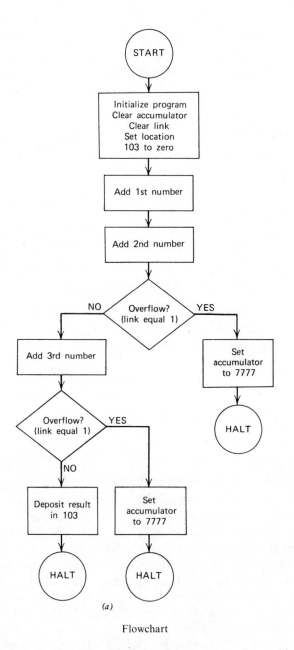

(a)

Flowchart

Figure 13-3. Flowchart and machine-language program to add three numbers and check for overflow.

Address	Instruction	Mnemonic	Comments
001	7300	CLA CLL	/CLEAR AC, L
002	3103	DCA 103	/SET 103 ZERO
003	1100	TAD 100	/ADD FIRST
004	1101	TAD 101	/TWO NUMBERS
005	7420	SNL	/OVERFLOW?
006	5011	JMP 11	/NO
007	7240	CLA CMA	/YES. SET AC to 7777
010	7402	HLT	/END
011	1102	TAD 102	/ADD 3rd NUMBER
012	7420	SNL	/OVERFLOW?
013	5016	JMP 16	/NO
014	7240	CLA CMA	/YES. SET AT to 7777
015	7402	HLT	/END
016	3103	DCA 103	/DEPOSIT RESULT
017	7402	HLT	/END
100	⟨data⟩		
101	⟨data⟩		
102	⟨data⟩		
103	⟨result⟩		

Machine-Language Program

Figure 13-3. (b)

Loops

A *program loop* is a set of instructions that are repeatedly executed on different sets of data from a given data set. Loops can make up a complete program or they can be part of a more general program. There are two basic types of loops, as illustrated by the flowchart shown in Figure 13-4.

The loop shown in Figure 13-4a is the DO-WHILE type loop and is the typical way a loop is implemented by a PL/I compiler when a PL/I DO statement is used. In this arrangement the exit condition is always tested before the body of the loop is executed. Thus, it is possible that the exit condition will be satisfied before the body of the loop is executed for the first time.

The loop shown in Figure 13-4b is the DO-UNTIL type of loop and is typical of the way a loop is implemented by a FORTRAN compiler when a FORTRAN DO statement is used. In this arrangement the body of the loop is always executed before the exit condition is tested. Thus the body of the loop is always executed at least once before an exit from the loop is made.

We will use both types of loop organization depending on the particular types of problems with which we are dealing.

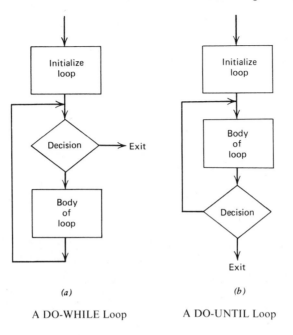

(a)

(b)

A DO-WHILE Loop   A DO-UNTIL Loop

Figure 13-4. Flowchart illustrating basic loop structures.

Counters

The simplest type of loop is one in which the body is executed a fixed number of times. In this case a DO-UNTIL loop organization can be used. A counter is used to count the number of times that the body of the loop has been executed. When the count reaches a predetermined value the computation is complete and the program exits from the loop.

Since SEDCOM does not include a special counter in the CPU, we must use an instruction sequence to simulate a counter. This can be done in the following manner.

Suppose that we wish to go through a given computational sequence N_8 times. To simulate a counter we select a particular memory location and load $-N_8$ into that location. Each time we complete the sequence of instructions that make up the loop body, we use the ISZ instruction to increment the contents of the counter memory location by 1. If this leaves us with 0 in this location, we know that we have completed the desired number of calculations. Thus we jump the next instruction and go on to the rest of the program. If the counter is not 0 this means that we must again repeat our sequence of instructions. Thus the next instruction following the ISZ instruction is a JMP instruction that takes us back to the beginning of our computational sequence.

The flowchart in Figure 13-5 illustrates how the counter would operate. It is assumed that the counter is contained in memory location MC and that memory

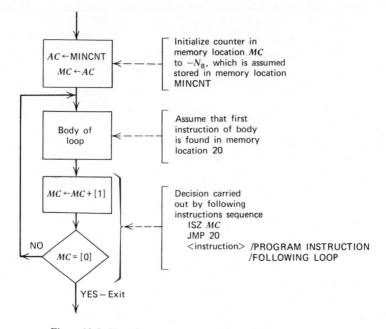

Figure 13-5. Use of a counter to terminate a DO-WHILE Loop.

location MINCNT contains $-N_8$. To initialize the loop we must initialize the counter by bringing $-N_8$ into the accumulator AC and then deposit this value into the memory location MC, which will be used as the counter. After this initialization step is completed, we execute the body of the program which we assume, for this example, to start in location 20. When we have completed the body of the loop, we must decide if we are finished. This decision is carried out by the following set of instructions.

ISZ MC	/INCREMENT COUNTER. IS IT 0?
JMP 20	/NO. GO BACK AND EXECUTE LOOP BODY AGAIN
⟨next Inst⟩	/YES. LOOP FINISHED. EXIT POINT

As an example of how a loop is used consider the problem described by PROGRAM 3.

The flowchart and machine-language program necessary to carry out this task is given in Figure 13-6.

The program of Figure 13-6b illustrates the necessity of fully understanding the tasks performed by each instruction. You should spend some time studying this program and making sure you understand what each instruction accomplishes. For example, we clear the accumulator as the first instruction, since we have no way of knowing what is initially in the accumulator. However, we do not need to use the CLA instruction just before we enter the body of the loop in statement 007, since the previous instruction DCA 16 serves to clear the accumulator.

Program Specification

PROGRAM 3

Task: Sum the numbers 1 through N modulo 2^{12}

$$Y = \sum_{I=1}^{N} I$$

Input: N is in location 100

Output: Y is placed in location 101

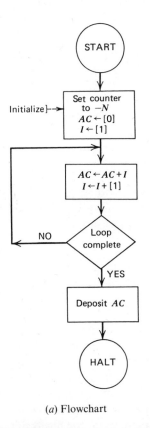

(a) Flowchart

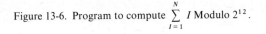

Figure 13-6. Program to compute $\sum_{I=1}^{N} I$ Modulo 2^{12}.

Address	Instruction or Contents	Mnemonic	Comment
001	7200	CLA	
002	1100	TAD 100	/GET N
003	7041	CMA IAC	/FORM $-N$
004	3015	DCA 15	/SET COUNTER
005	7001	IAC	/FORM 1
006	3016	DCA 16	/SET I $= 1$
007	1016	TAD 16	/PARTIAL SUM
010	2016	ISZ 16	/INCREMENT I
011	2015	ISZ 15	/TEST COUNT. IS IT 0?
012	5007	JMP 7	/NO. CONTINUE
013	3101	DCA 101	/YES. DEPOSIT RESULT
014	7402	HLT	/END
	/TEMPORARY STORAGE		
015	⟨counter⟩		
016	⟨value of I⟩		
	/INPUT-OUTPUT		
100	⟨value of N⟩		
101	⟨output value⟩		

Machine-Level Program

Figure 13-6. (*b*)

Note also that the Increment and Skip if Zero (ISZ) instruction is used in two different ways. Instruction 010 is used to increase the value of I by 1 while instruction 011 is used to increment and test the counter.

Pointers

Suppose that we wish to add N numbers. As long as N is a relatively small value we could use a straight line program such as **PROGRAM 1** or **PROGRAM 2** to do the job. However, consider what would happen if $N = 50$. A straight-line machine-language program would become so large that it would be unwieldy. To overcome this problem, we can make use of the indirect addressing option to create a *pointer* that can be used in a loop to access data.

When we deal with a block of data, the terms in the block are usually stored in sequential memory locations. If we wish to process this information we do it on a term-by-term basis. Thus, if we are to keep track of which term we are currently

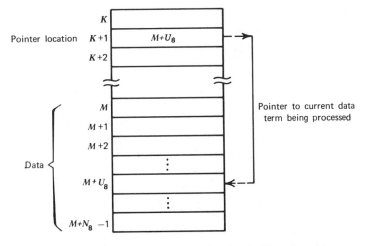

Figure 13-7. Memory organization illustrating the idea of a pointer.

working with, we need a "pointer" that points to that term. One way to do this is to use one particular memory location to store the address of the next data term to be processed. Then, whenever the data term is needed, the program can make use of this address information to retrieve the desired data. Figure 13-7 provides a graphical interpretation of the pointer concept.

In SEDCOM the indirect address feature allows us to use the pointer to access the desired data term. For example, assume that we wish to add a sequence of numbers between location 100 and location $100 + N_8 - 1$, where N_8 is an arbitrary octal number. To do this we could arbitrarily assign location 70 to be the pointer location. Initially we place the number 100 in location 70, since this is the address of the first data term. The program to carry out the desired computation would have the general form illustrated in Figure 13-8.

The instruction

$$\text{TAD I 70}$$

tells the computer to go to memory location 70 and use the number contained in that memory location as the address of the data term that should be added to the accumulator. The mnemonic I following TAD indicates that this is an indirect addressing instruction and the indirect address bit (bit 3 of the instruction word) is set to 1.

The next instruction

$$\text{ISZ 70}$$

is used to increment the value of the pointer by 1 so that it now points to the next data term. The rest of the program sequence then checks to see if we have completed

$$\left\{\begin{array}{l} \text{Program sequence} \\ \text{to initialize} \\ \text{program and} \\ \text{put 100 into} \\ \text{location 70} \end{array}\right.$$

050	TAD I 70	$\left\{\begin{array}{l}\text{Instructions to use pointer then}\\ \text{Increment pointer}\end{array}\right.$
051	ISZ 70	

$$\left\{\begin{array}{l} \text{Program sequence} \\ \text{to check if all} \\ \text{data terms have} \\ \text{been processed} \end{array}\right.$$

060	JMP 050
061	HLT
070	$\langle$Pointer$\rangle$

100	$\left\{\begin{array}{l}\text{Data}\\ \text{Terms}\end{array}\right.$
$100 + N_8 - 1$	

Figure 13-8. General program organization necessary to use a pointer.

Program Specification

PROGRAM 4

Task: Sum the N numbers A_I, $I = 1, \ldots N$, module 2^{12}

$$Y = \sum_{I=1}^{N} A_I$$

Input: N is in location 77 with octal value N_8

A_I—array is in location 100 through $100 + N_8 - 1$

Output: Y is placed in location 76

The value of the sum is also to be in the accumulator

the calculation. If we have, we halt. Otherwise, we go back to location 50 and go through another addition sequence.

To illustrate how a pointer is used consider the program described by PROGRAM 4.

The flowchart describing this program is given in Figure 13-9, and corresponding machine-language program is given in Figure 13-10.

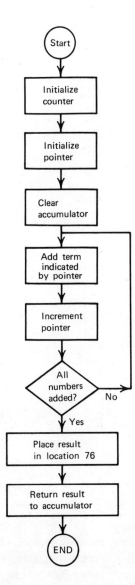

Figure 13-9. Flowchart to add *N* numbers.

Address	Instruction or Contents	Mnemonic	Comments
001	7200	CLA	/ZERO AC
002	1077	TAD 77	/GET N
003	7041	CMA IAC	/FORM −N
004	3070	DCA 70	/SET COUNTER
005	1072	TAD 72	/GET 100
006	3071	DCA 71	/SET POINTER TO 100
007	1471	TAD I 71	/ADD TERM INDICATED /BY POINTER
010	2071	ISZ 71	/INCREMENT POINTER
011	2070	ISZ 70	/INCREMENT COUNTER. /IS IT 0?
012	5007	JMP 7	/NO CONTINUE /ADDITION
013	3076	DCA 76	/YES DEPOSIT RESULTS
014	1076	TAD 76	/RESTORE VALUE IN /ACCUMULATOR
015	7402	HLT	

/TEMPORARY STORAGE

070	⟨counter⟩		
071	⟨pointer⟩		
072	0100		/INITIAL POINTER /VALUE

/INPUT-OUTPUT

076	⟨output value⟩		
077	⟨value of N⟩		
100			
⋮	} Input Array		
$100 + N_8 − 1$			

Figure 13-10. Machine-level program of algorithm shown in Figure 13-9.

Finite and Infinite Loops

A loop is a *finite loop* if we always make a decision to leave the loop after a finite, but not necessarily predetermined, number of steps. Otherwise, a loop is an *infinite loop*. It is often possible to have a loop that acts as a finite loop for one set of variables and as an infinite loop for variables that lie outside this set. We must, of course, insure that we never have an infinite loop. One way that we can do this, if necessary, is to introduce a counter in the loop so that whenever we go around the loop $N_{\max}$ times, we then go on to another portion of the program.

There are many variations that we find in program loops, but they all have the same property in that they allow us to carry out a calculation until we reach a condition that lets us know that the calculation is complete. We have concentrated on the DO-UNTIL type of loop. However, DO-WHILE types of loops are just as easy to realize. This class of loops are considered in the exercises.

Input/Output Programming

Information is read into SEDCOM by use of a reader, and output information is printed on a printer. Communication between the CPU and these devices takes place using the 8-bit ASCII code* given in Table 12-8 and Appendix 1. We now consider how these two units are used.

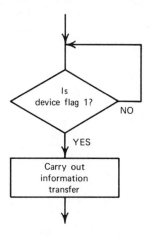

Figure 13-11. General flowchart illustrating information transfer routine.

Both the reader and printer are very slow compared with the speed of operation of SEDCOM. Thus whenever we wish to transfer information between SEDCOM and one of these I/0 devices, we must first check to see if the device is ready for an information transfer. If it is, as indicated by the device flag being set to 1, then the

---

* Remember that all references to the ASCII code in SEDCOM are to the modified 8-bit code.

information transfer can take place. If the device flag is 0, indicating it is not ready for the information transfer, we must go into a wait loop until the device sets its flag to 1. Figure 13-11 gives a flowchart representation of this check routine.

For an illustration of how the input and output tasks are accomplished, consider the program described by **PROGRAM** 5. The flow diagram and program for this is shown in Figure 13-12.

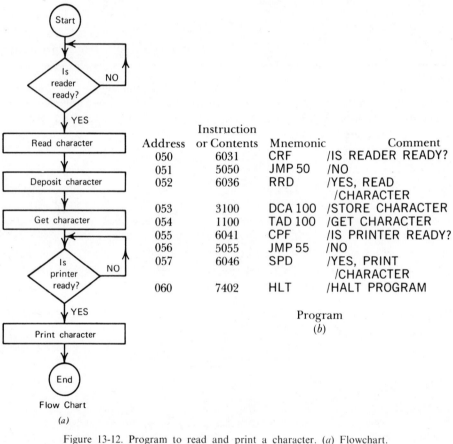

Address	Instruction or Contents	Mnemonic	Comment
050	6031	CRF	/IS READER READY?
051	5050	JMP 50	/NO
052	6036	RRD	/YES, READ /CHARACTER
053	3100	DCA 100	/STORE CHARACTER
054	1100	TAD 100	/GET CHARACTER
055	6041	CPF	/IS PRINTER READY?
056	5055	JMP 55	/NO
057	6046	SPD	/YES, PRINT /CHARACTER
060	7402	HLT	/HALT PROGRAM

Program
(b)

Flow Chart
(a)

Figure 13-12. Program to read and print a character. (a) Flowchart. (b) Program.

This example illustrates the ease with which we can use the I/0 devices. The biggest problem that we have with an I/0 device is that it is very slow compared with the speed of the rest of the computer. To get around this problem we can often carry out a large number of machine operations between each I/0 instruction.

Program Specification

PROGRAM 5

Task: Read a character from the reader, store the 8-bit ASCII Code corresponding to this character in location 100 and then print the character on the printer.

Input: ASCII character from Reader Buffer

Output: ASCII character in location 100
ASCII character in printer buffer

ASCII to Binary (Octal) Conversion

The 8-bit ASCII code used to represent character information must be used when information is read from the reader or when we transmit information to the printer to be printed. When we deal with character information inside the computer, we can retain this coding. However, if we wish to work with numerical information, the 8-bit ASCII code for the digits 0 through 9 must be converted to the binary equivalent of these digits. Similarly, if we wish to output a digit 0 through 9, the binary representation of the digit must be converted to an ASCII representation. This can be accomplished quite easily if we examine the structure of the ASCII code.

In ASCII the digits 0 through 9 are represented by the code 260_8, which corresponds to 0, through the code 271_8, which corresponds to 9. Thus if we wish to convert the ASCII character code to the binary equivalent, all we have to do is to subtract 260_8 from the code character. This relationship is shown in Table 13-1.

Table 13-1   ASCII to Binary Conversion

Digit (Decimal)	ASCII Code	Octal Equivalent After Subtraction 260_8
0	260	000
1	261	001
2	262	002
3	263	003
4	264	004
5	265	005
6	266	006
7	267	007
8	270	010
9	271	011

When we read a character, the 8-bit code appears in the rightmost 8 bits of the accumulator. Thus if we subtract 260_8, the resulting binary number appears in the rightmost 4 bits of the accumulator. If we restrict ourselves to working with the octal digits 0 through 7, then the rightmost 3 bits, which we obtain after subtracting 260_8, will be the binary equivalent of the input number.

In a similar manner we can convert a binary representation of a digit to its ASCII representation. Assume that the binary representation is in the rightmost 4 bits of the accumulator (3 bits if we are dealing with octal numbers) and all of the other bits are zero. Then by adding 260_8 to the accumulator, we will obtain the ASCII code for that digit. This code can then be sent to the printer if we wish to output the individual digit.

As an example of how we can use this conversion process, let us assume that we wish to implement a program to carry out the task described by PROGRAM 6. A flowchart representation of the algorithm necessary to carry out this task is shown in Figure 13-13. The corresponding machine-level program is given in Figure 13-14.

Program Specification

PROGRAM 6

Task: Read in a 4-digit octal number from the reader and store its binary equivalent in location 50.

Input: ASCII code representation of the octal number $D_1 D_2 D_3 D_4$ read from left-to-right

Output: Binary equivalent of $D_1 D_2 D_3 D_4$ in location 50

Notation for Figure 13-13

R3L[L, AC]   rotate contents of L and AC 3 bits to left

$M_{[46]}$ Memory location 46
            Counter

$M_{[47]}$ Memory location 47
            Temporary storage of data

$M_{[50]}$ Memory location 50
            Location of result

Assumption: Only ASCII codes for octal numbers are available to reader.

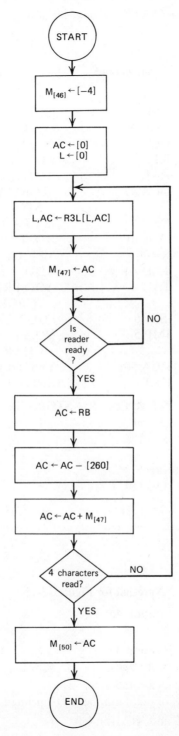

Figure 13-13. Flowchart of algorithm to load binary equivalent of a 4 digit octal number.

Address	Instruction or Contents	Mnemonic	Comments
001	7200	CLA	
002	1045	TAD 45	/GET −4
003	3046	DCA 46	/SET COUNTER
004	7100	CLL	/CLEAR LINK
005	7006	RTL	/ROTATE TWO LEFT
006	7004	RAL	/ROTATE LEFT
007	3047	DCA 47	/STORE AC IN TEMPORARY /STORAGE
010	6031	CRF	/IS READER READY?
011	5010	JMP 10	/NO. TRY AGAIN
012	6036	RRD	/YES. GET CHARACTER
013	1044	TAD 44	/ADD −260
014	1047	TAD 47	/ADD PREVIOUSLY INPUTED /INFORMATION
015	2046	ISZ 46	/FOUR CHARACTERS READ?
016	5005	JMP 5	/NO. PROCESS NEXT /CHARACTER
017	3050	DCA 50	/YES. DEPOSIT RESULT
020	7402	HLT	/END OF PROGRAM
		/TEMPORARY STORAGE	
044	7520	/−260	
045	7774	/−4	
046	⟨counter⟩		
047	⟨temporary storage⟩		
		/OUTPUT	
050	⟨result⟩		

Figure 13-14. Machine-level program to realize algorithm shown in Figure 13-13.

Notation for Figure 13-15

$M_{[46]}$	Memory location 46 Counter
$M_{[47]}$	Memory location 47 Temporary storage
$M_{[50]}$	Memory location 50 Location of octal number to be printed
RAL[L, AC]	Rotate L and AC 1-bit left
R3L[L, AC]	Rotate L and AC 3 bits left

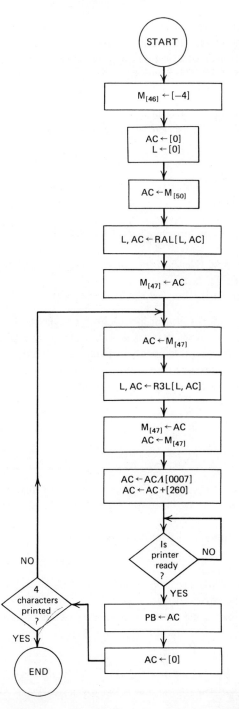

Figure 13-15. Flowchart of algorithm to print octal value of information in memory location 50.

A similar program can be developed to print out the octal representation of the contents of a memory location. The specifications for **PROGRAM** 7 describe this task. A flowchart representation of the algorithm necessary to carry out this task is shown in Figure 13-15. The development of the corresponding machine-language program is left as an exercise.

Program Specification

PROGRAM 7

Task: Print the octal representation of the contents of location 50 in memory

Input: The binary number (octal $D_1 D_2 D_3 D_4$) in memory location 50

Output: The ASCII code representation of $D_1 D_2 D_3 D_4$ sent to the printer buffer in that order

---

The programs and programming techniques presented in this section have illustrated the basic methods that are used to develop complex programs. It should be obvious that a considerable number of steps are needed to carry out some of the simplest tasks. In the next sections we study many of the basic information processing tasks and show how machine-level programs can be used to accomplish these tasks.

EXERCISES

1. Re-do the flowchart and program of Figure 13-6 using a DO-WHILE Loop. (*Hint*: the counter must be set to $-[N + 1]$. Explain why.)

2. Write the machine-level program necessary to realize the algorithm given in Figure 13-15.

3. How many seconds are taken each time the wait loop of Figure 13-11 is executed? If the information transfer device is a reader producing 10 characters per second, what is the maximum number of times that the wait loop can be executed?

3. SUBROUTINES

A program, which is sometimes referred to as a routine, usually performs a computation by breaking it up into a sequence of smaller component computations.

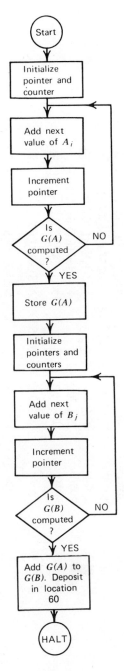

Flow Chart *(a)*

Figure 13-16. Flowchart and program to compute $Y = \sum_{I=1}^{N_A} A_I + \sum_{J=1}^{N_B} B_J = G(A) + G(B)$. *(a)* Flowchart.

Address	Instruction or Contents	Mnemonic	Comment
		/MAIN PROGRAM	
001	7300	CAL CLL	
		/FIRST OPEN SUBROUTINE: COMPUTE G(A)	
002	1100	TAD 100	/GET N_A
003	7041	CMA IAC	/FORM $- N_A$
004	3070	DCA 70	/SET G(A) COUNTER
005	1072	TAD 72	/GET AI POINTER VALUE
006	3074	DCA 74	/SET AI POINTER
007	1474	TAD I 74	/FORM PARTIAL SUM
010	2074	ISZ 74	/INCREMENT POINTER
011	2070	ISZ 70	/FINISHED SUM?
012	5010	JMP 7	/NO. CONTINUE ADDITION
		/END OF FIRST OPEN SUBROUTINE	
013	3050	DCA 50	/SAVE RESULT
		/SECOND OPEN SUBROUTINE: COMPUTE G(B)	
014	1200	TAD 200	/GET NB
015	7041	CMA IAC	/FORM $-$ NB
016	3071	DCA 71	/SET G(B) COUNTER
017	1073	TAD 73	/GET BJ POINTER VALUE
020	3075	DCA 75	/SET BJ POINTER
021	1475	TAD I 75	/FORM PARTIAL SUM
022	2075	ISZ 75	/INCREMENT POINTER

```
023   2071   ISZ 71        /FINISHED SUM?
024   5021   JMP 21        /NO. CONTINUE ADDITION
                           /END OF SECOND OPEN SUBROUTINE
025   1050   TAD 50        /ADD G(A)
026   3060   DCA 60        /STORE RESULT
027   7402   HLT           /END

             /STORAGE

050   ⟨temporary⟩          /TEMPORARY STORAGE
060   ⟨result⟩             /RESULT
070   ⟨counter⟩            /NA COUNTER
071   ⟨counter⟩            /NB COUNTER
072   101                  /START OF AI
073   201                  /START OF BJ
074   ⟨pointer⟩            /AI POINTER
075   ⟨pointer⟩            /BI POINTER
100   ⟨n_a⟩                /VALUE OF NA
101   ⟨ ⟩                  /AI DATA
 ⋮    ⋮
101 + NA ⟨ ⟩
200   ⟨n_b⟩                /VALUE OF NB
201   ⟨ ⟩                  /AJ DATA
 ⋮    ⋮
201 + NB ⟨ ⟩
```

Figure 13-16. (b) Program.

The program associated with each of these component computations is called a *subroutine*.

Some subroutines are so small that there is no loss in the efficiency of the program if the operations associated with the subroutine are included in the main body of the program whenever the calculation performed by the particular subroutine is needed. Subroutines of this type are called *open subroutines* or *in-line routines*.

As an example of an open subroutine, consider the flowchart for **PROGRAM 8** shown in Figure 13-16*a*. The machine-level program using open subroutines is given in Figure 13-16*b*. As shown this program makes use of two open subroutines, one to compute $G(A)$ and one to compute $G(B)$.

Program Specification

PROGRAM 8

Task: Compute, modulo 2^{12},

$$Y = \sum_{I=1}^{N_A} A_I + \sum_{J=1}^{N_B} B_J = G(A) + G(B)$$

Input: N_A in memory location 100, $N_A \leq 77_8$
N_B in memory location 200, $N_B \leq 77_8$
A_I in memory location 101 through $100 + N_A$
B_J in memory locations 201 through $200 + N_B$

Output: Result Y to be placed in location 60

In this program we use the subroutine to compute the sum of a sequence of numbers twice. The only difference between them being in the particular locations that the initial pointer and counter information are stored and the location of the beginning of each subroutine.

When the computation that we wish to perform requires that we repeat a complex subroutine involving many instructions a number of times, it becomes desirable not to include the program necessary to execute the subroutine in the main body of the program. Instead, a special location is set aside and the instructions associated with the subroutine are written down. Whenever it becomes necessary, during the execution of the main program, to perform the calculation represented by the subroutine, the main program transfers control to the subroutine. The calculation is then completed by the subroutine, and then control is passed back to the main program. Subroutines of this type are called *closed subroutines*.

Figure 13-17 illustrates the major difference between the use of open subroutines and closed subroutines. The in-line subroutine is easily implemented, since it is an integral part of the overall program. Closed subroutines, however, pose a number of special problems.

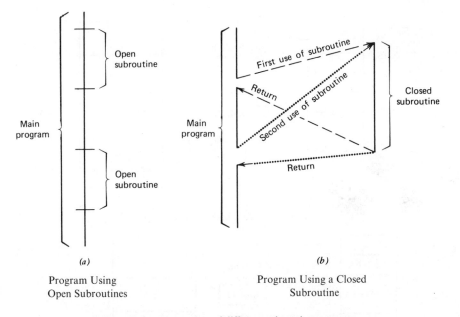

Figure 13-17. Illustration of different subroutine structures.

A closed subroutine consists of a self-contained sequence of instructions that carry out a given task. Thus the writing of the body of the subroutine is accomplished in the same manner as the writing of any other program. However, a closed subroutine can be called from any part of the main program. Therefore, there are four questions that we must answer if we are to use closed subroutines in a program. They are:

1. How do we call a subroutine?
2. How does the subroutine locate the data it needs to perform the given calculation?
3. How does the subroutine determine where it is to store the results of the computation?
4. How do we return to the main program after the subroutine has completed its computations?

Different computers have different ways in which to solve the linkage problem. In SEDCOM the Jump to Subroutine instruction

JMS AAA

where AAA is the address of the first location associated with the subroutine, provides one of the major tools that we need to create the linkage. Figure 13-18 illustrates how this instruction is used.

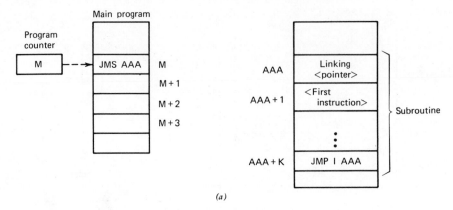

(a)

Contents Before Execution of JMS AAA

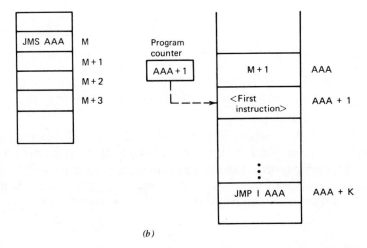

(b)

Contents Just After Execution of JMS AAA

Figure 13-18. Illustration of the action of the JMS instruction.

Just before the JMS instruction is executed, we have the condition shown in Figure 13-18a. We leave the main program at memory location M. When we return, it is assumed (at this point) that we will want to continue with the next instruction, which follows the JMS instruction. Thus we must have a pointer that indicates the next memory location following the JMS instruction. This pointer, called the *linking pointer*, is the first memory location in the subroutine (AAA in this example). The first instruction in the subroutine follows immediately after the pointer location (AAA + 1 in this example) and is the next instruction to be executed after the JMS instruction.

At the completion of the fetch cycle, during the execution of the JMS instruction, the program counter PC is set to the value $M + 1$. During the execute cycle the contents of the program counter is placed in location AAA and the program counter is set to AAA + 1. The result of executing the JMS instruction is illustrated in Figure 13-18b.

To return to the main program from the subroutine, we make use of the linking pointer. The information in location AAA at the completion of the subroutine is assumed to be the address of the next instruction that we wish the main program to execute. Thus we can return to this location by using the indirect transfer

JMP I AAA

The following examples will illustrate the various forms that a subroutine can take and the different ways that information can be passed between the main program and the subroutine.

Autonomous Subroutines

The simpliest types of subroutines are those that require no information transfer between the main program and the subroutine. This class of subroutines is rather limited, but the following example illustrates how the JMS instruction is used. Consider the subroutine described by the following subroutine specification. This subroutine is called PRAST. Note that PRAST represents both the address of the first memory location of the subroutine as well as the name of the subroutine.

Subroutine Program Specification

Subroutine PRAST

Task: Print a * without changing the contents of the accumulator

Input: None

Output: * printed by the printer

Calling Sequence: JMS PRAST

Figure 13-19a gives the flowchart of the algorithm, and Figure 13-19b gives the machine-level program that is found in memory locations PRAST through PRAST + 12. Note that in the example we assume that PRAST starts in location 100. Thus PRAST has a value of 100. Any other location could have been used.

We do not know the exact location of each memory location until we specify a value for PRAST. If we must refer to a particular location in the program, we can describe it by its address with respect to PRAST. For example, we could use

DCA PRAST + 11

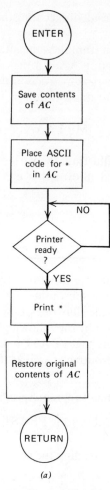

Flowchart of Algorithm

Figure 13-19. An autonomous subroutine.

to indicate that we wish to deposit the contents of the accumulator into the 12th (octal) memory location of the subroutine. Another approach is to assign a *mnemonic label* to indicate each memory location that we might wish to reference. For example, we might use

TAD AST

to indicate we wish to operate on the memory location indicated by the label AST. That location would be indicated by this label followed by a comma. (The comma indicates that the mnemonic is a label.)

The program in Figure 13-19 illustrates both types of references. The mnemonics PRAST, LP, and AST are all labels. LP is the label for the memory location PRAST + 3 while AST is the label for the memory location PRAST + 12.

Relative Address	Typical Code (PRAST = 100)	Mnemonic		Comments
PRAST	0000	PRAST,	0000	/LINKING POINTER /LOCATION
+1	3111		DCA PRAST + 11	/SAVE AC
+2	1112		RAD AST	/GET *
+3	6041	LP,	CPR	/READE READY?
+4	5103		JMP LP	/NO. TRY AGAIN
+5	6046		SPD	/YES. PRINT *
+6	7200		CLA	
+7	1111		TAD PRAST + 11	/RESTORE AC
+10	5500		JMP I PRAST	/RETURN
+11	0000		0000	/TEMPORARY /STORAGE
+12	0252	AST,	252	/* ASCII CODE

Machine-Language Program

Figure 13-19. (*b*)

To show how **PRAST** might be used, assume that the subroutine starts in location 100. To use **PRAST** in the main program, we could use the following sequence of instructions.

```
21    TAD 50
22    JMS 100    /PRAST STARTS AT LOCATION 100
23    DCA 51
        ⋮
```

when the JMS instruction in location 22 is executed the computer deposits 23 (the return address) in location 100 (the linking pointer) and then takes the next instruction to be executed from location 101. The final instruction of the subroutine is in location 112. This instruction, **JMP I PRAST** (i.e. JMP I 100), returns us to the main program at location 23, which is the location indicated by the value of the linking pointer.

The similar action could be indicated in mnemonic form as

```
21    TAD 50
22    JMS PRAST
23    DCA 51
```

In this case we do not have to define the value of **PRAST** until later.

The main use of a subroutine is to compute the value of a particular function $F(x_1, x_2, \ldots, x_n)$ for specific values of the arguments $x_1, x_2, \ldots, x_n$. Thus we must provide a way for the subroutine to have access to the particular values of the arguments at the time the subroutine is called. The sequence of operations that we use to do this is called a *calling sequence*. There are a wide variety of ways in which this transfer of information can be accomplished.

Local and Global Information

In many subroutines, we must use memory locations to store information that is needed only by that subroutine. The contents of these storage areas are of no interest outside of the subroutine. Information of this type is called *local information*, and the memory locations used to store this information is called *local storage*.

One way to pass information between the main program and subroutines or between subroutines is to define specific memory locations that will contain particular items of information. Each subroutine that uses that data can then reference it directly. Information of this type is called *global information*, and the locations used to store this information are called a *global memory locations*.

The accumulator can also be used to pass information to a subroutine. In this case, the calling sequence brings the information into the accumulator and control is then passed to the subroutine.

To illustrate how these ideas are used, consider the subroutine MAGN defined by the following subroutine specification. In this case, we assume that location 10 is a global storage location and that whenever B is to be used it can be found in location 10.

Subroutine Program Specification

Subroutine MAGN

Task: Compute

$$B \leftarrow |B - A|$$

Input: Value of B in location 10
           Value of A placed in accumulator

Output: Resulting value of B in location 10
           AC cleared upon return from subroutine

The flowchart and machine-level program needed to realize MAGN are given in Figure 13-20. Examining the program, we see that we do not have any local storage. Memory location 10 is a global storage location, and we pass the value of A to the subroutine by placing it in the accumulator just before we call the subroutine.

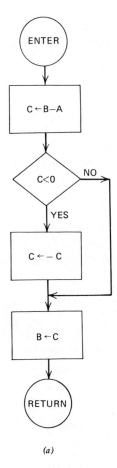

(a)

Flowchart

Relative Address	Typical Code (MAGN = 100)	Mnemonic	Comments
MAGN	0000	MAGN, 0	/LINKING POINTER
+1	7041	CMA IAC	/FORM −A
+2	1010	TAD 10	/ADD B
+3	7500	SMA	/RESULT NEGATIVE?
+4	5106	JMP LB	/NO.
+5	7041	CMA IAC	/YES. NEGATE RESULT
+6	3010	LB, DCA 10	/PLACE RESULT IN B
+7	5500	JMP I MAGN	/RETURN

Machine-Level Program

Figure 13-20. Subroutine MAGN which computes $B \leftarrow |B - A|$.

A typical calling sequence involving MAGN is shown below. It is assumed that MAGN starts in location 100, that a value of B is already in location 10, and the value of A is in location 50.

$$\vdots$$

25	CLA	/CLEAR TO START CALLING SEQUENCE
26	TAD 50	/BRING VALUE OF A TO AC
27	JMS 100	/TRANSFER CONTROL TO SUBROUTINE
30	⟨next instruction⟩	/AC CLEARED UPON RETURN FROM MAGN

$$\vdots$$

The use of global information to pass information to or from a subroutine is quite common. It does place a limitation on the programmer, since particular memory location must be reserved for this global data. This difficulty can be removed if we make use of the linking pointer to do more than just indicate the return address.

Parameter Passing Using the Linking Pointer

In the general case a subroutine may be used to evaluate a set of functions that can be represented, in general, as

$$z_1 = F_1(x_1, x_2, \ldots, x_n)$$
$$z_2 = F_2(x_1, x_2, \ldots, x_n)$$
$$\vdots$$
$$z_m = F_m(x_1, x_2, \ldots, x_n)$$

where m or n or both are greater than 1. If we are to use a subroutine to evaluate these functions, we must provide a systematic means whereby the subroutine can locate the values of the arguments $x_1, x_2, \ldots, x_n$ and a way by which the results $z_1, z_2, \ldots, z_m$ can be stored for later use in the program.

One way to do this is to make more extensive use of the linking pointer. In the memory locations immediately following the JMS instruction we can place the values used by the subroutine or the address of information needed by the subroutine. Similarly we can use these locations to receive values generated by the subroutine or to indicate the address of memory locations that are to receive this information.

Figure 13-21 illustrates the general organization of this particular linkage arrangement. After the JMS instruction is executed, the address of the following memory location is placed in the linking pointer. However, this location contains a parameter needed by the subroutine rather than the next instruction which is to

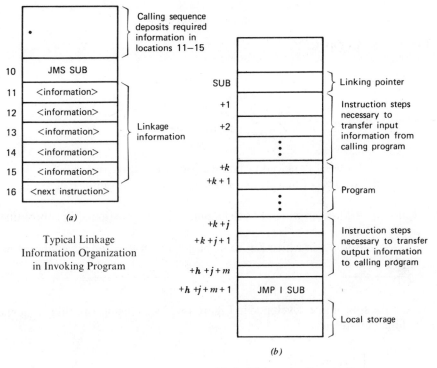

(a)

Typical Linkage
Information Organization
in Invoking Program

(b)

Typical Subroutine Organization

Figure 13-21. Illustrating general program organization when employing parameter passing using the linking pointer.

be executed upon return from the subroutine. Thus when the subroutine accesses that information the linking pointer must be incremented to point to the next location. This sequence of operations is continued until all of the information is used and the linking pointer is finally pointing to the next instruction to be executed.

As an illustration of subroutines of this type, consider the subroutine TWSUM defined by the following subroutine specifications. The flowchart of the algorithm used to compute these values is shown in Figure 13-22a and the corresponding machine-level program is given in Figure 13-22b.

If we examine the program in Figure 13-22b we see that statements 1 through 10 are used to transfer information from the invoking program to the subroutine. We use the linking pointer to read N. Then, after incrementing the linking pointer value, we read the address of the first term of the sequence A_I. The body of the subroutine consists of the statements in locations 11 through 26. The output information is transferred back to the invoking program by the statements 27 through 40 while statement 41 is the point at which we return from the subroutine. Statements 42 through 46 establish the local storage locations needed by the subroutine.

Subroutine Specification

Task: Compute

$$Y = \sum_{I=1}^{N} A_I \ (\text{modulo } 2^{12})$$

$$Z = \sum_{I=1}^{N} |A_I| \ (\text{module } 2)$$

Input: Value of N placed in 1st location after subroutine call
          Address of first A_I in 2nd location after subroutine call

Output: Address in which Y is to be placed in 3rd location after subroutine call
          Address in which Z is to be placed in 4th location after subroutine call

---

To use the subroutine developed in Figure 13-22 we must use a calling sequence of the following form.

```
001 ⎫
 ·  ⎬ Program before
030 ⎭ subroutine call

031    JMS 100                    /JUMP TO SUBROUTINE
032    ⟨N⟩                        /NUMBER OF TERMS
033    ⟨address of first A_I⟩
034    ⟨address of Y⟩
035    ⟨address of Z⟩
036    First Instruction after
       return to main program
 ·
```

In this example we assume that the subroutine starts in location 100. The information needed following the JMS instruction must be inserted by the programmer when the program is written, or another segment of the program must deposit the required values in the indicated location before the JMS instruction is executed.

A Complete Example

As a final example of the different ways of passing information between a subroutine and the program that invoked the subroutine, we use the subroutine SUM defined

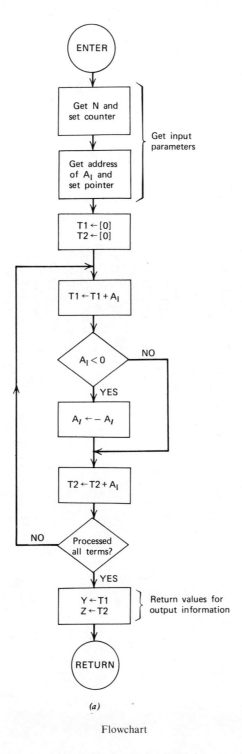

(a)

Flowchart

Figure 13-22. Subroutine TWSUM.

Relative Address	Typical Code (TWSUM = 100)	Mnemonic	Comments
TWSUM	0000	TWSUM, 0	/LINKING POINTER
+1	7200	CLA	/INITIALIZE AC
+2	1500	TAD I TWSUM	/GET N
+3	7041	CMA IAC	/FORM − N
+4	3142	DCA CNT	/SET COUNTER
+5	2100	ISZ TWSUM	/INCREMENT LINKING /POINTER
+6	1500	TAD I TWSUM	/GET POINTER
+7	3143	DCA PNT	/SET POINTER
+10	2100	ISZ TWSUM	/INCREMENT LINKING /POINTER
+11	3144	DCA T1	/SET T1 to 0
+12	3145	DCA T2	/SET T2 to 0
+13	1144	BEG, TAD T1	/GET T1
+14	1543	TAD I PNT	/ADD AI
+15	3144	DCA T1	/SAVE T1
+16	1543	TAD I PNT	/GET AI
+17	7500	SMA	/IS IT NEGATIVE?
+20	5122	JMP A	/NO
+21	7041	CMA IAC	/FORM − AI
+22	1145	A, TAD T2	/ADD T2
+23	3145	DCA T2	/SAVE T2

+24	2143	ISZ PNT	/INCREMENT AI /POINTER
+25	2142	ISZ CNT	/HAVE WE FINISHED /LOOP?
+26	5113	JMP BEG	/NO. CONTINUE /SUMMING
+27	1500	TAD I TWSUM	/YES. GET ADDRESS /OF Y
+30	3146	DCA ADST	/SAVE ADDRESS
+31	1144	TAD T1	/GET T1
+32	3546	DCA I ADST	/DEPOSIT T1 in Y
+33	2100	ISZ TWSUM	/INCREMENT LINKING /POINTER
+34	1500	TAD I TWSUM	/GET ADDRESS OF Z
+35	3146	DCA ADST	/SAVE ADDRESS
+36	1145	TAD T2	/GET T2
+37	3546	DCA I ADST	/DEPOSIT T2 IN Z
+40	2100	ISZ TWSUM	/INCREMENT LINKING /POINTER
+41	5500	JMP I TWSUM	/RETURN
		/TEMPORARY STORAGE	
+42	0000	CNT, 0	/COUNTER LOCATION
+43	0000	PNT, 0	/POINTER LOCATION
+44	0000	T1, 0	/T1 STORAGE
+45	0000	T2, 0	/T2 STORAGE
+46	0000	ADST, 0	/ADDRESS STORAGE

Figure 13-22. (b) Program.

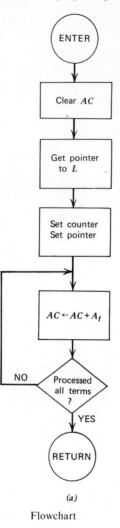

(a)

Flowchart

Figure 13-23. The subroutine SUM.

below. Figure 13-23 gives the flowchart and machine-level program for this subroutine.

The subroutine SUM can now be used to carry out the calculation called for by PROGRAM 8. This program computes

$$Y = \sum_{I=1}^{N_A} A_I + \sum_{J=1}^{N_B} B_J$$

where the data associated with A starts in location 100 and that associated with B starts in location 200. Figure 13-24 gives the flowchart and program necessary to compute Y by using the subroutine SUM, which starts in location 300.

Relative Address	Typical Code (SUM = 300)	Mnemonic	Comments
SUM	0000	SUM, 0	/LINKING POINTER
+1	7200	CLA	/INITIALIZE
+2	1700	TAD I SUM	/GET POINTER TO L
+3	3315	DCA PNT	/SAVE L POINTER
+4	1715	TAD I PNT	/GET N
+5	7041	CMA IAC	/FORM − N
+6	3316	DCA CNT	/SET COUNTER
+7	2315	ISZ PNT	/INCREMENT L POINTER
+10	1715	BGN, TAD I PNT	/ADD NEXT TERM
+11	2315	ISZ PNT	/INCREMENT L POINTER
+12	2316	ISZ CNT	/INCREMENT COUNT. /DONE?
+13	5310	JMP BGN	/NO CONTINUE
+14	5700	JMP I SUM	/YES. RETURN
			/TEMPORARY STORAGE
+15	0000	PNT, 0	/L POINTER
+16	0000	CNT, 0	/COUNTER

Machine-Level Program

Figure 13-23. (b)

Subroutine Program Specification

SUM

Task: Compute

$$Y = \sum_{I=1}^{N} A_I \text{ (modulo } 2^{12})$$

Input: Input information is stored in $N + 1$ locations L through $L + N$
Location L has the value of N. Locations $L + 1$ through $L + N$
contain the A_I values
Address of L is in 1st location after the subroutine call

Output: The value of Y is left in the AC

If we compare the program shown in Figure 13-16 which uses two open subroutines with the program shown in Figure 13-24, which uses one closed subroutine, we notice that we use six fewer memory locations using the closed subroutine. This savings would have been greater if the subroutine SUM were called

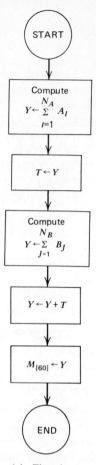

(a) Flowchart

Address	Instruction	Mnemonic	Comments
001	4300	JMS SUM	/COMPUTE FIRST SUM
002	0100	100	/ADDRESS A DATA
003	3011	DCA 11	/SAVE RESULT
004	4300	JMS SUM	/COMPUTE SECOND SUM
005	0200	200	/ADDRESS B DATA
006	1011	TAD 11	/ADD FIRST SUM
007	3060	DCA 60	/STORE RESULT
010	7402	HLT	/END
			/TEMPORARY STORAGE
011	0000	0	/TEMPORARY STORAGE
060	0000	0	/FINAL RESULT

Main Program

Figure 13-24. Program to compute $Y = \sum_{I=1}^{N_A} A_I + \sum_{J=1}^{N_B} B_J$ using subroutine SUM.

on to carry out a much more complex task. The price that we have to pay to use a subroutine is the extra steps to set up the linkage between the subroutine and the invoking program and the time necessary to transfer information between the two.

Subroutines take many forms, and many different types of calling sequences can be used to link a subroutine to the invoking program. Some of these techniques will be illustrated in the following sections.

EXERCISES

1. Convert PROGRAM 6 to a subroutine called OCTIN. On returning from OCTIN the binary number is to be in the AC. Use this subroutine in a program that will read in eight 4-digit octal numbers and store them in locations 200 through 207.

2. Write a subroutine that will print HELLO.

4. NUMERICAL CALCULATIONS

Numerical calculations play a very important role in many information processing tasks. It might, therefore, seem that we have imposed a considerable limitation on SEDCOM because we have only included the 2's complement addition operation in its basic instruction set. This limitation can be eliminated to a great extent by developing special subroutines that can be used to carry out the more complex numerical calculations. The penalty that we pay for using subroutines rather than hardware to realize a given numerical operation is one of time. This section illustrates how different types of subroutines can be developed to handle specific types of numerical calculations.

Fixed Point Multiplication

In Chapter 11 we saw that we could build a digital network that would multiply two r-bit positive numbers together. We accomplished this task by using three r-bit registers, an overflow register, and a sequence of shifting and addition operations that were determined by the network's control unit. To accomplish the same task with a subroutine we must simulate the same type of operation.

The subroutine FIXMUL defined by the following specification carries out the fixed point multiplication of two r-bit positive numbers. Examining this specification we see that memory locations 001, 002, and 003 serve as global memory locations. The calling sequence for this subroutine consists of first storing 0 in location 001, the multiplier in location 002 and the multiplicand in location 003. The link and accumulator are then cleared just before the JMS instruction is executed to enter the subroutine.

Subroutine Specification

FIXMUL

Task: Compute

$$Y = A * B$$

Input: A, the multiplier is a 12-bit positive number stored in location 002
B, the multiplicand is a 12-bit positive number stored in location 003
The Link L is set to 0. The AC is set to 0
Location 001 acts as a pseudo accumulator and is set to 0

Output: Y, the product is a 24-bit positive number. The higher order 12-bits are in location 001 and the lower order bits are in location 002

The flowchart of the algorithm to realize FIXMUL is given in Figure 13-25. The corresponding program is given in Table 13-2 where it is assumed that the subroutine starts in location 250. A similar program could be developed to carry out fixed point division.

Double-Precision Numbers

Up to this point we have taken the content of each word to be either a 12-bit positive binary number or a signed 11-bit number with the leftmost bit acting as the sign bit. In either case it is left up to the programmer to keep track of the binary point associated with the number. A number represented in such a manner is called a *single-precision number*.

In SEDCOM this means that we can represent positive integers between 0 and $2^{12} - 1 = 4095$ and regular integers between $\pm(2^{11} - 1) = \pm 2047$. If we wish to work with a larger range of numbers we can use two computer words to represent a given number. A number represented in such a manner is called a *double-precision number*. Figure 13-26 shows how both a signed and unsigned number can be represented in double-precision form.

Double-Precision Addition

It is obvious that if we wish to carry out the standard arithmetic operations with double-precision numbers we need a complete program to perform each arithmetic operation instead of a single instruction. We now develop a subroutine that will add two double-precision integers. This subroutine is defined by the following specification.

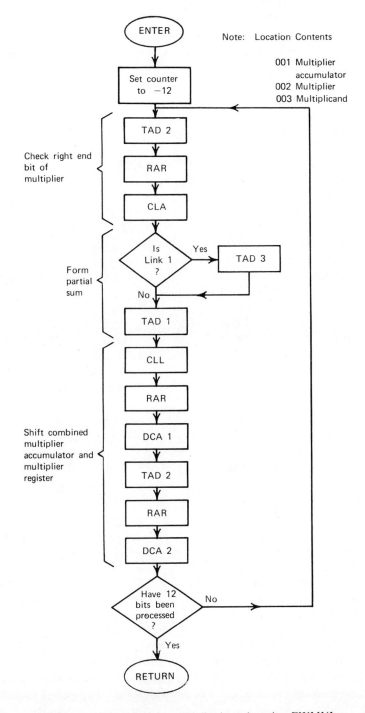

Figure 13-25. Flowchart for multiplication subroutine. FIXMUL.

Table 13-2

Subroutine FIXMUL To
Multiply Two Positive Numbers

Address	Instruc-tion or Content	Mnemonic	Comment
250	0000	FIXMUL, 0000	/LINKING POINTER
251	1274	TAD M12	/GET −12
252	3273	DCA CNT	/SET COUNTER TO −12
253	1002	BGN, TAD 2	/GET MULTIPLIER
254	7010	RAR	/SHIFT
255	7200	CLA	/PREPARE TO FORM /PARTIAL SUM
256	7420	SNL	/IS LINK 1
257	5261	JMP NX	/NO
260	1003	TAD 3	/YES. GET MULTIPLICAND
261	1001	NX, TAD 1	/FORM PARTIAL SUM
262	7100	CLL	/PREPARE LINK FOR SHIFT
263	7010	RAR	/CARRY OUT FIRST SHIFT
264	3001	DCA 1	/STORE SHIFTED RESULT
265	1002	TAD 2	/GET MULTIPLIER
266	7010	RAR	/SHIFT RIGHT
267	3002	DCA 2	/STORE SHIFTED /MULTIPLIER
270	2273	ISZ CNT	/ARE WE FINISHED
271	5253	JMP BGN	/NO. FORM NEXT PARTIAL /SUM
272	5650	JMP I FIXMUL	/YES. RETURN TO MAIN /PROGRAM
		/STORAGE	
273	0000	CNT, 0000	/COUNTER
274	7764	M12, 7764	/−12 IN 2's COMPLEMENT

From this specification we see that locations 001 and 002 are global memory locations that are assumed to contain the initial value of A. The calling sequence for this subroutine loads the address of the first word of B into the accumulator just before the JMS instruction is executed. The subroutine necessary to carry out this calculation is given by Table 13-3. It is assumed that it starts in location 200.

Similar subroutines can be developed to carry out the other standard arithmetic operations on double-precision numbers. If greater accuracy or range is required, we could also increase the number of words that we use to represent a particular number. Here again we would have to develop subroutines to handle numbers of this form.

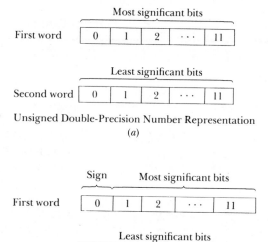

Unsigned Double-Precision Number Representation
(*a*)

Signed Double-Precision Number Representation
(*b*)

Figure 13-26. Double-precision number representation.

Subroutine Specification

DUBADD

Task: Compute

$$A \leftarrow A + B$$

Input: *A* is a double precision integer located in memory locations 001 and 002

B is a double precision integer. The address of the first word of *B* is loaded into the accumulator just before the JMS instruction

Output: The result is left in locations 001 and 002

The computer halts if there is an overflow

Floating-Point Number Representation

In the programming of computations involving noninteger single- or multiple-precision data, the position of the scale point (i.e., binary point in a binary number)

Table 13-3

Subroutine DUBADD To
Perform Double-Precision Addition

Address	Instruction or Content	Mnemonic	Comments
200	0000 DUBADD, 0000		/LINKING POINTER
201	3217	DCA 217	/SAVE ADDRESS
202	1217	TAD 217	/RETRIEVE ADDRESS
203	7101	IAC CLL	/FORM LOW ORDER /DIGITS ADDRESS. /CLEAR LINK
204	3220	DCA 220	/STORE ADDRESS
205	1002	TAD 2	/GET LOW ORDER /DIGITS OF FIRST /NUMBER
206	1620	TAD I 220	/ADD LOW ORDER /DIGITS OF SECOND /NUMBER
207	3002	DCA 2	/STORE RESULT
210	7004	RAL	/READ LINK INTO RIGHT /END OF /ACCUMULATOR
211	1001	TAD 1	/ADD HIGH ORDER /DIGITS OF FIRST /NUMBER
212	1617	TAD I 217	/ADD HIGH ORDER /DIGITS OF SECOND /NUMBER
213	3001	DCA 1	/STORE RESULT
214	7420	SNL	/IS THERE AN /OVERFLOW?
215	5600	JMP I DUBADD	/NO. RETURN TO MAIN /PROGRAM
216	7402	HLT	/YES. STOP PROGRAM
217	(Temporary storage of address of high order digits of second number)		
220	(Temporary storage of address of low order digits of second number)		

Note: First number is stored in locations 001 and 002 with higher order digits in location 001. Address of higher order digits of the second word is in the accumulator. The result is left in locations 001 and 002. The computer halts if there is an overflow.

must be kept track of by the programmer. Once numbers are entered into the computer, there is no hardware available to keep track of the location of the scale point. This point exists only in the mind of the programmer and only by keeping track of its imaginary position is he able to correctly interpret and control the computer's calculations.

One way to avoid this problem is to use a floating-point representation for numerical data. As discussed in Chapter 2, any binary number can be represented in the form

$$(. m_{-1}m_{-2} \cdots m_{-r})2^{\pm e_u e_{u-1} \cdots e_1 e_0}$$

where the exponent $(e_u e_{u-1} \cdots e_1 e_0)$ is an integer and the mantissa $. m_{-1}m_{-2} \cdots m_{-r}$ is a binary fraction. The mantissa is always stored in a normalized form with all of the leading 0's eliminated from the binary representation. Thus the highest order bit m_{-1} is always 1. The exponent represents the power of 2 by which the mantissa is multiplied to obtain the number's value when it is used in a computation.

For example, the floating-point representation of

$$101101.101 \text{ is } (.101101101) \times 2^{110}$$

while the representation of

$$.0010101 \text{ is } (.10101) \times 2^{-10}$$

In the above examples the number in the parentheses represent the mantissa and the exponent of 2 which is given in binary form represents the exponent of the number.

If a single computer word is large enough, it can store a floating-point number in a manner indicated in Figure 13-27a where the word has been divided into four

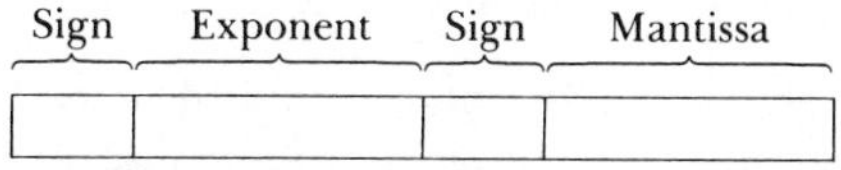

Sign	Exponent	Sign	Mantissa

(a) Single-word floating-point number

Sign	Mantissa

Sign	Exponent

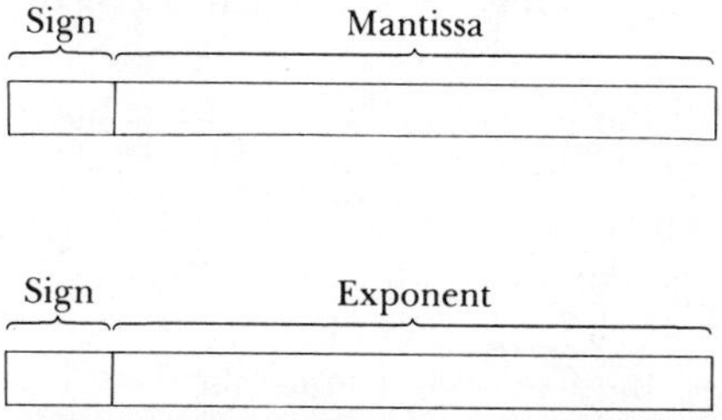

(b) Two-word floating-point number

Figure 13-27. Floating-point formats.

fields: sign of the exponent, value of the exponent, sign of the mantissa, and value of the mantissa. If a single computer word is not large enough to hold a floating point number, then multiple words can be used. Figure 13-27 illustrates how two words can be used. If greater precision is required two or three words are sometimes used for the mantissa.

For the following discussion we assume that all floating-point numbers are represented by two 12-bit words as shown in Figure 13-27b. Negative values of the exponent or mantissa are represented in 2's complement form. In making calculations with floating-point numbers we must use subroutines to carry out the standard arithmetic operations. These subroutines must deal with both the value of the exponent and the value of the mantissa of the floating-point numbers.

Multiplication of Two Floating-Point Numbers

To show how arithmetic operations can be performed on two floating-point numbers, we develop a multiplication subroutine that will multiply two positive floating-point numbers A and B. Assume that these two numbers have the following floating-point form.

$$A = m_a 2^{e_a}$$

$$B = m_b 2^{e_b}$$

Then the product is given by

$$AB = m_a m_b 2^{e_a + e_b}$$

Thus we see that we must add exponents and multiply the mantissas. But we can treat the mantissa of a number as an integer provided we keep track of the location of the binary point. Thus we can use the fixed point multiplication subroutine developed at the beginning of this section to carry out the multiplication of the mantissas.

If we examine this subroutine we see that it was designed to multiply two 12-bit unsigned numbers. However, if we examine Figure 13-27 we see that the leftmost bit represents the sign of the mantissa and the other 11 bits represent the magnitude of the mantissa. Therefore the calling sequence necessary to set up the information needed by the fixed-point multiplication subroutine must take this fact into account. Similarly when the fixed-point multiplication is complete, we will have a product term that is represented by a 24-bit number stored in two computer words. We must then convert this number into the standard form shown in Figure 13-27. With these observations we are now ready to develop the subroutine to carry out the multiplication of two floating-point numbers. The subroutine is defined by the following specification.

Subroutine Specification

FLMUL

Task: Compute

$$A \leftarrow A * B$$

Input: A is a floating point positive number stored in memory locations 004 and 005

B is a floating point positive number. The address of the first word of B is loaded into the accumulator and the link L is set to 0 just before the JMS instruction

Output: The result is left in locations 004 and 005

Subroutines Used: The fixed point multiplication subroutine FIXMUL is used

---

A flowchart describing the algorithm needed to realize FLMUL is given in Figure 13-28. The corresponding program, starting in memory location 100, is given in Table 13-4. From the specification we see that we use locations 004 and 005 as global memory locations that are assumed to contain the initial and final values of A. The calling sequence for FLMUL loads the address of the first word of B in the accumulator and clears the link L just before the JMS instruction is executed.

Examining the flowchart we see that we first set up the calling sequence for the fixed-point multiplication subroutine by rotating the mantissa of A and B one bit left and depositing the resulting terms in the multiplier and multiplicand locations of the subroutine. After we carry out the fixed-point multiplication we then add the two exponents of the numbers where, for simplicity, we assume that there will be no overflow. Finally we check the high order word of the product to see if there is a leading zero. If there is, we decrease the value of the exponent by 1 and use this leading zero to indicate the sign bit. If the leading bit is one, we must rotate the product one bit to the right to restore the sign to the mantissa. However, in this case, there is no need to change the value of the exponent. This completes the floating-point multiplication operation and we return to the main program.

In this section we have examined the different types of numerical representations that can be used in SEDCOM and how operations can be performed on data stored in the different forms. However, we must often deal with symbolic as well as numeric information. This problem is considered in the next section.

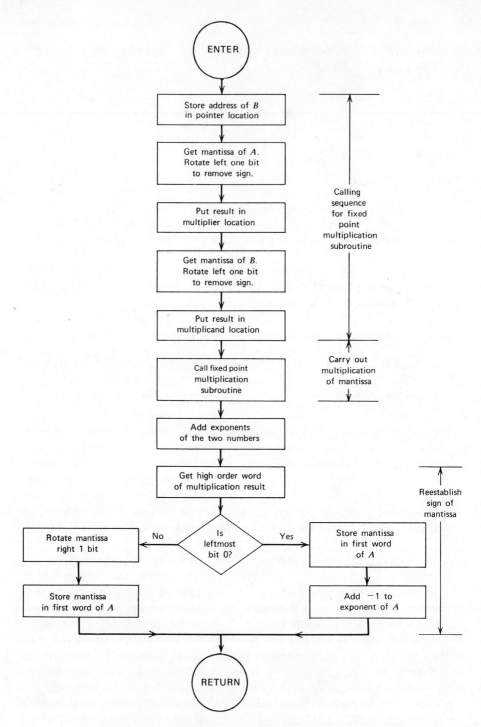

Figure 13-28. Flowchart of a subroutine FLMUL to form floating point product.

Address	Instruction or Content	Mnemonic	Comment
100	0000	FLMUL, 0000	/LINKING POINTER
101	3131	DCA PNT	/STORE ADDRESS OF B
102	1004	TAD 4	/GET MANTISSA OF A
103	7004	RAL	/REMOVE SIGN BIT
104	3002	DCA 2	/SET UP MULTIPLIER
105	1531	TAD I PNT	/GET MANTISSA OF B
106	7004	RAL	/REMOVE SIGN BIT
107	3003	DCA 3	/SET UP MULTIPLICAND
110	3001	DCA 1	/SET MULTIPLIER /ACCUMULATOR TO ZERO
111	2131	ISZ PNT	/INCREMENT ADDRESS OF B
112	4250	JMS 250	/GO TO MULTIPLICATION /SUBROUTINE
113	1005	TAD 5	/GET EXPONENT OF A
114	1531	TAD I PNT	/ADD EXPONENT OF B
115	3005	DCA 5	/SAVE NEW VALUE OF /EXPONENT
116	1001	TAD 1	/GET HIGH ORDER WORD /OF MANTISSA PRODUCT
117	7500	SMA	/IS LEADING BIT 1
120	5124	JMP A	/NO
121	7110	CLL RAR	/YES. INSERT ZERO IN SIGN /BIT
122	3004	DCA 4	/SAVE NEW VALUE OF /MANTISSA
123	5500	JMP I FLMUL	/RETURN TO MAIN /PROGRAM
124	3004	A, DCA 4	/SAVE NEW VALUE OF /MANTISSA
125	1005	TAD 5	/GET EXPONENT
126	1132	TAD M1	/ADD −1 TO EXPONENT
127	3005	DCA 5	/SAVE NEW VALUE OF /EXPONENT
130	5500	JMP I FLMUL	/RETURN TO MAIN /PROGRAM
131	0000	PNT, 0000	/POINTER TO STORE /ADDRESS OF B
132	7777	M1, 7777	/−1

Note: The first number is assumed to be in memory locations 004 and 005. The address of the first word of the second number is placed in the accumulator just before the subroutine is called. The result is placed in locations 004 and 005. This subroutine uses the multiplication subroutine of Table 13-1.

1. Write a subroutine that will subtract two double-precision integers A and B. The number A is assumed stored in memory locations 1 and 2 and the calling sequence must provide the initial address of B.

2. Modify the multiplication subroutine of Table 13-2 so that any two integers (positive or negative) can be multiplied.

3. Draw a flowchart for the program given in Table 13-3.

5. SYMBOLIC CALCULATIONS

Most of the examples that we have dealt with so far have involved numerical calculations. However, a computer is really a symbol manipulator, and it is just as easy to work with nonnumeric data as it is to work with numeric data. In this section we investigate some of the typical ways that symbolic data is handled.

Nonnumeric Data

Nonnumeric as well as numeric characters can be stored in a computer by assigning a binary code to each character with which we wish to deal. These coded characters can then be packed into a computer word by assigning a field to each character. This field is sometimes referred to as one *byte* of information. For example, each ASCII teletype character requires a field of 8 bits. Thus only one complete teletype symbol can be stored in one 12-bit word. Figure 13-29 illustrates how this information is stored.

As an example let us assume that we wish to store the character string

JMP ␣ 31

in memory starting in memory location 30. Then we would need six memory words that would contain the indicated ASCII coding.

Memory Location	Contents	Comment
030	0312	/J
031	0315	/M
032	0320	/P
033	0240	/␣
034	0263	/3
035	0261	/1

Character Field

0	1	2	3	4	5	6	7	8	9	10	11

Figure 13-29. One method of storing characters in a 12-bit word.

From this discussion we see that when we treat a number as a character, it is stored in a different manner than when we code it directly as numerical information. Whenever we wish to make computational use of numerical information in this form, we must either first convert it to fixed-point or floating-point form or we must develop special subroutines that operate on numerical information stored in character form.

Reading Character Strings

One of the common symbol manipulation operations consists of reading a sequence of characters from the reader and storing them in successive memory locations. We now develop a subroutine that will accept a sequence of characters from the reader until the carriage return character is detected. At this point the subroutine will store all zeros in the next memory location and return to the main program. The following specification describes this program.

Subroutine Specification

RDCHR

Task: Read a character string from the reader until a carriage return is detected. Place the characters in sequential locations in memory. The last location contains all zeros

Input: The character sequence from the reader. The address of the memory location that will receive the first character is placed in the accumulator before the JMS instruction

Output: The address of the memory location following the memory location containing all zeros is left in the accumulator when returning from the subroutine

---

The calling sequence consists of loading the address of the first memory location to receive a character into the accumulator and then executing the JMS instruction. A program to realize this subroutine is given by Table 13-5.

In this subroutine we note that we check each character by adding 7563, corresponding to -215, to the coded representation of the character. If the result is zero,

Table 13-5

Subroutine RDCHR To
Store a Character String in Memory

Address	Instruc-tion or Content	Mnemonic	Comment
050	0000	RDCHR, 0000	/LINKING POINTER
051	3071	DCA PNT	/USE ADDRESS /INFORMATION TO SET /POINTER
052	6031	BGN, CRF	/IS READER READY?
053	5052	JMP BGN	/NO, TRY AGAIN
054	6036	RRD	/YES, READ CHARACTER
055	3471	DCA I PNT	/DEPOSIT CHARACTER
056	1471	TAD I PNT	/RETRIEVE CHARACTER
057	1072	TAD M215	/SUBTRACT 215
060	7440	SZA	/IS CHARACTER A /CARRIAGE RETURN?
061	5066	JMP CP	/NO, CONTINUE /PROCESSING
062	3471	DCA I PNT	/YES, DEPOSIT 0
063	2071	ISZ PNT	/INCREMENT POINTER
064	1071	TAD PNT	/PLACE LAST MEMORY /ADDRESSES IN /ACCUMULATOR
065	5450	JMP I RDCHR	/RETURN TO MAIN /PROGRAM
066	2071	CP, ISZ PNT	/INCREMENT POINTER
067	7200	CLA	/CLEAR ACCUMULATOR
070	5052	JMP BGN	/GO READ NEXT /CHARACTER
071	0000	PNT, 0000	/POINTER
072	7563	M215, 7563	/−215

we know that the current character is a carriage return (i.e., code 215) and we terminate the subroutine. Otherwise, we continue the read sequence.

Tables and a Table Lookup Subroutine

In working with symbolic data we often store information in tabular form. For example, let us assume that we wish to translate the mnemonic symbols associated with a given instruction set into a corresponding machine-language code. We can do this very easily by developing a table lookup program that takes the given

Table 13-6

A Table Giving the Relationship
Between the Mnemonic Symbols and Their
Corresponding Machine-Language Representation

Mnemonic Input	Machine-Language Equivalent (Octal) Output
AND	0000
TAD	1000
ISZ	2000
DCA	3000
JMS	4000
JMP	5000

mnemonic term, looks it up in a table that is stored in memory, and then reads out the machine-language code corresponding to that symbol. Table 13-6 illustrates the type of correspondence with which we are dealing. Thus, for example, if the input was a suitably coded representation of TAD, then the output would be 1000. Before writing the program we must agree on how we will encode the information represented by this table for use by the computer.

Each line of the table can be represented in memory by four memory words. The first three words will contain the coded mnemonic information and the fourth will contain the value of the mnemonic term. Under this assumption we can encode Table 13-6 for storage in memory as shown in Table 13-7.

To use this table we now develop a subroutine that will take any mnemonic term $S_1 S_2 S_3$ and check to see if it is in the table. The following subroutine specification describes a subroutine SRCH, which will carry out this task. The flowchart indicating the major components of the algorithm to realize SRCH is given in Figure 13-30. The program corresponding to this flowchart is given in Table 13-8.

Subroutine Specification

SRCH

Task: Search the mnemonic symbol table to determine if the mnemonic term $S_1 S_2 S_3$ is in the table. If it is found return its value. Otherwise set the accumulator to 7777

Input: The symbols $S_1 S_2 S_3$ which make up the input mnemonic are stored in the consecutive memory locations 10, 11, 12. The accumulator is cleared before entering the subroutine. The mnemonic symbol table is in location 100 through 127

Output: If $S_1 S_2 S_3$ is found in the table, its value is placed in the accumulator. If it is not found, 7777 is placed in the accumulator

---

Table 13-7 Coded Mnemonic Symbol Table

Memory Location	Octal Content	Value Stored
100	0301	A
101	0316	N
102	0304	D
103	0000	0000
104	0324	T
105	0301	A
106	0304	D
107	1000	1000
110	0311	I
111	0323	S
112	0332	Z
113	2000	2000
114	0304	D
115	0303	C
116	0301	A
117	3000	3000
120	0312	J
121	0315	M
122	0323	S
123	4000	4000
124	0312	J
125	0315	M
126	0320	P
127	5000	5000

Table 13-8   Program for Table Lookup Subroutine

Address	Instruction or Content	Mnemonic	Comment
200	0000	SRCH, 0000	/LINKING POINTER
201	1010	TAD 10	/GET S_1
202	7041	CMA IAC	/FORM $-S_1$
203	3252	DCA MS1	/STORE $-S_1$
204	1011	TAD 11	/GET S_2
205	7041	CMA IAC	/FORM $-S_2$
206	3253	DCA MS2	/STORE $-S_2$
207	1012	TAD 12	/GET S_3

210	7041	CMA IAC	/FORM $-S_3$
211	3254	DCA MS3	/STORE $-S_3$
212	1255	TAD M5	/GET -5
213	3251	DCA CNT	/SET COUNTER TO -5
214	1256	TAD AD	/GET 100
215	3250	DCA PNT	/SET POINTER TO 100
216	1252	BGN, TAD MS1	/GET $-S_1$
217	1650	TAD I PNT	/MATCH IT TO FIRST TABLE /VALUE
220	7440	SZA	/DOES IT MATCH
221	5237	JMP 237	/NO, TRY NEXT TABLE ENTRY
222	2250	ISZ PNT	/INCREMENT POINTER
223	1253	TAD MS2	/GET $-S_2$
224	1650	TAD I PNT	/MATCH IT TO SECOND /TABLE VALUE
225	7440	SZA	/DOES IT MATCH
226	5240	JMP 240	/NO, TRY NEXT ENTRY
227	2250	ISZ PNT	/INCREMENT POINTER
230	1254	TAD MS3	/GET $-S_3$
231	1650	TAD I PNT	/MATCH IT TO THIRD TABLE /VALUE
232	7440	SZA	/DOES IT MATCH
233	5241	JMP 241	/NO, TRY NEXT ENTRY
234	2250	ISZ PNT	/YES, INCREMENT POINTER
235	1650	TAD I PNT	/READ VALUE OF $S_1 S_2 S_3$
236	5600	JMP I SRCH	/RETURN TO MAIN PROGRAM
237	2250	ISZ PNT	/INCREMENT POINTER
240	2250	ISZ PNT	/INCREMENT POINTER
241	2250	ISZ PNT	/INCREMENT POINTER
242	2250	ISZ PNT	/INCREMENT POINTER
243	7200	CLA	/CLEAR ACCUMULATOR
244	2251	ISZ CNT	/HAVE WE SEARCHED WHOLE /TABLE
245	5216	JMP BGN	/NO, TRY NEXT ENTRY
246	7240	CLA CMA	/YES, VALUE NOT FOUND /SET ACCUMULATOR TO 7777
247	5600	JMP I SRCH	/RETURN TO MAIN PROGRAM
250	0000	PNT, 0000	/POINTER
251	0000	CNT, 0000	/COUNTER
252	0000	MS1, 0000	/$-S_1$
253	0000	MS2, 0000	/$-S_2$
254	0000	MS3, 0000	/$-S_3$
255	7773	M5, 7773	/-5
256	0100	AD, 0100	/ADDRESS OF FIRST TABLE /ENTRY

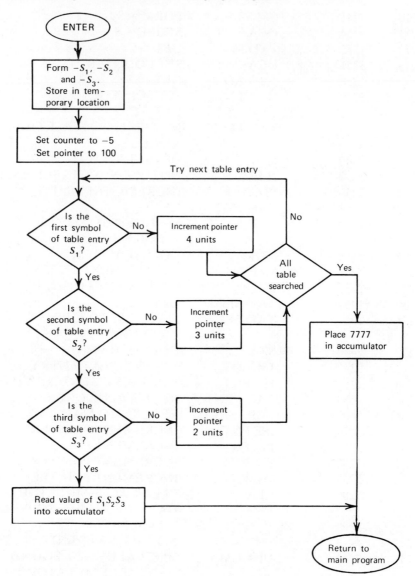

Figure 13-30. Flowchart of table look-up program.

Note that in this subroutine the locations of S_1, S_2, and S_3 as well as the location of the mnemonic symbol table are assumed to be global memory locations. The calling sequence must clear the accumulator before calling the subroutine.

From this discussion we see that the manipulation of symbolic data is as easily accomplished as the manipulation of numeric data. In the next chapter we use these concepts to show how we can develop higher level computer languages that will make it easier to program computers.

EXERCISES

1. Assume that a string of characters has been read into memory using the subroutine given by Table 13-5. Assume that the first character is stored in memory location 100. Write a program that will count the number of times the character *A* appears in the string of characters.

6. SUMMARY

Our main goal in this chapter has been to develop an understanding of how a computer actually carries out the computations associated with a program. To do this we have investigated how the basic operation of a simple computer can be used in carrying out the computations called for by a given algorithm. Using this background we were then able to write several machine-language programs to carry out various information processing tasks.

As we have seen from these examples, it is often a very tedious task to write programs in machine language. This is mainly because of the excessive detail that must be kept in mind as we write a machine-language program. However, since a computer is a symbol manipulating device, we can turn over many of these tedious tasks to the computer if we can write a program that will carry out the required information processing operations. Programs of this type are considered in Chapter 14.

REFERENCE NOTATION

As indicated, the SEDCOM computer is based on the PDP-8. A complete description of the PDP-8 can be found in [5]. A good discussion of the fundamentals of program organization and design are found in [1] and [2]. The relationship between machine-language programming and various other computer configurations can be found in [3] and [4].

REFERENCES

1. Booth, T. L., and Chien, Y. T. (1974), *Computing: Fundamentals and Applications*, Hamilton-Wiley, New York.

2. Forsythe, A. I., Keenan, T. A., Organick, E. I., and Stenberg, W. (1975), *Computer Science—A First Course*, Second Edition, John Wiley, New York.

3. Gear, C. W. (1974), *Computer Organization and Programming*, McGraw-Hill, New York.

4. Sloan, M. E. (1976), *Computer Hardware and Organization*, SRA, Chicago.

5. (1975), *Introduction to Programming*, Digital Equipment Corp., Maynard, Mass.

HOME PROBLEMS

The following problems all involve the writing of a SEDCOM program to carry out a specific information processing task. The complete solution of the problem should include:

(a)   A statement of the algorithm that is used to solve the problem.
(b)   A complete flow chart showing how the algorithm is implemented.
(c)   The SEDCOM program that will carry out the algorithm.
(d)   (Optional) If a SEDCOM simulator is available, proof should be submitted that the program actually carries out the claimed information processing task.

1.   Write a subroutine that will multiply two signed double-precision integers A and B.

2.   Write a subroutine that will subtract two signed floating-point numbers. Each floating-point number is represented by two 12-bit words.

3.   Write a program that will accept strings of symbols separated by blanks. Each string will consist of a four-letter name followed by a 0 or 1 followed by a three-digit octal number. Use these strings to calculate income tax where the three-digit number represents a man's salary and a 1 indicates he has dependents. If the man has dependents and his salary is between 0 and 177_8 his tax is 0 dollars, between 200_8 and 377_8 his tax is 050_8, between 400_8 and 577_8 his tax is 150_8, and between 600_8 and 777_8 his tax is 250_8. If he has no dependents, add 50_8 to his tax. On each line print out the man's name followed by a 0 or 1 (no dependents or dependents), followed by his salary, followed by his tax.

4.   Assume that data from a previous calculation is stored in locations 300_8 to 350_8. Write a program that will plot this data as a graph.

(a)   Give x and y axis.
(b)   Assume data are positive integers.
(c)   Assume that 7777 is full scale.

5.   Write a program that will read in a list of two-digit octal numbers between 0 and 25_8 and print out on each line the word OCT followed by the octal number and the word DEC followed by the decimal equivalent of that octal number.

6. Write a program to read in a list of 8 three-digital octal numbers and place them in storage in *descending* numerical order starting at location 370. The output will consist of two columns: the first a list of the registers from 370 to 377 and the second the contents of the register in the first column.

7. Write a program that will read in a list of words of varying length separated by a + sign. The end of the list will be indicated by an *. Each word should be stored one letter at a time in consecutive memory locations starting at location 330. Each line of the printout should consist of a word followed by its length followed by its starting address in memory.

8. Write a program that will scan an input sentence of any arbitrary length and count the number of times that a given word appears in the sentence. The word being looked for should be given as input data.

14

Assembler Languages and Assemblers

1. INTRODUCTION

As we saw in the last chapter, the programming of a computer to carry out a given computational algorithm can be tedious, time consuming, and subject to error if we must do all the programming using the computer's machine language. These difficulties are mainly a result of the following problems.

1. All instructions must be expressed in some form of numeric code that is usually difficult for a person to work with.
2. Every address reference must be absolutely defined. Thus, as a program is written the programmer must be able to define the locations of all data and program instructions that are referred to in the program. This is often necessary even though locations for these items have not been defined at the time this information is needed.
3. Changes in instructions, changes in data, or the insertion or deletion of instructions often lead to the necessity of reassigning the locations of instructions and data. This will usually result in the necessity of modifying other instructions in the program to account for changes in references to the new data and instruction locations.
4. The programmer must transform the coding into a machine-readable form, such as punched cards or punched paper tape, and check that this transformation is correct.
5. Parts of previously developed programs that are applicable to a new programming effort may not be usable without being completely recoded to conform with the address assignments of the new program.

In discussing the various programs that were used as an example in Chapter 13, we used a mnemonic term to indicate which basic operation was to be performed by the indicated octal representation of the instruction. This representation can easily be extended to indicate data terms and specific memory locations by assigning mnemonics to represent these quantities. All of these ideas make it much easier to write a particular program.

This advantage of using mnemonic symbols to represent the basic instructions was clearly evident to early programmers. Initially, programs were written in mnemonic form and then the programmer translated the mnemonics into the computer's machine language. However, it was quickly realized that this translation task was a purely mechanical process that could be carried out by the computer. Thus the idea of a simple program that would translate mnemonic terms into their equivalent machine-language coding was quickly evolved. These translation programs were named *assembler programs* and the corresponding set of mnemonics and their rules of use was referred to as an *assembler language*.

In this chapter we first introduce a simple assembler language and show how it can be used to help us in speeding up the programming task for SEDCOM. We then investigate the operation and structure of an assembler program that can be used to translate a program written in our assembler language into a SEDCOM machine-language program. This discussion emphasizes the important concepts used to design assembler programs rather than going through the details of actually writing a particular assembler program. In fact, the memory capacity of SEDCOM is not large enough to hold an assembler program. Thus any assembler for SEDCOM would have to be written for a bigger computer.

2. A SIMPLE ASSEMBLER LANGUAGE

Before we consider an exact definition of our assembler language let us briefly consider what form this language should have if it is going to simplify our programming task. To do this, suppose that we must write a program to add two binary numbers. If this is to be done in machine language we have to specify the exact locations of all the program statements and of the data. If we change any location we have to completely rewrite our program. For example, consider the two programs given in Table 14-1. Program 1 would result if the data and program were in the low part of memory and Program 2 would result if the upper part of memory were used.

Although both of these programs carry out the same computation using the same basic instructions they differ in the way they refer to the location of the data. This problem can become quite a nuisance, especially with large programs in which there are many references to a large number of different memory addresses. In particular, if it becomes necessary to change the location of the data and/or the instructions, it then becomes necessary to introduce these changes in all the instructions which reference the old addresses.

To overcome this problem we can as we did in Chapter 13 assign a *name* or *label*, to each memory location referenced by one of the program instructions. In addition, we can use the mnemonic representation for each of the basic machine-

Table 14-1 Two Simple Programs

Program 1			Program 2		
Address	Content	Mnemonic	Address	Content	Mnemonic
001	7200	CLA	100	7200	CLA
001	1004	TAD 4	101	1104	TAD 104
002	1005	TAD 5	102	1105	TAD 105
003	7402	HLT	103	7402	HLT
004	⟨Data⟩		104	⟨Data⟩	
005	⟨Data⟩		105	⟨Data⟩	

language instructions to indicate which operation is to be performed. With these conventions the above programs could be written, in mnemonic form, as shown in Table 14-2. In this program we labeled the two locations that contain data as DAT1 and DAT2 and then used these labels in the address portion of the mnemonic instructions.

When the labels DAT1 and DAT2 are used as identifiers of a memory location they are followed by a comma to indicate that they are the names associated with a particular location. However, when we use these labels in the address portion of an instruction no comma is required.

Table 14-2 A Simple
Assembler-Language
Program

CLA
TAD DAT1
TAD DAT2
HLT
DAT1, ⟨data⟩
DAT2, ⟨data⟩

Using mnemonics for each machine instruction and names as identifiers of particular memory locations makes it much easier to write a program. However, if we are going to use an assembler program to translate these mnemonics into machine-language instructions we must be very specific about the form that the assembler language takes.

Language Statements

The basic unit of any assembler or programming language is a line of symbolic code called a *statement*. A specific language is defined by giving a set of rules which specify how a certain set of symbols may be combined to form the statements of the language.

For our assembler language these rules are very simple and easily understood. We distinguish three classes of statements.

1. Machine Command Statements
2. Assembler Command Statements—called pseudo-operations
3. Data Statements

Machine command statements are statements that the assembler translates directly into the corresponding machine-language code. For example, the three statements

CLA
IAC
TAD DAT1

would be translated into the machine-language code

7200
7001
1104

if we assume that the label DAT1 is used to indicate memory location 104.

Assembler command statements or pseudo-operations do not lead to the generation of any machine-language code. They are used, instead, to provide information to the assembler program about how some portion of the assembly or translation process should be carried out. For example, the statement

END

must be the last statement of our assembler language program and it is interpreted by the assembler to mean that the end of the assembly language program has been reached.

Data statements are used to enter specific values into given memory locations. For example, the statement

DAT1,   1476

would cause the memory location identified by the label DAT1 to be loaded with the binary equivalent of the octal number 1476_8.

An assembler program processes one statement at a time. Thus the set of rules that define the different statements must provide a way for the assembler to classify the type of each statement and indicate how different types of information can be extracted from the statement. Therefore, before we can explicitly define our assembler language we must introduce a set of notational conventions that we can use to talk about the structure of the statements that make up the language.

Basic Types of Statement Terms

Each statement in our assembler language corresponds to a sequence of characters selected from a particular character set. In our case the character set corresponds to the set of teletype characters specified in Table 12-8. The information contained in a statement is not associated with the individual characters but with groups of characters called *terms*. For example, the statement

$$\text{TAD} \sqcup \text{I} \sqcup \text{PNT}$$

contains nine characters, where we have included the space character $\sqcup$ in the count, and three terms: TAD, I, and PNT. Since terms correspond to a sequence of one or more characters we must adopt certain conventions concerning the form that terms can take.

Terms that represent addresses, operation codes, or other special mnemonics are called *symbols*. Any sequence of from 1 to 6 letters (A, B, . . . , Z) or numbers (0, 1, . . . , 9) form a symbol provided the first character is a letter and the last character is followed by a space or other special nonalphanumeric delimiting character such as $+$, $-$, $=$, etc. Some typical symbols would be

$$\text{TAD} \sqcup \qquad \text{DAT1,} \qquad \text{B1165}+$$

The delimiting characters associated with these symbols are space ($\sqcup$), comma (,) and plus ($+$), respectively.

All numerical information is represented in octal form. A term is a *number* if it consists of a sequence of from 1 to 4 octal digits followed by a delimiting character. Some typical number terms together with the delimiter would be

$$1543 \sqcup \qquad 25+ \qquad 560/ \qquad 0036 \sqcup$$

In addition to symbols and numbers we must have some *special characters* to act as delimiters and to specify specific operations that the assembler is to perform upon the symbols and numbers contained in a statement. The special characters that we use are listed in Table 14-3.

The use of these special characters will be discussed shortly.

Now that we have identified the type of statement terms that we can use, our next task is to show how these terms can be used to form complete statements. To do this we use the notation

$$\langle \text{name of term} \rangle$$

Table 14-3 — Special Characters

Character	Name	Use
⊔	Space	Delimiting
⟩	Carriage return	Terminates statement
+	Plus	Combine symbols or numbers
−	Minus	Combine symbols or numbers
,	Comma	Assignment of symbolic address
.	Period	Has value equal to current location counter
/	Slash	Indicates start of comment

to indicate the different parts of a statement and the general function it serves. For example, the notation

$$\langle blank \rangle$$

serves to indicate a sequence of spaces that separates other terms and the notation

$$\langle command \rangle$$

is used to indicate a mnemonic symbol corresponding to one of the possible machine-language instructions. Using these ideas we can now investigate the structure of the various types of statements.

Command Statements

A command statement is translated by the assembler program into a machine-language instruction. The structure of these statements depends on the type of operation that they represent. For our simple assembler we assume that command statements can have the following general form

$$\langle label \rangle, \langle blank \rangle \langle command \rangle \langle blank \rangle \langle address\ information \rangle \langle blank \rangle \langle comment \rangle$$

Not every statement will contain all of these parts. The term

$$\langle blank \rangle$$

serves to separate the different parts of the statement and corresponds to any number of spaces between the indicated terms. The term

$$\langle command \rangle$$

is either a mnemonic for one of the possible machine-language instructions or the octal representation of a complete instruction. This term must always be present in any command statement.

The term

$$\langle address\ information\rangle$$

will be present if and only if the term

$$\langle command\rangle$$

is the mnemonic for a machine-language memory reference instruction. If the command is a direct memory address command then this term is either an octal number representing the absolute address of a memory location or the label used to identify some memory location. If the command is an indirect address command then the term is assumed to have the form

$$I\ \langle blank\rangle\langle address\rangle$$

where I is used to indicate that the address information involves an indirect memory reference and the term $\langle address\rangle$ is an octal number or label indicating the memory location in which the indirect address information is stored.

The term

$$\langle label\rangle,$$

will be present if we wish to attach an identifying label to the statement so that we can refer to the statement in some other command statement. The comma following $\langle label\rangle$ is included as a signal to the assembler program that the term $\langle label\rangle$ is to be used to identify the memory location that contains the indicated command statement. Labels, which may be omitted in any statement, cannot duplicate any command mnemonics, assembler command instructions or consist of the single character I.

The term

$$\langle comment\rangle$$

consists of a / followed by any sequence of symbols. This term can be appended to any statement or it can stand by itself. Comments are provided for the programmer's convenience and for documentation. Comments are ignored by the assembler program during the assembly process.

The following statements indicate the typical form of acceptable command statements.

(a)	BEGN,	TAD I VPNT	/GET VALUE FOR POINTER
(b)		TAD I PNT	
(c)		DCA DAT1	
(d)	M10,	DCA I 050	
(e)	MAX,	SMA	/IS RESULT NEGATIVE?
(f)	MAX,	7500	
(g)		CRF	/IS READER READY?
(h)		6036	/READ READER DATA

Data Statements

Data statements are very closely related to command statements. They are used to enter specific values of data into memory for use by the program. Statements of this type have the general form

$$\langle label \rangle, \langle blank \rangle \langle data \rangle \langle blank \rangle \langle comment \rangle$$

The terms $\langle label \rangle$ and $\langle comment \rangle$ have the same form as they do in command statements and they may or may not be present.

The term

$$\langle data \rangle$$

can take on a variety of forms. In the simplest case it is a one- to four-digit octal number. However, we often wish to use negative numbers or characters as data. If a minus sign precedes the term $\langle data \rangle$ then the assembler converts the binary representation of the data term to its corresponding 2's complement form. If a character is present and it is enclosed in parentheses, then the corresponding teletype code is placed in the indicated memory location.

The following statements indicate the typical form of acceptable data statements.

(a)	NPNT,	0100	/ADDRESS OF FIRST TERM
(b)		6666	
(c)	NCNT,	− 10	
(d)	STRT,	(A)	/SET 301 IN MEMORY
(e)	BEG,	−(A)	/SET NEGATIVE OF 301 IN MEMORY

Assembler Command Statements

For simplicity we only use two pseudocommands in our assembler language. They are the origin set and the END command. These command statements are defined as follows. The origin set statement is defined as:

$$\text{ORG} \langle \text{blank} \rangle \langle \text{octal address} \rangle \langle \text{blank} \rangle \langle \text{comment} \rangle$$

where the comment term may or may not be present. This statement tells the assembler program that the machine-language code corresponding to the first program statement following this pseudocommand is to be placed in the memory location indicated by the term $\langle \text{octal address} \rangle$. This term can be any octal number between 0_8 and 377_8. All subsequent machine-language instructions are placed in successive memory locations until another ORG pseudocommand is encountered. If ORG is not specified at the beginning of the program the assembler will take its value as 000.

The END command must be the last statement in the assembler-language program and it indicates to the assembler program that the end of the assembler-language program has been reached.

To illustrate how the ORG and END command is used consider the following simple assembler-language program.

$$
\begin{array}{l}
\text{ORG } 100 \\
\text{CLA} \\
\text{HLT} \\
\text{END}
\end{array}
$$

In processing this program the first statement encountered by the assembler is the pseudocommand ORG 100. This tells the assembler that the machine-language code for the first instruction CLA is to be placed in location 100, and that the machine-language code for the second instruction HLT is placed in location 101. The END pseudocommand tells us that we have reached the end of the assembler-language program. The complete machine language program that would be produced by the assembler program is given by the following listing.

Address	Content	Assembler Statement
		ORG 100
100	7200	CLA
101	7402	HLT
		END

This completes the definition of our simple assembler language. To show how this language can be used we now present two programs written in this language and show the machine-language program that would be produced if the first program were translated by an assembler program.

A Program to Form the Negative of a Sequence of Numbers

As our first example we develop an assembler-language program that forms the negative of each number in a set of numbers that are stored in consecutive memory locations. The following program specification describes the task to be performed by the program.

A flowchart describing this program is given in Figure 14-1, and the associated assembler-language program is given in Table 14-4.

In this program we have included a subroutine to form the 2's complement of a number. Normally this subroutine would be included in the main program. However, it is included in this example to illustrate how a subroutine can be handled in an assembler-language program. If this program is now translated by an assembler program, we would obtain the program listing given by Table 14-5.

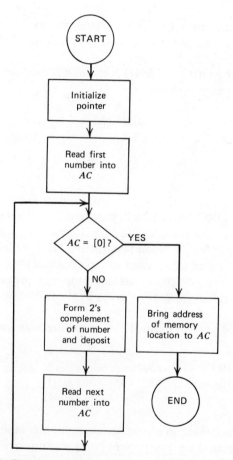

Figure 14-1. Flowchart of program to form the negative (2's complement) of a list of numbers.

Program Specification

PROGRAM 9

Task: Form the 2's complement of a set of numbers stored in memory

Input: The array of numbers to be processed are stored in memory starting at location 100. The end of the array is indicated by a memory location that contains 0000. This location is not part of the array

Output: Each element of the array is replaced by its 2's complement. The address of the memory location containing 0000 is left in the accumulator

Table 14-4   Assembler Language Program for PROGRAM 9

```
            ORG 10
            CLA
            TAD SPNT        /INITIALIZE
            DCA PNT         /POINTER
            TAD I PNT       /GET FIRST TERM
BEGN,  SZA                  /IS TERM 0?
            JMP NEXT        /NO. CONTINUE
            JMP OUT         /YES. EXIT LOOP
NEXT,  JMS NEG              /GO TO SUBROUTINE TO FORM
                            /2's COMPLEMENT
            DCA I PNT       /DEPOSIT RESULT
            ISZ PNT         /INCREMENT POINTER
            TAD I PNT       /GET NEXT TERM
            JMP BEGN        /GO BACK TO START OF LOOP
OUT,   TAD PNT             /BRING ADDRESS TO AC
            HLT             /END OF PROGRAM

            /2's COMPLEMENT SUBROUTINE
            ORG30
NEG,   0000                /LINKING POINTER
            CMA             /COMPLEMENT AC
            IAC             /INCREMENT AC
            JMP I NEG       /RETURN

            /DATA AND TEMPORARY STORAGE
            ORG35
SPNT,  0100                /ARRAY STARTS LOCATION 100
PNT,   0000                /POINTER
            END
```

Table 14-5

Listing of Assembled
Program for Program Table 14-4

Address	Content	Mnemonic Statement
		ORG 10
10	7200	CLA
11	1035	TAD SPNT
12	3036	DCA PNT
13	1436	TAD I PNT
14	7440	BEGN, SZA
15	5017	JMP NEXT
16	5024	JMP OUT
17	4030	NEXT, JMS NEG
20	3436	DCS I PNT
21	2036	ISZ PNT
22	1436	TAD I PNT
23	5014	JMP BEGN
24	1036	OUT, TAD PNT
25	7402	HLT
		ORG 30
30	0000	NEG, 0000
31	7040	CMA
32	7001	IAC
33	5430	JMP I NEG
35	0100	SPNT, 0100
36	0000	PNT, 0000
		END

This example illustrates the use of all of the different types of assembler statements as well as many of the mnemonics that are associated with the basic machine operations. As we can see by inspecting Table 14-5, the assembler-language mnemonic representation is very similar to the mnemonic representation that we use to describe programs in Chapter 13.

A Character Recognition Program

Many of the tasks that we use a computer for involve the processing of character sequences. As our second example we develop a program that will deal with character strings. The following program specification describes this program.

A flowchart describing the algorithm needed to realize this program is shown in Figure 14-2 and the corresponding assembler-language program is given in Table 14-6.

Program Specification

PROGRAM 10

Task: Print the sequence HELLO. Wait until a character is read from the reader. If the character is R print THANK YOU, otherwise print ERROR

Input: One character from reader. HELLO, THANK YOU, ERROR, character strings stored in memory

Output: The character strings HELLO followed by either THANK YOU or ERROR

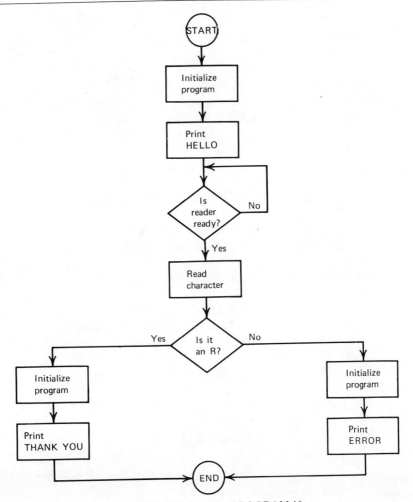

Figure 14-2. Flowchart for PROGRAM 10.

Table 14-6   Assembler Language Program for PROGRAM 10

```
              ORG 10
              CLA
              TAD VCNT1      /SET UP COUNTER FOR HELLO
              DCA CNT
              TAD VPNT1      /SET UP POINTER TO HELLO
              DCA PNT
              TAD CR         /GIVE A CARRIAGE RETURN
              JMS PRINT
              TAD LIFED      /GIVE A LINE FEED
              JMS PRINT
FIRST,        TAD I PNT      /GET CHARACTER
              JMS PRINT      /PRINT CHARACTER
              ISZ PNT
              ISZ CNT        /ARE WE FINISHED
              JMP FIRST      /NO
FLAG,         CRF            /YES. IS READER READY
              JMP FLAG       /NO. TRY AGAIN
              RRD            /YES. READ CHARACTER
              TAD MINR       /COMPARE INPUT TO R
              SZA            /IS THE CHARACTER R
              JMP ERR        /NO
              TAD VCNT2      /YES. SET UP COUNTER FOR THANK YOU
              DCA CNT
              TAD VPNT2      /SET UP POINTER TO THANK YOU
              DCA PNT
LAST,         TAD I PNT      /GET CHARACTER
              JMS PRINT      /PRINT CHARACTER
              ISZ PNT
              ISZ CNT        /ARE WE FINISHED
              JMP LAST       /NO
              HLT            /YES. STOP PROGRAM
ERR,          CLA            /INITIALIZE ERROR MESSAGE
              TAD VCNT3      /SET COUNTER FOR ERROR
              DCA CNT
              TAD VPNT3      /SET POINTER TO ERROR
              DCA PNT
              JMP LAST       /GO TO PRINT OUT ROUTINE
CNT,          0000           /COUNTER LOCATION
PNT,          0000           /POINTER LOCATION
/VALUES FOR DIFFERENT POINTERS, COUNTERS AND CONSTANTS
VCNT1, −6                    /NUMBER OF CHARACTERS IN MESSAGES
VCNT2, −12
VCNT3, −6
```

```
VPNT1, 100              /LOCATION OF MESSAGES
VPNT2, 110
VPNT3, 125
CR,     251             /OCTAL CODE FOR CARRIAGE RETURN
LIFED, 212              /OCTAL CODE FOR LINE FEED
MINR,  -(R)             /NEGATIVE OF R
/PRINT SUBROUTINE
PRINT, 0000
CHK,    CPF             /IS PRINTER READY
        JMP CHK         /NO
        SPD             /YES. PRINT CHARACTER
        CLA             /CLEAR ACCUMULATOR
        JMP I PRINT     /RETURN TO MAIN PROGRAM
ORG 100                 /CHARACTER SEQUENCE HELLO
        (H)
        (E)
        (L)
        (L)
        (O)
        ( )             /THIS PLACES A SPACE AFTER HELLO
ORG 110                 /CHARACTER SEQUENCE THANK YOU
        (T)
        (H)
        (A)
        (N)
        (K)
        ( )             /SPACE
        (Y)
        (O)
        (U)
        ( )
ORG 125                 /CHARACTER SEQUENCE ERROR
        (E)
        (R)
        (R)
        (O)
        (R)
        ( )             /SPACE
        END             /END OF PROGRAM
```

In this program we have used the fact that we can enter characters as data terms as well as the negative of these characters. Here again we encounter the fact that a computer can manipulate and test symbolic data as easily as numeric data. In the next section we make use of this ability to design an assembler program.

EXERCISES

1. Write an assembler-language program that will count the number of times the number N appears in any location between 100_8 and 177_8. N is initially stored in location 70 and can take on any value between 0_8 and 3777_8 specified by the programmer.

2. Translate the program of Table 14-6 into its equivalent machine-language program.

3. THE STRUCTURE OF A SIMPLE ASSEMBLER PROGRAM

In the last section we developed a simple assembler language that can be used to develop programs for SEDCOM. We now concentrate on the problem of specifying an assembler program that will transform an assembler-language program into a machine-language program. This is a separate operation from writing a program in the assembler language or of running the resulting machine-language program on the computer. The assembler-language program is called the *source program* and the resulting machine-language program is called the *object program*. Before we discuss the operation of an assembler program, let us consider some of the tasks that must be performed by the assembler during the translation process.

Tasks Performed by the Assembler Program

To process an assembler-language statement, the assembler must be able to recognize the various parts of the statement. The mnemonics for the machine-language operations and the pseudocommands are known a priori. Thus we can build this information into the assembler. However, the labels, which are recognized either by having the last character followed by a comma, or by finding it in the address of a command are assigned by the programmer. Thus the assembler must be able to recognize each label as it is introduced and locate the memory location corresponding to that label.

A second problem is to assign a unique memory location to each instruction and data term. This is done by using the ORG pseudocommand to indicate the starting address of the first instruction following this pseudocommand. All other instructions are placed in sequential locations until the END pseudocommand is encountered or until another ORG pseudocommand is encountered.

A third problem involves assigning the proper octal code for the address portion of the machine-language command. When we scan a source program we start at the top and work down. We often come to a label in the address portion of a command before the statement corresponding to that label has been reached. For example, consider the following program.

```
          ORG 10
          CLA
          TAD SPNT
          DCA PNT
               ⋮
          HLT
          ORG 50
SPNT, 0100
 PNT, 0000
          END
```

In this program the statement

TAD SPNT

is the third program statement while

SPNT, 0100

is the third from last statement in the program. Thus we cannot translate TAD SPNT into 1050 until we know that SPNT refers to location 50.

A fourth problem that must be considered is the detection and indication of errors in the source program. All programmers make errors and it is desirable to design an assembler so that it not only detects as many errors as possible but also indicates to the programmer the type and location of each error. The assembler will not be able to detect errors in the algorithm represented by the program but it should be able to detect such things as undefined labels, the use of the same label to indicate more than one memory location, improperly formed statements, or improper operation code mnemonics. For example, in the statement

STAN, JPM BEGN

The assembler would detect JPM as being an improper operation code. However if the statement

JMP BEGN

was mistyped as

JMS BEGN

the assembler would not be able to detect this error since both JMP and JMS are valid operation code mnemonics.

With these problems in mind, we now investigate the general structure of an assembler program and develop a flowchart representation of its operation.

Assembler Organization

An assembler program must be able to solve the four problems listed above. Thus before developing a flowchart representation of the assembler program itself, we investigate the operational organization of the processing that is carried out by the program. To do this we use the block diagram representation of the processor given in Figure 14-3. This block diagram is intended to represent the functional relationships that exist in the assembly process rather than the actual structure of the assembler program itself. This structure is discussed later.

If we examine Figure 14-3 we see that the assembler has three tables that are used to store information about the mnemonic terms that are used in the assembler-language statements. During the assembly process each term of a statement will be

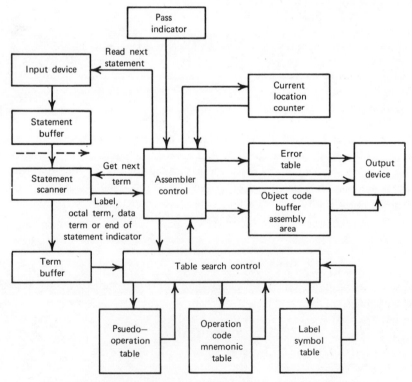

Figure 14-3. Flow diagram representation of general organization of the assembly process.

stored in the term buffer. If the term is a mnemonic term, the meaning or value of this term will be determined by looking it up in the appropriate table.

A numeric value or an instruction to the control unit will result when the term is located in the table. For our simple assembler we have three tables.

1. Pseudo-Operation Table T_P
2. Operation Code Table T_C
3. Label Symbol Table T_L

The pseudo-operation table will contain the two pseudocommands ORG and END. When the END mnemonic is found, the control unit is told that the end of the source program has been reached and the current phase of the assembly process can be completed.

During the assembly process each command and data statement must be assigned a memory location. The *current location counter* serves this function. The content of the current location counter indicates the memory location that is assigned to the command or data statement currently being processed. Since instructions are stored in sequential locations we use the ORG pseudocommand to set the current location counter to the value corresponding to the location of the first instruction. After each command and data statement is processed the count of the current location counter is increased by one to prepare for the next statement. This process is continued until the end of the program is reached or a new value is entered into the counter by the pseudocommand ORG. Thus when the term ORG is recognized the control unit is told to reset the current location counter to the value indicated by the ORG statement.

The operation code table contains the machine-language code for each of the operation code mnemonics. For example, if the term buffer contained TAD then the result of searching the operation code table would indicate that TAD corresponded to the operation code 1000_8. Similarly, the mnemonic CLA would produce 7200_8 as the corresponding operation code. On the other hand, if the term buffer contained the mnemonic HAT a search of the operation code table would show that HAT is not an operation code mnemonic and this conclusion would be so indicated to the control section.

Both the pseudo-operation and operation code mnemonic tables are completely determined a priori by the way the assembler language is defined. Thus these codes are entered into these tables at the time the assembler program is developed. The label symbol table, which gives the memory location associated with each label, does not have this desirable feature since a new set of label mnemonics are defined for each assembler-language source program.

This means that the label symbol table must be defined before we can start to carry out the actual assembly process. Thus we must make *two passes* over the input program. During the first pass we construct the label symbol table. Each time we encounter a new label we enter this label into the table. If the label is the first term in a statement, and is followed by a comma, we enter the value indicated by the current location counter into the table as the value of the label. If the label is in the address portion of a statement we check to see if it is already recorded in the table. When we find the label already recorded we continue our processing. Otherwise, we enter the label in the table and mark it as a label that must be assigned a value sometime during the first pass.

To illustrate how the symbol table is formed consider the following simple program:

```
            ORG 100
            CLA
BEGN,  TAD SAM
            CMA
            IAC
            DCA SAM
            HLT
SAM,     0111
            END
```

As the assembler scans this program during the first pass the first label encountered is BEGN. Since this label defines a memory location it is entered into the symbol table and it is assigned a value 101 corresponding to the value of the current location counter. As we continue to scan the statement we next encounter the label SAM in the address portion of the statement. SAM is entered in the symbol table and marked to indicate that it has not been assigned a value. The processing is continued until the label SAM is encountered as the label of the last statement. At that point SAM is assigned a value of 106.

As the assembler scans the object program it might find that the same mnemonic label has been used for two different memory locations. In this case we would want the assembler to print out an error message telling us that we have used the label twice and indicate the location of the two statements involved in this error. When the assembler reaches the end of the first pass all of the labels in the symbol table should have been assigned a value. If one or more of the labels have not been assigned a value we also want the assembler to generate an error message telling us which terms are not defined. These error-checking capabilities are very important aids to a programmer since they allow him to correct the errors before he tries to carry out the actual translation process.

Now that we understand the function of the various tables we can consider the complete operation of the assembly process. To start the assembly process we place the object program into the input device and set the pass indicator to pass one. This tells the control unit that we wish to scan the source program to define the contents of the label symbol table and to detect any detectable errors in the source program.

The First Pass

The processing is carried out one statement at a time. Each statement is read into the statement buffer. The statement scanner reads the contents of the statement buffer term by term under the control of the assembler control. When the control calls for the next term the statement scanner selects the term from the statement buffer and checks for special conditions such as a comma indicating a label term, an all-numeric octal term, a data term, or whether the statement buffer is either empty or the only remaining information is a comment.

The term buffer holds the current term while it is being processed. During the first pass all mnemonic terms must be checked against the contents of the proper table. The assembler control indicates to the table search control the type of term to expect. The table search control then checks to see if the term is in the proper table. In particular if the term is a label and it is not entered in the symbol table then the table search control enters the term into the table as described previously. At this point any errors are detected and an appropriate error message is entered into the error table, for later printing.

On completion of this phase of the processing the assembler control requests the next term. If the statement buffer is empty or only contains a comment, the control increments the current location counter and then requests the next source language statement.

The logical structure of the program that carries out the first pass processing is given by the flowchart of Figure 14-4. In this diagram we have omitted the exact details concerning the operation of many of the blocks of the flowchart since these details are of no particular importance to our discussion. Anyone concerned with the actual development of an assembler program would, of course, have to develop the operation of these blocks in greater detail.

Examining Figure 14-4 we see that the processing sequence is determined by the structure that we have assumed for the different types of statements. In processing a statement all comments are disregarded. They are retained during processing, however, so that we can obtain a final listing at the end of the translation process of both the object program and the complete original source program.

After we read a statement into the statement buffer we then check to see if the first character is a / which indicates that the sole contents of this buffer is a comment. If it is we read in the next statement. Otherwise we enter our processing sequence.

The first term that we encounter during the processing sequence will either be a pseudocommand, a label followed by a comma, a one- to four-digit octal number, a data term, or a mnemonic for a machine-language command. Pseudocommands are checked for first since they provide instructions to the assembler concerning the assembly process. Should the test fail, we next check to see if the term is a label that is used to indicate a memory location. If it is a label we check the symbol table to see if a value has been previously assigned to the label. Should we find a value associated with the label we know that an error has been made and we enter an error message in the error buffer. However, if there are one or more errors the programmer must correct the errors and repeat the first pass. If the corrected source program is now found to be error-free the programmer then goes to the second pass. Otherwise he repeats the correction process until he has an error-free program. As soon as he obtains an error-free output from the first pass he is ready to start the second pass.

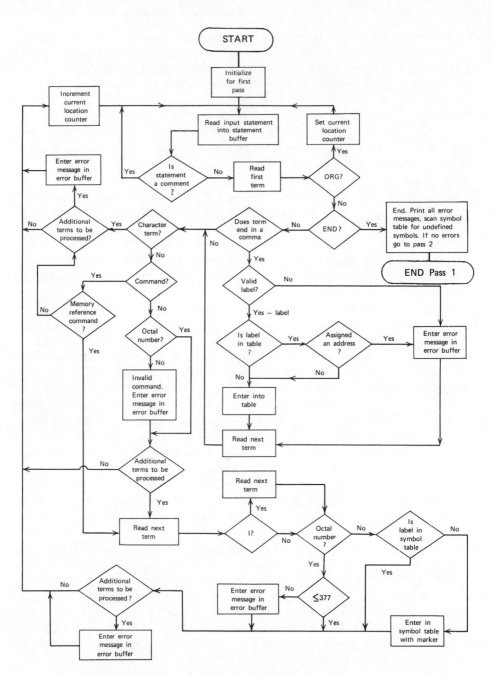

Figure 14-4. Flowchart of first pass of assembler showing assignment of label values and error detection.

The Second Pass

The second pass of the assembler program operates in essentially the same way as the first pass except that instead of checking for errors and forming the symbol table the assembler produces the object code equivalent of each source-language statement. The way that this is accomplished can best be illustrated by considering each type of statement.

The pseudocommands are handled in the same manner during the second pass as they were during the first pass. A statement such as

ORG 10

will be detected when ORG is found in the pseudocommand table. The assembler control will then take the term 10 and place this value in the current location counter. The pseudocommand END will be detected in a similar manner and this command will cause the assembler to complete the processing involved in pass two and leave us with the object program as the output.

Command statements are handled in a straightforward manner. Consider the simple program

```
        ORG 10
        TAD A           /GET NUMBER
        JMS BOB
        HLT
        ORG 150
BOB,    0000            /COMPLEMENT SUBROUTINE
        CMA
        JMP I BOB
        ORG 200
A,      0770
        END
```

The first statement sets the current location counter to 10. The next statement is read and the first term is read and found in the operation code table. The table shows that this term has the value 1000. This value is entered in the object code buffer and the next term is read. The term A is located in the symbol table and is found to have a value of 0200 corresponding to the fact that memory location 200 has been labeled A in the source program.

If we now add 0200 to the 1000 already in the object code buffer we have the result 1200 which is the complete object code for the source statement TAD A. This code is then outputed by the output device. Similarly we transform the source statement JMS BOB into 4150 and the following HLT statement into 7402.

The next statement, ORG 150 resets the current location counter to 150. Next we must process the statement

BOB, 0000

The term BOB is recognized as a label definition term and is skipped over since it is not needed in the generation of the object code for this statement. The term 0000 is then recognized as octal data and 0000 is entered into the object code buffer and then outputed by the output device.

The next statement consists of the single mnemonic CMA which is assigned the value 7040. The next statement

JMP I BOB

requires somewhat more work to process. First JMP is recognized in the operation code table and assigned the value 5000. This number is entered into the object code buffer. Next the indirect indicator term I is encountered. An indirect command corresponds to setting bit 3 to a 1. Thus 0400 is added to 5000 already in the object code buffer giving the intermediate result 5400. Finally BOB is found in the symbol table and assigned a value of 0150. Adding this value to the current content of the object code buffer gives the final object code representation of JMP I BOB as 5550. The processing of the program is completed by assigning the object code 0770 to location 200.

When the END statement is encountered the assembler control recognizes that the end of the second pass has been reached. It then terminates the assembly process and outputs any other additional information that might be required to complete the final object program in a form that can be executed by a computer. Most assembler programs also have an optional feature that allows the programmer to request a complete listing of both the object program and the source language equivalent of each line of the object code. This listing thoroughly documents the assembled program and is useful later if the program must be debugged or modified. For our example the listing would take the form shown in Table 14-7.

The logical structure of the second pass is given by the flowchart of Figure 14-5. If we compare this flowchart with the flowchart of the first pass we see that there is a great deal of similarity between the two. Consequently, we will only discuss

Table 14-7			Complete Listing for a Simple Program
		ORG 10	
010	1200	TAD A	/GET NUMBER
011	4150	JMS BOB	
012	7402	HLT	
		ORG 150	
150	0000	BOB, 0000	/COMPLEMENT SUBROUTINE
151	7040	CMA	
152	5550	JMP I BOB	
		ORG 200	
200	0770	A, 0770	
		END	

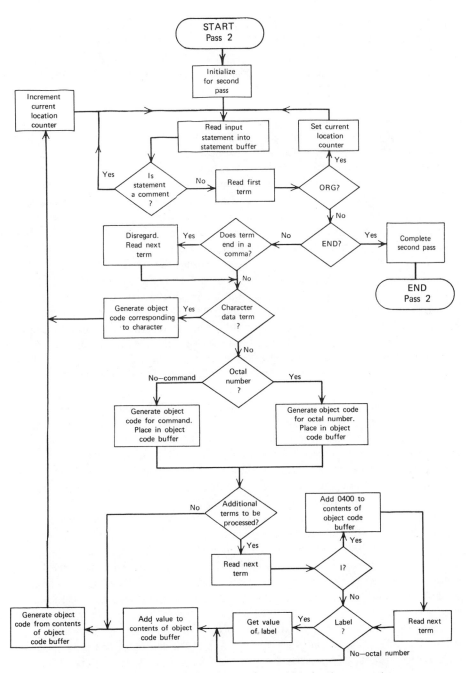

Figure 14-5. Flowchart of second pass of assembler showing generation of object code.

those parts of the flowchart that carry out operations which differ from those carried out during the first pass.

As each statement is read into the statement buffer, we check to see if it is a simple comment, a statement that must be translated, a data statement or a pseudo-command statement. Simple comment statements are ignored and the pseudo-commands are processed as they are during the first pass.

If the statement buffer contains a source statement that must be transformed into object code, we know that we can disregard any label term associated with the statement, since this information is only needed during the first pass. Thus we search the statement until we find the first nonlabel term. If this term is an octal number the corresponding object code is generated directly. If the term is a negative octal number or a character then the proper coding for this data term must be generated. If the term is a mnemonic it is checked to see if it is a memory reference command. The nonmemory reference mnemonics are translated directly by reading the value of the mnemonic from the operation code table.

When a term is recognized as a memory reference mnemonic a little additional work is required. We first locate the value of the mnemonic in the operation code table and temporarily store this information in an object code buffer. Next we check to see if an I is present. If it is we add 0400 to the contents of the object code buffer to set the indirect address bit. Finally we have the term indicating the address of the command. If this term is an octal number we complete the translation process by adding the value of this number to the contents of the object code buffer. When the address term is a label we first go to the symbol table to obtain the octal value of the address associated with this label. We then add this value to the contents of the object code buffer. The object code buffer now contains the object code corresponding to the current input statement.

After the processing of the statement is completed, we output the object code, increment the current location counter, and read in the next statement. We continue this process until we encounter the END pseudocommand. At that point we terminate the assembly process. The output of this pass is the machine-language object program ready for execution by our computer.

An object program in machine readable form on paper tape or punched cards cannot be easily interpreted by the programmer. If there are any programming mistakes, the programmer will need a listing of the object program in octal form and the corresponding source program. This listing can easily be provided by including a third pass option in the assembler program. The operation of the assembler program corresponding to this option is essentially the same as the operation of the assembler during the second pass. The only difference is in the output. Instead of generating a machine readable object program, the output routine generates the octal listing of the object program and the listing of the corresponding source program. The form that this listing takes is illustrated by Table 14-7.

The assembler program that we have been discussing is extremely simple because our main interest was in understanding the basic organization of the assembly process. There are, of course, many other routine tasks that could be handled by an assembler program. These tasks could be added to our assembler without too much added difficulty. In the next section we consider some of these additional features, but we will not discuss the changes in our program that would be required to implement them.

1. What will be contained in the symbol table and what error messages will be produced at the end of the first pass for the following source program?

```
              ORG 10
              CLM
      STRT, TAD I BOB
              ISZ TOM
              JMP SRT
              JMS STR
              HLT
              ORG 100
      STRT, 0000
              CMA
              JMP I STRT
      BOB,  0110
      TOM,  7774
              END
```

2. Explain what would happen during the first and second pass if the following statements were found in the statement buffer. JOE is assumed to be the label associated with memory location 50 while JOHN is assumed to be the label associated with memory location 100.

    (a) /THIS IS AN EXAMPLE
    (b) JOHN, JMP I JOE
    (c)   1000 I JOE
    (d)   AND 100

4. ADDITIONAL ASSEMBLER CONCEPTS

There are a variety of ways in which we can expand the capabilities of an assembler and thus reduce the amount of work required of a programmer when he is developing a source-language program. However, each new feature we add adds more complexity to our assembler program and results in a larger overall program.

In this section we investigate some of the possible extensions that could be added to our assembler language. First we investigate how the inclusion of arithmetic expressions in address terms can expand our programming flexibility. Then we consider some additional pseudocommands that would be useful. Our final discussion shows how the concept of a user-defined macro program can be used to eliminate the rewriting of frequently used open subroutines.

Arithmetic Expressions for Address Modification

One of the biggest problems that we encounter in developing an extensive source-language program is that we must use a large number of labels. Since the label symbol table in most assemblers is of limited capacity we often find, in large programs, that the number of labels in our program exceeds the space we have available in our symbol table for recording these labels. We now consider how the use of address modification techniques can reduce the number of labels we need in any given program.

As an example of how we can reduce the number of labels, consider the problem of adding data terms located in three consecutive registers. For our simple assembly language we would have to write the following program segment to accomplish this calculation.

$$\vdots$$

TAD DATE1
TAD DATE2
TAD DATE3

$$\vdots$$

DATE1, (Data)
DATE2, (Data)
DATE3, (Data)

During the assembly process we would need to provide space in our symbol table for the three labels DATE1, DATE2, and DATE3. This, of course, is a very inefficient use of our symbol table.

Let us consider the same problem if we could evaluate simple arithmetic operations during the assembly process. The following program segment could accomplish the same desired operation.

TAD DATE
TAD DATE + 1
TAD DATE + 2

$$\vdots$$

DATE, ⟨Data⟩
⟨Data⟩
⟨Data⟩

With this approach our symbol table would only have to store information about the label DATE. The address of the remaining data terms would be obtained by adding the indicated constant to the octal address assigned to DATE.

From the above example we see that if we allow the address portion of a memory reference instruction to contain arithmetic expressions, then we can reduce the number of labels we will need in our source-language program. These expressions are scanned and evaluated during the second pass to determine the exact address referred to in the address portion of the statement. In a normal assembler these arithmetic expressions consist of a sequence of symbols separated by arithmetic or Boolean operators. The value of any expression is assumed to be an unsigned integer number. If division is an allowable operation then the fraction part of the quotient is ignored. The following operations are often included as part of the assembler program.

$+$ addition
$-$ subtraction
$*$ multiplication
$/$ division (only integer part of result retained)
$\&$ AND
$!$ OR

Some typical address expressions involving these operations would be

$$A + 10$$
$$GET - 10$$
$$A + B * 15$$
$$A \& B$$

In these expressions it is assumed that the symbolic terms are assigned values in the symbol table.

Another convention often introduced is to use a special symbol to indicate the value of the current location counter. For example, let us use the period "." for this term. Then a program such as

```
          CLA
READ,  CRF          /IS READER READY
       JMP  READ    /NO. TRY AGAIN
       RRD          /YES. READ DATA
```

could be rewritten as

```
       CLA
       CRF          /IS READER READY
       JMP  .-1     /NO. TRY AGAIN
       RRD          /YES. READ DATA
       HLT
```

Thus by use of the "." to indicate the value of the current location counter we have eliminated the need to introduce the label READ.

The logical operation !, corresponding to the logical OR of the contents of two computer words, can be used to form combined microinstructions. For example, we form the 2's complement of a number in our simple assembler language by using the two statements

CMA
IAC

However, these two microinstructions can be carried out by one machine instruction if we OR the object code of CMA, 7040, with the object code of IAC, 7001. This gives a result of 7041. This result could be accomplished by the statement

CMA! IAC

Additional Pseudo-Operations

We introduced the two pseudo-operations ORG and END as part of our assembler program. It is often useful to define additional operations to reduce the amount of work that a programmer must do.

When we deal with data terms and constants in our assembler language we are required to express each of these terms as octal numbers. This is often very inconvenient. For example, we might wish to store the number 19_{10} in a particular location. Before we could do that we would first have to stop and convert 19_{10} to 0023_8. This is a process that could be easily accomplished by the assembler. Thus we could introduce the following two pseudocommands to tell the assembler the type of numbers we are dealing with.

OCTAL—All numbers encountered in a statement after this command are considered to be octal numbers.

DECIMAL—All numbers encountered in a statement after this command are considered to be decimal numbers.

As an illustration of how these two operations are applied consider the following program.

```
OCTAL
ORG 10
TAD 50
DCA 51
HLT
ORG 50
DECIMAL       /ENTER DATA IN DECIMAL FORM
598
761
END
```

On assembling this program, we would obtain the following object language program.

Address	Octal Content
10	1050
11	3051
12	7402
...	...
50	1126
51	1371

We can introduce pseudo-operations to cover each of the mechanical operations we encountered in writing an assembler-language program. However, it is also possible to provide the programmer with the ability to assign a name to a particular sequence of statements. He can then use this name in his program whenever he wishes to carry out the computation performed by this named sequence of statements. This capability also reduces the amount of effort necessary to write a program.

Macros

Programming at the assembler-language level often requires that we write a sequence of statements that perform essentially the same operation in many different places in the program. For example if we must form the 2's complement of a number in the accumulator we always use the instruction sequence

$$\text{CMA}$$
$$\text{IAC}$$

Macro facilities in an assembler allow the programmer to associate a name, called the *macro name*, with such a sequence of instructions and to subsequently use this name to denote that sequence. Whenever the assembler encounters the macro name in the program it substitutes the desired instructions in place of the macro name.

For example, if we wish to define the instruction sequence

$$\text{CMA}$$
$$\text{IAC}$$

as a macro we would first define it as a macro and give it a name by use of a *macro definition*. For the above instruction sequence this definition would have a form such as

```
MACRO     MINUS ← Macro Name
          CMA ⎫
          IAC ⎬ ← Macro Body
          FINISH ← Macro Terminator
```

The definition is introduced by the control operation MACRO followed by the *macro name* MINUS. The next two lines following this statement form the *macro body*. The MACRO definition is terminated by the pseudocommand FINISH.

Whenever the pseudocommand MACRO is encountered by an assembler during the first pass processing of the source program the assembler enters the macro name into a special macro table. Following the name, the assembler stores an encoded copy of the macro body. This macro body can then be used during the second pass of the source program through the assembly process.

Whenever the macro name is encountered by the assembler during the second pass it goes to the macro table and reads out the encoded macro body. The program corresponding to the macro body is then converted into object language code and inserted into the object program at the appropriate point. To illustrate how we would use the macro MINUS defined above, consider the program sequence shown in Table 14-8*a*.

If we use our macro capabilities, this program sequence would become as shown in Table 14-8*b*. During the sequence the assembler would recognize MINUS as a macro name and would substitute the instructions 7040 and 7001 in memory locations 12 and 13 respectively.

The usefulness of macros can be further expanded if we can associate parameters with the macro. In a macro definition we can introduce *formal parameters* for which different *actual parameters* can be substituted when the macro is used. For example we could define the following macro to form the 2's complement of a number stored in one location and place the result in a second location.

```
MACRO     MINUS X, Y
          CLA
          TAD X
          CMA
          IAC
          DCA Y
          FINISH
```

In this macro, X and Y are formal parameters.

A macro of this type would be useful in initializing counters in setting up a programming loop. For example, a program to count to 50 in steps of 5 would take the following form.

```
          ORG 10
          MINUS SCNT, CNT    /SET COUNTER
BEGN, TAD FIVE               /ADD 5
          ISZ CNT            /10 ADDITIONS?
          JMP BEGN           /NO
          HLT                /YES
SCNT, 0012
CNT, 0000
FIVE, 0005
```

Table 14-8   Use of Macro Programming

(a) Program Without Macro	(b) Program With Macro
ORG 10	ORG 10
CLA	CLA
TAD A	TAD A
CMA	MINUS
IAC	DCA B
DCA B	⋮
⋮	ORG 50
ORG 50	A, 0771
A, 0771	B, 0000
B, 0000	

In this program the macro MINUS SCNT, CNT would be handled by the assembler just as if we had placed

```
CLA
TAD SCNT
CMA
IAC
DCA CNT
```

in our source program at the point where we encounter this macro.

From this discussion we see that a macro definition has the following general form:

MACRO ⟨blank⟩⟨macro name⟩⟨blank⟩⟨formal parameter⟩, . . . ,
⟨formal parameter⟩
                    ⟨macro body⟩
                        ⋮
                    FINISH

This information is stored in a macro definition table when the macro is defined. Every time a given macro is called as part of the program, the assembler goes to the macro definition table, reads out the encoded body of the macro, substitutes the actual parameters for the formal parameters and then translates the encoded macro body into the appropriate machine-language instructions. The macro capability of assemblers provides very powerful aids to the programmers. Because of this, several variations and extensions of the macro concept are available.

However, further discussion of this concept is beyond the level of this treatment and the reader is referred to the references at the end of this chapter.

Standard Subroutines

Anyone who does a great deal of programming soon finds that there exists a set of standard operations or procedures that are used repeatedly. For example, it is often necessary to perform arithmetic operations on floating-point or double-precision numbers or it may be necessary to input or output numerical data in special formats. Each of these operations, and many others, can be handled by standard programs. Thus it is not reasonable to expect a programmer to write his own program every time he wants to carry out one of these standard operations. Instead, most computer manufacturers supply a set of standard subroutine programs that can be used in a program, where necessary, to carry out various standard operations.

These subroutines can be made available to the programmer in a number of different ways. Probably the simplest method is to have the subroutine written as a source-language program. The programmer then inserts the proper calling sequence for the subroutine in the main program and then appends the pre-programmed subroutine onto this program. In other cases pseudocommands are included in the assembler language so that the assembler program will automatically generate the calling sequence.

Some subroutines are so large that it would be impractical to reassemble the subroutine program each time it is needed. In this case, the subroutine is available as an object program and all the programmer must do is establish the proper subroutine call sequence in the main program. If the computer on which the assembler program is running has enough storage capacity, the object program corresponding to the referenced subroutines will be directly attached by the assembler to the object program produced when the main program is processed. Otherwise the object program for the referenced subroutines will have to be available in machine readable form. These programs are then loaded into the computer at the time that the main object program is loaded.

EXERCISES

1. Rewrite the following program sequences so that all labels are removed from the address portion of the statement.

    (a) BEGN, CLA
            CPF
            JMP BEGN
            SZA
            HLT

(b)   SUB, 0
              TAD I SUB
              ISZ SUB
              DCA TEMP
              TAD SCNT
              DCA CNT
          F5, TAD TEMP
              ISZ CNT
              JMP F5
              JMS I SUB
        TEMP, 0000
        SCNT, 7700
         CNT, 0000

2. Give the object program that would be generated if the following source program were assembled.

                    OCTAL
                    ORG 10
                    TAD DAT
                    TAD DAT + 1
                    TAD DAT + 2
                    SMA! SZA
                    HLT
                    DECIMAL
              DAT, 62
                    128
                    256
                    END

3. Define a macro TWNF X, Y, N that will add the number in location N to the number stored in location X and deposit the result in location Y.

5. SUMMARY

In this chapter we have investigated the techniques that can be used to relieve a programmer of many of the routine tasks involved in developing a machine-language program. The main concept is that a computer program can be used to translate statements that are meaningful to a programmer into machine-language instructions if we are careful in the way that we design these statements. In the next chapter we investigate how we can extend these ideas to the point where the programming language used by the programmer is essentially machine independent.

An assembler language is very closely related to the machine language of the computer that will process the object program. The statements of the language are easy to translate because we have imposed a very rigid limitation on the form that these statements can take. If we wish to have a language that can be used by a general user, we must make the statements in the language have a form that are easily interpreted by the user without requiring that he know how the computer operates. This requirement means that we need a much more complex program to carry out the translation process from the source program to the object program. Two levels of processing are required. The first level essentially transforms the source language statement into a sequence of assembler-language statements while the second level completes the process by translating these statements into an object program. Our next task is to consider how higher level languages can be defined and processed.

REFERENCE NOTATION

The use of assembler languages is covered in [2] and [5]. The SEDCOM assembler language is basically a subset of the PDP-8 assembler language described in [4] and [7]. Some of the advanced features of assembler programs are discussed in [1], [2], [3], [5], and [6].

REFERENCES

1. Aho, A. V., and Ullman, J. D. (1972), *The Theory of Parsing, Translation and Compiling.* Vol. 1: Parsing, Prentice-Hall, Englewood Cliffs, N.J.

2. Gear, C. W. (1974), *Computer Organization and Programming*, McGraw-Hill, New York.

3. Higman, B. (1967), *A Comparative Study of Programming Languages*, American Elsevier Publishing Co., New York.

4. Sloan, M. E. (1976), *Computer Hardware and Organization*, SRA, Chicago.

5. Stone, H. S., and Sieworek, D. P. (1975), *Introduction to Computer Organization and Data Structures: PDP-11 Edition*, McGraw-Hill, New York.

6. Wegner, P. (1968), *Programming Languages, Information Structures, and Machine Organization*, McGraw-Hill, New York.

7. (1975), Introduction to Programming, Digital Equipment Corp., Maynard, Mass.

HOME PROBLEMS

The following problems deal with developing specific subroutines to handle different portions of the assembly process. For each program give a flowchart to show the general organization of the algorithm used to carry out the specified task and an assembler-language program that implements the given algorithm.

1. Each statement in our assembler language consists of a string of ASCII characters. The end of a statement is indicated by the special delimiter character CARRIAGE RETURN (215_8). To process a statement an assembler program reads one statement at a time into the statement buffer. One of the simplest types of statement buffers is simply a sequence of consecutive memory locations that are used to store a single input character in each location.

   Write an assembler-language subroutine that will read a single assembler-language statement into the statement buffer and halt. This program should ignore all leading spaces (Code 240_8) and only retain one space between each term of the statement. The first location of the statement buffer is indicated by the label STBUF.

2. Each term in a statement buffer of the type discussed in Problem 1 is delimited by a space. Write an assembler-language subroutine NTERM that will read the next term to be processed from the statement buffer and place it in a term buffer consisting of 7 consecutive memory locations. The first location of the term buffer is indicated by the label TBUF. If all of the terms in the statement buffer have been read or if the rest of the content of the statement buffer is a comment all of the locations making up the term buffer are left zero.

3. Write an assembler-language subroutine called LATAB that will check the term in the term buffer to see if it is a label used to identify a memory location (i.e., is the first character a letter and does the term end in a comma?), or just a label (i.e., the first character is a letter and the last character is not a comma).

   If the term is not a label the accumulator is set to zero and the subroutine returns to the main program.

   If the term ends in a comma there are two possible actions. During the first pass the subroutine checks to see if the label is in the label table. If it is not, it is entered in the table (without the comma) and assigned a value corresponding to the value of the current location counter which is found in location CLC. If the term is found in the table, its value is checked to see if it is 7777 or an acceptable address. If the value is 7777 this indicates that the label was encountered in the address part of a previous statement. The label is reassigned the value corresponding to the value of the current location counter. Should the value of the label be other than 7777 an error message

$$\langle \text{term} \rangle \; \sqcup \; \sqcup \; \text{D2}$$

is outputted. $\langle \text{term} \rangle$ corresponds to the first six characters found in TBUF.

During the second pass the subroutine returns to the main program as soon as the comma is detected.

If the term is a label without a comma the subroutine checks to see if it is in the label table. If the term is found in the table it returns with the value of the term in the accumulator. Otherwise, the term is entered in the table and assigned a value of 7777 to indicate that the address associated with the label is not yet defined. The subroutine then returns to the main program.

4. Write an assembler-language subroutine called CMDCK to test if the term in the term buffer (see Problem 2) is an octal number, a character data term, or a command. If the term is an octal number or a character data term the program should transfer control to a subroutine TERST. If the term is not an octal number or a character data term it is checked to see if it is a command. Assume that a subroutine CMTAB can be used to carry out this check. CMTAB sets the accumulator to 7777 if the term is not a command, to X000 ($X \leq 5$) if it is a memory reference command and to the exact octal value corresponding to the term if it is a nonmemory reference instruction.

If the output of CMTAB is 7777 the error message

$$\langle \text{term} \rangle \ \sqcup \ \sqcup \ \text{UC}$$

is outputted and the subroutine returns to the main program.

If the output is of the form X000 ($X \leq 5$) indicating a memory reference command the subroutine also returns to the main program. Otherwise, the subroutine transfers control to the subroutine TERST.

5. Write an assembler-language subroutine called ENDST that will check the contents of the statement buffer to see if any additional terms are present that must be processed. If the statement in the buffer has been completely processed the current location counter, stored in location CLC, should be incremented. If there are additional unprocessed terms in the statement buffer an error message

$$\text{LOC} \ \langle [\text{CLC}] \rangle \ \sqcup \ \sqcup \ \text{SE}$$

should be outputted before incrementing the current location counter. The subroutine returns to the main program after the current location counter is incremented.

6. Assume that the subroutines described in Problems 1 through 5 are available. Write an assembler-language program that will implement the first pass of an assembler described by the flowchart of Figure 14-4.

15

Programming Languages and Compilers

1. INTRODUCTION

As we have seen in the last chapters, machine-language and assembler-language programming techniques are inherently tied in with the logical organization and computational capabilities of a particular computer. Consequently, anyone who uses these languages must spend a large amount of time and effort in becoming familiar with the particular characteristics of both the computer and the language before he can effectively develop programs for the computer. Even with this background, it is a very tedious process to write an extensive program in a machine or assembly language. This is partly because of the large amount of bookkeeping and related chores that must be done by the programmer, and partly because the structure of the language bears little resemblance to the structure of the information processing task that is being represented by the program.

These limitations were all too evident to the people who tried to use the first commercially available digital computers. In the early and mid-1950's this led several companies and research organizations to undertake the development of special translator programs that would take a source program written by a computer user in a language easily understood by the user and translate this program into an object program that could be executed by the computer. Since that time a large number of user-oriented rather than machine-oriented languages have been developed.

These languages, which are called *programming languages* or *procedure-oriented languages* share several features in common. Their design is such that they can be used by a computer user without requiring him to have extensive knowledge of how the computer actually carries out any given computation. Thus the user can concentrate on how best to solve a problem rather than on the problem of writing an efficient machine-language program. The task of transforming the program into a machine-language program that can be executed by the computer is left to a special translator program.

There are two types of translator programs that are in general use: compilers and interpreters. A *compiler* is a translator program that transforms an entire source-language program written in a particular programming language into a machine-language object program that can be run on a particular computer. An *interpreter* is a translator program that immediately transforms one or more source-language statements into a series of machine-language instructions and then executes these instructions before going on to the next sequence of source-language statements. An interpreter never generates a complete object program that can be saved for later use, since the translation and execution of each statement is continually interwoven.

Interpreters are of greatest value when the source-language program is to be executed only a few times. Situations of this type occur in many real-time applications where a computer user wishes to carry out a sequence of computations but must know intermediate results as he goes along. If a program is to be used a number of times it is much more efficient to use a compiler to generate a complete machine-language object program before making an attempt to execute the program. Compilers and interpreters share many features in common and both types of programs can be used to translate source-language programs expressed in all of the common programming languages.

In this chapter we concentrate on the structural properties of programming languages and how a source program written in such a language is transformed into an object program by a compiler. No attempt is made to develop a complete compiler program. However, each of the major operations performed by the simple compiler that we will discuss is explained in enough detail so that the translation process carried out by the compiler program can be understood.

2. PROGRAMMING LANGUAGES

A programming language should be as flexible as possible so that it can be used to program a wide range of problems. This can be accomplished by identifying the basic mathematical, logical, and procedural operations that are required in any program and then making these operations fundamental constituents of the language. Other special features can be added, as needed, to take care of special requirements imposed by the needs of particular classes of problems. Finally the language should be machine independent. That is, it should not rely on some special feature of a particular computer in order to be able to operate properly. A program written in a truly machine independent language can be run on any computer that has a compiler designed to handle that language.

Currently there are a variety of programming languages in various levels of general use. Jean E. Sammet, references [5] and [6], has compiled a summary of the characteristics and history of over 120 different programming languages that had been developed up to 1975. Each of these languages has been created to simplify a particular type of programming problem.

Probably the best-known languages are the procedure-oriented languages such as FORTRAN or ALGOL, which have been developed to handle scientific calculations. FORTRAN was first introduced by IBM in the late 1950's and has achieved wide acceptance for programs involving engineering and scientific calculations. At about the same time an international committee undertook the development of a programming language that would be used as an international standard for procedure-oriented languages. The resulting language was called ALGOL. It has achieved limited acceptance in the United States although it has proved popular among some university and mathematically-oriented computer people, particularly in Europe. FORTRAN proved to have many shortcomings and IBM has since introduced a new language, PL/I, which provided additional capabilities not found in earlier languages. This language is finding increasing use in the United States.

Other special purpose languages have been developed to handle special classes of problems. COBOL is a business-oriented language that was developed under the sponsorship of the United States government. It is designed to handle data of a type found in various business data processing problems. LISP, SNOBOL, COMIT, and IPL-V are languages that have been developed for processing lists and strings of symbols. These languages have their greatest use in research areas involving artificial intelligence, simulation of human cognitive processes, mechanical translation, information retrieval, and operations research. BASIC is a language that has been developed to facilitate numerical calculations on a time-sharing computer system. This language was designed so that it is relatively easy to learn how to use and to carry out calculations at a remote terminal.

None of the above languages are universal in the sense that they can handle every class of programming problem. In fact, they have a very artificial structure that resembles but does not have the range of natural languages. The study of artificial languages is a very important and active area of research, and it can be expected that future developments will provide languages that will make it even easier to program a computer.

In this section we investigate the general properties that a programming language must possess if it is to be both useful to a programmer and easy to process by a compiler. For the rest of this chapter we use statements from the FORTRAN language to illustrate the general properties of a programming language. It is assumed that the reader is already familiar with the techniques of writing programs in FORTRAN or some similar programming language. An ability to write FORTRAN programs is not required to understand the following discussions.

Basic Requirements of a Language

Programming languages differ quite radically from natural languages in that they are designed to perform a very narrow and well-defined function: that of providing an interface between a computer user and the computer. Thus, when a programming language is designed, it must be defined in an exact and unambiguous manner so that there will be no "misunderstanding" between what the programmer would like the program to do and what it actually does.

A programming language must be able to carry out two major tasks: it must describe the computation to be performed and provide information to the compiler program about how the object program should be organized. To handle the first task, the language must provide the programmer with the ability to define and operate on numeric and/or nonnumeric information. The second task can be carried out if specific conventions are adopted about the form that can be used to represent information and operations in the program and the way that the object program may be organized.

Every program that we write is for the purpose of carrying out some type of computation. The computation may be numeric where we compute a specific numerical value using numeric data, or it can be nonnumeric where we may be, for example, manipulating a list of names and addresses. In either case we must provide a means for defining, identifying, and assigning values to data variables that we either read into the computer while the computation is being performed or generate as part of the computation.

Data is combined or acted on by using operations. The set of operators that we include in a language will determine the types of computations that we can perform. Operators can be categorized roughly as *computational*, such as addition, subtraction, division and multiplication, *relational*, such as greater than, less than, or equal to, or *logical*, such as AND, OR, or NOT. These are not the only allowable operators and in some case we might wish to define special operations such as *write name as first element on list* or *read last name on list*.

To carry out a given computation we must be able to control the sequence in which the calculations that make up the computation are made. As we have seen from our discussion of programming in the two previous chapters we must provide methods to control the number of times that we execute a sequence of instructions, methods to test the value of a quantity and branch to a point in the program depending on the result of the test, methods to unconditionally transfer our execution sequence to another part of the program, and methods to call subroutines. In addition, we must provide a means to input and output data.

These tasks must be performed in carrying out a computation. However, if the compiler program is to perform the routine tasks necessary to generate a machine-language object program, it must have a way of obtaining information about the form that the machine-language program is to take from information contained in the source program. This is accomplished by specifying a well-defined set of rules that govern how the statements that make up a program can be written and by introducing special *compiler directives* that provide information directly to the compiler.

Language Structure

A program written in a programming language consists of a sequence of *statements* which are the smallest executable unit in a program. A statement is a command to the computer or the compiler to carry out a specific action. In dealing with any programming language we must deal with both the syntactic structure and the semantics of the statements that make up the language. The *syntax* of a language consists of a set of grammatical rules that tell us the acceptable ways to write the statements of the language. A statement that satisfies these rules is said to be an *acceptable statement* of the language while a statement that does not satisfy these rules is termed unacceptable. The *semantics* of a language consist of a set of rules that define how the compiler is to transform each statement into an appropriate set of machine-language instructions or how it is to extract information from the statement about the compilation process. The programmer must understand both the syntactic structure and the semantic meaning of each statement to effectively write programs in that language.

In order to provide examples of the concepts that we will be considering we use the FORTRAN statement type listed in Table 15-1. Since our emphasis is on the structure of languages rather than in writing programs in the language, this representative set of FORTRAN statements is sufficient for our discussions. In fact, a previous knowledge of FORTRAN is not required to understand any of the following material.

When the statements given in Table 15-1 are used in an actual program, they will often be preceded by a *statement number* so that we can refer to a particular state-

Table 15-1	Representative FORTRAN Statements

1. Assignment Statements

   General Form: ⟨identifier⟩ = ⟨expression⟩

   Definition: Assign the value obtained by evaluating the expression to the term indicated by the identifier.

   Example: $Z = W + X - Y$

2. Unconditional Transfer

   General Form: GO TO ⟨statement number⟩

   Definition: Transfer of control to the program statement indicated by the statement number.

   Example: GO TO 20

3. Conditional Transfer

   General Form: IF (⟨expression⟩) ⟨statement number 1⟩, ⟨statement number 2⟩, ⟨statement number 3⟩

Table 15-1 (*continued*)

Definition: Compute value of expression. Transfer control to statement number 1, 2, or 3 if the value of the expression is less than, equal to, or greater than zero respectively.

Example: IF (X + Y − Z) 10, 20, 30

4. Loop Control

General Form: DO ⟨statement number⟩ $i = m_1, m_2, m_3$

Definition: This statement is a command to execute repeatedly a group of statements following it up to and including the statement indicated by the statement number. The term i is an integer that is initially given the value m_1 and then incremented by m_3 each time the loop is executed. When the value of i reaches m_2 the loop is terminated. The terms m_1, m_2, and m_3 are either integers or identifiers representing integers.

Example: DO 25 I = 1, 20, 2

5. Input/Output Statements

General Form:

(a) Read

READ(⟨device number⟩, ⟨statement number⟩)⟨list of identifiers⟩
⟨statement FORMAT(⟨data field descriptions⟩)
number⟩

(b) Write

WRITE(⟨device number⟩, ⟨statement number⟩)⟨list of identifiers⟩
⟨statement FORMAT(⟨data field descriptions⟩)
  number⟩

Definition: The term ⟨list of identifiers⟩ is a list of terms that indicated data to be inputted or outputted by the device indicated by the device number term. The FORMAT statement indicates how the various data terms are to be interpreted.

Example: READ (1, 13) A, XMAX
        13 FORMAT (F 10.3, F 10.5)

6. Specification Statements
    Typical Statement Types

INTEGER   ⟨list of identifiers⟩
REAL   ⟨list of identifiers⟩

Definition: These statements are used to indicate the nature of each identifier. Unless otherwise indicated, identifiers starting with I, J, K, L, M, or N are assumed to represent integers and all other identifiers indicate real (floating-point) numbers.

Example: INTEGER X, Y
REAL IMAX, NO

7. Memory Reservation Statements

General Form: DIMENSION ⟨identifier⟩(⟨integer number 1⟩) . . .;
⟨identifier n⟩(⟨integer number n⟩)

Definition: This statement reserves a block of memory locations to store arrays of data associated with each identifier associated with the subscripted variable. The identifier term indicates the variable and the integer number term specifies the number of locations needed to store the array.

Example: DIMENSION A(5), B(6)

8. Compiler Directives

(a) STOP

Definition: This causes the computer to stop execution of the program. The program cannot be restarted.

(b) END

Definition: This statement tells the compiler that the physical end of the FORTRAN source program or of a user defined function has been reached.

(c) RETURN

Definition: Return to main program from a subroutine.

(d) Comments: C ⟨character sequence⟩

Definition: Any character sequence preceded by a C is assumed to be a comment and is disregarded by the compiler.

Example: C THIS IS A COMMENT

ment. For example, when we use a GO TO statement we must indicate the statement to which control is transferred by indicating that statement's statement number. A typical programming sequence would be

$$GO\ TO\ 10$$
$$\vdots$$
$$10\quad Z = X - Y + AMAX$$

Now that we have an example of a typical programming language, let us consider how information can be extracted from the statements that make up the language.

Fundamental Character Set

If we are to communicate with a computer we must have a device, such as a teletype, a typewriter, or a card reader, that will input information to the computer and a similar device to receive information from the computer. Each of these devices has a basic set of characters that form the *fundamental character set* of the computer.

There are three types of fundamental characters: alphabetic, numeric and special. The 26 alphabetic characters A through Z and the 10 decimal digits 0 through 9 are standard characters for all systems. However, the set of allowable special characters will vary from system to system. Some of the typical special characters that are used to indicate operators, delimiters, and punctuation in FORTRAN are

$$+ - */)(. , \$ = \text{'blank} \sqcup$$

Primitive Program Constituents or Tokens

The fundamental character set is of importance only in that it provides the building blocks from which we can form complete statements. However, it is not the individual characters but the way they are combined into primitive program constituents that is important in interpreting the statements of a programming language. The *primitive program constituents* or *tokens* are the basic units of information that form identifiable elements of a program statement. For example the character string

$$A\ B\ \# \ \$\ 1\ 5\ 6 = + ! ? ** C\ V$$

has, in all likelihood, no meaning. However in FORTRAN the character string

$$10\ ABLE = BIG + 256.5$$

has a definite meaning. In this case the tokens are 10, ABLE, $=$, BIG, $+$, and 256.5.

The set of tokens can be divided into two categories:

(a) System symbols
(b) Identifiers

System symbols can be either a single fundamental character or a string of these characters that have a fixed meaning specified by the programming language. Some typical single character system symbols are the operators $=$, $+$, $-$, $*$, and $/$. Multiple character system symbols are data constants such as 16, 12, 34, *key words* which are character strings such as DO, GO TO, IF, or FORMAT that have been assigned a specific meaning in the language, or multiple character operators such as $**$. Whenever any of these system symbols are encountered by the compiler, it knows how to interpret these symbols because the person who wrote the compiler program has included their meaning as part of the compiler program.

Identifiers

All the other basic character strings used by a programmer to name various terms and information structures are called *identifiers*. Identifiers serve as names of variables, of arrays of variables, and of mathematical functions. Most FORTRAN systems provide preprogrammed subroutines to evaluate several mathematical functions such as SQRT, SIN, and COS. The identifiers used to name these subroutines are assigned when the system is developed and the compiler is already programmed to handle these identifiers in a specific manner. Consequently, identifiers of this type are called *initialized identifiers*. Except for this special class of identifiers, all identifiers found in a FORTRAN program are created by the programmer at the time a FORTRAN program is written. Identifiers of this type are called *non-initialized identifiers*. For example, in the statement

$$JOHN = PA3 + BI5$$

the three tokens JOHN, PA3, and BI5 are non-initialized identifiers.

In FORTRAN, identifiers that are used to represent numerical data can have from one to six characters, the first of which must be a letter. However, when we deal with identifiers that represent numerical values, we must have a way to indicate to the compiler if these numbers are integers or real numbers that must be represented in floating-point form. This is necessary because the way each number is stored and operated on by the computer depends upon its type. This information is supplied by introducing a convention as to the way identifiers are formed or by using specification statements to indicate which attributes the compiler should associate with an identifier.

Expressions

An expression is a rule for computing the value of a quantity that is needed as part of the computation being carried out by a program. The expression might be used to either assign a value to or modify the value of an identifier or it can be used as part of a control statement to influence the course of execution of a particular program sequence. An expression can consist of a single identifier, or it can consist of a sequence of operators and operands which are consistent with the rules of syntax for forming expressions. For our discussion we will only consider the arithmetic operators

+   addition
−   subtraction
∗   multiplication
/   division
∗∗   exponentiation

Some typical expressions are:

36.5	single constant
A	single identifier
A∗B − DE∗∗2 + GT	sequence of operands and operators

To evaluate an expression the compiler must generate the sequence of machine-language coding necessary to accomplish the computations called for by the expression. To do this it is necessary to indicate the precedence of operations. Thus in evaluating an expression in which the hierarchy of the operations is not completely specified by use of parentheses, the following rules of precedence will be followed where it is assumed that the expression is scanned from left to right.

(a)   All exponentiations are performed first.
(b)   All multiplications and divisions are performed second.
(c)   All additions and subtractions are performed third.

Under this convention the expression

$$A ** B * C - A + D$$

would be evaluated as

$$((A^B)(C) - A) + D$$

The way in which a compiler actually generates the object code associated with an expression is discussed in the next section.

Functions

FORTRAN and most other programming languages provide for the use of certain common mathematical functions as part of the system. To use a function we give its name and follow it with an expression enclosed in parentheses. For example,

$$SIN (A ** 2 + B + C * D)$$

is such a function. To determine the value of this function the compiler first sets up the machine-language code necessary to compute the expression $A ** 2 + B + C * D$. The compiler then generates the calling sequence necessary to transfer operation to the subroutine that forms the sine of the resulting value of this expression. Functions such as the sine are generally evaluated by using a truncated series approximation fitted to the function.

Besides the functions supplied with the system, languages such as FORTRAN also have provisions for user-defined subroutines that will compute particular functions. In this situation the programmer assigns a name to the function by writing FUNCTION followed by its name. He then describes how the function is formed by writing the necessary programming statements. The definition of the function is terminated by writing END. The statement RETURN is used in every place in the function definition where it is possible to return to the main program.

A user-defined function has the general form

```
FUNCTION PI(X)
Body of Function Program
RETURN
END
```

When the compiler encounters the statement FUNCTION it generates a subroutine called PI that is defined by all the program statements between the statement FUNCTION PI(X) and the statement END. Whenever the function is used as part of a program the compiler generates the proper calling sequence for this subroutine.

A complete source program consists of a sequence of statements of the type given in Table 15-1. These statements are general enough to let us implement any algorithm that describes a numerical calculation. The next section investigates the different tasks that a compiler program must carry out to translate the source-language program into an object-language program.

1. Indicate the system symbols, key words, expressions, and identifiers in the following FORTRAN statements

(a)   A = 20
(b)   7 XN = X + ((FX + FMX)/2. + COSF(X) − 5.)
(c)   8 IF (X − XN) 5, 6, 8
(d)   GO TO 25
(e)   READ (5, 123) J, K, AX, BX
       123 FORMAT (16, 17, F6.0, F7.0)

2. Explain how a GO TO or an IF statement would be implemented using SEDCOM machine language instructions.

3. THE TRANSLATION PROCESS

The design of a compiler program is a complex and time-consuming process. However, the effort spent in developing an efficient compiler will pay off if the resulting object program is as good or better than the machine-language program that could be produced by an experienced programmer.

In the following discussion no attempt will be made to describe all the details that must be considered in writing a compiler program. Our interest is, instead, in examining the major parts of a compiler program and the task they must perform in the overall translation process. Although this discussion deals with the statement types associated with FORTRAN, the basic concepts presented are applicable to a wide range of translators.

Tasks Performed by a Compiler

One of the main features of programming in a procedure-oriented language is that it relieves the programmer of all the routine bookkeeping-type tasks used in writing a machine- or assembler-language program. In particular the programmer does not have to deal with such problems as the assignment of actual memory locations, the tying together of program segments, the setting up of calling sequences for subroutines, and the setting up of loops. Thus, if the source-language program is correct, the compiler will generate a machine-language program to carry out a given calculation much faster than even an experienced programmer could do it if he had to write the program in machine language.

Ideally a compiler would translate the source program directly into executable object code in one pass over the source program. Although it is possible to develop compiler programs with essentially this ability, most compilers carry out the translation process in two or more stages. This is particularly true for small computers with limited memory capacity. For the following discussion we assume that we are dealing with a two-stage compiler.

The general operation of a typical two-stage compiler can be understood by examining Figure 15-1. During the first stage of translation the compiler scans the input source program and produces an intermediate object program. This intermediate program is then processed during the second stage of translation to produce the final object code. In small computers the intermediate object program is often actually outputted on punched cards or paper tape. In this case the intermediate object program must be read into the computer as input data for the second stage.

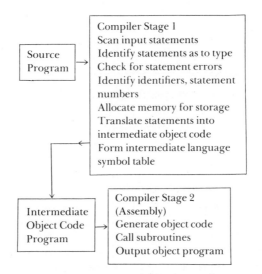

Figure 15-1. The major stages of a simple compiler program.

The intermediate object program is written in a form that strongly resembles an assembler-language program. Thus, for simplicity of understanding, we assume that the intermediate source language for our compiler is similar to the assembler language that we have been discussing in the previous chapters.

The tasks of the second stage of the compiler program are therefore very similar to the tasks of the assembler program discussed in Chapter 14. Consequently we do not consider this portion of the compiler program. Our main interest will be in the way that the intermediate object code is generated by the first stage of the compilation process. It is also noted that, as the intermediate object program is generated, we can concurrently establish the symbol table that we need for stage 2. Thus the stage 2 translation process corresponds to the second pass of the assembly process discussed in Chapter 14.

The first stage of the translation process essentially writes an assembler-type program that is equivalent to the original source program. As indicated in Figure 15-1, this stage must:

1. Classify each input statement as to type and detect any source language errors.
2. Identify all data terms and assign space in memory for those terms.
3. Assign space in memory for the segment of object code associated with each statement.
4. Generate the intermediate code associated with the statement.
5. Form the intermediate language symbol table.

To design this section of the compiler, we must make several assumptions concerning how the various statements will be translated and how the final object program will be organized in memory.

Statement Identification and Error Detection

Every language has a set of general statement types that are identified by the structure of the statement and the presence of one or more key words. Each FORTRAN statement given in Table 15-1 can be classified as one of six possible types. These types, the key words used to recognize each type and their general form are summarized in Table 15-2.

Although it is not indicated explicitly in Table 15-2, it is assumed that any executable statement can be preceded by a statement number.

Each statement is read into a statement buffer and scanned to find the key words that indicate the type of statement being processed, to find any errors present in the statement and to detect all of the identifiers used in the statement. When errors are found, the appropriate error message is generated; otherwise the information gathered by the initial scan is entered into appropriate tables and a statement processing subroutine of the proper type is called to translate the source statement into its corresponding intermediate object code.

Bookkeeping Tasks

Since we have assumed that the compiler is going to take over the bookkeeping jobs associated with writing the final machine-language program we must introduce conventions concerning the way the various types of data will be stored in memory and the way the actual program will be organized in memory. These conventions then influence the way the compiler handles the translation process. As the compiler scans the source program it must locate all identifiers, determine their type, and eventually assign memory locations to the items associated with each identifier.

Table 15-2   General Classification of Statements

(a) Assignment statements
⟨identifier⟩ = ⟨arithmetic expression⟩
key word =

(b) GO TO statements
GO TO ⟨statement number⟩
key word GO TO

(c) IF statements
IF (⟨arithmetic expression⟩) $\left(\begin{array}{c}\text{statement}\\\text{number}\end{array}\right),\left(\begin{array}{c}\text{statement}\\\text{number}\end{array}\right),\left(\begin{array}{c}\text{statement}\\\text{number}\end{array}\right)$
key word IF

(d) DO statements
DO ⟨statement number⟩$\left(\begin{array}{c}\text{integer}\\\text{identifier}\end{array}\right)=\left(\begin{array}{c}\text{integer}\\\text{identifier}\end{array}\right),\left(\begin{array}{c}\text{integer}\\\text{identifier}\end{array}\right),\left(\begin{array}{c}\text{integer}\\\text{identifier}\end{array}\right)$
key word DO

(e) Compiler Directives
STOP
END
DIMENSION ⟨list of dimensioned identifiers⟩
key words STOP, END, DIMENSION

(f) Input/output statements
READ (⟨device number⟩⟨statement number⟩)⟨list of identifiers⟩
WRITE (⟨device number⟩⟨statement number⟩), ⟨list of identifiers⟩
⟨statement number⟩ FORMAT (⟨specifications of identifiers⟩)
key words READ, WRITE, FORMAT

The way that data is handled in a computer depends on the size of each computer word, the instruction set of the computer and the form that the data takes. For our discussion we assume that integer numbers require one computer word and real numbers are represented in a floating-point form that uses one word for the exponent and two words for the mantissa.

Each compiler program has access to a standard set of subroutines that can be incorporated into an object program as needed. The particular subroutines that are actually included are determined by the initialized identifiers found in the source program. Subroutines to handle floating-point arithmetic, the evaluation of standard trigonometric and arithmetic functions and the reading and writing of information into and out of the program are standard in FORTRAN compilers. Most compilers also have a provision that allows the programmer to develop and use subroutines that are referenced in the source program.

The actual allocation of memory location assignments to specific parts of the object program is also a task that the compiler must perform. This task can be handled in a variety of ways. One method is to assign data and intermediate storage needed by the machine-language program to the higher order end of memory and to reserve a section of the lower end of memory for the permanent control programs and compiler subroutines used as part of the program. The program code is placed in sequentially increasing memory locations just above this reserved area. Figure 15-2 illustrates this general memory organization. The arrows on the right-hand side indicate the order in which memory locations are assigned by the compiler.

During the initial translation process all memory addresses are made with respect to an appropriate but undefined reference location. After the scan of the input source program is completed, the compiler determines how much memory must be reserved for each of the main portions of the object program and assigns absolute values to these reference locations.

There are three major classes of assignments that must be made.

1. The location of the main program and program-defined subroutines.
2. The location of the control programs and compiler supplied subroutines.
3. The location of data and intermediate storage associated with the program.

Before the compilation process starts, the compiler program has a table that lists the amount of room needed by the control programs and each compiler subroutine that may be called as part of the source program, but there is no information concerning the number of instructions that will be needed to realize the given program or the amount of memory that must be assigned to the storage of data and other

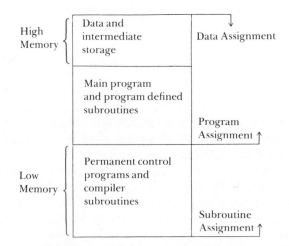

Figure 15-2. General organization of memory.

intermediate information. During the initial scan of the source program, the compiler gathers the following information about the program.

1. The names of the compiler subroutines that are to be used in the program.
2. A list of all identifiers and constants used in the program.
3. The type (real, integer) of each identifier and the number of storage locations that must be associated with each identifier. The DIMENSION statements indicate the space that must be reserved for subscripted identifiers.

This information is obtained as each source program statement is processed and entered into an appropriate table for use during the second phase of translation.

In addition to the identifiers contained in the source program, provision must be made for temporary data terms that are generated by the compiler as part of the translation process. Terms of this type must also be included in the compiler-generated symbol table.

General Organization of First Stage

The general operation of the first stage of the compiler process is indicated in block diagram form by Figure 15-3. Each of the major steps that are involved in the first stage translation process are indicated.

The source program is scanned statement by statement. When the compiler is ready to accept a statement, the statement reader loads the statement into a portion of memory that serves as a statement buffer area. The statement is then scanned to identify its type and to locate all the identifiers contained in the statement. The analyzer can make use of each of the specific statement type processors as well as the key words contained in the statement to identify the type of statement currently in the statement buffer.

As the statement is analyzed the various identifiers contained in it are recognized and entered in the identifier symbol table. This table is somewhat more complex than the symbol table used in an assembler. Besides keeping track of the memory location or locations assigned to the identifier, this table must also record information concerning the type of term that is represented by each identifier. This is accomplished by including a special field as part of each table entry to indicate the type of variable that is represented by the identifier associated with the given entry. The particular code found in this field will indicate if the identifier is a real number, an integer, the name of a subroutine, or a statement number.

After a statement is identified, it is then translated into its corresponding intermediate language code or, if it is a compiler directive, it is used to guide the compilation process. The assignment statements and IF statements both contain arithmetic expressions as part of the statement structure. Thus, in order to avoid duplication, a separate arithmetic statement processor can be called by either processor to translate arithmetic expressions.

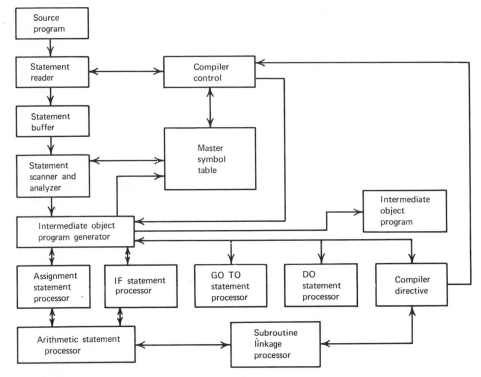

Figure 15-3. Organizational block diagram of a simple compiler first stage.

All of these translation steps are under the control of the compiler control section. As each statement is translated it is assigned a relative location in memory and the amount of space required in memory is determined. After the source program is completely processed the control section uses the data gathered from the various processors to assign particular memory locations to each portion of the program. This information is entered into the symbol table for use by the second processing stage.

Generation of the Intermediate Object-Language Program

The structure of the object program developed by a compiler from a given source-language program will, of course, depend on the particular computer that will be used to execute the object program. In the following sections we briefly consider some of the translation techniques that might be used in a compiler designed to generate an object program that could be executed on a computer that has an instruction set similar to the SEDCOM computer discussed in Chapter 9. We will use a mnemonic representation for each instruction and assume that the second stage of the compilation process can convert these mnemonics into an appropriate machine readable form. In this way we can concentrate on the translation process associated with each type of statement without having to worry about the computer dependent details that are involved with using a particular computer organization.

As we have seen, the compiler can call on a number of different subroutines that are designed to translate specific types of source statements. Probably the most important subroutine of this type is the subroutine that translates arithmetic expressions. Thus before we consider the complete translation process, we first consider the problem of translating arithmetic expressions.

4. THE TRANSLATION OF ARITHMETIC EXPRESSIONS

One of the most common tasks that must be carried out by a compiler is the translation of arithmetic expressions into an intermediate source-language representation. Unfortunately, the common mathematical methods for representing arithmetic expressions that were evolved as mathematics developed are not particularly suitable for computer processing. To understand the type of problem that we must solve, consider the following simple arithmetic expression

$$A * B + B * C$$
$$\uparrow \quad \uparrow \quad \uparrow$$
$$1 \quad 3 \quad 2$$

If we are to evaluate this expression we must first compute the product $A * B$, then store this product while we compute the product $B * C$ and then complete our evaluation by summing the two previously computed products.

The order in which we carry out each operation is indicated by the number under each operator. From this example we see that if we are to evaluate arithmetic expressions written in standard mathematical form, then we will have to provide a means of scanning back-and-forth along the expression to determine the next operation to be performed. To eliminate this problem it is possible to preprocess an arithmetic expression so that it is easier to evaluate. Thus before we investigate the translation process, we first consider how the compiler might restructure the form of the arithmetic expression before attempting to translate it.

Conventional Representation of Arithmetic Expressions

An arithmetic expression is said to be written in *infix* notation when each operator is written between the operands that it operates on. For example,

$$A + B \qquad C * D \qquad A ** 2$$

are some typical expressions written in infix form.

For more complex expressions we must be careful to define the conventions that we will use to define the order of evaluation of a complex expression written in infix notation. For example, the expression

$$A + B ** 2 * C$$

could be interpreted as

$$A + ((B ** 2) * C) \quad \text{or} \quad ((A + B) ** 2) * C \quad \text{or}$$
$$A + ((B) ** (2 * C)) \quad \text{or} \quad (A + B) ** (2 * C)$$

where each term inside a parenthesis is evaluated before the external operator is applied. To overcome this problem, we define an order of precedence in which the operators are applied. For FORTRAN, the rules of precedence listed in Table 15-3 are used.

These rules are applied below to produce the parentheses that lead to the correct evaluation of the indicated expressions.

$$A + B ** 2 * C = A + ((B ** 2) * C)$$
$$A * B/C = (A * B)/C$$
$$A + B - C + D = ((A + B) - C) + D$$

Table 15-3   Rules of Precedence for FORTRAN

1. All expressions contained in parenthesis are treated as a single term whose value is obtained by evaluating the expression inside the parenthesis as an independent expression.

2. All exponentiations (**) are performed first.

3. All multiplications (*) and divisions (/) are performed next.

4. All additions (+) and subtractions (−) are performed last.

5. Within a sequence of consecutive multiplications and/or divisions in which the order of the operations is not completely specified by parentheses, the evaluation is from left to right.

6. Within a sequence of consecutive additions and/or subtractions in which the order of the operations is not completely specified by parentheses, the evaluation is from left to right.

The conventions about precedents of the operators introduce a problem when we try to translate an expression into a sequence of intermediate object-language statements. In particular we cannot scan an expression from left-to-right and carry out the operation called for by each operator as it is encountered. Instead we must carry out the translation process in such a way that the precedent conventions are not violated. This problem can be overcome by introducing another technique for representing arithmetic expressions.

Polish Form Representation of Arithmetic Expressions

The Polish mathematician Lukasiewicz showed that it is possible to represent arithmetic expressions in such a way that all the operations appear in the order in which they are actually performed in the evaluation of the expression. This representation, which is often referred to as *Polish string notation* in honor of Lukasiewicz, also has the advantage that parentheses are not needed to set off subexpressions that must be evaluated as a single term.

The main idea behind Polish string notation is that the operator indicating the operation to be carried out on a set of operands is written *after* the operands. For example,

$$A + B \text{ is written as } AB+$$

and

$$A * B \text{ is written as } AB*.$$

An arithmetic expression represented in infix form can be manually converted to Polish form by the following two-step process:

1. Use the precedence rules of Table 15-3 to place parentheses around each pair of operands and their associated operator.
2. Convert the resulting expression, which is now independent of the precedence rules, to Polish string form. Eliminate all parentheses. Table 15-4 gives several examples that illustrate how this conversion process is applied.

To evaluate an arithmetic expression in Polish form we scan along the expression until we encounter an operator. The operator is then applied to the preceding operands that it acts on, and the result obtained by applying the operation replaces the operator-operand combination in the expression. The following example illustrates this evaluation process.

Let

$$A = 5 \quad B = 4 \quad \text{and} \quad C = 6$$

Table 15-4

Conversion of Arithmetic
Expressions in Infix Form to Polish Form

Infix Form of Expression	Parentheses Added	Polish Form
$A + B - C$	$((A + B) - C)$	$AB + C -$
$A * B + C * D$	$((A * B) + (C * D))$	$AB * CD * +$
$A + B ** 2 * C$	$(A + ((B ** 2) * C))$	$AB2 ** C * +$
$A * B/C$	$((A * B)/C)$	$AB * C/$

Then

$$AB\,2 ** C * + \ \rightarrow A\ 16\ C * + \text{ since } B\,2 ** = 16$$

$$A\ 16\ C * + \ \rightarrow A\ 96 + \qquad \text{since } 16\ C * = 96$$

$$A\ 96 + \ \rightarrow 101 \qquad\qquad \text{since } A\ 96 + \ = 101$$

FORTRAN arithmetic expressions are written in infix rather than Polish form. However, if we wish to translate a source-language arithmetic expression into its corresponding object-language code, it is much easier to work with arithmetic expressions in Polish form. Thus most compiler programs first translate all arithmetic expressions into Polish form before any attempt is made to generate the object code needed to evaluate the expression.

Translating From Infix to Polish Form

To mechanically translate an expression in infix form to Polish form we must adhere to the precedence conventions given in Table 15-3. To apply these conventions we can assign a *precedence number* to each operator where the higher precedence operators are assigned the higher numbers. There is a small problem involved in handling a $+$ or a $-$ sign that occurs as the leading term in an arithmetic expression or as the first character following an opening parenthesis. For example, consider expressions of the form

$$(-A + B) \qquad \text{or} \qquad -A + C * D$$

The minus sign is only applied to the term A. It is called a *unary minus*, and it must be distinguished from the regular minus operation on two operands. Therefore we indicate the unary minus by the special symbol $\sim$.

$$(\sim A + B) \qquad \text{and} \qquad \sim A + C * D$$

Table 15-5 Precedence Numbers Associated with Arithmetic Operators

Operator	Precedence Number
⊣, ⊢, (,)	0
+, − (binary minus)	1
~ (unary minus)	2
*, /	3
**	4

A similar unary + could be introduced but it is not needed. Thus it is assumed that no statement to be processed contains a unary +. If one is present, it is removed before the expression is processed.

In addition to the arithmetic operators, we need some special operators to indicate the beginning and end of expressions or subexpressions that should be treated as a single term. The special operators ⊣, ⊢ are used to delimit the beginning and end of complete expressions and the operators (,) are used to delimit the beginning and end of each sub expression that must be evaluated as a unit.

The precedence of each arithmetic operator and the string delimiters (,) and ⊣, ⊢ are indicated by the precedence number assigned to each operator in Table 15-5. The higher the number the higher the precedence of the operator.

The delimiter operators (,), which must always occur in pairs, convey information to the translator concerning how the translation process should progress. Expressions enclosed in (,) are treated as simple terms after the expressions are evaluated. Whenever the (delimiter is encountered the subexpression indicated by this delimiter is transformed before we continue with the processing of the terms outside of the delimiter.

Before we investigate the complete translation algorithm, let us first consider the steps that we would go through in translating a typical expression. Assume that we wish to translate the following expression

$$A * B + A * (B * D + C ** E)$$

If we were going to translate this manually we would first introduce additional parentheses to delimit the operands acted upon by each operator. This would give us

$$((A * B) + (A * ((B * D) + (C ** E))))$$

Next we would translate this expression into Polish form. This would give us

$$AB * ABD * CE ** + * +$$

as the desired Polish string.

To do this same translation using a program we can eliminate the need for adding the extra parentheses if we introduce the idea of a pushdown list to provide for the temporary storage of information during the translation process.

A *pushdown list* is a storage technique that places a sequence of items in consecutive memory locations. Items can be added and removed from only one end of this sequence, and an item lower down in the sequence cannot be utilized until all items above this particular item are removed. A pushdown list can be visualized as behaving in a manner similar to a stack of trays resting in a holder with a spring loaded false bottom. As each new tray is added to the stack, the other trays are pushed down into the holder and the new tray is at the level of the previous tray. The last tray placed on the stack is thus the first one removed. Storage of this type is thus referred to as last-in first-out storage.

To indicate the contents of a pushdown list, we write the symbols from left to right with a semicolon (;) between each symbol. The symbol at the extreme left will be taken as the top symbol and all the other symbols will be assumed further down the list. For example,

$$A; B; C; D \equiv \begin{array}{c} A \\ B \\ C \\ D \end{array}$$

represents a pushdown list with four symbols. The topmost symbol is A.

The actual translation process taking an arithmetic expression in infix notation and transforming it to Polish form can be represented pictorially by the system shown in Figure 15-4. The pushdown list is used to store operators which have appeared in the input sequence but are not immediately needed to form the output sequence. The arithmetic expression making up the input sequence is scanned from left to right. As each term is read, it is processed by the processor program which

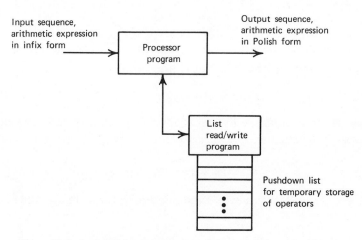

Figure 15-4. A pictorial representation of the translation of arithmetic expressions from infix to Polish form.

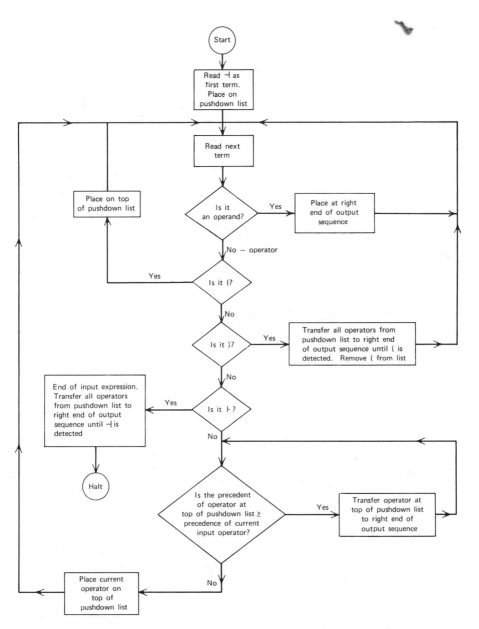

Figure 15-5. Flowchart representing translation of arithmetic expression from infix form to Polish form.

Table 15-6 Illustration of the Infix to Polish Translation of the Arithmetic Expression ⊣$A*B + A*(B*D + C**E)$⊢

Current Term	Contents of Pushdown List After Term is Processed	Current Output After Term Has Been Processed	Comments
⊣	⊣;		
A	⊣;	A	Operand
∗	∗;⊣	A	Precedence ∗ > precedence ⊣
B	∗;⊣	AB	Operand
+	+;⊣	AB ∗	Precedence + < precedence ∗ Precedence + > precedence ⊣
A	+;⊣	AB ∗ A	Operand
∗	∗; +;⊣	AB ∗ A	Precedence ∗ > precedence +
(	(; ∗; +;⊣	AB ∗ A	
B	(; ∗; +;⊣	AB ∗ AB	Operand
∗	∗; (; ∗; +;⊣	AB ∗ AB	Precedence ∗ > precedence (
D	∗; (; ∗; +;⊣	AB ∗ ABD	Operand
+	+; (; ∗; +;⊣	AB ∗ ABD ∗	Precedence + < precedence ∗ Precedence + > precedence (
C	+; (; ∗; +;⊣	AB ∗ ABD ∗ C	Operand
∗∗	∗∗; +; (; ∗; +;⊣	AB ∗ ABD ∗ C	Precedence ∗∗ > precedence +
E	∗∗; +; (; ∗; +;⊣	AB ∗ ABD ∗ CE	Operand
)	∗; +;⊣	AB ∗ ABD ∗ CE ∗∗ +	Remove all operators from list. Transfer to output.
⊢		AB ∗ ABD ∗ CE ∗∗ + ∗ +	End of input expression.

then generates part of the output sequence or temporarily stores the term on the pushdown list. A flowchart representing the major steps in this translation process is given in Figure 15-5.

The steps in the operation of this translation process are illustrated in Table 15-6 where the arithmetic expression

$$\dashv A * B + A * (B * D + C ** E) \vdash$$

is transformed into Polish form.

Now that we have developed a method for translating arithmetic expressions into Polish form our next task is to develop an algorithm that can be used to transform these expressions into a sequence of intermediate object-language statements.

The Intermediate Object Language Arithmetic Operations

For the following discussion we assume that the intermediate object language has the basic operations listed in Table 15-7. These operations are assumed to be one address operations where one operand is in the accumulator (ACC) and the other operand is in location A. In most machines some of these operations will be handled as subroutines. It is assumed that the second stage of the compilation process will generate the appropriate calling sequence for each such subroutine.

Table 15-7

Basic Mathematical Operations
Allowed in Intermediate Object Language

	Operation	Mnemonic	Action of Operation
1.	Load	LDA A	$ACC \leftarrow A$
2.	Deposit	DCA A	$A \leftarrow ACC \quad ACC \leftarrow [0]$
3.	Addition	ADD A	$ACC \leftarrow ACC + A$
4.	Subtraction	SUB A	$ACC \leftarrow ACC - A$
5.	Multiplication	MUL A	$ACC \leftarrow ACC * A$
6.	Division	DIV A	$ACC \leftarrow ACC / A$
7.	Exponential	EXP A	$ACC \leftarrow ACC ** A$
8.	Unary minus	NEG	$ACC \leftarrow -ACC$

Translation of Polish Expressions to Intermediate Object Language Code

Before giving a general algorithm describing how an arithmetic expression in Polish form can be translated let us consider a specific example. The final expression obtained in Table 15-6 was

$$AB * ABD * CE ** + * +$$

Table 15-8

Intermediate Object
Language Program Resulting
from Translating the Arithmetic
Expression $AB * ABD * CE ** + * +$

LDA A
MUL B
DCA TEMP1
LDA B
MUL D
DCA TEMP2
LDA C
EXP E
ADD TEMP2
MUL A
ADD TEMP1

To transform this expression into intermediate object code we scan from left-to-right and apply the appropriate operations every time we encounter an operator. Doing this we obtain the intermediate object program given in Table 15-8.

From the above example we see that we must temporarily store portions of the expression until we need them in the processing sequence. For example, we had to remember $A*$ while we were processing the subsequence $(B * D + C ** E)$. Similarly we had to introduce temporary storage locations TEMP1 and TEMP2 into the object program to account for the storage of intermediate results as the calculations called for in the object program are being performed.

Examining this example we see that as we scan the Polish expression we must save the operands until we encounter an operator. At that point the operator is applied to the appropriate operands immediately to the left of the operator. The result of this operation is an operand that must be remembered.

From this we see that we must provide a means for storing the operands that we read and do not immediately use to generate intermediate object code. In addition we see that each operator acts on the one or two operands that are immediately to the left of the operator. Therefore we must make provisions for storing these operands in such a way that they are immediately available for processing. These requirements can be satisfied by a system that has the general organization illustrated in Figure 15-6. The terms which represent the two latest operands are temporarily stored in locations OP1 and OP2. Terms representing all of the other operands that remain to be acted upon are stored in the pushdown list.

There are three types of operand terms that will appear in these storage locations. As we scan from left-to-right along an input expression, we may encounter identifier terms that represent particular operands that must be stored until we reach the operator that acts on the term. Each time we perform an operation on two operands we generate a result that is also an operand. During the execution of the object program, this result is contained in the accumulator. To keep track of this

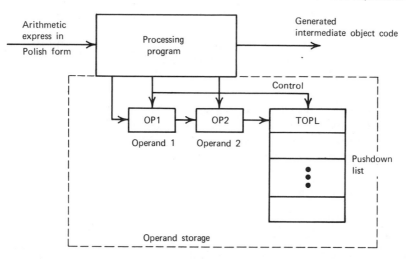

Figure 15-6. Block diagram representation of translation processes used to convert a Polish form arithmetic expression into intermediate object code.

fact during the translation process we use the special identifier ACC to indicate that the operand, which is formed by the indicated operation, is currently in the accumulator.

As we evaluate an arithmetic expression, we often find that we must evaluate several subexpressions before these subexpressions are used in the evaluation of the complete expression. During the translation process we must therefore provide for the temporary storage of these intermediate results by depositing the value of the operand corresponding to the evaluated subexpression into a temporary storage location. To do this we introduce special identifiers, that we denote by TEMPi, to indicate these special locations. The way in which these special terms are used is illustrated by the program of Table 15-8.

The particular translation operation performed by the processor program depends on the type of terms contained in the two operand storage locations OP1 and OP2 and the current input term being read by the processor program. There are two cases of interest.

The first case corresponds to the situation where the current input term is an operand. This operand is stored in OP1, and all the other operand information is pushed further down in the storage area. The three possible situations that must be accounted for and how they are handled are summarized in Part I of Table 15-9.

The second case occurs when the current input term is an operator. When this happens the processing program must generate the intermediate object language code necessary to perform the indicated operation. The different operator-operand combinations that can occur and the corresponding intermediate object language code generated by the processing program are summarized in Part II of Table 15-9. In examining this table, we see that whenever two operands are combined the result is left in the accumulator. This is indicated by placing the special

Table 15-9

Current Term	Initial Contents of OP1	Initial Contents of OP2	Form of Intermediate Object Code Generated	New Contents of OP1	New Contents of OP2	Other Action
I. Current Term An Operand						
OPRN	TERM 1	TERM 2	None	OPRN	TERM 1	TERM 2 placed on pushdown list
OPRN	ACC	TERM 2	None	OPRN	ACC	
OPRN	TERM 1	ACC	DCA TEMPi	OPRN	TERM 1	TEMPi placed on pushdown list. i increased by 1
II. Current Term An Operator						
~	TERM 1	TERM 2	LDA TERM 1 NEG	ACC	TERM 2	
~	ACC	TERM 2	NEG	ACC	TERM 2	
~	TERM 1	ACC	DCA TEMPi LDA TERM 1 NEG	ACC	TEMPi	Increase i by 1
+	TERM 1	TERM 2	LDA TERM 2 ADD TERM 1	ACC	TOPL	(a) TOPL-term that was on top
+	ACC	TERM 2	ADD TERM 2	ACC	TOPL	of pushdown list
+	TERM 1	ACC	ADD TERM 1	ACC	TOPL	(b) Any time a
−	TERM 1	TERM 2	LDA TERM 2 SUB TERM 1	ACC	TOPL	term used as operand is of
−	ACC	TERM 2	DCA TEMP Ø LDA TERM 2 SUB TEMP Ø	ACC	TOPL	form TEMPi decreased i by 1
−	TERM 1	ACC	SUB TERM 1	ACC	TOPL	
*	TERM 1	TERM 2	LDA TERM 2 MUL TERM 1	ACC	TOPL	
*	ACC	TERM 2	MUL TERM 2	ACC	TOPL	
*	TERM 1	ACC	MUL TERM 1	ACC	TOPL	
/	TERM 1	TERM 2	LDA TERM 2 DIV TERM 1	ACC	TOPL	

/	ACC		TERM 2	DCA TEMP Ø	ACC	TOPL
				LDA TERM 2		
				DIV TEMP Ø		
/	TERM 1	ACC		DIV TERM 1	ACC	TOPL
**	TERM 1	TERM 2		LDA TERM 2	ACC	TOPL
				EXP TERM 1		
**	ACC		TERM 2	DCA TEMP Ø	ACC	TOPL
				LDA TERM 2		
				EXP TEMP Ø		
**	TERM 1	ACC		EXP TERM 1	ACC	TOPL

indicator ACC in OP1. The term, TOPL, at the top of the pushdown list is then placed in OP2, and all of the other terms on the pushdown list are moved up one place.

A simplified flowchart representing the translation of an arithmetic expression in Polish form is shown in Figure 15-7. For simplicity, all the steps corresponding to the various translation tasks of Table 15-9 have been grouped together and not developed in detail. Using this flowchart and the operations indicated in Table 15-9, we can carry out the translation of any arithmetic expression in Polish form. Table 15-10 provides an illustration of how this translation process is accomplished.

The translation of arithmetic expressions in infix form into intermediate object-language code is necessary during the evaluation of a number of different types of

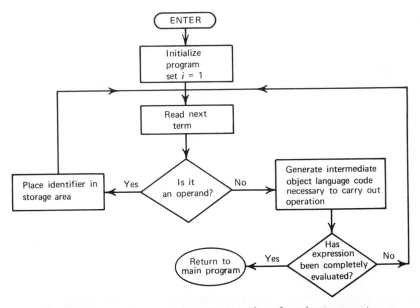

Figure 15-7. Simplified flowchart representation of routine to generate intermediate object language code associated with an arithmetic expression in Polish form.

Table 15-10 An Example of the Translation of $AB * ABD * CE ** + * +$ into Intermediate Object Language Code

Current Input	Initial Contents		Pushdown List	Generated Object Language Code	Final Contents		Pushdown List
	OP1	OP2			OP1	OP2	
A	—	—	—		A	—	—
B	A	—	—		B	A	—
*	B	A	—	LDA A MUL B	ACC	—	—
A	ACC		—		A	ACC	—
B	A	ACC	—	DCA TEMP 1	B	A	TEMP 1
D	B	A	TEMP 1		D	B	A; TEMP 1
*	D	B	A; TEMP 1	LDA B MUL D	ACC	A	TEMP 1
C	ACC	A	TEMP 1		C	ACC	A; TEMP 1
E	C	ACC	TEMP 1	DCA TEMP 2	E	C	TEMP 2; A; TEMP 1
**	E	C	TEMP 2; A; TEMP 1	LDA C EXP E	ACC	TEMP 2	A; TEMP 1
+	ACC	TEMP 2	A; TEMP 1	ADD TEMP 2	ACC	A	TEMP 1
*	ACC	A	TEMP 1	MUL A	ACC	TEMP 1	—
+	ACC	TEMP 1	—	ADD TEMP 1 END OF PROCESSING	ACC	—	—

statements. Therefore, this translation process must be accessible from a number of different points in the compiler program. In the next section, where we consider the translation of the other types of statements, we assume that whenever we encounter an arithmetic expression we go to the arithmetic translation subroutine to carry out this part of the processing. When we return from this subroutine, we assume that the generated object code represents the steps necessary to evaluate the original arithmetic expression and that the value of the expression will be in the accumulator at the end of the evaluation sequence.

EXERCISES

1. Find the Polish form for the following arithmetic expressions:

   (a) $A * B + C * D + E * F$
   (b) $(A * B - C)/(E - F) - (A - B) ** F$

2. Find the intermediate object-language code that would be generated by the translator discussed in this section for the two expressions of Exercise 1.

5. TRANSLATION OF COMPLETE STATEMENTS

In Section 4 we concentrated on one process that may be used to translate an arithmetic expression into its intermediate object-language representation. This discussion served to illustrate some of the techniques that can be used to transform a source-language program into an object program. In this section we briefly consider the operations that a compiler must perform to translate each of the different types of statements summarized in Table 15-2 into intermediate object-language form. A much more extensive discussion of compilers can be found in the references listed at the end of this chapter.

Translation of Assignment Statements

Assignment statements, which have the general form

$$\langle\text{identifier}\rangle = \langle\text{arithmetic expression}\rangle$$

are easily recognized by the = sign. The equal sign can be thought of as an operator and the algorithms presented in the last section can be modified to include the steps necessary to deposit the value calculated by the program sequence corresponding to $\langle$arithmetic expression$\rangle$ into the memory location associated with $\langle$identifier$\rangle$.

The intermediate object-language program generated when an arithmetic expression is evaluated is so arranged that the last statement in the object-language program leaves the result of the computation in the accumulator. To complete the translation of the assignment statement we must use an instruction to deposit the result into the memory location indicated by the identifier. This is easily done using the DCA instruction. For example, the assignment statement

$$X = A + B$$

would be translated into

LDA A	/Intermediate object code to
ADD B	/evaluate arithmetic expression
DCA X	/Intermediate object code to complete
	/translation of assignment statement

Translation of Functions

The evaluation of any of the system functions such as SIN (X) in a FORTRAN program is accomplished by using a standard subroutine that will be available as part of the object program. Thus whenever an initialized identifier representing a function is recognized, the subroutine linkage processor must generate the necessary sequence of intermediate object-language instructions to link the main program with the desired subroutine. The same process is used to call a user-defined function, except in this case the compiler must generate, at some point in the translation process, the object program corresponding to the subroutine.

If we assume that a function call has the general form

$$\langle \text{function name} \rangle (\langle \text{arithmetic expression} \rangle)$$

then the translation process consists of first evaluating the arithmetic expression, using the arithmetic expression translation algorithm of the previous section, and then calling the subroutine corresponding to the function specified by the function name.

For example, assume that the statement

$$X = SIN (A + B)$$

is encountered. When this statement is recognized as an assignment statement an attempt is made to translate the arithmetic expression on the right of the = sign. However, the initialized identifier SIN is recognized as the identifier for one of the standard subroutine calls. The compiler control transfers operation to the subroutine linkage processor. This processor then calls the arithmetic expression processor to process the arithmetic expression A + B. After this expression is evaluated, the subroutine linkage processor generates the necessary subroutine call and returns control to the assignment statement processor, which completes the translation sequence. The result of this processing would give us an intermediate object-language program of the following form:

$$\left. \begin{array}{l} \text{LDA A} \\ \text{ADD B} \end{array} \right\} \text{Evaluation of argument}$$

JMS SIN}Call SIN routine

DCA X}Assign value to X

If a function has more than one argument, a similar process must be followed except that a different calling sequence must be used. Suppose that we have a function of the following general form:

$$G (\langle \text{arithmetic expression 1} \rangle, \langle \text{arithmetic expression 2} \rangle)$$

This function could be translated as

$$\left\{\begin{array}{l}\text{Intermediate Object Coding}\\\text{to evaluate}\\\text{arithmetic expression 1}\end{array}\right.$$

DCA GS + 1
Intermediate Object Coding
to evaluate
arithmetic expression 2

GS, JMS G
(Value of arithmetic expression 1)
Rest of program

During the second pass, the assembler portion of the compiler program would assign the address of the instruction labeled GS and it would also generate the object machine language coding necessary to evaluate DCA GS + 1.

Any number of arguments can be handled in this general manner.

A user-defined function causes the compiler to generate a subroutine program corresponding to the statements which define that function. Thus when a statement of the form

FUNCTION PI (X)

is encountered, this tells the compiler to assemble the code for all of the statements up to the statement END as a subroutine. The compiler then assigns a location in the assembler program for this subroutine and then generates the subroutine program in the same manner as it uses to generate the main program.

Translation of Statement Numbers

Statement numbers serve the same purpose as labels in an assembler-language program. Thus the translation process associated with statement numbers is simply to attach them as labels to the sequence of intermediate object language instructions that they are used to label. For example, the statements

10   X = A + B
12   Y = A * B

would be translated into the sequence

10, LDA A
ADD B
DCA X
12, LDA A
MUL B
DCA Y

From this we see that the translation process associated with a statement number is simply to prefix each number with a # and to follow it by a ",". These two terms serve to mark the number as a label so that it will be handled properly by the assembler portion of the compiler program. Several different techniques can, of course, be used to mark statement numbers.

Translation of *GO TO* and *IF* Statements

GO TO and IF statements can easily be translated. The statement

$$\text{GO TO N}$$

where N is a statement number, is translated into the intermediate object language statement

$$\text{JMP } \#\text{N}$$

The IF statement is a little more complex to handle. A typical IF statement has the form

$$\text{IF } (\langle\text{arithmetic expression}\rangle) \text{ N}_1, \text{ N}_2, \text{ N}_3$$

where N_1, N_2, and N_3 are statement numbers.

The IF statement, which is recognized by detecting the key word IF, is translated by the IF statement processor in a sequence of steps. First, the processor calls on the arithmetic expression translator to generate the intermediate object-language program necessary to evaluate the arithmetic expression contained in the parentheses. The execution of this program sequence leaves the result in the accumulator. Thus the translation of the IF statement is completed by generating the instructions to test the contents of the accumulator and jump to the proper statement number as a result of this test. To illustrate the process consider the statement

$$\text{IF } (A + B - C) \ 16, 20, 32$$

This would produce the following intermediate object language program:

```
LDA A       /EVALUATE ARITHMETIC
ADD B       /EXPRESSION
SUB C
SMA!SZA     /IS THE ACCUMULATOR POSITIVE?
JMP #32     /YES
SZA         /NO. IS IT ZERO?
JMP #16     /NO
JMP #20     /YES
```

Translation of *DO* Statements

A typical DO statement has the form

$$DO \ N \ I = M_1, M_2, M_3$$

where N is a statement number and I is an identifier that represents an integer index variable that will be incremented from M_1 to M_2 in steps of size M_3. When a DO statement is used in a source program, the program has the following general form:

$$DO \ N \ I = M_1, M_2, M_3$$
$$\begin{cases} \text{Program segment} \\ \text{associated with} \\ \text{DO statement} \end{cases}$$
$$N \ \langle \text{statement} \rangle \begin{cases} \text{last statement} \\ \text{of DO loop} \end{cases}$$

The problem with implementing the DO statement is that the resulting intermediate object language program will have the following form:

```
            LDA M1          /SET UP I
            DCA I
    DST,
          ⎧ BODY           /THIS PART OF PROGRAM
          ⎪ OF PROGRAM     /IS GENERATED IN THE
          ⎨ INVOLVED       /NORMAL MANNER. THE LAST
          ⎪ IN DO          /STATEMENT IN THE SEQUENCE
          ⎩ LOOP           /HAS STATEMENT NUMBER N.

            LAD I           /INCREMENT THE
            ADD M3          /CURRENT VALUE
            DCA I           /OF I
            LDA M2          /CHECK IF
            SUB I           /END OF LOOP
            SMA             /IS I > M2?
            JMP DST         /NO CONTINUE LOOP
                            /YES
          ⎧ PROGRAM
          ⎪ STATEMENTS
          ⎨ FOLLOWING
          ⎩ LOOP
```

In examining this program, we see that in FORTRAN we must always execute the body of a loop at least once before we exit.

From this discussion we see that we cannot generate all of the intermediate object-language code for a DO loop at the time we are processing the DO statement. We must remember enough information about the DO statement so that the intermediate object-language code sequence which follows statement N can be generated after we complete the translation of this statement. This problem can be handled in a number of ways. All of these techniques essentially provide for the temporary storage of the end portion of the DO statement coding until the appropriate conditions are reached for its insertion.

The following example illustrates the type of intermediate language object program that would result from translating a segment of a source-language program that contains a DO loop. Consider the following program segment.

$$\text{DO 10} \quad I = K1, KM, KD$$
$$X = A + Y$$
$$10 \quad Y = A * X$$
$$Z = A + B$$

The resulting code would be:

```
         LDA K1      /SET UP
         DCA I       /VALUE OF I
DST,     LDA A       /FIRST STATEMENT
         ADD Y       /IN
         DCA X       /LOOP
#10,     LDA A       /ASSEMBLER LANGUAGE
         MUL X       /PROGRAM FOR STATEMENT
         DCA Y       /NUMBER 10
         LDA I       /INCREMENT VALUE
         ADD KD      /OF I
         DCA I
         LDA KM      /TEST FOR
         SUB I       /END OF
         SMA         /LOOP. I > KM?
         JMP DST     /NO. CONTINUE
         LDA A       /FIRST STATEMENT
         ADD B       /AFTER
         DCA Z       /LOOP
```

Processing of Compiler Directives

Compiler directives such as STOP and END are directions to the compiler to carry our certain tasks associated with the compiling process. The STOP statement generates the sequence of assembler statements necessary to stop the machine-language program and return control of the computer to the computer's general operating system while the END statement tells the compiler that it has reached the end of the source-language program and does not lead to the generation of any assembler-language code.

DIMENSION statements are used to inform the compiler that it must reserve the indicated number of memory locations to store an array of data. For example, the statement

DIMENSION A(10), B(20)

would tell the compiler to reserve ten memory locations for the ten data items that make up the array A and 20 memory locations for the 20 data items that make up the array B. This reservation of storage space is accomplished by entering the indicated information into the master symbol table of the compiler.

Translation of Input/Output Statements

The details of the input/output transfer of information to and from a computer involve very specialized programming techniques that are particular to a given computer and the device that is under consideration. Usually a set of subroutines are available for each computer which are set up to handle the given information transfer task. The translation process then consists of transforming the information contained in the READ or WRITE statements and the appropriate FORMAT statement into a calling sequence for the subroutine that is used to carry out the indicated information transfer. This calling sequence must indicate the type of information to be transferred, the form that it will take, and the location where it will be stored in memory. Because of the complexities and special programming problems involved, no attempt will be made in this discussion to present the inter-mediate object-language programming sequence necessary to translate input/output statements.

EXERCISES

1. Give the intermediate object language program that would be generated for each of the following statements.

   (a) $X = A * B + C * D + E * F/G ** H$
   (b)   IF (SIN(X) − Y) 20, 30, 40
   (c)   GO TO 20

2. Give the intermediate object language program that would be generated for the following source language program segment.

$$
\begin{aligned}
&K = 0 \\
&J = 1 \\
&\text{DO } 20 \text{ I} = 10, 20, 2 \\
&K = I + K \\
20 \quad &J = I * J \\
&IA = J + K
\end{aligned}
$$

6. SUMMARY

In this chapter we have briefly considered the problem of how a source-language program written in a higher level programming language can be translated into an object program that can be executed on a computer. Since our main interest was in obtaining an insight into the problems associated with these languages, no attempt has been made to present a complete language or to discuss all of the problems involved in designing a given language to handle a class of problems.

One of the reasons that we took this approach is that the development of programming languages and compilers for these languages is, at present a combination of an art and a science. The references at the end of this chapter present many of the details about the properties of artificial languages and the translator programs associated with these languages.

REFERENCE NOTATION

Many books on compiler design have recently been published. Reference [4] is a collection of many of the important papers that first presented a number of the ideas currently used in designing compilers. References [1], [3], and [8] discuss various aspects of the design of compilers while [2] and [7] give a general discussion of some of the theoretical principles behind the design of compilers. Sammet [5] and [6] discusses the basic properties of more than 120 programming languages.

REFERENCES

1. Aho, A. V., and Ullman, J. D. (1972, 1973), *The Theory of Parsing Translation and Compiling, Vol. 1 Parsing, Vol. 2 Compiling*, Prentice-Hall, Englewood Cliffs, N.J.

2. Aho, A. V. (1976), *Language Theory in Compiler Design In Applied Computation Theory: Analysis, Design, Modeling* (Yeh R. T., ed.), Prentice-Hall, Englewood Cliffs, N.J.

3. Gries, D. (1971), *Compiler Construction for Digital Computers*, John Wiley, New York.

4. Rosen, S. (ed.) (1967), *Programming Systems and Languages*, McGraw-Hill, New York.

5. Sammet, J. E. (1969), *Programming Languages: History and Fundamentals*, Prentice-Hall, Englewood Cliffs, N.J.

6. Sammet, J. E. (1976), "Roster of Programming Languages for 1974–75," Communication of the ACM, Vol. 19, No. 12, December.

7. Wegner, P. (1968), *Programming Languages Structures and Machine Organization*, McGraw-Hill, New York.

8. Wulf, W., Johnson, R. K., Weinstock, C. B., Hobbs, S. O., and Geschke, C. M. (1975), *The Design of an Optimizing Compiler*, American Elsevier Company, New York.

HOME PROBLEMS

1. Write an assembler-language subroutine for SEDCOM that simulates a push-down list. The quantity to be placed on the list is assumed to be in the accumulator and any item read from the list is assumed placed into the accumulator.

2. The Polish string representation of arithmetic expressions presented in this chapter is also referred to as *postfix notation* since each operator follows the operands that it is applied to. An arithmetic expression can also be expressed in *reverse Polish* or *prefix notation* where each operator precedes the operands that it is applied to.

   (a) Show that any arithmetic expression can be represented, unambiguously, in prefix form without the use of parentheses.
   (b) Give an algorithm that can be used to convert an arithmetic expression in infix form to an expression in prefix form.

3. Design a simple programming language that can be used to evaluate logical expressions.

4. Show all of the steps necessary to translate the following statement into intermediate object-language code.

$$T = B * C ** D - (A * B - C)$$

5. In most programming languages a provision is made for subscripted variables. For example in FORTRAN A(I) is used to indicate a variable with a single subscript. How might a compiler translate the following sequence of instructions:

$$X = 0$$
$$DO\ 5\ I = 1,\ 10$$
$$5 \quad X = X + A(I)$$

that are used to compute

$$X = \sum_{i=1}^{10} a_i$$

APPENDIX 1

Binary Codes for Character Representation

Standard binary codes have been developed to represent alphanumeric and special characters within a computer. Two such codes are the EBCDIC (Extended Binary Coded Decimal Interchange Code) code and the ASCII (American Standard Code for Information Interchange).

The EBCDIC code, which is an eight-bit binary code, is given in column one of the following table. This code is used extensively in IBM computer systems.

The ASCII code appears in a number of variations. The standard code is a seven-bit binary code. However in many computer applications a modified eight-bit code is used. In particular, the modified ASCII code given in column two of the following table is used extensively in minicomputer systems that use Teletypes or similar keyboard devices as the basic input terminal. This modified code adds a 1 as the leftmost bit to each code word. The standard ASCII code can be obtained from the following table by simply eliminating the leftmost bit from the given modified code. For example, the modified ASCII code for A is 11000001. Dropping the leftmost bit gives the standard ASCII code for A, which is 1000001.

	Character	EBCDIC representation	Modified ASCII representation
	Blank	0100 0000	1010 0000
.	Period, decimal point	0100 1011	1010 1110
<	Less than	0100 1100	1011 1100
(	Left parenthesis	0100 1101	1010 1000
+	Plus sign	0100 1110	1010 1011
|	Logical OR	0100 1111	
&	Ampersand	0101 0000	1010 0110
$	Dollar sign	0101 1011	1010 0100
*	Asterisk, multiplication	0101 1100	1010 1010
)	Right parenthesis	0101 1101	1010 1001
;	Semicolon	0101 1110	1011 1011
¬	Logical NOT	0101 1111	
−	Minus, hyphen	0110 0000	1010 1101
/	Slash, division	0110 0001	1010 1111
,	Comma	0110 1011	1010 1101
%	Percent	0110 1100	1010 0101
_	Underscore	0110 1101	
>	Greater than	0110 1110	1011 1110
?	Question mark	0110 1111	1011 1111
:	Colon	0111 1010	1011 1010
#	Number sign	0111 1011	1010 0011
@	At sign	0111 1100	1100 0000
'	Prime, apostrophe	0111 1101	1010 0111
=	Equal sign	0111 1110	1011 1101
"	Quotation mark	0111 1111	1010 0010

Character	EBCDIC representation	Modified ASCII representation
A	1100 0001	1100 0001
B	1100 0010	1100 0010
C	1100 0011	1100 0011
D	1100 0100	1100 0100
E	1100 0101	1100 0101
F	1100 0110	1100 0110
G	1100 0111	1100 0111
H	1100 1000	1100 1000
I	1100 1001	1100 1001
J	1101 0001	1100 1010
K	1101 0010	1100 1011
L	1101 0011	1100 1100
M	1101 0100	1100 1101
N	1101 0101	1100 1110
O	1101 0110	1100 1111
P	1101 0111	1101 0000
Q	1101 1000	1101 0001
R	1101 1001	1101 0010
S	1110 0010	1101 0011
T	1110 0011	1101 0100
U	1110 0100	1101 0101
V	1110 0101	1101 0110
W	1110 0110	1101 0111
X	1110 0111	1101 1000
Y	1110 1000	1101 1001
Z	1110 1001	1101 1010

Character	EBCDIC representation	Modified ASCII representation
0	1111 0000	1011 0000
1	1111 0001	1011 0001
2	1111 0010	1011 0010
3	1111 0011	1011 0011
4	1111 0100	1011 0100
5	1111 0101	1011 0101
6	1111 0110	1011 0110
7	1111 0111	1011 0111
8	1111 1000	1011 1000
9	1111 1001	1011 1001

APPENDIX 2

Answers to Selected Exercises

CHAPTER 2

Section 3

1. Add   001   Subtract 011   Clear 111
Multiply 010   Divide   100

2. $14.62_8 \equiv 1100.11001_2$
$123.61_{10} \equiv 1111011.1001110\ldots_2$
$A1B.F12_{16} \equiv 101000011011.111100010010_2$

3. BCD value of $145.64_{10} = 0001\quad 0100\quad 0101\quad .\quad 0110\quad 0100$

4. $14.65_{10} \equiv 16.5146\ldots_8$
$\equiv E.A666\ldots_{16}$
$1568.721_{10} \equiv 3040.5611\ldots_8$
$\equiv 620.B89\ldots_{16}$

5. $10110101_2 \equiv 11101111_{\text{Gray}}$
$1111111_2 \equiv 1000000_{\text{Gray}}$

6. (a) $.10110110\quad 2^{101}$
(b) $.10110\quad 2^{-110}$
(c) $.1\quad 2^{1101}$

7. (a) .00000000000101101
(b) 101101
(c) 1111100000

8.

$r = 2$	$m = 10$	$r = 5$	$m = 5$	$r = 16$	$m = 3$
$r = 3$	$m = 7$	$r = 8$	$m = 4$		
$r = 4$	$m = 5$	$r = 10$	$m = 4$		

Section 4

1. Resolution $= (\tfrac{1}{2})^8 = .00390625$
Range $= \pm 15.99609375$

	v			
	0	1	3	5
100100	-4	-2.0	$-.5$	$-.125$
110101	-21	-10.5	-2.625	$-.65625$
001010	$+10$	$+5.0$	$+1.25$	$+.3125$

Section 5

1. 10

2.

n	$.5 \cos(n\omega)$	$X = [b_s \cdot b_{-1} b_{-2} b_{-3} b_{-4} b_{-5}]$
0	.50000	010000
1	.49240	010000
2	.46984	001111
3	.43301	001110
4	.38302	001100

CHAPTER 3

Section 2

1. (a)

x_1	x_2	$x_1 \downarrow x_2$	$(\overline{x_1 \vee x_2})$	$\bar{x}_1 \bar{x}_2$
0	0	1	1	1
0	1	0	0	0
1	0	0	0	0
1	1	0	0	0

(c)

x_1	x_2	$x_1 \wedge x_2$	$\overline{((\overline{x_1 x_2})(\overline{x_1 x_2}))}$
0	0	0	0
0	1	0	0
1	0	0	0
1	1	1	1

2.

x_1	x_2	x_3	x_4	$f(x_1, x_2, x_3, x_4)$	$g(x_1, x_2, x_3, x_4)$
0	0	0	0	1	1
0	0	0	1	0	0
0	0	1	0	1	1
0	0	1	1	1	1
0	1	0	0	0	0
0	1	0	1	0	0
0	1	1	0	1	1
0	1	1	1	1	1
1	0	0	0	1	1
1	0	0	1	1	1
1	0	1	0	1	1
1	0	1	1	1	1
1	1	0	0	1	1
1	1	0	1	1	1
1	1	1	0	1	1
1	1	1	1	1	1

3.

x_1	x_2	x_3	$g(x_1, x_2)$	$f(x_2, x_3)$	$m(x_1, x_2, x_3)$
0	0	0	0	1	0
0	0	1	0	1	0
0	1	0	0	1	0
0	1	1	0	0	1
1	0	0	0	1	0
1	0	1	0	1	0
1	1	0	0	1	0
1	1	1	0	0	1

Section 3

1. $m_0 = \bar{x}_1 \bar{x}_2 \bar{x}_3 \bar{x}_4, \qquad m_{13} = x_1 x_2 \bar{x}_3 x_4$

$M_0 = x_1 \vee x_2 \vee x_3 \vee x_4, \qquad M_{13} = \bar{x}_1 \vee \bar{x}_2 \vee x_3 \vee \bar{x}_4$

2. $f(x_1, x_2, x_3, x_4) = m_0 \vee m_1 \vee m_4 \vee m_6 \vee m_7 \vee m_{11} \vee m_{13} \vee m_{14}$

$= M_2 \wedge M_3 \wedge M_5 \wedge M_8 \wedge M_9 \wedge M_{10} \wedge M_{12} \wedge M_{15}$

3. (a) $x_1 \uparrow x_2 = m_0 \vee m_1 \vee m_2 = M_3$

(c) $x_1 \oplus x_2 = m_1 \vee m_2 = M_0 \wedge M_4$

Section 4

1.

Gray Code			Binary Equivalent		
x_1	x_2	x_3	y_1	y_2	y_3
0	0	0	0	0	0
0	0	1	0	0	1
0	1	0	0	1	1
0	1	1	0	1	0
1	0	0	1	1	1
1	0	1	1	1	0
1	1	0	1	0	0
1	1	1	1	0	1

$$y_1 = m_4 \vee m_5 \vee m_6 \vee m_7$$
$$y_2 = m_2 \vee m_3 \vee m_4 \vee m_5$$
$$y_3 = m_1 \vee m_2 \vee m_4 \vee m_7$$

2.

i_1	i_2	Operation
0	0	$\overline{A \wedge B}$
0	1	$\overline{A \vee B}$
1	0	$A \vee B$
1	1	$A\bar{B} \vee \bar{A}B$

A_k	B_k	i_1	i_2	$f(A_k, B_k, x_1, x_2)$
0	0	0	0	1
0	0	0	1	1
0	0	1	0	0
0	0	1	1	0
0	1	0	0	1
0	1	0	1	0
0	1	1	0	1
0	1	1	1	1
1	0	0	0	1
1	0	0	1	0
1	0	1	0	1
1	0	1	1	1
1	1	0	0	0
1	1	0	1	0
1	1	1	0	1
1	1	1	1	0

$$f(A_k, B_k, x_1, x_2) = M_2 \wedge M_3 \wedge M_5 \wedge M_9 \wedge M_{12} \wedge M_{13} \wedge M_{15}$$

CHAPTER 4

Section 3

1. (a) $Z := [0, 1, 0]$
   (b) $Z := [1, 0, 0]$
   (c) $Z := [1, 1, 1]$

2. (a) $Z := [11010001]$
   (b) $Z := [00000001]$
   (c) $Z := [11111100]$

3. $Z := (\bar{t}_1 \bar{t}_2 \wedge (A)) \vee (\bar{t}_1 t_2 \wedge (\bar{A} \vee \bar{B})) \vee (t_1 \bar{t}_2 \wedge (A \oplus C))$
    $\vee (t_1 t_2 \wedge ((A \downarrow B) \oplus C))$

Section 4

1. (a) 2's 101010.01   1's 101010.00
   (b) 3's 2101.12   2's 2101.11
   (c) 8's 5056.15   7's 5056.14
   (d) 16's F59CEB   15's F59CEA

2. (a) 10.01101
   (b) 112.22
   (c) 8's 70777003
        7's 70777002 $= -70007.75$

Section 5

1. $', *, +, -, /, <, =, ?$

2. The network N has input a_i, b_i, d_{i-1}

$$d_i = \bar{a}_i \bar{b}_i d_{i-1} \vee \bar{a}_i b_i \bar{d}_{i-1} \vee \bar{a}_i b_i d_{i-1} \vee a_i b_i d_{i-1}$$

The input to the rightmost subnetwork must be 1. Note similarily to test for $A < B$.

3. $Z := ((T = [0]) \wedge X0) \vee ((T = [1]) \wedge X1) \vee ((T = [2]) \wedge X2)$
    $\vee ((T = [3]) \wedge X3)$

CHAPTER 5

Section 2
1.

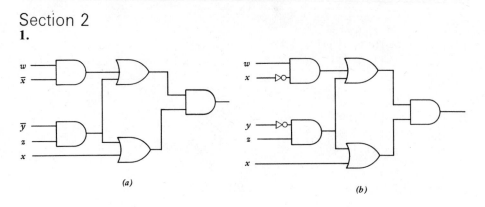

(a)   (b)

Section 3
1. (a) NAND   (b) NOR

2. $1.25

Section 5
$f(A, B, C) := (BC \vee \bar{B}A)A \vee \bar{C}$

CHAPTER 6

Section 2
2. (a) $(\overline{x_1 x_2 \vee \bar{x}_1 \bar{x}_2}) = (\overline{x_1 x_2})(\overline{\bar{x}_1 \bar{x}_2})$

$\qquad\qquad = (\bar{x}_1 \vee \bar{x}_2)(x_1 \vee x_2) = \bar{x}_1 x_2 \vee \bar{x}_2 x_1$

(c) $x_2 \bar{x}_3 \vee x_2 x_3 \vee x_1 \bar{x}_3 \vee x_1 x_3 \vee \bar{x}_1 x_2 \vee x_1 x_2 = x_2 \vee x_1 = (\overline{\bar{x}_1 \bar{x}_2})$

3. (a) $(x_1 x_2)(\bar{x}_1 \bar{x}_3) = (\bar{x}_1 \vee \bar{x}_2)(x_1 \vee x_3)$

$\qquad\qquad = (\bar{x}_1 \vee \bar{x}_2 \vee x_3 \bar{x}_3)(x_1 \vee x_2 \bar{x}_2 \vee x_3)$

$\qquad\qquad = (\bar{x}_1 \vee \bar{x}_2 \vee x_3)(\bar{x}_1 \vee \bar{x}_2 \vee \bar{x}_3)(x_1 \vee x_2 \vee x_3)$

$\qquad\qquad \wedge (x_1 \vee \bar{x}_2 \vee x_3)$

$\qquad\qquad = M_6 M_7 M_0 M_2$

$\qquad\qquad = m_1 \vee m_3 \vee m_4 \vee m_5$

(b) $m_2 \vee m_3 \vee m_4 \vee m_6$

(c) $m_5 \vee m_6$

Section 3

1.

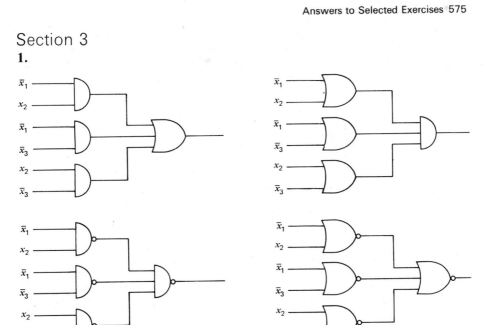

2.

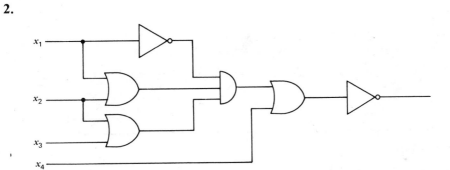

Section 4

1. Input $\quad x_1, x_2, x_3$

Output

y_1	y_2	
0	0	red light
0	1	green light
1	0	yellow light

$$y_1 = x_1 \bar{x}_2 \bar{x}_3$$
$$y_2 = \bar{x}_1$$

CHAPTER 7

Section 2

1. (a) $f(x_1, x_2, x_3) = \bar{x}_1\bar{x}_2 \vee \bar{x}_1 x_3 \vee x_1 x_2$ or $\bar{x}_1\bar{x}_2 \vee x_2 x_3 \vee x_1 x_2$

$$= (x_1 \vee \bar{x}_2 \vee x_3)(\bar{x}_1 \vee x_2)$$

(b) $g(x_1, x_2, x_3) = \bar{x}_2$

(c) $h(x_1, x_2, x_3, x_4) = \bar{x}_3\bar{x}_4 \vee x_1\bar{x}_2 \vee \bar{x}_2\bar{x}_4$

$$= (\bar{x}_2 \vee \bar{x}_3)(x_1 \vee \bar{x}_4)$$

2. Prime implicants of Figure 7-8

    (I) $\bar{x}_1\bar{x}_2\bar{x}_3\bar{x}_4$ (II) $\bar{x}_1\bar{x}_3$

         $\bar{x}_1 x_2 x_3$ $x_1 x_3$

         $x_1\bar{x}_2 x_3$ $x_1 x_2$

         $x_2 x_4$ $x_2\bar{x}_3$

         $x_3 x_4$

Section 3

1. (a) $\bar{x}_2\bar{x}_3 \vee \bar{x}_1 x_2 \vee x_2 x_3$ or $\bar{x}_2\bar{x}_3 \vee \bar{x}_1\bar{x}_3 \vee x_2 x_3$

(b) $\bar{x}_1\bar{x}_2\bar{x}_5 \vee \bar{x}_1\bar{x}_4\bar{x}_5 \vee \bar{x}_2\bar{x}_3\bar{x}_4\bar{x}_5 \vee x_1\bar{x}_2\bar{x}_3 x_4 x_5 \vee x_1 x_2 x_3\bar{x}_4 x_5$

$$\vee\ x_1 x_2 x_3 x_4\bar{x}_5$$

Section 4

4. $f_1(x_1, x_2, x_3, x_4) = \bar{x}_1\bar{x}_2\bar{x}_4 \vee x_2 x_3\bar{x}_4 \vee x_2\bar{x}_3 x_4$

$f_2(x_1, x_2, x_3, x_4) = \bar{x}_2\bar{x}_3\bar{x}_4 \vee x_1 x_2 x_4 \vee x_2\bar{x}_3 x_4$

$f_3(x_1, x_2, x_3, x_4) = x_1\bar{x}_3\bar{x}_4 \vee \bar{x}_1\bar{x}_2 x_3 x_4 \vee \bar{x}_2\bar{x}_3\bar{x}_4$

CHAPTER 8

Section 2

1. $X := [x_1, x_2, x_3]$

$S_1 = m_1 \vee m_2 \vee m_4 \vee m_7 = J_1$

$R_1 = m_0 \vee m_3 \vee m_5 \vee m_6 = K_1$

$D = S_1$

2. (a) *S-R* flip-flop

(b)

$x(t)$	$y(t)$	$y(t + \tau)$
0	0	0
0	1	0
1	0	1
1	1	0

Section 3

1. Repeat the following transfer r times for an r-bit register

$$\tau: X \leftarrow SR(X), \ A \leftarrow SR(X_1, A)$$

2. T is a 1-bit signal

$D_i = \bar{t}\bar{a}_i \vee ta_i$

D_i is the input to the ith bit of the B register

Section 4

$X \leftarrow f_1 g_1 X \vee f_2 g_1 Y \vee f_3 g_1 Z$

$A \leftarrow f_1 g_2 X \vee f_2 g_2 Y \vee f_3 g_2 Z$

$B \leftarrow f_1 g_3 X \vee f_2 g_3 Y \vee f_3 g_3 Z$

Section 6

1. $A \leftarrow ((T = [0])(\bar{A})) \vee ((T = [1])(A \vee X)) \vee ((T = [2])(B \wedge X))$
$\vee ((T = [3])(X))$

2. $D_i = \bar{t}_1 \bar{t}_2 \bar{a}_i \vee \bar{t}_1 t_2 (a_i \vee x_i) \vee t_1 \bar{t}_2 (b_i \wedge x_i) \vee (t_1 t_2 x_i)$

CHAPTER 9

Section 2

1.

$[y_1 y_2]$ $\quad^x$	0	1
$[0, 0]$	$[1, 0]/[1, 1]$	$[1, 1]/[0, 0]$
$[0, 1]$	$[0, 0]/[1, 1]$	$[0, 1]/[0, 0]$
$[1, 0]$	$[1, 0]/[0, 1]$	$[1, 0]/[1, 0]$
$[1, 1]$	$[0, 0]/[0, 1]$	$[1, 1]/[1, 0]$

2. (a) $[0,0] \xrightarrow{1} [1,1] \xrightarrow{0} [0,0] \xrightarrow{1} [1,1] \xrightarrow{1} [1,1] \xrightarrow{0} [0,0] \xrightarrow{1} [1,1] \xrightarrow{0} [0,0]$ state
                                                                    sequence

    $[0,0]$ $[0,1]$ $[0,0]$ $[1,0]$ $[0,1]$ $[0,0]$ $[0,1]$ output
                                                                        sequence

(b) $[1,0] \xrightarrow{1} [1,0] \xrightarrow{0} \cdots$ all transitions   state sequence
        $[1,0]$ $[0,1] \cdots$ etc.   output sequence

Section 3

1. (a) $S_1 = \bar{y}_1 \bar{y}_2 x \vee y_2 \bar{x}$ $S_2 = \bar{y}_1 \bar{y}_2 \bar{x} \vee y_1 x$
         $R_1 = y_1$ $R_2 = y_2$

(b) $D_1 = \bar{y}_1 \bar{y}_2 x \vee y_2 \bar{x}$
        $D_2 = \bar{y}_1 \bar{y}_2 \bar{x} \vee y_1 x$

(c) $J_1 = y_2 \bar{x} \lor \bar{y}_2 x$ $J_2 = \bar{y}_1 \bar{x} \lor y_1 x$
     $K_1 = 1$ $K_2 = 1$

2. All have the same number of logic elements.

Section 4

1. Let $[y_1, y_2, y_3]$ be the contents of the counter register.

$J_1 = y_2 y_3$ $J_2 = y_3$ $J_3 = 1$
$K_1 = y_2 y_3$ $K_2 = y_3$ $K_3 = 1$

2.

State \ Input	0	1
q_0	q_1	q_3
q_1	q_2	q_0
q_2	q_3	q_1
q_3	q_0	q_2

3. Let $q_0 = [0, 0]$, $q_1 = [0, 1]$, $q_2 = [1, 0]$, $q_3 = [1, 1]$
   in general $q = [y_1, y_2]$, $i =$ input
   $J_1 = y_2 \bar{i} \lor \bar{y}_2 i$
   $K_1 = y_2 \bar{i} \lor \bar{y}_2 i$
   $J_2 = 1$
   $K_2 = 1$

CHAPTER 10

Section 2

1. .0999 sec/character. Thus 99.9% of the time is spent waiting for a character.
2. See the discussion of serial transfer in Chapter 8.

Section 3

2. (a) $5.128 \, 10^4$
   (b) 5.128 kHz

Section 4

1. Core 11

CHAPTER 11

Section 2

1. (a) $A \leftarrow ((T = t_0) \vee (T = t_4))A \vee ((T = t_1) \vee (T = t_2))X \vee (T = t_3)Y$
$B \leftarrow ((T = t_0) \vee (T = t_1) \vee (T = t_4))B \vee ((T = t_2) \vee (T = t_3))X$
$C \leftarrow ((T = t_0) \vee (T = t_3))C \vee ((T = t_1) \vee (T = t_2))Y \vee (T = t_4)X$

(b) $B \leftarrow (T = t_0)B \vee (T = t_1)(X + A) \vee (T = t_2)(X - A) \vee (T = t_3)X$

2.

$A \leftarrow (T = t_0)A \vee (T = t_1)(X + A) \vee (T = t_2)X$
$B \leftarrow (T = t_0)B \vee (T = t_1)A \vee (T = t_2)(A + B) \vee (T = t_3)X$
$S: = (A = B)s_1 \vee (A < B)s_2 \vee (A > B)s_3$

Section 4

2. Drill hole 1
(a) 00100000
00010101
(b) 01000000
00010101
(c) 10000010
(d) 01100000
01010000
(e) 10100000
etc.

CHAPTER 12

Section 2

1. (a) Read. The memory word $M_{[MAR]}$ will not be cleared at τ_2 thus it does not have to be rewritten at τ_3.

(b) Write. The old information does not have to be cleared at τ_2.

Section 3

1. $2^{10} = 1024$. Thus a word size of at least 14 bits is needed.

Section 4

1. (a) [PC][151]   (b) [PC][151]
[AC][0224]   [AC][2220]
(c) [PC][151]   (d) [PC][152]
[AC][0144]

2. 7360

3. The letter E will be printed by the printer.

CHAPTER 13

Section 2

3. (a) 6 microseconds
(b) 16666 executions

Section 3

2.

Address	Instruction or Content	Mnemonic	Comment
010	7200	CLA	/CLEAR ACCUMULATOR
011	1026	TAD 26	/GET − 5
012	3030	DCA 30	/DEPOSIT IN COUNTER
013	1027	TAD 27	/GET POINTER
014	3031	DCA 31	/DEPOSIT POINTER
015	7200	CLA	/CLEAR ACCUMULATOR
016	1431	TAD I 31	/GET LETTER
017	6041	CPF	/PRINTER READY?
020	5017	JMP 17	/NO
021	6046	SPD	/YES. PRINT LETTER
022	2031	ISZ 31	/INCREMENT POINTER
023	2030	ISZ 30	/INCREMENT COUNTER
024	5015	JMP 15	/REPEAT LOOP
025	7402	HLT	/END OF PROGRAM
026	7773		/− 5
027	0100		/ADDRESS OF FIRST /LETTER
030	(counter)		
031	(pointer)		
100	0310		/H
101	0305		/E
102	0314		/L
103	0314		/L
104	0317		/O

Section 4

1. This subroutine must first form the 2's complement of A and then add the result to B. The double-precision addition routine can be used for addition except that the overflow condition must be changed.

The formation of the 2's complement requires particular care. The 1 is added only to the word corresponding to the lowest order digits. A carry, if present, must however be propagated to the word containing the higher order digits.

2. The simplest, but not the most elegant method of multiplying two signed numbers is to first determine the sign of the result and then convert all negative numbers to positive numbers. Multiplication is then carried out on the positive numbers and the result is adjusted to have the proper sign.

Section 6
1.

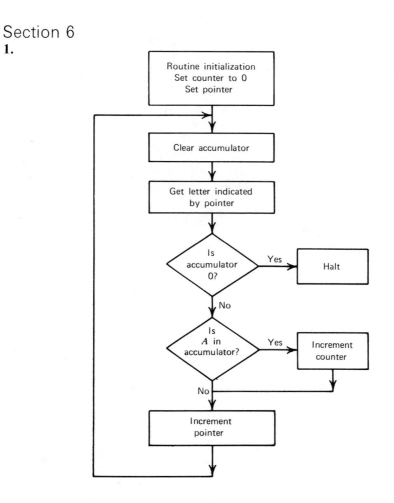

Section 2

1. ORG 10

```
        CLA
        TAD   VCNT    /SET COUNTER
        DCA   CNT     /TO −100 (BASE 8)
        DCA   NCNT    /SET NUMBER COUNTER TO 0
        TAD   VPNT    /SET POINTER
        DCA   PNT
        TAD   N       /GET N
        CMA           /FORM −N
        IAC
        DCA   MN      /STORE −N
BEGN,   TAD I PNT     /GET NUMBER .
        TAD   MN      /COMPARE TO N
        SZA           /DOES IT COMPARE?
        JMP   NXT     /NO
        ISZ   NCNT    /YES. INCREASE COUNT
NXT,    CLA
        ISZ   PNT     /INCREMENT POINTER
        ISZ   CNT     /FINISHED?
        JMP   BEGN    /NO
        HLT           /YES
VCNT,   −100
VPNT,    100
CNT,       0
NCNT,      0
PNT,       0
MN,        0
        ORG 70
N,         0          /CONTENTS TO BE SPECIFIED
        END
```

Section 3

1. Symbol Table

STRT	11
BOB	103
TOM	104
SRT	Marker
STR	Marker

Error Messages
STRT   Defined twice
SRT   Undefined address
STR   Undefined address
CLM   Undefined command

2. (a) Disregard—comment

(b) First pass   JOHN   entered in symbol table with value 100.

JOE   entered in symbol table and marked if it is not already there. Otherwise it is ignored.

Second pass   Assembled   JMP 5000

I   0400

JOE <u>0050</u>

5450

(c) First pass   1000   and I are passed over.

JOE   entered in symbol table and marked if it is not already there. Otherwise, it is ignored.

Second pass   Assembled   1000   1000

I   0400

JOE   <u>0050</u>

1450

(d) First pass   No action

Second pass   Assembled

AND 0000

100   <u>0100</u>

0100

Section 4

1. (a) CLA   (b) 0
CPF   TAD I .−1
JMP .−2   ISZ .−2
SZA   DCA .+7
HLT   TAD .+7
DCA .+7
TAD .+4
ISZ .+5
JMP .−2
JMS I .−11
0000
7700
0000

2. Address   Contents

     010   1015
     011   1016
     012   1017
     013   7540
     014   7402
     015   0076
     016   0200
     017   0400

3. MACRO   TWNF X, Y, N
                  CLA
                  TAD X
                  TAD N
                  DCA Y
                  FINISH

CHAPTER 15

Section 2

2. (a)   GO TO   JMP statement

     (b)   IF set up a test sequence by first calculating the expression and then testing the value to see if it is positive, zero or negative.

Section 4

1. (a)   AB * CD * + EF * +

     (b)   AB * C − EF − /AB − F ** −

2. (a)   LDA A   (b)   LDA A

(a)	(b)
LDA A	LDA A
MUL B	MUL B
DCA TEMP1	SUB C
LDA C	DCA TEMP1
MUL D	LDA E
ADD TEMP1	SUB F
DCA TEMP1	DCA TEMP∅
LDA E	LDA TEMP1
MUL F	DIV TEMP∅
ADD TEMP1	DCA TEMP1
	LDA A
	SUB B
	EXP F
	SUB TEMP1

Section 5

1. (b) LDA X   (c) JMP #20
       JMS SIN
       SUB Y
       SMA!SZA
       JMP #40
       SZA
       JMP #20
       JMP #30

2.   LDA N10
            DCA I
       DST, LDA I
            ADD K
            DCA K
       #20, LDA I
            MUL J
            DCA J
            LDA I
            ADD N2
            DCA I
            LDA N20
            SUB I
            SMA
            JMP DST
            LDA J
            ADD K
            DCA IA

In an appropriate place the following locations are set aside and loaded with the following information (all numbers are decimal).

       J,   0
       K,   1
     N10, 10
     N20, 20
      N2,   2

Index